THE MIND

OF THE

MIDDLE AGES

AN HISTORICAL SURVEY

Interior of Amiens Cathedral.

FREDERICK B. ARTZ

OBERLIN COLLEGE

The

MIND

of the

MIDDLE

AGES

A.D. 200-1500

AN HISTORICAL SURVEY

Third Edition, Revised

The University of Chicago Press
Chicago and London

The University of Chicago Press, Chicago 60637
The University of Chicago Press, Ltd., London

Copyright 1953, 1954 © 1980 by Frederick B. Artz
All rights reserved. Published 1953
Phoenix Edition 1980
Printed in the United States of America

ISBN: 0-226-02839-9 (cloth); 0-226-02840-2 (paper)

TO

IRVING BABBITT

AND

PRESERVED SMITH

NOW BEYOND THE REACH OF THESE WORDS

Acknowledgments

I am indebted for help to the following persons, first among my friends and colleagues in Oberlin: Andrew Bongiorno, Ernest Brehaut, Francis W. Buckler, Edward Capps, Jr., Ellsworth Carlson, Charles D. Cremeans, Julian S. Fowler, Emma Frank, Lucius Garvin, James H. Hall, Oscar and Recha Jászi, Frances Keller, William E. Kennick, Thomas S. Kepler, John C. Lapp, John D. and Ewart Lewis, Donald M. Love, Herbert G. May, Charles T. Murphy, Robert D. Murray, Jr., Charles P. Parkhurst, Jr., Helen Senour, Chester L. Shaver, Wolfgang Stechow, Forrest G. Tucker, Jennie Tucker, Mary Venn, Clarence Ward, Seldon S. Wolin, and Hermina Zortz; next to the staff of the Bibliothèque Nationale, Paris, and those of the Widener and Oberlin libraries; and finally to these scholars of other institutions: Milton V. Anastos, Dumbarton Oaks Library; Gray C. Boyce, Northwestern University; Marshall Clagett, University of Wisconsin; Ernest E. Dawn, University of Illinois; Sydney N. Fisher, Ohio State University; Erwin R. Goodenough, Yale University; Henry E. Guerlac, and Charles W. Jones, Cornell University; Theodore E. Mommsen, Princeton University; John C. Murray, Woodstock College; Sidney Painter, Johns Hopkins University; Robert R. Palmer, Princeton University; Anton C. Pegis, University of Toronto; Gaines Post, University of Wisconsin; Dorothy M. Quynn, Frederick, Md.; Raymond de Roover, Wells College; Douglas V. Steere, Haverford College; Anselm Strittmatter, St. Anselm's Priory, Washington, D. C.; and Harold R. Willoughby, University of Chicago.

The aid I received ranged all the way from helping me to get books to reading the entire manuscript and proof. Most of the persons listed read and commented on at least one chapter. I am deeply grateful to all these fellow-workers. They have saved me endless time and have rescued me from divers mistakes. The errors that remain are my own.

F. B. A.

Oberlin, Ohio

Preface to First Edition

I approach the reader like St. Denis, with my head in my hands. I know that no specialist would write a book that ranges from Moses and Homer to Erasmus and Machiavelli. Yet, as Preserved Smith has said: "The need is now, surely, for a return to synoptic writing. Here is a map of a large region, not a geological chart of a square mile or a plan of a single city." As on a general map one looks in vain for some special river or road, so here, as I know, omissions will occur to every reader. But no two writers will agree on what to omit; any discussion of so vast and complex a subject must necessarily involve many lacunae. Perhaps a better name for this book might be "Selected Topics in the History of Mediaeval Thought." A discussion of this sort tends to dwell on the achievements of exceptional individuals. The broad stream of mediaeval cultural life flowed in muddier and slower currents. For the earlier Middle Ages, it would be impossible to write a history of the ideas of the masses because of the lack of adequate sources; for the later Middle Ages there are an insufficient number of monographic studies on which to base an adequate general account. So I have confined this book to the history of the interests of the intellectual classes. In the Byzantine world from its beginning, and in Islam, after about 800, the intellectual classes included large numbers of the laity, especially in the larger towns. In the more backward Latin West, the intellectual classes before the Twelfth Century consisted largely of that part of the clergy who had received some education. After about 1100, each century found more of both clergy and the laity reading, and, thus, doing more thinking for themselves. This is certainly the cause for the great diversity of views on many subjects evident from the Twelfth Century on. By the Fourteenth Century, one is no longer surprised to find devout mystics like Wyclif side by side with witty worldlings like Chaucer. The prevailing views of the church were, after 1300, criticized by mystics, nationalists, rationalists, humanists, and men of a most secular outlook, men who had little in common except the air they were breathing. The rapid increase in the numbers of those in the Latin West who may be included in the intellectual classes is basic to the understanding of the history of ideas in the later Middle Ages.

The account is inevitably very succinct; every section of every chapter could be expanded into a book. Oversimplification has been unavoidable, and in trying to follow main currents, minor influences had to be sacrificed. Also, in view of the scale on which the book is written, brief dogmatic formulations must often be substituted for full discussions. Most of the subjects herein discussed are so interrelated that they should, at least in any given century, be treated together. This survey often divides things that ought to be united, but the author has found these divisions, into chapters and sections, a stubborn necessity. I must beg the reader to unite what here is put asunder. The arrangement of the chapters is partly based on sequence in time, though basically the whole plan is topical. In the second half of the book, I may seem to have given too large a space to imaginative literature. This is done because there are no accounts available which treat the European literatures of the Middle Ages from an international point of view, and a fuller discussion seems, thus, more justified than in other fields. I do not mean to imply that mediaeval literature has greater value than the philosophy, political thought, and art of the period. The "Epilogue" may be read either as an introduction to the book, or as a conclusion, or as both.

These chapters are heavily factual, with perhaps too many names. They are more descriptive than interpretive, more annals than analyses. But some interpretation undoubtedly runs through the exposition. This must be the case, since one of my colleagues, after reading one chapter, told me I was too favorably disposed to all things mediaeval, and shortly after, a Jesuit scholar, who read the same chapter, wrote me that I was so unsympathetic to all things mediaeval that I could never have any real understanding of the period. I have tried to avoid interpretations that generalize the significance of ideas beyond their particular historical context. Even the most radical and the most original of mediaeval thinkers never ceased to maintain vestiges of their own time and they were never wholly modern. Moreover, it should always be borne in mind that in such a condensed account it is not possible to show the mediaeval centuries in all their diversities. Even in any given century there were differences not only from decade to decade, and from one nationality to another, but even from one district to the next, for, unlike the culture of modern times, that of the eleven centuries between A.D. 400 and 1500 was tied to the soil. Communication was difficult, and there was little political or economic interdependence of one area on another. Hence all these generalizations can never be more than approximate. It should, likewise, be added that in an account that is as objective as this one tries to be, there is perhaps too little emphasis on what was always present in the minds of mediaeval Jews, Christians, and Mohammedans, namely, God and his influence in this world and the next.

This survey is the outgrowth of a quarter century of teaching. Besides the stimulus of my students, who, like the wedding guest in the "Ancient Mariner," "could not choose but hear," I have had the help of a number of scholars who have read parts of the manuscript. To them my immense gratitude; they must not, though, be reckoned responsible for my errors. The critical apparatus has been reduced to a minimum, though an extended bibliography is attached. Nearly every quotation and many titles in the bibliographical notes have been condensed, and, to aid the reader, I have deliberately omitted the customary three dots. References in the footnotes will nearly always indicate where the full quotation may be found. For the important men mentioned I have given the date of death, where it is definitely known, or, where the exact year is uncertain, I have used what seemed to be the best estimate. Inaccuracies must persist despite care and patient checking. The author hopes to bring out a second edition; he would appreciate comments from his readers.

FREDERICK B. ARTZ

Oberlin, Ohio: October, 1952

Note to Second Edition

A new edition being called for in less than a year, the author has taken the occasion to make a large number of changes in phrasing, to correct misprints, to extend the description of Aquinas' philosophy, to bring the bibliography up to date, and to make a new and fuller index. He is indebted to a number of colleagues and correspondents for valuable suggestions.

F. B. A.

January 15, 1954

Note to Third Edition

In this edition, the section on universities has been recast, a second bibliographical note has been added, and a number of minor changes made.

F. B. A.

May 1, 1958

Note to 1965 Printing

A few changes have been made in the text, and a third supplementary bibliographical note has been added.

F. B. A.

December 15, 1964

Note to 1980 Printing

A few changes have been made in the text, and a fourth supplementary bibliographical note has been added.

May 1, 1979 F. B. A.

x]

Contents

✿

PART ONE: THE DOMINANCE OF THE EAST

[xi

Contents [xiii

Illustrations

❦

ACKNOWLEDGMENTS

Illustrations Nos. 2 and 3 are from Kenneth J. Conant, A BRIEF COMMENTARY ON EARLY
MEDIAEVAL ARCHITECTURE. Copyright 1942 by The Johns Hopkins University Press. Re-
printed by permission of The Johns Hopkins University Press. No. 5 is from Clarence Ward,
MEDIAEVAL CHURCH VAULTING. Copyright 1915 by Princeton University Press. Reprinted by
permission of Princeton University Press. No. 6 is from James Westfall Thompson and
E. N. Johnson, INTRODUCTION TO MEDIAEVAL EUROPE. Copyright 1937 by W. W. Norton and
Company, Inc. Redrawn by permission of W. W. Norton and Company, Inc. No. 8 is from
F. Bond, AN INTRODUCTION TO ENGLISH CHURCH ARCHITECTURE (London, Humphrey Milford,
1913). Copyright 1913 by F. Bond. Reprinted by permission of the executors of the F. Bond
estate.

PART ONE

The Dominance of the East

CHAPTER I

The Classical Backgrounds of
Mediaeval Christianity

I. TRADITIONAL RELIGION IN THE GRAECO-ROMAN WORLD
2. THE IMPACT OF PHILOSOPHY
3. THE MYSTERY RELIGIONS

SOCIOLOGISTS usually begin with the Flood and the Fijis; writers of history, with the Greeks. These "spoiled darlings of the historians," as they have been called, may often be allowed too dominant a place in world history, but their role in the story of mediaeval culture is fundamental. Indeed, present views not only tie modern times closer to the Middle Ages, but, at the other end, make mediaeval civilization a long chapter of later antiquity. There is, in this view, something of a return to the estimates of mediaeval men who, long before the Renaissance, thought of themselves as part of the world of the ancients. From Philo the Jew, in the days of Jesus and Saint Paul, to Pico della Mirandola in the fifteenth century it was commonly believed that the Greek philosophers—above all Plato—had imbibed their first inspiration from Moses and the Hebrew prophets. Mediaeval men, thus, were deeply aware of an organic relation among the various currents of history, though their chronology was usually muddled, and, like the wife of Disraeli, they never could remember "which came first, the Greeks or the Romans."

[3

The civilizations of Greece and Rome influenced mediaeval culture in a multitude of ways, in religion and philosophy, in law, government, and social usage, in art and technology, in science and education, in language and literature, and in music. It is on the side of religion and philosophy that the connections between antiquity and the Middle Ages are deepest and the debt of mediaeval thinkers to their Greek and Roman ancestors is most profound. Interest here centers in the long story of the growth of asceticism, mysticism, and monotheism in the religious and philosophical experience of antiquity. So, like mediaeval men, who used from the riches of classical culture those parts that seemed germane, the author has, at this point, selected from the whole Graeco-Roman heritage only that part that influenced mediaeval religion and philosophy. Later on, he will have frequent occasions to discuss many other Greek and Roman influences in mediaeval civilization. The men of the mediaeval centuries were the inheritors of a long evolution of Greek and Roman culture, a culture that in spite of many common elements changed greatly in the eleven centuries between Homer and St. Augustine. In the fields of religion and philosophy, as in nearly every other branch of culture, the history of Roman civilization after about 300 B.C. began to merge with that of Greek culture; hence there is much justification for treating the story of Graeco-Roman civilization as a single development.

I. TRADITIONAL RELIGION IN THE GRAECO-ROMAN WORLD

GREEK and Roman religion started independently with simple interpretations of the forces of nature which included methods of trying to make these forces work for man's good. The thought of primitive men everywhere lacks a sense of natural causation. There are no laws of nature, there are only unpredictable forces. These forces are in trees and springs and stones and animals; they are everywhere, and these forces are like men. If a primitive man hits his head against a tree in the dark, he says: "that tree meant to do me harm. It must be propitiated." So by prayers and ritual forms, the performance of certain acts, like a libation of milk or wine or burning a cake or an animal, and by taboos (the avoidance of other acts) the spirits that dwell in all things may be made to work for man and not against him. Here, close together, are the beginnings of religion, art, and music. These attitudes and experiences of primitive man are older than logic, and, even in highly civilized men, often remain stronger than logic.

Among all primitive peoples, a vast polytheism of many gods is built up, so numerous the ancients often said there were more gods than men. In the course of time these forces of nature were given personalities, and stories about them grew. Still later, some gods became more important than others and a hierarchy of divine forces was developed with Zeus or Jupiter as the chief of the great gods of Olympus. Besides the family gods of the fireside and the fields, and the gods of the city-state, there was added by Alexander the Great the worship of the ruler, and this cult was continued in the Hellenistic states and still later in the Roman Empire. Both these high gods and the innumerable lesser spirits are superior to men, not in spiritual or moral qualities, but only in outward gifts, strength, beauty, or immortality. There was no inward and spiritual relation of the individual with a moral force as in later religions and philosophies; it was a sort of contractual relation, to every god and spirit its due. Such a religion, common among all primitive peoples, knew little of the dark by-ways of mysticism. If men acquitted themselves of their obligations to these deities of the hearth, the field, and the marketplace, they would enjoy divine favor, or, at least, be unmolested.

The fight of Christianity was less against the great gods who dwelt on Olympus or, among the early Germans, in Walhalla, less against Zeus and Apollo, Odin and Thor, than against this vast multitude of lesser deities, a fight that the church lost. For the early Christian missionaries soon found the belief of the people in these spirits that would help in specific situations so deeply rooted that they early developed the cult of the saints and the cult of relics to take its place. "Remember," said Pope Gregory the Great, "you must not interfere with any traditional belief or religious observance that can be harmonized with Christianity." The theologians of the church never gave these saints any role except that of mediators between man and his God, but the masses made no such fine distinctions; they took the heroes of the new faith to their hearts, embraced them, and worshipped them as deities.[1]

The view of life of the average man of classical antiquity was confined to this world. It accepted this world and was largely indifferent to the promise of a future life. The growth of conscience, a sense of sin and shortcoming, and any great longing for a future life were of slow development. The traditional religion of the family and the state had no founder, no prophets, no inspired leader, no sacred books, no fixed theology or rules of orthodoxy, no religious caste. It did not produce a comprehensive code of ethics nor did it place emphasis on the need of right living. It was largely concerned with forms and outward acts of devotion. The need of peace with the gods produced a sort of religious legalism. Only in minor religious currents connected with the cults of Dionysus, of Orpheus, and of Demeter was there any indication of a mystical desire for moral purity and for union with the god. The formal and legal side of religion is what is meant by paganism. The old traditional religion of the family and the state lived on, at least among the masses, for centuries; it even survived the fall of the Roman Empire in the fifth century A.D. When St. Benedict in the sixth century climbed the hill at Monte Cassino to found what was to become the mother house of his great monastic order, he discovered the inhabitants of the village all turned out for a feast of Apollo, and his eyes fell on a scene similar to the one Keats saw on the Grecian urn. The persistence of the ancient cults was due to the natural conservatism of all men in matters of religion and to the great inertia which any long-established usages possess. The old cults recalled the glories of the past, the ritual was attractive, and the state worship was the mother of art, literature, and music, and was all tied up with them.

In the course of centuries these traditional religious ideas and practices were modified by the poets, artists, and philosophers, and by a steady growth of mystery cults. The writers and the artists, for example, created the concept of Zeus as the creator and sustainer of a moral order in the universe and connected the gods with ethical ideals. As a result of these currents of art and literature, and of philosophy and the mystery religions, the old traditional paganism was overlaid, but it never disappeared. The old cults failed to satisfy certain classes who reached out toward a monotheistic view of religion; they were inadequate in that they paid little attention to matters of morality; they showed little concern for the problems of an after life and they failed to touch the hearts of many individuals or to satisfy their minds. Religious thinking came to exist on a number of levels at once, and the story of Greek and later Roman religion, from about 600 B.C. on, must be considered as proceeding in a sort of polyphonic manner. The new comes in alongside the old, but the old does not disappear.

2. THE IMPACT OF PHILOSOPHY

THE LEGACY of Greek philosophy to the Middle Ages was enormous, and in the long centuries when Greek science, art, and literature were as good as forgotten throughout much of the West, the work of the Greek philosophers and of their Roman commentators formed the basis of Christian theology and the learning of all mediaeval schools.

Greek and Roman philosophy, like the rest of classical culture, went through a long evolution; its story from Thales of Miletus and Pythagoras to St. Augustine and Boethius is the greatest single chapter in the history of man's adventurous mind. Philosophy and science among the Greeks began together about 600 B.C., over two centuries later than Homer. They began together as an approach other than religion to explain the nature of things. Thales of Miletus was the first of a series of thinkers who were interested in astronomy, physics, and mathematics, and who tried to explain man and the universe on purely mechanical and rational lines. Thales believed "all came from water and to water all returns." The universe is explained chiefly on the basis of the processes of the weather. Ignoring old ideas, these thinkers were indifferent rather than hostile to religion. They explained the universe in the processes familiar to the farmer, the smith, and the sailor. They were eminently practical; Thales, for example, was later (falsely) reputed to have foretold an eclipse, and to have introduced from Egypt the methods of land measurements and founded geometry. Anaximander probably invented the sun-dial. Practical as they were, they were also the first thinkers who raised the basic questions of philosophy: What, in the final analysis, is real? What is the character of being?

This school of Miletus founded not only Western philosophy in general but, more specifically, a current of that philosophy that has remained more or less mechanistic in outlook. This mechanistic current came to its first adequate presentation in the philosophy of Democritus, an older contemporary of Plato, who reduced all reality to atoms and a void. In him we have the first clear statement of philosophic materialism in its modern meaning. His reduction of all reality to quantitative difference ultimately made possible that application of mathematics to the treatment of phenomena which is essential to the modern notion of scientific law. These theories of Democritus were later taken over by the Epicurean school and formed the basis of the magnificent philosophic poem of Lucretius, the *De Rerum Natura* of 55 B.C. This mechanistic current in ancient philosophy, important as it was, had no great influence on thought until the sixteenth century.

Contemporary with the work of Thales and his followers was that of Pythagoras, who is the founder of the great current of ethical and religious philosophy out of which ultimately came the Jewish, Christian, and Mohammedan philosophy of the Middle Ages. Ernest Barker once remarked: "The Middle Ages begin with Plato"; he might better have said: "The Middle Ages begin with Pythagoras." Pythagoras grew up in Ionia from whence had come the philosophy of Thales and his followers, and he was thoroughly trained in the best science of the period, in mathematics, physics, astronomy, music, and medicine. From these studies he conceived of a great world order, apart from man, perfect and harmonious in form and embodying principles of order and justice. It was the work of the Greek idealist philosophers to find a way of life for man that accorded with this world order. The early success of the Greeks in mathematics, physics, and astronomy is the determinant element in the growth of Greek idealism from Pythagoras to Plotinus.

Besides the influence of Ionian science, Pythagoras was also early influenced by Orphism, an ascetic and mystical Greek religious movement. Orphism held that the soul (the life-breath) was imprisoned in the body, that "the body is the tomb of the soul," and that this life is a preparation for life hereafter. The aim of life is redemption from the wheel of rebirth by a system of purifications. The soul can escape and rejoin the original divine essence only by death. It is possible, however, to anticipate this reunion by virtue of a religious mystery or ceremony that temporarily delivers the soul from its bodily prison and brings it into communion with the divine essence. What men call life is really death. The soul is divine and immortal, but through the sins of his ancestors, the Titans, man has fallen from his earlier high estate and must be released through a series of reincarnations. The mystic union with the hero Orpheus, including the eating of an animal which embodied his spirit, was one of the means of purification and of an eventual return to a higher level of existence. The initiate enjoyed the privilege of knowing divine things. Wicked souls live after death in men or in darkness under the earth; good souls, after many reincarnations, go to a blessed land. Here is the idea of the war of the soul on the body, a sense of weakness, sin, and shortcoming, and the idea of winning immortality partly through the moral effort of the individual, as, for example, abstaining from eating meat, and partly by a mystic identification with a divine savior. Here was a religion that could satisfy both the head and the heart. Orphism, in its various forms, not only inspired Pythagoras but it had a deep influence on Plato, and through him on Stoicism, Neo-Platonism, and early Christian theology—systems in which knowledge is no longer a desire for power over nature, but a means of virtuous living identified with the well-being of the soul.

Pythagoras combined the science of his time with elements of the various religious currents he knew and created something that he was the first to call philosophy, literally "the love of wisdom." He founded a religious order in southern Italy and for it laid down elaborate rules for the study of science and music, for a life of stern renunciation on the one hand, and on the other, a contemplation of the divine order of the world in which all was law, proportion, order, and harmony. Pythagoras' aim was to find a way of life by which the soul could escape from the body and return to its maker. With all the Greek philosophers before Plato, including Pythagoras, we cannot be certain that we have anything they themselves wrote, and we must reconstruct their thought from fragments they are supposed to have written and from descriptions of their ideas in the writings of Plato, Aristotle, and later Greek philosophers. From such sources we can see that Pythagoras had an elaborate philosophic system that included a metaphysics and a system of ethics. He was the first to discover, by experimenting with a vibrating cord, that the intervals of the scale which seem to the ear concordant are associated with definite proportions of one string to another. He had a strange theory that everything could be explained in a system of numbers that corresponded to the tones in a musical scale, which in turn corresponded with a pre-existing harmony in the universe. This number symbolism had a great appeal to mediaeval men and was much used for centuries as a means of attempting to solve ethical and scientific problems. In Pythagoras we see the beginning of an idealistic, mystical, and ascetic philosophy that was later developed by Plato, the Stoics, and the Neo-Platonists, and from them entered Jewish and Christian thought.

The intervening generations between Thales of Miletus (d. *ca.* 546 B.c.) and Pythagoras (d. *ca.* 497 B.c.) and Socrates and Plato (d. 347 B.c.), a period of about a century and a half, saw a brilliant series of Greek thinkers concerned with trying to adjust the rival claims of science and ethics, of popular religious ideas, and purely mechanical explanations. Philosophy now became the center of education, where it remained through all the later phases of Greek and Roman antiquity and during the Middle Ages. The idea of a single force — the *logos* Heraclitus called it, Parmenides named it the *One,* and Anaxagoras *nous* or mind — that created and sustained the universe, and the idea of an ordered cosmos were the chief contributions of the thinkers between Pythagoras and Socrates. As Xenophanes wrote: "One God there is, midst God and men the greatest; in form not like to mortals; he without toil rules all things; ever unmoved in one place he abideth."

The political and social upheaval caused by the Persian wars, soon followed by a bitter internal strife between Athens and Sparta, caused a sort of moral anarchy in Greek thought in the fifth century B.c. Ideas of all types poured into Athens. The old and the new were in conflict, and the result was often skepticism, cynicism, and defeatism. Many of the intellectual classes rejected all attempts to explain the world; orthodox religious ideas were declining, and old notions of right and wrong were called into question. In this world, travelling teachers, the Sophists, taught young men the arts of rhetoric and oratory, one of the chief roads to success in the democratic cities of the time. We know the Sophists chiefly through Plato, who disliked them. Most of them seem to have placed the emphasis of their teaching not on fundamental problems of science or philosophy or ethics but on the art of getting on and the ability to argue for any point of view irrespective of its truth. Aristophanes makes a Sophist say, in effect, that nothing is either good or bad, but thinking makes it so, or as Protagoras put it, "man is the measure of all things"; everything is relative. There are no values, no standards of right and wrong, no objective truth or morality can exist; all is relative, all is flux. In some ways the Sophists stood for emancipation and freedom. Most of the Sophists did not pretend to be philosophers and they probably reflected rather than created a certain elegant contemptuousness toward conventional religion and morality, but they deeply exasperated the noblest soul of their age, Socrates (d. 399 B.C.), and were the first cause of his life-work.

"Saint Socrates, pray for us," wrote Erasmus in the sixteenth century, and that may stand as the judgment of history on this extraordinary teacher and spiritual leader. No one in the history of philosophy so changed its course simply by what he was. In the midst of confusion, disintegration, and cynicism, this humble stone-cutter's son set out on an earnest quest for a knowledge of the good life. Personally he was ugly of countenance and shabby of dress, but he possessed enormous physical and intellectual vigor and a warm temperament. He was a stimulating talker, full of irony and earnestness. Those who knew him adored him. He seems to have begun as a Sophist, but soon broke with them; like the Sophists, he rejected many of the commonly held ideas of his time, and he questioned all the common concepts of the good and the true. But he rejected the facile cynicism of the Sophists. Among conflicting opinions he tried to find a solid core of truth, particularly in matters of ethics. His method was that of close questioning of those about him, insisting all the while on a consistent and exact use of words, and on clarification of all concepts used. All of Plato's abstracts were developed from Socrates' basic definitions. Man's first need is to take care of his soul, which he defined as the whole intellectual and moral personality, the responsible agent in all man's actions. After Socrates, his conception of the soul and his conviction that the development of the soul is the most significant thing in life become central in philosophy. Socrates' teaching on the soul stands for one of the great changes in the history of thought and is the most significant development in Greek philosophy in preparing the way for Christianity.

Along with his interest in the growth of the soul, Socrates taught that the universe is ruled by intelligent and moral forces. Something of this good world order can be known by the soul, though the chief guidance for the soul is knowledge of sound principles of ethical action. Virtue lies in knowledge, by which he seemingly meant full comprehension, of the good. To act rightly one must first know the right; all wickedness is due to ignorance. Socrates, though he left no writings, accomplished a revolution in Greek thought. He turned away from scientific to ethical and metaphysical problems. Before his time, philosophy had been chiefly concerned with the origins of all things. Socrates turned philosophy around and bade it look to the end for which the world existed; he turned from facts to values. The result of his teaching was that the later systems of Greek philosophy looked for the nature of things no longer in simple materials but in some final perfection toward which all things aspire. The effect on science was, in the long run, disastrous. The world of fact began to recede into the background, and, in the end, the Greek mind became too entranced with its own creations.

Socrates' moral doctrine is self-contained; it is the old Greek "know thyself"; it requires no support from older religious beliefs. His distinction between good and evil must be known directly; no supernatural sanction is needed. Socrates is said to have met an East Indian to whom he declared that he sought to understand human life, and the Hindu replied that man cannot know himself without knowing God. This story may show that some of Socrates' successors were aware that the recognition of right and wrong demanded by the master could not be separated from the recognition of an ultimate force who made and sustains the universe and a great moral order.

Aristotle states positively that Socrates was chiefly a teacher of ethics, who did not "occupy himself with the general nature of things" and that Plato was responsible for his own metaphysics. In any case, Plato as Socrates' leading disciple is our chief source for the master's ideas. Plato (d. 347 B.C.) himself is the first philosopher whom we can know well through his surviving works. He came of a well-to-do Athenian family, received an excellent education, and early fell deeply under the influence of Socrates. He was twenty-eight years old when Socrates was put to death; at the age of forty, Plato established a school, "The

Academy," which lasted from 387 B.C. to A.D. 529, a longer time than any university has endured.

Plato's mind ranged widely, and he worked over the ideas of the earlier Greek philosophers. From Thales and the School of Miletus he drew his interest in mathematics, physics, and astronomy; from Heraclitus he got his belief in the transitoriness of all sensible things; from Parmenides came his vision of eternal being; from Anaxagoras came the idea that the moving cause of all things is mind. From the Pythagoreans he drew his ideas of the nature and destiny of the soul, his belief in order in the universe and in an eternal reality transcending our senses, and some of his asceticism and mysticism. All of these conceptions inherited from his predecessors were transformed and reordered in the light of the teaching of Socrates.

Plato outlined the great problems of philosophy, including a metaphysics, and, based on this, a psychology, an ethics, a theory of education, a system of aesthetics, and a philosophy of politics. He left gaps in his system; it is often difficult to find his final solution of some of the great metaphysical problems he raises, and he frequently contradicts himself. Nevertheless, his philosophy is the first elaboration of a theistic philosophy of a divinely made and directed universe. Plato's basic doctrine holds that there exists a world of eternal realities, of Forms or Ideas, entirely separate from the world our senses perceive. These Forms make up an organic and harmonious structure, the world of real being. Above all these separate Forms is the highest Form of the Good, the first principle of reality. This Form of the Good is not God in the Hebrew-Christian sense, for the Form of the Good does not include all the other Forms. Plato, thus, approached the monotheistic conception of the Old Testament but he never reached it. In the *Timaeus* he shows the Divine Force in three aspects, a sort of Trinity: first, the Divine Craftsman, then the Forms or Ideas, and finally the World Spirit, a deputy or agent of the Divine Craftsman. Christian theologians were at a later period to find this useful.[2]

The notions men have of the eternal Forms, which lie behind all the things we can see and know, are but feeble copies of these spiritual realities. But that men are able to know these Forms at all is due to the fact that the soul knew the Forms before it entered the body and is reminded of them by perceiving, through the senses, those things in this world that participate in them. The world of the senses is a world of flux; it is but half real. Things and events are but symbols of the great realities that lie behind and beyond this world. He who is willing to undergo the appropriate discipline can come to conceive Justice itself and Beauty itself, realities that are real as nothing in this world is real. It is only of these wholly immaterial and unchanging realities that man may have knowledge; all the rest is mere sensation and opinion. The purpose of man's life is to bring into the state and the life of man, the microcosm, something of the moral order and purpose that exists in the universe, the macrocosm. Man's highest faculty is reason, which should be fully trained, but the life of reason is insufficient: it is only a ladder up to a religious experience in which man surveys all time and all existence.[3]

Plato's fundamental position is bottomed on an act of religious faith in a divinely directed universe. It is, as we have seen, a conception of all existence that approaches monotheism. It is a view of life that is mystical in that Plato wishes to help men identify themselves with the divine forces. A philosophy or a religion is not mystical when it is inspired merely by reverence and loyalty and even love for a divine being or force. It becomes mystical when, in addition to these sentiments, there is an inner sense of insufficiency and a desire for a union and fusion with the divine.[4] Plato's view of life is super-rational in that it aims at achieving a knowledge that is beyond perception and reason. His system of education shows how a man may aim at mystical heights by toiling up a long hard road of physical and intellectual discipline. Plato's is also a view of life that is somewhat ascetic. The joys of this world are evanescent and delusive. He protests that men confuse a round of pleasures or the pursuit of power and wealth with true happiness. Philosophy can deliver men from false and shallow judgments, and it can teach men to avoid an inner division in the soul by showing them that the goods of fortune are worth little; goods of the body are worth more, but goods of the soul are worth most. The way of the fullest life is also a way of renunciation. Finally, Plato's view of life is no longer the man-centered view that we commonly associate with the classical Greeks. It is a view of life that is centered, if not in God, at least in an immaterial and spiritual world, and the measure of time and space is not man or this world but eternity. For Plato life is only secondarily a series of events in this world; for him life has become primarily an adventure in eternity.

The weaknesses of Plato's philosophy were the weaknesses of much of Greek philosophy. He does not distinguish between illustrations and brilliant analogies and real argument. He indulges frequently in mere abstraction detached from either concrete observation or precise definition. Plato, like many Christian theologians later, seems, at times, to think that the greater the abstraction the more profound the truth. The Greeks made remarkable progress in mathematics, especially in geometry, and they wrongly supposed that a system of thought explaining the universe and man could be built as easily. So they were always hunting for unchanging reality, the elements, the truth, the moral law, and the absolute. Hence, Plato's system did not deal adequately with the finite world and had no method of expanding factual information about man and the world. Finally, his philosophic system is not only incomplete and often vague but over subtle, and these defects became exaggerated in the work of his successors, the Neo-Platonists and the Church Fathers.

But Plato's greatness has transcended many of these limitations. His superb literary style, which is the greatest of all the philosophers', gives his work, as Milton would say, "a life beyond life." And his great system has a superlative sweep, offering an explanation of man's destiny matched only by some of the greatest Jewish prophets and by Jesus of Nazareth. His enormous influence was on the side of a super-rational, though not an anti-rational, mysticism, and on the side of monotheism and of a reasonable asceticism. Men were particularly interested in his conception of human life as a pilgrimage to our true home. This last current, which came chiefly from Pythagoras, was passed on by the Stoics and the Neo-Platonists from which sources it entered Christianity.

The measure of Plato's influence on the whole history of Western thought is shown in Whitehead's statement: "The safest general characterization of the whole Western philosophical tradition is that it consists in a series of footnotes to Plato." [5] Only the "Timaeus," the most obscure of Plato's dialogues, was available in Latin translation during the Middle Ages; yet, through his influence on Cicero and on the Church Fathers, the system of Plato dominated the whole theology of the Christian Church from the first century through the twelfth, when the influence of Aristotle came in alongside that of Plato. Beyond this, the ideas of Plato were so diverse and so protean and they have so penetrated all Western thought that, on many subjects, to think at all means to think in terms of Plato. Emerson once loaned a Vermont farmer a copy of *The Republic*; later the farmer told Emerson: "that book has a great number of my ideas."

The philosophy of Plato was deeply modified, though not replaced, by that of Aristotle (d. 322 B.C.). Aristotle's father was the physician of Philip of Macedon, and later Aristotle became the tutor of Alexander the Great, though this relation seems to have had little influence on either teacher or pupil. The earliest influence on Aristotle was that of Ionian scientific thought. He began his intellectual career as a biologist; it is important to remember that he had a different beginning from that of Plato. At eighteen, he became a pupil of Plato, who was then sixty years old, and he remained a member of Plato's Academy until Plato's death twenty years later.[6] Jaeger has shown that Aristotle's thought went through a long development. His earlier works were critical of Plato; then he tried to combine his ideas with those of Plato, and from this he finally constituted his own philosophy, which is basically a reconstructed Platonism. He is known for a long series of treatises on metaphysics (called by Aristotle "first philosophy"), on logic, on physics (in which he was very reactionary), on anatomy and physiology (in which he was forward-looking), on politics, ethics, rhetoric, and poetics. No other man made such important contributions to so many branches of knowledge. Nothing, it seems, was too great or too small to arouse his curiosity. The enormous range of his interests, his passion for classification, his orderliness, and, finally, his inspired common sense, which made him able to see both sides of most questions, give his philosophy a range possessed by no other in history.

Aristotle, being of a definitely scientific turn of mind, was greatly interested in what had been found out and what might be discovered by careful and objective investigation. In this he possessed a temperament fundamentally different from that of Plato. He accepted many of the ideas of Plato, but he objected to Plato's radical separation of the eternal Forms from the actual things of experience. Aristotle believed in Plato's Forms, only he maintained that they exist in this world and are in things and have no independent existence apart from them. Matter and Form are relative terms; only God has any real existence apart from matter. It is only the mind that separates them, and Form is grasped only after a prolonged study of individuals. The purposefulness of things is bound up with them, though this purposefulness is directed toward a transcendent end.

At the bottom of the great chain of being which constitutes the universe, stands pure matter, though, as one finds matter, it is always in some rudimentary form. The first stage upward from pure matter, in which matter has already taken on form, is to be found in the four elements: earth, air, fire, and water. Unfortunately for the future of science, Aristotle rejected the contemporary theory of matter of Democritus. From these four elements, we pass upward, through level after level of inorganic life, to organic life. In organisms, we advance from the vegetable life of the simplest plants to the animal soul, which is capable of sensation and motion, and from the animal soul to man, the rational being, each step being governed by an upward impulse which constitutes the goal toward which it is striving. At the top of the great chain of being is the first cause, God, who is pure form without matter. Unmoved himself, he is the first mover of the universe. God is the ideal toward which the whole of creation moves as by an inner necessity. Each ascending existence or reality in this great chain, made up of its own form and matter, becomes, in turn, the matter of a higher form: a brick is form given to clay, the brick in turn becomes matter for the form of the wall, the wall becomes matter for the form of the temple. In Plato's universe there was just one world of forms sharply set off from one world of matter, and Plato gives no adequate explanation of the relation of these two worlds. In Aristotle's world there is an interlocking hierarchy of forms from lowest to highest.

The Aristotelian idea of a great chain of being dominated the thought of the West down into the seventeenth century. It is extremely important for the theology, philosophy, and science of the Middle Ages. What was to be the common mediaeval conception of this hierarchy of being is summed up by the Neo-Platonist Macrobius. Writing in the fourth century A.D., he says: "Since from the supreme God, mind arises, and from mind, soul, and since this, in turn, creates all subsequent things and fills them all with life, and since this single radiance illumines all and is reflected in each as a single face might be reflected in many mirrors placed in a series; and, since all things follow in continuous succession, degenerating in sequence to the very bottom of the series, the attentive observer will discover a succession of parts from the supreme God down to the last dregs of things, mutually linked, and without a break." [7]

In ethics, Aristotle took the position that emotions like anger, envy, love, and hatred, and actions like eating and drinking are, in themselves, neither good nor bad. Any emotion or action in excess will throw a man's soul off its balance. It is measure that a man needs, not mere suppression. Act always midway between two extremes; follow the "golden mean"; "nothing in excess."

In each part of Aristotle's philosophy there is a closely co-ordinated and organic structure of scientific fact, common sense, and this-world activity. His metaphysics is much more tightly knit than Plato's, and this world and the world of ideas are more integrated. For example, Plato regarded the soul as an entity separated from the body; he compares the soul to a rider controlling the horse on which he is mounted; with Aristotle the soul and body are united; the soul is the form by which the substance of the body is actualized and without the body the soul would have no existence. Both Plato and Aristotle believed the soul immortal though Aristotle rejected Plato's belief in a personal immortality and his idea of successive reincarnations.

Aristotle had a system of philosophy; Plato had created only the outlines of a philosophy. With Aristotle, however, there are some gaps. All seems closely knit; then, suddenly, we find that the structure has towered out of this worldly atmosphere and we are in a world of pure spiritual being, with forms that are divine, eternal, and transcendent. Aristotle was for twenty years in the closest contact with Plato. Though he usually seems determined to avoid the transcendental, the influence of the older teacher is always there. This is shown by the fact that when he comes to the farthest point to which his own system will take him, he then takes refuge in metaphors of a mystical character for which the reader is not prepared; this is especially true when he is dealing with the soul and with the First Mover. At heart, Aristotle always remained a good deal of a Platonist in spite of himself. He is, however, far less mystical and less ascetic in outlook than Plato, though he is more clearly monotheistic in his centering of all creation in God.

Plato's philosophy is set forth in a style that charms and sometimes bewilders the reader as does a great poem. Plato's writing casts a spell. Aristotle's philosophy, in the form in which we have it, is written in jottings, rather like telegrams, sometimes giving the barest bones of his thoughts, sometimes in epigrams and brilliant turns, occasionally in repetition or in mere confusion. Cicero, who knew some of Aristotle's original dialogues, speaks of his "golden stream of speech." But the extant writings of Aristotle seem to be skeleton memoranda prepared for his students.

Aristotle, in 335 B.C., founded a school, the "Lyceum," which ran parallel with Plato's Academy until A.D. 529. Plato's influence on later antiquity and on the Middle Ages down into the twelfth century was greater than that of Aristotle. During much of this long period, out of all of his works only two of Aristotle's logical treatises, the *Categories* or classes of propositions, and the *De Interpretatione* on parts and kinds of sentences, both elementary treatises, were available in Latin translations of Boethius. But in the twelfth and thirteenth centuries the rest of Aristotle's writings were translated into Latin; his philosophy captured the schools, and he became, for many besides Averroës and Dante, the "master of those who know."

The Jewish, Christian, and Mohammedan theologians who used Aristotle found three great stumbling blocks in their way. Aristotle's system denied the idea of divine providence and the possibility of God's sudden intervention in an ordered universe; no miracles were possible for Aristotle's unmoved First Mover. Aristotle, also, did not believe in a special creation of the universe as described in Genesis; with him matter is eternal. And, finally, Aristotle denied personal immortality. But the Jews, the Christians, and the Mohammedans used his system, and for the orthodox he is still the basis of their theology. In artistic, literary, and musical criticism many of Aristotle's concepts like that of form and matter have remained the stock in trade. Many of the ideas of the great trinity of Greek philosophy, Socrates, Plato, and Aristotle, reached the early Christian Fathers and the writers of the Middle Ages through later schools of Greek philosophy, especially through

Stoicism and Neo-Platonism, and through Latin Works of popularization, above all those of Cicero and Seneca.

After 350 B.C. Alexander the Great destroyed the free self-governing
Greek city-states and set up a dictatorship. At the same time, his conquests and the trade developments that followed him went far to wipe
away the old differences between Greeks and barbarians and to spread
the language and culture of the Greeks through the whole of the Near
East. Old national groups and old distinctions between classes of society were blurred or wiped out. But Alexander, having swept away
the old order, did not live long enough to establish a new one. For the
next three centuries—from about 300 B.C. to the time of the founding
of the Roman Empire by Augustus, just before the beginning of the
Christian Era—there were nearly incessant wars and insurrections
through the Graeco-Roman world. These constant upheavals throughout the whole Mediterranean area swept away the old landmarks;
nowhere was there any longer a stable society where men knew and
respected one another and where the details of life were controlled by
the opinion of a compact body of citizens. The civilized world for
much of the time in the three centuries before Augustus and Jesus
was a vast scramble where millions of men, each on his own, struggled
for themselves. In such a world, a man would often rise to great
power and riches and then suddenly be flung into the mire. There
seemed to be no reason or sense or principle of order any longer. The
individual often found himself uprooted, isolated, and alone. Men
were hurled along like sticks in a torrent.

The old Greek city-state had had its weaknesses; it offered its
marvellous opportunities to only a few; the states had much internal
strife, and they often fought one another. But to Plato and Aristotle
the old Greek city-state was not merely a government; it was also a
training school for youth and a place in which the citizen could in his
own work and in service in the army, the navy, the courts, and the
assembly realize the highest possibilities of his being. The state was a
moral and spiritual corporation; it had an ethical function. It was not
merely an institution that collected taxes, built roads, and furnished
police protection. It was a great spiritual bond for the perfecting of its
members. An individual citizen could only realize himself in and
through the state. The old Greek city-state was, then, something like

the mediaeval church and like the state in the philosophy of Hegel; there was little idea of a conflict between the interests of the individual and the interests of the state.

The destruction of freedom in the Greek city-states, the gradual loss of faith in the old gods, and the long succession of wars and disorders raised the whole question of self-perfection apart from the group. How could one achieve fullfilment and peace and the good life outside the state? The state was now considered evil; it was widely regarded as a great killing machine, an engine of might without right, in which unprincipled adventurers and tyrants scrambled for rich prizes. Likewise, to many men life itself seemed bad. Everything depended on whim and chance. Men came to fear life. Every interest a man had was like a filament going out from his heart and attaching itself to some object. If this object was unstable, he was pulled miserably this way and that after it. The way of freedom and peace was to reduce the field of interest, to cut all these strands going out in all directions and attaching one to family, property, honors, riches, and the state. Confidence was shaken; aspirations were lowered; there was a withdrawal from high endeavor. Men were turning to philosophies and religions of renunciation and consolation. There was a gradual "failure of nerve." [8]

All these changes in the ways of life led to a search for new philosophies and religions. Some sought to revive old Greek mystery cults; others in both the eastern and the western ends of the Mediterranean turned to mystery religions from Egypt, Asia Minor, Syria, Persia, and finally Palestine. Others revived Pythagoreanism and Platonism or turned to new philosophies. Everywhere men were no longer at home in this world; they felt themselves wayfarers seeking peace.

To Plato and Aristotle the origin of philosophic inquiry had been a desire to forge ahead to know more about man and the universe. To the Stoic Epictetus the source of philosophy is "a consciousness of one's own weakness and inadequacy"; to Cicero "philosophy is the healing of the soul"; to Plutarch it is "the only medicine for spiritual diseases." The philosopher is no longer the bright star going before the earnest seekers after truth; he has become a stretcher-bearer following in the wake of the struggle for existence and picking up the wounded. The philosopher has become the physician of the soul.

New religions and philosophies now offered schemes of personal development and personal salvation entirely independent of the fate of any earthly state, independent even of the fate of the great Roman Empire. All were highly cosmopolitan; they were for all men everywhere, for the whole of humanity, and were not confined to any nation or any class of society. The community is redefined, and it becomes world-wide. At the same time that the new philosophies and religions became cosmopolitan, they also became highly individualistic, appealing directly to the mind and heart of the believer.

One of the most attractive of these philosophies was that of Epicurus (d. 270 B.C.). The Cyrenaics, a group that stemmed from Socrates, had earlier developed a philosophy that showed men how to avoid distress by forgetting the gods and the soul and thereby finding a key to inner peace. Epicurus developed these ideas into a doctrine and founded a school called the "Garden." The Epicureans were largely indifferent to learning; they took up the materialism of Democritus to rid themselves of any belief in the soul, in immortality, and in God. The gods exist, but they live a life apart from this world. Don't bother about them. Most of the evils men fear can be avoided; if they come, they can be endured. It is anticipation of pain that makes men wretched and saps their courage. Death is like sleep, an unconscious forgetfulness. Reject the world and its prizes. Be unambitious.

> *There is nothing to fear in God*
> *There is nothing to feel in death;*
> *What is good is easily procured*
> *What is bad is easily endured.*[9]

Epicurus, desirous of removing every disturbance from without, advised men not to take part in public life, to avoid marriage, to withdraw from the world and live a hidden life. Pleasure, as he defined it, is mainly negative, avoiding the world so as to gain a peaceful state of mind. Like Heine's Englishman, Epicurus seems to have "taken his pleasures sadly." There is an essential distrust of life, an escapism, about this faith that warns one not to attract the world's attention and then the world will not hurt one. Its essential hedonism and its materialism made Epicureanism, after 200 B.C., popular among intellectuals and the well-to-do of the Graeco-Roman world. It inspired the greatest philosophic poem of antiquity, the *De Rerum Natura* (55 B.C.) of Lucretius, but its materialism and atheism had no attraction for the early Christians or for the men of the Middle Ages. It came back into vogue in the sixteenth century and later, and appealed deeply to thinkers like Montaigne, Thomas Hobbes, and Holbach.

Much more influential than Epicureanism, both in later antiquity and in the Middle Ages, was Stoicism, which derives from another group of Socrates' followers, the Cynics. Poor men who were never organized in a school, the Cynics were at war with established ideas and institutions. They used ridicule and witty abuse, and, foreswearing all the comforts of civilization, they travelled from place to place, making public harangues and giving moral advice to individuals. The Cynic and later the Stoic teachers moved about like missionaries ministering to men. They were consulted for advice on moral problems; a Stoic teacher was often attached to a Greek or Roman family as a sort of chaplain. The discourses he delivered were like the sermons of the Christian church of a later time. The cardinal point of the teaching of the Cynics was the supreme value of virtue and the utter insignificance and worthlessness of all else. Desire and the world must be set aside. Possess nothing; fear nothing except evil; desire nothing but virtue. They allowed no distinctions between men except on the basis of virtue alone; Greek and barbarian, rich and poor were words that meant nothing to the Cynics. It was a strongly ascetic creed; one Cynic said: "Look at me, I am without house or city, property or slave. I sleep on the ground. I have no wife, no children. What do I lack? Am I not without distress or fear? Am I not free?" [10] It all sounds like St. Jerome or one of the early Christian ascetics. The life of virtue they loved to compare with the life of an athlete, a figure of speech often used by Seneca and St. Paul.

The activity of the Cynics forms the background for Stoicism, whose founder, Zeno (d. 263 B.C.), opened a school, the "Stoa" or "Porch," in Athens some years before Epicurus founded his school. Zeno's doctrine is severe. He accepted Socrates' idea that knowledge is virtue, and the general theory of Plato about the universe. The universe is not a place where senseless atoms swirl chaotically about. It is a great moral order created by God and governed by "natural law."

This "natural law" is independent of popular conventions and of human legislation; it is the rule of reason and justice that lies at the heart of the universe. Men and institutions should strive to follow it. Reason is man's highest faculty and he must use his reason to suppress his emotions and to attain temperance, courage, and peace. Man may then come to live in harmony with God's ordered universe.

The strongest forces in Stoicism that influenced later thought were, first, its emphasis on duty, duty to family, to friends, and to all obligations; second, its belief that a man must listen to his conscience, his inner light; third, its injunction to join with men of good will everywhere to extend justice among mankind; and, finally, its great doctrine of "natural law." Maintain your soul as a fortress. You have to fight alone. Listen to your conscience, follow your duty not your desires, attune your spirit to a great world order, be just to your fellowmen, and live a life of inner strength, of stern self-sufficiency, inaccessible to grief and undisturbed though the heavens fall. As with other schools of Greek philosophy, there is no reliance on a loving God or on a personal savior.

Few early Stoic writings survive, and the chief sources are Roman writers after 100 B.C., Cicero, Epictetus, Seneca, and Marcus Aurelius. The earlier Stoics were interested in metaphysical problems, but the surviving Stoic writings are chiefly concerned with ethics. Stoicism, like Epicureanism, is more significant in history as a way of life than as a philosophy. The spirit of Stoicism is deeply religious. "Have courage to look up to God," wrote Epictetus, "and say, 'deal with me as thou wilt. I am thine. I flinch from nothing so long as thou thinkest it good. Wouldst thou have me hold office or eschew it, be rich or poor? For all this I will defend thee before men.' " [11] Cicero wrote, regarding the brotherhood of man: "and there shall no longer be one law at Athens, and another at Rome, one law today another tomorrow, but the same law, everlasting and unchangeable, shall bind all nations, and there shall be one ruler of all, even God, the creator of this law, and he who will not obey it shall be an exile from himself." [12] Seneca compared the world of the spirit and the world of material things to two cities; one is the everyday world of transitoriness and discord, the other, the real and spiritual world: "each of us owns two fatherlands, one the country in which we happen to be born, the other an empire on which the sun never sets." This concept evidently became common centuries before Augustine wrote his *City of God*.

The Stoics first denounced the myths about heroes and gods, but in time, though they were monotheistic in outlook, they took over the whole classical polytheism, and they began the use of allegory in explaining myths. For example, Homer's story of how Hera was fettered by Hephaistos and liberated is said to show that the order of the universe depends upon the balance of the elements; when Zeus hangs Hera suspended in the air, this points to the origin and succession of the elements. Everything in mythology could be given a physical or moral meaning. This method was passed on to the Jews and the Christians and played an enormous role in the interpreting of the Scriptures. The Stoics also accepted many superstitions about astrology and a whole system of astral religion that came to flourish in the Greek and Roman world after 200 B.C.

They taught submission to authority in politics. In general, doing one's duty meant submission to anything that comes to you. Stoicism made a strong appeal to many of the statesmen, judges, lawyers, administrators, and businessmen who held together the Roman Empire. It profoundly influenced the Roman law both in legislation and in legal interpretation in the courts, pushing law always in the direction of the ideal of justice embodied in the concept of "natural law." It improved the treatment of women and slaves and helped to bring justice to the peoples Rome conquered. The most famous figure in Latin literature, Virgil's Aeneas, is a Stoic who follows the stern road of duty. Stoicism influenced St. Paul and some of the early Christian writers. So close was the spirit of Stoicism to Christianity that Seneca was considered almost a Church Father by the Middle Ages, and a curious legend arose that he had a long correspondence with his contemporary, St. Paul.[13]

Marcus Aurelius said, "our days are a pilgrimage and a sojourning," but the journey, unlike Christianity, had no clear goal. Stoicism throve because it was a philosophy of suffering; it fell because it was a philosophy of despair. For Stoicism held out no hope for the future of mankind. In this dead air of later antiquity one of the many things Christianity brought was a hope for the future of both the individual and society. Often the Stoic made a desert in his heart and called it peace;

the price is excessive. But Stoicism still remains as the nearest approach to an acceptable system of ethics for those who cannot accept revelation but still keep some faith that there is a purpose in things. Finally it should be observed that in Epicureanism, and still more in Stoicism, we see the ancient world slowly turning from the "nothing in excess" of the famous inscription of Delphi and the golden mean of Aristotle's ethics to an ascetic view of life. Passions and desires, which were in themselves neither good nor bad except in the manner of their use, are now declared evil. For the earlier classical ideas of temperance there is gradually substituted a doctrine of renunciation.

Faith in reason had in one phase or another characterized Greek philosophy through all its changes from Thales of Miletus down, though from the time of Pythagoras on, reason was often subordinated to ethical ideals and values, and, at the same time, was related to some sort of a vast spiritual world order. This second current of moral philosophy steadily got the upper hand, and the older Greek interest in scientific problems gradually declined. The last great works of Greek science, Ptolemy on astronomy and Galen on medicine, appeared about A.D. 160. A decline in Greek science parallels the growing interest in ascetic and other-worldly philosophies and religions that offer ways of self-perfection or even of self-annihilation outside the state and beyond the bounds of men.

The first three centuries of the Christian Era saw many rival schools of philosophy and many religions flourishing side by side. The old philosophic schools—the Platonists, the Aristotelians, the Cynics, the Skeptics, the Cyrenaics, the Stoics, and the Epicureans—were still active. Alongside them grew up new schools of Neo-Pythagoreanism and Neo-Platonism, and, in addition, philosophic sects of astral theology, of Gnosticism, and of Hermes Trismegistus, strange mixtures of philosophy, traditional religion, science and pseudo-science, mystery religions, and plain superstition. These philosophies and religions borrowed extensively from each other's ideas and rites. Eclecticism and syncretism became so extended that all of the philosophies and religions shared many ascetic and mystical ideas, and their differences frequently lay in the emphasis placed on one philosophic theory or on one religious rite as against another.

Most interesting and significant of these currents for later history is the Neo-Platonic school. The philosophy of this famous school is one of the last creations of the Greek philosophic spirit, the other being early Christian theology. No schools of Greek philosophy carried abstraction further. Both were characterized by an extreme subtlety and an abuse of analysis which ended in mazes of innumerable distinctions, but all the analyses were heated by a deep emotional fervor and exaltation. Alexandria was the greatest commercial and cultural center of the eastern Mediterranean world, and it was there the Neo-Platonic school was founded by a Christian, Ammonius Saccas, who had deserted the faith. Among his pupils were the philosopher Plotinus, Longinus, and Origen, the greatest of the Greek Fathers of the church. The presence of the young Plotinus and the young Origen in the same school inevitably reminds one of a later day when John Calvin and St. Ignatius Loyola were both students together in the University of Paris. Plotinus (d. A.D. 270), after studying in Alexandria, stayed for a time in Persia, and finally settled in Rome, where he founded a school. From his youth, he seems to have been filled with a consciousness of sin and a need for achieving peace. He was an extreme ascetic and mystic; tradition has it that he was ashamed he had a body and that he could never remember the names of his parents or the date of his own birthday.

At the center of Plotinus' system is a transcendent force, the One God. All flows out of the One by a series of emanations and to him everything returns. Though everything flows out of the One, he is never diminished. The One is apart from the world, is all powerful but is essentially indefinable, for to define the One is to limit him. The God-head, to Plotinus, is a trinity. From the One, the first emanation is universal Mind, the world of ideas, containing the archetypes of all things in the phenomenal world. From Mind comes the next emanation, Soul, which manifests itself in individual souls and gives existence to all things in the world of phenomena. By study, by prayer, and by ascetic practices we may attain to some knowledge of the One. The world of phenomena is due to a falling away from the One, but there persists in every human soul a longing to return to it. Man may rid himself of some of the restrictions of matter, and, rising above the world of the finite, penetrate to the universal. Evil is an illusion, as in modern Christian Science; evil is a matter of misguided mortal man

On the heights of a mystic experience, the distinct conceptions of the intellect fade into the haze of an immediate identity with the One. So the philosopher—the faith is for the few, not for the many—rises first above the life of the senses, then above the life of the intellect to a sort of cosmic consciousness, "the flight of the alone to the alone." Plotinus is super-rational but not anti-rational. He does not despise the intellect, for man's intellect is nearest of all exalted things to the One. The cultivation of an intellectual insight into the structure and purpose of the universe and into the values of all types of existence is an essential preliminary task on the road to the good life of contemplation. On this road the philosopher hopes for an occasional ecstasy in which personality and consciousness are left behind and in which he feels a fusion with the divine, a union in which there can be no shade of separation. Plotinus had an ascending ladder of virtues in which the highest form of existence possible to man is a life of pure contemplation. His biographer tells us that he was himself warmed by the divine presence three or four times in a long lifetime. (This ecstasy with Plotinus is of a corroborative character, and is not, as with some of his followers, a substitute for philosophic inquiry.) We already begin to breathe the atmosphere of the catacombs and the cloister.

Plotinus' great work, the *Enneads*, presents a very subtle and complicated metaphysics warmed by a pulsating religious faith. He is everywhere absorbed with the problem of how the soul can pierce the curtain about it and escape from this charnel house of the flesh and the world. It is a philosophy of the intellect enraptured, a system of thought based on Plato and on Aristotle's chain of being, but much more other-worldly. Matter becomes almost an illusion. His system, unlike that of Plato, provided a vast hierarchy of intermediate beings or existences who bridged the distance from God to this world. There were also some evil spirits, powers of darkness, scheming man's misery. All these concepts squared with popular notions of good and evil spirits active in the world. In his elaborate and detailed descriptions of spirits in his hierarchy of the emanations from God, Plotinus and his followers contributed mightily to the vogue of angelology, demonology, magic, and astrology of all the later Christian centuries.

Neo-Platonism profoundly influenced Christian theology and philosophy. Origen in the East and Augustine in the West were both immersed in Neo-Platonism. Augustine's conversion to Neo-Platonism was the last step of a long spiritual Aeneid before his final conversion to Christianity. He finally renounced Neo-Platonism because it was too cold and impersonal, could not reach the masses of mankind, and above all because it lacked a religious leader like Jesus.[14] Writing in the eleventh century, Psellus, the Byzantine scholar, defined God in purely Neo-Platonic terms: "God is not the sky, nor the sun, nor anything that can be perceived, nor the best possible mind, nor a Platonic form apart from matter. God is of an unfathomable nature." [15] Western Christian thought got a second great infusion of Neo-Platonism through the writings of John Scotus Erigena in the ninth century and a third infusion through the works of Ficino and Pico della Mirandola in the fifteenth century.

The Christian thinkers all recognized that both Plato and the Neo-Platonists had a great conception of the Divine, but by the time of Plotinus, Christianity was two centuries old. By the third century, both inside and outside Christianity the goal of life was salvation in another world, a world far beyond the power of mortal mind to comprehend or mortal effort to attain. Only a sublime and supernatural strength coming down from God could assure weak mortals of attaining their goal. These assurances came to men, through philosophy or through religion or through both, as a "gift of the spirit," "a radiant vision," or "an illumination." Union with the divine came only through experience of Him. The soul, in its essential nature, is capable of coming into contact with the One, for it is akin thereto, but is hindered by its connection with the corporeal. The soul must train itself to wait in holy stillness in which all sense-perceptions are set aside; the soul must be taught to turn in upon itself and reject all consciousness, even self-consciousness. Then in the soul's depths there is a union with the One. This union with the One must be experienced; it cannot be described. This union is an illumination which gives assurance of the existence of the One but not full knowledge of its nature. By this union man becomes divine. Knowledge is no longer obtained by mental effort alone but by revelation.

The weaker sides of Plotinus were carried further by some of his followers. Porphyry was a great popularizer; he edited the *Enneads* and prepared them for publication. In his own writings he introduced a lavish amount of allegorizing and laid great emphasis on ascetic practices. His best known work, *An Introduction to the Categories of Aristotle*, was translated into Latin by Boethius in the sixth century and became of enormous importance for mediaeval philosophy. Another Neo-Platonist was Iamblichus the Sublime, whose works are a tedious collection of remarks on all sorts of subjects with masses of quotations from every kind of writer, at once diffuse, commonplace, and confused. He admitted all the pagan deities to his system, allegorized them, mixed magic, superstition, and bits from the philosophers of the past to make a sort of united front against the Christians. Julian the Apostate made Iamblichus' synthesis of religion, philosophy, and magic the official doctrine of the empire for a time in the fourth century. With Iamblichus one is groping in a murky atmosphere of theosophical fantasies. Iamblichus believed that the divine powers that emanate from the One can animate that which has no soul and set in motion that which cannot move—pebbles, bits of wood, and the like. The wheel has come full circle and we are back where we started with a belief in the forces that lie in all things in nature. Old seeds that had long lain dormant put forth new shoots. The philosopher now yearns for magic and sorcery and is credulous on principle. In this mystic atmosphere of late antiquity strange ideas shot up like weeds in a hot house. Iamblichus' life, as told by his Neo-Platonic biographer, is as full of miracles as the contemporary life of St. Anthony by Athanasius. The common superstitions of the masses had now wound themselves into the systems of thought of the highest philosophers.[16]

The last of the Pagan Neo-Platonists was Proclus (d. A.D. 485), who tried to systematize the whole body of Neo-Platonic writing and joined it with the cults of paganism. His work is a sort of metaphysical museum with all the stages of being catalogued and laid out on their proper shelves. He was so eclectic that he is said to have practiced the ceremonial abstinences prescribed for the sacred days of all religions. Proclus' works are very well organized and systematic and he was much studied by the Greek Fathers of the church. The whole system of Dionysius the Areopagite was built on that of Proclus, and, through Dionysius, Proclus deeply influenced the thought of both the Greek East and the Latin West throughout the whole mediaeval period.

When in A.D. 529 Justinian closed the schools of ancient philosophy (because they were not Christian), they were all deeply under the influence of Neo-Platonism.

3. THE MYSTERY RELIGIONS

THE POPULAR mystery religions did much more to modify the traditional religious ideas of the Greeks and Romans than did art, literature, or philosophy. As the intellectuals lost faith in the old gods and as the worship of the ruler seemed but an empty rite, they often turned to philosophy. When this loss of faith affected the masses they usually looked to the mystery religions. Back of these mystery religions was a long evolution about which little is known. The only persons who could have left us information about these cults were the initiates themselves and they were pledged to secrecy. So historians have had to depend on scattered literary references, on archeological finds, and on the descriptions of the mystery religions in the early Christian writers who regarded these religions with a somewhat jaundiced eye. Each cult seems to have begun as a nature rite connected with the change of the seasons, but, in the course of time, the old myths had been reinterpreted and the rites reorganized to turn on the birth, death, and resurrection of man.

The oldest cults in the Graeco-Roman world were those in Greece that were connected with the worship of Dionysus, of Orpheus, and of Demeter. With these very interesting cults there were myths that explained that man had a twofold nature; he was part divine and part earthly. In the beginning the rites connected with the cult of Dionysus were of a barbaric nature, characterized by ecstatic transports and erotic excesses, processions with torch bearers at night, shrieks and howls, tearing to pieces of animals, and the eating of their still palpitating flesh. Thus the initiate might have the feeling that he shared in a larger life and shared too in the spirit of the god embodied in the animal eaten. He became "enthusiastic," literally the state in which "God is in man." As early as the sixth century B.C. there was connected with the cult of Orpheus (a spiritualized Dionysian cult) the idea that ritual purity was not enough. Through some ascetic practices a moral purity must also be striven for, and the lower world, where dwelt the spirits of men after death, was transformed into a place of punishment.

Much the most is known about the rites of Demeter, first celebrated at Eleusis in Attica and spreading from there to other centers. The ceremonies there included a dramatic passion play and a communion service in which the initiate shared the sorrow of Demeter in giving her daughter to the king of the underworld each autumn, and her joy in her daughter's return in the spring. The old cult rites had been given a higher spiritual meaning at least as early as 500 B.C. The initiate felt his soul lifted from the body in which it had been imprisoned, and he gained an inner assurance of salvation. Besides the ceremonies, the initiate had to perform various ascetic acts such as abstaining from certain foods. Here we can see, as in other mystery religions, an old act of ritualistic purification being transformed into an act of moral purification.

The Greek mystery cults, which undoubtedly influenced deeply the philosophies of Pythagoras and Plato and their followers, were never much extended either in Greece or outside Greece. The great changes in popular religion after 300 B.C. were due to the spread of mystery religions originating in the Near and Middle East of which the most important were those of Magna Mater from Asia Minor, of Isis from Egypt, and of Mithra from Persia. The story of the spread of these and similar cults lies chiefly between 300 B.C. and A.D. 300. In the Greek and Roman world before 300 B.C. one finds currents of Orphism and cults like that of Eleusis and of some foreign mystery religions and the philosophic schools of the Pythagoreans and the Platonists. At the other extremity, in A.D. 300, Christianity is about to become the official religion of the Roman Empire. To find these cults accepted among large numbers of people, and to find a wholesale borrowing of gods, of rites, and of religious ideas until syncretism had made practically one religion in the vast Roman world, one would have to come down to A.D. 100. The two centuries between A.D. 100 and 300 constitute the period of most rapid change, and they form the most fascinating chapter in the history of the West. Everywhere men were saying: "Here on earth we are under tension and trial; how deep is the pain, of what worth is the act; what must I do to be saved?"

One of the oldest of the non-Greek cults was that of Magna Mater, which spread from Asia Minor through the Greek world from the sixth century B.C. on, and reached Rome in 204 B.C. According to her myth, the Great Mother, the source of all life, was infuriated at the unfaithfulness of Attis, her lover. She drove him mad so that he emasculated himself beneath a pine tree into which his spirit passed; at the same time his blood was transformed into violets. The Great Mother mourned over her dead lover and brought him back to life. It is a nature myth: Attis, the god of vegetation, is loved by Mother Earth, but vegetation fades. The mother mourns in autumn and winter, but in the spring she is able to restore Attis (vegetation) to life. In the rites of the cult, the annual festival was celebrated in March. After preliminary ceremonies, a pine tree was felled on the 21st of March and taken, wrapped like a corpse in woolen bands and garlands of violets, to the temple of the goddess. After some days of mourning, the pine was buried amid highly emotional ceremonies in which the priests made shrill cries, clashed cymbals, played piercing notes on flutes, and flagellated themselves. Those who intended to join the priesthood in the height of the ceremonies emasculated themselves with stones, repeating the experience of Attis, and, at the same time, giving the goddess all their fertility. Then followed a vigil during which the worshipper was supposed to be united with the goddess. On the 25th of March there was a wild jubilation, the pine was dug up, Attis had come to life. The ceremonies ended on the 27th of March with a procession through the streets of the town.

Connected with the rites of Magna Mater was a baptismal ceremony, the *taurobolium*. Widely spaced planks, or an iron grill, were placed over a ditch in which stood the candidates for baptism. A bull was then slain, the blood ran down like red rain onto the naked initiates; this act was supposed to wash away human sin and weakness and to give initiates a second birth. The pit probably signified the kingdom of the dead; the initiate who entered the pit is thought to die; the bull is Attis, and the blood that rains down is his life principle. When the initiate leaves the pit he is said to be born again, and to symbolize this regeneration, he is, as a newborn infant, given milk to drink. After twenty years the ceremony was repeated. There was also a sacred meal at which the initiates ate bread, sacred to Attis and embodying his spirit. The bread and other food eaten were served from a drum and a cymbal, instruments sacred to Magna Mater. The rites of Magna Mater were crude, though a highly spiritual interpretation came to be given to them, and the rites became vehicles for a deep religious experience.

The cult of Isis from Egypt seems to have been more refined. It too involved a supreme female deity and her lover, Osiris, who gave the arts and laws to men. Osiris is killed and is reborn by the efforts of Isis. As one text says (the words refer to an initiate of the cult): "As truly as Osiris lives, he also shall live, as truly as Osiris is not dead shall he not die." [17] Isis, like Demeter and Magna Mater, was a mother goddess personifying the force of life in nature and the human hope for a final triumph of life over death. The ceremonies of the cult were elaborate and to the worshipper deeply impressive; the cult of Isis had a great attraction for women in the Greek and Roman world. The public services included a daily liturgy in the morning and a benediction in the afternoon; these were accompanied by chanting, the ringing of bells, the sprinkling of holy water, and the burning of candles and incense. As with the official cults and the other mystery religions, the shrines were left open, and the faithful could come at any hour to meditate and pray. "Indeed," says Frazer, "the stately ritual with its shaven and tonsured priests, its matins and vespers, its tinkling music, its baptisms as aspersions of holy water, its solemn processions, its jewelled images of the mother of god, presented many points of similarity to the pomp and ceremonies of Catholicism." [18]

The keenest competitor of Christianity and the most moral of all the mystery religions—and several have been omitted from this account—was Mithraism from Persia. Here was a form of old Zoroastrianism, a dualistic system in which the powers of light and darkness were contending for mastery over the universe and over the soul of man. Mithra was an agent of light, the upholder of truth and virtue, and the implacable enemy of evil. His legend represents him as a mighty hunter who slays the bull. To a nation of herdsmen, the wild bull stood for the idea of unrestrained power, needing to be brought under control for the service of man. Mithra is represented as chasing the wild bull and finally mounting his back and slaying him. The birthday of Mithra was celebrated on the 25th of December, and his sacred day was the first day of the week. Mithra was an unfailing help to mortals in their struggle for a life of virtue. He strengthened his followers against the spirit of evil and the temptations of the flesh. For those who merited it, he assured a happy immortality. Sacred rites and ceremonies, including a baptismal rite with water and later the *taurobolium* (borrowed from the cult of Magna Mater) and the eating of a sacred repast of bread and wine identified the worshipper with a hero-savior. Moral living deepened this identification. Mithraism seems to have had no woman devotees, and its great appeal was to soldiers; from one end of the Roman Empire to the other, from Scotland and the Rhineland to the sands of Africa and the borders of Persia, often in the most out-of-the-way army posts as well as in the big cities, shrines of Mithra have been dug up. As in the other mystery religions the worshippers were gathered into organized companies bound by ties of secrecy, brotherhood, and mutual help.

The Church Fathers denounced the mystery religions as inventions of the devil to trick the unwary. Modern scholarship is not in agreement on the subject of how much Christianity drew from the mystery religions. At one extreme scholars hold that the borrowing of the Christians was extensive; at the other extreme, the critics believe that what influence on Christianity was exerted by the mystery religions was indirect, through the general atmosphere diffused by them. On one aspect of the subject there is widespread unanimity: the mystery religions, through their teachings, their ceremonies, and the moods they invoked, helped to prepare the masses and smooth the way for the acceptance of Christianity.

The range of the mystery religions was as great as that which lies between Greek Orthodoxy or Roman Catholicism and Quakerism or Unitarianism in modern times. And in any given religious cult there was evidently a great interval between the highest and lowest manifestations, a long gamut in the spiritual life. But in spite of all such differences and contrasts, all the mystery religions and Christianity had much in common. All embodied an imaginative and emotional appeal that the old traditional paganism of Greece and Rome lacked. Like the later schools of Greek philosophy, but in much simpler terms, they offered full explanations of the meaning of life. All appealed, at once, to both the head and the heart. All borrowed freely from each other and each, except Christianity, identified its deities with those of another, so that the Phrygians recognized their Great Mother in the Syrian goddess, the Greeks and Romans saw Dionysus or Bacchus in the person of Osiris and Hercules in the Hebrew Samson; in the Persian sun god, the Greek and Roman saw Apollo, and in Magna Mater and in Isis they recognized Demeter or Ceres. So the varied religions became translatable one in terms of another. This syncretism is shown in the frequent assertion in mystery documents that a given deity represented the totality of the divine nature. Rites, formulae, and ritual passed freely from one religion to another. All, except Christianity, were tolerant, and a person could belong to several mystery cults at once. They all taught, however, that without initiation into a mystery, there was no hope of immortality for the individual. All were supported by volunteer brotherhoods recruited mostly, though not entirely, from the lower classes. Unlike the official religion, they received no state support.

Each of these cults had a long and venerable tradition as old as that of classical paganism or older, and each had a set of sacred writings, stories, ideas, and ritual practices that were capable of a lofty and spiritual interpretation. The oriental mysteries and Christianity had each a professional priesthood which ministered to the needs of the individual and usually conducted missionary work. Only the priest could administer the sacred rites. All were, at the same time, both monotheistic and polytheistic; one deity made the world and sustains it, but other divine forces are at work—saviors, heroes, spirits, or saints.

All of these religions were God-centered, not man-centered in outlook; all were other-worldly and regarded life as an adventure in eternity. All were filled with a sense of the weakness and shortcoming of man, but all believed there was a divine element in man which could be released. All were indifferent to or belittled reason. Man could not save himself; only some force outside this world could start man upward. All satisfied a demand for a future life and regarded this life as a preparation for a more real existence beyond the grave. Man's rebirth and salvation was the result of a quasi-magical and quasi-spiritual operation. All, except Mithraism and Christianity, were primarily religions of faith rather than of works; the divine was released by correct ritual, and correct knowledge (*gnosis*), and communion with the divine was secured by emotional rather than by ethical means. Most were colored by some ascetic ideals and practices. All were supernatural and rose above reason, above man and above the world. Each had a place for a savior-mediator between the individual and the supreme divine force. The individual achieved a mystic union with the savior by prayer, by ascetic practices, by the eating of some symbol of his being, by the passionate contemplation of the spectacle of his suffering death and his resurrection, and, finally, in certain religions, by living a more moral life. All had impressive rites and ceremonies with candles, flowers, holy-water, chanting, bells, and incense. All were international, for all peoples and all classes, and all were highly individual, speaking directly to the heart of the worshipper, and all laid emphasis on the dignity and value of the individual.

By A.D. 300 this variety of religions in the Roman Empire had become so impregnated by Stoicism, Neo-Platonism, astrological myths, and Oriental mysteries that there seemed to be only a single religion whose doctrines were the following: adoration of the elements, the rule of one god with many spiritual attendants, assurance of salvation by sacred rites, punishment for the evil ones, and an eternal life for the saved. The temples of the old gods still stood open and the official priests, supported by the state, still performed the ancient rites. The traditional routine of ceremonial worship was still performed, but crowds no longer thronged these temples. The day of the old gods was passing. "Let us suppose," says Cumont, "that in modern Europe the faithful had largely deserted the Christian churches to worship Allah or Brahma, to follow the precepts of Confucius or Buddha; let us imagine a great confusion of all the races of the world in which Arabian mullahs, Chinese scholars, Tibetan lamas, and Hindu pundits should all be preaching fatalism and predestination, ancestor-worship and devotion to a deified sovereign, pessimism and deliverance—a confusion in which all those priests should erect temples of exotic architecture in our cities and celebrate their disparate rites therein. Such a dream would offer a pretty accurate picture of the religious chaos in which the ancient world was struggling before the age of Constantine." [19]

Slowly the classic world had turned, during a millennium, from animism and a simple type of nature religion through rationalism to monotheism, asceticism, and mysticism. Steadily the ancient world was turning mediaeval long before it became Christian. Slowly ancient culture had swung from the primitive religious animism of early ages through clear channels of logical thought to a sense of world worthlessness and from belief in man as man to an emotional immolation to the supersensuous and the super-rational. It had changed from the love of the beauty of the human body and of this world to flight from this world and condemnation of all that was corporeal. The Greek word for athlete, "asketés," has become the word for ascetic. So the old wisdom had become foolishness and the old foolishness wisdom. The world of Homer had become, at long last, after nearly twelve centuries, the world of Constantine. Here, if anywhere in man's long history, was a re-evaluation of all values.

CHAPTER II

The Jewish and Early Christian Sources

of Mediaeval Faith

1. JUDAISM AND THE OLD TESTAMENT

2. THE DIASPORA AND PHILO THE JEW

3. THE NEW TESTAMENT AND THE BEGINNINGS OF CHRISTIANITY

THE OCCIDENT is the heir of a double antiquity; alongside the classical background of mediaeval Christianity and culture lie the great traditions of Judaism and early Christianity. These two strands of culture must have had many things in common, or, later on, they could never have fused. But they started from different premises; the Greeks sought after knowledge, the Jews sought after righteousness. In the quest, however, each culture ranged over the whole of existence and independently discovered nearly all the worlds of thought and emotion knowable to the mind and heart of man.

1. JUDAISM AND THE OLD TESTAMENT

THE OLD traditional religions of the Greeks and the Romans were not embodied in sacred books. Judaism and Christianity and, later, Mohammedanism were religions of the book. The name, Bible, may come from *biblion,* papyrus rolls, or from Byblus, a town in Syria famous as a papyrus market; as we have it, the Bible was written down between 1000 B.C. and A.D. 150. The longest part of this holy book, the Old Testament, is a collection of what the ancient Jews regarded as their best religious literature, a very small selection collected and extensively edited out of a huge mass of material. It reached its present form about A.D. 100. The Old Testament, as we know it, covers many centuries and embodies a long evolution. It resembles a book that would comprise the best of Greek literature from Homer through Proclus—*ca.* 850 B.C.–A.D. 500—or the best of Latin literature from the *Laws of the Twelve Tables* through Gregory the Great, the last of the Latin Fathers of the church—*ca.* 450 B.C.–A.D. 600. The Psalms, for example, are an anthology that covers hundreds of years, from about the ninth century B.C. to the third century B.C. If the Greeks and the Romans had no sacred books, the Jews, in their turn, produced no scientific or metaphysical works. The Hebrew vocabulary remained very concrete; it had few abstract terms. This meant that the Jewish writers usually kept their ideas within the understanding of the masses.

Tradition attributed the first five books of the Old Testament, the Pentateuch, to Moses, the Psalms to King David, the Proverbs and the Song of Songs to his son, Solomon, and the various books of prophecy to the prophets whose names they bear. The higher criticism of the nineteenth and twentieth centuries has greatly modified these views. On the basis of discoveries in archeology, anthropology, and philology, it is evident that the Old Testament was the work of many minds, and that besides those who wrote it originally were numerous editors who later rewrote much of it. For centuries it was edited and re-edited, parts were deleted, and new parts written in to make the text fit into later schemes; the Pentateuch, for example, seems to be the work of writers and editors between about 850 and 400 B.C. But for slow centuries men believed that the authors of these books were the ones mentioned in them or those whose names had become attached to them, and this belief is in itself very important in the history of religion, literature, art, and music.

The books of the Old Testament were regarded as messages from God, so they were considered very differently from the way in which the Greeks and the Romans looked at their literature. God had centered history around the Hebrew people, and he had created for them a code of ethics which was to be found in their holy writings. Among the Jews, as later among the Christians and to some extent among the Mohammedans, the books of the Bible came to be more revered than understood. Often, too, they were not read as wholes but were considered as vast collections of oracular sayings which had to be illuminated by theological subtleties, allegorical interpretations, and ritualistic formulas. These were usually in the hands of the priests, a sacred caste which the traditional religions of Greece and Rome did not have.

The Old Testament shows that the Jews were originally polytheistic in religion and that their monotheism and their idealism were the results of a long evolution. Sin was a half-material pollution, largely divorced from considerations of morality. The earliest concepts of a single god were those of a local god of Mt. Sinai, then of a war god, and then of an agricultural god. It was Moses (about 1200 B.C.), who introduced the distinctive elements in Hebrew religion and made Yahweh the Hebrew God. Moses' God was human in form and thus was not a mere name for an impassive natural force; his God was a person, though he was invisible; he was the creator of the universe and the source of justice. Moses' God was dictatorial, jealous, and resentful like an Oriental despot. From him, the faithful sought material benefits such as the destruction of one's enemies, new lands, the multiplication of flocks and of children, and a long and plentiful life on earth with little concern about another world. Moses set up the idea of a covenant between the Hebrews and Yahweh, a contract of obedience and protection. All in all, Moses not only enlarged the Hebrew conception of God but he also gave the Jews a sense of destiny as God's people and furnished them the basis for national unification. He stands in history as the creator of Judaism. During the period of the exile in Babylon (586–536 B.C.), the Jewish leaders deepened and broadened the concept of God until the Jewish idea of God had a moral grandeur unmatched by any other conception of the divine in history.

The Hebrew tradition from Moses onward shows that there was frequently a deep conflict between the point of view of the priests and that of the religious teachers, the prophets. The priestly tradition tended to represent a rule of ritualistic observance and an elaborately regulated rule of conduct. The prophetic tradition leaned toward a

personal, spontaneous, and immediate approach to God, often in conflict with the ritual and the ceremonial rules of the priestly caste. To
the general populace and to their leaders sin was often only a neglect
of ritual regulations; to the prophets it was a violation of the moral
law. Amos, the first of the prophets whose writings have been preserved (eighth century B.C.), says: "Now therefore hear thou the word
of the Lord: I hate, I despise your feast days. Though ye offer me
burnt offerings, I will not accept them. Take thou away from me the
noise of thy songs. But let judgement run down as waters and righteousness as a mighty stream." [1] Isaiah put the whole idea in two words,
"wickedness and worship." "Hear the word of the Lord," says Isaiah,
"to what purpose is the multitude of your sacrifices unto me; I am full
of the burnt offerings. Bring no more vain oblations; incense is an
abomination unto me; your appointed feasts my soul hateth. Make
you clean; put away the evil of your doings; relieve the oppressed;
plead for the widow." "What," says Micah, "does the Lord require of
thee, but to do justly and to love mercy and to walk humbly with thy
God." [2] Or, as Jesus said: "Ye shall know them by their fruits." This
conflict between the priestly and the prophetic traditions carries
through the whole history of Judaism, and from Judaism the conflict
extended into Christianity and Mohammedanism.

The Hebrew word "prophet" means one who is called or given a
vocation by God. The Hebrew prophets were forth-tellers rather than
fore-tellers; they saw visions and spoke with superb confidence, courage, and intensity. They attacked the polytheistic religions and what
they called "false gods" about them, and they insisted that purity of
heart is of more avail than ritual purity. "Rend your hearts and not
your garments." There must be an inner and personal righteousness
and a direct relation of the individual to God. They condemned not
only those who had too much faith in ceremonies, but also those who
did not build their lives on sound principles of justice. The prophets
denounced luxury, immorality, self-indulgence, and cruelty. Especially
were some of them severe on those who oppressed the poor. "Some remove the landmarks," we read in Job, "and they violently take away
flocks; they drive away the ass of the fatherless; they take away the
widow's ox; they cause the naked to lodge without clothing; they
pluck the fatherless from the breast." [3] The prophets were always the

voice of a minority; they usually worked against common ideas and practices. They were generally unpopular, and, to a large extent, were failures in their own time, "despised and rejected of men." But they are the crucial figures in the development of Judaism. Their mark is everywhere in the Old Testament; the history of the Jews was edited under their influence, and the law was modified to embody their ideals. As Greece revered her philosophers and Rome her statesmen and soldiers, the Jews came to exalt their prophets.

The prophets conceived of God as a god of power and transcendence, far above the world, but also as immanent, in the world and interested in men. With the Jewish prophets, God is the creator and controller of nature; he is also the creator and sustainer of a lofty moral law. At the same time that he is all-powerful, he is interested in every man who seeks him. God is above all creation yet active in men's affairs; he dwells not only in the sky and on earth but in the heart of man. He is the unseen partner in the fortunes of the nation and of the individual who follows his will. The great achievement of the Hebrew prophets was to have combined God's transcendence and his immanence at once. They did not, on the other hand, work out a theology, and later the Jews, the Christians, and the Mohammedans had to borrow from the Greek philosophers to create a reasoned defence of their religious ideas.

Later Judaism (especially in Hosea) conceived of a loving God as well as a God of justice, though as in Greek and Roman religion, all stages of religious development existed side by side. One stage did not supplant the other, but the whole complex proceeded in a contrapuntal fashion; the new came alongside the old but never supplanted it entirely. In the last centuries before the beginning of the Christian era some of the Jews accepted ideas from Persia: the concepts of Satan and of a fiery hell and of a glowing heaven, of a last judgment when all would be called again before God, and of hierarchies of angels and demons. The Persian influences, however, seem to have had little effect except where such beliefs had already started in Judaism. Most of the fundamental ideas and attitudes of the Jews were taken over by the Christians and still later by the Mohammedans.

Mediaeval men saw in the Old Testament a vast collection of stories, and they accepted these stories without any feeling for their historical setting. They took these tales to their hearts, allegorized them, and meditated upon them. These stories begin with the tale of creation, of Adam and Eve in the Garden of Eden, of their temptation and fall, then the fatal story of Cain and Abel, followed by the tale of the flood and of Noah's Ark. Next comes the story of the Tower of Babel, followed by tales of the early patriarchs, Abraham (about 1800 B.C.), Isaac, and Jacob, of how Joseph was sold by his brethren into slavery in Egypt, of the oppression of a community of Jews in Egypt. This brings the reader to the story of how Moses reformed the religion of his people and led them to the borders of Palestine. Then Joshua conquered Palestine. Next follows the Book of Judges, named for the Jewish religious and political leaders, wherein are the great human tales of Samson and of Ruth. Then there is the story of the Jews under Samuel, followed by an account of the growth of Jewish power in the days of David and Solomon (1010–937 B.C.) when all the Jews were united and their earthly power was most magnificent. Then the tale goes on with good kings and bad, in which times the Jewish state was split, until defeat leads to exile. The northern kingdom of Israel fell in 721 B.C., and the southern kingdom of Judah was overthrown in 586 B.C. From these times on, the Jews were often under the foreign rule of Babylonians, Persians, and Romans. The later books of prophets denounced the sins of men and set forth the wisdom and power of God. All these writers preached a stern morality for which, unlike any philosophy, the prophets claim the authority of God. God first revealed himself to the Jews, but, in the end, some of the prophets believed he would reveal himself to all men and bring all men to righteousness. Those who look up to God need never despair. Nothing can really defeat them. God's cause will always win—though in God's time. The story of the chosen people, through happy years and years of misery, is brought, in the Old Testament (including the Apocrypha [4]) down to the beginning of the Christian Era. Most of the great stories of the Bible were, for many centuries, far more familiar to men than the history of their own forebears.

Throughout the Old Testament there runs a tone of grandeur, solemnity, and power rarely if ever reached by the writers of Greece and Rome, even by Plato, Virgil, Lucretius, or Plotinus. The style of the great Hebrew writers was influenced by that of Egyptian, Canaanite, and Mesopotamian religious literature, but it far surpassed them. Indeed, there are parts of the Old Testament that, in their grandeur, reach beyond anything in world literature. In making any selection, one is embarrassed by riches. "It is the day of the Lord's vengeance," says Isaiah, "and the streams shall be turned into pitch, and the land shall become burning pitch. It shall not be quenched night and day; from generation to generation it shall lie waste, the bittern shall possess it and the owl and the raven shall dwell in it, and he shall stretch out the stones of emptiness. They shall call the nobles thereof, but none shall be there, and thorns shall come up in her palaces, and it shall be an habitation of jackals and a court of owls." [5] Even grander poetry is found in Psalms like The One Hundred and Fourth. This sublime tone of the Old Testament runs through the New Testament and from these sources it entered early Christian and mediaeval literature.

The Old Testament, then, is the great sacred book of the Jews, of the nation and the faith "chosen of God." It contained the classic account of their national history, from the beginning of the world through nearly the whole of antiquity. It comprised also the statement of the divine laws of God, which they must revere and obey. It treasured for them a body of sublime poetry, deep aphorisms of wisdom, and immortal stories of their heroes. Its prophecies denounced their sins, healed their wounds, promised God's help, and foretold the triumph of righteousness. The Jewish priests and teachers interpreted all this. Every faithful Jew revered it. Few outside the little region of Palestine knew much about it; it was all the possession of a small but intensely earnest, self-assured, and at times self-righteous nation. The unique thing about this Old Testament was its connection of a stern morality with a lofty religion. It was the most profoundly moral book that the Occident produced before the beginning of the Christian Era.

In view of the influence of Judaism, it is important to notice some of the later ideas and attitudes that are hardly, if at all, present in the Old Testament. It contains little mysticism; it is one thing to adore God, to talk with him, to walk with him, and to try to do his will; it is still another to desire to merge oneself with him. The mysticism in the Christian and Mohammedan traditions came from Greek philosophy and from the mystery religions. Likewise, the Old Testament contains little asceticism, little of the war of the body on the soul. The Hebrew writers condemned sensuality; they were more Puritan than the average Greek and Roman writers, and, unlike the Greek and the Roman law, the Hebrew law held that there should be no sex relations except for the procreation of children. But the Old Testament is far less ascetic than Pythagoreanism, Stoicism, and Neo-Platonism. The Old Testament contains no references to a glowing heaven as the abode of the dead; all persons on their death went to Sheol, the land of no return, beneath the earth. The messianic hope in the Old Testament is usually not centered on a person, but on a day when the Jewish state shall be purged of its unworthy members and a righteous remnant shall flourish. When the messiah was conceived of as a leader there was no agreement as to when or how he would come. Finally, the Old Testament contains little or nothing about the Holy Ghost, the Trinity, or the Virgin Birth as these doctrines appear in the New Testament.

What then of the Old Testament survived in later Judaism, in Christianity, and to a lesser extent in Mohammedanism? Above all there survived the Jewish concept of an all-powerful, just, and loving God; the idea of a holy book which reveals God's ways and his will; the use of a sacred caste set aside to direct religious services, the concept of an orthodoxy to which all should conform, the close interpenetration of state and religion, but hostility toward foreign governments and emperor worship, and an unwillingness to take part in state ceremonies and to appear in the gymnasium, the theater, and the arena. There survived also the idea of a divine plan in history. The Greeks and the Romans regarded the whole world process as an eternal repetition and a vain recurrence; the Jews introduced the idea of history moving from God's mighty act of creation toward the fulfillment of God's will on earth. This divine plan was associated with a divine community, a people chosen to be the vehicle of God's purpose. The Christians and Mohammedans took over this idea of a grand design, modified it, and used it for their own ends. The later faiths likewise adopted the idea of a vital connection of public and private morality and religion, and the belief that, though the king is God's anointed one, government is bound by a divine law, and authority in the family and in the state and the ownership of property are all trusts from God. The Christians and the Mohammedans took from the Jews the idea that all others were wrong. Most Jews believed that their faith was for the Jews alone; a few Jewish teachers wished to make converts. From Judaism, Christianity and Mohammedanism took their belief in the creation of the world, and in God's continuing ability to change the forces of nature at will. The Hebrews were a great miracle race and the Old Testament is full of inconsistencies, contradictions, and absurdities: the statement that the world was created in six days, that a flood destroyed all living creatures except those that were on the ark, that the sun was stopped, and stories of talking serpents and asses and of Jonah three days in the belly of the whale. These, together with the occasional glorification of violence, cruelty, and bigotry came over into the later faiths derived from Judaism. Finally, some of the forms in the Christian and Mohammedan services came from Judaism: the reading of the holy book, chanted prayers, congregational singing, and preaching.

2. THE DIASPORA AND PHILO THE JEW

THE JEWS were a small nation surrounded by large and powerful states which frequently conquered them, and yet it is amazing that, down to about 175 B.C., they remained little influenced by the cultures about them. That the Jews escaped assimilation and submergence was due to their stubborn and inextinguishable loyalty to Yahweh, to their stern code of ethics, and above all, to their powerful consciousness of a special, divine mission. Even in their darkest periods this sense of a mission animated some of their leaders who, in turn, could always rally a saving remnant to stand on the Lord's side against all compromise with heathendom.

The Jewish dispersion (the Diaspora) had begun back in the sixth century B.C. with the removal of an elite of the nation to captivity in Babylon. Gradually, from this time on, the Jews had become settlers all over the Mediterranean basin. In scattered centers, they no longer lived on the land, but dwelt in the cities as merchants, moneylenders, craftsmen, and intellectuals. In the eastern half of this area Greek was the *lingua franca,* and, wherever the Jews went, they learned and used the popular Greek language (*koiné*). They held on to their religion, though they were more liberal in their interpretation of Jewish ideas and were naturally more influenced by Greek philosophy and the mystery religions than the Jews who stayed in Palestine. Outside Palestine, the Jews made converts among the Gentiles. In a world craving spiritual regeneration, Judaism attracted men by its appeal of a venerable antiquity, always an important item of apologetic in the Graeco-Roman world, by its lofty conception of God, and by its stern morality. Inevitably these converts in accepting Judaism brought with them, from the gentile world, the current philosophic and religious ideas. So, from two sides, the outlook of the Jews of the Diaspora began to show the influence of the outside, gentile world.

It was in this world of the Diaspora, particularly in some of its great urban centers like Alexandria and Antioch, that traditional Judaism was most deeply modified. In Alexandria, in the third century B.C., the Pentateuch was translated into Greek; this version was called the *Septuagint* because it was traditionally supposed to be the work of seventy-two translators. Some time later the rest of the Old Testament was translated; this version became widely known in the Jewish communities all over the Mediterranean area. Outside Palestine the average Jew thought and spoke Greek, although he religiously kept the Sabbath, took part in the services of the synagogue, and practiced circumcision. At the same time the Jews learned to regard God in Platonic terms or as the Aristotelian "unmoved mover." Some of them identified Moses and Osiris and conceived the idea that the Greek philosophers had received their first inspiration from the great Hebrew teachers. It was from such Hellenized Jews, who had laid aside some of their older ideas, that Christianity largely took its early converts.

Typical of the currents of thought in Judaism at the beginning of the Christian Era is the work of Philo the Jew (d. *ca.* A.D. 50), a contemporary of Jesus and St. Paul. Philo belonged to the wealthiest Jewish family of Alexandria, the greatest commercial port and the most important melting pot of ideas of the time. As a youth he came into contact with Greek philosophy and the mystery religions. His experience must have paralleled, in part, that of St. Paul, the other great Jewish writer of the Diaspora. One can imagine the effect on the sensitive and gifted young Philo, whose mind was filled with the solemn words of the Old Testament law and the glowing utterances of the prophets, when, for the first time, he read the sublime pages of Plato. He may also have known some Stoic who told him of the worthlessness of all things but virtue and inner strength. These ideas were quite different from anything in his own books, and yet they were just as stirring in their passion for justice and for truth and in their faith that behind this world there was a universal force that cared for good. Here, surely, the young Jew found ideals that drew him by their similarity to his own. Philo must, too, have early come under the influence of older Jewish writers and teachers who had tried to combine Judaism and Greek culture—thinkers who did not regard themselves as going out of Judaism but only deeper into it.

The great desire of Philo's life was to further this work of uniting Hebrew ideas and Greek philosophy. Like other Jews of his time, he borrowed from the Stoics their allegorical method of explaining away all that was absurd and vulgar in the Greek myths, and he applied the method to some of the stories and ideas of the Old Testament. By the use of allegory he tried to explain away those things in Judaism that would be repellent to the Greeks: circumcision, the distinction of clean and unclean foods, and the use of the Sabbath. Philo explained that the whole Pentateuch (the only part of the Old Testament in which he showed much interest) was an allegory of the virtues and vices and the processes of the soul. More specifically, he tells us that the Jews in Egypt represent man in the body; Egypt is the material world; when the Jews went to Palestine they moved away from a purely material existence toward a higher and more immaterial world. Philo not only wished to show his fellow Jews the wisdom of the Greeks, but, by his system of allegory, he wished to prove to the Greeks the excellence of the Old Testament.

Earlier Hellenistic Jews had made extraordinary claims about their ancestors, namely that Moses invented writing, that Abraham taught the Egyptians astrology, and that Pythagoras, Socrates, and Plato had derived their wisdom from Moses. Philo elaborated on these ideas. Reading the Jewish Scriptures through Greek spectacles, he identified Plato's world spirit with the divine utterances of Moses, just as the Christian writers were very shortly to identify Plato's world spirit with the Christ, the second person of the Trinity. Thus the Platonic idea of the spirit or utterance or deputy of God, the expression of divinity that was itself divine, was at nearly the same time being worked into both Jewish and Christian thought. This explanation made it possible to retain the idea of the uniqueness and transcendence of God but, at the same time, to make God manifest to men. Moses, in Philo's system, is not only the Platonic world spirit but he is also, at the same time, the holy mortal of the mystery religions. Christian writers were shortly to make the same claims for Jesus.

Philo's message to his fellowmen is to suppress the flesh and identify oneself with God. The aim of all human experience is to live as little as possible the life of the body, of the senses and of the passions, and as much as possible the life of reason and of the spirit. His God is a transcendent abstraction with little relation to the traditional God of Judaism. God is placed far above the world so that he can never conceivably come into contact with matter. The soul of man can only approach the highest divinity by moving upward through the emanations of God: the realm of angels and powers, then, higher to that of the world spirit, or divine reason, and at last to God himself, whose existence man may realize but whose being man can never grasp. Man's highest aim is this knowledge of God, and man's highest experience is an ecstatic contemplation of God which culminates in a mystical union with him. Much of this mysticism derives from Plato and the mystery religions. Philo's system is definitely a syncretism, but a very mystical one. On the heights of contemplation, he is lifted out of his ordinary round of successive thoughts and feelings; the flow of time vanishes, the soul is absorbed in an eternal Now. The universe lies before the soul like an open book, and the soul is swept with a marvellous uplift and joy.[6] Philo's writings are vague and often confused, and his work is a mixture of learning, pedantry, insight, and naïveté; it is already definitely mediaeval in tone. As a philosophic thinker, he anticipates many of the ideas of the Neo-Platonic School two centuries later, but his writings lack the power, depth, and scope of those of Plotinus.

In the thought of Philo the Jew, as in later religious philosophies, the philosopher starts with the conviction that there is one infallible source of truth, God, and that he is revealed in the Bible. In these holy writings, the religious philosopher finds a description of the world, with references to earth, water, air, and fire, the heavens and the stars, and all material things and living creatures; with these materials the philosopher may begin to understand the world. He finds, too, in these sacred books, divinely ordained rules of conduct. God has furnished a great revelation to man; he has also endowed man with reason. And man has discovered many useful truths with his reason; many of these truths are embodied in Greek philosophy. The divine books and Greek philosophy are, thus, two collections of writings which contain all knowledge and truth: the first, the wisdom made known by revelation; the second, the wisdom discoverable by reason. Since God is the source of both these types of truth, there can be no contradiction between them. If a conflict should appear it is due either to man's misunderstanding of the divine writings or to man's mind being misguided by the vile body in which his mind is imprisoned. So in practice the Jewish, Christian, and Mohammedan religious philosophers begin with the Bible's story of creation, the belief in divine providence, and the belief in God-given rules of conduct. Then, assuming these divine truths, they search the writings of the pagan philosophers to illustrate the divine principles. When a conflict arises, the religious philosopher may explain it away by allegory; more frequently he denied the statements of the Greek philosophers. From Philo and other Jewish thinkers of the Diaspora much of all this entered into Christianity, first in St. Paul, then in the Fourth Gospel, and, more significantly, in the Church Fathers. At the same time, Philo's writings set the pattern of the religious philosophies of Judaism, Christianity, and Mohammedanism. From Philo came both the predecessors and the successors of Averroës, of Maimonides, and of St. Thomas Aquinas.

3. THE NEW TESTAMENT AND THE BEGINNINGS OF CHRISTIANITY

Out of Judaism came Christianity, and out of the Old Testament grew the New Testament. The Jewish Old Testament covers about two thousand years of Hebrew history; the New Testament covers only about a century. To the early Christians the Scriptures were the Old Testament, and only about A.D. 110 did they commence to think of their writings as constituting the beginning of a New Testament; not until about A.D. 185 was there any agreement on the canon of the New Testament. The selection finally made was chiefly based on the age of the books and on how they conformed to what was considered to be the teaching of the first followers of Jesus. Until the invention of printing in the fifteenth century, both the Testaments were used in parts rather than as a whole.

The New Testament is the record of how a small Jewish sect, the followers of Jesus, laid the foundation of a new religion. It is a record of beliefs more than a narrative of events. The New Testament, as finally arranged, opens with four accounts of Jesus: his birth, his youth, his preaching of from one to three years, his trial, crucifixion, and resurrection. The first four books bear the names of the "Evangelists," the bearers of good tidings; all seem based in part on an oral tradition. At first no one seemed to think it necessary to write down anything, for the second coming of Jesus was momentarily expected. As the years passed, this hope waned, and it was deemed necessary to have records to carry on the Christian teaching. By this time, various ideas seem to have crept into the tradition of what Jesus had said and had done.

The earliest of the four Gospels is probably that of Mark, which seems to have been written (in Greek) in Rome just before A.D. 70, more than a generation after Jesus' death. It is a strongly dramatic account, which shows Jesus as the son of God, coming with miraculous powers. Much of Matthew and Luke was taken out of Mark. Matthew, written about A.D. 85 to 90, presents Jesus as a great teacher, the successor of Moses, and Jesus is made to fulfill ideas of some Jewish groups about the Messiah. Most valuable in Matthew are five reconstructions of Jesus' sermons. Luke is the work of a physician who had been converted; the author seems also to have written the Book of Acts. Christianity is presented as a logical outgrowth of Judaism. The last gospel, that of John, written between A.D. 95 and 110, links Jesus to Platonism and presents him as a philosopher. The Acts of the Apostles lays emphasis on the career of Paul. After these five books of narrative, there are twenty-one pastoral letters, most of them addressed to special bodies of Christians; some discuss specific points of ethics and doctrine, others are general expositions of the faith. Nine or ten of these letters are the work of St. Paul. The last book of the New Testament, the Book of Revelation or the Apocalypse, differs from all the others. It is a vision, resembling Ezekiel, chapter 1, and Daniel, chapters 7 and 8, written to encourage Christians being persecuted in Asia Minor about A.D. 95. Symbol is piled on symbol, and the whole is composed in the most ecstatic style. All that is clear is that there is to be a last judgment, whereupon this world and all that is in it will pass away and the faithful will enter the New Jerusalem. The interpretation of this book in the last two thousand years has shown that nearly anything can be read into it. As in the case of the Old Testament, certain works of lesser inspiration were collected into a Christian Apocrypha, though, unlike the Jewish Apocrypha, these books were never included by the later Christians in their canon of the Bible. No part of the New Testament seems to have been written by anyone who ever saw Jesus or heard him speak. The earliest book, in the form in which we have it, is probably St. Paul's First Epistle to the Thessalonians of about A.D. 50, and the last, the Second Epistle of Peter of about A.D. 150.

The central figure in the New Testament is Jesus of Nazareth. Jesus' immediate background in Palestine was one of restlessness and of hatred of Roman rule and a revival of an old idea of the return of a golden age when the Jews would again be united, free, and prosperous. For some Jews, there was hope of a new leader, a personal messiah, the anointed one, though even in such circles there was no agreement whether he would be a warrior, a king, or a spiritual leader. Many Jews of the upper classes did not share these dreams and hopes. Jesus, in the spirit of many Jewish prophets before him, proclaimed the coming of a spiritual kingdom where righteousness would prevail. He denounced the selfish, those who did not love God nor follow his teachings, and who did not love their fellowmen. Jesus was especially severe on the religious leaders of the Jews whom he regarded as self-righteous hypocrites, deceivers of the Jewish people, " blind leaders of the blind." Like the Hebrew prophets, Jesus was a revolutionary in revolt against the established religion in the name of a more strenuous faith and religious life.

He evidently had a high estimate of the moral powers of the common man. He did not have the gloomy pessimism, either of the current philosophies and religions of his time outside Palestine or of some of the later Christian leaders. Man needed God, but man could do much for himself; and, through the efforts of men of good will, a better society could be built. There is no indication that Jesus was particularly ascetic, and he was certainly a simple unlearned man. All the later, elaborate theories of original sin, of free will versus predestination, of the nature of the Trinity, of the Virgin Birth, and many other dogmas of the church would probably have amazed him. In the surviving accounts of him, Jesus showed no interest in organizing a church, in a theology, or in a system of ritual, liturgy, and sacraments, though he himself observed most of the traditional Jewish rites. Nor did he present a theory of property or a political program.

Jesus expressed many of his moral ideas in parables to illustrate some particular point. His parables and his other sayings reflect country scenes: ploughing, sowing, reaping, lost sheep, the beauty of wild flowers. He knew little of city life, as did Paul, and little of the world outside Palestine. Unlike Paul, he seems to have known nothing of the history, philosophy, art, literature, politics, and religions of the Greeks and the Romans. All he knew of what we call science was the simple belief that God did everything and was so near to earth he numbered the hairs on men's heads. Jesus was a man of the people, virile, vivid, and forceful. His teaching is not systematic; it dealt chiefly with particular situations, though occasionally he preached a general sermon. There are many aspects of his life and teachings of which we have no record; we know, for example, of only about sixty days out of his life of over thirty years.[7]

Jesus' basic idea seems to be, first, to observe God's law, in spirit rather than merely in the letter. This law was in the Old Testament, but it needed a new interpretation: "I come not to destroy the law, but to fulfill it." Man must love God and he must have an inner communion with God. God will do his part in this relation, but man must also strive to meet God. Second, Jesus taught that every man must love his fellows as himself and do unto them as he would that they should do to him. His first interest evidently lay in reforming Judaism and in breathing new life into old forms. The love of God and the love of one's fellowmen is to supersede much of the Jewish ceremonial law, though it carried on the most important moral and spiritual elements of Judaism. Jesus apparently believed himself "the Son of God" and "the Messiah," and he believed he would suffer death at the hands of his own people, the Jews.[8] These ideas, however, are never clearly defined in what we know about him, and they are subordinated to his message of loving God and one's fellows and so aiding to bring in a reign of justice here below.

To the populace, Jesus did not speak in the terms they anticipated; he preached the love of God and of one's fellows and of building the kingdom of God on earth, when they expected an appeal to revolt. To the learned, Jesus must have seemed an ignorant pretender; to the priests and the upper classes he seemed a dangerous agitator who might stir up the masses to one of those violent revolts which had always been sternly put down by the Roman authorities. They also disliked him for his denunciation of their riches and their hypocrisy. Others he merely bored. The Roman authorities regarded him as another Jewish crank. The Jewish religious authorities accused Jesus of blasphemy in pretending to be the Messiah, and of subverting civil authority by calling himself "King of the Jews." So to please certain classes among the Jews, the Roman authorities agreed to his crucifixion, then considered the most ignominious way of putting a criminal to death. To his followers, his suffering for his beliefs on the cross became the glorious crown of his life.

The miracles connected with the story of Jesus seem to have been colored by those who passed on the oral and, later, the written tradition. Without any intention to deceive, they interpreted events in his life in terms of ancient heroes and in terms of the myths of the mystery religions.[9] But the stories of the New Testament, like those of the Old, were believed literally for centuries and were known to millions who pondered on them and made them subjects for literature, art, and music. The greatest of all miracles, however, remains: the deep impression of the personality of Jesus and of his message on the history of the future. If we find little in the New Testament with which to reconstruct the story of his life, the New Testament nevertheless reveals a personality of unmatched insight into the roots of human nature. His teachings are paralleled in those of Oriental, Jewish, and Greek teachers, but nowhere in history has there appeared such a personality to drive these ideas home. As a teacher he is beyond Moses and Isaiah and Plato, though in the same great tradition; moreover, he was crucified as they were not. His personality and his teaching about God and the love of man are many times more important than all the rest of Christianity. Jesus has been rightly called by Loisy "the highest manifestation of the human conscience seeking justice." All this makes him the supreme miracle of history.

Jesus' first followers were so impressed by him that they believed him to be divine and believed him the promised Messiah, and they began to worship him accordingly. They believed he had risen from the tomb and had ascended to heaven. The insistence on the resurrection and the ascension is central in the preaching of the first Christians. His followers explained that he did not reign at once because the Jews were not ready for him. No one thought of founding a new organization; they all expected his second coming, and, if they wanted to do anything immediately, it was to try to reform Judaism as Jesus had done before them. Jesus had devoted his teaching to a reform of men's lives; his earliest followers asked men to worship him. Jesus had insisted first on a right attitude toward God; his first followers insisted first on the right attitude—their own—toward Jesus.

Most of his earliest followers, who came from the lower classes among the Jews of Palestine, had no idea of spreading their beliefs among the Gentiles. It was impossible for them to conceive of the acceptance of the gospel by the Gentiles without its acceptance first by the Jews. But some followers did carry the story of Jesus and his teaching outside Palestine to Jewish communities of the Diaspora. Those Jewish groups were less strict and more willing to accept new ideas than the Palestinian Jews. And among these communities the influence of Greek philosophy and of the mystery religions had been profound. Here Platonic idealism and metaphysics, Stoic ethics, and the idea of a Savior God had penetrated Judaism. It was this transformed Judaism that prepared the way for the spread of Christianity; this is the world in which Philo the Jew and St. Paul grew up. This Hellenistic Judaism of the Diaspora is the great bridge between traditional Judaism and the early Christian church.

The Christianity to which Saul of Tarsus was converted on the road to Damascus was already in existence in Jewish communities outside Palestine.[10] Paul modified it and passed it on through his writings. He did not create it. Paul, however, left so deep an impress on Christianity that he is often called its "second founder." He began his career in a large Greek city of Asia Minor as a devout Jew, "a Jew of the Jews," a rigid observer of the Jewish law. He found no peace in his strict practices and was unsatisfied. He must have learned early about Greek philosophy and the mystery religions, which may have helped toward his conversion, as they were to help in many other conversions to the new faith. Exactly how this vivid and driving man heard about Jesus we do not know. After his conversion, at about the age of twenty-five, he turned to spread the new faith among all men.

Those outside Jewish circles would have no interest in a purely Jewish Messiah who would be intelligible only in connection with the nationalist hopes of the Jewish people, nor would they respect a spiritual leader who had met the most disgraceful of deaths. But outsiders were interested in Jewish and Christian monotheism and ethics, and they were acquainted with the idea of saviors who died and were reborn and with whom men could be united in a mystical way. To meet this situation some converts, including St. Paul, conceived of Christianity in a new light. They believed the new faith was for all men everywhere, that the old Jewish ceremonial law was no longer necessary, and that Gentiles could become Christians directly. Paul, who was of an authoritarian temperament, quarreled with some of the other Christion leaders, especially the group in Jerusalem. They insisted that any outsider who joined the new faith must first become a Jew and observe the Jewish law. Paul's view finally prevailed, and he did more than other leaders to cut the new Christian faith off from Judaism and launch it as a world religion.

In his Epistles, written between A.D. 50 and 62, Paul is commenting on Christian ideas and doctrines already in existence in an oral tradition. Paul shows himself a man of deep feeling and burning conviction and a magnificent stylist. There is no evidence that the Epistles were written for publication; but they so impressed those who received them that they were later collected and published. Paul had, as few men in history, that quality Aristotle called "greatness of soul"; he possessed enormous energy, an iron will, and a genius for leadership and organization. He was convinced that Jesus was a divine being, who by his death and resurrection saves those who are united with him by a mystic faith—"salvation by faith," as the doctrine was to be known in history. This mystic union with the divine one, the Christ, replaced the observance of the old Jewish law. It was the result of moral living, of worship, of prayer, of works of charity, and of the rites of baptism and the Lord's Supper. These last he considered as sacraments, acts that in and of themselves are effective in changing the relation of God and men.

Paul's Christ had existed with God through all eternity. God had sent him to take on the form of man, and he had died to soften God's wrath against sinful men. Paul quotes Jesus only once; otherwise he never refers directly to Jesus' sermons or teachings. He preached, as he said, "Christ crucified." This interpretation of the life of Jesus as a divine sacrifice was the great contribution of Paul to Christian thought. Here, in addition to the old Jewish dogma of the fall of man in Eden, we have the doctrine of the incarnation of God in Christ, and of the atonement, that is, of Christ's suffering for the sins of man. The Christian believer must die in the flesh, and, by moral living and the sacraments, be reborn in the Christ. Paul created the Christian view of history by placing the Crucifixion and the Resurrection as the central events in all time and all existence. The drama that began in Eden reached its climax on Calvary and will culminate in a Last Judgment.

In ethics, Paul was ascetic but less so than some schools of Greek philosophy and less so than the Jewish Essenes and the Church Fathers. He prefers continence to marriage, but he accepts marriage—"it is better to marry than to burn." His ethics are essentially those of Judaism with some elements of Stoicism. He has no specific social gospel; he tells you to stay where you are—if you are a slave make no effort to be free. "In the condition in which God has called each let him walk." Not the amelioration of society, but one's own salvation is the end of life. But, in a broader sense, Paul has a social gospel in his insistence that all men are brothers, and in his preaching of the ideal of justice. "Ye are all children of God; there is neither Jew nor Greek, neither bond nor free, neither male nor female, but all are one in Jesus Christ." [11]

Paul's ideas are a vast synthesis of divergent elements; his ideas come from many sources, and they contain the seeds of future confusion and conflict. He combines, for example, the Jewish, Greek, and Roman ideas of certain religious laws and duties that must be fulfilled with the Platonic idea and the ideas of Gnosticism and of the mystery religions of a mystical experience that lifts one up to and identifies one with God. He conceives of baptism and the Lord's Supper not as pieces of magic, but as necessary aids to a mystical identification with Christ and through him with God. Neither the sacraments alone nor good works alone will save man. Not till Ignatius and Irenaeus are the Christian rites transformed into sacraments, *ex opere operato,* wrought by the act independent of the merits of the priest or the worshipper. Paul also identified the old pagan deities with demons. Only the seeds of these later ideas are in Paul. Christianity issues from Jesus of Nazareth, but its real foundation as a world religion independent of Judaism is due to the early Christian leaders outside Palestine, above all to Paul.

The writers of the four Gospels move beyond Paul in their emphasis on the miracles of Jesus. The authors of the Fourth Gospel, of the Epistle to the Hebrews, and of First John emphasize the knowledge (*gnosis*) of God as the crown of religious experience and identify the Old Testament "wisdom" and the platonic "logos" or world spirit with Jesus, repeating what Philo had done in Judaism with the personality of Moses. The fourth Gospel begins: "In the beginning was the Word [logos] and the Word was with God, and the Word was God. All things were made by Him; in Him was life, and the life was the light of men." [12] The Fourth Gospel, with its logos interpretation of Jesus, was written soon after A.D. 100 for non-Jewish Christian intellectuals. It makes no mention of the Sermon on the Mount or of the Lord's Prayer and contains none of Jesus' parables. Indeed, there is little realistic setting; it is all about Light and Life and Darkness. Even the story of the last days of Jesus is modified. He becomes the "Lamb of God who taketh away the sins of the World." The book shows it was written not to supplement the first three gospels but to supplant them.

The author of the Fourth Gospel lays more emphasis on sacramentalism than does Paul. He first disparages the emphasis on religious rites—"whosoever liveth in me shall never die"—yet in other places, he promotes sacramentalism—"except ye eat the flesh of the Son of Man and drink his blood, ye have no life in you," and "whoso eateth my flesh and drinketh my blood hath eternal life." He lays great emphasis on the knowledge of God and of Jesus and urges the reader to believe that Jesus is the anointed Son of God, and that in believing one may live in his name. One of the great ideas of the Fourth Gospel is that one "must be born again." [13] The whole of this book is written on the

Platonic and Stoic basis that, while most men think and live on the physical level, there are some who are capable of understanding and of living on a higher and spiritual level. There is no longer much sympathy with traditional Judaism; Christianity is a fuller and better dispensation. If one is a mystic by temperament he will prefer the Fourth Gospel to the other three.

The later books of the New Testament lay emphasis on the idea that all Christians belong to one vast spiritual community; they lay emphasis also on the authority of the clergy and the earthly corporation, the Christian Church. There is a considerable contrast between the free, unfixed, and creative Christianity of Jesus and Paul in the first century and the organized, controlled, formalized, and much less creative Christianity of the second century. One has only to compare the Sermon on the Mount or Paul's First Corinthians with the later non-Pauline epistles to realize this. The Christian life had to be organized; it was the price of survival, but it was a heavy price and much was lost.

Heresies arose in the church, particularly with those who denied Jesus' humanity. They maintained that Jesus was only human in appearance; his soul was never really united with matter. These teachers, who were declared heretical, also believed that all matter was an illusion and that the Old Testament should be abandoned because it was either evil or outmoded. These heretics, who disagreed fiercely among themselves, came mostly from Gnostic circles. Gnosticism was a Greek philosophic cult and was of non-Christian origin. There seem to have been as many varieties of Gnosticism as there were Gnostics. Only some of the adherents of Gnosticism came into contact with Christianity which they, in turn, tried to make over. With the Gnostics, the principal basis of salvation is *gnosis* or knowledge of the divine order. Only a few are capable of this knowledge, for *gnosis* was a secret revelation given only to the initiates of the cult. Gnosticism was, for many individuals in later antiquity, a way of life. It was very ascetic and renounced the world and the flesh as nothing but change and corruption; it issued in a heavenly illumination that satisfied the intellect and touched the emotions. In some forms it was a lofty ideal; in others, it was nothing but occultism, magic, and superstition. Gnosticism in the first three Christian centuries threatened to overwhelm Christianity. This threat did not materialize, but Gnosticism deeply influenced Christianity in the direction of asceticism, mysticism, and super-rationalism. The Christians continued to fight Gnosticism into the fifth century A.D.

Before the end of the New Testament, about A.D. 150, there was arising a catholic or universal church, a state set off from the Roman state. The church was a body of scattered religious societies held together by common beliefs and a common hope. Not until the seventh century were the Christian societies of the West finally brought together by the bishop of Rome, a process that was never paralleled in the East where there never was a pope. The church had a special religious caste of bishops and priests set off from the laity, a set of ascetic, mystical, and philosophic traditions, a body of sacred writings, and a slowly forming theological orthodoxy. A liturgy and a ritual were growing, all centering in the Lord's Supper in which men believed the bread and wine were miraculously transformed into the body and blood of Jesus. Men were coming to believe that the sacraments worked a kind of magic, and their use could be divorced from morality. A Christianity institutionalized, rationalized, and ritualized was coming into existence, an amazing syncretism of Judaism, Greek philosophy, Graeco-Roman paganism, and the mystery religions. Christianity came to have in it something for everyone. "Primitive Christianity," said Harnack, "had to disappear in order that Christianity might remain."

The Christian church was at war with the old classical paganism, with the mystery religions, and with Roman government. The Roman government was usually easy going about foreign religions and admitted many strange gods to its pantheon, but it persecuted the Christians because they seemed a vast conspiracy against the law. Like the Jews, the early Christians, who by A.D. 250 formed about one-tenth of the population, would take no part in pagan public ceremonies, would not bow before the statue of the emperor, and, sometimes, refused to take an oath in a court of law or serve in the army. But persecution strengthened the church, and, in the fourth century, long after the close of the New Testament, Christianity became the official religion of the Roman state. This "Peace of the Church" meant a great change in its wealth and prestige; it became fashionable to be a Christian; large numbers crowded into the church membership and the moral tone of the church was lowered. The Roman Empire was partially Christianized and the church partly paganized. For those who found this new spiritual climate unsatisfactory, there was now an escape into the growing world of monasticism. The fight against differences and heresies in the church was never to be finished. As late as A.D. 325 there were ninety Christian sects; by the end of the fifth century this number was reduced probably to as low as twenty, most of them small in comparison with the four or five leading sects.

The reasons for the triumph of Christianity in the ancient world are various. The new faith, from the beginning, showed an enormous capacity to borrow from other philosophies and religions. Indeed, Christianity is the supreme syncretism of antiquity. This general borrowing helped to make for a worldly success, but it often obscured the personality and teaching of Jesus. Likewise, the early Christians, within a century after the death of Jesus, had developed a remarkable organization. Judaism had given the Christians a sense of exclusiveness, and the persecutions helped to give them a strong sense of solidarity. Working out from this, the early Christians organized themselves into congregations and then into large areas involving a number of congregations called dioceses, each under a bishop, and above all the bishops, a general church council. This strong but flexible organization was unmatched in any of the mystery religions. This organization was one of the chief reasons why Constantine turned to the church as a means of holding together the disintegrating imperial state.

Another reason for the triumph of Christianity was that it had back of it the whole Hebrew religious tradition and literature. In them morality and religion were bound together. None of the mystery religions could match this noble tradition. Judaism, too, presented a God whom man could seek as did some Greek philosophies and the mystery cults, but it was unique in presenting a God who was seeking man. Christianity, with its promises of salvation, also strongly appealed to the masses, especially to those who were weak, troubled, and downtrodden; the four Gospels are explicit on this. But it brought to all who sought Jesus a great cause, that of building a better world. Greek philosophy and the mystery religions offered help for the individual in a dark world that would never be better. Christianity, like Judaism, held out the hope and promise of social justice and a better society;

it held out to men a social cause for which to live and die. Certainly no Greek philosophy and no mystery religion could match the heights and depths of this faith, this hope, and this love. Finally, at the center of Christianity stood the personality of Jesus of Nazareth. He was no myth like Attis, Adonis, or Mithra, nor was he the form of a Platonic idea. He had walked the earth and was a vivid and personal force among men. His personality had a greater power of arousing enthusiasm and releasing human spiritual powers than any other in history.

The triumph of Christianity, as the residual legatee of many of the ways of feeling and thinking in later antiquity, marked a great change in the ideals of life. A new act had slowly been added to the drama of man's life, and this extra act had been put over into another existence, as Lucretius said, "beyond the flaming ramparts of this world." Life was, as Augustine said, merely the "via" on the road to the "patria," the true fatherland, in Heaven. Excellence and right was no longer a matter of the rational and strenuous endeavor of the enlightened man. Man's life was no longer in his own hands; only the grace of God could save man. Not man but God was the pattern of human righteousness: "Be ye perfect, even as your Father in Heaven is perfect." One turned to him for help and strength; the sinful self found itself only by losing itself in God and his causes. This seeking for a righteousness never reached, and this reaching up to God with the aid of his divine grace, was to be the deepest inspiration of mediaeval faith. For centuries life had been slowly wrenched off its old foundations and rebuilt on new. Roman literature had celebrated the forum in Cicero, the state in Virgil, Livy, and Tacitus, urbanity, measure, and proportion, "nothing in excess," in Horace. If one turns to Jerome and Augustine in the fourth century all this has passed away. The Church Fathers turn their backs on this world and all its ways. Society is evil, the state, property, and the family are all founded in sin; the flesh is weak and should be mortified. The last word in wisdom is to flee from the world, "for," said St. Paul, "the wisdom of this world is foolishness with God." [14]

CHAPTER III

The Patristic Age, 2nd–5th Centuries

1. THE GREEK FATHERS OF THE CHURCH

2. THE LATIN FATHERS OF THE CHURCH

3. THE BEGINNINGS OF CHRISTIAN POETRY, ART, AND MUSIC

THE ANCIENT world had been slowly turning toward other-worldliness, mysticism, and asceticism long before the beginning of the Christian Era. This transformation steadily became more marked in the three centuries between Augustus and Constantine, in the centuries that cover first the Apostolic and then the Patristic Ages of the Christian church. "Our fathers," writes Nock, "could quote Swinburne's

> *Thou hast conquered, O pale Galilean;*
> *The world has grown grey from thy breath*

and could think in terms of an antithesis between a free, untrammelled Greek mind and a dogmatic mediaevalism, or between clean-limbed models for Pheidias and unwashed hermits. That is all past now. We know that paganism had of itself gone far in the direction of grayness, asceticism, and mysticism." [1] Everywhere there was a growing sense of world-worthlessness.

Men of the highest education were no longer ashamed of being superstitious; the unpardonable sin was to be a materialist and an atheist. Sorcery, magic, astrology, sun-worship, other-worldly philoso-

64]

phies, and salvation religions were in the air. Men had turned away from the world of natural phenomena because they could see nothing in this world but change, deterioration, and decay. Only by taking refuge in their inmost consciousness with what they regarded as reality, in a spiritual world, eternal, unchanging, and divine, could they find satisfaction. Interest in science was declining. For a thousand years the eyes of men were largely closed to nature.

Typical of these centuries is the *Physiologus*, a series of popular animal stories written in Greek by a Christian in the second century A.D. Everything is moralized and allegorized. The lion brushes his footprints with his tail; this signifies the secret of the Incarnation, of the Lion of the tribe of Judah. The lion sleeps with his eyes open, so slept Jesus on the Cross, while his Godhead watched at the side of the Father. Finally, we are told, the baby lions are born dead, on the third day after birth the father breathes on them; this signifies the resurrection of Jesus on the third day. And so on through stories of pelicans, unicorns, phoenixes, and other animals, both real and fabulous, all the accounts are shaped by considerations of religious dogma. No distinction is made between the actual and the fantastic, nor did the readers make any distinction. It is true, this is a book for the masses and not for the learned; yet Origen in the East and Ambrose, Jerome, and Augustine in the West draw material from it. These stories were read, during the mediaeval centuries, from the Nile to Iceland, they were quoted by popes and scholars and wandering minstrels, and they appeared on castle walls and cathedral carvings.

From A.D. 100 on, the early Christian writers produced many books that were never included in the New Testament. There are pastoral letters, accounts of Jesus and his early followers, stories of martyrdoms, and apocalypses with elaborate descriptions of heaven and hell; in most of this writing miracles bloom with a wild luxuriance.[2] There is also a mass of early Christian writing which concerns itself with controversies over heretical movements: Docetism, Marcionism, Montanism, and Gnosticism. The most important part of the post-New Testament writing is that devoted to construction of a theology for the church. This early Christian theology, in both the Greek East and the Latin West, is the last product of Greek philosophy which may be said to have died in giving it birth.

The atmosphere of the Patristic Age (second to fifth centuries) is very different from that of the preceding Apostolic Age. The new religion was becoming institutionalized; it was rapidly developing an elaborate organization and a great ecclesiastical caste. Enthusiasm and spontaneity were passing; priests and bishops and patriarchs now took precedence over prophets. The right of appeal to individual conscience was set aside, and an authoritative dogmatic system was being formulated with a rigid organization, a sharply defined orthodoxy of belief, a fixed liturgy and ritual, laying the emphasis on grace through sacraments. Christian experience was gradually labelled, catalogued, and standardized. By the end of the fourth century all this had the official backing of the Imperial Roman government, whose full resources were now available for persecuting heretics. Christian schools were established in Antioch, Alexandria, Athens, Carthage, and Rome, schools set up to teach the correct faith, though actually they differed among themselves in what was taught. Complete standardization proved impossible. At the same time, asceticism developed rapidly and led in the second and third centuries to a great growth of monasticism. It was under these circumstances that the Greek and Latin Fathers of the church did their writing. Nearly all that is still alive in Greek and Latin literature after about A.D. 200 is to be found in these Christian writers. In both the East and the West the syntax and the vocabulary continued to undergo great changes. But, with few exceptions, it was only the Christian writers who used Greek and Latin with warmth, vigor, and conviction. Most of the later writers of pagan outlook in both languages, as far as one may judge from their surviving works, were "idle singers of an empty day."

The earliest Christian Fathers, both Greek and Latin, were disdainful of classical culture. Justin Martyr tells the Greeks that "the compositions of your poets are monuments of madness and intemperance," and Tertullian is even more contemptuous: "What indeed has Athens to do with Jerusalem?" Both men, however, show a good deal of knowledge of pagan literature. As time went on, the Fathers spoke more favorably of the great classic writers. Clement and Origen find some good in them, and the standard attitude came to be set by Origen in the East and Augustine in the West. The pagan authors might be pillaged—as the children of Israel in the Mosaic story borrowed ornaments and vessels from the Egyptians—to find arguments and literary adornments for Christian writings. Later writers would revert to an attitude of wholesale condemnation of the pagan writers. Jerome tells, in a famous passage, a story of how Christ reproached him, in a dream, for being a better Ciceronian than he was a Christian. Another often-cited passage is that from a letter of Pope Gregory the Great of the late sixth century, in which the last of the great Latin Fathers denounces a clergyman for reading the pagan writers and condemns those who would "fetter the language of the Holy Spirit with the rules of Donatus"; "the same mouth should not sing of both Jupiter and Christ." Later on Peter Damian, St. Bernard, and the Spiritual Franciscans damned those who loved the classics. These critics have too often been taken as typical of the attitude of the church toward pagan culture. The prevailing attitude, however, is that characterized by the words of Paul, "Prove all things and hold fast that which is good," or by those of John of Damascus, "Like a bee I shall gather all that conforms to the truth, even extracting help from the writings of our enemies." Actually, all the Fathers of the church down to the death of Augustine in the fifth century, and much later in the Byzantine Empire, showed the influence of their classical training in literature and rhetoric, and they showed also extensive reading in the great writers of pagan antiquity. And from Clement of Alexandria in the East and Ambrose in the West, the Christian writers respected the pagan classics, and, as far as they could, they used them.

The attitudes of the Church Fathers are so removed from modern ways of thinking and feeling that it is difficult to read them with understanding. The ancient world was disintegrating politically, economically, and morally. The hope for the future was much less in evidence with the Fathers than it had been with the Christians of the Apostolic Age and than it was to be in later phases of Christianity. One may catch something of the mood in which they wrote, at least the mood of those who lived after A.D. 200, in these remarks of Cyprian on the decline of the world:

> The world itself announces its approaching end by its failing powers. In the winter there is not so much rain for nourishing the seeds, and in the summer the sun gives not so much heat for ripen-

ing the harvest. Less and less marble is quarried out of the mountains, and the veins of gold and silver are dwindling day by day. The husbandman is failing in the fields, the sailor at sea, the soldier in the camp. Honesty is no longer to be found in the market place, nor justice in the law courts, nor craftsmanship in art, nor discipline in morals. The setting sun sends out rays that hardly warm, the old tree that once was green and hung with fruit grows gnarled and barren, and every spring in turn runs dry. The whole world is failing and is about to die.[3]

The Church Fathers wrote in the mood of Christina Rossetti's poem, "Passing away saith the world, passing away."

I. THE GREEK FATHERS OF THE CHURCH

THE EARLIEST attempts, after the New Testament, to construct a theology are found in a group of second-century writers called the Apologists. They began by defending Christianity against the accusations of pagan writers and the Roman government. Both had accused the Christians of atheism—the ancients could not conceive of a theistic religion without images—of cannibalism, infanticide, incest, the worship of an ass's head, and the adoration of a criminal who was crucified. The writers of the Apostolic Age had written chiefly for the faithful; the writers of the second century tried to influence the opinion of the world outside. The Apologists presented the Christian faith in the guise of a new and superior philosophy which claimed to supersede the rival philosophies and religions of the pagans about them. They maintained that the Christians had a faith older than any other and that Moses had inspired Plato; and they poured scorn on the idolatry and the immoral myths of the pagans. They often used the language and the concepts of Greek philosophy and of the mystery religions, repeating what Hellenistic Jews, like Philo, had done for Judaism.

The first important Apologist was Justin Martyr (d. A.D. 165), who came to Christianity from Platonism and Stoicism. His *Apology*, addressed to the emperor and the senate, asks the authorities to observe that the Christians are neither atheists nor idolaters and that they are decent law-abiding people. Ignorance of the truth is the cause of sin, and the purpose of both philosophy and religion is to know God. Justin is conciliatory toward Greek philosophy, but he insists on the belief in the Virgin Birth of Jesus and on the dogmas that Jesus is both the Messiah and the Logos. His work is not original, and the thinking in it is confused. It shows the steady growth of syncretism in Christian thought, though the author, unlike Origen in the next century, is not abreast of the best culture of his day.

Slightly younger was Irenaeus (d. A.D. 200), who was born and educated in Asia Minor, spent a period in Rome, and finally became a bishop in Gaul. Thus he knew both the East and the West. His *Against the Heretics* is the first attempt, on an extended scale, to standardize the doctrines of the church. His importance lies, first, in combatting Gnosticism and saving the Old Testament for the church, thus tying up Christian religious feeling and theology with its Jewish origins; second, in his clear exposition of the human and the divine sides of Jesus—Jesus as an ethical teacher and as God's anointed— showing how, though all men fell through Adam, they can be saved through Jesus; and, finally, in his insistence that Christian teaching must be in harmony with the teaching of the twelve Disciples and Paul. If there are questions of doctrine and discipline, they must be referred to the bishop or to a church council. He condemns many writers as heretical and his quotations from them are often all that has survived of their writings. Irenaeus was a pillar of orthodoxy and the first formulator of a comprehensive Christian theology.

In the third century Alexandria was the great center of Christian learning, and the first Christian school of which we have any knowledge was established there. The leading teacher was Clement of Alexandria (d. A.D. 215), a Greek who came to Christianity as a convert from Platonism. Clement lays great stress on a thorough training in Greek philosophy as a proper preparation for a full understanding of the Christian faith. Faith is more important than knowledge, but faith should be fortified by knowledge. "Philosophy," he wrote, "serving as a guide, prepares those who are called by Christ to perfection." Like Philo and others, he believed that God had inspired the Greek philosophers; the Logos has been active in all ages though it was only revealed fully in the Christ. Clement's principal works are the *Address*, directed to pagan readers to whom he points out the failure of all earlier philosophies and religions before Christianity, and the *Tutor*, a handbook of Christian ethics. The way of the Christian is a way of contempt of the world, of stern mortification of the flesh, and of prayer; the aim of the Christian is to know God. As with the Gnostics, it was a form of knowledge that ended with an effortless dwelling in God. Clement's toleration for pagan culture was very great. He taught that what the law was to the Hebrews, philosophy was to the Greeks; God is the source of both. He used both philosophy and allegory to iron out contradictions and to find hidden meanings. Clement had a large and luminous mind; he was a great stylist and wrote with a magnificent sweep and a glowing imagery.

More significant than Clement was his pupil Origen (d. A.D. 254), the greatest of the Greek Fathers and the most prolific Christian writer of antiquity. Harnack said of Origen that "he made Christianity part of the civilization of the world, and orthodox philosophy has never advanced beyond the circle mapped out by his mind." [4] Origen was born a Christian; as a youth he studied literature, philosophy, and science in the same pagan school where Plotinus was a student. He then went to study with Clement. In both schools, all the Greek philosophers, except the Epicureans, were freely taught. His father was martyred, and the young Origen had to teach rhetoric to support his mother and six brothers. Later he established a school at Caesarea; he died a martyr. In the school where Origen taught, all subjects were freely discussed; as one of his pupils writes: "No subject was forbidden; we were allowed to be acquainted with every doctrine, investigating the whole circle of knowledge." [5]

Origen was the first great Christian scholar who had been thoroughly trained in Greek philosophy. He also mastered Hebrew and prepared a critical edition of the Old Testament with five parallel versions in Greek, a huge work, long the wonder of the library in Caesarea. He wrote commentaries on every book of the Bible and a prodigious series of theological treatises. His best-known work, *Concerning Principles*, was the basis of all later Christian theology. Besides systematizing and explaining Christian ideas along Neo-Platonic lines, he did much to promote the elaborate deductive method later used both in theology and in scriptural exegesis. He takes a simple statement, sets forth its obvious import, then goes on to analyze and draw out all its implications. For example, the Bible says, "God is spirit"; then Origen discusses whence spirit comes, how it has been revealed to man, and how it acts. The fundamental truths are revealed in the Bible; they are not discovered by man. But to ferret out all their meaning was the work of reason. Origen made this the standard method in theology.

His God is a Platonic abstraction, out of the second book of the *Republic* and the tenth book of the *Laws*, worlds apart from the personal God of the Bible. God is pure, invisible, incorporeal intelligence. Origen, like his contemporary Plotinus, believed that all attempts to define God limit him. Moreover, if there is introduced into God the slightest particle of matter, he will partake of the perishable. Origen's God is moved into a hyper-transcendence; it is hard to see how he has any relation to the world and to struggling humanity.[6] Yet, like Plato and Plotinus, Origen believes that man may rise to God by contemplation and that some men even live in God. He combines a subtle intellectualism with a mysticism of incredible fervor. It is all more Platonic than Christian; the God of Jesus, Origen hardly understood. He identifies the angels of the Bible with the intelligences that God created in a hierarchy beneath himself. There are, also, at work in this world evil intelligences who rebelled against God. There is a vast chain of being from God that stretches from the transcendent world through Christ down through hierarchies of spirits to the ultimate confines of the visible.

The souls of men come from God and may, with his help, return to him. Redemption consists in the return of the divine elements that have gone astray into impure matter, which, as in the system of Plotinus, is near to being an illusion. He believes strongly in man's free will to choose his destiny; if a man chooses to go upward toward God, Christ will help him. Almost nothing is said about the life of Jesus or the crucifixion and the resurrection. Origen knows the Bible thoroughly, but he uses it only to illustrate his own system of Christian Neo-Platonism. From Philo and others he borrows the allegorical method of interpreting scripture, and he often carries it to great length. Truth in the Bible, he says, "is sometimes conveyed in what one might call literal falsehood." Every line in Scripture has three meanings, a literal meaning, a moral one, and, finally, an allegorical significance, and only in this last is the heart of truth. All this is part and parcel of the Platonic idea that all things visible are but blurred copies of the invisible, so the theologian, like the Christian artist and poet, must first look at all things to see what they are not.

Origen's Christ, like his God, is abstraction. As God is the divine transcendent, Christ is the divine immanent. He seems never to have understood the Jesus who lived and taught and suffered. His philosophy, at many points, is close to that of both Philo and Plotinus. We can well understand the bitter lament of Porphyry, who deplored the fact that so remarkable a thinker as Origen should have wasted his time explaining Jewish fables. Later on, Origen, after having been used by other Church Fathers, was condemned for heresy, and the most original Christian thinker of antiquity was misjudged and nearly forgotten for centuries. Yet Origen's range of speculation is only matched in the whole of Christian theology by that of Aquinas and of Calvin, who lived a thousand and more years later.

Among the Greek Fathers of the fourth century, interest centered in defining the nature of the Trinity and then of Christ. The savior must be both human, sharing man's weakness and death, and, at the same time, divine, sharing the eternal existence of God. If he were not fully human, he could not have atoned for human sin, and if he were not divine, the individual could not be saved through a mystic union with him. The insistence on Christ's humanity was to resist various currents of heresy that were always exalting his divinity, and, in so doing, minimizing or denying his humanity. The interminable discussions of the exact nature of Christ finally so penetrated the mass of the population that in cities like Antioch, Alexandria, and Constantinople, it was said, a person could hardly buy a loaf of bread without hearing these matters discussed. Defining Christ's nature followed on the earlier question of defining the Trinity. Is God one, or three, or both? From whence does the Holy Ghost proceed—from God or from both God and Christ? Nearly all the writers take it for granted that Jesus was the Messiah, the Christ, the Divine, Anointed One who was sent by God from Heaven and had returned there after his earthly work was finished. The great difficulty only came with his humanity, with his involvement with matter.

Some of those who limited Christ's divinity, like Arius, the heretic, did so because they considered it a limitation on the reverence due to God to believe that Christ had existed from all eternity. In the early fourth century a great controversy between Arius and Athanasius, an ardent Trinitarian, rocked the whole Christian world. Finally the emperor intervened, and, at the Council of Nicaea (A.D. 325) Arianism was condemned, though it lasted in certain areas into the sixth century. Arius' writings have not been preserved, but Athanasius is known from a series of polemical tracts and for a famous life of the hermit St. Anthony.

The Trinitarian position was elaborated by the three Cappadocian Fathers, St. Basil, his brother Gregory of Nyssa, and their friend, Gregory Nazianzus. These theologians were all well-trained in Greek literature and philosophy; their theology resembles that of Origen but is far less original. They went beyond Origen in clarifying the concept of the Trinity by admitting in God only one substance, but distinguishing in it three persons. Their writings had great literary qualities and appealed to cultivated readers as had none of the writings of earlier Greek Fathers. St. Basil is best known as the author of the most influential monastic regulations of the Eastern churches, and Gregory of Nyssa, the ablest of the three, had a great influence, through his writings, on Ambrose and Augustine in the West. The most popular Greek Father of the fourth century was St. John Chrysostom ("the golden mouthed"). He was the leading representative of a school of theologians of Antioch who defended a literal and thus less allegorical and theological interpretation of scripture. He was an eloquent writer and a brilliant coiner of phrases. Style carried him far, as it had Cicero; Chrysostom was much admired and imitated by Jerome, Augustine, Cassiodorus, Alcuin, Aquinas, Erasmus, and Melanchthon from the fourth century through the sixteenth. Contemporary with this group was Eusebius (d. A.D. 340) of Caesarea whose *Chronicle* is the great source of church history from New Testament times through the Age of Constantine.

The interest in theological questions in the Greek East was enormous, and the literary output very extensive. Among the later Greek Fathers the strangest is the unknown author who calls himself Dionysius the Areopagite. The name is that of a man converted by Paul and mentioned in the Book of Acts, though the writings that bear his name were evidently written just before A.D. 500. The dominant theme of this writer, whoever he was, is the method of attaining a mystic union with God. The chief end of man is to forget himself and this world and to lose himself in God. There are three roads to God: the *linear,* in which we pass directly from observing the external world of unreality to the real world of spirit behind it, an intellectual process; the *spiral,* in which we reach God through elaborate reasoning, also an intellectual process; and, finally, the best way, the *circular,* in which, turning away from all things earthly and material and abandoning reason, we emotionally lose ourselves in the Absolute Being, God. It is all very mystical, and it is not only super-rational, but also definitely anti-rational. The author, like all Neo-Platonists, cannot find words to express the greatness of God; he is above all being and above all knowledge, an abstraction above all definition. Man can only say what God is not; he can never say what he is. Our surest way to a union with God is by reading the Scriptures, by prayer, and by suppressing every human desire.

Dionysius' *Celestial Hierarchy* is a description of all the higher spiritual beings that emanate from God: Seraphim, Cherubim, Thrones, Dominations, Virtues, Powers, Archangels, and Angels. All of his descriptions are full of fanciful conceits, endless symbolism, and the mystic significance of numbers like 3, 7, and 33. His *Ecclesiastical Hierarchy* is a similar discussion of the clergy and the sacraments, their symbolism and their hidden and secret meanings. He also wrote a treatise on the *Divine Names of God* and a *Mystical Theology.* In these four books, filled with a fantastic religious emotionalism, philosophy is melted into a hymn.[7]

These works, during the mediaeval centuries, were very popular throughout the whole Christian world. The Eastern emperor sent a copy of Dionysius' writings to Louis the Pious, who gave them to the Abbey of St. Denis near Paris. This St. Denis, the patron saint of France, was popularly confused with the man mentioned in the Book of Acts, and when the manuscripts arrived it seemed very appropriate to send them to the monastery of St. Denis. So, from the ninth century on, the three men, the convert spoken of in Acts, the Byzantine author of these mystical works of theology, and St. Denis of France were commonly believed to be the same person. John Scotus Erigena translated the four works of Dionysius the Areopagite into Latin in the ninth century, and from then on, they had an enormous influence on the theologians, poets, mystics, and artists of Latin Christendom. The deeply recessed portals of the Gothic churches arranged their statues of holy beings in the order of the *Celestial Hierarchy*, and these strange books influenced men as different as Robert Grosseteste, Hugo of St. Victor, Peter Lombard, Vincent of Beauvais, Bonaventura, Aquinas, and Dante. They are the great fountainhead of much of the mysticism in the Latin Church after the ninth century, and, through the Roman Church, of the Protestant world after 1500. Even the sanest, most systematic, and most orthodox of theologians did not disdain to warm themselves at the fires of Dionysius the Areopagite. His vast fame is shown by the fact that Dante placed him high in the gleaming heavens of his *Paradiso*.

The last important Greek Father, who carries one far down into the Byzantine period, is John of Damascus (d. 754). He is known as a theologian and a great writer of mediaeval Greek hymns; his *Fount of Knowledge* is the final, great summary of Greek theology. He was a far less original writer than Origen or Augustine, on the one hand, or Aquinas, on the other, and his temper was very conservative. He writes, "I say nothing of my own," though this is not true, for he is the first Father, East or West, to make a considerable use of the philosophy of Aristotle. The first division of the *Fount* is a treatise on logic following Aristotelian lines; the second part is a history of heresies, and the third and most important section is a very comprehensive and systematic treatment of the whole of theology. Justinian had formally closed the ancient and mostly moribund schools of Greek philosophy in A.D. 529. In its later phases ancient philosophy had become in these schools an adjunct of religion and the slave of popular superstitions. The schools closed by Justinian had taught a strange mixture of the highest and the lowest in which the sciences were rejected for the secret wisdom from the East, and in which dogma had replaced reason and investigation. All that was alive in Greek philosophy was now to be found in Christian theology. With the death of John of Damascus, just past the middle of the eighth century, the sun of Greek philosophy that rose with the school of Miletus about 600

B.C., over thirteen centuries earlier, set forever in eastern Europe. It was western Europe, through the Latin Fathers and their successors, that carried on the great philosophical traditions of the Occident.

2. THE LATIN FATHERS OF THE CHURCH

THE EARLY Latin Fathers of the church overlap the greatest of the Greek Fathers; Tertullian, the first important Latin Father, was a contemporary of Origen. In the Greek East, Christianity was conceived of as a way of life that, through a special knowledge and wisdom, would unite man with God. So would man be raised up from the corrupt and mortal to the eternal. In the Latin West, Christianity was likewise construed in this way, but, in addition, it was interpreted in legal terms, requiring obedience to law. The Greek Fathers were interested in theological subtleties of all sorts, and the theology of the church was mainly their work. The Latin Fathers took over this theology and added an interest in practical ethics and church organization. The ideas of the Greek Fathers reached the churches of the West through the Latin Fathers, so that the Latin Fathers play something of the same role in relation to their Greek predecessors and contemporaries that Roman writers, like Cicero, Seneca, and Marcus Aurelius, had played in relation to the Greek philosophers.

Latin Christian literature had its first great center not in Rome but in North Africa and its first important writer in Tertullian (d. A.D. 222). As a youth he studied law; then, for a while, like Augustine, he taught rhetoric. His conversion to Christianity turned him to theological studies. He read deeply in the Greek Fathers; he knew both Greek and Latin and wrote in both languages. His was a curious mentality, at once highly emotional and legalistic, and he wrote in a violent, bitter, intolerant, but often eloquent style. In his ethics he was a Puritan of the Puritans, and in his faith a strong obscurantist. He says: "The Son of God was crucified; that is not shameful because it is shameful, and the Son of God died; that is credible because it is absurd. And he rose from the dead; that is quite certain because it is impossible!" [8] He once boasted that Christianity made it possible for the common laborer to answer all the questions that had puzzled the minds of the greatest philosophers. He is violent against the reading and study of Greek and Latin literature and philosophy, in which attitude he is far from the broad humane views of Clement and Origen. It was unfortunate that this vindictive legalism got rooted in the Latin West; not Antioch or Alexandria, with their finer Hellenic mentality, but Carthage and Rome set the mode for Western Christianity.

The most important surviving work of Tertullian is his *Apology*, which was much influenced by a similar work of Irenaeus. Here in a vituperative but glowing style he defends the Christians against all the charges made against them and asserts the superiority of Christianity over all the philosophies and religions of antiquity. He boasts to the Romans: "We are multiplied every time we are mowed down; the blood of martyrs is seed!" Tertullian takes a dark view of human life. Man is born in sin; God is a pitiless judge. God is vengeance; virtue is rooted in fear. One of the chief delights of the saved in paradise is to witness the tortures in hell of those who once persecuted them. Though he denounced philosophy and helped to keep alive stories that besmirched the memory of Socrates and Plato, he was very learned. Tertullian helped to create the Latin Christian vocabulary by coining new words and by giving a new theological meaning to many words in common use. As might be expected from one of his temperament, he quarreled with the church authorities and joined a heretical sect. The church of his time rejected him not for his puritanism but for his protestantism, his extreme individualism and his self-will. Though he was declared a heretic, his writings continued to be read.

A second outstanding Latin Christian Father was Cyprian (d. A.D. 258). Like Tertullian he was trained in the law, and he was a convert to Christianity. He later became the Bishop of Carthage, and, like Origen, died a martyr. Cyprian was much less original and less eloquent than Tertullian but better balanced. And he was particularly well fitted to pass on most of the stock ideas of the Greek Fathers. He is best known for his clearly formulated theory of the church set forth in his *On the Unity of the Catholic Church.* Cyprian conceives of the church as a vast community headed by Christ. As only those on Noah's Ark escaped drowning, so only those in the church will be saved; all pagans and heretics are lost. He insists on the necessity of conformity to a standard of belief and on obedience to the bishop and the church authorities. His theory of the church shows the old Hebrew idea of exclusiveness which had cut the chosen people off sharply from all others. It manifests, likewise, the influence of the mystery religions, which maintained that no one not initiated into a mystery could win salvation. Finally, Cyprian's theory shows the traditional Roman interest in law and political organization and Rome's long experience in controlling a huge empire. No earlier writer had so elaborated the basis for church unity and conformity, and, in a true sense, Cyprian was the founder of the Roman Catholic Church of the West.

Of the four greatest Latin Fathers, Ambrose, Jerome, Augustine, and Gregory, whom mediaeval men regarded as only a little lower than the four Evangelists, Ambrose (d. A.D. 397) was the oldest and the life of Gregory (d. A.D. 604) belongs to a much later period. Ambrose was the son of a Roman official, was educated for the law in Rome, and then was in government service at Milan. There in a controversy over Arianism—Milan remained the great center of the Arian heresy for several centuries—Ambrose spoke so eloquently that the orthodox group made him their bishop. Though he was at the time not yet a baptized Christian, he decided to follow an ecclesiastical career, and he devoted several years to intense study of the Bible and of theology. We know from his later writings that he was a well-educated man and that his favorite authors were Plato, Aristotle, the Greek and Latin poets, Cicero, Philo the Jew, Origen, and the Cappadocian Fathers. His best-known works, the *Hexameron* ("Six days of Creation"), shows the range of his reading, though it is unoriginal and is loaded with allegorizing and miracles. "To discuss the nature and position of the earth," he says, "does not help us in our hope of the life to come. It is enough to know what Scripture states, that He hung up the earth upon nothing. Why then argue whether He hung it up in air or upon the water? Not because the earth is in the middle, as if suspended on even balance, but because the majesty of God constrains it, does it endure, stable upon the unstable." [9] The great emphasis of his writings is on ethics, mostly Stoic and borrowed from his admired Cicero's *De Officiis*. His dogmatic treatises were, like those of the other Fathers, undertaken to instruct the faithful and to refute heretics.

Ambrose got into a controversy with the empress, who had accepted

Arianism. He wrote defiantly: "If you demand my person, I am ready to submit; carry me to prison or to death, I will never betray the church of Christ." In this controversy he insisted that the church must be protected by the state, that the state must respect the moral laws as interpreted by the church, that the state must aid the church to suppress all rival sects, and finally that the clergy are to be tried in church courts. The writings of Ambrose that came out of this controversy are of great importance for fixing certain ideas of the relations of the church and state. Here the emphasis is on the autonomy of the church in spiritual matters. There is, though, already in embryo the idea that the state is in certain respects subordinate to the church. "Bishops," he wrote, "are wont to judge of Christian emperors, not emperors of bishops." He also wrote some great hymns, and he may have arranged the music that still bears the name of Ambrosian chants. Ambrose was a vigorous man of action, rather than a scholar or an original thinker. He had a very Roman and authoritarian manner, and he stands among the Church Fathers primarily as a powerful personality and as the model bishop and administrator of the church.

Jerome (d. A.D. 420), the second of the four great Latin Fathers, was the son of a wealthy Christian family. He was not a convert; "from the cradle," he writes, "I was brought up on the milk of the Christian faith." As a youth he went to Rome, where he studied rhetoric with the great Donatus. Of all the Latin Fathers he was the most nurtured on the Greek and Latin classics, and later on he added to his other accomplishments a knowledge of Hebrew. After travelling widely all over the Roman Empire he fell ill of a fever. During this period he resolved to devote himself to Biblical studies. "David is henceforth to be my Simonides, my Pindar, and my Catullus." He then went to the desert and took up the life of a hermit.[10] This experience led him later to write the lives of various hermit saints, one of which, Jerome's *Life of Paul the Hermit*, became a Christian classic. Then, for a time, he studied with Gregory Nazianzus at Constantinople. Finally, the bishop of Rome set him to revising the Latin text of the Bible.

For this work Jerome settled in Bethlehem, where he spent the last thirty-nine years of his life. He made an entirely new translation of the Old Testament, translating into Latin directly from the Hebrew; for the New Testament he revised an existing translation. The resulting work, the Latin Vulgate, is a superb achievement. He used the common, everyday language of the fourth century, his style is easy and flexible, and he naturalized a good deal of Eastern imagery and modes of expression. Long after men could no longer understand the artificial language of the Latin classics, those who spoke a Romance language could understand the Vulgate. It had a great influence on later Latin poetic and prose style and it entered into the liturgy of the church, where it is still used. Mediaeval men could not think, or write, or pray without falling into the language of Jerome's great translation. He is also known for a series of theological treatises, for commentaries on a number of books of the Bible, for a Latin translation of Eusebius' history, and finally for his collected correspondence. Jerome was a sensitive and temperamental man, a gifted translator and stylist rather than an original thinker. He became the great patron of Christian scholars, and men loved to remember him, as Dürer and others represented him in art, in his quiet study at Bethlehem. His writings show him irritable and unreasonable at times, brilliant and bitter in polemic, but the most fascinating writer among the Latin Fathers. Like Chrysostom among the Greek Fathers, Jerome could turn a phrase. When he heard of the sack of Rome by Alaric the Visigoth in A.D. 410, he wrote: "My tongue cleaves to the roof of my mouth and sobs choke my utterance when I think that the city that led captive the world is now led captive." [11] Jerome still loves Homer and Virgil and Horace, and he still shows the great charm of an ancient and aristocratic culture, like a last flower on a shrunken tree. He could flay a heretic with an epigram of Horace; yet he is mediaeval in being subject to great gusts of passion and emotion and in trying to turn them all to God.

The giant of the Latin Fathers and one of the great figures of history is Augustine (d. A.D. 430). Though his mother was an ardent Christian, Augustine came to Christianity only at the age of thirty-two. According to his *Confessions,* his youth in North Africa was wild. For a time he studied at Carthage and Rome and then taught rhetoric. His education was not very thorough; he learned some Greek, but he read the Neo-Platonists and, later, Origen in Latin translations. In his style of writing he always remained the grammarian and rhetorician of the Roman decadence. During these formative years Augustine tried all the creeds of his day: traditional paganism, Manichaeism, and Neo-Platonism. He was always looking for a solution to the riddle of existence and for the meaning of life. This passionate search for a spiritual peace long preceded his conversion to Christianity. "Thou hast made us for thyself," he wrote, "and we cannot rest till we rest in thee." His progress from a Carthaginian libertine to Christian sainthood was largely the result of his studies in pagan philosophy.

He went to Milan to teach and there he heard Ambrose preach; "I came to damn and stayed to praise." Ambrose's allegorizing of parts of the Old Testament cleared away the last difficulties to his becoming a Christian. The most important element in this conversion, however, was the personality of Jesus.[12] Like Luther, a thousand years later, he was also deeply impressed with the ideas and the life of Paul. Augustine then entered the priesthood and spent the best years of his life as bishop of Hippo in North Africa. Like Luther he shaped his "ideas on the anvil of discussion," and most of his treatises were the outgrowth of controversies with non-Christians and with Christian heretics. His hottest controversies were with the Manicheans who, following the teachings of Zoroastrianism, believed that evil was a positive principle in the world, independent of God, and with the Donatists, who believed the sacraments ineffective if the priest were a man of bad character. In this controversy Augustine worked out his ideas on the nature of the sacraments. Finally he combatted the Pelagians, who believed that human nature could not but do good, and that any man has the free will to choose his own way of life. In one treatise after another, in which he treats the most abstruse questions in a fascinating and personal style, he demolished his opponents.

Augustine's theology, though much of it was based on that of the Greek Fathers, remained important for the whole future of Christianity. At the center of his system is his concept of God. God is complete being; all other beings, because they are not self-sufficient, only partake of being, and thus are only partially real. God is, also, the only adequate object of knowledge, though no man can ever completely know him. God reveals himself to man through nature and through the Bible. Nature is a key to unlocking some of the hidden meanings of Scripture, and this is the only reason why man should study nature; for example, God in the Bible is called "Light"; the better we understand what light is the better we can understand what God is. So the Christian lives only to discover the creator behind his handiwork. Augustine rejects the Neo-Platonic idea of the universe being an emanation from God. The universe was created by God in a voluntary act and in six days. There are spiritual beings inferior to God as in the Neo-Platonic system, but they were created in time by him. The universe has no stability in itself; it would lapse into nothingness unless God cared for it continually.

Evil, according to Augustine, is not a positive principle; it is the absence of true good. God permits evil to exist to make the good more evident to men. On the other hand, he believes in Satan and the revolting angels and the evil they continue to work. In ethics, he is very ascetic and puritanical; he equates love with lust and believes the highest life is that of monastic renunciation and contemplation, that without grace man can only will and do evil. Human nature is so bad that man can do nothing to save himself unless God's grace comes to him. Only a divine operation can start man upward. After God has planted the love of the good in a man's heart, then what he does with his life from that point on depends on him. Everything here is thought out in terms of Augustine's own experience. He had had personally a bitter fight with evil, and he regarded himself as a brand snatched from the burning; he is sure that only God's grace could have saved him. Augustine believed certain men were predestined by God for salvation and others for damnation. Most mediaeval churchmen rejected the theory, but it was later to be revived by Luther and Calvin.

God, in Augustine's system, not only made the universe and continually governs it, but he can, at any time, change the course of events. Miracles are always possible. Any distinction between the natural and supernatural does not exist. Miracles need no special explanation; they are no more ordinary or extraordinary than the phenomena of everyday existence. Augustine believed in astrology and in dreams as a means of finding God's will. At the same time he denounced witchcraft and sorcery as evil, though he never makes it clear where to draw the line. Like all the Church Fathers, he rejected the theory of Aristarchus that the sun was the center of the universe because Genesis was based on the theory that this earth was the center. "Nothing," he says, "is to be accepted except on the authority of Scripture, since greater is that authority than all powers of the human mind." [13]

Augustine's doctrine of the church was like that of Cyprian; the church is the Christian community organized. It is the earthly outpost of the city of God whose head is Christ in heaven. The state exists to keep the peace; it is in God's plan, but the state must be used to guide men toward righteousness. So also does God permit the family, slavery, and property if each be used to further God's work here below. The state must be subject to the religious powers and must persecute the church's enemies. We have here theories that later produced the papacy and its hierarchical theory of the state and the mediaeval Inquisition.

Augustine wrote profusely; there are over one hundred and eighteen separate titles in the list of his works. The two most read of his books are his *Confessions* and the *City of God*. The *Confessions* is a tremendous outpouring to show the evil in man and the working of God's grace. As a spiritual autobiography it has never been surpassed, and it made the incidents of Augustine's life, especially in the earlier part of it, as familiar to mediaeval men as the stories of the Bible. It is overshadowed, however, by the *City of God*. This work was called out by the sack of Rome by Alaric in A.D. 410, and the belief of the pagans that this catastrophe was due to the desertion of the altars of the pagan gods. Augustine spent thirteen years on the work, though he finally published it without the thorough revision and editing that would have cleared out the repetitions in it and given it unity. Of the twenty-two books, the first five are occupied in refuting the idea that the misfortunes of the Roman Empire are due to the desertion of the old altars; the next five are against those who believe that any but the Christian God can assure immortality. The author then goes on to explain the origin and destiny of the two cities of God and of this world. Cain, who founded the first state, and Romulus, who founded Rome, were both murderers; from this he concluded that all earthly states are founded in sin. The true state is the City of God, which extends from Eden through Calvary to the Last Judgment. All history he divides into seven ages to correspond to the days of Creation: 1) Adam to the Flood, 2) the Flood to the Tower of Babel, 3) Abraham to David, 4) David to the Babylonish Captivity, 5) the Babylonish Captivity to the Crucifixion, 6) the Crucifixion to the Last Judgment, and, finally, 7) an eternal sabbath with the damned in hell, the saved in paradise, and this earth uninhabited. In all ages, God punishes the evil and rewards the good. The work is uneven, partly due to its piece-meal method of construction. To appreciate the rolling periods and the sublime oratory of the *City of God* one should hear parts of it read aloud as did Charlemagne and many generations of mediaeval monks and scholars.[14]

Augustine encouraged his pupil, Orosius, to fill out this story with a fuller account of secular history. In *Seven Books against the Pagans*, Orosius divided history into the story of four monarchies: 1) the Babylonian of the East, 2) the Macedonian of the North, 3) the African of the South, and 4) the Roman of the West. He ignores all the cultural achievements of the past and presents a lugubrious, unbroken procession of wars, pestilences, earthquakes, and floods, a red tale of carnage, and a horrible history of devil-worshipping heathendom that preceded Christianity, all loaded with allegory and moralizing. The work was written in less than a year; it is hurriedly done, based on poor authorities, and dull, though broken now and again with eloquent and glowing passages. These fantastic distortions of ancient history by Augustine and Orosius began to be cleared up only in the sixteenth century, though they still dominate Bossuet's *Universal History* in the seventeenth century. On the other hand, Augustine's *City of God*, carrying on the Hebrew tradition, found a real grandeur in history, a divine epic. His seeing humanity as a unit, in one vast sweep, was a great contribution to thought taken over from Judaism and passed on to the future.

St. Augustine, in the whole history of Christianity after Jesus, holds a position second only to that of Paul. He is the greatest mind revealed to us in Latin literature, and he is the most powerful stylist who ever used the Latin language. He is the only Roman who can be compared with Plato. He knew all types of human beings and had unusual insight into them; he has been called "the first modern psychologist." Many of his ideas shaped the daily life of millions of Christian clergymen and laymen. His theology dominated the Middle Ages in the West, and it was the rediscovery of the Bible and Augustine in the early modern period that formed the doctrinal basis of the Protestant Reformation and of Jansenism. (There is a Spanish proverb which says that every good house contains a wine cellar and every good sermon must contain a quotation from St. Augustine.) Augustine is important in the later history of theology, philosophy, psychology, history, political thought, and ethics. He indeed fulfilled Dido's prophecy in the *Aeneid* that there would come from the land of Carthage an avenger who would give a law to Rome.

3. THE BEGINNINGS OF CHRISTIAN POETRY, ART, AND MUSIC

GREEK Christian poetry, except for some scattered fragments, begins with Clement of Alexandria in the late second century. Clement wrote a number of religious poems influenced by the Psalms but based on the classic Greek metrical system of quantity, that is, of long and short syllables. Following his example, a great deal of Christian Greek poetry was written in the succeeding centuries, the best of it, before A.D. 450, being the work of Gregory Nazianzus. His output of ethical and dogmatic verse was enormous; a few of these poems, which speak of his own religious experience, have a great beauty and vividness, qualities lacking in any of the pagan poetry of the time and in most of the Christian didactic verse. In the fourth century, the old distinction between long and short vowels went out of use. This opened the Greek language to the possibility of a new verse convention that entered Greek from Syriac. Ephraim (d. A.D. 373), a Syrian, wrote the first Christian hymns and these were immediately translated into Greek verse. The originals were written in a verse with a stress rhythm, and the translations reproduced this in Greek; the Syriac melodies were also adopted, along with the stress rhythm, and helped to fix this new rhythm in Greek usage. From this time on, Greek Christian poetry used both these conventions side by side; some of the poets wrote verses based on quantity, some wrote poetry based on a stress rhythm.

Something of the same process went on in the early development of Christian Latin poetry. Early Latin verse used a stress rhythm. About the middle of the third century B.C. the principles of Greek versification were introduced. So great was the prestige of all things Greek that the old type of poetry was considered beneath the attention of cultivated writers. But it lived on among the people, and as Christianity spread among the lower classes some of the Christian writers began to use this popular form of verse rhythm.[15] The use of this stress rhythm in Latin was delayed because, at first, the Christian communities in the West used Greek, and not until the middle of the third century was Latin commonly used in church services. About A.D. 250, Commodian wrote a series of crude poems, full of the worst sort of grammatical barbarisms, in which he attacked the Jews and the gods of the heathen, and admonished the Christians to follow the road of faith and virtue. Commodian used a stress rhythm, and he also occasionally introduced the deliberate use of rhyme, a practice hitherto unknown in Latin verse. The same use of a clumsy rhythmical scheme in Christian Latin verse is found in inscriptions from North Africa; these also occasionally add rhyme and assonance, and an acrostic construction, that is, the first letters of the verses, taken in order, form the title of the poem. None of these early Christian Latin poems are of great value as literature but they are important linguistically, for in them is to be seen a new style of versification which was, in the course of time, to change poetry. This process of change from a type of verse based on quantity to one based on a regular stress rhythm was hastened because, from the second century on, the Latin language itself was changing and long and short vowels were being pronounced more alike. By the end of the fourth century, the difference had disappeared entirely in ordinary speech.

From Commodian's time on, exactly as in Greek Christian poetry, verses written in quantity paralleled verses written with a stress rhythm. This usage continued through the mediaeval period both in the Byzantine world and in Latin Christendom. In the fourth century there was an extensive body of Christian Latin poetry; besides shorter pieces there was a long narrative poem on the resurrection called the *Phoenix* and a Christian epic on the Gospels. Both were written to provide educated Christian readers with a substitute for the perilous beauties of the pagan poets. In the same period appeared a number of anonymous hymns, notably the *Te Deum* and the *Gloria in Excelsis*, though the *Te Deum* is written in a rhythmical prose. The great Latin hymns in verse of the fourth century were mostly the work of Hilary of Poitiers and Ambrose. Hilary's hymns were didactic; those of Ambrose, while also didactic, were much simpler and touched with a poetic fire and were intended for congregational singing. His hymns are strictly quantitative but his divisions of four-line stanzas and his general style of writing fixed the form of Latin hymnody for centuries.[16] Writing rather for the educated middle class than for the people was Prudentius (d. A.D. 405), the first great Christian poet. He wrote long hymns, more like odes, using material from the Bible instead of classical mythology, lives of martyrs in the form of short epics or ballads, and didactic and theological essays in verse. The most famous of his long poems, the *Psychomachia* (the Soul's Conflict), was an epic in which the personified virtues, modesty, humility, and patience fight against the vices, lust, and anger. The work became a great favorite of the Middle Ages and deeply influenced mediaeval literature and art. Prudentius' poems are more strictly correct than those of Ambrose and are written in verse based on quantity. His output was varied and quite extensive. A few of his poems rise to the level of great writing; in these his love of Rome and of classical culture and his intense Christian fervor blend harmoniously. Although there are a few notable exceptions, Greek and Latin Christian poetry, taken as a whole for the period before A.D. 450, rarely rises above mediocrity. Its chief interest lies first in creating the type of hymn that was later to prevail, second in introducing the use of stress rhythm into the practice of poetry, and, with Prudentius, in showing the way to treat Christian history, legendry, and allegory in verse.

Architecture was to be the dominant art of the Middle Ages. Though sculpture, painting, and the minor arts all flourished, they were usually, at least until the fourteenth and fifteenth centuries, subordinated to architecture. And in the field of architecture, religious building is of first importance. The church had the wealth and could command the best talent, and it built prodigiously. The changes in church building dominated nearly all basic features of styles in secular architecture. In considering mediaeval architecture one studies the aesthetic designs of the building in relation to their uses in the services of the church, but one must also study their engineering: the methods of handling foundations, walls, and roofs. For these various reasons, most of the accounts of mediaeval art are rightly concerned chiefly with engineering problems of the vaults and domes of churches. Alongside these concerns, emphasis must also always be placed on the transcendental and other-worldly quality of nearly all mediaeval architecture, sculpture, and painting. Christianity as a view of life, and as an organization, controlled the general habit of mind and the culture of the West; it permeated all the processes of life. This religious character gives the mediaeval styles of Early Christian, Byzantine, Romanesque, and Gothic art their unity and sets them off from the art of ancient and of modern times.

Early Christian art is a phase of later Hellenistic and Roman art. After the first century of the Christian Era the traditional forms of classical art had been deeply modified, first along the borders of the Roman Empire and then inside the Empire itself. Greek and Roman painting and sculpture had been interested in a realistic, three-dimensional style, and their art was done to the measure of man and this world. In the eastern borderlands of the Roman Empire, especially in centers like Antioch and Alexandria, Oriental ideas of all-powerful gods and of a mysterious universe, and different techniques of architecture, painting, and sculpture deeply modified the prevailing Graeco-Roman style. The penetration of styles of art from the East parallels the movement westward of Gnosticism, Neo-Platonism, and the mystery religions, which represented many of the same ideas and attitudes in philosophy and religion. These Oriental styles from Egypt, Mesopotamia, Persia, and, above all, Syria, showed less interest in realism than did Roman art. They were indifferent to perspective, to the anatomy of the human body, and to realism in the representation of natural objects. Men and objects stand flat and disembodied, like an abstract pattern, on a single plane with a blank background of undefined depth; the whole thing is removed from the sphere of actual life and from this world. These new ideas and new techniques steadily penetrated the Roman Empire after about A.D. 100; the effects varied from one part of the Roman world to another, but everywhere there was a steady change in style. We begin to find in Roman art new subjects and new handling of old subjects. On reliefs, the emperor is borne to the skies by angels, on tombs men are presented no longer as soldiers or civic dignitaries but as philosophers with scrolls in their hands and far-away looks of suffering and of hope on their faces. A stiffness and awkwardness of attitude, a shift from the old classical proportion in the bodies, figures in a composition standing isolated and unrelated to one another, staring into space, and not seeming to belong to each other, and a flat two-dimensional effect—all these new features seem to show a deliberate protest against realism and against old ideals of beauty. The world of nature is growing less interesting than a higher supernatural and transcendental reality out of and beyond this world. Architecture shows the same change. Alongside traditional post and lintel constructions like those of the classical temple, there were built huge domed and vaulted buildings like the *Pantheon* and later the *Basilica of Maxentius,* both of which give the beholder a sense of infinitude. The de-naturalizing of style in sculpture goes hand in hand with a decline of skill in craftsmanship. The change is due still more, however, to a new attitude of indifference toward man and the world of nature. Men were seeking escape to a higher world, and their art, like their philosophies and religions, became other-worldly. A veil of transcendentalism hung between the artist and nature; the vocabulary of art became conventionalized and stylized. The classical style of Greece and Rome was being transformed into the transcendental style of the Middle Ages. Art, like much of the rest of classical civilization, became mediaeval before it became Christian.

The earliest Christian painting and sculpture, which dates from about A.D. 200, is found in the Catacombs. Here, in underground passages built as burial places for the dead, for whom Christian ideas forbade cremation, are found stone and stucco sculptures and crude paintings. The style is classical, but the subjects are Christian, though sometimes, as in the case of the fish and the anchor, the Christian intent was hidden. In the third century are found the Good Shepherd with the lamb across his shoulders (as in sculptures of the Greek Hermes), winged angels (from the Roman figure of victory), the fish (whose name in Greek, *ichthus,* spells out the first letters of "Jesus Christ, Son of God, Savior"), doves, sheep, a ship (the ship of life), an anchor (the Christian faith is an anchor in life, and the anchor also contains the cross), the peacock (because its flesh was supposed to be incorruptible), the olive branch (peace), the palm (victory), and praying figures. The earliest stories presented are from the Old Testament, Moses striking the rock, Noah and the Ark, the sacrifice of Abraham, Jonah and the whale (the favorite subject), David conquering Goliath, the three Hebrews in the fiery furnace, and Daniel in the lions' den. When New Testament stories were introduced, the favorites were those of the

Good Shepherd surrounded by sheep, the marriage at Cana, the multiplication of the loaves and fishes, the healing of the paralytic, and the raising of Lazarus. Nearly all of these stories represent the idea of deliverance from sin and death. These became the stock subjects for Christian art in the next thousand years. The first representations of Jesus present him as a beardless youth, like a young Greek god; this was soon paralleled by a bearded Jesus modelled on Jupiter or the type of the Greek philosopher. The Gnostics were the first to represent Jesus with a crown.

The fourth century brought the "Peace of the Church"; Jesus now begins to appear enthroned as a monarch with a court of angels about him and the halo of a Mesopotamian god or of a Roman ruler about his head. In the fifth century appeared the first representation of Jesus on the Cross and of the symbols of the four Evangelists. These symbols were derived, by Jerome and others, from the four beasts of Ezekiel's vision; to Matthew was assigned the angel, to Luke the ox, to Mark the lion, and to John the eagle. The catacombs about the city of Rome are the best places to study this early Christian iconography, though the symbols and the method of handling the subjects all seem to have come from Syria and Egypt. All this Christian material is mixed with the cupids, griffins, tritons, the seasons, garlands, and other stock Roman decorative motifs. They were all produced in a pagan environment; the artists undoubtedly worked for both a Christian and a pagan clientele. The only thing in this early Christian art that is peculiar to it is the subject matter; the style is that of late Graeco-Roman art.

The first extensive building done by the Christians was at the time of the "Peace of the Church"; before this they had worshipped wherever they could find a room, which was usually in the home of one of the faithful. In the fourth century, with wealth and state patronage available, the Christians built basilicas and round memorial churches all over the empire. They took over and modified the basilica type of Roman court or assembly hall, because the Roman temple interior was too small for the congregation, and the Christians followed the Jewish idea that religious rites should take place in the presence of the faithful.[17] One basilica form was a simple rectangular hall with a broad central nave separated by rows of columns from the side aisles which were about half the height and half the width of the nave. The build-

ing was too wide to vault and was covered with an open beamed
ceiling.

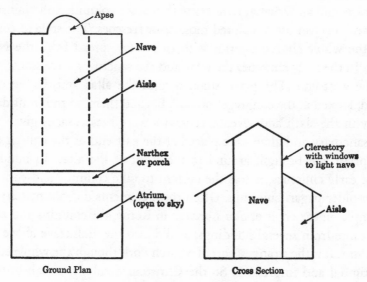

BASILICA (ONE TYPE)

Besides basilicas, various types of round and polygonal churches and
memorials were built; some of these were vaulted, some were covered
with a wooden roof. Out from the round or polygonal center, arms
were occasionally added. The churches of this type were usually
erected as shrines over sacred spots, and they were most common at
the eastern end of the Mediterranean basin. This class of churches and
memorials, which showed great variation in plan as did the basilicas, meant, for the interior, new spatial effects. The basilica interior was low and broad, quite earthly and classical in feeling. The
round and polygonal churches and baptistries laid emphasis on the upward lines of the building. By the fifth century buildings of this type
were almost always vaulted to help resist the effects of fire and earthquake. The first extensive use of vaulting, with squinches and pendentives to carry round domes over square or polygonal bases, occurred
in Asia Minor or farther east in Armenia or the borders of Persia. It
was found that the high rounded surfaces were excellent for liturgical
song and for rich mosaic or fresco decoration. Out of this style of early
Christian architecture came the great achievements of Byzantine times.

The outside of the early Christian churches was usually severe and undecorated except on the façade or about the main doorway. But the interiors had an Oriental richness with marble columns and wainscoting and a lavish use of colored mosaics or frescoes. The style of covering the whole church interior with rich color spread from the Near East. In the early churches the altar and the sanctuary were sometimes at the west end. The priest stood behind the altar and, facing eastward, looked at the congregation and, beyond them, to the front door. Only in the sixth and seventh centuries were these usages given up; the sanctuary and altar were placed at the east end of the church and the priest was brought around to the front of the altar. In building these early churches, it was the custom to take columns and cornices from older pagan buildings. Often these elements did not match; for example, in the choir of *San Lorenzo* in Rome, the columns and capitals came from several buildings, as did also the architrave above the columns. It is the strangest sort of a patchwork though the whole effect is original and impressive. So the Christian theology, ritual, liturgy, art, and music, and the church organization and discipline came from many sources and were combined into a new and original synthesis.

Christian music begins with the earliest Christians. The Bible says Mary praised God in song before the birth of Jesus; his birth was heralded by angelic chorus, Jesus intoned a song at the Last Supper, and his Apostles, especially Paul, reminded the faithful to sing Psalms and to praise the Lord with music. The earliest Christians took over the Hebrew idea that music was a proper form of worship. The first Christian music was probably that of congregational singing of the Psalms and Canticles, and, as the first Christians were Jews, the music they used was from the Jewish synagogue. From converted readers and precentors of the synagogue came the first leaders and teachers of singing in the earliest congregations. From Judaism also came an elaborate style of chanting which often used a number of notes to one syllable and also adorned the chant with ornaments like the repeated Alleluias at the end of a Psalm. There is no reason to suppose that any extensive change took place, at first, in transferring the music of the synagogue to the Christian church. As the Christians spread outside Palestine their music came into contact with Greek music, first in Syria and Egypt, and then beyond. This contact seems to have simplified the

Christian song and to have moved its style toward a method of singing in which the melody followed the metre of the text with usually just one musical note to a syllable of text.

After the earliest style of congregational singing, the next step in church music was probably a sort of antiphonal singing in which the congregation was divided and sung alternately. In the course of time, the liturgy and the church organization developed to the point where the clergy took over much of the service. The final step was the introduction of the choir, a group of clergy or a group of laymen under clerical direction. In this final form of the liturgy of both the Greek East and the Latin West, the singing took place between the officiating clergy and the choir or between two parts of the choir. In the early church, the music was unharmonized and usually entirely vocal; instruments were rarely used. Some of the early church leaders were puritanical; they could not, in view of what the Old and the New Testaments say about music in worship, ban it from the services of the church, but they would limit it. Clement of Alexandria would allow only the "lyra" and the "kithara" because there was a legend that David had used them, but Clement preferred voices alone. St. Basil defends church music as a means of attracting men to the church; it has a value in propagating the faith. Music, like the learning of the pagans, could be used by the church only if it served the purposes of the church. In the West, Ambrose and Augustine, on the other hand, were ardent believers in the value of music in Christian worship. Ambrose either wrote or edited musical settings for the liturgy, and he composed a series of hymns. Augustine speaks eloquently of the influence of music in his spiritual life. During the same fourth century a series of liturgies with varying types of music was in use; in the East there was a Syriac liturgy centering in Jerusalem, an Egyptian liturgy used about Alexandria, and, finally, a Byzantine liturgy with Constantinople as its center. In the West, there was an Ambrosian liturgy, reorganized by Ambrose, about Milan, a Gallican liturgy in Gaul, a Hispanic (later called Mozarabic) liturgy in Spain, and finally a Roman liturgy centering in Carthage and Rome. The music of these liturgies was all based originally on Jewish chant; each had, however, been modified by local influences. The two great styles of Constantinople and of Rome were only in formation by A.D. 450. In the end, they supplanted most of the other liturgies. These liturgies all contained three types of singing: first a style of solemn chant used for reading the Gospels, then a freer style from simple chant to full-fledged song for the Psalms and Canticles and hymns, and, finally, the ecstatic and freer singing of the single word *Alleluia*. These were all sung in melodic formulas appropriate to their liturgical function. Eventually the theorists assigned the melodies to the modes. Each melody is supposed to comply with a unique form within the octave; the sequences of tones within the octave are without sharps or flats, and they differ among themselves in the relative position of the five tones and the two semitones. Most of our knowledge of church music before A. D. 600 is based on literary descriptions and on later use of liturgical music. Of secular music in the first four Christian centuries, we know even less than is known about Graeco-Roman religious music. In the chant of the church, especially in that of Constantinople and Rome, there were developing some magnificent melodies and a general style of cantillation that was neither purely Hebrew nor purely Greek, but was an original creation of great range and expressiveness, a new form of musical art as fine as the mosaics at Ravenna or the church of *Hagia Sophia* at Constantinople.

With the death of Augustine in A.D. 430, during the siege of his city of Hippo by the Vandals, the Patristic Age in the West came to a close. Soon all of western Europe was over-run by the Germanic barbarians; the ancient system of Roman government, communication, and commerce broke down, and western Europe sank slowly into a backward agricultural localism and into a twilight of culture. Only in the eastern end of the Mediterranean did the Byzantine Empire carry on the old Greek and Roman ways of life and thought.

CHAPTER IV

Byzantine Civilization

1. THE NATURE OF BYZANTINE CIVILIZATION

2. THE CHURCH AND LEARNING

3. LITERATURE, ART, AND MUSIC

4. THE INFLUENCE OF BYZANTIUM

GIBBON dismissed Byzantine civilization with mordant epigrams; he could find in its history nothing but "a tedious and uniform tale of weakness and misery. The subjects of the Byzantine Empire, who assumed and dishonored the names both of Greeks and Romans, present a uniformity of abject vices, which are neither softened by the weakness of humanity, nor animated by the vigor of memorable crimes." [1] The twentieth century has at last revised this judgment.

I. THE NATURE OF BYZANTINE CIVILIZATION

For over a thousand years, from the later fourth century to the middle of the fifteenth, the old city of Byzantium, the largest and greatest Christian city, was the center of a brilliant culture. The empire about it was the home of art, literature, learning, manufacture, and commerce when Latin Christendom in the West was sunk in a backward economic localism with a low level of intellectual culture. The Eastern Empire had a strong army and navy, a great merchant marine, and a regular system of tax collection and of law enforcement when the Latin West was, for long centuries, practically without any of these.

Byzantium gathered the elements of her civilization from the West and the East and combined them into a unique culture. From Greece came her language, which replaced Latin in the sixth century as the language of the court. The Attic idiom was acquired in her schools with grammar and lexicon, and the Greek literary and philosophical classics were the basis of her education. Every educated Byzantine could catch an allusion to Homer, and many were familiar with Pindar, Thucydides, Sophocles, Plato, and Aristotle. Greek, likewise, was the clarity in her designs in architecture, painting, and sculpture. From Rome came her legal and administrative machinery, her ability to assimilate many cultures, and her system of taxation, which held the empire together through incredible vicissitudes. Roman, too, were her system of commerce and shipping and her extensive army and navy, though she put most of her soldiers on horseback. Her cities, with their great parks, public buildings, and state institutions, were constructed on the Roman model. And her great engineering achievements were also Roman. From the Orient, Mesopotamia, Persia, and, above all, from Syria came the pomp of her imperial court and the great ceremonial of both the court and the church, the love of color and magnificence in architecture and costume, the transcendental character of her art, and, finally, an emotionality and a mystical attitude toward life.

In the culture of Byzantium and in her political and economic history there were changes and conflicts and long periods of stagnation and aridity followed by striking revivals. But, until the twelfth century, the Latin West showed nothing like her art, her learning, her administrative, legal, and fiscal organization, or her great cities or her commercial activity. The story of Byzantine civilization is divided into three great epochs, first the Golden Age of Justinian, which saw extensive conquests all over the Mediterranean basin, and, at home, the building of *Hagia Sophia* and the codification of the law. This was followed by a period of struggle at home over the use of Christian images, the Iconoclastic Strife, and, abroad, with the effort to hold some of her old empire against the successful onslaughts first of the Persians, then of the Mohammedan hordes. A second great age of political, economic, and cultural revival ran from the ninth through the twelfth centuries. This was interrupted by the Fourth Crusade, and the Venetian Occupation from 1204 to 1261. The last revival, in the fourteenth and fifteenth centuries, lasted until the Empire fell to the Ottoman Turks in 1453.

At the center of the Empire was its capital city, which Constantine had renamed for himself in the fourth century. By the tenth century this great city had a million inhabitants; no other Christian city could be remotely compared with it. Here was the residence of the emperor and of the patriarch; here were palaces, churches—above all *Hagia Sophia*—and monasteries, baths, theaters, orphanages, and parks. When Paris, London, Vienna, and Rome were dirty villages, Constantinople had miles of paved streets, policed at all hours and lighted at night. On the one hand, one found incredible splendor, and on the other, in the dark alleys of the capital, poverty and vice, often a world of dogs, dirt, and thieves. In the harbor were the vessels of Syrians, Egyptians, Russians, Scandinavians, Persians, and Venetians, and in the streets and on the quays one found half the nationalities of both Europe and Asia, a motley and cosmopolitan horde. There was here a vast confusion of every tongue and every religion.[2] The Byzantines called it the "city protected by God," and the whole mediaeval world dreamed of Constantinople as the great center of magnificence and wealth. "She is the glory of Greece, she is even richer than is reported," wrote a Frenchman in the twelfth century. Another wrote: "Two-thirds of the world's wealth is in Constantinople, and the other third is scattered throughout the world." "Men dreamt of her," says Diehl, "amid the chilly mists of Norway, and on the banks of the Russian rivers; they dreamt of her in western strongholds, where trouvères sang the marvels of the imperial palace. Men dreamt of her amid the barbarian Slavs and the needy Armenians. Men dreamt of her in Venice and the commercial cities of Italy, and calculated the magnificent revenues yearly derived from this city." The life of the capital centered around the great ceremonies of the church of *Hagia Sophia,* where the pomp of feast days was most brilliant, around the palace, where the etiquette was incredibly elaborate and where the luxurious display of marble, mosaics, precious metals, stones, and fabrics defied all description, a world worthy of the Arabian Nights, and around the Hippodrome, where games and races and riots entertained the mob. "For God," says one historian, "there was *Hagia Sophia,* for the emperor the sacred palace, and for the people the Hippodrome." ³

As in modern France, the provincial cities and the country districts formed a striking contrast to the capital. Both were less luxurious and elegant, but also less turbulent and corrupt. Life was simpler, more robust, and far less agitated. The lesser cities, again, as in modern France, were often smaller imitations of the capital. In literature, education, learning, and art they followed Constantinople, often at a considerable distance. In the country districts the nobles often lived in great luxury, and the peasants, though thrifty and usually hard-working, were poor. The commercial life of the empire brought in enormous wealth to the government and the upper classes in spite of continual wars, of an inadequate credit system, of over-elaborate government supervision, and of granting too many commercial privileges to the Venetians and other Italians. The Byzantine state everywhere was a kind of political and economic dictatorship. Situated at the meeting place of Europe and Asia, and of the Black Sea and the Mediterranean, money-making was inevitable.

Naturally, in the ten centuries of its history, Byzantine civilization showed many changes and differences; though being a conservative culture, dominated by an absolute monarchy and an authoritarian church, and always on the defensive against outside attacks, there were many continuing features. Among these was the Byzantine character. This was essentially Oriental. It delighted in shows and magnificent ceremonies even if they were bloody and brutal. When the Byzantine individual or the Byzantine mob became excited with religious or political hatred, these mercurial and impressionable people were capable of violence. When calm, the Byzantines could be reasonable and generous. They, very much like mediaeval men in Latin Christendom, lived in the mystic heights or in the most brutal depths. Capable of great religious exaltation and of terrible brutality, they lacked balance. Intellectually they were very curious and very subtle at once; they loved refined and complicated arguments and gossip and witty raillery. They believed passionately in miracles, astrology, and magic. Family ties were strong, but private vice and political corruption were common. The Latin Christians from the West found the Byzantines too supple, too calculating, too ingenious, too cunning, and too untroubled by scruples. The final impression is one of more admiration for their intelligence than for their character.⁴

Perhaps the most amazing thing about Byzantine civilization was its long endurance. It was repeatedly attacked by Vikings, Russians, and other Slavs from the North, from the East and South by the Persians and the Arabs, and from the West by the Venetians. The Empire sometimes included the whole of the Balkan Peninsula, Asia Minor, Armenia, Syria, Palestine, and rich outposts in Italy and North Africa; and then, at other times, it would shrink to a small area about Constantinople. What a history of repeated sieges, of catastrophic defeats, and of stunning victories! But its capital was only taken twice in its long history—in 1204 by the Venetians and in 1453 by the Ottoman Turks. There are various reasons for this phenomenal recuperative power and this extraordinary persistence; first was the military strength and the commercial importance of Constantinople. It was the most vital trade center of the whole Mediterranean area, and, at the same time, so placed on a tongue of land, with water on three sides and a huge set of walls on the fourth, that it was nearly impossible to capture. Then, what would today be called a sense of nationality held the Byzantines together. In some periods they called themselves Romans and at other times, Greeks, but they proudly thought of themselves as the bearers of a great classical tradition and, more important, as a nation willed by the Christian God, standing together against the onrush of barbarians and infidels. The dictatorial government that controlled the church and regulated economic life with an iron hand gave them strength in a world where they were continually under threat of siege or actually besieged. The part played by the citizen was never a matter of his own election or initiative; the state assigned the individual his place. The subject, his ideas, and his activities were all ever available to the state, which remained always a sort of vast frontier garrison. The church might quarrel with the state, but it could never hope to master the state as the pope did in the West. Finally, the emperorship remained open to men of ability; critics call attention to the pages of Byzantine history red with blood and black with crime and accumulated horror, but the system tended to bring strong leaders to the fore. So Byzantium, like Venice in Wordsworth's sonnet, for over ten centuries "held the gorgeous East in fee, and was the safeguard of the West."

2. THE CHURCH AND LEARNING

RELIGION held a central place in Byzantine civilization. As in the Latin West, and as in the Islamic states after the seventh century, religion penetrated the whole of life, and civil and religious institutions were so intertwined that one cannot understand any one without the others. Every writer on Byzantine history points out how the masses carried this interest in religious and theological questions into the streets. In the fourth century, Gregory of Nyssa complained that the baker and the bath-keeper would argue the subtleties of Arianism; by the sixth century this popular interest veered from theological to liturgical issues; still later it shifted to the use of images and to such questions as the use of leavened or unleavened bread in the eucharist. Everyone from the emperor down loved to distraction controversies about all of these church matters. Behind these disputes, however, there were often deep political and economic enmities, but the real reason for all this interest in religious issues was a genuine piety of a people who lived in a constant state of mystical exaltation, who believed passionately in miracles, and who were ever ready to make great sacrifices to support and defend their religion.

The head of the church in Constantinople and surrounding territories was the patriarch. He was appointed by the emperor and could be deposed by him. The emperor was the representative of God and was the head of the church as well as of the state, supreme in every walk of life. The state was a divine institution; all its officers, their functions, and even the buildings where they lived and worked were "sacred" or "divine" or "holy." So, although the patriarch was the appointee of the emperor, because of the high prestige of the office of patriarch and often of his own person, he dared defy the emperor and could sometimes get him to change his course. The patriarch's power in relation to the secular state was, however, much less than that of the pope in the Latin West; and even among the Eastern Christians the patriarch did not control the faithful in areas far removed from Constantinople. Just as the nationalities in the Near East—Copts, Syrians, Armenians, Georgians, and Slavs—did not speak Greek, but maintained their national languages, so did they also maintain their separate church organizations. The complete Latinizing of the West, followed by the centralized control of the bishop of Rome, had no counterpart in the East, either in language or church organization. In the West, Anglo-Saxons, Irish, French, Germans, Poles, Magyars, and the rest used Latin in their services and their schools and followed the direction of the pope in Rome. In the East, the service books were translated into the many vernaculars. In the same way, the patriarch controlled only the area about Constantinople, and the other churches in the East were separately organized.

Parish priests were allowed to marry, usually before they were ordained; they could not remarry. Bishops were required to be celibate; they were usually chosen from the monastic clergy. Sometimes a civil servant with administrative experience, if unmarried or a widower, would be appointed to a bishopric. This system, which amazed Latin Christians, seems to have worked well in that it occasionally recruited able men for the church who would otherwise not have been available. The monks were in popular regard the most respected of all the clergy. As a result, promotion in the church depended more on spiritual qualities and even on intellectual attainments and less on political and legal skill than in the Latin West. The tradition of charity was well established and an interest in it was, like the interest in liturgy and theology, interwoven in men's daily lives. The church directed many charitable enterprises, such as hospitals for the sick and the aged, hostels for pilgrims and travellers, maternity homes, orphanages, and schools, which were served by secular clergy and laymen rather than by monks and nuns. The elaborate church ritual and decoration was taken over from the luxurious and Oriental ceremonial of the imperial court, and the religion of the average man was thus far removed from the personality of Jesus. The typical Byzantine icon presents Jesus as the *Pantocrator,* the Lord Omnipotent on his heavenly throne. There was small place in this religious system for the New Testament or for the real personality and teaching of Jesus. The Byzantine Christ, whom men worshipped, was seemingly much like the heavenly saviors of the mystery religions.[5]

The Byzantine church was torn with many internal dissensions; the most serious and protracted one was over the use of images, the Icono-clastic Struggle which went on from 725 to 843. The emperor forbade the use of carved and painted religious figures to satisfy certain groups who regarded such figures as idolatrous. The protest was due to ex-cessively superstitious practices; images played the role in the Byzan-tine church that relics played in the Latin church. People prostrated themselves before images, kissed them, and lighted candles before them, wrote hymns to them, and attributed to them miracles and mar-velous cures; the populace regarded the images as real deities. These practices, often favored by certain clerical circles, especially among the monastic clergy, brought down the disgust of other church groups. At the same time, the craze for image worship called out the bitter raillery of Jews and Mohammedans. Besides attacking the use of images, the reformers opposed the excesses of the cult of relics and the over-elabo-ration of rituals. It was a genuine reform movement aiming to restore a primitive purity to Christianity. A similar movement made little headway in the West until the sixteenth century. The monks took up the traditional side against the reforming party and the emperor. The party in favor of the use of images had the able help of John of Da-mascus and Theodore of Studius. In defending their use, Theodore held iconoclasm a heresy in that the iconoclasts were trying to deny the human side of Christ and the necessity of earthly symbols in his worship. To deny the legitimacy of icons of Christ was to deny God's incarnation in Jesus. The emperor, at the time, also believed that the cloister was attracting too many men from agriculture, industry, the navy and the army, and that the monasteries were acquiring too much tax-exempt property. The controversy thus in the end raised the most fundamental questions of the relations of church and state. The final outcome was a defeat for the reforming party and a restoration of the use of images and other outlawed practices. The whole controversy rocked the Byzantine state for over a century, and it led—through try-ing to force iconoclasm on the Roman church—to worsened relations with the papacy and the world of Latin Christendom.

The Latin church had received its theology, its liturgy, and its ideas of church organization from the churches of the Greek East. But it had cared less for theological subtleties; it longed to have the decisions of the early church councils regarded as authoritative and final, and it disliked the continual quibbling over refinements of theology of the Eastern Christians. The theological differences between Constantinople and Rome, at any given time, were the ostensible cause of quarreling, but the real reason for dissension lay deeper. The bishop of Rome and the patriarch of Constantinople each tried to assert his authority over the other. Constantinople regarded its Christian tradition as older and superior and would not accept the Roman decretals as canon law; in the view of Rome the patriarchate had no apostolic tradition of Peter and Paul and was a mere upstart. This was one basic point at issue; others were the differences in language and culture between Rome and Constantinople. In theory the church was one, but after the fifth century this remained only an ideal. Each church went its own way. In 1054 the pope and the patriarch mutually excommunicated each other; these differences made trouble aplenty during the period of the Crusades (1095-1291). And, though on a number of later occasions the churches agreed to unite, the last time in 1439, the Byzantines were finally left to face the Ottoman Turks alone, and the old differences between pope and patriarch did much to bring on the final downfall of the Byzantine Empire. And beyond, this ancient cleavage has meant grave misunderstanding and suspicion between eastern and western Europe which has lasted into modern times. In the sixteenth and seventeenth centuries the Latin Christians are represented in hell in the frescoes of churches of Moldavia, while writers of the Latin church declared that the enslavement of the Greek Christians to the Ottoman yoke was a divine punishment as well merited as the dispersion of the Jews. The split in the world of Christendom cut off eastern Europe from the results of the Renaissance, the Reformation, and the Enlightenment, and its marks are still evident in the twentieth century.

It would be difficult to overemphasize the role played by the monks in the religious life of Byzantium. It was on the lands of the empire that this institution had first arisen, though not until the church was nearly two hundred years old. The origins of Christian monasticism go back to certain injunctions of the New Testament; "if thou wilt be perfect, go and sell that thou hast, and give to the poor, and thou shalt have treasure in heaven." [6] Other sources of monasticism were the ascetic Pythagorean communities of the Greek world, the recluses of Isis in Egypt, and the Essene fraternities among the Jews.[7] Those early Christians who accepted this call did not, at first, separate themselves from the body of the faithful, but continued to live in the world, practicing celibacy, fasting, prayer, and charitable works. The first hermits about whom anything is known were St. Anthony and St. Paul of Thebes who lived in Egypt, about sixty miles south of Alexandria, in the second half of the third century A.D. These first anchorites or hermits were soon followed by many others who went out alone into the desert, making the "exodus of despair." The climate in Egypt favored this sort of life; nowhere else could a hermit's life be so easily maintained. Caves were numerous and little clothing was needed. Hermits usually raised their own vegetables (they ate no meat) and found honey. They made mats and baskets from rushes, spun and wove linen, and sold these products to travelling commercial agents.

The hermits, whether like St. Anthony they dwelt in caves in Egypt or like Simeon Stylites they lived on a pillar in Syria, attracted enormous prestige and veneration from the faithful.[8] By A.D. 350 there were thousands of hermits in eastern Mediterranean lands. At the same time, cenobite communities arose from the system of a number of hermits building cells around the abode of a particularly holy man. A group of these, called a *laura*, would often have a common church and a wall to protect those whom the Church Fathers loved to call the "athletes of God." Some of the earliest monastic churches still exist in Egypt; they use pointed arches of brick from which the Mohammedans later got their pointed arches. St. Pachomius (d. A.D. 346) is the first important leader of a cenobite community. He wrote the first monastic rule. Those who wished to join the community had to undergo a probation of three years and then agree freely to follow all the rules of the community as laid down by the founder. By the time Pachomius died he had founded nine monasteries for men, with 3,000 monks, and two convents for women, all in Egypt. In these communal houses, work was assigned in the fields and workshops, hours were fixed for prayer, for study of the Scriptures, and for rest. Pachomius' monasteries were well-organized, self-supporting agricultural colonies. From Egypt, the monastic movement spread rapidly, first to Palestine, Mesopotamia, and Syria, where it took on very exaggerated forms; soon it had extended all over the Roman Empire. Anchorites and cenobites—in great numbers of both men and women—were found throughout the Mediterranean world by A.D. 400.

The first important writing on monasticism was Cassian's *Collations*, written about A.D. 425; they give an interesting exposition of the aims and purposes of the monastic life. It here becomes clear that monasticism was giving organization to two of the deepest urges of the time: mysticism and asceticism. The mystic wishes to suppress the flesh, to forget himself, and to merge his life with God. Asceticism helped in this suppression of self; asceticism proceeds on the idea that human desire not only in its excess but in its normal operation is evil; not gluttony, but normal eating, not sexual intercourse, but sexual desire are evil. Asceticism, by suppressing the senses, frees the soul from all desire and prepares it for a mystic union with the divine. The rapid increase in the number of hermits and cenobite monks in the fourth and fifth centuries was partly due to the "Peace of the Church," which had made it fashionable to become a Christian and had driven the more ardent ascetic souls to take unto themselves a heavier yoke and which, also, had ended persecution and the chance for marytrdom. Another reason for the rapid increase in the number of monks was the hardship and the uncertainty of the times.

The father of later Greek monasticism was the Cappadocian, St. Basil (d. A.D. 379). He had travelled widely and visited both hermits and monasteries in Egypt, Syria, and Palestine before he wrote his rules. He was much opposed to the extravagant and often ostentatious austerities of some ascetics, and, like Pachomius, he wished to organize monastic life around a program of devotional exercises, work, study, and charity. Fasting and austerities were not to interfere with prayer or work. Moreover, to do charitable work, monasteries were to be established near towns. In the system of Pachomius, the monks lived in different houses, ate at different hours, and gathered in the church only for the greater services; the communities were large, with as many as a thousand monks. But Basil established a common roof and a common refectory and limited membership in any house to about thirty. A period of probation had to be passed before a man could be received as a full member of the community. No vows were taken, but the virtues of poverty, chastity, and obedience to the superior were insisted on. The Council of Chalcedon passed several canons regarding the monastic life which embodied Basil's ideas and helped to spread them. The two rules attributed to St. Basil are, together with other of his writings, all descriptions of the monastic life as he conceived it rather than a body of regulations. He never founded an order, but his writings made such an impression that they have ever since been the basis of monasticism in the Greek and Slavonic churches, and, through his influence on St. Benedict, he has also deeply influenced the monasticism of Latin Christendom.

In the fifth century, Palestine, under the inspiration of St. Sabas, became a great center for monastic activity; alongside houses that followed the ideas of St. Basil, many were founded in which the monks lived in separate cells within an enclosure. There were few monasteries in and around Constantinople before the fifth century. Then they increased rapidly, and the government in the sixth century began to regulate them. The Council of Chalcedon (A.D. 451) had already decreed that no new monasteries could be founded without the permission of the bishop, that the bishop should supervise the monasteries in his diocese, that monks must stay in their houses, that a slave might not be made a monk without his master's consent, and that no regularly established monastery could be secularized nor its property alienated. The regulations passed by the state supplemented these rules, and the government used every effort to force the monasteries to conform. In the Code of Justinian of the sixth century there is a whole section on monastic law; part of this confirms earlier decrees of church councils and regulations of the state. New regulations were added; they are quite detailed and show that the number of monasteries must have been very large and the abuses therein numerous.

In the eighth century, extensive reforms were undertaken by Theodore of Studius in the house of which he was head in Constantinople, from whence their influence spread. Theodore set out to restore Basil's spirit to its primitive vigor, but to accomplish this and to gain permanence for the reform, he saw there was need of more specific regulations for the daily details of monastic life. Theodore laid out a plan to improve the power and discipline of the abbot by creating a whole hierarchy of functionaries, each with his exact duties. The monks were divided into the choir-monks and the lay-monks. The monks were to meet together three times a week to be instructed on the virtues demanded by the cloistered life: devotion, self-discipline, and obedience. Minute rules for the communal life were laid down; everything was rigorously disciplined, but it was all reasonable and it deliberately avoided ascetic exaggerations. Unlike the *Rules* of Basil, Theodore's *Constitutions* make no provision for charitable work outside the monastery. Most of his regulations are highly specific, such as a rule forbidding entrance into a monastery, not only of women, but even of female animals. This was done to remove the temptation of animal raising in connection with the monastery, as breeding would oblige the monks to hire lay servants from outside the monastic walls. Thus the *Rules* of Basil and the *Constitutions* of Theodore of Studius, along with the enactments of early church councils, constitute the basis of Greek and Slavonic monastic law. In the last four centuries of Byzantine history the greatest monastic centers were on Mount Athos. A large number of monastic rules for this period after 1000 have survived, but they show little change beyond the system of Theodore of Studius. Much of the evangelization of the Slavs was undertaken by monks, and the first monastery established in Russia (in Kiev about 1050) was founded by a monk from Mount Athos.

The influence of monks in Byzantine civilization was enormous. Men looked up to the monastic calling as the highest form of life. The monasteries possessed miracle-working images and saints' relics, which the masses venerated. They usually distributed alms among the common people to the very limit of their resources. The patriarch and the bishops were nearly always chosen from the monastic clergy, and, finally, the monks maintained a great reputation as preachers, as prophets, and as confessors and spiritual advisors of the high and the low. There are even many examples of the emperor asking simple monks for advice and the benefit of their prayers. Gifts were heaped on the monasteries, and their endowments expanded enormously century by century. The wealth of the monks, their popularity, their fanaticism, and their continual interference in state affairs, including wild riots they sometimes incited, often made them a great problem to the government.

The story of Byzantine monasticism abounds in quarrels and abuses. The state regulations that put every monastery more or less under the direction of the local bishop led to endless squabbles. Often the monastery appealed to the emperor, the protector of the faith, for immunity, and sometimes the emperor granted it. Many used the monastery as a convenient refuge; politicians, soldiers, scholars, wealthy merchants, and nobles, and even the emperor himself would enter a monastery, stay for awhile, and then depart. Some entered the cloister to escape taxes or to evade the law, others to avoid service in the army or merely to find an easy means of living. Persons were sometimes confined in the cloister by their own kin. Often the novices were improperly trained, and many who were admitted to the house had no real calling for the monastic life. Sometimes the bishop would grant monasteries to laymen with the condition that they be repaired; this was made a mere pretext for giving away religious houses. In some monasteries, strange hysterical practices such as *hesychasm* took place wherein the mystic by holding his breath and gazing fixedly at his navel would fall into a swoon in which he believed himself united with God. Absentee monks constituted another abuse; for one recluse who remained for forty years without leaving his house there were hundreds of restless monks passing from monastery to monastery and roaming the highways of the whole empire. The unit of Byzantine monasticism was the single monastery; there were no orders as in the Latin West. A house would be founded, flourish, and fall into decay or even be abandoned. Instead of trying to rehabilitate it, the next donor would found a new monastery. The whole system was utterly without order or effective organization. The number of monasteries grew so large that they weakened the state by withdrawing too many men from active life and by depriving the state of much needed income. The state tried in vain to remedy some of these abuses, but reforms were either not enforced, or, soon after they were started, a new emperor would be persuaded to reverse the course of his predecessor. Eastern monasticism never knew a development parallel to that created in the Latin West by the variety of large religious orders, each responding to a special need. In some cases the monasteries looked after hospitals and orphanages and other charitable institutions, supplementing the work done by the state. In other cases the monastery owned such charitable institutions but turned them over to lay clergy to run. Nearly every monastery distributed alms; this seems to have been the chief reason why the masses so venerated the monks. The downfall of the Western Empire in the fifth century and the slow reconstruction of political, economic, and cultural life had no counterpart in the East. Society in the East had its unbroken traditions of secular learning and secular education. Thus there was never a need in the Eastern Empire for monasticism to come to the rescue of civilization itself as it did in western Europe. So eastern monasticism, in spite of its great extent and its enormous influence, did not achieve any contribution in the fields of learning comparable to that achieved by the monks of the West.

Byzantine education was a joint enterprise of church and state. Alongside state schools of various types were church schools. Primary education was largely in the hands of private teachers supported by the fees of the pupils; the higher schools were run by the church or the state. Unlike the Latin West, there was no special intellectual distinction connected with the word *clerk*. In the West, the cleavage between the clerical and lay classes was deepened by the fact that the separation between these two classes for centuries coincided with the distinction between educated and ignorant. In the Byzantine world, cleric and layman were on common ground. There were as many learned laymen as learned priests and monks. And even in theology, the layman was not at the mercy of the priest, for his education included some theology.

The Byzantines believed strongly in education; lack of training was considered a misfortune, and continual jibes were made at the ignorant, especially if they were in high places. Writers constantly lauded the value of a well-trained mind. Parents made great sacrifices to send their sons to school. The teachers in both church and state schools were highly respected and were usually well trained and well paid. The first subject taught a child at the age of six, either by a tutor or a member of the family, or in a primary school supported by the fees of the pupils, was Attic Greek, which included the basic subjects of reading, writing, spelling, and the parts of speech. Homer was the first author read, and large sections were committed to memory; other classical poets and some prose writers were also studied. At the age of ten to twelve the pupil passed to rhetoric, which was simply a continuation of the reading of standard classical Greek authors and the writing of original compositions; to this were soon added arithmetic, geometry, music, astronomy, and philosophy. By the age of eighteen, the boy was ready to enter the university or some other higher type of school to study law, medicine, or theology. The education of girls was never carried far in school. Through all these stages, religious education was given by ecclesiastics. Children learned the Bible with some thoroughness; next to Homer it is the chief source of allusions and quotations in Byzantine literature. In practice, the monastic schools usually confined themselves to educating those who intended to enter the monastic life. The monasteries were more interested in saving the souls of the members of the corporation and in producing saints than they were in learning or teaching, and the preservation of learning was largely in other hands.⁹

The highest schools or universities were scattered through the empire in the larger cities: Constantinople, Antioch, Ephesus, Nicaea, Edessa, Alexandria, Salonica, and Athens; a few were in small towns. Some were run by the central government, some by the church, and a few by the municipalities. The advance of higher education was seriously handicapped by incessant wars, which in many cases crippled or destroyed the schools, and by the ever-changing policies of the emperor. The University of Constantinople is representative of the changing fortunes of most of the highest schools. Founded in the fifth century, with thirty-one professors, it soon became famous for its instruction in law. Advanced instruction was also given in classical literature, philosophy, and mathematics; school and university subjects overlapped. In the eighth century, after four centuries of successful instruction, the University was closed for opposing the emperor's policy of forbidding the use of images. Re-opened in the ninth century, the University slowly recovered. The revived institution flourished from about 1045, when it was divided into a school of law and a school of philosophy—the latter under the great scholar Psellus—until the sack of Constantinople by the Venetians in 1204. Admission was easy for men of capacity who were allowed to study without payment of fees, and the University trained many of the most important lawyers, judges, and state administrators of the empire. In 1204, the remnant of the University was moved to Nicaea; after it was taken back to Constantinople in 1261 it never regained its former position. For the training of ecclesiastics, other than monks, some of the bishops maintained schools; the highest and most esteemed of these was the patriarch's school at Constantinople, founded in the seventh century. It became a sort of university, where instruction was given not only in theology but in literature and other subjects. From the eleventh century on, the patriarch and the church authorities dominated both what was taught and the methods of teaching in nearly all the state schools.

From top to bottom, Byzantine learning was traditional. The descriptions and catalogues of libraries show that they were richly stocked with all the wealth of Greek literature, including many important works which have since disappeared. And the extent of reading shown in Byzantine writers indicates a thorough knowledge of the whole range of Greek literature and learning. Among the great encyclopedic collections that have survived are the *Palatine Anthology* of Greek epigrams of the tenth century, Photius' *Bibliotheca* of the ninth century, an extended and schematic digest of 280 prose works he had read, many of which have now perished, and *Suidas*, a huge lexicon of the tenth century, containing summaries of many fields of Greek learning. The fortunes of learning, like those of literature and art, followed closely the political and economic fortunes of the empire. In times of internal struggle and foreign wars, learning and the schools languished. The most backward centuries were the seventh to the middle of the ninth, after which there was a renaissance of learning, literature, and art. The second golden age, the first having been in the sixth century in the Age of Justinian, continued till the opening of the thirteenth century. A last revival took place from about 1300 to the fall of the empire in 1453. In spite of the interest in learning, the results were out of proportion to the effort. The Byzantine scholar was held down by the overwhelming prestige and authority of the ancients and by an authoritarian church and state. The Byzantine scholar, like the scholars in the Latin West until the twelfth and thirteenth centuries, commented endlessly on the learning inherited from the past, but almost never doubted this learning or tried to move beyond it. One of the worst features of Byzantine learning was its passion for compends, abridgements, and anthologies; they even abridged the *Iliad*. In theology the great and fundamental writers had been Greeks like Origen and the Cappadocian Fathers. The last of the great theologians, John of Damascus in the eighth century, had written a huge summary of theology, and after him theologians either re-thrashed the old material, or, like Photius, in the ninth century and later, they discussed chiefly the relations with the Roman church and the advisability of a reunion with Rome. At its worst, this Byzantine theological literature, like that of Latin Christendom, is monotonous, repetitious, and stereotyped, with endless quotations from the Bible and the Church Fathers. Byzantine theology never produced an Abe-lard, a Bonaventura, or an Aquinas. The greatest of all Byzantine scholars, Psellus in the eleventh century, tried to bring Aristotle and Plato together in a new philosophy; his work resembles that of Fi-cino and Pico della Mirandola in fifteenth-century Italy. Three of the later Byzantine philosophers, influenced by Psellus' writings, Chryso-loras, Gemistus Plethon, and Bessarion, came to Italy in the days of the early Renaissance, and they form a link between Byzantine and Italian Renaissance Platonism.

No contributions of great importance were made to astronomy, mathematics, and medicine, though the Byzantines always had avail-able the best Greek works. "It is notorious," says Bury, "that the Byzan-tine world, which produced many men of wide and varied learning, or of subtle intellect, such as Photius and Psellus, never gave birth to an original and creative genius. Its science can boast of no discovery, its philosophy of no novel system. Age after age, innumerable pens moved, lakes of ink were exhausted, but no literary work remains which can claim a place among the memorable books of the world. To the mass of mankind Byzantine literature is a dead thing; it has not left a single immortal book to instruct and delight posterity. The classical tradition was an incubus rather than a stimulant; classical lit-erature was an idol, not an inspiration. Higher education was civilizing but not quickening; it was liberal but did not liberate." [10]

3. LITERATURE, ART, AND MUSIC

BYZANTINE literature is not a great literature, but it forms a marvel-ous mirror of Byzantine history and civilization. In this literature, as in the language, there is less break with the ancient world than there was in western Europe. The language used was still Greek, but like every living language the colloquial form changed in pronunciation, vocabulary, and grammar; for example, the New Testament was written in the current Greek (*koiné*) of the first and second centuries. As early as the first century B.C., an Atticist movement had started with the avowed purpose of returning to the classic Greek of the fifth century B.C. This movement went on century after century but it never succeeded in stopping writing in the changing vernacular. In Byzantine literature some important works were written in the language currently in use. This might have led to a new vernacular literature as in the case of French, Spanish, and Italian in the West. But by the eleventh century, a purist movement of great force was under way in the Byzantine world, and nearly all the writers used classical Greek. Thus the language of most Byzantine writers of the period after the eleventh century was quite unrelated to the spoken tongue; it was artificially learned from grammar and lexicon and from reading the Greek classics. This tendency grew, so that in determining the date of a work, the more ancient the language used the more recent the author. The divorce of the written and spoken languages, always marked in Byzantine writing but more evident after 1000, separated much of the literature from the world about it. It lacked roots in the life and speech of the people. This gave it a certain artificiality and proved to be a bad heritage passed on by the Byzantines to the modern Greeks. Thus some Greek writers in the twentieth century use grammatical forms that were obsolete long before the tenth century.

Like some mediaeval Latin literature, Byzantine literature shows the baneful influence of an over-elaborate training in rhetoric. Not only is the language artificial, but also the style is often badly mannered and affected; ingenuity is substituted for inspiration. This slavish devotion to rhetorical models often deprives even the better works of individuality and trenchancy. All of Byzantine literature that survives comes either from the court in Constantinople or from the monastery. Popular literature has left few remains, and the centralization of all life in the capital did not favor the growth of literature in the provincial cities. It is only in the popular saints' lives, in sermons and orations, and in some of the correspondence of the great writers that one finds any details of the daily life of the middle class and of the common people in town and country.

In bulk, theology takes first place in surviving Byzantine prose writing, although after the period of the Greek Fathers, there is little that is new except in the field of mysticism. Here, besides the fabulous writings of Dionysius the Areopagite, there were the more sober reflections of Maximus the Confessor, one of whose works, in the ninth century, was translated into Latin by John Scotus Erigena. With these Byzantine mystics we enter a world of introspection and silence in which severe discipline had fashioned an attitude wherein worldly temptations have lost their power. The mind has been taken captive by another's strength, and the soul has gained a sense of joy ineffable, and in that ecstasy has forgotten itself and all things terrestrial. The Byzantine mystics, unlike those of the Western church, did not attack the forms and ritual of the church; they were neither actual nor potential heretics.

The most effective prose writing is in the field of history, which the Byzantines much cultivated. Most of their historical writing falls into two groups: first, works by learned authors who wrote in a more or less classical Greek and who described their own times and the period immediately before them, and, second, chronicles of a more popular nature—usually the works of monks—often written in the current vernacular, and usually recapitulating the history of the world since the Creation. The learned historians were deeply conscious of being the inheritors of a great tradition, and they imitated Herodotus, Thucydides, Xenophon, and Polybius. Most of the learned historians were lawyers, and this, added to their deliberate imitation of ancient Greek models, made them careful in collecting their facts and judicious in interpreting them. The Byzantine historians also, unlike those of the Latin West, were not dominated by the church and by theological concerns. This resulted in a type of historical writing that was at once accurate and concrete although some of it is wanting in independent judgment.

There is, with only one break from about 650 to 850, a continuous line of able Byzantine historians from the time of Justinian in the sixth century through the fall of the empire in the fifteenth. In the age of Justinian, Procopius, the secretary of the general Belisarius, wrote a long history of the wars against the Persians, Vandals, and Goths. The work is of great value especially for the light it sheds on geography and on the peoples outside the empire. He also wrote a *Secret History*, full of scandalous details about the court and with much criticism of Justinian, and, finally, a descriptive account of the buildings erected under Justinian. The great influence on Procopius was Thucydides, whose reconstruction of speeches and whose interest in accuracy he imitates. He lacks, however, the philosophic outlook of his master. Constantine VII in the tenth century was not only a great patron of historians but he also wrote several valuable books himself. His *Ceremonies* contains a mass of information on the Byzantine government and the elaborate court and church ceremonial. Here one may find out all the regulations about court robes, baptisms, marriages, coronations, burials, and tombs, about the reception of foreign ambassadors, the equipment of military organizations, and state officers and all their functions. Still further information about the government, about foreign affairs, and about the peoples bordering on the empire is found in his *Concerning the Imperial Administration*. All through the later history of the empire there were produced a number of this type of legal, administrative, diplomatic, military, and agricultural handbooks which, though of no great literary value, are extremely useful for reconstructing the history and the life of the empire. Two other historians, among many, are outstanding: Psellus, the great scholar of the eleventh century, who, out of his experience as a secretary to the emperor, wrote a very well-balanced history of the years 976 to 1077 that shows a first-rate talent for bringing past scenes to life, and Anna Comnena, an emperor's daughter, who wrote the *Alexiad*, an excellent history of the reign of her father Alexius I (d. 1118). Anna was a very able writer, though something of a blue stocking. She aimed at accuracy, but she managed always to place her father in the best light. She is too impressed with externals and in language is an extreme purist. Her descriptions of the Western leaders and the soldiers of the First Crusade are etched with acid, but they show extraordinary insight. Historical work of high quality continued to be written down past the end of the empire in 1453.

The historical chronicles were usually the work of monks, and many that have survived are anonymous. Most of them can lay no claim to literary merit, and the poorest ones are full of inaccuracies and miracles. We learn that Sophocles, Herodotus, and Pythagoras were contemporaries of Philip of Macedon, and we hear of a peddler's dog who could find buried rings and return them to the owners and could distinguish coins of different emperors. The fall of an empire and the tricks of a travelling clown are related with the same seriousness. Other chronicles are of a higher quality. Their chief value to the modern historian lies in filling in gaps left by the learned historians and in furnishing many glimpses of Byzantine life. Closely allied to the chronicle in spirit and style was the saint's life; it was written to interest and to edify the masses. The great model of Byzantine hagiography was Athanasius' *Life of St. Anthony*. Byzantine churchmen wrote these works by the hundreds; the taste for them was apparently insatiable. They reflect the Byzantine love for wonders and miracles and the Byzantine admiration for the life of the monks. At their worst they are mechanical and dull, but they often have humor and vividness and give a first-hand picture of daily life not elsewhere found in Byzantine literature. Out of this genre came one extraordinary religious novel, *Barlaam and Josaphat*. This popular story is a Christianized version of the life of Buddha written by a monk in the seventh century. A great pagan king is told by a soothsayer that his son is to be a Christian, and so he orders this son to be brought up in a secluded palace where he is to learn nothing about suffering and death. Finally, the father allows the son to venture outside the palace gardens. Here the youth discovers all sorts of human misery, is much distressed, but finally finds a Christian hermit who explains the spiritual meaning of all these things. The son, at last, dies a venerated saint. The character drawing is excellent, and the story had a great vogue. It reached the West in various translations by the twelfth century and had an enormous popularity; it even furnished incidents to Boccaccio and Shakespeare.

The beginnings of Byzantine religious poetry go back to the accentual poems of Gregory Nazianzus in the fourth century. From this time on down to the end of the empire some poetry was written with a stress rhythm, while other poetry was composed employing the old Greek quantity system of versification. The full glory of the religious lyric appears in the hymns of Romanos in the sixth century. Like Ephraim, he came from Syria, and he is said to have written over a thousand poems celebrating the festivals of the year, the stories of the

Bible, and the lives of the saints. Eighty of his poems have survived; the longest runs to thirty-three stanzas, each of twelve to twenty-one lines in length. Some have a strong dramatic quality and are sermons in verse. They vary greatly in metrical structure and show enormous technical capacity. His faults lie in too great a use of rhetorical devices and in an over-fondness for long digressions into abstract theology; both often becloud the flow of his thought. At his best, Romanos is one of the greatest of all Christian poets. The music for Romanos' hymns has been mostly lost; some of his longer poems seem like the words for an oratorio. A number of the hymns of John of Damascus are nearly as fine as those of Romanos. In the best Byzantine religious poetry, the genuineness and the intensity of religious feeling break through the barriers of rhetorical convention to reach a sublime greatness equal to the wonders of *Hagia Sophia*. Later hymn writers became more mannered and elaborate, but they lack vitality, and Byzantine hymn writing practically died out in the eleventh century. Besides religious lyric poetry, some secular lyric poetry was produced; it is largely conventional in quality, pleasant but rarely vivid:

> *The soft narcissus springs joyful from the earth*
> *And the gracious, golden-flowered crocus and the anemone,*
> *The swallow pours forth its untiring song,*
> *And, in its nest at dawn, chatters like a maiden.*[11]

Popular forms of lyric poetry were satires, parodies, panegyrics, and didactic and begging poems—a genre the Byzantines invented. But the liveliest form of the lyric in Byzantium was the epigram, which satisfied the Byzantine taste for ingenuity and which links this culture to the refined and sophisticated Hellenistic civilization. Many of the leading writers wrote epigrams as a diversion, and some Byzantine authors made their reputations entirely as writers of epigrams.

> *Thou talkest much, but soon reft of breath;*
> *Be silent, and yet living study death.*[12]

Didactic poems and descriptive poems had a vogue; the most remarkable of the latter is Paul the Silentiary's contemporary description in verse of Justinian's reopening of *Hagia Sophia* in A.D. 563 after an earthquake had damaged it. The poem gives an accurate and detailed description of the great church; in places the author breaks through his frigid tone into deeply impassioned verse.

The Byzantines had a religious drama like that of the Latin West, which arose out of the custom of putting dramatic dialogue into sermons. It remained as a part of the church service until the twelfth century when an independent religious drama arose. One religious play, *Christ's Sufferings*, of the eleventh or twelfth century, has been preserved, but this is a learned work and it was probably never acted. About a third of the lines are borrowed from ancient plays, chiefly Euripides. The Virgin Mary uses many lines from Aeschylus, Sophocles, and Euripides in her stilted speeches. It is evidently the work of an ecclesiastic trained in the classics; the play has little literary or dramatic value. Secular plays, vaudeville shows, and pantomimes ran through the whole history of the empire; descriptions of all these exist, but none has survived. The Greek classic plays were read, but never acted. There are a number of second-rate romances, all of them influenced by the chivalric romances of the West. Finally, one admirable epic, *Digenes Akritas*, of the eleventh century, survives. This Byzantine *chanson de geste,* written in the current Greek vernacular, tells the story of the love and adventure of a mighty warrior who fights the Saracens in Asia Minor. It had no classical model or prototype, and it skillfully combined Byzantine history and a mass of ancient folklore. It gives a vivid picture of the life of the great noble on the frontier of Islam. It shows him living in wealth and splendor in a lavish palace, all aglow with marble and gleaming mosaics and set amid charming gardens. There are brilliant feats of arms and violent and brutal combats with the Mohammedans. It has been compared to the nearly contemporary *Chanson de Roland*. It is less dramatic, has more of a love interest, and is more vivid in description and more subtle in character portrayal. Actually it is fully as close to a Western chivalric romance as to a mediaeval epic.[13]

Byzantine literature has the same limitations as Byzantine learning. Except for a few outstanding works in theology and history, for the hymns of Romanos and the story of *Digenes Akritas*, Byzantine literature is reminiscent. It lacks spontaneity; nearly every literary work looks backward, and this fact served to draw always more tightly the threads that linked the present with the past. The authors often seem aloof from their own age; they no longer possess the ardor and curiosity of youth or even the more mature desire to fathom the secret of nature and of the universe. "Find what interest one may in mediaeval Byzantium, and it is full of interest," says Henry Osborn Taylor, "still it is a tale of what has reached its zenith, of what has passed its best strength, a tale of decadence postponed with skill and energy, and yet only postponed." [14]

Byzantine art grew out of early Christian art, and it is difficult to find an exact dividing line between the two. It is an art that drew on many sources, East and West, but achieved nevertheless a very distinct individuality. From its Greek past came the clarity, balance, and logic of its architectural designs and its mural decorations. From the Near East came the love of grandeur, luxury, and color, and the emphasis in the great mosaic and fresco compositions on the underlying meaning and significance of the subjects rather than on the surface forms. From its Christian background came the idea that the great reality was a spiritual world far beyond the present and beyond the littleness of man to grasp, but toward which man must ever reach upward. Finally, from its Roman past came the elaborate Byzantine engineering schemes and the ability to handle arches and vaults of the most complicated sorts. These Roman engineering devices had in the third and fourth centuries been used in new forms in Syria, Asia Minor, and further east into Persia, and, in turn, were brought back west after Constantine moved his residence to the Bosphorus in the fourth century. From the Roman imperial court also came the lavish display of marble, mosaic, precious metals and stones, and rich fabrics used in church interiors, and the complicated church ritual. At the same time Jesus became the "Emperor of the World," and the Virgin Mary became "the Queen of Heaven." The influence in all this was from the state to the church, not the other way about. By the late fifth century these various elements had been fused into a definitely Byzantine style centering in Constantinople. The three great periods of this art were, first, the sixth and seventh centuries, then a revival from the ninth through the twelfth centuries, and, finally, a last revival in the fourteenth and fifteenth centuries.

The first great achievements of Byzantine architecture are the great churches of the sixth century; in fact, the whole story of this architec-

ture is largely one of church building, for few Byzantine secular buildings survive and these present no important features of their own. The
first great churches followed a number of designs; the old Roman
basilica type continued to be built; then domed churches where the
domes rose either over round walls, or, more typically, were built over
polygonal or square foundations with the use of either squinches or
pendentives to carry the weight of the round dome down onto its
square base; [15] and, finally, combinations of the basilican and domed
types of plans, usually in some sort of a cruciform design. The favorite
building material was the flat, thin Roman brick with courses of mortar as thick as the bricks. In some regions, like Syria and Armenia,
where stone was easily available, it was used. The methods of construction varied enormously: for example, some types of domes were built
with the use of wooden centering; other types were erected, course by
course, without any support, so put together that each successive layer
rested on the one below. The domes and vaults were shells of stone or
brick or of hollow earthenware jars homogeneous with the walls and
covered outside with lead or tiles. The exteriors were left bare, but the
interiors were lavishly decorated with mosaics above, and marble columns and wainscoting below. The sculpture was in low relief and was
largely confined to carvings on the capitals of columns and to decorative bands, usually about the doors. Sculpture in the round practically
disappeared after the eighth century. The sculpture, like the designs
in the mosaics, had a totally unplastic, flat character. It avoided human forms, at first because of Christian dislike of pagan sculpture, and
later because of the Iconoclastic Struggle and of influences from Mohammedan art, which entirely rejected human and animal forms. The
sculpture of the capitals was of wonderful variety of design; the most
typical style of carving was to cover the four sides of a capital with a
lace-like and deeply undercut flat design. Above the capitals there was
often added a second capital or impost block to help carry the heavy
weight of the masonry onto the slender columns below and to lighten
the aesthetic effect of the arches. Usually this impost block was much
less elaborately decorated than the capital below it.

The great glory of these churches was in their glowing mosaics,
each made of tiny squares of glass or stone (*tesserae*) fitted into huge
designs and set in cement. The backgrounds were usually of gold made

by putting gold-leaf between two sheets of glass and cutting it after the glass cooled. The designs of these vast wall mosaics are highly transcendental; the figures seem to float in an other-worldly atmosphere. These Byzantine figures have travelled far from Graeco-Roman nature; they hardly have bodies at all; there is no flesh, no bones, no breath in these ghostly symbols. The figures, however, are all carefully related to one another, to the services of the church, and to the congre-

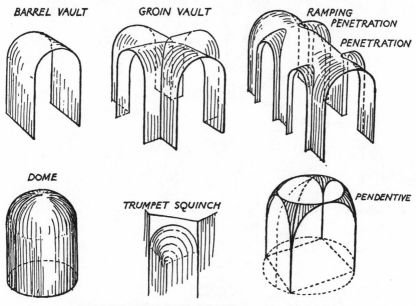

BARREL VAULT   GROIN VAULT   RAMPING PENETRATION
PENETRATION
DOME
TRUMPET SQUINCH
PENDENTIVE

ROMAN AND BYZANTINE VAULT FORMS

gation of the faithful. The designs are planned on the idea that the church interior "is heaven on earth, in which lives and moves the heavenly God," as one Byzantine writer said.[16] So the figures in the mosaics are related to one another, but they must also, as far as possible, face the congregation. Images on walls were not separated from the beholder, who was himself enclosed and surrounded by the congregation of the saints and taking part in the events he saw. The many curved surfaces of the Byzantine churches made it possible to have the figures both face each other and face the faithful, as for example, the Virgin Mary and Gabriel in the Annunciation face each other on two sides of a squinch, but at the same time they are able to face the congregation below.

The idea of a strict frontality of the figures as expressing the awful presence of the sacred persons and as furnishing a means of commun-

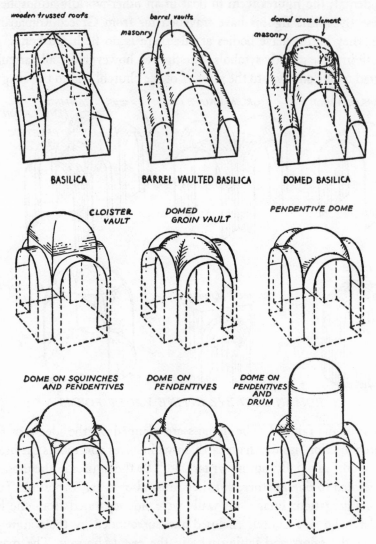

ROMAN AND BYZANTINE VAULT FORMS

ing with them through their images came from Mesopotamia or Iran. It appears clearly in the paintings of Dura Europos and was common in early Christian and Byzantine art. The figures, also, were always placed so that they did not cut across structural lines and they respected the basic frame of the building. And, from the point of view of architectural decoration, this was one of the most effective styles, for there was no attempt to knock a hole in the wall by driving through a perspective. The figures lie flat on the surface and never work at cross

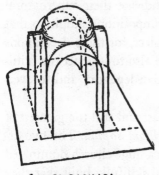

DOMED BASILICA
WITH CRUCIFORM
NAVE

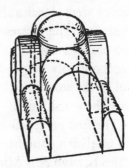

CRUCIFORM DOMED BASILICA

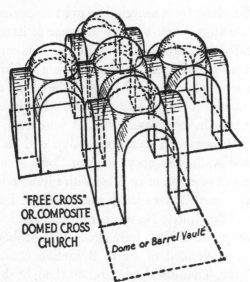

"FREE CROSS"
OR COMPOSITE
DOMED CROSS
CHURCH

Dome or Barrel Vault

ROMAN AND BYZANTINE VAULT FORMS

purposes with the architecture. The figures say the same thing that the building says: "I am wall, or vault, or dome." The curved surfaces of most Byzantine churches also were much better for catching the light on the glass mosaics than the flat side and back walls of the basilica type of building. Mosaics have a luminous richness not possible with frescoes or tapestries. The designs were usually flat and little attempt was made to model the figures in the round. The settings were simple and conventionalized; the landscapes were unreal and airless; all forms were denaturalized so as better to indicate their supernatural meaning. The figures were large and the compositions simple so that the observer could easily understand the subject, for these decorations were not only to glorify God, but they were also to instruct the faithful in the stories of the Bible and of Christian legendry and to overawe the worshipper.

The first great achievement of Byzantine art and still the greatest of all Christian churches is the sixth-century *Hagia Sophia*. The two architects, from Asia Minor, planned and built a huge church dominated by a vast central dome 179 feet high, and so skillfully built that they were able to put forty windows about the base of the dome. This gave to the dome, as Procopius said, "an effect so light it seemed rather to hang by a golden chain from heaven than to be supported by solid masonry." [17] Within all was aglow; the poet wrote of its marbles, "fresh green as the sea, or emerald stone, or again, like blue cornflowers with here and there a drift of fallen snow; there is a wealth of porphyry too, powdered with white stars." [18] Justinian hired ten thousand men to work five years on this vast sanctuary, and when it was finished in 537, he declared: "I have surpassed thee, O Solomon." One can only imagine how it all looked on great festival days with its glorious marble columns and walls, and above a great cloud of witnesses on a golden sky, the vast reservoir of air filled with a luminous golden haze, while into this unearthly haze there rose clouds of incense and the moving chants of the church. No wonder the ambassadors from Vladimir, the Russian prince of Kiev, were astounded, spellbound, and then overwhelmed, and decided to accept Byzantine Christianity rather than that of Rome. That day these Russians thought they saw angels descending to join in celebrating the mass. "The Greeks led us," they said, "where they worship their God and we knew not whether we were in heaven or on earth. For on earth there is no such splendor or such beauty, and we are at a loss to describe it. We only know that God dwells there among men." We saw things "transcending human intelligence." [19] Everything about *Hagia Sophia* was done not to the measure of man and this world but to the measure of God and of eternity.

Belonging to this same sixth century are the great churches of *San Vitale* and *San Apollinare Nuovo* in Ravenna; *San Marco* in Venice is a later copy of a sixth-century church in Constantinople that has disappeared. *San Marco*, next to *Hagia Sophia*, gives the best existing impression of what the great sixth-century churches once looked like. The mosaics in *Hagia Sophia* have been recovered from under the Turkish whitewash and paint, and the great church has regained much of its ancient glory. These buildings, remarkable as they are as feats of engineering, are more than brick and stone and glass and marble; they seem to exist outside the time and space of this world and seem still, what their builders intended them to be, outposts of eternity in this world of mortal men and transitory things.

The Iconoclastic Struggles of the eighth and ninth centuries drove many artists into exile; some went to southern Italy, others worked for the Mohammedans on such buildings as the *Dome of the Rock* at Jerusalem and the *Mosque of Damascus*. The arts and crafts, however, were kept alive at home, where churches and palaces continued to be built and where the decoration now consisted of historical and secular subjects, and flowers, animals, and landscapes. A great revival of art followed in the ninth through the twelfth century. Much more has survived from this period than from the art of the Age of Justinian. The churches now were usually much smaller, and the common type of church plan became a Greek cross inscribed in a square, with four small chambers at the four corners of the building. A central dome on a high drum rose above four lesser domes, also on drums, set at the four corners. The exterior was now no longer bare, but picturesque, decorated with arcades and with bricks and stone laid in elaborate designs: crosses, lozenges, circles, stars, and chequers. These church plans and the exterior decoration show great inventiveness and variety. In Russia the domes were covered with wooden or metal onion-shaped cupolas to shed the rain and snow. These were often brightly painted or gilded. In some areas, especially in Roumania, it later became the custom to fresco the whole outside of the church with huge religious designs. Within, the interior was lightened by substituting columns for piers, and the mosaics or frescoes had now come to be ar-

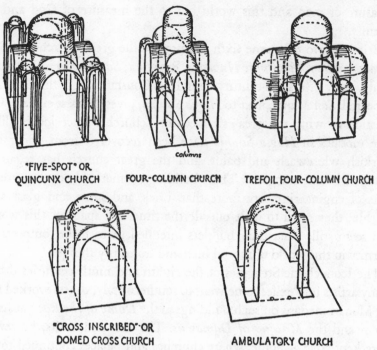

"FIVE-SPOT" OR
QUINCUNX CHURCH   FOUR-COLUMN CHURCH   TREFOIL FOUR-COLUMN CHURCH

"CROSS INSCRIBED"-OR
DOMED CROSS CHURCH   AMBULATORY CHURCH

LATER BYZANTINE VAULT FORMS

ranged in a fixed order. The decoration takes on a more liturgical and dogmatic plan; for each part of the building a certain subject is reserved. In the central dome is Christ, the world ruler, the *Pantocrator*, with angels and prophets about him; in the apse is usually the Virgin Mary praying for humanity, and on the four pendentives, supporting the central dome, are the four Evangelists. A correspondence is made between incidents of the Old and the New Testaments. This scheme of decoration not only told stories from the Bible but also illustrated the great dogmas of the church as they had been formulated by the church councils and the writings of the Fathers. For example, after the sixth century, the Virgin Mary in the scene of the Nativity is represented, not seated by the cradle, but lying down flat on a bed to emphasize the idea that Jesus really had a human birth, that "the Word" really "became flesh."

The decoration of both churches and palaces became more elaborate. Silver and ivory doors, purple curtains sliding on silver rods, silk fabrics and tapestries embroidered with gold, great golden lamps swinging from palace roofs and church domes, and furniture and fittings encrusted with mother of pearl, ivory, and gold—all became common.[20] It is from this period, from the ninth through the twelfth centuries, that much of the surviving Byzantine art comes. Besides churches and mosaics there has also come down a large amount of ivory carving where the use of human figures survived long after it had been given up in stone sculpture, magnificent metal work of all sorts, enamels, fabrics, embroideries, illuminated manuscripts, and also a great deal of panel and fresco painting. In much of this work, the craftsmanship is of so expert and subtle a quality that it could only have been the result of a tradition centuries old. Alongside the official art of Constantinople and the large centers, there flourished a more sentimental, more dramatic, and more popular art in the monasteries. The mosaics and paintings done in the cloisters are full of carefully observed bits of contemporary life; Jesus suffers on the cross, and Mary is worn from weeping. Much of the art connected with the monasteries was in the form of fresco painting and of icon painting of small wooden panels done in tempera. The basic arrangements for sacred pictures were fixed in manuals; as the Second Council of Nicaea (787) stated it: "the composition of religious imagery should not be left to the initiative of the artists, but formed on principles laid down by the church and by religious traditions." [21] But in spite of such rules, there is a much greater variety in Byzantine painting, especially in the popular art of the monks, than one would, at first, imagine. Western painting is familiar through numerous superb examples in our galleries, but to understand Byzantine mosaics and paintings one has to go to Venice, Ravenna, Rome, and further east. Even good color reproductions of Byzantine mosaics and paintings are rare.

The last flowering of Byzantine art in the fourteenth and fifteenth centuries came at a time when the empire was very reduced in size and when it was impoverished. Hence, fresco painting almost entirely supplants mosaics for the decoration of churches, monasteries, and secular buildings. During this Indian summer of the old empire some artists became, like the painters in Renaissance Italy, interested in problems of representing movement and dramatic action; others deliberately attempted to imitate old classical models. From the ninth century on, this art of Byzantium influenced profoundly the art of both

East and West. Workmen went from Constantinople, travelled into the Balkans, Russia, and the Mohammedan states, and into the lands of Latin Christendom. At the same time, Western missionaries, pilgrims, crusaders, and traders carried Byzantine ivories, manuscripts, textiles, embroideries, metal work, and panel paintings from one end of Europe to the other. Scandinavian rulers were crowned and buried in Byzantine silks, with lions, elephants, eagles, and griffins woven in them; they kept their Byzantine jewels and enamels on gold in Byzantine-carved ivory chests. The same was true of the Russian princes of Kiev, the doges of Venice, the abbots of Monte Cassino, the Norman kings of Sicily, and the wealthy merchants of Amalfi. It was always to the fabulous city on the Bosphorus that men turned for centuries for craftsmen or for *objets d'art* and *articles de luxe*.

Byzantine music developed out of the same combination of Jewish and Greek musical styles that formed the music of the Patristic Age. The Byzantine chant—about secular music nothing is known—had many features in common with the Syrian, Ambrosian, and, later, the Gregorian chant. The melodies were put together out of short traditional formulae; the composer combined these little bits of melodies with connecting passages, the whole being constructed to fit the words. People liked to hear these well-known short melodies arranged in different ways and connected by new transitional passages. Only after these longer melodies were composed did the theorist find that the notes of these elaborated melodies belonged to a mode, that is, to a consistent series of whole and semi-tones. But these modes were far from containing all the twelve semi-tones of a modern scale. Four or five tones provided all that was needed for a satisfactory leading of the voice. Such a scale was enough to support the more common modes.

The melodies were unharmonized and were probably sung without accompaniment. While the Latin Church adopted the Psalms as the textual basis of their chants, the Eastern Church developed its style for the musical presentation of original hymns. In the sixth century, the long ode-like hymns of Romanos, with from twenty to thirty stanzas of varying length, came into wide usage. For these long hymns, which became longer by the eighth century, elaborate melodies were written. The earlier Byzantine notation before about 1100 has never been deciphered. After 1400 the traditional chant, which was largely syllabic, was enriched by the introduction of elaborate rapid passages with runs and trills which, owing to uncontrolled license, led to a complete decadence of the style. Some of the old Byzantine melodies have been preserved in the Eastern churches of Russia and the Balkans and by the community of Uniate monks at Grottaferrata near Rome.

4. THE INFLUENCE OF BYZANTIUM

BYZANTIUM's services to civilization, in both the east and the west of Europe, were enormous. For centuries she preserved the Greek classics and Roman law until the barbarians from the worlds of Latin Christendom, Islam, and Slavdom were sufficiently civilized to take them over and develop them. The matchless city at the meeting place of East and West kept open a commercial exchange and a flow of ideas with all the ends of the then known world. She was for a millennium the great clearinghouse between Europe and Asia, and between antiquity and all later times. She had created a great art and a magnificent engineering from which men borrowed from Spain to India and from Greece to Norway, and in eastern Europe Constantinople played the role of civilizer taken by Rome in the Latin West.

As Latin Christendom slowly emerged from the backwardness and barbarism that followed in the wake of the Germanic migrations, it was to the Byzantine world that she turned for ideas. The art of the Carolingian and of the Ottonian Renaissance and, still more, the art of the Romanesque were all deeply indebted to the designs of the Byzantines which frequently reached them either through Greek craftsmen who came west or through small ivory carvings, reliquaries, illuminations, and icons which came to the West through trade. In many cases the Byzantine object was not merely copied, but its whole spirit was assimilated and it became the inspiration for a new creation. So it is not merely the Romanesque churches of France and of the Rhineland that resemble Byzantine buildings or are almost copies of them that show this influence. It entered into and deeply permeated all the artistic styles of the West for centuries in iconography, in color and design, and in the techniques of building, of painting, and of sculpture. The influence of Byzantium reappears in the West in the beginnings of

Italian Renaissance painting of men like Duccio and Giotto and in the humanism of the Florentine Academy of the fifteenth century.

At the same time, there was hardly an aspect of the Islamic culture of the Middle Ages that did not show Byzantine influence. It was from the Byzantines, directly or indirectly, that the Mohammedans procured the great works of Greek science and philosophy, which they were to develop in original ways. From Byzantium came, also, some of the inspiration of Islamic art. Byzantine architects, painters, mosaic workers, sculptors, and craftsmen found employment at Bagdad, Damascus, Cairo, and the other great Mohammedan centers. The beginnings of Islamic building and decoration, of cloth-making and other crafts, show them, at first, only as borrowers. Later on Islamic art, in turn, influenced the art of Byzantium. But even after the fall of Constantinople, the Ottoman sultans continued to build palaces and mosques in the Byzantine style.

The greatest influence of Byzantium was in the Slavonic world of eastern Europe. About 864 the Tsar of the Bulgarians was converted to the Greek Church, and in the early tenth century a separate Bulgarian patriarchate was established. The Serbs were converted in the eleventh century, though they remained under the patriarch of Constantinople. In the meantime, about 989, the prince of Kiev was baptized, the "third Rome" was born, and the transformation of Russia began. And soon the larger towns in Russia had each its *Hagia Sophia,* its *Golden Gate,* and its palaces, churches, and monasteries, all copied after those of Constantinople. In the ninth century two Greek missionaries, Cyril and Methodius, modified the Greek alphabet for use by the Slavs and translated the Bible into one of the Slavic dialects, doing something of the same work that Ulfilas had done in the fourth century for the Goths. Byzantine Christianity, including its monasticism, its theological literature, and its art and music spread all over the Balkans and northward toward the Arctic Circle in vast Russia. The first books written in the Slavic languages, Bulgarian, Serb, and Russian, were translations of the Bible, of the Greek theologians, and of popular Byzantine chronicles, saints' lives, and devotional treatises. The Byzantine church made no attempt to impose its language on the daughter churches as had the Latin church in the West. The church in the East had long been polyglot and remained so. The Byzantine Empire has disappeared, but the Byzantine church remains, and among the Slavs it still has on its side the force of numbers. Despite the anti-religious persecutions of the Communist regimes in the twentieth century, and despite the multiplicity of the languages in which its ancient liturgy is celebrated, it has kept a character as distinct and unique as that of Islam, and one much more traditional than that of the Church of Rome which has been profoundly changed, since mediaeval times, by the Counter-Reformation and Jesuitism.

CHAPTER V

Islamic Civilization

1. THE NATURE OF ISLAM

2. EDUCATION, LAW, PHILOSOPHY, AND SCIENCE

3. LITERATURE, ART, AND MUSIC

4. ISLAM AND THE WEST

ON the outer edge of Latin Christendom, in Spain, Sicily, and North Africa, and around the heart of the Byzantine Empire, in Egypt, Palestine, Syria, and Asia Minor, and farther on to the east stood the world of Islam. For centuries, Islam was both a threat and a source of commerce and ideas to both the Greek East and the Latin West. Its great cities and the courts of its princes became, from the eighth century through the twelfth, the centers of a brilliant material civilization and of a great scientific, philosophic, and artistic culture.[1]

When the Arabs began to expand in the first half of the seventh century they brought with them only one marked cultural trait: a love of poetry. Soon, though, they learned from the Byzantines, the Jews, the Persians, and the Hindus the basic elements of culture, and, as the Arabs extended their religion and their language, the conquered peoples, in turn, passed on their civilization to their Mohammedan conquerors. Spreading both eastward and westward, Islam embraced, before the Christian missions of the nineteenth century, more different national groups than any other world religion; these included Cau-

132]

casians, Chinese, Malayans, and Negroes—peoples dispersed halfway
around the globe—and Mohammedanism still represents about one-
seventh of mankind, and its adherents are spread out from Morocco
to the Philippines.

I. THE NATURE OF ISLAM

ARABIA, the home of Islam, is about half the size of Europe. In such
a huge area there was naturally a variety of climate and soil and a great
diversity of cultural traditions. At the time of Mohammed, around
A.D. 600, there was no strong government controlling any large part of
the country, and, in some areas a prolonged period of dessication was
causing economic stagnation, misery, and restlessness. In the central
areas of Arabia were nomad tribes, the Bedouins, who subsisted largely
on the milk of their camels and on dates. Their simple tribal organization was for the defense of date-growing oases and their flocks or for
attack on similar possessions in the hands of their neighbors. The practice of blood revenge of one tribe on another and endless tribal wars,
broken only for the four spring months which were sacred, was the
rule among these hardy tribesmen. Along the coasts, commerce was
carried on, and there were more cultural influences from the world
outside Arabia.

Mecca, the birthplace of the Prophet, was a focus of trade, on the
main route from the Mediterranean to the Red Sea and the Indian
Ocean. The town was strong enough to protect its wealth and freedom
from the Bedouin raids; part of the income of Mecca came from the
pilgrims who flocked to its great collection of shrines. Most of the
Arabs were polytheists, and many of the gods of the peninsula were
represented in the sacred *Ka'bah* or cube, a small square building near
the center of the town. The ceremonies of the annual feast at Mecca
and the *Ka'bah*, with its sacred black stone, were taken over by Mohammed into his religious system, and both have survived to the present. Among some of the Arabs the existence of a single supreme deity,
Allah, was a common conception; this idea probably had a native origin independent of outside influence, but it had been strengthened by
ideas from Jewish and Christian circles. Allah, the lord of men, had

no cult; he might be the creator of all things, but this was no argument against the existence of other divine beings. These monotheistic ideas had become so familiar in Mecca in Mohammed's time that he seemingly had no difficulties in converting the common people to the creed of one god, meeting opposition only from those who had vested interests in the *status quo*. The Koran never goes into the matter of the existence of Allah; what it does insist on is that Allah is the only god. Scattered through the Arabian peninsula were communities of Jews, Christians, and Persian monotheists. Many Arabs had joined these religious groups, and beyond these converts, the ideas of these surrounding faiths were undoubtedly widely known, at least in the larger Arabic centers.

The personality of Mohammed remains obscure in spite of his sayings and the many legends about him. There have been almost as many theories about the Prophet as there are biographers. According to tradition, he was born in A.D. 570, about five years after the death of Justinian, into a cadet branch of one of the leading families of Mecca. His father died before Mohammed was born, and his mother died when he was still a small child. First his grandfather, then an uncle, who was in the caravan trade, reared him. As a youth in the busy center of Mecca he probably learned to read and write enough to keep commercial accounts; he also heard Jewish and Christian teachers and early became interested in their religious ideas. Mohammed must have suffered, in these early years, from hardships, and he evidently became aware of the misery of many of his fellowmen. These early experiences were later to be the basis of his fervent denunciations of social injustice. At the age of twenty-five, he married a wealthy widow and probably went on some long caravan trips, at least to Syria. This gave him further contacts with Jewish, Christian, and Persian religious teachers. At the age of forty, after spending much time in fasting and solitary meditation, he heard a voice calling him to proclaim the uniqueness and power of Allah. Mohammed seemingly did not, at first, conceive of himself as the conscious preacher of a new religion. It was only the opposition from those about him at Mecca that drove him on to set up a new religious community with distinctive doctrines and institutions.

Mohammed's teaching, from the beginning, shows strong Jewish and Christian influence. He probably could read and write some Arabic, though later when he wanted anything recorded he employed a secretary. But the question of his reading and writing Arabic is of little moment, for at this time no religious books seem to have existed in Arabic. That Mohammed could read a foreign language is incredible. So what he knew of other monotheistic religions must have been acquired by hearing their preachers and by talking with their adherents. In any case, Mohammed learned the great stories of the Old Testament; especially was he impressed with the life of Abraham whom he later considered one of his own predecessors and who he claimed had founded the *Ka'bah* at Mecca. He, likewise, learned of the Christian Trinity whom he understood to be God the Father, Mary the Mother, and Jesus the Son. He learned about the Last Judgment and also about Jewish homiletic literature and the Jewish law of the *Talmud*.[2] Mohammed believed that both Jews and Christians were right about the idea of one god, the Last Judgment, and other matters, but also that Judaism could never be a religion for his people, and that Christianity had got mixed up with too much idolatry. He was looking for common ground on which to found a faith for all monotheists. He had a profound respect for Jews and Christians, especially for the Jews, though when they refused to join him and when later they thwarted him, he attacked them fiercely.[3] Mohammed took from Jewish, Christian, and also Persian teaching only what he wanted, and he combined all he borrowed in a set of ideas that always bore his own mark. In the Koran, for example, he uses the characters of the Bible as successful advocates in the past of the doctrines of Mohammed in the present. Mohammed called the Jews and the Christians the "People of the Book,"[4] and he came to believe himself called to give his own people, the Arabs, a book.

Mohammed began, with great vigor, to try to make converts, but at first his followers included only his wife and a few members of his own family and a handful of others. From indifference toward Mohammed the attitude of the local leaders turned to hostility because it was feared that acceptance of his teaching would change the government of Mecca and would destroy the income from pilgrimages. Some of his followers fled to Abyssinia. In the city of Medina, 200 miles to the north of Mecca, where many of the citizens were Jewish, some factions, weary of continual quarrels, turned to Mohammed as an arbitrator. He sent some of his followers to Medina, and thither he went himself in A.D. 622. This migration or Hegira, which became the Year One of the Muslim calendar, marked a turning point in Mohammed's fortunes and in the history of the world. At Medina, Mohammed became a political and social as well as a religious reformer. The Jews in Medina rejected him, and so he turned for converts to the Bedouins. He assured his followers that warfare on the unbelieving was holy, holding out to them, at once, the prospects of plunder and of salvation if they followed his leadership. At Medina he proved to be the great political and moral leader of Arabia, and he turned his people from raiding one another to a great raid on all the world outside. Mohammed now saw clearly that he was founding a new religion distinct from Judaism and Christianity. Friday was made the holy day, instead of Saturday or Sunday, the call from the minaret was decreed in place of the Jewish trumpet and Christian bells, a month of fasting and the pilgrimage to Mecca were instituted, and a great many regulations for the life of the faithful were established. After a few years, Mohammed was able to take Mecca. Only a few of his personal enemies were put to death, and though the idols of the *Ka'bah* were destroyed the building itself was preserved, declared venerable, and incorporated into the new religion of Islam. In 632 Mohammed died, the last of all the founders of great world religions. "Serious or trivial, Mohammed's daily behavior has constituted a canon which millions observe at this day with conscious mimicry. No one regarded by any section of the human race as Perfect Man has been imitated so minutely." [5] "Within a brief span of mortal life Mohammed had called forth out of unpromising material a nation never united before in a country that was hitherto but a geographical expression, established a religion which still claims the adherence of a goodly portion of the human race, and laid the basis of an empire." [6]

Mohammed's most precious legacy to his followers was the Koran, the sacred book of his teachings, compiled some years after his death. According to tradition, the Koran was put together from "scraps of parchment and leather, tablets of stone, ribs of palm-branches, camel's shoulder-blades and ribs, pieces of board and the breasts of men." [7] The passages were not arranged chronologically, or according to content; but, so far as there seems to be a principle, according to length.

As it was finally edited, the Koran consists of a hundred and fourteen chapters (*suras*); the whole is somewhat shorter than the New Testament. The style of the various parts differs; the passages dictated at Mecca are in a vivid, brief, and oracular style replete with prophetic feeling; the chapters dictated later are verbose and filled with legislative details and theological dogmas.

The Koran is presented as the inspiration of Allah dictated to Mohammed by the angel Gabriel; each passage opens with "In the name of Allah." This faith was first revealed to Abraham, the founder of monotheism as well as of the sacred *Ka'bah* of Mecca. From Abraham's eldest son had sprung the Arab race. God had also revealed himself to other Jewish teachers and later to Jesus, but the Jews and Christians had strayed away from true religion and had now rejected God's latest revelation through his prophet Mohammed. Islam was God's final revelation and must inevitably win all men. Mohammed's Allah resembles the God of the Jews; his god is not all wrath or cold justice; he is also a merciful god, "the compassionate one." In the same spirit, Mohammed emphasized the duty of forgiving injuries instead of avenging them.

Some of the insistence on detailed injunctions in the Koran is due less to a certain dictatorial character possessed by Mohammed than to his strong reaction from the social anarchy of Arabia in his time. Mohammed's legislation about women, marriage, and the family, the care of orphans, the poor, the slaves, and the insane does not suffer in comparison with the Roman and the Christian standards set by the codes of Theodosius and of Justinian. "The equality of all Mohammedans before the law, the absence of antagonistic class distinctions in Mohammedan society, the absence of any priestly caste—for in Islam every man is his own priest—the freedom of Mohammedan society from the evils of an ambitious and avaricious clergy like the bishops and abbots of the Byzantine Empire—these qualities stamp early Mohammedanism with a new and refreshing vigor." [8] This sacred book, the Koran, became the most widely-read book ever written; besides its use for worship, it was for centuries and still is the textbook from which practically every Mohammedan learns to read Arabic.

The regulation of the life of the faithful depends partly on the Koran and partly on tradition (the *Sunna*). This body of tradition was handed down in the form of short narratives told by someone who knew the Prophet. But not until over two centuries after Mohammed's death was any thorough work of editing undertaken. The whole history of this traditional literature has been of value to historians as a mirror in which is reflected the controversies and the changes in the political and religious history of Islam. Thus out of the Koran and out of the tradition of Mohammed there was early formed a doctrine of Islam. The first duty of the Mohammedan is to believe that "there is but one God, Mohammed is the Apostle of God." [9] In its unqualified monotheism and in allowing nothing to stand between man and his God, and in making men trust in God, has lain the strength of Islam. Whatever comes, the Muslim says: "It is the will of Allah; I am content with his decree." This belief brings comfort in sorrow and lessens the bitterness against wrongs, and it may be one reason why suicide has always been rare in Islamic lands. The worship of any other god in any possible form is idolatry; the Christian Trinity was as detested by Mohammed as the polytheism of the Arabs. No images of men, animals, or plants were allowed lest they become objects of worship. The angels are God's messengers, they bring God's inspiration to the prophets, they record the actions of men, receive their souls when they die, and appear as witnesses for them at the Last Judgment. Alongside the angels are the devils, who have rebelled against God and are ever ready to lead men astray.

Another aspect of this first duty of the faithful is to believe that God has sent prophets at all times to warn men of his power and of the judgment to come. The Koran mentions twenty-five prophets of God including three earlier Arabians, the patriarchs and prophets of Israel, and Jesus. Many of these messengers were rejected by their fellows who were punished for this sin of apostasy. The last or "Seal" of the prophets is Mohammed. Mohammed, however, disclaims all divinity for himself; he is very explicit in insisting that he is only God's mouthpiece. But his revelations of God, dictated to him by the angel Gabriel, must be accepted in all matters of faith and conduct. In God's time will come the Last Judgment. The trumpet will sound, the heavens will be opened, and the mountains turned to dust; out of their graves all men will rise; the deeds of each will be weighed. The blessed will go to a paradise of gardens and running waters where they will enjoy the company of lovely maidens and wives of perfect devotion. The evil shall be cast into a burning hell of fearful torments. On no subject did the Prophet so love to dwell as on that of the Last Judgment and the delights of Heaven and the horrors of Hell. God's judgment is based partly on right belief and partly on the careful observance of religious rites and duties by the faithful.

The second of these religious duties is prayer. Neither the ceremonies for prayer nor the five set times for devotions are stated precisely in the Koran, but tradition maintains that these usages were fixed before Mohammed's death. For each of the five prayer times the worshipper must face Mecca and the prayer must be made in Arabic. Ablutions in water or sand, of the face, feet, and hands, must be made before prayers. In times of sickness or of danger the ritual may be relaxed.[10] On Friday, the faithful men must gather at noon for prayers in the mosque. Here the leader, the *imām,* takes the direction in timing the prayers. Like the Jewish rabbi, the *imām* is not a consecrated person; he has only the prestige that his own learning, character, and personality command. There are no sacraments and no priestly ordination or apostolic succession. In neither the Jewish nor Mohammedan religions may anyone stand between the worshipper and God. Such a relation, if established, can only be direct. The unison prayers in the mosques help to give a sense of social equality and of solidarity among the community of the believers. These services have been called "the first drill ground of Islam." The Friday prayers are usually followed by a sermon.

A third duty is the giving of alms. This came to be fixed as a tax, though in theory it was always regarded as a loan made to God, which he would repay many fold. The proceeds were used to support the poor, to run the charitable institutions of the community, and to build and repair mosques. A fourth religious duty is to fast during *Ramadān,* the ninth month of the lunar year; no food or drink can be taken between sunrise and sunset.[11] The sick or those on a journey are exempted, though they are expected to fast an equal number of days later. Mohammed always insisted that, though essential for religious discipline, ceremonial practices were secondary. "If a keeper of the fast does not abandon lying, God does not care about his leaving off eating and drinking." A fifth duty is to make, once in a lifetime, a pilgrimage to Mecca, to follow there the traditional ceremonies. The Mecca pilgrimage has long been one of the greatest unifying influences in Islam. It offered and still offers (for Mohammedanism is a great living faith) a chance for high and low, men of many nations, to meet together on a common basis before God. Of all world religions Islam has been most successful in overriding barriers of color and nationality. No line is drawn except between believers and unbelievers.

Almost as important as these five sacred duties, "the five pillars of faith," was sacred war—all wars were sacred—against those "who ascribe partners to God," that is, the non-Mohammedans. "Fight against those who believe not in God nor in the Last Day, who prohibit not what God and his Apostle have prohibited, and who refuse allegiance to the True Faith." [12] Besides these major obligations, the Koran and the tradition of the Prophet contain a large body of religious and ethical teachings and of legal injunctions. For example, the use of wine and pork, gambling, usury, and the making of images of men and animals are forbidden. Rules are laid down for marriage, divorce, and many aspects of the life of the family; penalties are fixed for crimes like stealing, murder, fraud, perjury, slander, and many minor offences. In fact the Koran is the great source of all law in the Islamic states. Everywhere Mohammed substituted the moral fellowship of religious belief and ethical conduct for tribal union through blood kinship. He rejected the nationalist side of Judaism, and accepted the universalism of Christianity. His personality and his teachings left an enormous impression on men of many generations; in the history of mankind only Buddha and Jesus are to be compared with him in influence.

Soon after Mohammed's death in 632, a wave of conquest gathered in all of Arabia, Palestine, Syria, Egypt, and part of Persia. In less than a century all of North Africa, Spain, Asia Minor, and Central Asia to the Indus River were swept by the conquering armies of Islam. These conquests were as orderly as they were speedy; little damage seems to have been done, and immediately after the Arab armies entered an area they organized it. The Arab annexation, at first, meant little more than a change of rulers. Life and social institutions went on as before with little interference and no forced conversions; the conquered peoples could even keep their own religion by paying a tax. But gradually the culture patterns of both the conquerors and the conquered changed. The Arab colonies planted in each new territory became the centers from which Islamic religious ideas spread and in which, at the same time, a new culture developed. Like the Roman conquests, the Arab conquests were based on the ideas, first of subduing a country and setting up an administration for it, then of waiting for the populace to become converted to the new order. Not until the new peoples, like the Seljuks, who were outside the Graeco-Roman tradition, were converted to Mohammedanism did Islam become fanatical. Indeed, no such militant intolerance as characterized the Christian attack on paganism was normally shown by the Mohammedans until into the eleventh century. The reasons for these fantastic conquests were various. To his own people, especially to the desert tribes, Mohammed offered war and booty, and to those who lived in the Arab towns he offered the extension of commerce. Caravans travelled in the midst of the Muslim armies. For those who died, Islam promised a glowing paradise. One drop of blood shed in battle, even a single night spent under arms would count for more than two months of prayer or fasting.

The campaigns began as raids for warring tribes now forbidden by religion to fight among themselves. The immediate object was booty rather than permanent expansion, but the whole movement acquired drive as it passed from one victory to another until finally more organized campaigns were undertaken, and the great Arab empire was launched. As the plundering armies moved on from the bare and sandy lands of Arabia into the fruitful countries of Syria, Persia, and Egypt, they were joined by thousands of others, many of them not Arabs, who assisted in the plunder of rich cities. Both the Byzantine and the Persian Empires were thoroughly exhausted because of a long struggle that had been going on between them. This helped to make both states an easy prey to conquest. In addition, those peoples under Byzantine rule frequently hated the Byzantine tax collector and the orthodoxy of the Byzantine upper clergy. In Syria, the Christian Byzantine auxiliaries went over en masse to the conquerors. Everywhere the Jews were favorable to the Mohammedans who would persecute them less than did the Byzantine Christians; moreover the Arabs who believed in one god were, to the Jews, inevitably better than the wicked "who were trying to persuade the world that Three is One." The Persian cities fell as easily as had Antioch, Damascus, and Alexandria; many apparently believed a change of masters might be better and could hardly be worse. The Muslim creed in Persia offered to make all men brothers, whereas Zoroastrianism condemned the industrial classes and the artisans as impure and unclean. Many of the conquered could now follow their religious practices with less interference than before. Prosperity rose in all the regions subdued, and the taxes were lighter and were more fairly collected.

Actually the Arab penetration of the areas about Arabia had begun before Mohammed. Arabs had been admitted in numbers into the Byzantine and Persian states as soldiers and settlers, pushing their way from their barren homelands into the fertile crescent, much as the Germans had earlier been allowed to push their way into the Roman Empire. Some historians believe that the Arabs would inevitably have expanded into the surrounding lands without Mohammed; the over-population and the dessication of Arabia, and the known wealth of the lands round about are sufficient to account for some of the expansion. The sanctions of a religious crusade only added zest and direction to these basic causes. Finally the brilliant generalship of some of the Muslim commanders and the use of troops on horse- and camel-back against the foot-soldiers of their enemies counted in the total situation. The Arab conquests, however, constitute one of the most fantastic chapters in human history and one that will always remain something of a mystery. The Mohammedans wanted to close the crescent by driving up through Gaul from the west, and up the valley of the Danube from the east, but they were finally checked, almost at the gates of Constantinople, in 718, and at the Battle of Tours in the valley of the Loire in 732. After their first century of rapid expansion, the Muslims never won much or lost much.[18]

Mohammed left no male heir, nor had he designated a successor or even a method of selecting one. His friends made his father-in-law caliph (meaning successor or vicar), the political and religious head of Islam, because the Prophet had asked him to lead prayers during Mohammed's last illness. He died shortly, and they chose in turn two disciples who had fled with Mohammed to Medina in 622. The second, Othman, was a member of the important Ommiad family. A movement to keep the caliphate in the hands of Mohammed's own family and to set up the Koran as against the tradition of Mohammed opposed the rule of Othman. Othman was murdered in 656 and Ali, the husband of Mohammed's daughter, Fatima, became caliph. He, in turn, was murdered and a member of the Ommiad family again became head. The capital was moved from Medina to Damascus which, under the Ommiad rulers, became a great commercial and cultural center. Their state was modelled on that of Byzantium.

A descendant of Mohammed's uncle, Abbas, in 750, overthrew the Ommiads, set up the Abbasid Dynasty (750–1258), moved the capital further east to Bagdad, close to old Persia, and made the Persian oriental despotism the model for the state. But the Abbasids could not maintain the political unity of Islam. The last surviving Ommiad in 756 set up a state in Spain with Cordova as its capital. Other small independent states were established in North Africa; one of these held Sicily from 831 to 1090. The Fatimites, named for Mohammed's daughter, in 909 began a caliphate in Tunis, and in 972 took Egypt from the Abbasids and founded a new capital at Cairo. The Arabs had never developed a powerful state in Arabia, and the new states they established never held together as had the Roman Empire. In all the Arab states there was always a conflict between the landed aristocracy and the ruler as there was in the states of Latin Christendom. Nevertheless, though the Arabs never built an enduring state like the Roman Empire, they did spread a common religion, a common language, a common economic life, and a common culture that cut across all the divisions of these political states and made a cultural unity of the whole world of Islam.

Mohammed had warned his followers against religious divisions: "Do not part in sects, you were enemies and God made friendship between your hearts." But he, nevertheless, anticipated that there would be factions among the faithful, for he once said: "My people will be divided into seventy-three sects, of which only one will be saved." [14] The first great division came after the Prophet's death. One group, the *Sunnites,* wanted to keep the headship (the caliphate) elective, and, in doctrine, they accepted the ideas of the *Sunna,* the body of traditions of Mohammed. A minority group, the *Shī́ites,* wished to keep the headship in the family of Mohammed, and in doctrine held only to what was in the Koran, though, in time, they developed an elaborate religious tradition of their own. The *Sunnites* came to predominate in Arabia, Turkey, North Africa, Afghanistan, North India, and Malaysia; the *Shī'ites* have their main seat in Iran, but there are others in India and some in all the regions of Islam. From these two main divisions about a hundred sects have broken off, and Islam has been divided by political, economic, and theological differences, resembling—though not so sharply diversified as—the Christians. The Muslims, never having had any machinery for formal excommunication, have always been slow in recognizing that a group of dissenting believers has broken off.

The most significant religious movement inside Islam was the rise and spread of mysticism. The term *Sūfism* is used by the Muslims to denote any variety of mysticism, the word being derived from the rough woollen garments worn by Christian ascetics and taken over from them by religious enthusiasts of Islam. On one side of his nature, Mohammed was himself a mystic. He practiced certain methods of inducing a trance-like state borrowed from the mystics of Judaism, from Christianity, and even from the Persian religious mystics. Mohammed often felt very close to God; typical of his ideas are the following: "Wherever ye turn there is the face of Allah; we (God) are nearer to him (man) than his neckvein." [15] And he always preached the religious value of prayer, vigils, and fasting. Though the Prophet spoke unfavorably of the life of the monk—the Koran says: "Ye that are unmarried shall marry"—his own example in the practice of mystical devotion, and the influence of surrounding religions, started, by the eighth century, a mystical and ascetic movement inside Islam. The movement was further stimulated by the terrors of hell as depicted in the Koran, by the upheaval and misery of civil and foreign wars, by the lavish display and worldliness of the upper classes, by the easy and mechanical piety of many of the faithful, and, finally, by the growth of rationalism and free-thought. All of these induced a counter movement toward asceticism, mysticism, and a desire to discipline the soul beyond the merely formal observance of ritual forms.

The earlier *Sūfis* wandered from place to place, either alone or in small groups, living by begging or by their own labor. Most of them came from the artisan classes in the towns; many became popular preachers and missionaries who took the lead in carrying the faith to the masses and in spreading it into new lands. The strength of these mystics lay in the satisfaction they gave to the religious craving of the common people, who found the teachings of the theologians cold and abstract. Thus, gradually, the mystics gathered to themselves much of the vital religious energy of the Muslim world, and they created therein a great fount of self-renewal. The early *Sūfīs* preached a simple gospel, which urged man to renounce all earthly ambition, and showed them a way of prayer, fasting, and good works that would lead them to a rebirth in God. In the ninth century, *Sūfīsm* became penetrated with Hellenistic doctrines of *gnosis* through ecstasy and self-annihilation. At the same time, the *Sūfīs* grafted onto the main stem of Islam masses of traditions, some of which came from Christian sources, like the belief in the second coming of the Prophet, and the belief in miracles connected with the life of Mohammed and of other holy men of Islam. In all of this there is evidence of Gnostic, Neo-Platonic, Jewish, Christian, Hindu, and Persian influences. Indeed, mysticism is the common ground where Judaism, Christianity, Mohammedanism, and the religions of Persia and India touch each other most closely. All believe in a knowledge imparted in ecstasy and in a wisdom that differs altogether from intellectual understanding. With all the mystics language becomes inadequate, and they all fall back on symbolism. Some of the mystics protested not only against the common religious practices of Islam but also against the political and social abuses around them, abuses that appeared to be condoned by the official *Ulamā*. These radical social views, and ideas that seemed too pantheistic for the orthodox, led to persecution of some of the mystics. But the high esteem in which many of the *Sūfīs* were held by the mass of the faithful rendered the opposition useless.

By the ninth century, a few of the mystics were organized into monastic communities, though this became more common from the twelfth century on. It was out of these communities that there came some important treatises which laid down a method by which the soul could return to God through a series of "stations" which included repentance, abstinence, and renunciation. Purifying exercises of meditation, prayer, and fasting help to exalt the soul, but love is the guiding principle of the seeker after God. The return to God is achieved partly by man's own effort and partly by God's grace.

The *Sūfīs* never formed a completely separate sect with sharply defined ideas. They comprised many shades of opinion, and out of *Sūfism* came a variety of religious currents and of religious orders, somewhat like the monastic orders of Christendom. The movement included men of genuine conviction and some great scholars and poets, but also some charlatans and fanatics. Some introduced the worship of Mohammed as a deity, and brought into Islam an elaborate cult of saints and relics. There was no papacy to control these matters, just as there was no organized way to canonize the heroes of ascetic ideals, except the informal canonization of popular acclaim. The whole *Sūfīc* movement in Islam has been, from the beginning, varied and protean in character.

It was al-Ghazālī (d. 1111) in the eleventh century who provided a metaphysical basis for *Sūfism,* and grafted it onto the main current of Islamic theology and life. As a youth, he studied law, theology, and philosophy. He was then a teacher of law, and he became famous throughout Islam for his eloquence and learning. When he was nearing the age of forty, he had a violent religious conversion. He found himself in revolt against the dry formalism of the theologians, and he set out to find reality through examining all the Muslim religious ideas of his time. He was deeply learned in Greek and Mohammedan thought, but, after a long struggle, he fell back on the *Sūfīc* doctrine of a personal experience of God, of a relation to the divine that can never be learned from books. Like Luther, he led men back of an elaborate theology to the simple experience of the founder of the faith. He felt himself called to save the faith from the slow destruction of outward attack and inward dessication by infusing into it a new spiritual life. Thus, al-Ghazālī broke the yoke of Islamic scholasticism somewhat as Luther was later to break that of Christian formalism.

The religion al-Ghazālī preached was a vivid one, full of the love of God on the one hand, and of the horrors of sin and hell on the other. His most influential books were the *Destruction of Philosophy* and the *Revival of the Science of Religion.* In these he argues that sensation is illusory, and that reason, based on sensation, is deceptive and leads only to doubt. Logic and science cannot prove God the only great reality. Only a life of prayer and good works can bring man to know God. At the same time, without a belief in God and a desire to do his will there can be no moral order in society. He accepts the Islamic religious practices, but he interprets them only as a guide to direct the soul upward toward a union with God. He succeeded in bringing *Sūfīsm* into the main current of Muslim theology and religious usage. From now on, the orthodox accepted the idea that the revelations given to the mystics supplement and clarify those given to Mohammed. He created a marvellous synthesis of the old and the new and stirred Islam with a new fervor. Next to the Prophet, al-Ghazālī remains the most influential religious force in the Muslim tradition. He influenced deeply the greatest of mediaeval Jewish philosophers, Maimonides, and even Christian writers—above all Aquinas, Dante, and Pascal—found an inspiration in his translated works and used his ideas in the defense of their religion.

What al-Ghazālī could not foresee was that by bringing *Sūfīsm* into the main current of Muslim religious practice and theology he was opening the door to some ideas and practices that would later debase the faith. *Sūfīsm* and *Sūfīc* religious orders, in the twelfth century and later, swept over the whole of Islam somewhat as the Franciscan movement stirred the Latin Church in the thirteenth century. Some of the later mystics moved far from the faith of Mohammed and set up a pure monist system, on Neo-Platonic lines, where all flows out of God and all returns to him. Mohammed becomes identified with the Platonic logos, the perfect man who was the outward manifestation of God, in a way that resembles the doctrine of Paul and of the Fourth Gospel concerning Christ. These ideas, especially with some of the Persian poets of the twelfth and thirteenth centuries, were wafted into a fantastic and esoteric theosophy in which the whole of the visible world becomes a vast illusion. Religious rites and duties count for little with God. All that matters is an ardent faith, a heart full of prayer, and a mystic union with God. The one great center of resistance to some of these vagaries was to be found in the orthodox schools, *Madrasas,* in connection with the mosques. These schools strove to hold the whole Islamic community fast to the essentials of its belief and to a continuing sense of their own unity as Muslims. They tried to offset the abuses of *Sūfism,* but they came finally to hold a dead hand over the growth of Muslim thought.

2. EDUCATION, LAW, PHILOSOPHY, AND SCIENCE

THE SOURCES of Islamic culture in part resembled the sources of Byzantine civilization, but, for the rest, the Muslims drew much more from the ancient cultures of Arabia, Mesopotamia, Persia, and India. At the time of the rise of Mohammedanism in the seventh century, the first great age of Byzantine civilization had not yet passed, and the Graeco-Persian culture of the Sassanian period in Persia was still at its height. This Persian culture, besides having a strong native tradition in art and literature, had taken over Greek science and philosophy (though not Greek literature) from schismatics and pagan philosophers driven out of the Byzantine Empire. By the middle of the sixth century Persia had become a great repository of Greek science and philosophy, the cultivation of which had greatly declined in Europe. By A.D. 641, the Arabs had conquered Persia, and they fell heir to this rich Greek and Persian heritage. Within two centuries most of these works were available in Arabic translations, and the culture of the Persians had conquered the conquerors. In the meantime, the great Byzantine centers of culture in Syria, Palestine, and Egypt had been taken over by the Muslims, and their power had reached into the river valleys of North India. In bringing early Islamic culture into contact with Greek science and philosophy, the conquest of Syria was as important as that of Persia. From all these sources in the Near and Middle East, the Islamic world, in the course of the two centuries following the death of the Prophet, produced a new and original culture that was spread from the Pyrenees eastward to the Philippines.

The greatest centers of this culture, as far at least as it was to influence the civilization of Europe, were Damascus, Bagdad, Cairo, and Cordova. Damascus, the first to develop, was already an ancient city before the Arab conquest. Built at a point where five streams converge, it was well supplied with parks, fountains, and public baths. It became a great commercial and manufacturing city and by the tenth century had a population of 140,000. In the middle of the Muslim city stood the huge palace and the gardens of the caliph and, beside them, the greatest of all Islamic mosques built on the site successively occupied by a Roman temple and by a Christian cathedral. Twelve thousand workmen were employed for eight years to build this mighty sanctuary whose ground plan, engineering, and decoration were Byzantine. The vast mosaic floor was covered with rich carpets, the walls were faced with marble and tiles, and the interior was lighted with seventy-four stained glass windows and thousands of hanging lamps of metal and of enamelled glass. In its construction, the master masons used for the first time in a Muslim building the horse-shoe arch, and one of its three minarets is the oldest that survives in all Islam. As in the Byzantine cities, there were splendid parks and public buildings, and great charitable foundations for the care of the sick, orphans, and the aged. Each craft had its quarter. The poorer sections of the city were as squalid as other parts were magnificent. Outside the city the landed aristocrats and the wealthier merchants had magnificent homes surrounded with gardens.

Bagdad came to be even larger than Damascus; in the tenth century it had at least 800,000 inhabitants and was, after Constantinople, the largest city in the world. The Tigris River and a system of canals gave the city access to the sea, and its trade and manufacture brought an enormous accumulation of wealth. Its palaces, mosques, schools, and public buildings were the wonder of the world. The upper classes loved luxurious display; they lived in houses incrusted with marble, mosaics, tiles, and arabesques in plaster or stone. They loved polo games, and horse-racing was a mania with them. They dressed in the richest silks and gold brocades, perfumed their clothing, hair, and beards, and loaded themselves with jewelry on ears, necks, wrists, and ankles. Women were usually excluded from men's social gatherings, as they were not in the Byzantine world, and their place was taken by poets, musicians, and dancing slave girls. Life in Cairo and Cordova, and in the lesser cities, was very much the same. In the eleventh century Cordova is said to have had 200,000 houses, 600 mosques, and 900 public baths. The streets of all the larger towns were paved with stones, and were cleaned, policed, and illuminated at night. Water was brought to the public squares and to many of the houses by conduits. The tooled leather work, the work in metal, glass-making and silk-weaving, the tile and ceramic creations, the illuminated manuscripts, and the wrought jewels made in these Islamic centers found markets all over Asia and Europe.

The great Islamic cities of the Near East, North Africa, and Spain were supported by an elaborate agricultural system that included extensive irrigation and an expert knowledge of agricultural methods. By the ninth century, the agricultural methods used in Islamic lands were the most advanced in the world. The Muslims had the finest horses and sheep and the best orchards and vegetable gardens. Through Sicily and Spain they introduced into Europe for the first time (or reintroduced after they had been lost in the West) oranges and lemons from India and Syria, roses and peaches from Persia, strawberries, figs, quinces, spinach, artichokes and asparagus, cotton, rice, sugar-cane, hemp, the mulberry and the silk worm from the Near and Middle East. They knew how to fight insect pests, how to use fertilizers, and they were experts at grafting trees and crossing plants to produce new varieties. By these means areas that have since become lands of low agricultural production were able, from the ninth through the thirteenth centuries, to support huge populations.

The larger cities were the centers of important schools. The first school connected with a mosque, about which anything is known, was one set up at Medina in 653; the first one in Damascus dates from 744. But by 900 nearly every mosque had an elementary school for the education of both boys and girls. These and other schools were run by private tutors who lived from the fees of their pupils. Children usually started to school at five; those in the poorer classes ordinarily did not continue for more than three years. As education apart from religion was to the Mohammedan mind an anomaly, the young pupils were first taught to read and write Arabic so that they could understand the Koran. One of the first lessons in writing was to learn how to write the ninety-nine most beautiful names of God and simple verses from the Koran. After the rudiments of reading and writing were mastered, the Koran was then studied thoroughly and arithmetic was added. According to the Muslim writers, reading, writing, and grammar were primarily for the study of the sacred texts, arithmetic for working out the shares of inheritance according to the Koran, and astronomy for the orientation of mosques toward Mecca and for compiling the calendar. It was assumed, of course, that these studies would also be useful in other fields. For those who wanted to study further, the larger mosques offered instruction in Arabic grammar and poetry, logic, algebra, biology, history, law, and theology. *Madrasas,* or houses of learning, mostly in connection with mosques, were set up by princes and high officials, and these schools grounded the upper classes—and such poor boys as the foundation or wealthy patrons supported—in the traditional ideas of Islam and in the rudiments of secondary education. For those who wished to specialize in theology, the instruction in the larger mosque schools was more advanced. These primary and secondary schools and lectureships connected with the mosques were supported by the income of lands and buildings belonging to the mosques and by the fees of the pupils. By 900 learning was held in high esteem, and both teachers and pupils were greatly respected by the mass of the population. The large libraries collected by the wealthy landed aristocrats and merchants showed that learning—as in the Italian Renaissance—was one of the marks of a gentleman.

Among higher and more advanced schools that of Medina first came into prominence. In Medina the Koran had received its final form, and the *Sunna* was here first organized. So, from an early period, students flocked to the school connected with the chief mosque of Medina. The teachers strove to maintain the unity and orthodoxy of Islamic thought after the breakup of the caliphate and the rise of sects among the faithful. Paralleling this famous school of higher studies, others arose in the great Muslim centers. In 830, one of the caliphs founded the *House of Wisdom* in Bagdad; it was primarily a research institute like the old Alexandrian Museum; it contained a library, scientific equipment, a translation bureau, and an observatory. Instruction was given in rhetoric, logic, metaphysics and theology, algebra, geometry, trigonometry, physics, biology, medicine, and surgery. An encyclopedic course of study arranged by a Muslim society called the *Brothers of Sincerity,* written about 1000, lays down an elaborate program of graded studies beginning with elementary subjects and proceeding to the most advanced. It survives as the most complete educational system that the mediaeval world produced. The judge and the theologian were expected to be experts in Islamic tradition, canon law, and scholastic theology. The state administrator, the civil servant, and the educated noble or merchant were supposed to be thoroughly trained in grammar, rhetoric, and history, a universal if somewhat superficial type of learning. Among these groups facility and distinction in written expression, mastery of etiquette, and a fine command of handwriting were considered the great accomplishments. In 1065 a great university was founded at Bagdad. Other universities developed, including important ones at Damascus, Jerusalem, Cairo, Alexandria, and Cordova. A second university founded in Bagdad in 1234 became the largest of all. It had magnificent buildings, including quarters for four law faculties, one for each of the four main schools of the *Sunnites*. The students who were admitted were, in part, supported by the endowments. The university also maintained dormitories, a hospital, and a huge library, where it was easy to consult the books, and where pens and paper and lamps were supplied free to the students. In this second Bagdad university, though it had fine equipment, the teaching was severely restricted by religious orthodoxy.

Besides the study of Mohammedan religious and legal ideas, the study of poetry ranked very high, as it had with the Greeks and Romans. In the tenth century, a writer considered the native Arabic studies of poetry, grammar, history, law, and theology as higher in value than the imported, foreign subjects of logic, medicine, mathematics, astronomy, music, mechanics, and alchemy. In most of the higher schools the sciences were studied, and much publication in all fields came out of the higher schools. Scientific and rationalistic studies were always frowned upon by some of the learned, and the great intellectual development in the chief centers was, in large part, due to the patronage of a few caliphs of large vision. After the eleventh century, the reactionary orthodox got the upper hand everywhere except in Spain and North Africa. Here scholars driven from the East found a refuge, just as schismatic and pagan scholars driven out by the Byzantines found refuge with the Muslims. Finally, after the thirteenth century, the conservatives everywhere got control and from then until the nineteenth century no important new intellectual currents developed inside Islam.

The Muslims were great book collectors, and in all the larger towns there was a flourishing book trade. The employment of paper rather than papyrus or parchment made books relatively cheap. Besides great libraries attached to the mosques and the larger schools, princes, nobles, and merchants had extensive private collections which they were usually willing to open to qualified scholars. We hear of a private library in Bagdad, as early as the ninth century, that required a hundred and twenty camels to move it from one place to another. Another scholar of Bagdad refused to accept a position elsewhere because it would take four hundred camels to transport his books; the catalogue of this private library filled ten volumes. This is the more astonishing when it is realized that the library of the king of France in 1300 had only about four hundred titles. In the thirteenth century before the Tartars sacked the city (1258), Bagdad had thirty-six public libraries and over a hundred book-dealers, some of whom were also publishers employing a corps of copyists. Descriptions of both public and private libraries speak of the classification of books and their arrangement in separate cases or even in separate rooms. Elaborate catalogues were kept, and the larger libraries were staffed with educated librarians, copyists, and binders. The most extensive public library of which there is a record is a tenth-century foundation in Cairo; it originally contained a hundred thousand volumes. These were later moved into a larger research foundation called the *House of Wisdom* which, by the eleventh century, claimed to have over a million volumes on its shelves. By 1250 the most valuable material in the Islamic libraries had become available to European scholars in translation. This transference came just in time, for, shortly after the middle of the thirteenth century, the Mongols in the East and the Christians in Spain began to destroy Islamic books in a wholesale manner. Spain was so stripped of Muslim books that when Philip II, in the sixteenth century, founded the Escorial library, he was unable to find many Arabic books in Spain. Some survived in Morocco, and gradually a collection was built up, though a seventeenth-century catalogue of the Escorial library, then the largest in Spain, showed only 4,000 Islamic titles, lorn survivors of one of the worst holocausts of books in history. Fortunately, a large number of Islamic books survived in Egypt, Persia, and India, from whence most of our knowledge of Muslim civilization has come.

Islamic law has always been rooted in the religious system of the Koran; the religious leader and the law-giver were never distinct in the personality of the Prophet himself. His aim from the beginning was to comprehend life in its totality so that from birth to death there would never be a moment unprovided for by religious regulation. The legal and the religious were all interwoven. The divine inspiration as set forth in the Koran and in the tradition of Mohammed regulated such diverse matters as belief and religious practice, the family, many types of political and commercial relations, the calendar, diet, dress, sexual intercourse, weights and measures, legitimate and prohibited musical instruments, and many other matters both great and small. Islamic law became the most fundamental force in moulding the whole social order of the Muslim world. This law differed in the interpretation of different schools of thought, but, in its essentials, it was uniform and all pervasive. Law, rather than theology, has been the most significant and the most highly developed subject of Muslim study.

The Koran and the tradition of Mohammed offered not a complete and systematic body of law but only the general principles out of which a legal system could be evolved. This law was much less severe than the religious law of the Jews and Christians. It allowed the believer to enjoy the good things that Allah had provided for men, though restraint and due measure had to be observed. It favored practical activity in agriculture, industry, and commerce and believed that labor was good. Human nature was full of evil impulses and the law was to restrain these, so that men would co-operate for the common good. All men were equal before God, and all were equal before the law, though in social relations elaborate differences in rank were everywhere recognized. To make the law adequate for varied situations "the principle of analogy" was developed; this applied to new problems, principles that the legalists derived from the original deposit of faith. After a few centuries of growth, "the principle of consensus" was set up to find a common core of opinions among the early interpreters of the law. A class of *Ulemā,* learned interpreters of the law, grew up, corresponding to the "scribes" of Judaism and having some of the same religious prestige as the clergy among the Christians. Within three centuries after the death of Mohammed, the Islamic law, as laid down in the Koran and the tradition of the Prophet, and as interpreted by analogy and by the consensus of early decisions, came to be a very rigid system. The doctrine of consensus fixed the law about as the early councils of the church had defined the Christian faith. In both cases the tendency was to freeze the whole system into a fixed form. Thus the right of individual decision for later scholars was restricted to making commentaries on the legal principles evolved in the first centuries of Islam.[16]

The political theory of Islam defined the community as the body of the faithful. Mohammed substituted for a real or fictitious family relationship among the Arabs the Jewish idea of the holy people entrusted by God with divine knowledge and a special destiny among all mankind. "The Muslims," says one of the traditional narratives about the Prophet, "are a single hand, like a compact wall whose bricks support one another." [17] A corollary of this concept of religious brotherhood is equality; all Muslims are equal before God.[18] The Muslim state was a theocracy, and no distinction, in theory, was drawn between the temporal and the spritual. The split in Latin Christendom between church and state was unthinkable in the Islamic world. God is the supreme ruler of the Muslim community; thus the state treasury is "the treasury of Allah," the public officials are the "employees of Allah," and the armed forces are the "army of Allah." The community under God will set a bound to men's evil natures. The Koran says: "Men are the enemies of each other and law and government are ordained of God to curb men's evil instincts, to prohibit certain acts and to enjoin others. The object of government is to lead men to prosperity in this world and to salvation in the next." At the beginning of mankind, the human race had been a single group. Men were then ignorant of evil and lived according to the precepts of the natural law in a sort of peaceable anarchy. This golden age had ended suddenly with the murder of Abel, when social disorder arose, and laws and governments had had to be instituted. Since then every right that man has as a member of the group needs some restraint for the common good. The right of property, for example, means that the wealthy must not squander their riches without a worthy purpose or according to a whim, nor must they be negligent in bestowing alms and helping others. Property is a trust from God, an idea derived from Judaism.

The same reasons that make it imperative that men live under law likewise make it necessary for them to have a ruler. All power belongs properly to God and is to be exercised by the ruler here below only as a trust from God. Men owe obedience to the ruler whom God sends, for without order in the state there would be no proper religious observances or stable social life. The ruler, the caliph, should be a free man not a slave; he should be a man, for "a people whose chief is a woman cannot prosper"; he should be of good judgment and moral character, of physical soundness, with the wisdom and courage to maintain the state in war and peace according to the laws of Islam. The selection of the ruler should be entrusted to the civil and military notables, "the men of the pen and of the sword." The caliph is the supreme administrator, judge, and general, but he has no priestly character and has no right to change the law of Islam. He is a trustee of the body of the faithful and will have to answer to God for the conduct of his office. Only in cases where there is no positive law is his power, at least in theory, unlimited. The caliph, unlike the pope, was never considered the depository of divine truth; his position was much nearer to that of emperor. The caliph must defend the faith, make war on those who refuse to accept Islam, collect and distribute taxes, punish wrongdoers, and direct the administration of the state. In theory, the office was elective; in practice, each caliph usually nominated his successor, though the fiction of election was kept up by having the highest nobles and officials take an oath to the new caliph at the time of his succession. It was never necessary in the Islamic states that the succession should follow in the direct line. When the caliph did not fulfill the law or when he became incapacitated or was taken captive, a new caliph had to be chosen.

It is open to doubt whether the caliphate as conceived by the theorists ever had a real existence; certainly by the eleventh century the separation between the ideals and the facts became very marked. As only the first caliphs were related to Mohammed or to his tribe, the part of the theory which demanded that the ruler be of the tribe of the Prophet was dropped by many of the faithful. The influence of the absolute monarchy of Persia also changed the ideas and usages of Islam. But some of the old theories of rulership always survived, though alongside of them came defences of the absolute right of the ruler even if his rule were based on violence and even if it were not in accordance with divine law, the difference being that any effective rule was better than anarchy and private violence.[19] But, just as with the

Christian political theorists, the Islamic writers held onto political and legal theories that were thoroughly unreal, or at least quite out of touch with the world of living men. Indeed, by the eleventh century, when the caliph's position had become much reduced, the theorists set up for him the most extensive claims ever made, just as the papal theorists did for the pope during the Babylonian Captivity of the fourteenth century.

Islamic philosophy [20] is not marked by the highest originality, but certainly Avicenna and Averroës are more than "mere commentators" as Bertrand Russell has called them. [21] And as transmitters of thought the Muslim philosophers are of first-rate importance. Early in their conquests the sons of Islam came into contact with Greek philosophy and science in Syria and in Persia. Greek philosophical and scientific works had begun to be translated extensively into Syriac as early as the fourth century A.D. A school opened at Edessa in 363 became the chief center of this work; it was closed in 489 because of the Nestorian heresy that flourished there. Some of the scholars betook themselves to Mesopotamia and to Persia and continued their work of study and translation of Greek writings. In Persia these Syriac Christian scholars were joined by some Greek philosophers forced into exile by the closing of the philosophic schools of Athens in 529. Converts from Judaism and Christianity, and, later, Mohammedans born in the faith, in the course of time translated many of the important works of Greek philosophy and science into Arabic. The history of these translations shows that some were translated from Syriac versions and some directly from the Greek. Among the translations of philosophic works some Neo-Platonic works of Plotinus and Proclus were attributed to Aristotle. And most of the Aristotelian works came over into Arabic with Neo-Platonic commentaries. As a consequence, Islamic philosophy, from the beginning, tried to harmonize Aristotle and Neo-Platonism. The result of the contact between Muslim religion and Greek philosophy was the creation of an Islamic scholasticism.

The earliest important school of Muslim philosophy appeared in the eighth century at Bagdad. Its major concern was the defence of free-will against the determinism taught by the orthodox theologians. The first outstanding figure in the school was the Arab, al-Kindi (d. 873). He translated part (Books 4 to 6) of Plotinus' *Enneads* and entitled his translation and interpretation the *Theology of Aristotle*. He or some other member of the school also translated a work of Proclus under the title of the *Book of Causes*; this also came to circulate as a work of Aristotle. So there early arose in Islamic thought a confusion as to just what Aristotle did teach. Al-Kindi was a thinker of great range; his interests included mathematics, astronomy, and medicine, but he never constructed a consistent philosophy. His first interest in Greek philosophy, like that of nearly all the later Muslim philosophers, was in the logic of Aristotle. He tried to harmonize Mohammedan religious ideas with parts of Greek philosophy. He believed that religion and philosophy should not contradict each other and that even revealed truth could be proved by reason alone since natural religion had —among men—long preceded revelation. In spite of his efforts, al-Kindi was vigorously attacked by the orthodox theologians. Al-Fārābi (d. 950) continued the work of trying to harmonize Platonism and Aristotelianism and orthodox Mohammedanism. He translated parts of the work of Porphyry and the *Organon* of Aristotle; this was important in extending the use of Aristotelian logic in the Muslim world. It was this work which gave him the name of the "second Aristotle" as Avicenna was later to be called the "third Aristotle." Al-Fārābi also tried to integrate with Muslim thought the Neo-Platonic theory of the world as a series of emanations from God. He believed that theology and philosophy should be separated. Like the Muslim philosophers after him, he did not mean to undermine Islamic theology; rather he wished to make logic and philosophy more serviceable to theology, and he was trying to make the Muslim faith more understandable to the intellectual classes. Thus, long before the Christian scholastics tried to harmonize Aristotle and the Christian religion, Muslim thinkers were endeavoring to bring together into one system Aristotelianism and a revealed religious system. The work of the early Islamic philosophers won neither the confidence of the average educated Muslim nor the approval of the theologians. The orthodox held tenaciously to the idea that God had created the world and that it was not, as Aristotle believed, something that had always existed. The orthodox also taught the possibility of miracles, the idea of a last judgment, and the dogma of personal immortality.

In the tenth century a group of thinkers called the *Brothers of Sin-*

cerity carried on the ideas of al-Fārābi that philosophy could amplify and support religious revelation and that rational speculation could even rectify the faith in some particulars. Members of the group, like the other Islamic philosophers, wrote on a wide range of scientific and philosophical subjects. The most remarkable man who came from this current was the Persian, Ibn Sīna, known in the Latin West as Avicenna (d. 1037); his interests included medicine, geometry, physics, and law, as well as theology and metaphysics. His reputation in the West was even greater as a medical authority than as a philosopher. Among the Muslims he has always been regarded as the real creator of Islamic scholasticism. He had the gift of popular writing; his works were more generally read than those of any other Muslim scholar, and he was translated in the twelfth century and widely read in Latin. As a young man, Avicenna tells us in his autobiography, he had immersed himself in the *Metaphysics* of Aristotle, but he only arrived at understanding the master when he read the commentary of al-Fārābi. In his *Healing*, Avicenna's best-known philosophical work, he interprets Aristotle in a Neo-Platonic manner. From God comes the first Intelligence, and this, in turn, gives birth to an intelligence under it and so down through the whole scale of being. God knows only universals; it is impossible for God to create material things directly. He leaves to all the inferior intelligences of a vast hierarchy the knowledge and control of their respective spheres. The orthodox attacked this idea that God did not concern himself with individual persons because it denied the omniscience of God and the efficacy of prayer.

In his metaphysics, Avicenna arrived at a compromise between Platonism and Aristotelianism that resembles somewhat Aquinas' eclecticism. Avicenna's formula, "thought brings about the generality of forms," was repeated by Averroës and by some of the thirteenth-century Christian scholastics. In amplifying this statement Avicenna makes it clear that Plato's universals are *before* things (*ante res*) in God's understanding. God decides to create men; this requires that the idea, man, is anterior to particular men. Universals are *in* things (*in rebus*); when a man is created, mankind is in each man. Finally universals are *after* things (*post res*) in our thoughts, because when we have seen many men we notice their likeness and arrive at the general idea, man. Avicenna believed that the individual soul was not immortal; only the higher part of the soul returned to the universal intelligence in which it lost its individuality. He likewise followed Aristotle in believing in the eternity of the world, and so he denied the Biblical story of the creation. These beliefs were further causes for attacks from the orthodox. The views of Avicenna which denied the creation of the world by God, the possibility of God's interest in individuals, and the idea of personal immortality were attacked, with great insight, by the mystic al-Ghazālī in his *Incoherence of the Philosophers* and a number of other works.

The last great philosopher of Islam was the Spanish Ibn Rushd, of Cordova, known in the West as Averroës (d. 1198). He did not know Greek and was obliged to depend on Arabic versions of the Greek philosophers. Averroës worshipped Aristotle, though he could not read him in the original, and he tried to clear Muslim philosophy of some of its Neo-Platonic concepts so as to bring it closer to the doctrine of Aristotle. "Aristotle," he wrote, "was the wisest of the Greeks, and constituted and completed logic, physics, and metaphysics. All the works on these subjects previous to him do not deserve to be mentioned. None of those who have succeeded him, during fifteen hundred years, have been able to add anything to his writings or to find in them any error." [22] Only in Spain would Averroës have been allowed to publish at all, and even there he was finally forced into retirement. He believed in the eternity of the world and so did not accept the Biblical story of the creation; but he developed an earlier Muslim theory of creation. Out of a universe of undefined matter God is continually creating an ordered world; God's vigilance and action is never abated. Only God, the prime mover, is both eternal and without cause. Like Avicenna, Averroës denied the interest of God in individuals and the idea of individual immortality.

Averroës seems to have believed sincerely that religion and philosophy could exist together. In the interest of preserving both, he tried to define the exact knowledge that should be possessed by different classes. In his first class were the philosophers who should have all truths rationalized; in the second class were those with a general education who needed some explanation, though not too thorough a rational explanation, of truth; and finally, in the third class, were the masses who needed only poetic and emotional explanation of all things. The Koran contained various kinds of truth; beneath an external sense for the layman there was, in the sacred book, a hidden meaning for the philosopher. A mind ought never to try to interpret the Koran from a point of view above its own powers, and a philosopher ought never to divulge to the masses his interpretation of truth. What may be understood clearly in philosophy must often be expressed allegorically in theology. This puts philosophy above theology, for it leaves it to the philosopher to decide just which theological doctrines need to be interpreted literally and which allegorically. These ideas later circulated in Latin Christendom as "the doctrine of the double truth." According to this theory contradictory conclusions could exist simultaneously; a proposition could, at one and the same time, be true in philosophy and false in theology and vice versa. Actually Averroës never held this idea in so crude a form.

The Muslim philosophers were the masters of the mediaeval Jewish philosophers who lived among them. From the beginning of the Christian Era, the Jews had cherished the philosophy of Philo, who had sought to combine the Jewish religious faith with Platonism. Out of this current had developed the *Cabbala*, the first part of which, the "Creation," had reached its present form by the ninth century, though the second part, "Brightness," was probably not committed to writing till about 1300. The first part of this cryptic and mystic work shows clearly that Jewish thought was deeply influenced by Philo and by Neo-Platonism long before it was affected by the philosophy of Islam. In the writings of Muslim thinkers, however, later Jewish philosophers found certain concepts which they used in trying to bring together Greek philosophy and the truths of the Old Testament.

Israeli (d. 955), a physician at the court of one of the caliphs, is the first important mediaeval Jewish thinker. Like most of the other Jewish philosophers of the Middle Ages, he wrote in Arabic and shows a thorough knowledge of Muslim learning. Israeli had the same desire as the Islamic thinkers to fuse Aristotelianism and Neo-Platonism, though he apparently made no attempt to harmonize his philosophical ideas with Jewish religious teaching. The first important attempt at such a harmony appears in the works of Saadiah (d. 942). Anything that contradicts Jewish religious ideas, like the concept of the eternity of the world, he rejects, and he uses the Greek philosophers to buttress an orthodox Jewish position. The same process was carried further by the Spanish Jew, Solomon Ibn Gabirol, or Avicebron (d. 1058) as he was called in the Christian West. His best-known work, the *Source of Life*, which is strongly Neo-Platonic in outlook and method, and which won him the name of the "Jewish Plato," does not mention Judaism, and the thirteenth-century Christian scholastics always thought it was the work of either a Mohammedan or a Christian. Avicebron has an interesting interpretation of the Neo-Platonic theory of emanations. Except for God, matter is universally existent. Everything below God is composed of both matter and form. In this way the author obviates a serious break in the Neo-Platonic system, according to which there were, beneath God, a series of purely spiritual beings, and then, suddenly descending in the hierarchy, beings that contain matter. Avicebron avoided this dilemma by positing the idea of the existence of some matter at all levels of creation below God. The doctrine was taken over by St. Bonaventura. The type of bold speculation shown by Avicebron vexed the orthodox Jewish theologians and brought on a reaction led by Halevi (d. 1141) in defence of traditional Jewish beliefs. Halevi was also a great poet and he resembles al-Ghazālī among the Muslims, distrusts much of philosophy, though he uses philosophic terms and arguments, and is a subtle and forceful thinker. The philosopher makes God a mere object of study, whereas the religiously minded man wishes a more complete consciousness of God. Halevi is less severe on the philosophers than is al-Ghazālī; he merely wishes to point out their limitations.

In the twelfth century, the Aristotelian current that had become more marked among the thinkers of Islam also became more pronounced among the Jewish philosophers. It was the work of the Spanish Jew, Moses Maimonides (d. 1204), the greatest of Jewish mediaeval thinkers, to try to harmonize the Jewish faith with the thought of Aristotle. His *Guide to the Perplexed*, his best-known work, is an attempt to meet the religious problems raised by the study of philosophy. He starts with the belief that God made the world and the laws of nature, and, having brought them into being, God can change them to create miracles, to answer prayer, and to give men revelations of his will. He departs from Judaism in believing that only the intellectual part of the soul is immortal and that only those who have formed some union with God will have this partial immortality. If statements contained in the Old Testament contradict what is plainly established by reason, then such statements should be interpreted allegorically. Beliefs of this sort led the Jews to consider Maimonides heretical, and the Jews in southern France appealed to the Christian authorities against him. He was a profound thinker, one of the great mediaeval philosophers.

None of the Muslim or Jewish philosophers constructed as comprehensive a philosophic system as that of a number of the Christian scholastics of the thirteenth century. But, at a time when there was little philosophy in either the Byzantine or Latin Christian worlds, the philosophers of Islam and of Judaism kept alive the great philosophic traditions of the Occident, and in the revival of philosophy in Latin Christendom their writings played an important role. As in science, so in philosophy, the Muslim and Jewish thinkers were the great bridge between antiquity and the "Renaissance of the Twelfth Century."

In no field did the Mohammedan world, in the years 850 to 1100, shine so brightly as in that of science. Like the Christians, the Muslims were hedged about by many misconceptions inherited from Greek learning and were retarded by over-reverence for the work of the Greeks and by religious prejudices against scientific investigation. Also they found it difficult to work their discoveries into general laws, and they never created any great new hypotheses in science like those of Copernicus and Newton. But they kept alive much of the Greek scientific heritage, and, in some cases, added important new discoveries of their own.[23] At the same time, they developed, at certain points, an experimental technique which was ultimately of greater importance than their specific discoveries. In the eighth and ninth centuries, the works of Hippocrates, Galen, Dioscorides, Aristotle, Archimedes, Euclid, Ptolemy, and of the other great Greek scientific writers became available in Arabic translations. Other materials, such as astronomical tables and mathematics, came from Persia and northern India. Soon Muslim writers began to add to this body of inherited science. Their work was, at first, supported not by the schools, which taught the Koran and theology and law, but by the patronage of rulers and the well-to-do and by the professional activity of the scientists who supported themselves as physicians, lawyers, and state officials. Later on many scientific subjects were taught in schools. From the ninth century to the twelfth the Muslims were the curators of the scientific knowledge of the world.

The output of general treatises and special studies in medicine was enormous. The first great Muslim writer on medicine was a Persian, al-Rāzi, known to the West as Rhazes (d. 925). He, like other Muslim students of medicine, used little human dissection; because of religious objections he did some experimenting with animals. Rhazes, like many other Islamic scientists, wrote on many subjects. His reputation was based on his writings in chemistry and on the *Comprehensive Book*, which summarized Greek and Syriac medicine and added some discoveries of the author. Much of his anatomy and physiology follows Greek precedent; his originality lies in his descriptions of diagnoses and in his methods of treatment. He knew that certain diseases were contagious, and his clinical observations are acute. In a monograph he gives the first good descriptions of smallpox and measles.[24] Rhazes, in selecting a site for a hospital in Bagdad, is said to have hung up shreds of meat in different quarters of the town, and where the meat showed least signs of decay the hospital was built. The most influential work of Muslim medicine is the famous *Canon* of Avicenna. Its encyclopedic sweep and its systematic arrangement, bringing together the biology of Aristotle, the medical ideas of Galen, and their Muslim commentators, gave it a unique reputation. Besides the compends of the type written by Rhazes and Avicenna, Islamic physicians produced a large number of special studies on various types of diseases and their treatment. Their most advanced work was done on the maladies of the eye. At the same time, the Muslim physicians improved the *materia medica*. In the larger cities instruction came to be given in medical schools, and there were public hospitals which also offered courses in medicine. The cities had excellent pharmacies, and both physicians and pharmacists had to pass state examinations to be licensed.

There is an interesting contrast between Muslim and Christian medicine in a twelfth-century account written by a Muslim:

They brought to me a knight with an abscess in his leg, and a woman troubled with fever. I applied to the knight a little cataplasm; his abscess opened and took a favorable turn. As for the woman I forbade her to eat certain foods, and I lowered her temperature. I was there when a Frankish doctor arrived, who said, "This man cannot cure them." Then, addressing the knight, he asked, "which do you prefer, to live with a single leg, or to die with both legs?" "I prefer," replied the knight, "to live with a single leg." "Then bring," said the doctor, "a strong knight with a sharp axe." The doctor stretched the leg of the patient on a block of wood, and then said, "cut off the leg with the axe, detach it with a single blow." Under my eyes the knight gave a violent blow. He gave the unfortunate man a second blow, which caused the marrow to flow from the bone, and the patient died immediately. As for the woman, the doctor examined her and said, "She is a woman with a devil in her head. Shave her hair." They did so; she began to eat again—like her compatriots—garlic and mustard. Her fever grew worse. The doctor then said, "the devil has gone into her head." Seizing the razor he cut into her head in the form of a cross. Then he rubbed her head with salt. The woman expired immediately. After asking them if my services were still needed, and after receiving a negative answer, I returned, having learned from them medical matters of which I had previously been ignorant.[25]

Modern chemistry grew, in some measure, out of Islamic alchemy. Alchemy seems to have begun in China as early as the fourth century B.C.; the chief goal of Chinese alchemy was the prolongation of life. It is next heard of in Egypt in the first Christian centuries. The Muslim alchemists seem to have derived their inspiration mostly from Egypt. In its beginnings, alchemy was mixed with sheer superstition and magic. The ideas and the recipes of the alchemists were drawn from religion, Greek science and philosophy, from folklore, and from industrial processes such as the making of mercury, ammonia, alum, soda, arsenic, steel, cloth, leather, and glass. It had many connections with astrology and other branches of occultism and with fraudulent deception. The basic beliefs of the alchemists were the idea of Aristotle that all matter consists of the four elements: earth, air, fire, and water, in various combinations, that gold is the "noblest" and "purest" of all metals, silver is next, that the transmutation of one metal into another is possible by an alteration in the admixture of the elements, and, finally, that "base" metals may be turned into "noble" ones by means of a precious substance often called the fifth element or quintessence. Along with much experimenting that followed these theories, and the belief that they could discover an "elixir of life" that would prolong life, there was a great deal of practical experimenting done in the making of glass, leather, and cloth, the working of metals, and in the preparation of drugs. The first laboratories in history, about which much is known, were those set up by the Islamic alchemists; they practiced distillation and sublimation and developed much of the chemical apparatus in use up to about 1650.[26] The alchemistic treatises usually describe clearly the apparatus employed, but they deliberately treat of the substances used in an obscure fashion, and it has been nearly impossible to decipher most of their recipes. The commonest excuse given for this mystification is that a plain exposition would result in political upheavals, due to the inevitable fall in the price of gold which would follow a revelation of the secret of transmutation.

The greatest name in Islamic alchemy is that of Geber (Fabirihn-Hayyān), who may have lived in the ninth century, though many later works of alchemy were also attributed to him.[27] He improved methods for evaporation, filtration, sublimation, distillation, and crystallization. Geber described scientifically the two principal operations of chemistry: calcination and reduction. He knew how to prepare chemical substances like sulphide of mercury, arsenious oxide, and lead carbonate. A large part of his writings were devoted to chemical theories that have since gone with the wind. But the by-products of his work have endured; and his emphasis on the value of experimentation was passed on to later scientists. "The first essential," he wrote, "is that you should conduct experiments. For he who does not conduct experiments will never attain to the least degree of mastery. It must be taken as an absolutely rigorous principle that any proposition which is not supported by proofs is nothing more than an assertion which may be true or may be false." [28] Rhazes improved on Geber's classification of substances. In place of Geber's traditional classification of mineral substances into "bodies" (as gold, silver), "souls" (as sulphur and arsenic), and "spirits" (as mercury and sal-ammoniac), Rhazes classified substances as animal, vegetable, and mineral, a concept much more basic. He held on, however, to the common theory that sulphur and mercury were the primary principles of things. This lasted as one alternative to the four elements of Aristotle until well into the seventeenth century. Avicenna wrote some chapters on alchemy in one of his longest works. He flatly denies the possibility of transmuting metals, but, in spite of his protests, the alchemistic theories lived on. The work of the Islamic alchemists yielded some positive results, but they never freed themselves from a lot of scientific and metaphysical preconceptions taken over from the Greeks and superstitions inherited from later periods, and, without thermometers, barometers, accurate watches, or air-pumps, their work could never really move into modern conceptions of science. It is as transmitters, rather than as innovators, that they take their place in the long history of science.

The Muslim contribution to the fields of astronomy, physics, and mathematics was higher than in medicine or chemistry. Astrology, like alchemy, was a false science but one that yielded varied scientific by-products. The Muslims gathered some astronomical knowledge from India, and they translated the great work of Ptolemy, the *Almagest* as the Latin West called it. The greatest of the Muslim astronomers were al-Battāni (d. 929) of the Bagdad observatory, and Yūnus of Cairo of the eleventh century. They did not hesitate to criticize parts of Ptolemy, and they added many tables about the movements and positions of the heavenly bodies. They twice measured a degree, based on the assumption that the earth is round, but their measurement was too great by 2,877 feet. This would make the circumference of the earth only 20,400 miles and its diameter 6,500 miles. These dimensions were less accurate than those of Eratosthenes (d. 194 B.C.). But they achieved more accuracy than the Greeks in measuring the length of the solar year and in calculating solar and lunar eclipses. They perfected the astrolabe (for taking altitudes of heavenly bodies), the armillary sphere (a set of brass circles representing the paths of the sun and planets in relation to the celestial equator), the celestial globe, Jacob's staff, and the quadrant.

In physics the Muslims' most outstanding achievement was in optics where they clearly surpassed their Greek masters. Alhazen (d.

965) of Cairo opposed the theory of Euclid and Ptolemy that the eye sends out visual rays to the object of vision. Rather, the form of the perceived object passes into the eye and is transmuted by its lens. He found the relation between the positions of a source of light and its image formed by a lens. He discussed the propagation of light and colors, optical illusions, and reflection of light, and gave methods for measuring the angles of incidence and refraction. Muslim physics also included the determination of the specific gravity of certain metals and precious stones, and work on meteorology, on tides, and on such problems of applied mechanics as the following: windmills and water-wheels (which the Muslims were the first to develop), balances, wells, water clocks, agricultural methods, irrigation, canal and road building, the preparation of iron and steel, methods of working metals, constructing scientific instruments, paper-making, leather work, and silk and cotton cloth manufacture.

Finally, in mathematics the Muslims made their greatest scientific contributions. From the Greeks and the Hindus, they learned geometry and trigonometry, and from the Hindus, arithmetic and algebra. The first great work of Muslim mathematics was the arithmetic of the Persian al-Khwarizmi (d. 830), whose name is the source of our word, algorism. In this treatise the author used the Hindu system of numbers in which the digits depend for their value on their position. His *Algebra* (*al-Jabr*) is the first work in which the word appears in a mathematical sense, meaning "restoration," that is, the transposing of negative terms of an equation to the opposite side. This work of al-Khwarizmi, while not original, made arithmetic and algebra more useful because of the use of what we now call "arabic numbers" and because of his skill in applying mathematics to physical and astronomical problems. Other Muslims developed geometry and plane and spherical trigonometry.

Some detailed studies in botany, zoology, and geology were written; the best ones were of a detailed and monographic nature, but brought forward no essentially new basic hypotheses. The Muslims went on long voyages by sea and travelled far and wide on land to make the pilgrimage to Mecca and to carry on commercial enterprises, and they made some additions to geographical knowledge. They early had a translation of Ptolemy's *Geography*, though they usually treated the work with the over-zealous respect with which they regarded the writings of Aristotle, Galen, and Ptolemy (*Almagest*). It was, therefore, in descriptive rather than in theoretical geography that they excelled. A long series of detailed works were written about many parts of the known world describing their climates, religions, trade, agriculture, coinage, weights and measures, and general manners and customs. These works are often very valuable, less because of their scientific character, for they are sometimes vague and inexact, than for the fact that they contain information nowhere else available. The greatest of all the Islamic geographers, al-Idrīsi (d. 1166), who lived at the court of Roger II, the Norman king of Sicily, wrote a huge encyclopedic description of all the known parts of the earth, based on Greek, Hindu, and earlier Muslim writers and on information he gathered in Sicily, the great cross-roads on the Mediterranean. He too dared to criticize Ptolemy and other earlier writers, and his work contained a mine of excellent information even about remote parts of Asia and Africa. Strangely enough, none of the Muslims added much to Greek methods of map-making, and cartography made little advance till the end of the Middle Ages, when it was started on its modern course in Latin Christendom. The Muslim and Jewish ship-masters and pilots by the tenth century commonly believed the earth to be spherical. They passed this belief on to Spanish and Catalan Christian sailors, so that the idea of a round world became no longer a monopoly of the learned.

In trying to sum up the contributions of the Muslims to philosophy and science, we think first of how they attempted to harmonize Aristotelianism and Neo-Platonism with a revealed religious system, and of how they passed on the Greek scientific heritage, combining it with certain elements borrowed from Persia and India. They improved mathematics by the use of arabic numbers and by enlarging the uses of algebra, and by developing plane and spherical trigonometry. They improved the experimental methods used in chemistry, and they partly freed both chemistry and physics from Greek metaphysical notions and from magic. They added to the previously existing knowledge of optics, astronomy, medicine, and geography. The Muslims did all this without basically altering the theoretical background of the material they took over, but they gave to western Europe in the

twelfth and thirteenth centuries the impetus out of which the Latin
Christians began modern science.

3. LITERATURE, ART, AND MUSIC

THE ARABIC language and the Muslim religious faith were the great
bonds of union in Islamic culture. The Arabic language, as it spread to
become the language of religion and of culture for a seventh of the
human race, proved to have a rich vocabulary to which extensive additions could readily be made so as to be capable of every shade of
meaning. Arabic came to be a language suitable both for poetry and
eloquence and for exact science and philosophy. The oldest surviving
literary works in Arabic are pre-Islamic poems of the early sixth century. Their metrical schemes, based on quantity and a single rhyme
that runs through the whole poem, are very elaborate and imply a
long earlier development about which nothing is known. These early
poems consist of battle pieces, elegies, praise of the poet's tribe and
satires on other tribes, various kinds of occasional verses, and longer
odes of sixty to one hundred lines. The odes follow a pattern that tells
of a homesick warrior who revisits a camp site where he was once in
love with a fair maiden; inside this framework there is a series of pictures describing various aspects of Arabian life. The construction of
these odes attains a degree of refinement unknown to any other Se-
mitic language; and early as they are in the history of Islamic poetry
they set the poetic style for later centuries. These oldest poems were
transmitted orally for two centuries and were probably somewhat
modified before they were finally written down. They show clearly
the taste of the Arabs for poetry; poetry was the one highly developed
art among the early Arabs, a people otherwise very primitive in culture.

The first work in the Arabic language to be written down was the
Koran, which was composed in rhymed prose. The utterances of the
Prophet show a growing command of the language and a striking
ability to mould it into varied forms of expression. Few achievements
in literary history are more remarkable than the development in a
single book of a prose style out of a poetic dialect. The work had an
enormous effect on Islamic literature because it was in connection

with the Koran that the majority of the branches of Muslim literature had their origin and because later it became a basis of Arabic prose style. Due to the respect for the Koran the various dialects of the Arabic-speaking peoples did not fall into distinct languages, as Latin, in spite of the church, broke into the Romance tongues.

Mohammed had criticized the morals of the poets, and poetry was, for a time, under a ban. A new urban influence first at Medina, later at Damascus and Bagdad, and the patronage of the caliphs brought poetry back into favor. Bagdad after 750 was the great center of literature, as it was also of philosophy and science. In every field subject peoples were now bringing to Islam their own cultural contributions. Poetry shows much Persian influence; it is more elaborate, more urbane, more worldly, and more erotic than the oldest Arabic poetry. The conventional ode is given up in favor of shorter verse forms: love songs, revel songs, hunting pieces, and mystical religious verse. Long narratives in verse became popular. The finest poet of the Bagdad period was abu-Nuwās (d. 810). His shorter lyrics, which have often been compared to those of Heine, are regarded as the great masterpieces of Muslim lyric poetry. The most popular of all Islamic poets, however, is al-Mutanabbi (d. 965) of Aleppo, whose style is extremely ornate and precious.

Various types of prose developed—specialized styles to suit the exposition of theology, philosophy, law, history, and science. Other literary forms developed in familiar essays, novels, and short stories, which were written in quantities for the upper and middle classes. The one important example of this type of literature that reached the West was the *Arabian Nights*, a collection of matchless tales from many sources.[29] After A.D. 900 many of the secular writers imitated the rhymed prose used in the Koran. The literate public, which by the ninth century was very extended, read works in all fields, the most popular of which, next to short stories and poetry, were history and biography. The greatest historical work was that of al-Tabari (d. 929), who had travelled widely in Persia, Syria, and Egypt, and whose fifteen volumes covered the history of the Muslim peoples year by year in an annalistic way. Besides histories of huge dimensions, there were histories of separate states, dynastic histories, and histories of various cities, and a rich biographical literature. The last important Muslim historian, ibn-

Khaldūn (d. 1406) of Tunis, has been called "a founder of sociology" because he combined his general history with theories of the growth and decay of states and with discussions of climate and geography and their influence on human affairs. There is no evidence that the Muslims ever translated or studied the Greek historians; the chief outside influence in their historical writing was Persian. In both history and biography, the accuracy and insight of the Muslim historians was as outstanding as that of the Byzantine writers. By the end of the eleventh century, when the whole culture of Islam entered into a decline, the old literary unity was breaking up and regional literatures were developing. By this time, the greatest days of Islamic letters and learning were over.[30]

The art of Islam, like the rest of Muslim culture, showed borrowings from the civilizations round about, but these borrowings, chiefly from Byzantium and Persia, were fused into a great and original style. In architecture, the principal buildings erected were mosques and palaces. The small primitive dwelling, built in 622 at Medina under Mohammed's direction, was the model for most of the later mosques. The whole was a square enclosure, entirely surrounded by walls of brick and stone. One side of the enclosure was roofed with palm branches covered with mud and supported by palm trunks.[31] The next mosque, built in Mesopotamia in 639, was erected on exactly the same plan, but the roof was supported by marble columns. Within eighty or ninety years of the building of the Prophet's house at Medina, all the features of the congregational mosque had been evolved. Inside this basic square plan was a large open fore-court with a fountain for ablutions in the center and a shaded colonnade around the sides. Within, everything was arranged for the central act of worship: prayer. This religious act was supposed to have greater force if performed in union with others of the faithful. The worshippers lined up in parallel rows facing Mecca; the first row being nearest Mecca, and, as everyone wished to be near the front, the prayer area of the mosque was usually rectangular; in the *Great Mosque at Damascus* the prayer chamber is 131 meters wide and only 38 meters deep. In the middle of the wide side of the interior, toward Mecca, was a small apse, the *mihrāb* (borrowed from the Christians), and near it an elevated pulpit, the *minbar*, for reading from the Koran and for sermons. Rising above the low roofs of the mosque enclosure was the *minar,* a tower from which was sent out the call to prayer. The annual pilgrimage to Mecca, from all parts of Islam, contributed greatly not only to the standardization of the form of the mosque and of other types of building, but also to the standardization of all the decorative arts.

The structural materials used in both mosques and palaces, whether brick, stone, marble, or clay, depended on what was available in the particular locality. Styles also varied somewhat; in Syria the influences of ancient Rome and Byzantium were strong; in Mesopotamia and Persia the traditional local styles lived on inside of a larger synthesis; in Egypt many decorative features were derived from the work of the local Copts; in Spain and North Africa, Roman and Visigothic influences are in evidence; in India, the style was modified by the indigenous Hindu art. Muslim minarets, for example, followed, with some modifications, the traditional shape of the towers of the countries where they were built. The Muslims early adopted a horseshoe type of arch from Mesopotamia or from Spain which they spread everywhere, and they did the same with pointed arches which may have been borrowed from the Visigoths. They used less vaulting and more wooden roofs than the Byzantines, though in Persia and India they built huge brick domes. In Muslim palaces great emphasis was laid on the use of gardens with shaded porticos about them; in the *Alhambra* nearly all the main rooms have water running through them in a marble groove in the floor. The garden of the *Generalife,* the summer palace in Granada, is typical of the love of gardens with walks and fountains, all arranged in close relation to the living quarters.

The mosques and the palaces were severe without, but within were lavishly decorated with glazed tiles, low flat carvings known in the West as arabesques, rich marble, and carpets; the mosques also had stained-glass windows. Human and animal forms were forbidden by the Koran. Mohammed had said that, on the Day of Judgment, the artist will be called upon to breathe life into the figures he created and he will be condemned to eternal punishment if he is not able to accomplish this, and he had also said that angels will never enter the house of a Muslim if there are images in it. The artist must never try to make imitations which might seem to have a likeness to the creations of Allah; also, men must have no images about that might tempt them to idolatry. In practice, carpets could show figures because one trod on them, and cushion covers, because one sat upon them. Many Muslim patrons had paintings put on their walls that represented men and animals, and both were very common in manuscript illuminations. In some cases where human or animal figures were used, the artist avoided three-dimensional effects and made his figures very flat, or he added wings and beaks to animals, or covered animals with flat designs that have nothing whatever to do with the animal, like the flowers scattered over porcelain cows and pigs in eighteenth-century Western porcelains, all of which show that the creature could never be counted as a living being.

The typical Islamic decoration, however, was one based on interlacing lines and geometric designs and one that used much color. As one thinks of marble and mosaic as the typical decoration of Byzantine churches and palaces, so one thinks of the colored tile and the carved and painted arabesque as the common decorative means of Islam. These were combined with the use, in ceilings, of stalactite forms and types of complicated coffering. The designs of both tiles and arabesques showed marvellous taste, ingenuity, and inventiveness. They used inscriptions in the wonderful Arabic calligraphy, the most beautiful that man has devised, as a common decorative motive. In all their designs—on walls, on leather, and on cloth—they liked patterns that were not centrally organized but that went on, in all directions, without either a beginning or an end. The Koran and the tradition of Mohammed were not only against the use of any forms that might seem idolatrous, but they were also against luxury. "He who drinks from gold and silver vessels drinks the fire of Hell," says one of the Mohammedan traditions. So to circumvent these injunctions, the Muslims made vessels and tiles of earthenware and covered them with gold luster; they inlaid steel, brass, copper, and bronze objects with fine bands of gold and silver; and they often carved their complicated arabesques in plaster, even in a place like the *mihrab,* where one would expect stone or marble. The taste for luxury being too human to suppress and the vast accumulation of wealth offering opportunity for "conspicuous waste," the Muslims spent vast sums on objects where the greatest cost was not in the material but in the workmanship lavished on it.[32] Like the Byzantines, the Islamic peoples were splendid craftsmen, and they shipped the products of their handiwork over much of Europe, Asia, and Africa. These products included carved ivories, enameled glassware, tooled leatherwork of all sorts, tiles, pottery, paper, carpets of which the finest came from Persia, illuminated manuscripts, an art that developed late and was at its height in the fifteenth century in Muslim Persia, metalwork including damascened swords and vessels, fine cotton cloth, and rich silk fabrics. Today the Islamic sections of our museums cherish these matchless objects of expert and exquisite craftsmanship.

In no nation in history was music so honored and so cultivated as among the Muslims. Mohammed had frowned on musicians chiefly because he disliked the heathen elements in the words of their songs and because he distrusted the sensuous element in music. He is said to have declared that instrumental music was the devil's call to prayer. Time was to set aside these injunctions; music accompanied the Muslim from the cradle to the grave. Every occasion in life had its particular music to express the joy or sorrow of the moment. Every well-to-do household had to have its singing girl, and the homes of the very wealthy had groups of musicians and dancers. Vocal music was more appreciated than instrumental music, probably because of the ardent taste for poetry, and the highest awards, often of fabulous amount, went to the singers attached to the courts of the caliphs. Early Islamic music resembled Hebrew and Greek music. In the seventh century, the Muslims began to write mensurable music, their notation indicating both the pitch and the duration of the note, an advance not known in Latin Christendom before the twelfth century. Different parts of the Muslim world used different scales, but after various trials with varied types of scales, the Greek Pythagorean scale became nearly universal. Their music was usually unharmonized, though they occasionally adorned a melody with companion notes, striking a note simultaneously with its fourth, fifth, or octave that gave a sort of harmony. The common instruments used were all types of lutes, flutes, rebecs (one ancestor of the violin), drums, horns, tambourines, cymbals, castanets, harps, and organs. The Islamic peoples carried the manufacture of musical instruments to a high art, and they improved nearly every type of instrument that they had early borrowed from the Byzantines, the Persians, the Hindus, and other peoples. Large groups of players were organized into bands; no great military or civilian event was complete without a band. For these large groupings of instruments, the Muslims introduced the custom of having the conductor keep time with a baton. The Muslim writers all point out the important influence of music on men's emotions. We hear of one famous singer whose art "warmed and chilled more than a hot bath"; al-Ghazālī says, "ecstasy means the state that comes from listening to music," and the *Arabian Nights* remarks that "to some music is meat, to others medicine." [33]

The enormous interest of the Islamic peoples in music is shown in the many references to the art in their literature and in the extended writings on music. Among the theoreticians, al-Kindī, al-Fārābi, Avicenna, and Averroës, four philosophers, were the best known. They commented on what the Greek writers on music had said, criticized their ideas, and added their own discoveries. Al-Fārābi's *Grand Book on Music* is superior to any earlier work on music. The most important new theoretical advance the Muslims made dealt with the problem of the spherical propagation of sound.

4. ISLAM AND THE WEST

ISLAMIC civilization borrowed wholesale from the cultures about it, but it tried to admit nothing that it could not assimilate. Its originality consisted in the capacity to adapt alien ideas to its own needs, to reject the unadaptable, and to recreate in its own synthesis all that it had borrowed. From the eighth century through the eleventh, Islam maintained a great unity in its culture and a high level of civilization, brilliant in intellectual achievement, wealthy in its economic activity, and cemented by religion, law, and the Arabic language. During this time Islam remained amazingly receptive, flexible, and tolerant. The striking decline that followed this golden age was due to a number of causes. In the middle of the eleventh century, the backward Seljuk Turks, lately converted to Mohammedanism, took Bagdad and much of the Near East. The Seljuk authorities were repressive against all who did not agree with the orthodox Muslim theologians; in the long and bitter fight of orthodoxy against freedom of thought, the orthodox now, at last, won the upper hand. At the same time the Seljuks could not maintain order; constant revolts and general anarchy, broken rarely by a strong and enlightened ruler, brought devastation, depopulation, and stagnation. Muslim civilization had, from the eleventh century on, something of the same problem of being overrun by inferior cultures that the Roman Empire had had in the fifth century. Only in North Africa and in Spain did the old lights of Islamic learning still burn brightly. After the Seljuks, and much more destructive, came the Mongols in the thirteenth century. Whereas the Seljuks had retarded culture in the Near East, the Mongols nearly wiped it out. After the thirteenth century, the only important centers of Muslim culture were in India, Persia, Egypt, and Spain, and in these areas a less dramatic but steady decline set in from the middle of the thirteenth century.

The great centuries of Islamic culture, the eighth through the eleventh, were those of backwardness in Latin Christendom. The Muslims kept alive the philosophy, science, and music of the Greeks and added to them, and they created an original art and music of their own. To all of these the Latin West, as it began to recover in the tenth and eleventh centuries, turned to learn and to imitate. Latin Christians began to visit the Islamic world in the tenth century, and in the eleventh there began to flow from Spain and Sicily a stream of translations of Greek and Arabic works. By the thirteenth century the Latin Christians knew most of the great works of Greek philosophy and science, together with their Muslim and Jewish commentators.[34] As a result, nearly all the great Christian philosophers and scientists show the pronounced influence of the Muslim writers. At the same time, Muslim literature, art, and music were influencing the West. From Muslim literature came not only some of the themes of the troubadours, trouvères, and minnesingers, but also their view of life and love.[35] In music, the West owed Islam the lute, the drum, and other musical instruments, the conductor's baton, and something of theoretical acoustics, the idea of measuring consonant lengths of strings (especially in the lute and rebec), and, perhaps, the idea of harmony and mensural music. Finally, in art and craftsmanship, the West, in some degree, got from Islam the machicoulis, the running defence balcony at the top of a castle or town wall, the use of pointed arches, ribbed vaults, cluster columns, and of engaged shafts and multifoil arches, the covering of architectural surfaces with low reliefs, the use of inscriptions as decorations, the use in windows of both plate and bar tracery and of stained glass, the employment of striped courses of dark and light marble, as in the *Cathedral of Siena,* and a multitude of designs for textiles, glass, tile, metal, and leather-work.

The whole story of Islamic influence on the West is very extended. Space forbids a full discussion, but the extent of this influence can, at least, be symbolized by a random list of words that have come into the English language from Arabic: chemistry, alcohol, alkali, alembic, elixir, nadir, zenith, cipher, zero, algebra, root, almanac, cupola, camphor, orange, lemon, syrup, lute, guitar, coffee, lilac, sumach, jasmine, saffron, muslin, damask, satin, admiral, arsenal, tariff, ginger, rice, cotton, artichoke, ream (of paper), and, finally, sherbet, julep, candy, and sofa.

CHAPTER VI

The Latin West, 5th–10th Centuries

1. THE SURVIVAL OF THE CLASSICS IN THE WEST

2. THE TRANSMITTERS OF CLASSICAL AND PATRISTIC LEARNING

3. POETRY AND HISTORY

4. ART AND MUSIC

WHILE the lights of Byzantine and Islamic culture burned most brightly, the Latin West was, by comparison, sunk in economic and cultural backwardness. The Barbarian Migrations of the fifth century broke down the Roman political regime in central and western Europe and in North Africa, and the universal rule of Rome was replaced by a multitude of small and weak states. Warring tribes produced a fearsome chaos, and inside each of these weak political units, family carried on blood-feud against family. At the same time the old Roman economy, in the next four centuries, went to pieces; the towns and the Roman roads and bridges slowly sank into ruin; the old urban economy eventually gave way to a crude agricultural order tied to the soil and to the immediate locality, and so constituted that it was self-sufficient. The writers were full of woe; "every colony is levelled to the ground," wrote Gildas. "The inhabitants are slaughtered, and the flames crackled around. How horrible to behold the tops of towers torn from their lofty hinges, the stones of high walls, holy altars, mutilated corpses, all covered with lurid clots of blood, as if they had been crushed together in some ghastly wine press." Famine and sometimes pestilence added to the misery. "The flocks remained alone in the pastures," wrote Paul the Deacon. "You see villas or fortified places filled with people in utter silence. The whole world seems brought back to its ancient stillness: no voice in the field, no whistling of shepherds. The harvests were untouched. Human habitations became the abodes of wild beasts." "For centuries," says Trevelyan, "the Roman ruins stood, a useful stone quarry sometimes by day, but at night haunted in the imagination of the peasant by the ghosts of the race that his ancestors had destroyed." [1]

This economic backwardness steadily became more marked; the West was cut off from contact with Byzantium, and the lingering towns were starved out. The use of money steadily declined from the fifth century on and symbolized the slow descent to economic and social localism and stagnation. At the same time, the schools of the towns slowly sank, the knowledge of Greek died out except in isolated areas like Britain and parts of Italy, where it was revived for short periods. Without schools, Latin became barbarized. The lack of educational facilities and of intellectual communication, except as they were maintained in some monastic centers, brought on a tremendous drop in the intellectual level. Culturally Latin Christendom, like a ruined family that could no longer maintain its old dwelling, came to live in a few rooms of the cellar. Later on, in the memory of posterity, the Latin writers from the fifth to the eleventh centuries—especially Gregory, Isidore, Bede, Alcuin, and Rabanus—gained a certain aureole that they never would have commanded had they lived either earlier or later. Their influence and the glory attached to their names far surpasses the value of what they wrote. Some signs of a cultural revival appear in the eighth century, but there is no very marked turn upward till the tenth and eleventh centuries.

I. THE SURVIVAL OF THE CLASSICS IN THE WEST

THE MIDDLE AGES created many ideas and institutions of its own—parliaments, the common law, Gothic cathedrals, chivalric romances, scholastic philosophy, and universities, to mention only a few—but central in mediaeval culture, in both the East and the West, was the knowledge of Greek and Roman civilization. Having described the survival of the knowledge of classical culture in the civilizations of Byzantium and of Islam, let us now briefly consider the survival of classical writers in the Latin West in the ten centuries between Augustine and Erasmus.

Homer, the father of Greek literature, remained only a name. Many of his stories of the siege of Troy and of the adventures of Ulysses came down through Virgil and through Latin prose versions. Though he was greatly admired and often referred to, Homer was still a closed book to Dante and Petrarch in the fourteenth century. In the fifteenth century, Homer was again read in Greek and was translated into Latin and the vernaculars. Sappho, Pindar, and the Greek lyric poets were barely known by name; they exerted an indirect influence in the West through the Latin verses of Virgil, Ovid, and Horace. Like most of the rest of Greek imaginative literature, the lyric poets were recovered in the fifteenth century. Herodotus, Thucydides, and the later Greek historians exerted only an indirect influence through Livy and the Roman historians. The great Greek dramatists, Aeschylus, Sophocles, Euripides, and Aristophanes, had influenced the Romans, Plautus, Terence, and Seneca, but the Latin West knew little more about them than their names. Demosthenes, the Greek orators, the Hellenistic poets, and Plutarch remained undiscovered and without influence in the West till they were recovered, studied, and translated in the fifteenth and sixteenth centuries. In the sixteenth century, in the world of Tasso, Montaigne, Ronsard, Shakespeare, and Cervantes, all these Greek imaginative writers were widely known and lavishly admired and imitated.

Of Plato, the guiding star of the Church Fathers, nothing was known widely except a Latin translation of the *Timaeus*. Plato's indirect influence through Cicero, Neo-Platonism, the Church Fathers, and the Muslim and Jewish philosophers was enormous. When all the original Plato was recovered by the Italians of the fifteenth century, enthusiasm rose so high that candles were burned before his bust in the palaces of Florence and Rome. Of Aristotle, two of the logical treatises were available in the Latin translation of Boethius. Most of the rest of Aristotle, along with the great Greek writings on medicine, astronomy, mathematics, and physics came into western Europe in Latin translations from Byzantium, Sicily, and Spain between the eleventh and the thirteenth centuries. All this material dominated the schools of Latin Christendom from the later twelfth century on. In the fifteenth and sixteenth centuries the influence of Aristotle waned. But while his philosophical dictatorship declined, his aesthetic works, the *Poetics* and the *Rhetoric,* grew in esteem. All in all the direct Greek influence, between 500 and 1400, except in philosophy and science, was small, though its indirect influence was large.

The Latin element was immediate and first-hand in its influence; for Latin remained a living language in both church and state. Men prayed, and preached, and sang, and wrote, and spoke in Latin from one end of Western Christendom to the other. Not until the purists of the sixteenth century tried to arrest its growth did Latin as a living language for the learned begin to atrophy and to die.

Among the poets, Virgil, "the courteous soul of Mantua whose fame shall last as long as the world endures," as Dante speaks of him, held first place. In his *Fourth Eclogue,* Virgil was supposed to have foretold the coming of Christ. His *Aeneid* celebrates the greatness of Rome, and it could be interpreted as a moral allegory of the return of the human soul to God. Virgil remained the great model of style and the heart of school instruction. On the stall of a twelfth-century cathedral he is carved along with Moses and Isaiah. Century after century he was copied, cited, and imitated. Next to Virgil, in reputation, stood Ovid, though his popularity dated only from the twelfth century. His *Art of Love* was translated by Chrétien de Troyes and was the basis of Andreas Capellanus' *Art of Courtly Love.* It was quoted by the Goliardic poets, by the trouvères, and by Abélard and Héloïse. Ovid's *Metamorphoses,* the great anthology of classic myths and a sort of golden legend of antiquity, was much used by artists and poets. Horace was sometimes quoted, but his polished urbanity made him a prime favorite only in the Renaissance. Something of the same is true of the elegiac poets, Tibullus and Propertius, of the satirists, Juvenal, Persius, and Martial, and of the two very gifted yet totally different poets, Catullus and Lucretius. On the other hand, two second-rate epic poets, Lucan and Statius, had a high reputation with Dante, with the writers of chivalric romances, and with Chaucer. The plays of Plautus, Terence, and Seneca were, at different stages of the Middle Ages and the Renaissance, greatly esteemed.

Of the Latin prose writers, Cicero, the "king of eloquence," was the favorite. His Platonic and Stoic ideas and his elegant style were vastly admired. In his *Confessions*, St. Augustine says it was Cicero's *Hortensius* that turned his mind to religion. Seneca's essays on morals were often quoted; his plays did not become popular before the Renaissance. Pliny's *Natural History*, with its strange combination of insight, learning, and superstitious nonsense, was much read. Two important Latin writers neglected by the Middle Ages were the rhetorician Quintilian and the historian Tacitus. Many Latin authors were lost; pagan writers were less likely to survive than Christian authors. Informative writers had the best chance of being passed on; thus the writings of many second-rate geographers and encyclopedists survive, but very little poetry and drama.

2. THE TRANSMITTERS OF CLASSICAL AND PATRISTIC LEARNING

THE GREAT creative Patristic effort in the Latin West ended with the death of St. Augustine (430). The tremendous influx of barbarians into the empire greatly reduced the assimilative power of Roman civilization and pushed ahead processes of disintegration that had long since been under way. The changes in the Latin language are symptomatic of the transformation of the whole culture. At the beginning of the Christian Era, the Latin of the upper classes did not differ extensively from that of the masses. By the time of Constantine (about A.D. 300), there had come to be two languages: the speech of the upper classes and the educated and that of the masses. With the masses the distinction between long and short vowels had disappeared, and there had come to be also other differences in pronunciation, vocabulary, and syntax. After the Barbarian Migrations of the fifth century, very few schools taught grammar (that is, the rules of Donatus or the syntax of Cicero). By 800 Latin ceased to be a spoken language except among the clergy; and in the parts of western Europe Rome had ruled, the Romance dialects were already well developed.

The period after St. Augustine is marked not only by the almost universal disappearance of a knowledge of Greek, and a steady change in the type of Latin used, but also by a great decline in intellectual culture. We enter an age of transmission; all independent desire for new knowledge is gone, and the old straw is rethrashed and tied in new bundles. First among the transmitters were the grammarians. Donatus, the teacher of St. Jerome, who lived in Rome in the middle of the fourth century, wrote two popular texts with quotations from the Latin classics. His books were simple and direct, and the *Ars Maior* and the *Ars Minor* remained the most-used Latin grammars for more than a thousand years. They were so well-known in Chaucer's day that any grammar was to him a "donat." A longer grammar, Priscian's *Institutes* (written about 515), also had wide circulation. It contained copious quotations from Latin prose and poetry which the pupils had to learn by heart. In mediaeval art, Donatus or Priscian usually represent grammar.

A typical textbook of the early Middle Ages in the West was the work of Martianus Capella (d. 429), an African Neo-Platonist. His *Marriage of Philology and Mercury* is a dull compend in nine books, of which the first two tell of the marriage of Mercury with a virgin, Philology. All the gods are assembled to discuss the marriage; this allows the author to display his knowledge of classical mythology. The next seven books treat of the Seven Liberal Arts (a term first used later by Cassiodorus). First, there are grammar, rhetoric, and dialectic, called after 600 the *trivium*, then, arithmetic, geometry, astronomy, and music, later named the *quadrivium*. These abstract discussions are linked to the story by personifying each of the liberal arts as a courtier of Mercury and his bride. The book contains a statement that the earth is round and that the sun is the center of our universe—ideas repeated by Isidore of Seville, Bede, and John Scotus Erigena. The actual information conveyed is often slight; for example, Book VI is entitled *Geometria*, but it begins with some elementary geography, followed by a few propositions of geometry, whereupon it is announced that the person who personifies the subject presents unopened the books of Euclid. Apparently they had never been opened. The whole work is written in a clumsy and involved style, combining prose and verse; but it has a sing-song quality that makes its rules easy to memorize. "A sterile union of pedantry and fancy, sapless as the rods of a mediaeval schoolmaster," Taylor calls it; and C. S. Lewis says of it: "I have heard the scholar defined as one who has a propensity to collect useless information; in that sense Martianus is the very type of the scholar. The philosophies of others, the religions of others—back even to the twilight of Republican Rome—have gone into this curiosity shop of the mind. He piles them up all around him till there is hardly room for him to sit in the darkness of the shop; and then he gloats and catalogues but never dusts them, for even the dust is precious in his eyes." [2] Yet the *Marriage of Philology and Mercury* was still widely circulated in the sixteenth century. Indeed it was one of the most successful textbooks ever written.

More significant than the preceding transmitters of thought are a number of intellectual leaders in the period 500 to 750, first among whom is St. Benedict of Nursia (d. 543). Benedict was by no means the founder of monasticism, but he is its great legislator and is easily the most important figure in the monasticism of the West. [3] Monasticism was already centuries old when he drew up his famous rule for the house of Monte Cassino, which he founded about 520. Benedict's rule was noted for its reasonableness; it combined about six hours of work, four of prayer, and three a day of devotional reading; it did not demand extraordinary austerities. The rule describes the monks' vows of poverty, chastity, and obedience; emphasis is laid on humility, and the "twelve stairs of humility" are described as the road up to God. But Benedict also gives specific instructions about many practical matters such as how to elect an abbot, what to eat, when to work, and when to pray. The monk is to fight the allurements of the devil with prayer, pen, and spade. "Idleness," says the rule, "is the great enemy of the soul." Therefore monks should always be occupied, either in manual labor or in sacred reading.

In practice, monasteries came to follow a more or less uniform design. The central building was the church, which from the ninth century on was usually built on a cruciform plan. Inside the church a wooden or stone screen separated the choir from the nave, which often formed the church of a parish. Usually the monastic buildings lay to the south of the church, and these were built around an open court surrounded by cloisters. About the cloisters, and built in a solid square, were the refectory, the chapter house for meetings of the monks, the dormitory from which they descended once in the night for services in the church, an infirmary, a library, and other common rooms. Beyond the main structure were such buildings as the kitchen, bakery, stables, storage places, and workshops. A monastery was a little world in itself.

A typical monastic day, as organized after St. Benedict's time, began at midnight with the services of *Matins* and *Lauds,* each taking about half an hour. The monks then returned to bed. They rose with the sun. In the Middle Ages the day was reckoned from sunrise to sunset, and this period was divided into twelve hours; so the times of services and duties, in mediaeval times, varied with the season. At daybreak, there was the service of *Prime* followed by a regular mass. Then the monks went to the chapter house where tasks for the day were assigned; a sermon might be preached, and those who desired might confess. The monks gathered again at the third hour of daylight for *Terce,* followed by High Mass and *Sext,* with short intervals between. It was now mid-day and the monks entered the refectory for dinner, their first meal, which, in a strict house, consisted of bread, soup or meat, and fruit. On fast days, fish or eggs replaced meat. The monks then worked or read until the ninth hour when they gathered for *None,* a short service. At the tenth hour *Vespers* was sung; then came supper. Later *Compline* was said, and the monks retired.

The abbot, who governed the house, was elected by the monks for life; he appointed and removed all the officials of the monastery. The abbot consulted with all the monks in matters of great moment, in lesser matters with a few of the older members. He was bound to listen to them, but the final decision was in his hands, and all had to obey. The abbot, however, had to govern according to the rule. This is the system that, though not laid out in exactly this form by St. Benedict, came to prevail in Western monasticism.

The monastic orders from the sixth through the twelfth centuries were the wealthiest, most venerated, and most learned part of the church. The monasteries were founded to save the souls of the monks and to set an example of virtuous living to all mankind, not to foster learning, to further craftsmanship, or to improve agriculture, though all of these were significant by-products of monasticism. The later history of monasticism was a tale of backsliding and revivals. The great revivals connected with Cluny in the tenth century, and with the Cistercian and Carthusian orders in the eleventh century, used the Benedictine rule with improvements. Monasticism became one of the great mediaeval institutions; on the bad side it gained for celibacy an exaggerated importance, and, by establishing a double standard of conduct for monks and for the laity, it may have tended to lower the standard of Christian conduct for ordinary men and women. To the modern man it may seem a social waste. Moreover, many houses became corrupted by wealth, by their unseemly quarrels with the secular clergy, and by immorality, inertia, and dryrot. On the good side, the monks believed in the dignity of labor—"to work is to pray" says the Rule of St. Benedict; they emphasized the equality of rich and poor; they definitely improved agricultural methods; they undertook charitable work in the countryside and in the towns; and, finally, the monks kept learning alive. The copying and reading of books was intended, as we have seen, to keep the brothers from mischievous idleness. It was sometimes the occupation of writing, rather than what was written, that was valued. There were, of course, many monks truly devoted to learning; yet, while they were preserving learning, other monks were neglecting to care for valuable texts. Learning was a byproduct of monasticism; still, without the monks there would have been very little learning in Latin Christendom down, at least, into the twelfth century. At its best the monastery was what Peter Damian said of it in the eleventh century: "a paradise watered by the streams of the four gospels, a garden of delights, a spiritual field where earth and heaven meet, a ground in which, as in a wrestling school of the spirit, the frailty of flesh contends with the powers of the air."

Contemporary with St. Benedict was the great scholar Boethius (d. 524). Born of a noble Roman family, he had evidently been well educated. He served Theodoric the Ostrogoth at Ravenna, but disagreed with him on political issues. He may also have intrigued with the Eastern emperor. In any case, he was thrown into prison for treason and later executed. Boethius shared the lofty idea of Theodoric—later the ideal of Charlemagne, of Alfred the Great, and of the German Ottos—of trying to fuse the best of Roman, Christian, and Germanic culture. As a part of such a program, Boethius hoped to translate all of Plato and Aristotle into Latin and to harmonize the systems of the two philosophers. Unhappily he only got as far as part of the *Organon*, that is, two of Aristotle's logical treatises, and Porphyry's *Introduction to the Categories of Aristotle*. This translation of Aristotle by Boethius was the only part of the master's writings used in the West until the twelfth century.

Besides "launching this lifeboat from the sinking ship of Greek thought," Boethius wrote some treatises of his own. His *Tractates*, which show that he was a trinitarian Christian, are concerned with theological questions. He also composed a series of short treatises on arithmetic, geometry (only part of which survives), music, and probably astronomy. His most admired work was a little book written in prison, *The Consolation of Philosophy*. In his dark cell the noble lady, philosophy, visits him, lifts him from despair, and calms his spirit. The work is Neo-Platonic and Stoic in tone; it contains no reference to Jesus. The mood is one of resignation, untormented by a sense of sin or a yearning for salvation. It is written in alternate verse and prose, and the style is direct and unadorned in contrast to the over-ornate and diffuse style common among the writers of this period. The author's sincerity and depth of emotion seem to have moulded his expression. Gibbon speaks of the *Consolation* as a "golden volume, not unworthy of the leisure of Plato or Cicero, but which claims incomparable merit from the barbarism of the times and the situation of the author." [4] It became one of the most popular books of the Middle Ages and was one of the most translated of all mediaeval books. Alfred the Great, in the ninth century, translated it into Anglo-Saxon, it was turned into German in the eleventh century, and into French (by Jean de Meun) in the thirteenth. Chaucer translated it into Middle English in the fourteenth century. It was well known to Dante, Thomas More, Shakespeare, Queen Elizabeth, and Milton, all of whom quote it. Boethius has been called "the last of the Ancients" because of his knowledge of Greek and his understanding of Greek philosophy; he has likewise been named "the first of the Scholastics" since he tried to fuse the doctrines of the church with Aristotelianism and helped to create a new Latin vocabulary for philosophy, bequeathing to later Scholasticism some of its terminology and definitions. It is fascinating to speculate on the probable development of mediaeval thought in the West had Boethius lived to complete his program of making Plato and Aristotle available in Latin.

Cassiodorus (d. 583), like Boethius, was a Roman who served Theodoric. At the age of about sixty he retired to family estates in Calabria and established two monasteries. His great interest was in higher education. He had proposed to the bishop of Rome the establishment of a sort of university in Rome; times were too unsettled for this to be realized. But in his two monasteries, one for cenobites, and one for a group of hermits, he was able to introduce some of his ideas. For each house he wrote a rule, resembling in part that of St. Benedict. He also wrote a *History of the Goths* which has survived only in a summary of Jordanes and in a number of theological treatises.[5] His best-known work is his *Institutes*, a plan of study for the Scriptures and the Church Fathers and the order in which books should be read, with elaborate instructions on how to study the seven liberal arts, how to copy books, and how to organize a library. His program is very intelligent and laid out on most liberal lines and includes both pagan and Christian authors. Cassiodorus was deeply impressed with the need of an educated clergy, and he also saw clearly how the vast leisure and peace of the monastery could be used to further learning. The *Institutes* were widely read, and the Benedictine Order took them up and helped to spread their use. Without the influence of Cassiodorus' *Institutes* the Carolingian Renaissance would have been less than it was, just as the Italian Renaissance would have been less without the labors of the Carolingian scholars.

By the end of the sixth century, great confusion and barbarism prevailed in western Europe. To try to offset this the church had undertaken a second Christianization of the West. The first Christian missionaries had spread the new faith before the Barbarian Migrations began. Then these Migrations, in the fifth century, drove a great wedge of heathendom and savagery from Germany down into Spain and North Africa. In the second evangelization of the West, the missionaries worked principally from Ireland and from Rome. They converted the barbarian chieftains, baptized the masses, founded monasteries, established dioceses and parishes, and began to train a native clergy. The new religion offered the new peoples a loftier religion, a greater culture, and a better ordering of life. Theirs was an attitude of ignorance and docility towards recognized wisdom. Usually the barbarians caught, at first only faintly, the meaning of the new faith. When, according to legend, Clovis, the Frank, heard the story of the Crucifixion, he told the missionary that that miserable business would never have occurred if he and his men had been there! Then Clovis and three thousand warriors were baptized in one afternoon. The missionaries in their "peregrinations of God" showed splendid courage, devotion, and resourcefulness. Not only did they bring back Christianity to the Roman lands in the West, but they began also to carry the faith beyond the borders of the Roman Empire till, by the eleventh century, they had brought Latin Christianity to Scandinavia and across the continent from the east side of the Baltic and Poland through Bohemia and Slovakia to Croatia on the Adriatic. Some of the Barbarians who came into the Roman Empire in the fifth century were converted to Arianism, but, finally, by the eighth century, all the Latin Christians were Trinitarians and were in communion with the bishop of Rome. In the minds of the missionaries they were converting the heathen to save them from hell; to the mind of the modern historian the missionaries were also saving the barbarians from savagery and were bringing them into contact with the ancient civilization of the Mediterranean world.

In the midst of this backwardness and confusion lived Gregory the Great (d. 604), a contemporary of Mohammed, and the last of the great Latin Fathers of the church. Like Boethius and Cassiodorus, Gregory came of an old Roman family. He served, as a young man, in the town government of Rome, which by his time had shrunk to a village. Surrounded by the mountainous ruins of the Colosseum, the Forum which had become a cow pasture, the Palatine, and the Baths of Caracalla, now the dwelling places of bats and owls, snakes and lizards, the few remaining inhabitants made their living through service in the court of the bishop of Rome and through looking after a stream of pilgrims who came to visit the sacred shrines. The city of the Caesars, referred to by a tenth-century poet as "red with the blood of the martyrs," had become a vast and picturesque wilderness, murmurous with the prayers of Christian pilgrims. For a time Gregory was in Constantinople, and when he returned to Rome, he entered a monastery from whence he was called to the papacy. "Being upon a certain day overwhelmed with the trouble of worldly business," he writes, "I retired to a solitary place congenial to grief. After I had sat a long time in affliction, Peter the deacon joined me. When he saw me overwhelmed in languor of heart, he questioned me, "What is the matter?' To him I answered, 'O Peter, the grief I endure is with me both old and new; old through long use, and new by continual increase. Truth it is that my unhappy soul, wounded with worldly business, is now calling to mind in what state it once was when it dwelt in my monastery, how it would soar above things corruptible, and though enclosed in mortal body would yet pass beyond its fleshy bars. I sigh as one who turneth back his eyes to a forsaken shore. For thus it is that the mind lapseth. First it is faithless to the good which it held, though it may still remember that it hath forsaken it. It cometh, at length, to such a pass that it cannot so much as behold in memory what before it had actively practiced. So we are carried so far out to sea that we lose sight of the quiet haven whence we set forth." [6]

Gregory in his own time was known as a great church administrator, the backer of missionaries like St. Augustine, whom he sent to found the see of Canterbury in 597, the protagonist of monasticism, the patron of a reorganized church liturgy and music, and the prelate who did more than any other to bring all the churches of Latin Christendom under the bishop of Rome. More than any other man, Gregory is the founder of the mediaeval papacy with one doctrine, one liturgy, and one earthly head. Fear of revolts had prevented the state and church authorities from suppressing pagan rites in rural districts. The church regarded the organization of the population under priestly control as a first step toward the introduction of the Christian ethical code. In accordance with this traditional policy, Gregory urged the taking over of the pagan holy places and dedicating them to Christian usages so as to gather to the church the reverence attached to the old pagan shrines. In the whole process it meant that the church also took over legends and superstitions and ways of feeling and thinking to create a new religious syncretism often removed from the spirit of the Gospel, a type of Christianity removed also from the syncretism of the first four Christian centuries.

Gregory's best-known works are his letters, of which over six hundred survive, his *Pastoral Care*, on the duties of the bishop, a comprehensive survey of how to run a diocese (a parallel for the secular church to the rule of St. Benedict for the monastic church), a series of *Dialogues* or edifying moral discussions concerning the lives of holy men, and, most important of all, the *Moralia*, a long and most discursive commentary on *Job*. Gregory's writings, with their clumsy Latin and their poor organization and their general dimness, show the intellectual decline since Augustine. He says of his bad Latinity that he will despise the laws of case and declension because he deems it unfit "to submit the words of the divine oracle to the rules of Donatus." In the seventh century, Latin style had separated into debased provincial dialects, all of which had in common the neglect of declensions of nouns and conjugations of verbs, wretched spelling, and a messy word order. It is often difficult to make out just what the author is trying to say, and the best authors cannot put order into their ideas or clarity into their expression of them. Even the handwriting is uniform only in its disorderliness. While Gregory's learning was based on that of the greatest of the Latin Fathers, he was not able to understand much of Augustine, for he lacked the knowledge of ancient literature, of Greek philosophy, and of the Greek Fathers that Augustine possessed. His enthusiasm for far-fetched and sometimes unintelligible allegory, his tendency to moralize everything, and his superstition, as when—at least according to legend—he was convinced he had prayed the Emperor Trajan out of hell, and his uncertainty as to whether the moon received its light from the sun— all show the depths to which learning had sunk by the end of the sixth century. The Christian faith, he declared in the *Moralia*, is "a kind of river, which is both shallow and deep, wherein the lamb may find a footing and the elephant float at large"; and in the name of allegory and interpretation he sometimes introduces the most fantastic explanations of things earthly and divine. There is no originality, and sometimes very little reason, in his work. His faith is mystical, though deeply rooted in the fear of hell. Gregory had the mind neither of an ancient Roman, nor of a converted pagan, but of a mediaeval monk, and so he represents almost a complete break with ancient culture. He contributed to current ideas about angels, demons, purgatory, miracles, the use of relics, the cult of the saints, and the belief in the magical value of the sacraments. The converging currents of barbarism and classical decadence meet in him. Yet Gregory the Great was widely read for centuries and was an important medium through which all of early Christian thought was passed on to the later Middle Ages.[7] As an administrator, Gregory was a Roman of the Romans, and not only the organization of the papacy, but even the survival of the church in the confusion of the times owes much to him. He gave to the papacy a policy and a position which have never been lost, and he would be a man of great significance in history even if he had never written a line.

In a world of equal intellectual murkiness lived Isidore of Seville (d. 636), a Visigothic bishop before the Muslim inundation. His best-known work was a popular encyclopedia, the *Etymologiae*, a huge work which he left incomplete. Books I through III are devoted to the several liberal arts; Book IV is on medicine, V on law and on divisions of time, VI on the Bible and church services, VII concerns God, angels, and saints, VIII the church and sects, IX languages, races, kingdoms, armies, X is a miscellaneous etymological word list, XI concerns men and fabulous monsters, XII animals, XIII the universe, XIV the earth and its parts, XV buildings and lands, XVI stones, minerals, and metals, XVII agriculture and botany, XVIII wars and games, XIX ships, building materials, dress, and, finally, XX food, drink, and furniture. It must have been an enormous task to have compiled such a work with the few books available in seventh-century Spain. The actual information on most subjects is unusually slight and often wrong: "the fruits of the much decayed tree of ancient learning." The spell of words on Isidore is strong; he strings them along and one wonders how much he understood some of his own vocabulary. It remained, however, until Vincent of Beauvais composed his *Speculum* in the thirteenth century, the most accessible book in which one could find information about many subjects—a sort of "old lumber room in which had been stored away many of the cast off clothes of antiquity."

With the Venerable Bede (d. 735), in this process of selecting only a half-dozen men over nearly as many centuries, we come to a writer who is able to put order into his ideas and to express them with clarity and correctness. Behind the career of Bede was a great development of monastic learning in Ireland extending back into the fifth century, followed by a still more remarkable growth of learning in English monasteries beginning in the sixth century. In some of the larger monasteries of the seventh century, Greek was taught and some Greek books were available. Bede spent his whole life at a monastery in northern England, writing and teaching. For the period in which he lived, he must have been well supplied with books; he speaks of "searching through the pantries of the Fathers" and again of "culling the sweetest flowers from the patristic meadows." In addition, Bede was evidently a man of powerful intellect. He wrote admirable textbooks on some of the seven liberal arts, a series of Biblical commentaries which were highly esteemed and widely read for centuries, works on chronology which are among the highest achievements of the West in natural science between 500 and 1200, and, finally, the greatest historical work in Latin of the whole period 450 to 1200, *The Ecclesiastical History of the English People.* The learning and the spirit of Bede and of a number of English schoolmasters of his time dominate much of the learning of the Carolingian Renaissance.

Back of the Carolingian Renaissance stands also the tenacity of monastic learning, not only in Irish and English centers, but also in some of the great Italian foundations like Monte Cassino, all of which had kept learning alive in spite of the general disorder that followed the great migrations. Also back of this revival was the earlier work of Irish and English missionaries. The Irish missionaries had founded mission stations on the islands of Iona and of Lindisfarne on either side of northern England. From here they had established parishes and monasteries in England; and, landing on the Continent, these intrepid Irishmen, like St. Columbanus, had founded a series of monasteries across the continent as far as St. Gall in Switzerland and Bobbio in northern Italy. Pushing into central Germany, they founded more monasteries and churches. By the eighth century many Anglo-Saxon missionaries were also at work on the Continent; one of them, St. Boniface, sent into Germany by the pope and Charles Martel, reorganized the see of Mainz and founded the great Benedictine house of Fulda.[8] Boniface was also a scholar, and he used his influence to improve older monastic schools and to start new ones. A third important element in the background of the Carolingian Renaissance was the steady growth of the Frankish state. The Franks had, in the fifth century, moved across the Rhine into the tottering Roman Empire. Without ever losing contact with their homeland, and never, like all the other Germanic Barbarian peoples, planting themselves as an alien island among strange peoples, they had expanded southward into Gaul and Italy and northward into Germany. By the time of Charlemagne, at the end of the eighth century, the Franks controlled the largest state built up since the fall of Rome, a state that included a section of northern Spain, all of old Gaul, part of the Low Countries, western Germany, and Italy as far down as Rome—indeed, most of Latin Christendom. Through all of this expansion, the Frankish rulers, since the end of the fifth century, had usually worked in close co-operation with the bishop of Rome.

Charlemagne conceived of a fusion of Roman, Christian, and Germanic culture.[9] His plans included the consolidation of a centralized state with local officials, according to a system inherited from his ancestors, and travelling inspectors (the *missi dominici*), whom he introduced. He depended greatly on help from the clergy, and he saw clearly that their training had to be improved. Every monastery and cathedral was ordered to run a school, and Charlemagne called to Gaul, where learning languished, the best scholars he could find in England and Italy, where the cultural level was higher. Besides extending education, he wished to further the work of copying manuscripts and of improving the style of handwriting. Also through his influence artists turned to the Mediterranean world for inspiration in the art of ancient Rome and of Byzantium. So the Carolingian Renaissance was a revival at once of good government, of education and learning, and of art.

Central in Charlemagne's plan was a palace school to train his children and to supply leadership in learning. He inherited this school from his predecessors, but he completely reinvigorated it.[10] To this school he invited Alcuin (d. 804), who had been trained at York by a pupil of Bede. York in Alcuin's youth had the best school in England and the largest library in Latin Christendom. Most of the books copied during the Carolingian Renaissance came from York and other English centers and from Italy. Alcuin himself was primarily a grammarian interested in the improvement of Latin style. For a time he was head of the palace school; later he was the abbot of a famous house of secular canons at Tours. From this monastery at Tours spread an improved style of handwriting, based on a clear Merovingian book-hand. The Carolingian hand used round uncial letters, differentiated between the capital and the small letters, and separated one word from another. It was a better book-hand than anything the Romans or the earlier Middle Ages had known, and it proved to be one of the leading contributions of the whole Carolingian Renaissance. Besides Alcuin there were at the palace school, Paul the Deacon, a Lombard, Peter of Pisa, an Italian mathematician, and Einhard, a German educated at Fulda. It was, as we have seen, part of Charlemagne's plan to have every bishop run a school; this was an attempt to universalize a practice that was already developing. But as the monastic clergy were more interested in learning than the secular clergy, he had greater success in founding and improving monastic scholarship, especially in the area between the Loire River in Gaul and the Weser in Germany. When the great emperor died in 814, the leading centers of erudition in Europe were no longer in the British Isles and in Italy; they were in Orléans, Tours, Corbie, St. Denis, St. Wandrille, Fulda, St. Gall, Reichenau, and Lorsch.

The patronage given to learning by Charlemagne was continued by his son, Louis the Pious, and by his grandson, Charles the Bald. Rabanus Maurus (d. 856), a pupil of Alcuin, later abbot of Fulda, and, finally, archbishop of Mainz, was an unoriginal writer, but a very important influence in spreading learning in western Germany. His pupil, Walafrid Strabo (d. 849), though he died young, was the author of some widely-used compends, the most important of which was an anthology of writings from the Church Fathers on the various books of the Bible. It is no more than a compilation, but it had an enormous vogue throughout all the rest of the Middle Ages. Walafrid was also known for his Latin verses.

The greatest figure of the whole Carolingian Renaissance was the Irishman John Scotus Erigena (d. 877), probably driven out of Ireland by the Viking raids. He had learned Greek, probably in Ireland, before he came to the court of Charles the Bald in France.[11] He first attracted attention through a controversy he had with Gottschalk of Fulda over predestination. Later he began to study the works of Dionysius the Areopagite which had been sent to a Frankish ruler by the Byzantine emperor and which he had deposited in the monastery of St. Denis near Paris. Erigena translated these works and other Greek writings and then devoted years to the composition of his own *On the Divisions of Nature*. Its five books are written in the form of a dialogue between teacher and pupil; they show not only the influence of some of the Greek Fathers, but also a profound knowledge of the writings of St. Augustine.

The term "nature," for Erigena, means not only the natural world but also God and the supernatural; it denotes all reality. The divisions of nature are four, namely: nature that creates and is not created (God), nature that is created and creates (logos and Platonic ideas), nature that is created and does not create (all earthly things), and finally nature that neither creates nor is created (God as end and purpose of all). Basically his system is the Neo-Platonic and pantheistic monism where all parts of creation emanate from God and return to him. He believes that reason and revelation both come from God and cannot contradict each other; if they do contradict, reason should dominate. "Authority proceeds from reason, but reason never from authority. True reason, since it rests on its own strength, needs no reinforcement by any authority." [12] He strives to avoid pantheism and tries to separate God and his creatures, and it is evident that he considers himself quite orthodox. His book is profoundly Neo-Platonic in his basic belief that all universals are anterior to particulars. Only God has essential being, though God is unknowable to the finite mind of man. Sin has no positive existence, nor does evil have its ground in God. Sin and evil are only the absence of reality and are caused by men's misdirected will. The whole system of Erigena, in spite of its Neo-Platonic antecedents, is one of surprising originality. The church found it unorthodox because of its pantheistic tendencies and condemned it in 1225. Actually, Erigena had no immediate predecessors and no direct followers. When philosophy in the West again moved ahead in the writings of Anselm, its problems were formulated in somewhat different terms. Among the important later mediaeval philosophers only Abelard shows his influence. Erigena thus remains the loneliest figure in the whole history of European thought.[18]

The originality of the learning of the Carolingian Renaissance, except for John Scotus Erigena, is so slight that some writers have dismissed the whole concept of a renaissance. It is true that there was a greater tendency to transmit the existing tradition than to put independent questions, to make selections from available works, and to imitate the ancient poets rather than to create anything new. But such studies gave a literary training, purified and clarified style, and helped to develop intellectual faculties. Charlemagne's cathedral and monastic schools fought, at once, the bad morals, the bad learning, the bad Latin style, the bad handwriting, and the bad singing of the preceding age. It was all purely clerical. Lay society no longer made use of Latin as it had in the Merovingian Age. Latin was now the possession only of the priestly caste; the clergy were also now the only ones who could read. The masses spoke a series of dialects and read nothing. Latin Christendom, like a schoolboy, was now making a new beginning after the near breakdown of ancient civilization in the West. Thanks to the Carolingian Renaissance, many of the Latin classics survived; over ninety per cent of the writings of ancient Rome that have come down to us exist in their oldest form in a Carolingian copy. Though political and social anarchy returned, learning never again sank so low as it had been in the preceding age.

Otto I, elected king of the East Franks in 936, took the title of "Roman Emperor of the German People" in 962, and he, his son, Otto II, and his grandson, Otto III, were patrons of learning in Germany during most of the tenth century. They had the help of the new monastic order founded at Cluny in Burgundy in 910. The Cluniacs used the Benedictine rule, but they added provisions that tied up the daughter houses to the mother house; they stiffened discipline in the monasteries they founded or took over, and they brought a general quickening of all monastic life. The Ottos, like Alfred the Great, the Anglo-Saxon king of the ninth century, and Charlemagne earlier, worked in closest co-operation with the church. All regarded the clergy as the great civilizing force in their several states, and all took pains to try to get worthy men into the positions of abbots and bishops. The church did not always serve these rulers well; many churchmen were less fitted to feed their flocks than to fleece them; the clergy sometimes were too much interested in increasing their power even at the expense of the state that backed them. Some churchmen wasted their best efforts in theological disputes over such questions as free-will and predestination, a controversy that waxed hot in the later ninth and through most of the tenth century. On the other hand, it must always be remembered that the church had to work through the personnel it could recruit in a turbulent and backward time. Under the patronage of the Ottos learning flourished in some of the great German monasteries and in a few cathedral schools. There were scholars and poets like Notker of St. Gall, Roswitha, the nun of Gandersheim, and Widukind of Corvey, and there was a revival of stone architecture and sculpture which gives the Ottonian Renaissance in Germany something of the same character as the earlier Carolingian Renaissance in Gaul.

In the tenth century, once called by the fifteenth-century humanist Laurentius Valla "the century of lead and iron," there began to be some cultural and commercial contacts with the superior civilization of Islam. The Carolingian Empire had gone to pieces, and western Europe was being continually raided by the Vikings from the north, the Magyars and Slavs from the east, and the Mohammedans from the south. In spite of the difficulty of the times, the cultural level, at least in Germany, was not as low as it had been in the seventh and eighth centuries, and there remained good schools in Gaul, in Switzerland, and in northern Italy. Details are lacking, but some knowledge of Muslim science appears in the monastic and cathedral schools of Lorraine.[14] This cultural contact with Islam seems to lie back of the career of the greatest scholar of the tenth century, Gerbert of Aurillac (d. 1003). He spent three years as a student in Christian Spain, and later he was in the service of the German emperors Otto I and Otto II who made him the abbot of Bobbio in Italy. Then he took service with Hugh Capet, the first important ruler of his line in France, and was made archbishop of Rheims. Otto III then made him archbishop of Ravenna, from whence he was called to Rome as pope, under the title of Sylvester II. Gerbert was so learned that he was said to be a magician in league with the devil. His chief interests were in literary studies and in mathematics; he wrote a treatise on the abacus and introduced the Arabic numbers (though not the zero) into western Europe. He taught his pupils to identify musical tones by means of a vibrating string and showed them how to represent the universe with balls, rods, and bands. He may have had an astrolabe for use in celestial and terrestrial measurements. He seems to have inspired in his pupils a great enthusiasm for dialectical arguments that later reappears in Roscellinus and Abelard. He undoubtedly helped to create a desire for Greek and Arabic scientific knowledge. At the same time, Gerbert was a humanist who urged his students to read the Latin classics instead of condensations and to imitate the styles of Horace and Cicero. We know that, like a Renaissance humanist later, he had agents all over western Europe collecting Latin manuscripts for him. The great cathedral school of Chartres, under Gerbert's pupil Fulbert, was the heir to the master's teaching of the Latin classics and his humanistic enthusiasms. No Latin translations from the Arabic scientists and philosophers circulated in the West until the time of Constantine the African in the next century, the eleventh, but the career of Gerbert represents the beginning of cultural contacts with Islam and, through Islam, with the science and philosophy of ancient Greece. Gerbert's interest in science and in humanistic studies represents, thus, the beginnings of new chapters in the history of Western culture.

3. POETRY AND HISTORY

EVERY mediaeval century produced a large volume of Latin poetry, and, even for the earlier mediaeval centuries, much of this has been preserved. Over all this poetry hangs the spell of the ancient Roman poets and the spell also of Roman rhetoric. The ancient classical models and the grammatical writings of Donatus and Priscian kept Latin verse from becoming as corrupt and even as nearly unintelligible as, for some centuries, was Latin prose. Some of the early mediaeval poetasters went far beyond any ancient models in their rhetorical tricks, such as writing poems every line of which began with the same letter, or in which the initial letters of succeeding lines spelled some special word, or poems in the form of the cross, of a pyramid, of trees, or of animals, or lines of verse that read nearly the same either way, as "Roma tibi subito motibus ibit amor" (Sidonius).[15]

For the peoples who now lived in parts of the old Roman Empire of the West, Latin remained something of a living language. This was particularly true in Italy, but the Germans and the Celts had neither made Latin culture nor grown up in it, and their Latin poets had to woo the muses in a foreign tongue. On these new peoples the spell of rhetorical studies lay heaviest; they had painfully to acquire the rules and could write only with the grammarians and the Roman and early Christian poets at their elbow. Everywhere, though, the mediaeval Latin poets went to school to the poets and rhetoricians of ancient and early Christian Rome. Not until the twelfth century was there much secular Latin poetry that bore the marks of genuine originality. All through the history of mediaeval Latin poetry, verse written in the classical Roman meters based on quantity paralleled poetry written with an accented rhythm; some poets used both metric devices in their verses.

St. Ambrose and Prudentius, as we have seen, were the first great mediaeval Latin poets; their originality lay in their ability to handle Christian subjects in an effective way, and their works were later the great models of religious poetry. Parallel with them, and extending down into the age of the Barbarian migrations, were a number of other early Christian poets whose verse is, however, more secular in outlook. None of them are men of the first order, but they were highly considered by mediaeval writers and were widely imitated. Ausonius (d. 400) has been called "the first mediaeval secular poet." His great interest is in himself; his verses are the poet's autobiography. He wrote a delightful series of verses, the *Ephemeris* (or diary of day's business), in which the poet takes the reader through a typical day from the moment of awakening. He liked to play poetical tricks with words; one poem of forty-two lines, each line consisting of five words, has the first word of a single syllable, the second word of two syllables, and so on up to the fifth word of five syllables. Another poem has 164 hexameter verses, each one ending in a different mono-syllabic noun. Ausonius, who was always the schoolmaster, set all kinds of homely themes to verse, and he loved to compose epigrams. His best-known poem is a long one, the *Mosella*, in which he describes a trip up the river with effective word-pictures of its vine-clad banks, its ships, its fish, and the country estates along its sides. Ausonius passed on the device of borrowing phrases, whole lines, and figures of speech from earlier poets. He strung together tags of Virgil and other ancient poets, often with great ingenuity. Beneath his rhetoric, his pedantry, and his artificiality, there is often a flash of real poetic feeling.

Ausonius' pupil, Paulinus of Nola, was of a more serious turn of mind. Though he began as an elegant versifier on trifling themes, in later life he turned his talents to devotional themes and to poems in praise of saints and martyrs. Sedulius tried to turn those who loved the fables of Ovid to an interest in the miracles of Jesus. His most esteemed work is a long poem, *Carmen Paschale*, which relates the miracles in the Bible connected with Jesus and ends with a description of the Resurrection and the Ascension. The allegory and symbolism of this work assured it a great popularity in all the mediaeval centuries. Apollinaris Sidonius of Gaul (d. 480) was known later through his collected letters and his verses, which presented him as a Roman "gentleman of the old school," who, in a world of growing barbarism, kept the elegancies of a fallen day about him. His graceful though mediocre poems are full of the dying echoes of Roman urbanity and the love of gracious living. Claudian of Alexandria, who remained a pagan, was the greatest master of verse form in the group; his best-known work was a poetic retelling of the story of Proserpine and Pluto. Also belonging to the period around A.D. 400 is the great hymn *Te Deum Laudamus*, the authorship of which is uncertain. It is written in rhythmical prose and became part of the service of *Matins* whenever the *Gloria* was said at mass. It has also long been used for special occasions of rejoicing. The impression made by most of these poets of the end of antiquity and the beginning of the Middle Ages is that they are skilled rhetoricians rather than great poets. They rarely move much beyond the schoolroom where they have learned to turn their verses, and only rarely do they capture something of the manner and magic of their great models. But later on, mediaeval men cherished the Latin writers who were nearest to them in time and in spirit, and this group of Latin poets who lived during the great migrations were highly regarded and held up as models by all the later mediaeval generations.

After the storm of the migrations had passed, and there was some return to a quieter way of life, Latin poetry again flowered with Fortunatus (d. 600). It is true the muses had not been stilled, and both

Boethius and Cassiodorus had written poems of a religious and philosophic tenor. Indeed, there is hardly a prose writer of importance who
did not write verses that have been preserved. Fortunatus, however,
made his reputation entirely as a poet. Though born in Italy, most of
his life was spent in Gaul, where he finally became bishop of Poitiers.
Here he met Radegund, a Frankish queen, who had retired to a nunnery. Many of his poems were written at her behest or in her honor.
His adoration of the queen, now a nun, represents the beginning of a
style that flowers in the poetry of the troubadours. The sensual desire
of the pagan poets has been sublimated to a mystical devotion. Fortunatus wrote voluminously: occasional poems on the pleasures of the
table and on this and that, saints' lives, letters in verse, and devotional
verses. His poetry abounds in grammatical faults and often lacks genuine inspiration, but some of his verses addressed to Radegund and
the best of his religious poetry are admirable. One of the well-known
is on the true cross, a relic of which had been sent to the nunnery at
Poitiers by the Eastern emperor. The poem is developed on the theme
that as sin and death had entered the world by the tree in the Garden
of Eden, so by a tree, in the Crucifixion, the redemption of the world
was assured. One of his poems that celebrates the elevation of one of
his patronesses to the position of abbess sings of the cloistered life in
the form of a mystic epithalamium in which angels, prophets, patriarchs, and saints come in a ceremonial procession to assist at the rites;
the spirit is no longer that of early Christianity, but is thoroughly mediaeval. His best religious poetry is filled with the Catholic spirit and
with Catholic symbolism and mysticism.[16] The form is still classical,
but in his use of stress rhythm and of occasional rhyme, and in the
emotional quality of his inspiration, he is mediaeval and he contributed toward the growth of a new tradition that was to blossom in the
great religious poetry of the twelfth and thirteenth centuries.

Gregory the Great, Isidore of Seville, Bede, and nearly all the well-
known scholars of the Carolingian and Ottonian Renaissances also
wrote verses. Only rarely does this poetry rise above the level of rhetoric as in the magnificent hymn *Veni Creator Spiritus*, probably by
Rabanus Maurus. With the exception of the *Te Deum*, there has been
no other hymn so extensively used as the *Veni Creator Spiritus*. Nearly
as fine are the earlier *Ave Maris Stella* and *Gloria Laus et Honor*, the

last the work of Theodulf, the ablest of the poets at the court of Charlemagne; it is now part of the Palm Sunday service. The number of Latin hymns greatly increased after 500.

In the field of secular poetry a great deal of occasional verse, versified riddles, eclogues, epigrams, and poetical epistles survive. Most of it smells of the lamp and shows the hand of the schoolmaster. When the monkish spirit objects to the study of the pagan poets, there is always someone at hand, like the Spaniard Theodulf, who can allegorize away all the objectionable elements. So Proteus becomes Truth, and Hercules an example of the power of virtue; to that sort of thing there is no end. Alcuin writes of spring; the cuckoo's note sounds in the forest, flowers appear in the meadows, the vine begins to turn green, and the nightingale sings again. It is all in terms of the Latin poets; it is doubtful whether Alcuin had really looked at nature. Walafrid Strabo in his *Hortulus* describes the herbs and flowers, their beauties and healing virtues, in the monastic garden at Reichenau. Some of the Carolingian poets continue a tradition, started earlier by Irish and Anglo-Saxon poets, of introducing some alliteration and assonance in their Latin verses, a usage probably borrowed from vernacular poetry. The Irish poets, too, did much to further the development of verse with an accented rhythm, the love of which passed from the Anglo-Saxon poets onto the Continent in the eighth century. In all of this verse, one sees a dim and only partly conscious humanism struggling with mediaeval murkiness, a strange mixture of individualism and rules, of the secular and the devout. These poets not only lacked inspiration, but, even with all their rhetorical studies, they seem to us often to have had a defective sense of quantity and a lack of taste in the selection of words. But they helped to keep alive for better days the love of letters and of the old poets.

The poetry of the Ottonian Renaissance of the tenth century in Germany shows that the Roman and early Christian poets were less thoroughly studied than during the Carolingian Renaissance a century earlier; the observance of quantity is poorer, and the style and taste are cruder. However, some important new verse forms came in, two of which were the liturgical sequence and the trope, probably invented in Gaul but first described at the monastery of St. Gall. Both were destined later to be among the great literary forms of the high Middle

Ages. The sequence arose out of the singing of the final "a" of the *Alleluia* in the mass. It was customary to prolong this "a" into a long melody or *sequentia* whose singing required considerable skill. The *sequentia* was divided into parts, and, probably in the eighth century in Gaul, priests began to compose words for these melodies. The trope was another addition to the liturgy which first arose in Carolingian times; it was originally an introduction or addition to some part of the liturgy completing it or commenting on it. Tropes range from a few amplifying words interpolated between *Kyrie* and *Eleison,* to lengthy explanatory sentences, and even to entire poems or plays placed between two words of a liturgical text. Out of the trope came the first Latin Easter play, the tenth-century *Quem Quaeritis,* and ultimately the whole mediaeval Latin and vernacular drama.

Ekkehart I (d. 973) of the monastery of St. Gall may have been the author of a hexameter narrative of 1,465 lines, the *Waltharius,* a stirring tale of adventure and fighting in the days of Attila the Hun. Its vogue shows the growth of national feeling, a consciousness of history, and the popularity of vernacular epics. Charlemagne had collected the latter with loving care. The *Waltharius* also shows the influence of the *Aeneid* and of Prudentius; it is a well-constructed and lively tale, and moves along without the creaking of machinery. There is, too, a sense of proportion and artistic maturity generally lacking in the literature of the time. Its readers must have known the story in German; the large number of surviving manuscripts attests its popularity. Also, probably from Toul, comes an anonymous beast-epic, a moral tale in which the characters are all animals. The chief figures, the calf (the narrator), the lion, the leopard, the wolf, the fox, the nightingale, and the swan, are all really monks. They fast, go to mass, and feast in the refectory; all is written for the edification and warning of young monks. This *Ecbasis Captivi* is inferior from a literary point of view but is interesting as an early example of a literary form that was to become very popular in the later Middle Ages.

The most interesting figure among the Latin writers of the Ottonian Renaissance is Roswitha (d. 970), the nun of Gandersheim. Daughter of a noble Saxon family, she was given a good education and early wrote poems on saints and martyrs; one contains a tale of a priest who made a contract with the devil, the earliest poetic treatment of the

Faust-type of legend. She also wrote two mediocre historical poems, one on the life of Otto the Great and the other on the founding of the monastery of Gandersheim. Her fame, however, rests on six plays in rhymed prose and based on a rather unintelligent study of the comedies of Terence. The subjects are taken from Biblical and Roman history; and the intention is to treat the·material as a series of moral lessons, especially to inculcate the virtues of chastity. To this end, she is obliged to portray the evil temptations that have to be overcome. They seem dull in comparison with the comedies of Terence, which they try to imitate; indeed, they are hardly more than legends in a dialogue form. The plays, however, show some insight into character, and, considering the age in which they were written, have often a surprising naturalness and liveliness.

From the period just before 1000 there survives an interesting anthology of about fifty Latin lyrics preserved in Cambridge and called now the *Cambridge Songs*. The most interesting poems in this strange collection are several short narratives and the love songs; one of these, the "Nun's Complaint," is one of the loveliest of all mediaeval lyrics.

Spring comes forth in wanton play,
Dons his coat of colors gay,
Strews the fields with flowery sheen
Decks the woods with foliage green.

Beasts dig out their summer lair;
Little birds their nests prepare,
Singing welcome to the spring
'Neath their leafy covering.

All I hear and all I see
Breathes enchantment; but—ah me!
While the world is full of gladness,
I am full of tears and sadness.

Sitting in my lonely cell,
Pale with thoughts I dare not tell,
If perchance I lift my head,
Eyes and ears in trance are dead.

Hearken, hearken, gracious spring,
And some comfort to me bring.
Bright each flower and fresh each leaf,
But my soul is faint with grief.[17]

Mediaeval vernacular literature and secular music have been much less well-preserved than have mediaeval Latin literature and sacred music. The church was a continuing organization that, unlike a family, did not die out and have its possessions dispersed. Moreover, the church often had stone and brick buildings in which to keep its manuscripts, and, though these buildings were sometimes burned or sacked, they were much less likely to be destroyed than the homes of the nobles. And so while the history of Latin letters and of church music can be traced with only a comparatively few breaks, the story of vernacular literature and of secular music, at least before the twelfth century, is a thing of shreds and patches.

The first surviving works of mediaeval vernacular literature show a highly finished art into which must already have gone centuries of development. The oldest large body of vernacular literature that is still extant is that of the Anglo-Saxon peoples. This literature is the work of clerics who, if they did not create it, are at least responsible for its preservation. This explains why most of the surviving Anglo-Saxon literature is elegiac in form and spiritually edifying in content. Actually, works composed centuries later, like the Scandinavian *Poetic Edda* and the sagas and the German *Nibelungenlied*, contain much more of pagan northern myth and savage realism than do these much earlier Anglo-Saxon works. The verse form used by the Anglo-Saxon poets is made up of lines containing a varying number of syllables; each half line has two stressed syllables. Usually two or three of these syllables are alliterated, that is, they begin with the same consonant or group of consonants, as in the following line:

"Stéap stánhlitho—stíge nearwe"
(Steep stone-slopes—paths narrow.)

Sometimes the repetition is formed by vowels. A second poetic device used by all the early Germans was assonance, that is, an incomplete type of rhyme depending on the identity of vowel sounds, as in "main" and "came." The Anglo-Saxon language was complicated in vocabulary and grammar. Endless compounds were used: battle may be "spear-play," sword may be "battle-gleam," and blood may be "war-sweat," the sea may be "pathway-of-sails," "whale-way," or "swan-path." Grammarians count for each noun four cases and a variety of declensions, for adjectives two sets of inflections, and many conjugations for verbs. Complicated as is the language, Anglo-Saxon verse in accent, style, and metre is monotonous, and in the five centuries of Anglo-Saxon literature, from the eighth through the twelfth centuries, there was no change in style and no new differentiation of literary genre.

Among the longer surviving poems are *Widsith*, dealing with the life of a wandering scop, or poet, and his patrons, and the *Complaint of Deor*, a tale of a man estranged from his lord, who comforts himself with the thought that fate is unkind to all men. With somewhat more Christian coloring are a number of elegies: the *Ruined Burg*, the finest of the elegies, which laments a ruined city, probably Roman Bath, the *Wife's Complaint*, a sad tale of malicious tongues that separate a woman from her beloved, the *Wanderer*, wherein a young man mourns the passing of his lord, and the most original, the *Seafarer*, a tale of dark northern seas, of cold blasts and the tumult of storm waves, followed by a lovely description of spring. Riddles were a favorite verse form; the poet describes, without naming it, some familiar thing, a bird, an animal, a utensil in daily use, as, for example, a shield which, in one riddle, recounts its own life on the battlefield. Among a large number of these riddles, many of which have a fine poetic quality, is one in which a hurricane sings of its deeds as a bringer of terror to earth and sky and sea. In its deep feeling for nature, one is reminded of Shelley's *Ode to the West Wind*.

Less interesting is a mass of religious poetry, paraphrases of books of the Bible or of Latin poems based on the Bible, in which, amid long stretches of lifeless moralizing, will suddenly appear vivid descriptions of persons and scenes. One of the earliest of these, according to Bede, was the work of a cow-herd, Caedmon, who was called one night, by a divine voice, to sing the story of Creation. He dictated what came to him, and a translation of Bede has preserved one of his pieces, a few lines of no great literary merit. In general, these paraphrases of the Bible are full of fire and force; some of them branch out and add to Biblical incidents other apocryphal incidents. One of these religious poets, Cynewulf, wrote, among other pieces, part of a long poem on Christ and a number of saints' lives. Some of his poems are diffuse and confused; at his best, however, his style is flowing and melodious. Also Christian in outlook are two anonymous poems, the *Dream of the Rood*, in which the tree on which Jesus died tells its own story from its forest home to Calvary, where it received "the young hero, strong and brave," and the *Phoenix*, based on an early Christian poem, in which the phoenix, rising from its ashes, symbolizes Christ and the Christian soul. The *Phoenix* has a wonderful picture of the Holy Land, full of radiant sunlight and strewn with flowers, as remarkable a description as that of the northland in the poem of the riddle of the hurricane. Among the most characteristic Anglo-Saxon poems are stories of fighting. One short and powerful piece, the *Battle of Branunburh*, tells of a victory of the King of Wessex in 937; the lines ring with exultation over a fallen foe as the sun rises on the blood-stained field where birds and beasts devour the corpses. Another fragment, the *Defeat at Maldon*, wherein is told the story of men outnumbered but fighting to the last, is the most heroic bit of Anglo-Saxon verse.

The great glory of Anglo-Saxon literature, however, is the epic *Beowulf*, probably written, in the form we have it, by a Northumbrian monk about 700. The story centers in Denmark and Sweden; England is not mentioned.[18] The epic is more a series of episodes, interspersed with long digressions, than a continuous tale. Beowulf crosses the sea from Sweden to help the Danish king fight a man-eating giant, Grendel. After some magnificent fights, Beowulf slays both the monster and his mother. Fifty years later, when he is king in his homeland, he defeats another monster, but dies of his wounds, happy that he had saved his people. The monsters represent what primitive men most feared—the strength and stealth of wild animals, the poison of serpents, the destructiveness of fire, the mystery of lonely waters, and the nameless dangers that walk in darkness. The audience knew all the allusions so that the author could take many things for granted. *Beowulf* was evidently intended for a chanted recitation, for it is full of stock epithets and repetitions needed to keep the attention of the hearers. The style is already so over-elaborated that it has become stereotyped and, to some degree, decadent, but in its best passages the poem has great power.[19] The only thing naïve about *Beowulf* is its Christian theology, which the author does not always treat with technical assurance. Some of the Christian material is not well integrated with the story and seems dragged in. On the other hand, the moral grandeur of the character of Beowulf shows that it is, in part, based on a real understanding of the heroes of the Old Testament. The hero combines Germanic and Christian ideals; he does what he ought to do with fine heroism, and he finds therein his life's satisfaction. He acts, too, with a sense of duty and of loyalty that may show some influence of the Stoic hero of the *Aeneid*. His is an ideal of gentleness and honor united to strength, and of heroic valor ennobled by virtue. It is a story of a vanishing age in which the pagan gods are fading, and though there are still echoes of the day of Thor's thunder, the bolt is spent, and there is dawning a time of Christian faith and new ideals.

Anglo-Saxon prose was slow to develop. It has survived in collections of laws, in the *Anglo-Saxon Chronicles* kept in various monasteries and in the translations of Orosius, Boethius, Gregory the Great, and Bede, made either by Alfred the Great or at his order. The clearest and most musical Anglo-Saxon prose is that of Aelfric, once a student in a great Benedictine school at Winchester, the Anglo-Saxon capital, who wrote, in the eleventh century, a series of *Catholic Homilies* based on the Latin Fathers. At the time of the conquest (1066), Anglo-Saxon prose had become much more flexible, closer to the speech of the common man and even to Latin prose, than was the verse style which remained full of obsolete words and of archaic alliterative expressions. Hence, after the Norman Conquest, Anglo-Saxon poetry practically disappeared, whereas prose continued to develop and suffered no sharp break with the past, to reappear in the fourteenth century as the English prose of the age of Wyclif and Chaucer.

As it is doubtful whether any existing text of old Scandinavian poetry dates before A.D. 1000, this literature will be discussed later. In the case of Spanish and Italian vernacular literatures, there are no texts in which the language is really freed from Latin before the eleventh and twelfth centuries. The earliest extant text in a Germanic tongue is a fragment of Bishop Ulfilas' fourth-century translation of the New Testament into the Visigothic dialect. From later centuries come fragments of Isidore of Seville, parts of the Bible, and other religious works in Germanic dialects. From the ninth century is a German text of the *Strasbourg Oaths*. These early texts are of linguistic rather than of literary interest. The oldest original German literary work is the fragment of the *Hildebrandslied* of about 800, composed, like the Anglo-Saxon poems, in alliterative verse. The old Hildebrand meets a man in battle who proves to be his own son. The fight begins but the manuscript breaks off, and one can only guess that the close is tragic. It is a rough and uncouth poem with few literary graces, but the work has power, through its directness, its dramatic intensity, and its grim irony, all characteristics of primitive literature. Probably the original formed part of the collection of early German poetry which Charlemagne, according to Einhard, ordered collected, but which has unhappily all disappeared. About 830, a monk, probably of Corvey, wrote the *Heiland*, the story of Jesus, in West Germanic dialect. The author is a master of the dramatic; the story is told for its human interest, and the personages live. From the same period dates the *Muspilli*, a spirited account in the Bavarian dialect of the battle at the Last Judgment between angels and devils for the souls of the dead, and the *Evangelienbuch* of Otfried, a pupil of Rabanus Maurus. Otfried's tale of Jesus is written in a verse that uses rhyme, the first known German poem that uses this poetic device. From the literary point of view it is much weaker and less vivid than the *Heiland*. Its influence, however, upon both the language and the metrical forms of German poetry, was great during the two succeeding centuries.

The earliest text of any importance in an Old French form is a version of the *Strasbourg Oaths* of 843 in the *lingua romana*. From the same century is a twenty-nine line religious poem, the *Sequence of St. Eulalie*, the story of a martyr, written in strophes of two lines linked by assonance. The *Homily on Jonah*, a part of a prose sermon in the vernacular, and the poetic *Life of St. Leger* (of 240 lines) date from the tenth century. The dialects used in these early texts are really ancestors of Old French, which does not appear till the tenth or eleventh century in the *Life of St. Leger*. None of these early works has any notable literary value.

History stands next in importance to poetry in the literary development of the centuries between Boethius and Anselm. The great changes due to the Barbarian Migrations, followed by the wars of the Barbarian Kingdoms, left a deep impression and led writers to record these stirring events. The early mediaeval historians were all ecclesiastics and their outlook was always deeply influenced by the historical writings of Jerome, Augustine, Orosius, and Salvian. Cassiodorus wrote a long *History of the Goths*, which has only survived in a poor condensation of Jordanes of the sixth century. It has, however, some value as being the first history of any of the Barbarian Migrations. The *History of the Franks* was written by Gregory of Tours (d. 594). His style is barbarized, but less so than the civilization he describes in sixth-century Gaul. Gregory gives marvellous pictures of a violent society; his narrative is full of vigor and force and is a mine of political and social history. His greatest talent is that of delineating personalities. Like all mediaeval histories, Gregory's account gains in both accuracy and interest as he approaches his own time. In the eighth century, Bede wrote in his *Ecclesiastical History of the English Nation* the most remarkable history before the twelfth century. Bede knew the sixth-century story of the Anglo-Saxon conquest written by the Welsh monk, Gildas, and a number of other chronicles, histories, and saints' lives only a few of which are now extant. He knew not only the history of Britain, but somehow he had acquired knowledge of the history of Italy, Gaul, Germany, and Christian Spain. Before he wrote his history he had published his important work on chronology, the *De Temporum Ratione*, a work of great erudition and originality. His great history is unmatched in all early mediaeval literature for its breadth of information combined with its splendid organization and lucid style.[20] The last of the histories of the Barbarian peoples is Paul the Deacon's *History of the Lombards* of the late eighth century. It is a useful source, but it lacks the colorfulness of Gregory of Tours and the accuracy and insight of Bede. For the period after Charlemagne, there is an admirable account, the *Four Books of History* by Nithard, carrying the history of the Frankish Empire down to 843. In Germany, Widukind wrote a *Saxon History* through the reign of Otto I.

Part of the same period is covered by the historical writings of Luit-prand of Cremona (d. 972), a worldly and witty prelate, who also wrote a fascinating account of a trip he made to Constantinople in 968. The chief historical sources, however, for all the western European states after about 650 are the collections of laws and the mass of annals and chronicles that survive.

Besides the histories that have survived for the period 600 to 1000, there is a large number of these annals and chronicles. Both grew out of adding bits of information to Easter tables prepared long in advance to assure the uniform celebration of all the movable feasts of the church. Their contents vary from the briefest mention of events to extended accounts of happenings. The annals were primarily a yearly record set down by a contemporary; a chronicle usually summarized the story of a considerable period on the basis of a number of annals and of other sources, written and oral, put down by years. Annals and chronicles are often of value to the modern historian, although they lay disproportionate emphasis on church matters and purely local events such as the transfer of the bones of a saint or the birth of a two-headed calf on the monastic farm. What is today the most famous of early mediaeval chronicles, the *Anglo-Saxon Chronicle*, is the oldest historical work in any vernacular language. It seems to have been be-gun in Winchester in the seventh century. In the ninth century, other chronicles were combined with it, and the compilation was widely distributed. After Alfred the Great's death in 900 it was continued in different monasteries into the twelfth century; hence it survives in a number of versions. This *Anglo-Saxon Chronicle* is uneven, but parts of it are rich and racy, forthright and vigorous.

Biography mostly took the form of saints' lives, the pattern for which had been set by the early Christian writers, especially by the very popular *Life of St. Anthony* by St. Athanasius of the fourth cen-tury. Every mediaeval century produced a substantial number of these works, which are usually rather stereotyped and of greater his-torical than literary interest. Their chief value is to the historian be-cause the hagiographer regarded it as his duty to relate every incident of the actual or alleged career of his subject, and so he usually put in many valuable details of the daily life of all classes. Thus the lives of the saints picture mediaeval life as do the manuscript illuminations and the paintings of the later Middle Ages and the Renaissance. The finest biography of the whole period, however, is Einhard's *Life of Charlemagne*, written in imitation of Suetonius. It tells us something of the great emperor's predecessors and of his activities as conqueror and statesman and does not fail to describe vividly the personality and character of Charlemagne himself. It is a little masterpiece.

4. ART AND MUSIC

THE ART of the early Middle Ages (500–1000) shows two marked currents: the first descends from the primitive crafts of the Celts and the Early Germans, while the second comes from the art of the Mediterranean basin—Roman, Byzantine, and Near-Eastern. Some of the Germanic peoples, before they moved in numbers into the Roman Empire, were used to constructing buildings in wood. After the great migrations of the fifth century, they built houses of two or three stories; occasionally the first floor was of stone as a precaution against fire. The homes of the nobles, both before and after the migrations, centered in a great rectangular hall like Heorot, the hall of the chieftain described in *Beowulf*. The hall figures in all the early literature of the Celts and of the Germanic peoples, and it was the center of life, later on, in the feudal castle. The Early German churches were often built of wood; one type had a high, tower-like central structure with a low, single story built around it on four sides. Tower churches of this type still survive in Norway.

The Early Germans, and the Celts also, decorated their wooden structures with interlacing low reliefs that used, often with great effectiveness, abstract and highly conventionalized plant and animal forms. These were often brightly painted. (In these arts of the Barbarian Peoples representations of human forms were rare.) The same sort of designs were used on the prows of ships, in metalwork, and later in manuscript illuminations. The Celtic designs are usually more elaborate and complicated than those of the Early Germans. The Celts loved patterns made up of endless curving lines that covered a flat background with a network of circles and spirals. The involved line designs that run in enchanting exuberance over the pages of the *Book of Kells* (ninth century) show this Celtic art in its fullest flowering.[21] Both the Celts and the Early Germans have left a great deal of fine metalwork, above all jewelry. On belt-clasps, ear-rings, brooches, cups, and book-covers, often with enamels or with large semi-precious stones incrusting them, are found patterns from far-away Egypt, Persia, and the Near East. Some of these designs were acquired by the Goths during their stay in southern Russia, and from thence these patterns moved westward. Other designs in textiles and metalwork came west through trade channels. This Celtic and early German metalwork gives the impression of a rude barbaric vigor combined often with great skill in craftsmanship. Later on, many of the designs of the Celts and of the Early Germans reappear in Romanesque reliefs, metalwork, and manuscript illumination. The few buildings that survive from the period 500 to 750 are small and rude stone constructions. From literary descriptions it is evident that, while much has perished, there was, to begin with, little brick or stone construction. One of the important features of the churches were tall bell-towers of wood or stone, sometimes at the front of the building, and sometimes built like a lantern over the center of the structure.

The crafts of the Barbarian Peoples were of little use to the church for teaching religious stories and ideas. It was all an abstract and inarticulate art, incapable of conveying any religious instruction, and unable to depict the stories of the Bible and the legends of the saints. The art of the Carolingian and of the Ottonian Renaissance, thus, shows a deliberate attempt to revive the figural art of Rome and also to revive Constantinian church architecture. Building now came to be on a larger scale, and the designs became more elaborate. In some cases, as in the *Cathedral of Aachen,* Byzantine stone masons and mosaicists may have assisted in the work, and Byzantine plans were certainly studied in designing the building. Most churches built between 750 and 1000, however, followed the ground plan of the old Roman basilica. This basilican design, with arms added as transepts, formed a ground plan in the shape of a Latin cross. As the ground plans became more elaborate, some churches had two apses, and, more rarely, two sets of transepts. In the tenth century an ambulatory, with radiating chapels built as part of the apse, became popular. This was done to display saint's relics and to make them available for private devotions and for pilgrimages and church processions. Other new features began to appear. A porch and a two-towered façade, arcading and designs in the stone or brick work, and low reliefs about the doors gave variety and picturesqueness to the exterior, which in the early Christian basilicas had been very bare. Within, piers of various designs replaced round columns to support the roof, the windows were arranged together in groups of two or three and sometimes had stained glass, and bright frescoes and mosaics with human figures decorated the walls. It has now been discovered that many of the new structural features in western European buildings, from the eighth century on, came from Syria, Egypt, Asia Minor and even farther east, rather than from ancient Rome. The craftsmanship is often clumsy—the best stone masons came from Lombardy—and vaulting was ordinarily confined to crypts and apses. The wall paintings were usually better than the large-scale sculpture; in both there are interesting evidences of borrowing from Roman and Byzantine models. Among the finest objects of Carolingian and Ottonian craftsmanship are carved ivories and manuscript illuminations in which the flat and transcendental Byzantine style is combined with reminiscences of Roman art and the arts of the primitive Celts and Germans. The courts of Otto II and Otto III maintained close connections with the Byzantine world, and Byzantine influences on the West became more pronounced after 900.

Modern investigation has shown that the flowering of Romanesque art after 1000 was not sudden; it grew slowly out of methods of building and decoration developed during the Carolingian and Ottonian Renaissance, especially in Gaul. The total amount of stone and brick building in Latin Christendom between 500 and 1000 was amazingly small in comparison with the Roman period earlier or the Romanesque and Gothic ages afterwards. Of what was built, only a few buildings remain, and nearly every one of these has suffered from reconstruction. The backwardness of the five centuries, at least in the building arts, is shown by the fact that Charlemagne, the richest and most powerful monarch of the whole period, lived in a big wooden compound much like the stockade trading posts of the American frontier. The interest of the art of Latin Christendom from 500 to 1000 lies in the flowering of the decorative crafts of the Celts and the

Early Germans and in the beginnings of a great new style, the Romanesque.

The early Christian centuries had set the pattern of church music, a style adapted principally from the Jewish chants used in the synagogues. Before the fall of the Roman Empire in the West, this Christian chant, with certain vocal variations, had spread all over the Mediterranean basin. Then the Barbarian Migrations in the West lowered the standards of performance in the services of the church, and, by making more difficult communication among the Christian communities in the West, produced a diversity of usages. To bring order and unity into the musical life of the church the bishops of Rome for several centuries strove to correct these abuses and to disseminate the Roman rite. Central in this story is the *Schola Cantorum*, which may have been established by Gregory the Great after his return from Constantinople. All that is definitely known is that, sometime before 600, this school was set up in two buildings near the Lateran; in one of them singers and priests lived; in the other was an orphanage that educated boys for the choirs of the churches in Rome. In the course of the next centuries, these reforms, which seem to have been spread over some time, were attributed to Gregory the Great. The result of this reforming effort was a uniform method of singing the chants, a method that still serves the Roman church and is the trunk from which most later music grew. The excellence of this chant springs from the richness and diversity of its melodies, from the flexibility of its rhythm which is not definitely marked but is like the rhythm of prose, and from its lofty impersonal style which fits the exalted words of the liturgy. The melodies are not divided into measures but are given in a free recitative manner, such as an orator would use. The earliest of these chants had been written in four modes, which differ in the sequence of the semitones and in the cadences used. To the original four modes, four others had been added sometime between Ambrose and Gregory. These modes use no sharps or flats, except in the cases when, at a later time, "b" came to be flatted to aid the singers. The Gregorian melodies assume a somewhat different character according to the mode in which they are composed.

For centuries Gregorian chant was the only music recognized by the church and taught in its schools. Spreading from Rome, it was carried from one end of Latin Christendom to another, and it entered into the life of the people, high and low. The church sought to suppress every other type of music, and, in its extension, Gregorian chant either wiped out or assimilated nearly all the local styles. However, the chaotic situation that had led originally to the Gregorian reforms continued to plague the Roman church, and it remained difficult to preserve a common usage throughout Latin Christendom. In the twelfth century, St. Bernard wrote, probably with great exaggeration: "Take the antiphonal of Rheims and compare it with that of Soissons, Amiens or Beauvais, if you find any similarity, render homage to God!" [22]

By the tenth century the notation of Gregorian music had come to be fairly complicated. Small marks, *neumes,* above the words indicated the rise and fall of the voice and the manner of singing, but they gave no idea of the exact pitch of the notes or of their duration. Nearly everything in the style of the performance depended on the traditional usage in which one generation of singers after another was trained. In practice, the pitches used were relative, as the single melodic line of the chant made any absolute pitch unnecessary, and the different ranges of the singers, men and boys, made it impossible. Not until the eleventh century were lines representing a fixed pitch commonly used; the first lines were made merely by a stylus, and then by a red line to designate the tone "f."

The unharmonized chants began to be modified, perhaps as early as the eighth century, by simple harmonic schemes which may have been borrowed from Celtic and early German usages. In this first harmonized style, *organum,* the voices move ahead at intervals of a fourth or a fifth. Both voices could be duplicated at the octave, thus leading to a performance in four parts. So a harmonized musical style began to arise, though the great possibilities in polyphonic music did not begin to be realized until the twelfth century. In the ninth and tenth centuries, the development of the sequence and the trope in the liturgy meant the use of old or new melodies as musical settings for these new liturgical forms. The sequence set words to the elaborate vocalization over the last "a" on the *Alleluia* in the mass in order to facilitate the memorizing of the music. The trope, in the beginning, merely added explanations between parts of the liturgy as "Kyrie (fons pietatis a quo bona cuncta procedunt) eleison"; later longer explanatory sentences or even entire poems were interpolated into parts of the liturgy. The style of the melodies supplied for the sequences and tropes differs from that used in the older chants because of the length of the passages to be set to music and the use of formal devices in the Latin text, such as repetition in sections of a sequence or a trope. These new additions to the mass opened up a new phase in mediaeval music, that is, the beginning of independent composition.

The music of the church was primarily vocal, though organs were used. These were usually small, with a short range, and of no great force. They were ordinarily built so that each slide was answered by two or more pipes. Such a combination consisted of the note desired and notes from one to four octaves higher, and, after the ninth century, of fifths between several of the octaves. Organs began to be larger and more elaborate after the eighth century. A famous organ finished in 980 at Winchester had 400 pipes, 26 bellows, and two manuals. Ten pipes sounded to each slide. The pipes were not in tune and were too loud; no wonder that contemporaries compared the sounds of these large organs to the roar of thunder.

Secular music, which probably found its way into church music by way of sequence and trope, has left its only traces in literary descriptions and in survivals in music written after 1000. Apparently the traditional music of the Celts and Early Germans did not follow the modal style of the church. Instead, it seems to have organized its tunes in thirds. The use of harmonized arrangements in early organum may have come from the musical usages of the Celts and Early Germans. The commonest musical instruments in use in Latin Christendom before 1000 were, besides the organ, the lyre and the harp, both of which mediaeval men believed came from Ireland, various types of fiddles and wind instruments, and bells, which before 1100 were usually small and cup-shaped and must have given a dull tone.

Early mediaeval writers did some theorizing about music. The most widely-read of these works, written before 1000, were treatises by St. Augustine, Boethius, Cassiodorus, and Odo of Cluny. Augustine declares he will, following the Greek writers, treat music as a matter of mathematical law, but his treatise is largely devoted to questions of metre and versification with some attention to Pythagorean number symbolism. Boethius' *De Institutione Musica* begins by reiterating the idea of some of the Greek philosophers that music is a science. This became a dogma of later mediaeval theorists. He then considers the effect of music on man, following Plato's discussion of the influence of music on character and the relation of music to the Pythagorean concept of the motion of the spheres, the organization of the universe, and the alternation of the seasons. His actual discussion of the practice of music mentions various musical instruments and methods of singing. Boethius attached the old Greek names of the modes to the ecclesiastical scales, in which he made the mistake of assuming that the scales he knew were identical with those of the Greeks. He recommends, in teaching, the use of the monochord, a long narrow sound box with a single string under which a movable bridge can be moved along a graduated scale, thus allowing the tester to read the mathematical ratio for each portion of the bridge. The monochord was later widely used for pitch identification. Cassiodorus' *Institutes* contains a detailed discussion of instruments that he classified as percussion, tension, and wind instruments, and an elaborate description of fifteen keys. These early theoretical writings were filled with vague generalities, and the definite information they contained was sometimes incorrect, but the prestige of the authors gave them great authority; the respect in which they were held retarded musical development.

About 935, Odo of Cluny wrote his *Dialogue on Music*. It contains the first systematic use of seven letters for pitches and the first clear discussion and illustration of organum. The whole book is much more specific than any earlier work on music, and it shows that musical theory is moving away from philosophy and that it is beginning to consider, in a more first-hand way, actual musical production. Musical change from 500 to 1000 was slow. The chant of the church was better organized than it had been in the early Christian centuries, new elements in the sequence and the trope were added to the liturgy, notation began to be improved, and polyphony took its first steps in organum.

The achievements of Latin Christendom in the five centuries from the fifth through the tenth centuries are overshadowed by the Byzantine and Islamic attainments, which paralleled them, and by the accomplishments of the high Middle Ages, which succeeded them. The

Roman Empire had been weakened first by internal decay and then by the Barbarian Migrations. The old Roman political unity, the life of the Roman towns, and the whole Roman economy all gradually sank into ruin. The Mohammedan conquests of the seventh and eighth centuries brought a further descent into economic backwardness, and they shut in Latin Christendom on itself. It was now removed by barriers of religion and of cultural stagnation from the ancient Greek sources of civilization and removed by great distances from its own brilliant contemporaries in the Byzantine and Islamic worlds.

Culture in the West was further retarded by incessant fights of little kingdoms and of feuding families warring on each other. Then in the eighth century, when conditions seemed more calm, there began new raids of Vikings, Slavs, and Magyars. These were troubled centuries; long stretches of them are, as Trevelyan says, "like Macbeth's battle on the blasted heath. Prophecy hovers around. Horns are heard blowing in the mist, and a confused uproar of savage tumult and outrage. We catch glimpses of giant figures—mostly warriors at strife. But there are ploughmen too, and we hear the sounds of forests crashing to the axe." [23] The rude vigor of the Early German settlers of the fifth century and of the later Viking invaders of the eighth and ninth centuries rings in these verses of a Norse saga:

We have fought with the sword! I was yet young when in the East we caused a river of blood to flow for the wolves, and invited the yellow-legged birds to a great feast of corpses. The sea was as red as a newly opened wound, and the crows swam in blood.

We have fought with the sword! I saw near England innumerable corpses loading the decks of the ships. Torrents of blood rained from our weapons at Pesth; there was none left in the carcasses for the vulture; the bow twanged and the arrows buried themselves in the coats of mail; sweat trickled down the blades of the spears, and we mowed down the warriors like the hammer of Odin.

We have fought with the sword! Death clutches me. My sons will groan at the news of my death; their faces will flame with anger, such bold warriors will not rest until I am avenged. Here

*he is whom Odin sends to conduct me to his glorious palace. I go
to drink mead in the place of honor. The hours of my life glide
away, and my smile braves death.*[24]

Strange it is that the same centuries that glorified brutality should
also have produced an exquisite creation like the *Book of Kells*. One
must agree with Rabelais that the Middle Ages were both "monstrous
and delicate."

In these backward and troubled times, the leaders of culture were a
few enlightened monarchs like Theodoric the Ostrogoth, Charlemagne, Alfred the Great, the German Ottos, and the statesmen and
scholars of the Roman Church. With a few hundred books at best,
most of the early mediaeval scholars worked in rustic isolation. In a
brutal and poverty-stricken society these struggling scholars kept
learning alive, while bishops and priests were busy consolidating the
organization of the church under Rome and founding the mediaeval
papacy. In no period of its long history does Western civilization owe
so deep a debt to the Church of Rome as in these first five mediaeval
centuries. By the eleventh century the greatest days of Byzantine and
of Islamic civilization were over and Latin Christendom began to
move ahead as the leader in Western civilization.

PART TWO

❧

The Revival of the West, 1000–1500

CHAPTER VII

Learning (I)

1. THE IMPETUS TO A NEW LIFE

2. SCIENCE AND TECHNOLOGY

3. PHILOSOPHY FROM ANSELM TO FICINO

I. THE IMPETUS TO A NEW LIFE

THE TENTH and eleventh centuries show western Europe everywhere awakening to a new life. No longer does the story of Latin Christendom seem to be merely later chapters of a dying antiquity. On all sides, one sees western Europe, in politics, in economic affairs, in religious activity, and in culture, reaching out to produce an original civilization of its own. Centralized national governments in Germany, France, and England began to show progress in curbing feudal anarchy, and they began to develop systems of local administration that brought the king's law, the king's ability to raise troops for his army, and the king's right to collect taxes into the local district. Already there is underway, by the end of the eleventh century, that process of the "conquest of a kingdom by its kings" which Lavisse made a central thread in the history of a mediaeval France. At the same time that the king's power is extended into the local district there is taking place a reorganization and departmentalization of the administration of the central government. The process of royal and national consolidation went on, with many advances and many setbacks, in the six centuries between 900 and 1500, until, by the close of the mediaeval period, most of the states of western Europe were highly-centralized national despotisms. The process of consolidation took place on a large scale in France, England, and Spain, and on a smaller scale in the petty states of Italy and Germany. By 1500, the earlier feudal state where the king had only a title and a shadowy power, and the real control was in the hands of a quarrelling lot of feudal landowners, is passing.

Alongside the growth of strongly centralized government went a striking growth of the middle class. In all the mediaeval centuries, the overwhelming majority of the population were peasants closely attached to the soil. But in this backward agricultural society, towns began to grow rapidly, beginning in Italy in the tenth and eleventh centuries. Italian merchants made commercial contacts with the Byzantine and Islamic urban centers and, at home, developed the mechanisms of modern banking. Western Europe not only began to expand commercially, but it reached out to extend its own boundaries. In 1085 Toledo fell into the hands of the Christians, in 1095 the Crusades began, and in the same eleventh century the Muslims were driven out of southern Italy and Sicily. Like the ascent of spring in the great basin of the Mississippi River, this revival of town life spread from Italy westward and northward till all of Latin Christendom was affected. The town offered new careers in business, in the professions of medicine, law, and teaching, and in government administration. As the breakdown of town life and the practical disappearance of the middle class in the West is the great watershed between the last phases of Roman civilization and the early Middle Ages, so the revival of town life and the growth in wealth and power of the middle class marks the great transition from early mediaeval into later mediaeval and modern times. The town was a great center for the growth of the new ideas and attitudes. The townsman learned in the town meeting the rudiments of self-government, and, in the life of trade, he came to have a more worldly and less transcendental view of life. Often the townsman and the monarch joined hands to curb the power of the feudal noble, for both the middle class and the ruler wished to maintain internal peace, good roads, and uniform courts and coinage. As a result of the growth of the middle class, in the period from 900 to 1500, western Europe could no longer be divided by ecclesiastical writers into the nobles who governed and fought, the clergy who prayed, and the masses who tilled the soil.

In a world where strong and well-administered states were developing and the middle class was extending its activity, its wealth, and its influence, the Roman Church was trying to guide the whole of society. The papacy had been of slow growth, but in the eleventh century it found itself able to try to direct the whole of Western society. The church since Augustine had conceived of a single universal society with Christ as its head. Gregory VII undertook, in the eleventh century, to give this entire society a unified control under the pope. And, from the time of Gregory VII to the Protestant Reformation, the church stood enthroned over Western society. It made a great and gallant attempt to unify all life under the direction of a single Christian rule. Politically the church rebuked kings for mismanagement of the state and of their private lives; economically the church sought to regulate industry and commerce by preaching the idea of a just price, by prohibiting usury, by teaching that property is a trust from God held for the general benefit, and by its inculcation of charity; intellectually it developed a single culture in the schools and universities; and in the last resort, when everything else failed to achieve conformity, it invoked the Inquisition. Finally, through the sacramental system, the church largely controlled the life of the individual and the life of the family. The church was the true state of the Middle Ages; it not only commanded the first loyalty of the individual, which in modern times goes to the state, but it had, better than any state, the ability to collect its taxes and enforce its laws over a wide area. The mediaeval church was more like the Roman state and the modern state than was the mediaeval secular state. All in all, and affecting every range of life, the mediaeval church was a magnificent attempt at a synthesis of the whole of life by a sovereign wisdom.

As the state and the middle class grew stronger, so did the church, and there were bound to be clashes between state and church. In each of the later mediaeval centuries from the eleventh to the sixteenth, one expects to find the church, the state, the feudal nobility, the peasants, and the townsmen. But over the whole period it is clear that an earlier type of culture that was agricultural in economic and social organization, feudal in government and in its social sanctions, and ecclesiastical in its outlook has growing up within it a new culture that is urban, national, and secular. The new comes in alongside the old; the balance from the old to the new shifts very slowly. The old never disappears and only slowly does the new come to have the upper hand.

While western Europe moves toward a civilization in which the secular state and the middle class play a larger role, it produces at the same time a phenomenal cultural revival. The science and philosophy of the Greeks are recovered, and with them admirable Muslim and Jewish writings. And, unlike Byzantium, the thinkers of Latin Christendom took these writings and finally used them as the basis for the founding of modern science and philosophy. There was, at the same time, a phenomenal development of all types of Latin and vernacular literature. And, finally, in the art of the Romanesque and the Gothic, Latin Christendom produced two of the greatest styles of history. In the first phases of this development, from the eleventh century through the thirteenth, northern France took the lead, so that in every field of culture from Iceland to the Holy Land, Latin Christendom was made up culturally of a series of provinces of northern France. The center of culture in the fourteenth century began to shift to Italy, until by the sixteenth century all of the Latin West had become, culturally, a series of provinces of Renaissance Italy. In the whole history of the civilization of the West, the great turning point from mediaeval to modern is not the Italian Renaissance of the fifteenth and sixteenth centuries; it is, rather, the revival of philosophy, science, education, literature, art, and music that centered in northern France in the twelfth and thirteenth centuries. All of these changes brought Latin Christendom into the position of the leader of Western civilization.

In the centuries from the Crusades to the Reformation the means of transmitting ideas were various. The old Roman roads and bridges had fallen into decay, and beyond the Rhine and the Danube there were no good roads until well into modern times. Everywhere communication remained difficult until the eighteenth century. Besides, the extreme economic localism, which was at the basis of mediaeval civilization, made communication largely unnecessary. In comparison with either ancient Roman times or with the modern centuries, there was less movement of men and ideas. Mediaeval life was marked by many localisms in types of building, in costume, in dialects, saints legends, and in local feudal rulers. The oldest type of intellectual center was the monastery; for centuries the monasteries stood like scattered islands in a sea of ignorance. Even in the most confused of the earlier mediaeval centuries they were centers where old books were copied and new ones were written. The monasteries exchanged books among themselves, and the later orders, the Cluniacs, the Cistercians, and the Carthusians, with their more centralized types of organization, made intellectual interchange easier. There was, later on, still more coming and going among the conventual houses of the Franciscan and Dominican Friars. The monasteries not only played a role in preserving learning; they were also important centers for creating and disseminating styles of art and music, and for collecting legends that influenced sculpture, painting, and vernacular poetry. The monastery, all during the Middle Ages, was the meeting place of the monk, the trader, the pilgrim, the jongleur, the musician, and the skilled craftsman and artist. The monasteries educated very few secular priests and almost no laymen, but they remained important centers for the development of learning, literature, art, and music.

Alongside the monastery as a center of culture was the cathedral school, run by the local bishop. Some cathedral schools went back into the period before 1000; from the eleventh century on, a number of them became great educational centers. To them was brought most of the science and philosophy recovered by the West from the Byzantines and the Saracens. The bishops collected libraries, patronized scholars, poets, artists, and musicians, and made their cathedral centers the cultural lighthouses of western Europe. There was much cultural interchange between these episcopal centers from the eleventh century on. In the twelfth century the most important cathedral schools in Latin Christendom were those of northern France at Paris, Chartres, Rheims, Orléans, and Laon. Out of the cathedral school of Notre Dame in Paris grew the greatest of mediaeval universities. The bishop's court and the bishop's school thus are, after 1000, even more important than the monastery in the history of learning and in all other aspects of culture. After the founding of universities there was an immense commerce of ideas between one university center and another. The use of Latin as the common language of learning and the custom among both students and teachers of travelling about meant that the university was unmatched by any other medium in the spread of ideas in the later Middle Ages. It was this universality of the learned world that gave a great unity to later mediaeval learning.

A third important center of patronage for writers and artists was the noble or the princely court. As in the bishop's court, the noble and the prince brought together scholars, poets, artists, and musicians. All had to live on patronage of some sort. The nobles were the great patrons of vernacular poets, troubadours, trouvères, and minnesingers. From the court of one nobleman to that of another there spread, throughout Latin Christendom, the southern French lyric and the northern French chivalric romance, and the northern French language became the courtly language of most of the Latin West. Lay patronage of scholarship was less universal than that of the church. There was always a chaplain, at least, to say mass, keep records, and write the necessary correspondence. More important noblemen might have astrologers or learned priests as aides. Some noblemen liked to be surrounded by learned men. The jongleur or minstrel would usually be a transient, at one castle then at another. Courtly patronage was a necessity for those who lacked assured ecclesiastical income. Nobles were often great builders and hired stone-masons, stone-carvers, and painters to decorate the walls of their castles and to illuminate their manuscripts.

A last type of cultural center was the town. Here church and lay schools taught boys the rudiments of reading, writing, and arithmetic needed to run a business. The town became, in the twelfth century, the home of two great literary forms, the *fabliau* or *novella,* and the mediaeval drama. It was also the place where heresies grew, the Waldensians, the Cathari, the Albigensians, the Lollards, and, later, the German Evangelicals, and the Swiss, Dutch, French, and British Puritans. Besides the bishop's court, as a patron of all types of learning and art, the town offered patronage to the masons and artists who built and decorated its town hall, its guild halls, and its fine town houses like the one Jacques Coeur built at Bourges in the fifteenth century. In the later Middle Ages, the wealthy bourgeoisie, especially in Italy, built town houses on a sumptuous scale, and the tyrants, who came to control the Italian city-states in the fourteenth and fifteenth centuries, were lavish patrons of the fine arts and of literature. The towns likewise influenced one another in government. Charters and town constitutions often left their marks on towns far away.

Some records survive of the rapidity with which news travelled. In the twelfth century, it took four months for the news of Frederick Barbarossa's death in Asia Minor to reach Germany although only four weeks were required to carry the story of the capture of Richard, Coeur de Lion, from Vienna to London. In the twelfth century, the normal time for news to reach Canterbury from Rome was seven weeks, but urgent news sometimes travelled this same road in four. All in all the economic localism and the rustic character of mediaeval life seems to have furnished fewer hindrances to the movement of ideas than one might have imagined. "One of the most singular phenomena of mediaeval literary history," writes Renan, perhaps with exaggeration, "is the intellectual interchange, and the rapidity with which books spread from one end of Europe to another. The philosophy of Abelard, during his lifetime, had reached to the bottom of Italy. The French poetry of the trouvères, in less than a century, had been translated into German, Swedish, Norwegian, Irish, Flemish, Dutch, Czech, Italian, and Spanish. A book written in Morocco or Cairo was known in Paris or Cologne in less time than it takes in our day for a significant German book to cross the Rhine." [1] And what Renan says of the spread of learning and literature is true also of the spread of styles of art and of music.

After the Barbarian Migrations of the fifth century, the Latin West spent most of the next thousand years slowly assimilating the heritage of antiquity, both classical and Christian. The ancient material was gradually appropriated, intellectually and emotionally, and then reexpressed in new forms. In any century, besides what is inherited from the preceding century, we find men reaching back into still earlier periods, searching for treasures, trying to understand what they find and to use it as the basis of a new creation. So by a very slow process, mediaeval men made their classical and Christian heritage dynamically their own. They came to have, through the depth of their penetration into the heritage of the past, an understanding that made their own works creative. In this intellectual and emotional reappropriation of the past, three great stages stand out, a first culminating in the Carolingian and Ottonian Renaissances, a more vital appropriation in the twelfth and thirteenth centuries, and a re-expression of classical civilization in mediaeval terms in the fourteenth and fifteenth centuries. In the first age, we find, as typical, the scriptural commentary and the beginnings of the understanding of classical and Byzantine art; in the next great age, the great theological *Summas*, Romanesque and Gothic art, the activity of the Friars, and the poetry of Dante. Finally, in the last phase, came the classical Renaissance and the Protestant Reformation.

2. SCIENCE AND TECHNOLOGY

BACK of all mediaeval science and philosophy—Byzantine, Islamic, Jewish, and Latin Christian—lay a common set of preconceptions that came down from the last centuries of antiquity. All agreed that the great truths were revealed by God and were contained in certain sacred books. All agreed, too, in accepting a common set of ideas about the nature of the universe and of man that were largely the creation of the ancient Greeks, and, finally, all accepted a mass of traditional folklore.

The ancient Greek interest in science had, as we have seen, declined sharply in the later centuries of antiquity. The Greek thinkers had become fascinated and absorbed in problems of metaphysics and ethics. The best of Greek science was vitiated with speculations about "unchanging reality," the "elements," the "truth"—and the "absolute." Such a point of view, even in the great days of Greek science, interfered with a careful and continuous accumulation of factual knowledge about man and the world. At the same time, the Romans never took much interest in theoretical science. Indeed, Cicero praised his countrymen that they were not as the Greeks, and were able "to confine the study of mathematics to the domain of useful applications." So the growth of ancient science stopped short in the second century A.D.; it stopped short long before the Greeks had developed the modern means of accurate measurement. Watches, thermometers, telescopes, microscopes, and barometers had to wait until the sixteenth and seventeenth centuries. At the same time, the Greeks produced no mathematical means for describing matter in motion. They developed logic; but without the technique for assembling factual information, logic could be very misleading. The Greeks combined all this with the belief that labor is degrading, mechanics a vile art, and that contact with matter is corrupting to the spirit. Indeed, at its best, the Greek genius largely failed to understand the nature of science and of technology. Later on, with little of the inquiring spirit that had started Greek science on its way, men took over, for nearly a millennium and a half, the general results of this science, as understood in the second century A.D. By this time what passed for science had often taken unto itself a mass of astrology and popular superstition. Thus, if we except a few scholars who kept alive an interest in science in the last centuries of antiquity, there was in the highest circles of learning, which were mostly Neo-Platonic in outlook, little distinction between purely physical facts and events, moral truths, and spiritual experiences. Ideas on God, on nature and on man, on the moral world, the material universe, the spheres, the four humors, on the soul, and on the resurrection of the dead were all closely interwoven. The modern mind separates its ideas into categories, scientific, ethical, philosophical, and theological, and counts it a virtue to keep its concepts clearly defined. To later antiquity and to the Middle Ages, the segregation of ideas in this manner would have been incomprehensible. All learning was not only ethical and theological in outlook, but it was also always encyclopedic.

The mediaeval centuries, in one way or another, inherited the whole body of Greek thought, together with many ideas from the Old and the New Testament, and then a mass of religious ideas, folklore, and superstitions from a more immediate background. This body of material varies, depending on whether one is dealing with Byzantine, Muslim, or Latin Christian thought. Mediaeval men compiled, arranged, and commented on all this inherited material. With the mediaeval mania for order, and the mediaeval taste for grandiose ideas, they arranged all this traditional wisdom in vast schemes. Some of the Muslim and, later, some of the Latin Christian scholars added details here and there and so extended the bounds of knowledge by investigation. But, almost without exception, they failed to criticize the basic conceptions they inherited. Nearly all mediaeval writing on science is not only encyclopedic and theological in method and outlook, but it is also very verbose. An immense amount of attention was paid to the mere arrangement of the material which frequently occupied the author more than did the ideas he had to convey. Great stress is also laid on argument, usually in a syllogistic form, and on extended appeals to ancient authorities.

The religious authorities, both in the East and the West, began by condemning magic, divination, and astrology. But their condemnation did no good, and they finally had to accept these false sciences, with the limitation that in some parts they were good and in some bad. In the Latin West, the church took over magic and astrology, about as the missionaries had taken over the pagan groves, hills, stones, and wells of the heathen and had given them saints' names. Some churchmen, for example, said that astronomy was a subject worthy of study, but that astrology was evil, and then turned around and said that the stars did influence men's lives, but not their souls. So the Jewish, Christian, and the Muslim religious authorities never really made up their minds about scientific studies. They were usually uneasy about them, some condemned them *in toto,* some accepted them in part, and some were even enthusiastic about scientific studies.

Mediaeval men shared common ideas about the nature of the universe and the nature of matter. The universe according to the Old Testament had been created by God in six days. The philosophers, both Muslim and Christian, had a hard time harmonizing this with Aristotle's idea that the universe had always existed. At the center of this God-created universe was our world, which was fixed and stationary and consisted chiefly of earth, the grossest and heaviest of the four elements. The earth was covered by the other three elements: water, air, and fire. Most scholars believed the earth was round; the idea of a flat earth surrounded by water was a popular idea. The round earth was divided into five zones, the polar areas, two temperate zones, and an equatorial zone. Whether anyone lived on the opposite side of the earth or in the equatorial zone was much debated; the general belief was that both areas were uninhabited. Beyond the earth and moving about it, in a series of spheres, are the moon, the sun, and certain fixed stars. These all move, at different speeds, as they revolve about the earth from east to west. Each is guided by an angelic intelligence just as the human body is directed by the soul. Outside all this is the unmoved empyrean in which dwell God and the blessed in paradise.

Since the intelligences that move the spheres about the earth are immaterial and the stuff of which these spheres are made is superior to anything built up out of the four elements, it is profitable for man to contemplate the heavenly part of the order of nature. There is an element in man, the soul, which has an affinity both with the immaterial intelligences that guide the spheres and with God. The movements in the heavens determine all changes on earth. This universe, made by God in six days, will not last forever. Just as it was created in time and as Adam and Eve were placed in the Garden of Eden, so it will proceed through all human history, in which the central events for the Christians were the Crucifixion and the Resurrection, to the Last Judgment. Then all that was on the earth will be consumed by fire; the souls of the damned will be bound eternally in hell under the earth, and the souls of all the saved will be gathered in paradise; the spheres will stop revolving and the chief heavenly bodies will shine seven times more brightly. The whole marvellous mechanism of the universe will stand motionless forever as a monument to its creator. It was all a view of a universe that was closed, and it was all as clear and simple as the vast painted clocks run by machinery of which the men of the Renaissance were so fond. It was this universe that Copernicus upset in 1543.

Basic in the mediaeval idea of the nature of matter were the Aristotelian and Neo-Platonic ideas that from God everything exists in a vast hierarchy, that superiors always rule inferiors, and everything on earth is related to some force in the sky. Everything below God is arranged in a huge chain of being. At the bottom of this chain are objects like stones which have no soul; then plants with the most rudimentary kind of soul that takes care of growth and reproduction; then animals, which have the power of motion; then man; then the orders of angels who are able to apprehend universal truth, on up to God, who is pure soul, pure actuality, and the very essence of being. Man is the highest of the animals, and, at the same time, the lowest of intellectual beings. Man is superior to the animals in that he can know something of universal truth, but he is inferior to the angels in that he can attain such knowledge only by abstracting it from sense images. Man's highest faculty, reason, is to work on the data that sensations, memory and imagination supply so as to abstract the spiritual forms above them. There was much disagreement among Christian, Muslim, and Jewish thinkers as to the exact role of reason, but there was general agreement that though man must begin with his senses, he must rise above them to apprehend truth and reality. For men all values are hierarchical; there are, for example, three kinds of law: the highest, God's law of nature, next, the law of nations applicable to all states, and finally, civil law for particular communities. Society is also a hierarchy of clergy, nobles, and people.

The common mediaeval view of the nature of matter took over Aristotle's idea that matter takes four common forms: earth, air, fire, and water. Each of these forms had two qualities, heat and cold, moisture and dryness; thus earth might be cold and moist, or cold and dry, and so on. According to this type of classification, a thing first had "substance," for example, man, bread, house; then it had "qualities" or "accidents"—heaviness, wholeness, whiteness. In man, the Greeks believed, there were four humors: blood, phlegm, black bile, and yellow bile. For perfect health these must be kept, by diet, drugs, or bleeding, in proper balance. All these ideas about the nature of the universe and of man were highly rational, too rational and insufficiently experimental. They show mediaeval men ignoring nature, hunting for moral and allegorical meanings, and, in general, trying to understand physical phenomena by showing, not what they are, but what they are not. Most mediaeval men had no conception of nature having a reality of its own. That is why in trying to explain all things great emphasis is laid on showing that nothing is what it appears to be. Reality is immaterial; what the senses know is only a reflection of reality.

The nature of the universe and the nature of matter were always conceived together and there was found a profound correspondence between the nature and structure of the one and the other—an idea that came down from early Greek philosophy. The structure of man, the microcosm, followed the structure of the universe, the macrocosm; for example, the four elements of the universe corresponded to the four humors in man.[2] The stars moving regularly in circles controlled the ordered course of nature, day and night, winter and summer, in growth and decay; the erratic planets governed the variable elements. To determine the relations of man and his affairs with the forces in the universe was the work of the astrologer. Combined with all of this, and also an inheritance from Greek thought, was the science of the symbolism of numbers. The number two means diversity and antithetical pairs; three represents all, beginning, middle, and end, the three theological virtues, and the Trinity; four stands for the four directions, the four winds, the four seas, the four elements, the four humors, the Four Evangelists, and the four cardinal virtues, and so on. According to Pythagorean philosophy, to certain passages in the Old Testament, and to later writers like Philo and Augustine, things occurring in the same number possessed inner relations. No branch of mediaeval thought entirely escaped this interest in number symbolism; it affected theology, science, literature, art, and music. There was built up out of Greek science, religious ideas, and folklore an immense and intertwined tangle of astrology, alchemy, chemistry, geography, and other sciences. In this rich, lush jungle of science and pseudo-science, rather than in an open plain of ignorance, the seedlings of real science had to grow.

One of the best ways to see how all these ideas were held by mediaeval men is to look at the large number of popular books on science that, before the twelfth and thirteenth centuries, represented the sum of science in Latin Christendom, and after the twelfth century still remained the commonly-held ideas of science. These popular science books were, according to their main emphasis, concerned with animals (bestiaries), plants (herbals), and stones (lapidaries). The contents of these books do not differ much from the contents of the *Physiologus* of early Christian times and some of the most exaggerated tales come from Pliny. Nearly everything is allegorized and moralized. On the other hand, such works occasionally contain shrewd observations made directly from nature.[8]

The most outstanding contributions to science were found in the herbals. From the thirteenth century on, these not only are concerned with the healing qualities of plants, but Albertus Magnus and a number of other writers contributed careful and detailed observations of plants. These writings, and the herbals which popularized them, give excellent descriptions of the stalks, leaves, and flowers of plants and their relation to other flora, but no mediaeval botanist discovered the minute structure of plants, their mode of reproduction, or any basic method of classifying them. In the fourteenth century the herbals were illustrated with drawings. These became more detailed and more accurate in the fifteenth century when they were done not only in manuscript, but also in woodcuts in the early printed books. This interest in representing plants exactly appears in the fifteenth-century paintings of men like Botticelli, Leonardo da Vinci, and Dürer. The same artistic concern for representing animals and men exactly, greatly contributed to the late mediaeval advancement of anatomy and physiology.

The first important steps beyond an elementary type of scientific writing had been taken by the Muslims. They had returned to the Greek sources of science, had added certain ideas from the Hindus, and then had gone on to push out the bounds of knowledge.[4] In the eleventh century, Latin Christendom began to receive, from Spain, Sicily, and Constantinople, translations of these works, as well as of the philosophical writings of Aristotle. This recovery of Greek learning, usually accompanied by important Muslim works, marks a great turning point in the history of Western thought.

The first contacts between the Latin West and the learning of the Muslims was in the tenth century, but the earliest translations known date from the eleventh century. Constantine, the African (d. 1087), who lived just south of Naples, translated a Jewish-Arabic work, *On Fevers*, and some other medical treatises used in the medical school of Salerno. He either conceals the names of the authors from whom he borrows or gives them incorrectly, a common trick with later translators. Several contemporary translators from the same neighborhood, in which Constantine worked, also did some translating directly from Greek medical works. Another early translator was Adelard of Bath (d. 1150), who spent time both in Spain and Sicily. He turned the *Arithmetic* of al-Khwarizmi with its use of Arabic numerals and Euclid's *Elements* into Latin, and wrote also a popular compendium of Arab science, the *Natural Questions*. Robert of Chester (d. 1160) translated the Koran, a text on alchemy, and the *Algebra* of al-Kwarizmi, and he calculated tables of latitude and longitude for London based on Arabic writers. By the middle of the twelfth century,

Toledo had become the most important center of translation. Here were translated Aristotle's *Physics* as well as a whole series of astronomical treatises. The greatest of all the translators connected with Toledo was Gerard of Cremona (d. 1187); he is credited with translating ninety-two Greek and Arabic works, including the *Almagest* of Ptolemy, the huge *Canon of Medicine* of Avicenna, and a long list of other mathematical, medical, alchemist, and astronomical books.

A less important group in Sicily, which was active into the thirteenth century and included Michael Scot (d. 1235), not only translated other Greek and Arabic books, but made parallel translations of works, like Ptolemy's *Almagest*, that had already been translated in Spain. In the meantime, the philosophic works of Aristotle and his Muslim and Jewish commentators were being turned into Latin. The first versions of Aristotle's *Metaphysics*, his *Ethics*, and others of his works came from Constantinople, and soon translations from the Arabic were also available. The first interest of the West was in Greek and Muslim science; the interest in Aristotle's philosophy and his Islamic followers came later. By the end of the thirteenth century, much of the surviving corpus of Greek science, the best Muslim scientific works, and most of Aristotle was circulating in the West in various translations.

The difficulties in the way of the early translators from either Greek or Arabic into Latin were enormous. There were no lexicons or grammars available, and it was usually both difficult and hazardous to find a teacher of either language. Another great obstacle was the scientific and philosophical insufficiency of the mediaeval Latin vocabulary, as a result of which many Greek and Arabic terms were taken over into Latin. A common way of translating from the Arabic was to find a Jew who knew Arabic. He would dictate the work to be translated in the local dialect, and as he slowly dictated, the Christian put the vernacular version into Latin. The greatest weakness of the translations, as a whole, was less in their inaccuracies than in their too great literalness. As time went on, better translations became available, but the older translations continued to circulate alongside the newer and better versions.

These new Greek and Arabic works circulating in western Europe were usually the starting points for fresh developments in philosophy and in the various sciences. Before 1000, western Europe knew scarcely anything of medicine; its astronomy and mathematics were very rudimentary; chemistry and physics hardly existed. The only books concerned with anything resembling alchemy were certain collections of technical recipes for dyeing, the making of pigments, and the handling of metals. Alchemy had its first great growth in the West following the translations of Geber and some of the Muslim alchemists into Latin beginning with those of Robert of Chester and Gerard of Cremona. As in Islam, alchemy involved a grandiose system embodying vast fields of astrology, occultism, and practical recipes for making chemical combinations. The alchemists postulated the theory of the unity of all matter and the belief that a "philosopher's stone" would transmute base metals into gold. One of their favorite theories was the sulphur-mercury theory of the composition of metals; sulphur represented combustibility and mercury represented fusibility; they were often depicted as masculine and feminine principles. The theory that sulphur and mercury were the basic elements of all things runs parallel to the four-elements theory of Aristotle until the later seventeenth century. Pure sulphur and gold were linked with the sun, and pure mercury and silver were linked with the moon. Another theory connected seven leading metals with seven prominent heavenly bodies; still another held that all matter is sensitive and endowed with life. The combination of two bodies the alchemist saw as "marriage," the loss of their usual activity as "death," the production of something new as "birth," the rising of vapors as "spirit leaving the corpse," and the formation of a volatile solid as "the creation of a spiritual body." In their formulae, great importance was attached to form, odor, and color; for example, in preparing the philosopher's stone, four colors, black, white, yellow, and red were supposed to make their appearance successively. These colors were, in turn, associated with the four elements and the four humors. The alchemists loved to use cryptic expressions and allegory, and a multitude of signs in their writings: the sun, the moon, symbols for the four elements, a crow for black, a swan for white, a phoenix for red, a dove in upward flight for white sublimate, a bear for a still, an ostrich for a flask, and a stork for a retort. Actually they made great play with a limited stock of ideas upon which they rang an unending series of trivial changes.

The alchemists ranged from pure charlatans to devoted scholars. They did take over from the Arabs a large number of chemical techniques that were of use later in turning chemistry into a real science. Most of the great intellectual leaders of the later mediaeval centuries believed in alchemy. But Albertus Magnus, after making some experiments, found that alchemical gold turned to ashes. He concluded, as had Avicenna, that the alchemist produced imitations of gold but did not bring about a true change. Still, he believed that such a change was possible. Roger Bacon distinguishes between speculative alchemy and practical alchemy which is of use in manufacture. Aquinas believed in the alchemist idea that gold could be produced by the alchemist. Chaucer, by the fourteenth century, is skeptical and he satirizes the alchemical swindlers in the *Canon's Yeoman's Tale*. Many famous writers, including Aristotle, Avicenna, Albertus Magnus, and Thomas Aquinas had works of alchemy attributed to them which they never wrote. The alchemist had great difficulties in conducting his experiments. It was not a good thing to be known as an alchemist; the religious suspected him of being in league with the devil, and the civil authorities did not want to have anyone active who might upset the economic situation by making gold. It was, too, an expensive pursuit, and many wasted fortunes looking for the "philosopher's stone" and the "elixir of life." The instruments were made by glassmakers and potters, and by small manufacturers of drugs, pigments, and chemicals who made products like mercury, sulphur, alum, and vitriol, mainly for apothecaries and physicians. Though the alchemists produced an enormous body of writings, chemistry remained in 1500 no more advanced than it had been with the Muslims in 1100.

Astrology and astronomy had begun together in ancient Babylonia; by the second century B.C. astrology had been elaborately organized. The Stoics were the first school of ancient philosophy openly to espouse its ideas, but by the beginning of the Christian Era all schools of Greek philosophy had come to accept astrology. Plato's *Timaeus* became a breviary for astrologers and magicians; the myth of the Demiurge, creating the world as a living organism, every part of which is intimately related to every other, came to be used as the great justification of ideas of the macrocosm and the microcosm and of the influence of the heavenly bodies on the lives of men. By A.D. 160, all that the ancients knew about astronomy was summed up by Ptolemy, the first great Greek scientist to accept astrology. Further work on astronomy was done by the Muslims from the ninth through the eleventh centuries; they had likewise kept astrology alive; indeed the two were never clearly separated until modern times. In the course of the twelfth century, nearly all the ancient Greek and Muslim astronomy and astrology became available in Latin translations.

The complexity of astrology was as great as that of alchemy. The sun, which moved regularly in a circle, controlled the more ordered events of nature, such as night and day and the four seasons. The planets, on the other hand, less certain in their motion, governed the more variable events in the world, the happenings that make life so uncertain. It was to the assessment of the factors governing these events, in a zone between the sure and the unsure, that astrology set itself. The signs of the zodiac were connected with the four elements, the four qualities, the four humors, and the four winds. The human body was divided into twelve sections each one under the control of one of the signs of the zodiac. The seven planets were connected with the seven days of the week, the seven ages of man and of the world. Everything in the life of man and of nature was believed to be governed by the stars. In making predictions, astrology dealt with the following: *nativities,* the determination of a person's temperament from the positions of the constellations at the time of his birth; *revolutions,* the predictions of general events, weather, crops, and political changes; and *elections,* the art of selecting the right moment to do anything from planting a bean to deposing a king. The belief in all this sort of thing was so ardent, and the possible combinations of the movements of the stars and the actions of men so immense, that generations of astrologers were kept busy figuring out all these possibilities. Every prince hoped to have an astrologer at his court.

Among both the Muslims and the Christians there were some who attacked astrology as being against common sense, as against the use of man's free-will, and as generally immoral. The early Christian attack on astrology drove it, and with it almost all knowledge of astronomy, out of Latin Christendom from the fifth century to the twelfth. Isidore of Seville, following Augustine, represents the cautious attitude of these centuries; to him astronomy is a legitimate science, but astrology is a superstitious evil. If the heavenly bodies have any influence over men it is only over men's bodies and over material things that this influence is exerted; over men's souls the heavenly bodies have no power. With the introduction of Greek and Islamic astronomy and astrology in the twelfth century, they were widely studied by both charlatans and scholars in the West. Aquinas accepts the idea that men may study astronomy and they may use it for medical and meteorological purposes. Astronomy came to be taught in the universities, especially in Italy, though one of Bologna's most famous professors of astronomy was burned at the stake, in 1327, for the crime of sorcery.

As the knowledge of astronomy in Latin Christendom increased, so did the vogue of astrology. But in the fourteenth and fifteenth centuries, both scholars and literary men attacked astrology. Petrarch declared that the astrologers were worse quacks than the physicians. There was also a revival of the patristic attack on astrology as being immoral. No final disproof of astrology was ever written; among the learned the idea of astrology slowly died of its own. In the field of astronomy itself, the later Middle Ages added little beyond what the Islamic scholars had discovered. The Latin Christians after 1200 had celestial globes, astrolabes, and quadrants for determining positions and angular distances between the heavenly bodies. Two Spanish Jews prepared for King Alfonso the Wise the famous *Alfonsine Tables*, the most accurate tables of the movements of the heavenly bodies made up to the thirteenth century. They continued in use for three hundred years as the best planetary tables. No basic advances were made in astronomy till the sixteenth century. But even after Copernicus, old ideas lived on; in the early seventeenth century Kepler, a great astronomer, was still casting horoscopes.

In mathematics and physics the starting point of new developments in the West was again the introduction of Greek and Islamic writings. Leonard of Pisa (d. 1245) is, in part, responsible for spreading the use of Arabic numbers and the knowledge of Islamic arithmetic, algebra, geometry, and trigonometry in Latin Christendom. In spite of all this, some calculations were still being made in Roman numerals in the sixteenth century. In the fourteenth century, a group at the University of Paris, as we shall see, laid the foundations of modern physics.

Medicine by 1500 had made little advance beyond the system of Galen. Many physicians had never seen a dissection though, beginning at the University of Bologna in the fourteenth century, dissection was used in most medical teaching. Few knew how to make a logical diagnosis. The ordinary method of diagnosis was to examine the blood and the sputum as to its color, density, and odor; more commonly the urine was inspected. From the layers of sediment, the urine was supposed to show in what region of the body lay the cause of the disorder, thus turbidity of the upper layer indicated a disease of the head and so on through four layers. Blood letting from the side of the body opposite where the disease was located, and undertaken to bring the four humors in balance, was one of the commonest forms of treatment. Astrology determined the favorable days and hours for all treatments. Baths, diet, and elaborate medication were used in treating the sick. From the descriptions it would seem that the cures were often worse than the maladies. The church and the municipalities, from the twelfth century on, supported hospitals in most of the larger towns. Most towns, too, had elaborate regulations controlling the practice of medicine inside the town limits. By the thirteenth century many diseases had come to be considered contagious, and those who suffered from them were isolated—a definite advance in the history of medicine. Surgery was usually in the hands of men of less education and lower status than that of the physicians, and some surgery was undertaken by barbers. In spite of their lack of theoretical training, many mediaeval surgeons were extremely skillful. Some real progress began in the fifteenth century in a more objective study of anatomy and in the treatment of diseases in some of the Italian universities, especially at the University of Padua. In the fourteenth century, the Ockhamites at the University of Paris, especially Buridan and Oresme, had attacked the traditional scientific learning of the schools; in the fifteenth century a materialistic Averroism, transferred from the University of Paris, led to a similar attack on old ideas in some of the Italian universities. In both Paris and Padua there was a growing emphasis on the idea that the principles of all science are strictly mathematical in character.

For the growth of science two factors are essential: careful and controlled observation and bold and imaginative synthesis. This combination rarely appeared in the Middle Ages, and if one looks for important scientific achievement in Latin Christendom in the centuries between the Crusades and the Reformation he is almost certain to feel that, even in spite of the recovery of Greek and Islamic science, the scientific life of the West marked time. When examined more closely, however, the period 1200 to 1500, proves to be an important seed time wherein some thinkers are re-examining the past and are reaching out toward new methods and new concepts that were to make revolutionary changes in science in the early modern centuries after 1500. A few representative thinkers may be cited to show that inside the old respectful repetition of inherited scientific ideas a revolutionary ferment was working. The chief center of this re-examination of old ideas in the thirteenth century was Oxford, and here the leading figures were Robert Grosseteste (d. 1253) and Roger Bacon (d. 1292). Grosseteste had pointed out the necessity of applying mathematics to physics. He criticized some of the theories of Aristotle and did some experimental work on optics. Bacon, in his *Opus Maius*, discusses the causes of ignorance and error, the relations of philosophy and theology, the importance of studying foreign languages, the usefulness of the study of mathematics, perspective and optics, experimental science, and, finally, moral philosophy. Bacon dared to attack the uncritical reverence paid to earlier authorities, even to Aristotle, and he had some glimpses of the gains for mankind in the possible applications of science. He believed strongly in the study of Hebrew, Greek, and Arabic so that the student could find out what the Bible said and what the Greek and Islamic writers really thought. To aid in this study he himself wrote a Hebrew and a Greek grammar. Bacon also saw dimly the value of mathematics in the study of all sciences, and he had a vague notion of the value of experimentation. His *Opus Maius*, the most representative of his writings, contains some religious and scientific nonsense, many digressions, and too many quotations. He is very careful, therein, to insist on his religious orthodoxy, but in spite of all this, Bacon's *Opus Maius* is one of the greater works of human genius, and it remains today more readable than any other work of mediaeval science or philosophy.[5] His own experimental work was chiefly on optics, though his general perception of the meaning of scientific method, dim as it was, was revolutionary. "Future generations will know much that we are ignorant of, and a time will come when our descendants will wonder that we were blind to things so obvious to them." In spite of the fact that he insisted that the Bible contained all truth and that in religious matters he yielded to the church, Bacon was imprisoned, probably for criticizing the morals of churchmen. In legend, he became a necromancer who "by condensation made a bridge thirty miles long over the sea from the Continent to England, and after passing over it destroyed it by rarefying the air; and he made a mirror in which you could see what people were doing in any part of the world." [6] Nonetheless, Bacon was much studied and much quoted after his death.

At the other end of Europe, in Palermo, Frederick II (d. 1250), the Holy Roman Emperor, was, at the same time, revealing the value of an experimental method in science. He lived at the place where Islam, Byzantium, and Latin Christendom met, and he gathered ideas from all three sources. Unlike Bacon, he seems to have been a skeptic, and, according to tradition, he wrote a tract, *The Three Impostors, Christ, Moses, and Mohammed.* The Emperor loved to write verses and he is one of the first Italian vernacular poets. He was also an enthusiastic patron of art and, in his highly centralized and efficient government, prefigures the early modern type of ruler. His contemporaries called him "Stupor Mundi" (the wonder of the world), and because of his scientific, aesthetic, and political outlook, modern historians have named him the "first modern man." Frederick's scientific interests show him, on the one hand, a student of Greek and Muslim science, and, on the other, a keen, if somewhat naïve, investigator. He had young children isolated to see what language they would talk, and found they would talk none. He had men cut open to see how fatigue affected digestion. He ordered a man put into a sealed cask; later when it was opened he found only a corpse and no soul; this apparently confirmed the Emperor's disbelief in immortality. Frederick, like some Mohammedan rulers before him, and like Christian rulers later, maintained a menagerie with elephants, camels, panthers, lions, leopards, monkeys, birds, and even a giraffe. His interest in the animals was entirely scientific. His *Art of Falconry*, with its beautiful drawings on the nature of the falcon and its training, is preserved in the Vatican Library. The work is very methodical and thorough; it shows a knowledge of the Greek and Muslim writers whom he does not hesitate to criticize, and it contains many new facts about the anatomy and physiology of birds. The whole work is first-hand and filled with a spirit of free inquiry. It is hard to realize that Frederick II was a contemporary of St. Francis of Assisi, Aquinas, and of the builders of the thirteenth-century cathedrals. His influence on scientific change was less than that of Roger Bacon and others of the thirteenth-century Oxford group.

In the fourteenth century the University of Paris became the center for new scientific ideas. Here took place a vigorous re-examination of the inherited scientific ideas of Aristotle and others. The leaders were Ockhamites, who believed that there was no heresy in a free examination of scientific concepts. The theory of the diurnal rotation of the earth, a basic emendation of Ptolemaic cosmology, was proposed by Oresme, who is also a remote precursor of Descartes in the invention of analytical geometry. Oresme and Buridan carried out a fundamental revision of Aristotle's theory of motion, establishing in its stead the theory of impetus. Oresme perceived vaguely the principle of inertia and the law of falling bodies. Oresme, Buridan, and Albert of Saxony began to envisage the necessity of careful measurement in science. They likewise came to new conclusions about what were later to be the fundamental concepts of force, motion, volume, density, and causation. They still conceived of all these concepts, however, inside a theological frame of reference. And though they believed their scientific concepts to be capable of measurement, and though they laid some emphasis on the idea of precision in the manufacture and use of instruments, little measuring was done. At the same time, some scholars at Merton College in Oxford for the first time analyzed accelerated movement kinematically, that is on the basis of distance and time. As a result they developed the theorem describing uniform accelerated motion in terms of uniform mean velocity, a theorem to be used later by Galileo. These and many other obscure workers of the fourteenth century were the great precursors of Copernicus and Galileo, and, in that sense, one may say modern science began in the Universities of Paris and Oxford in the fourteenth century. This work was continued in northern Europe in the fifteenth century by men like Pierre d'Ailly and Nicholas of Cusa, who rejected the grosser aspects of alchemy and astrology, attacked the excessive devotion to Aristotle, and began to criticize the Ptolemaic system. Nicholas of Cusa (d. 1464) believed that the earth rotated on its axis and that it was not the center of the universe. In the fifteenth century the leaders were the Averroist professors in the University of Padua. They were aware of what had been done in the previous century, and they moved on, under men like Cajetan (d. 1534), to formulate a mathematical as against a qualitative physics. Improved work was also being done in Padua in anatomy and physiology. The University of Padua remained into the seventeenth century the leading scientific school in Europe; Nicholas of Cusa, Purbach, Regiomontanus, Vesalius, Copernicus, and Harvey all studied there.

Typical of a new day in science are the writings of Leonardo da Vinci. All science interested him, and he has left notes on anatomy, physiology, geology, botany, physics, and practical inventions. In all of them he shows himself an independent investigator, ready to criticize the ancients when he found them wrong. So far as is known, no one before him ever made so many dissections on human bodies; he is the first man to give an accurate description of the human skeleton and the first to give a correct picture of nearly all the muscles of the human body. No one before him had drawn the nerves and the blood vessels so correctly. In spite of his care he made some errors, usually because he gave too much weight to Greek and Muslim authorities; he looked closely, but sometimes he did not look closely enough. Leonardo's theoretical writings on physics are vague. On the other hand, his descriptions of how to build bridges, irrigation works, harbors, armored cars, lamp chimneys, lifting cranes, water mills, locks and canals, and all types of instruments of war and fortifications are revolutionary. He was the first man to make studies of the tensile strength of building materials, one of the factors that is basic in modern engineering. He also designed a flying machine and other mechanical devices. He studied fossils and had a vague idea of the geological evolution of the earth. He remarks that "the sun does not move," and "a weight falls toward the center of the earth by the shortest path," but followed up neither comment with proof. All through his scattered notes runs the basic idea that all scientific work should start with experiments and end with conclusions. Leonardo's varied scientific writings are illustrated by vivid and exquisite drawings of his own. He liked to keep his notes in back-hand mirror-writing to prevent their being stolen and to avoid difficulties with the religious authorities. As most of his writings were not published until the nineteenth century, Leonardo is less an influence than a weathervane to show which way the winds of ideas were moving.

By the end of the fifteenth century modern science was rapidly unfolding. It was still held back by too great a respect for Greek and Muslim science which led scientists to try to fit new discoveries into outworn hypotheses, by the lack of adequate scientific instruments for accurate measurements, and by the contempt of the fashionable humanism for all scientific work. But even if Erasmus and Vives found the disputes about motion, falling bodies, and infinitesimals "silly discussions," modern science was well on the way to transforming the world.[7] Common to all the outstanding geniuses of mediaeval science from Grosseteste and Bacon through Leonardo da Vinci is a desire to reduce man's search for knowledge to a principle of unity that would lead to a mastery of nature. Though they all showed too much lingering respect for basic concepts of ancient and Islamic science and for theological preconceptions, they also were men of great shrewdness and common sense, and they had a talent for pulling together scattered ideas of other thinkers; they were men with prophetic vision.[8]

Alongside the different kinds of scientific books, both popular and learned, which circulated in Latin Christendom from 1000 to 1500, were a number of encyclopedias, covering many subjects. Some were chiefly factual, others were highly allegorized. From the number of surviving manuscripts they must have had a wide circulation. The oldest ones in use were Pliny's *Natural History*, the *Physiologus*, the *Etymologiae* of Isidore of Seville, Bede's *On the Nature of Things*, and Rabanus Maurus' *Concerning the Universe*. In the twelfth century three mystical writers, Hugo of St. Victor (d. 1141), Bernard Sylvester (d. 1150), and Hildegard of Bingen (d. 1180), wrote allegorized accounts of the universe and of man based on the doctrines of the macrocosm and the microcosm. None of their works is as generally comprehensive as that of Isidore of Seville. They explain creation as a series of symbols and they are more interested in edifying than in teaching. The alphabetical classification was known to the Middle

Ages; this is shown in the indices prepared for encyclopedias, but, for fundamental arrangement, alphabetical classification was rejected in favor of more general plans. Among a number of Latin and vernacular encyclopedias, the two most famous that circulated after the thirteenth century were Bartholemew the Englishman's, *Concerning the Properties of Things*, and Vincent of Beauvais' (d. 1264) famous *Speculum Maius*. This huge work was divided into four parts, the *Mirror of Nature*, the *Mirror of Doctrine*, the *Mirror of History*, and the *Mirror of Morals*. The first three parts were done by Vincent and a staff of helpers, the last quarter was compiled after his death and was mostly taken from Aquinas. The whole work would fill forty large modern volumes; it contains material not only on theology, science, and history, but also on art, music, education, industry, agriculture, government, and a multitude of other subjects. It is interesting to note that neither the Greeks nor the Romans ever produced a similar work on such a scale; and, in turn, it was not equalled again until the eighteenth century. Like the Gothic cathedrals and their ten thousand figures in glass and stone, like the great theological *Summas* of the thirteenth century, and like the *Divine Comedy* of Dante, the *Speculum* of Vincent represents the vast ranging and all-inclusive character of mediaeval thought and its deep passion for order.

While scientific work moved ahead slowly, technology advanced rapidly. Indeed, the phenomenal technological change that is one of the most characteristic features of modern civilization had its real beginnings in the Middle Ages. None of the important skills of the Romans seems to have been lost in the early Middle Ages. And, from the eighth century on, new machines, devices, and techniques multiplied. Without entering the debated field of the origin or the earliest dates of these discoveries, we find western Europeans making things the Romans had either not known at all or had barely known, such as felt, trousers, soap, butter, barrels and tubs of wood, wheelbarrows, fiddle bows, spinning-wheels, and the wheeled plow which made ploughing easier and more effective and made it possible to work wet bottom lands. North of the Alps and north of the Loire, the old Roman two-field system, which was very wasteful in allowing half of the cultivatable land to lie fallow each year, gave way to a three-field system which set aside each year only a third of the arable land for fallow—an epoch-making improvement in agriculture. By the thirteenth century many other new things had come into use—spectacles, the functional button, which revolutionized clothing, paper, the mechanical clock, from which later came many other precision instruments, the compass and gunpowder, the last two being now believed to be European rather than Chinese inventions, the crank, unknown to the Greeks and Romans, first used on machines to grind grain, then on rotary grindstones, and finally applied to all forms of machinery. The crank proved to be an invention second only in importance to the wheel. Almost as important was the spread of the vertical windmill, useful for grinding of grain and for pumping water and much cheaper to build and more convenient than mills run by water. One of the great technical achievements of the later Middle Ages was the production of cast iron. This depended on building bigger furnaces and working large bellows, usually by waterpower, so as to attain high temperatures. The greatest pieces of iron casting were cannon and other ordnance. In addition to this, traditional methods of wrought-iron making and of the manufacture of small pieces of crucible steel continued. The Italians from the twelfth century on learned from the Muslims to manufacture, for export, nitric, sulfuric, and muriatic acid, fine glassware, silk and woollen goods, and glazed pottery: faience and majolica.

Shipping was transformed by the use, after the thirteenth century, of the compass and by the gradual spread of use of the rudder and of fore and aft sails which made possible larger and more seaworthy ships, which were more maneuverable. Before 1000 the Vikings had gone on long voyages, but they had never developed commercial shipping. After 1000 the earliest long trips were those made by land to the Orient, in the thirteenth century, by missionaries, and by traders like Marco Polo. By the end of the fourteenth century, the best ships and nautical instruments were in the hands of the Portuguese who pushed out to discover islands in the Atlantic and began a long series of attempts to round Africa, which by 1488 led to the discovery of the Cape of Good Hope. The incentive of these extensive voyages was partly commercial, to break the Italian monopoly on trade with the East, and partly religious. Men were searching for spices, slaves, and souls. The improvements in methods of ship-building, navigation, and map-making of the last two mediaeval centuries led to the discovery and exploration of the Americas and the opening up of European trade in Asia and Africa.

The invention of printing was fully as significant for civilization as the geographical discoveries. Papermaking reached the West from Islam by the twelfth century. Here was a material for making books much cheaper and easier to handle than parchment. In the fifteenth century devotional books and playing cards, printed from carved wooden blocks, became very popular. But the great invention was printing from movable metal type seemingly invented by Gutenberg, a goldsmith of Mainz, just before 1450. The background of the invention was the fine metalwork of the later Middle Ages which made possible the casting of pieces of type exactly calibrated. From Germany this invention, comparable in man's history to the discovery of fire, spread throughout Europe. By 1500, nine million books and pamphlets had been printed, and their price had sunk to one eighth of what it had been before printing. As an early French printer boasted, "with twenty-six metal soldiers I have conquered the world." Printing brought the book to the common man, and produced what Spengler calls a "Buch-und-Lesen Kultur."

Some modern scholars have found in the improved use of the horse the most representative of mediaeval technical changes. The Romans used only yokes for harness, and so the load could not be heavy or the horse would choke. The Romans had no method of harnessing more than one horse at once, and, as they usually did not shoe their horses, they frequently rendered them useless through broken hoofs. Some time before 1000 men learned to shoe horses with nailed-on shoes and invented the horse-collar, tandem harness, and the stirrup. With a collar a horse could pull three or four times what the ancient could get out of him with a yoke; and, with tandem harness, a number of horses could pull on a single load. With shoes the danger of breaking the horses' hoofs was greatly reduced, and with the stirrup, riding and controlling the horse were both made easier. Formerly all heavy loads had to be moved by manpower; now they could be moved by horse-power. "The chief glory of the later Middle Ages," says one modern writer, "was not its cathedrals or its epics or its scholasticism; it was the building, for the first time in history, of a complex civilization which rested not on the backs of sweating slaves but primarily on non-human power." [9]

3. PHILOSOPHY FROM ANSELM TO FICINO

To the mediaeval thinker, Jewish, Christian, and Mohammedan, all knowledge was one, and it is only for the sake of convenience that the modern student separates one branch of mediaeval learning from another. Since all learning was considered as one, it was always assumed that at the foundation of learning were theology and philosophy. The system of Jewish, Mohammedan, Roman Catholic, and, later, of Protestant thought, in which the revealed truth of certain holy books stands first, but in which there is a continuous effort to give religious ideas a rational demonstration, has long gone by the name of Scholasticism. In it may be seen the faith of the Middle Ages seeking reason, just as in the twentieth century, men, grown weary of reason, are seeking faith.

In later antiquity, outside the ranges of Jewish and Christian thought, philosophy had steadily grown more like a religion, a refuge for the disconsolate and a guide for the perplexed. Most of the asceticism and superrationalism usually connected with the Middle Ages was, as we have seen, the creation of later Greek and of Roman antiquity, and Greek philosophy continued to dominate the philosophy of the Middle Ages. If one considers the whole range of Christian philosophy from its beginnings in the New Testament to the end of the fifteenth century, this thought may roughly be divided into three periods. First is a Platonic and Neo-Platonic period down to the thirteenth century; in this period, philosophy is subordinated to revealed religion. In a second period in the thirteenth century Aristotle is the dominant influence, and there is an alliance and co-ordination of revelation and philosophy. Finally, in the fourteenth and fifteenth centuries, scholasticism failed in its task of rationalizing the revealed dogmas of the church, and theology and philosophy separate. During the mediaeval centuries, the questions oftenest raised were as to how much of the basic doctrine of the Bible could be proved by the unaided reason of man; how much of it, while not subject to complete proof by the human intellect, could be approached and interpreted by reason; how much of it is altogether beyond the power of reason to interpret or explain; how could Greek and Muslim philosophy be used to buttress the Christian faith; and, finally, what fields of knowledge, if any, might be studied apart from revelation?

The foundation of mediaeval Christian theology and philosophy had been the work of the Church Fathers, who had based their theology on the elaborate systems of Platonic and of Neo-Platonic metaphysics. The Fathers of the church were convinced that, since both reason and revelation were from God, they could never really contradict each other. Faith must come first—"I believe in order that I may understand" was said by Augustine long before it was repeated by Anselm—but reason is also a divine gift to help men to grasp God's truth. True philosophy and true religion should work together. From this point of view, philosophy's task is to explain the doctrines of the church, to deduce their consequences, and to demonstrate their truth. This aspect of mediaeval thought, which by no means characterizes all its phases, led Bertrand Russell to dismiss all mediaeval philosophy with the remark, "the finding of arguments for a conclusion given in advance is not philosophy but special pleading." [10] Russell's remark fails, however, to indicate how mediaeval philosophy produced the seeds of modern science and philosophy.

In the West the first Christian philosophical effort had largely stopped in the fifth century with the death of Augustine. Except for the work of John Scotus Erigena, an isolated thinker in the ninth century, and some discussions involving purely theological doctrines, there is almost a blank in the history of philosophy in the West between Augustine in the fifth century and Anselm in the eleventh. Besides the writings of the Latin Fathers and of Erigena, there circulated in the West two translations of one dialogue of Plato's and that the most obscure, the *Timaeus,* two of Aristotle's logical treatises translated by Boethius, an *Introduction to the Categories of Aristotle* of Porphyry, and also translated by Boethius, a work commonly called, by mediaeval writers, the *Isagogue.* Porphyry had given to Aristotle's logic a special metaphysical orientation which Aristotle had avoided. At one point, Porphyry states: "Next, concerning genera and species, the question whether they have a substantial existence, or whether they consist in bare intellectual concepts only, and whether they are separable from the sensible properties of things I shall forbear to determine. For a question of this sort is a very deep one and one that requires a long investigation." [11] The passage sums up not only the difference between Platonism and Aristotelianism, but also the later differences between the mediaeval Realists and Nominalists. These lines of Porphyry play, from Erigena on, as important a role in the history of thought as any passage of equal length in all literature outside the Bible.

The Church Fathers, and later Erigena, had taken the Neo-Platonic position that truth or reality consists of a series of forms in the mind of God, and what we see and know are only reflections of these realities and are of secondary importance. Human ministers of justice may fail, but Justice never fails. The idea or concept of Justice, in other words, as it is set forth in the Bible, the Greek philosophers, and the early writers of the church, is the great reality. Men's motives and actions that are just are so only because they partake of the fundamental idea of Justice. The general theory that all parts are absorbed in a transcendent whole fitted the purposes of the church, first, because it was mystical in placing the source of truth outside this world and beyond the grasp of reason alone, second, because it proved the necessity of the union of the church under the hierarchy of the clergy culminating in the pope, the representative of God on earth, and finally, because it implied the subordination of the individual to a divine authority. Some form or other of this philosophic Realism, summed up in the formula, *universalia ante rem,* has always been the basis of orthodox philosophy in the Roman Church.

Before the eleventh century these ideas, except in the writings of Erigena, usually appear only in purely theological arguments on such subjects as free will versus predestination, the nature of the Trinity, and the meaning of the Eucharist. [12] In a famous argument on the Trinity, in the eleventh century, Roscellinus (d. 1122) attacked the Realist attitude of the church and made an extreme statement of the opposite position. In insisting that the Trinity represents three gods, Roscellinus says that the whole idea of universals consists in merely giving names to abstractions and that such abstractions have no existence or reality outside the mind of the thinker. Individuals alone are real; in Roscellinus' position the sole reality is difference. His statement, *universalia sunt nomina* (universals are names), while it did not create the idea, which is old, gave to his position the name Nominalism. The Nominalist point of view came to be summed up in the formula *universalia post rem*. Roscellinus' ideas were condemned as heretical and do not again become important until the fourteenth century.

The orthodox Realist point of view was powerfully restated by Anselm (d. 1109), the Archbishop of Canterbury and, after the death of Augustine, the next important thinker in orthodox Catholic thought. Anselm's first principle, "I believe in order that I may know," which he took from Augustine, holds that the unbeliever will never understand, exactly as the blind man cannot conceive of light, nor the deaf man conceive of sound.[18] The doctrines of the church are true, but they are also rational, and it is the business of human reason to understand these doctrines. In Anselm there is no such fusion of the philosopher and the passionate religious mystic as in Augustine, and he sought after philosophical argument to buttress his faith. He always remained certain that he could find such arguments. Reason and revelation are both from God, and they must be in accord. In attacking Roscellinus, Anselm said: "Reason is so confused with corporeal ideas in their souls [the souls of the Nominalists], that they find it impossible to separate from such material ideas that which ought to be considered independently of all corporeal intermixture. They cannot understand that man is something more than an individual."[14] Anselm's arguments are mostly his own creation, rather than citations from the Bible and the Church Fathers, as is usually the custom with ecclesiastical writers. Typical is one of his proofs of God: Man has the ability to conceive of an infinitely good and infinitely powerful being; therefore God exists. He tells us that this problem pursued him for years, caused him to forget his meals, brought him sleepless nights, and pursued him even in the most solemn moments of the Mass. Anselm's well-known work, *Why God Became Man*, remains one of the best brief introductions to mediaeval Scholasticism. One may see clearly in Anselm the basic aims of Scholasticism which are threefold: first, to defend the traditional doctrines of the church against heretics, both when they taught doctrines hostile to the creed, as did Roscellinus, and when later, like the Averroists, they held theories inconsistent with dogma; second, to establish a unified and articulated system of theology, harmonizing statements in Christian thought and in philosophy which seemed to contradict each other; and finally, to build up a system of philosophy that could stand by itself and could also support the theological system. Thus each single doctrine had to be bound inseparably to the others and welded into a whole. The method used was that of deductive logic inherited from the schools of antiquity. The mediaeval philosopher did not set out to discover new worlds; knowledge for him was buried in the pages of authoritative writers from whom it had to be quarried by arduous study.

A more original and more controversial figure than Anselm was Abelard (d. 1142). He studied first with the rebel Roscellinus, and then with the orthodox William of Champeaux, but he became dissatisfied with both and slowly worked out his own philosophy. Abelard was a vain, restless, and contentious man who got into difficulties with the church authorities more by the way he stated his views than because of the views themselves. His famous love affair with Heloise was also used by his enemies against him. Judging from the surviving records, Abelard must have been born to fascinate or repel. His teaching in the schools of Paris, which was clear, witty, and eloquent, attracted students in great numbers; twenty of his pupils became cardinals and over fifty became bishops. Abelard greatly admired Greek thought, but he lived before translations had made most of Aristotle available in Latin versions. He found all the essential doctrines of Christianity, its conception of God, the Trinity, and the Incarnation, in what he knew of Greek thought, and he declared that the distance between paganism and the Gospel was not so great as that between the Old and the New Testament. Hence, why should we deny the pagan thinkers eternal bliss because they did not know Christ? Like Roger Bacon in the next century, Abelard was disgusted with "the presumptuous credulity of those who indiscriminately and hastily accept any doctrine whatsoever before considering its merits." His famous *Sic et Non*, following the methods of the canon lawyers who lined up authorities for and against a given idea, quotes the Church Fathers and shows them by no means in agreement. Abelard supplies one hundred and fifty-eight problems, sets forth the authorities pro and con, and leaves the reader to solve the problems for himself.[15] This doubtless shocked many of his contemporaries. Abelard's determination to think for himself comes out most clearly in his ethics. Here his analysis of human motives led him to formulate the theory that intention alone should be our criterion of guilt.

Abelard saw clearly the need of axe-work through a jungle of earlier authorities and the value of using reason and logic. He had, however, an exaggerated belief in the power of reason alone, and his passion for dialectic sometimes resulted only in an ingenious jugglery of words. His was an age in which logic was regarded as the principal road to truth, the way by which men passed from the known to the unknown. With intellectuals logic had the same standing, from the twelfth into the sixteenth century, that the scientific method had in the nineteenth century. Abelard drew his belief in logic from his own age, but he undoubtedly helped to deepen it for his successors.

His own doctrine, Conceptualism, was a compromise between the earlier Realism and Nominalism; his formula was *universalia in re*. He conceded the affirmations of both sides while denying the correctness of their negations. The main tenet of the Nominalists, the absolute existence of the individual, he accepted. On the other hand, if the universals were the creations of the intellect, they were its necessary creations, they corresponded to realities in the mind of God, and they existed there before the creation of the world. Therein he accepted the main tenet of the Realists. Abelard had Boethius' translation of Aristotle's *Categories* and his *De Interpretatione*; he also used a twelfth-century translation of Aristotle's *Topics, Analytics*, and *Sophistic Questions*. But it remains amazing that, without a knowledge of Aristotle's *Metaphysics*, which was not yet available in Latin translation in his time, Abelard should have approached Aristotle's own position on the nature of reality. Abelard's compromise of Conceptualism was the basis of the thought of the great philosophers of the thirteenth century, especially that of Albertus Magnus and Aquinas. There was no trace of the religious mystic about Abelard; St. Bernard, his contemporary, denounced him: "Abelard is trying to make void the merit of the Christian faith when he deems himself able by human reason to comprehend God altogether. The man is great in his own eyes. He sees nothing as an enigma, nothing as in a glass darkly, but looks on everything face to face." [16] Abelard was not, as he has been sometimes represented, a mediaeval Voltaire. He believed in a divine revelation and he recognized the authority of the Bible, but he refused to accept ideas he was told to believe whether they were reasonable or not, and—like Ramon Lull later—he opposed all compulsion in matters of belief; faith should be the result of a personal experience and should never be forced. He deprecated the practice of reading all sorts of things into the sacred text, and, finally, he took a broad view of inspiration which he thought was not confined to Biblical authors alone but was shared by many others. He was, in these attitudes, so far out of his own age that his contemporaries and his followers were able to take from him only a part of his ideas. In the twelfth century, his influence was felt in making Paris the great center of philosophical studies, in showing a way to solve the earlier controversies of Realists and Nominalists, and, in the *Sic et Non*, in setting forth a new method of philosophic presentation.

While Abelard was turning the schools of Paris to dialectic and philosophy, a humanistic revival dominated the Cathedral schools of Orléans, Laon, and Chartres, where the great luminary was John of Salisbury. These humanists were interested in improving Latin style in poetry and in prose and had a literary rather than a philosophical approach to the Christian tradition. Scholars at Chartres like Gilbert de la Porrée (d. 1154), who were primarily interested in philosophic questions, were strongly Platonic and Augustinian in outlook. Most of the humanists of the school of Chartres thought the scholars of Paris were wasting their time in vain and fruitless dialectical controversies. This was also, as we have seen, the view of St. Bernard, the greatest of twelfth-century mystics, and the attitude, too, of the community of mystics in the monastery of St. Victor of Paris. The mystics, while not opposed to learning, insisted that God is known by experiencing him. He is never to be reached by dialectic or logic, but in a mystic experience through the activity of the soul. These currents of humanism and of mysticism, however, could not stem the rising tide of philosophical and scientific studies, which was soon augmented by the recovery of a mass of Greek and Muslim learning.

The philosophical tradition of Abelard in Paris was continued by his very orthodox pupil, Peter Lombard (d. 1164). He composed a famous manual of philosophy, the *Sententiae* ("Opinions"). As did Abelard in *Sic et Non*, he borrowed his method from the writers on canon law like Gratian, and on each basic doctrine he set down the authorities for and against, but, unlike Abelard's *Sic et Non*, the *Sententiae* of Peter Lombard gives a reasoned harmony of these opinions. The work contains a summary of the seven sacraments; he adds, more definitely than any earlier writer, ordination and extreme unction. Later Aquinas stated that Christ instituted all of the sacraments. Henceforth the sacraments are regarded as necessary intermediaries between God and man. It was this new emphasis on the role of the sacraments in the life of the Christian that was disputed by the Waldensians, Wyclif, Hus, and Luther. The comprehensiveness of the *Sententiae*, its clarity, its simplicity, and its careful orthodoxy made it a favorite textbook for centuries.

By the second half of the twelfth century, a large number of Greek and Muslim scientific and philosophical works were circulating in Latin translations; the flood of translations increased in the thirteenth century. Some time usually elapsed between the translation of a Greek or Muslim treatise and its wide diffusion. The first theologian who made any extended use of Aristotle's *Metaphysics* was William of Auxerre, writing between 1215 and 1220. Much of Aristotle's writings, however, must have been circulating earlier or the church's prohibitions of 1210 and 1215 against teaching them would have been meaningless. So far as can be ascertained, the new Aristotle, the most important book of which was the first part of his *Metaphysics*, was introduced at both Oxford and Paris between 1206 and 1209.[17] So there was turned into the stream of Western thought a huge patrimony, mixed and often confused, of the intellectual treasures of Greece, Rome, Syria, the Muslims, and the Jews. Over all this mixed heritage rose the towering figure of Aristotle, and the principal philosophic currents from the thirteenth into the seventeenth century were determined by the position taken by different thinkers toward Aristotle. In addition, Christian thought was deeply influenced by the Mohammedan and Jewish attempts to harmonize religious revelation and Aristotelianism. To the Jewish, Mohammedan, and Christian thinkers, Aristotle's philosophy was a static thing. None of them understood that the original Aristotle was a thinker who corrected his opinions continually. If Aristotle contradicted himself, his followers had first to harmonize Aristotle. The true nature of Aristotle's thought was only discovered after men stopped idolizing him.

In the thirteenth century, three main schools of philosophy, all centering in the University of Paris, are clearly discernible. The first, led by Alexander of Hales and his pupil, Bonaventura, leaned heavily on traditional Neo-Platonic and Augustinian thought. A second school, of whom the leading thinker was Siger of Brabant, accepted most of Averroës' interpretations of Aristotle. Finally, the third school, led by Albertus Magnus and Aquinas, tried to create a Christian Aristotelianism. Besides these three main currents there were numerous minor eddies. The University of Paris remained the center of these controversies, but they extended into most of the universities and cathedral schools of Latin Christendom. These schools show a great variety of points of view, for example Albertus Magnus and Aquinas differed in many ways. At the same time, it is hard to find any important philosophical question that has ever occupied the mind of man that was not raised and subjected to a thoroughgoing analysis by the philosophic writers of the thirteenth and fourteenth centuries. This variety of ideas and attitudes makes it impossible to portray Scholasticism as a homogeneous development with an organic doctrinal unity.

The first great thirteenth-century *Summa Theologiae* was that of Alexander of Hales (d. 1245), an English Franciscan at the University of Paris. He used the new Aristotle and followed the expository method of Peter Lombard. Though he tried to harmonize Aristotle with Christian thought, his leanings were strongly toward Augustinianism. The same was true of Bonaventura (d. 1274), an Italian Franciscan in Paris. He sought to combine Plato and Aristotle with religious thought as had been suggested by Plotinus and Augustine. Bonaventura assigned to Plato the realm of wisdom and the eternal, and to Aristotle the realm of science and the changing. He was of a mystical turn of mind, and he never had Aquinas' veneration for Aristotle. While he knew Aristotle and used his ideas, his philosophical synthesis ends in a contradiction and condemnation of Aristotle. Bonaventura's attitude is illustrated by his statement that Aristotle spoke the language of science and Plato the language of wisdom; Augustine, under the inspiration of the Holy Spirit, spoke both languages. Bona-ventura's philosophical system is the most comprehensive one along mystical lines that the Middle Ages produced. In general, the Franciscans preferred Plato to Aristotle, Bernard to Abelard, and Augustine, Bonaventura, and Duns Scotus, to Aquinas.

A second great current in the schools of the thirteenth to the fifteenth centuries was Averroism, of which one of the leading thinkers was Siger of Brabant (d. 1281), a teacher in the University of Paris. The Muslim attempts to harmonize Aristotle with the Mohammedan religious system deeply influenced most Christian thinkers, but the Latin Averroists claimed the right to philosophize apart from religion. "We have nothing to do with the miracles of God," Siger insisted, "since we treat natural things in a natural way." The Averroists aimed to separate philosophy from theology and to allow reason complete freedom to work without any control of religion, though, on the other hand, they opposed Averroës' view that exalted reason above revelation, and always acknowledged the superiority of revelation. The church, however, found other errors in their views, and certain propositions of Siger were condemned in 1277, especially his denial of divine providence, his belief in the eternality of the world, and his denial of personal immortality. In spite of the condemnation, Averroism remained for centuries a powerful influence in the schools.

The dominant school of thirteenth-century philosophy was that of Albertus Magnus, and his pupil, Thomas Aquinas, two Dominicans at the University of Paris. The church authorities, having first condemned the teaching of Aristotle's natural philosophy and metaphysics, had found that students insisted on reading him anyway, and so the ecclesiastical authorities came to allow the study of Aristotelianism provided it was harmonized with Christian thought. Under the direction of the pope, a new translation of Aristotle, directly from the Greek, and without any Muslim commentaries, was prepared. It was this improved translation that was used by Aquinas. By the later thirteenth century, Aristotle had become the great philosopher of the church, "the precursor of Christ in natural things, as John the Baptist was his precursor in matters of grace," and Aristotle could not, at many points, be contradicted without the danger of a charge of heresy. Down to the time of Albertus Magnus (d. 1280), philosophic thought had enjoyed a relative independence. Its object was to prove the agreement between a dogma and natural reason. Henceforth the object was to prove the agreement of a dogma with the teachings of Aristotle. This brought into the philosophy of the church a taste of science and a spirit of rational analysis that the church ultimately could not control.

The writings of St. Thomas Aquinas represent the most comprehensive and the most profound system of philosophy since Plotinus. Aquinas, the son of a powerful nobleman, was born, near Naples, in 1224, or early in 1225. He began his education, at the age of five, at the old Benedictine Abbey of Monte Cassino. When he was fourteen, he entered the University of Naples which had been founded only a few years before by the Emperor Frederick II. At the age of twenty, he decided to enter the Dominican Order, and he was ordered to go to the University of Paris to study theology. On the way there, two of his brothers seized him, and he was detained by his family a year in the hope that he would change his mind. But all efforts to dissuade him from following a religious career having failed, he was allowed to proceed to Paris. Here, he soon fell under the spell of the great Dominican teacher, Albertus Magnus, who was making the first thorough study of the uses of Aristotle's writings for Christian philosophy. The young Aquinas studied diligently the commentaries on which his teacher was working, and he accompanied his master to Cologne in 1248, returning to Paris four years later. By 1256, Aquinas was giving instruction in the University of Paris, and had published several works. He took the degree of Master of Arts in 1257, according to tradition, the same year in which this degree was conferred on the Franciscan scholar, Bonaventura. Aquinas' contemporary, William of Moerbeke, a Dominican, was, as we have seen, making a new version of Aristotle's writings. William, evidently with some help, either made new translations of all Aristotle's works, except the *Poetics* and the *Rhetoric*, or revised the existing versions. These improved translations of Aristotle's writings were used for all but the earliest of Aquinas' writings. In 1259, Aquinas was called to teach at the Papal Court, and while there he composed his first long treatise, the *Summa contra Gentiles*, a summary of theology and philosophy for unbelievers.

He returned to Paris in 1268 and was soon deeply involved in disputes with rival teachers: with the traditional Augustinians, who would have little or none of Aristotle, and with Siger of Brabant and the Averroists, who, in following Aristotle too closely, were believed to be undermining the Christian faith. Four years later (1272), Aquinas was recalled to Italy where he was entrusted with the direction of the theological curriculum of the Dominican schools. Here he worked strenuously at his *Summa Theologica*, a summary of theology and philosophy for students. The first *Summa* had treated natural and revealed theology separately. In this second *Summa* the two are combined; also in the later work the illustrative material, especially in the form of divergent opinions, is much extended. The *Summa Theologica* was left unfinished, but it was carried through to completion after Aquinas' death by one of his students who seems to have followed carefully his master's outline and plan. After only two years in Naples, Aquinas started north to take part in the Council of Lyons. On the way, he fell ill, and died (1274) in a monastery near Rome at the early age of forty-nine. All through his busy years as a teacher, Aquinas was extraordinarily productive, and he left a surprising body of writings which, beside his two *Summas*, include a large number of shorter treatises and commentaries on books of the Bible. In his own time, many thinkers considered Aquinas a dangerous modernist. Some of his ideas were even condemned, in 1277, by the Archbishops of Paris and of Canterbury. But his critics were silenced through his canonization by Pope John XXII in 1323. Aquinas was proclaimed a Doctor of the Church by Pius V in 1567, and was set up as a guide for Catholic theologians and philosophers by Leo XIII in the Nineteenth Century. In the whole history of Christian philosophy, none of Aquinas' predecessors and few of his successors equal him in the ability both to synthesize and to analyze their ideas.

The stones of the vast structure Aquinas built were the basic dogmas of the Christian church, and these he fitted together with the *Metaphysics*, the *Logic*, and most of the other writings of Aristotle. At one time or another, Aquinas commented on nearly all of Aristotle's writings. Aristotle, moreover, is quoted or referred to in almost every chapter of the two *Summas*, often several times in a chapter. Of course,

Aquinas was neither a biologist, nor a physicist, nor yet an astronomer. Hence, he could not independently criticize Aristotle in these fields, even when Aristotle had gone hopelessly astray. Also, in spite of his effort to get a correct text of Aristotle, and to understand the real Aristotle, Aquinas, to some extent, always saw Aristotle through a Neo-Platonist haze. Aquinas' system, as we shall see shortly more in detail, is closely reasoned from beginning to end; and it demands the closest attention. One may see, at once, how Scholasticism trained men in close reasoning and in the making of fine distinctions. One may see, also, why Rashdall speaks of Scholasticism as being "at once too dogmatic and too disputatious." Everything is carefully reasoned, but the premises are never adequately examined. The foundations had been fixed by the Bible, the Church Fathers, and the early councils of the church, and these foundations are accepted and never doubted. In their own time, both Albertus Magnus and Aquinas were liberals, liberal in the sense that the theologians who accepted Darwinism, political and social radicalism, and the Higher Criticism in the Nineteenth Century were liberals. Both Aquinas and his teacher were convinced that Aristotle had come to stay, and that Christianity must make terms with him if the church was not to lose the confidence of the intellectual classes. Like the Averroists, Aquinas realized fully the value of a thorough study of Aristotle, but he was early determined to get the best text possible of Aristotle's writings, and he was equally determined to study these writings without becoming Aristotle's slave.

Aquinas' vast synthesis of Aristotelian philosophy and Christian thought was accomplished by drawing two sharp distinctions. The first was between natural and revealed theology. Natural philosophy comprises all those truths about God and the world that may be discovered by sense, experience, and unaided reason. "The origin of our knowledge," he says, "is in sense, even of those things above sense." Other ideas must be accepted on faith. "Now in those things which we hold about God," he writes, "there is truth in two ways. For certain things that are true about God wholly surpass the capacity of human reason, for instance that God is three and one; while there are certain things to which natural reason can attain, for instance that God is, which even the philosophers proved, being guided by the light of natural reason." Revelation and reason are both from God, and should be in accord; whenever a philosophical conclusion contradicts dogma it is a certain sign that this conclusion is false, "though the truth of the Christian faith," he declares, "surpasses the ability of human reason, nevertheless those things which are naturally installed in human reason cannot be opposed to this truth." At the opening of the Fourth Book of the *Summa contra Gentiles,* Aquinas elaborates this view. "Man may have a threefold knowledge of divine things; the first is what he gains by the material light of reason when he ascends through creatures to God; the second, when divine truth exceeding human understanding descends to us by way of revelation; the third is when the human mind is raised to a perfect insight into the things that are revealed." Among "the certain truths which wholly surpass the capability of human reason," Aquinas includes such doctrines as those of the Creation, of the Trinity, of the Incarnation, of the Atonement, and of the last Judgment.

A second distinction that Aquinas draws sharply is between the conditions of inadequate knowledge in this life and a fuller knowledge in the life hereafter. The highest end of man is the knowledge of God; and Aquinas redefines Aristotle's doctrine that the highest wisdom for man is to concern himself with the end and purpose of the universe. So with Aquinas, the supreme happiness of man, which is also man's highest end, lies not in bodily pleasures, in earthly wealth, or power, or glory. This knowledge of God, which alone brings to man happiness and fulfillment, cannot be rationally demonstrated, nor is it the result of faith and prayer in this life as many of the mystics believed. It can come fully to man only from a direct vision in the afterlife when man has left his corporeal nature.

Thus in Aquinas' system faith and reason has each its own field, but they must work together. Faith and the realm of revealed theology begin with the love of God and the desire to know him and his ways and descend to the creature. Reason and the realm of natural theology begin with the creature and ascend to God. The revealed truths, while not contrary to reason, are yet beyond reason, and, on the other hand, a whole world of natural phenomena, even of natural religion and ethics, can be discovered by reason unaided by revelation. As for those doctrines that are beyond reason, Aquinas does not try to prove their truth by reasoning, but only uses reasoning to repel objections that have been brought against them. Thus he tries to show these dogmas are reasonable if not demonstrable. His whole method is less to seek new truth than to draw all the possible consequences from truth already known, and, at the same time, to defend this truth from all possible objections to it. Aquinas' acceptance of divine revelation as the source of knowledge about certain truths seems to contradict Aristotle's idea that all human knowledge has its origin in the senses. But Aquinas draws a distinction between the religious prophet who received an inspiration from God directly through his senses and ordinary men who must accept these truths on the authority of the prophet. The prophets were different from ordinary men. As in the future life, when the soul is freed from the body, its way of knowing will be entirely different from its way of knowing when it was on earth, so the prophet's means of gaining knowledge was different from that of ordinary men. The prophet was illumined from above; his experience was a foretaste of that of the saved in the life eternal. Thus Aquinas provides for divine revelation without contradicting Aristotle's theory of knowledge. Here, as elsewhere, he shows great skill (and perhaps some sophistry) in using Aristotle to serve his ends.

Among the ideas that could be proved by reason alone without the help of revelation is the existence of God. Aquinas rejects Anselm's proof from the idea of a perfect being. Instead, he follows Aristotle's belief that motion implies an unmoved mover for "all objects are not self-moved but remain at rest unless moved from without." Aquinas then goes on to use other arguments to prove the existence of God: all things must have a first cause; the existence of beings of various degrees of perfection implies a perfect being which is God; and, finally, from the order evident in the universe, there must be an intelligent governor. Having proved, by reason alone, the existence of God, Aquinas goes on to define and describe God. God is eternal, he was never created nor is he ever moved, he is unchanging since he contains no passive potentiality; he is the good of all goods. God not only knows general truths, but also all particular things because he is their cause. God also knows the future because he sees everything in time as if it were the present. God is manifested everywhere and in all things; he is the only cause of all activity. He rules the world though he exercises this rule through subordinate agents, both angels and men. By these means, Aquinas saves the idea of providence and the continual possibility of miracles. At the same time, in describing the ways of God, he rejects Aristotle's belief in the eternity of matter. God created the world out of nothing, and will continue to sustain it eternally. Aquinas' God is, in general, made to square with Aristotle's absolute and unchanging First Cause.

For both Aristotle and Aquinas, all that exists and all that happens, exists and happens for the sake of some final cause and for some outcome, near or remote. The explanation of all things and events lies in the end which they subserve and toward which they move. All this change and becoming are actuated by ends implicit in them, and presuppose something which does not change and does not become. Everything below God, the first cause, and below the angels, partakes of matter, the underlying element of which all things are made. Matter is purely passive and requires form for its actual expression. Matter is being continually transformed into determinate shapes. The form which matter takes is the principle of completion; thus health is determined by a form of health, cold by a form of cold. Form gives reality to matter, but form is not dependent on matter and form may, as with God and the angels, exist without it. All this which is basic to Aquinas' metaphysics he takes from Aristotle, though as elsewhere, he moulds it all for his own purposes.

Reason could prove, not only the existence of God, but, with Aquinas, it could also prove the immortality of the soul. Aquinas accepts Aristotle's idea that the soul is the form of the body, but unlike Aristotle he believes that the soul can be separated from the body. For the soul is capable of knowing all possible kinds of objects, and is not restricted to knowing one body. In addition, the soul can know immaterial objects and can reflect on itself. It must, then, itself be immaterial and separable from the body, and since each man has his own soul, immortality can be a personal immortality. So Aquinas uses Aristotle again, but he rejects Aristotle's conclusion, as well as that of Averroes, that there is only a general and impersonal immortality. Having established the separability of the soul from the body, Aquinas then goes on to prove immortality, and his basic reason is that, since nature does nothing in vain, it is impossible to suppose that any natural human desire will be permanently disappointed. Thus immortality must exist.

Aquinas' greastest work, the *Summa Theologica*, is divided into three parts. Part one opens with a short introduction on the nature of theology, then proceeds to treat of the existence of God, of God's nature and attributes, of the trinity, of creation, of angels, and of the divine government of the world. Part two deals with man in all his aspects and relations: virtues, vices, and the laws of society. Part three discusses Christ and the sacraments. The second part, which is devoted to ethics, includes Aquinas' political and economic theories discussed in the next chapter of this book. Personal ethics are, likewise, given detailed attention; indeed, Aquinas' treatment of ethics is the fullest and the most systematic of that of any Christian writer up to his time. He leaves many acts to be regulated in such ways as may best express the essence of God's law: i.e., the spirit of love for God. The value of any act depends jointly on its motive and on the act itself with its attendant circumstances. To live the Christian life is not to keep the law merely because it is a law and demands obedience, but because man must love and follow God from whom the law proceeds. Details of right behavior for the group and for individuals are often given. Fornication and divorce are forbidden, because the father should stay with the mother to help rear the children and maintain a home. Birth control is denied as against nature (though on this account, it may be noted, Aquinas does not forbid celibacy). Incest is forbidden as it would complicate family life. All these arguments on sexual ethics are based on purely rational considerations and are not founded on divine commands alone. Often Aquinas is detailed in his ethical injunctions, but everywhere he lays emphasis on the inner disposition, and he insists that formal correctness and legal righteousness can never make up for the lack of a love of God.

Aquinas believed strongly in free will. "Man has free will,' he asserts, "otherwise counsels, exhortations, commands, prohibitions, rewards, and punishments would be in vain. Some things act without judgment, as a stone moves downward. And some act from judgment, but not a free judgment, as brute animals. But man acts from some act of comparison in the reason, therefore he acts from free judgment and retains the power of being inclined to various things." But man, because of the Fall in Eden, is capable of error and sin, and if he will not be persuaded he must be coerced. Unbelievers may be tolerated, and Christians, already strong in their faith, may associate with them and may perhaps arrive at converting some. Heretics, though, if they will not change their views, must be punished for, says Aquinas, "they have merited by their sin not only excommunication but death; for it is much worse to corrupt the faith through which the soul lives than to counterfeit money which supports the temporal life. If the offender persists, the church abandoning hope of his conversion provides for the safety of others by excommunicating him and finally gives him up to the secular judge that he may be put out of the world by death."

So Aquinas pursues his subject article by article with the most orderly method and an encyclopedic thoroughness. First there is a general statement of the subject to be dealt with including the various subdivisions and parts of the subject. Then for each of these Aquinas gives opinions with which he does not agree or agrees only in part. He runs down all such with great persistence and thoroughness, and with amazing frankness. Then the author's own position is set forth, and the article is concluded with answers to the objections cited earlier. Occasionally these answers are omitted as unnecessary. He then turns to the next thesis, each time playing four parts, plaintiff, defendant, judge, and court of final appeal. For example, at the beginning of his *Summa Theologica* he discusses, in order, whether God exists, whether he is perfect, whether he is the highest good, whether he is infinite, and whether he is eternal. Nothing misses his keen glance, and the range of his work, especially that of the *Summa Theologica* is enormous. Beside it all other works of scholastic philosophy pale. Aquinas' faith, unlike that of Augustine, seems to have been a willed faith and one that was constantly struggling with a multitude of difficulties that reflection threw in its way. Some parts of the whole do not seem to fit, and his greatest work has been characterized as less a synthesis than "a mosaic built by a man who had a desire for a synthesis." [19] (This, however, may also be said of the philosophies of Plato and of Aristotle.) From Aquinas on, theology and philosophy begin to move apart, each slowly coming into a realization of differences in principles and interests. Aquinas did not, in the minds of some thinkers, succeed in reconciling Aristotle and Christian theology, but, rather, in the long run, won an epoch-making victory for reason. He led reason as a captive into the house of faith, but, in so doing, he helped to bring the age of faith to an end. As Lord Acton, paraphrasing Dr. Johnson, said, "Not the devil but St. Thomas Aquinas was the first Whig." [20]

The systems of the Dominican, Aquinas, and those of a number of other thirteenth-century thinkers were severely criticized by their younger Franciscan contemporary, Duns Scotus (d. 1308). Duns Scotus was an acute critic, though a quibbler over words, and a thinker who seems to have been determined at all hazards to differ from Aquinas and some of his predecessors. The Franciscans took him up vigorously and pushed his philosophy as against that of Aquinas. His subtleties carried him into unlimited analyses, sometimes corresponding to no real differences in the nature of things, and into an elaboration of terminology beyond what was required for distinguishing ideas. This was to be a bad heritage passed on to the Scholastics of the last mediaeval centuries, and, when Scholasticism went out of fashion, the name of Duns Scotus became the source of the word "dunce." "The philosophers and divines," wrote Erasmus in his *Praise of Folly*, "are deeply in my debt, as it is I who bestow upon them that self-love in which they look down upon the rest of mankind, while they are themselves protected by so vast an array of magistral definitions, conclusions, corollaries, and propositions, and have so many loopholes of escape that no chain can hold them but they will contrive to extricate themselves." Erasmus, at another point, speaks of Scholasticism as an attempt "to discover in thick darkness what in reality has no existence whatever." [21] To assume that this was true of the whole of Scholastic philosophy is a grossly biased view cultivated by the Renaissance humanists.

Among all the intricacies of the thought of Duns Scotus there was opened a door, through which Duns Scotus himself did not pass, to philosophical agnosticism on the one hand, and to a mystical conception of theology on the other. And this led to a revival of Nominalism in the fourteenth century. The thirteenth century had been an age of synthesis; Latin Christendom was directed along religious, educational, political, and economic lines by the powerful papacy; the unity of life and thought was symbolized in the plan and decoration of the Gothic Cathedral, in the Summa Theologiae of the great Scholastics, and in the *Divine Comedy* of Dante. The fourteenth century, on the other hand, was full of strife and controversy. The pope became, at Avignon, a puppet of the king of France, and the unity of Latin Christendom was split. On all sides old institutions were attacked from a variety of points of view: mystic, humanist, rationalist, and nationalist. The critics usually had little in common except their restlessness. Certainly the society of the time was becoming more diversified, and the unity of the Age of Innocent III, St. Francis, Aquinas, and Dante was waning.

Typical of the new age is the philosophy of the English Franciscan, William of Ockham (d. 1349). According to Ockham, the great religious truths could never be proved by reason and could be really understood only as the result of a mystical religious experience. So, like Duns Scotus, whose philosophy he had studied thoroughly, Ockham attacked the use of Aristotle to explain the divine mysteries. It is impossible to demonstrate the existence of God, or the fall of man, or the workings of providence. Moreover, the universals of both the Platonists and the Aristotelians are not real, but are only names used for the sake of convenience to designate things that are similar. From its very nature, the human mind can grasp only realities that are individual. On the other hand, to understand the world of nature, she must be studied directly for her own sake. Part of Ockham sounds like Descartes and Francis Bacon. Gilson and de Wulf agree that he helped to destroy traditional Scholasticism by merciless criticism and by taking a religious refuge in mysticism. Had William of Ockham drawn from his first premises the logical conclusions to which they led he would have moved into a modern positivist position. But he lacked such thoroughness, and he often restated all that he seemed to destroy. In the long run, Ockham's system implied an interest in scientific and worldly concerns, in individualism, nationalism, and democracy. Nominalism, with its emphasis on the variety of phenomena and its interest in the affairs of this world, came to be the natural ally of the secular and of the scientific points of view. It became, too, the natural ally of individualism as against group control, and of nationalism against the control of the papacy.

In the later fourteenth and the fifteenth centuries, Scholasticism often descended into a mass of vain subtleties, and many of the best minds were attracted to humanistic and scientific studies. Followers of Ockham at the Universities of Paris and Oxford in the fourteenth century laid the foundations of early modern astronomy and mechanics. Nicholas of Cusa (d. 1464), a leading philosopher of the fifteenth century, is difficult to classify. He derives in part from the school of Ockham and in part from Italian humanism, but the deepest influence on him was that of the German mystics. God is only knowable by a negative approach which he calls "learned ignorance." Aristotelianism, with various scholastic interpretations, still dominated the schools and controlled the teaching of theology and medicine, and, to a lesser extent, of law. At the University of Padua, where an Averroist interpretation of Aristotle prevailed, the philosopher, Pomponazzi (d. 1524), was trained; later he taught at the University of Bologna. In the northern universities, the philosophers were either theologians or teachers of natural philosophy and logic in the faculty of arts where they had to defend themselves against a powerful theological faculty. The Italian universities were long without faculties of theology, and from the beginning schools of Aristotelianism developed as part of the preparation for medicine rather than for theological studies. This forms the background for the development of legal, medical, philosophical, and humanistic studies in Italy in the fourteenth and fifteenth centuries. Pomponazzi tried to give natural explanations for supposedly miraculous happenings and insisted that immortality cannot be proved on rational grounds.

The revived interest in the study of Greek and Latin literature, grammar, history, and moral philosophy in Italy in the fourteenth and fifteenth centuries also brought a great revival of Platonism. The humanist leaders of this movement came to dominate the north Italian secondary schools, found high places in the local governments, and even pushed their way into the universities. The humanists made Latin translations of all of Plato, of the Neo-Platonists, of Plutarch, and of some of the great Stoic writers. Their writing in philosophy is often literary and superficial, but their worldly interests came to affect the few first-rate philosophers the movement produced. The greatest center of revived Platonism was the Platonic Academy in Florence, founded in 1462 when the two leaders were Marsilio Ficino (d. 1499) and Pico della Mirandola (d. 1494). Pico was an eclectic who dreamed of combining the best of Christian, Greek, and Jewish thought. He even harmonized Aquinas and Duns Scotus. All religious and philosophical doctrines, he believed, contain some true ideas, for all share in one universal truth.[22] Ficino, after doing a complete translation of Plato and Plotinus, wrote his *Platonic Philosophy* in which he sought to fuse the teachings of Plato, Neo-Platonism, and Christianity. The central concern of his thought is the return to God by means of the contemplative life. Since the goal of such a quest cannot be attained in this life, he postulates the immortality of the individual soul. Ficino was not only influenced by ancient Platonism, but also by the theories of Dante and the Tuscan poets. He connected the spiritual love between two human beings with the quest of the human soul for God and invented the term "Platonic love" for this relationship. Ficino's "philosophy of love" had a great effect on the poetry and art of the Renaissance both north and south of the Alps. The Platonism of the Florentine Academy, likewise, had a great influence north of the Alps among men who believed in a renewal of religion. The emphasis on Christianity as a way of life rather than as a creed appealed to Reuchlin in Germany, Lefèvre d'Etaples in France, Zwingli in Switzerland, Colet and More in England, and, above all, Erasmus of Rotterdam. All show later the desire of Ficino and Pico to revitalize religion and bring it close to what Erasmus called the "philosophy of Christ."

In spite of the literary and philosophic Platonism of the fifteenth and sixteenth centuries, the Scholastic teachings still continued. Out of Scholasticism came the philosophies of Descartes, Spinoza, and Leibniz, the founders of modern philosophy in the seventeenth century. Something of the general continuity in philosophic thought is shown in the fact that the favorite book of Descartes, which he carried in all his travels, was Aquinas' *Summa*. Neither the learning of the Greek Christians nor that of the Muslims contained, as did the science and Scholasticism of the Latin West, the seeds of modern philosophy and science. As Condorcet said in the Age of the Enlightenment, "logic, ethics, and metaphysics owe to Scholasticism a precision unknown to the ancients themselves." In Protestant circles, Melanchthon and, later, others reworked something of Aquinas and something of Ockham and other Scholastics into a Protestant Scholasticism. Calvin's *Institute of the Christian Religion,* the most important single work in the history of Protestant theology, was created largely out of mediaeval materials.

On the Catholic side, the system of Aquinas was reconstructed in the sixteenth century by the Spaniard, Suarez, who is still considered by the Roman Church as, next to Aquinas, the greatest of all the Scholastics. The Counter-Reformation raised the reputation and prestige of Aquinas. Leo XIII, in the nineteenth century, gave his system a status in the Church of Rome possessed by that of no other philosopher, and since 1880 there has been a great Neo-Scholastic movement. So, in both Roman Catholic and Protestant circles mediaeval scholasticism, modified somewhat by modern thought, lives on parallel with purely secular schools of philosophy that are also its descendants.

CHAPTER VIII

Learning (II)

I. BACKGROUNDS OF MEDIAEVAL POLITICAL

AND SOCIAL THOUGHT

LIKE the hero of Tennyson's *Ulysses* who was part of all that he had met, mediaeval political and social thought showed everywhere the results of a long historic experience. From Plato and Aristotle mediaeval thinkers derived the idea of the state as having a moral purpose, and, from the same sources, they conceived of all political and social thought as forming a part of an all-inclusive ethical and metaphysical system. From the Stoics descended the idea of the whole universe conceived as a single intelligible unity, pervaded by reason, and ruled by God. From the Stoics, likewise, came the idea that there should be one universal society among all men and one state ruled by just laws attuned to the laws of the universe; in such a society there was an equality and a brotherhood of all men under God.

The Stoics also conceived and handed on the idea that all power ought to justify itself in the light of a higher ethical law. According to the Roman Stoic writers, whatever might be the powers of the ruler, he should always remember that his power is derived from the people and that he should always be bound by the laws of the state. As Ulpian, a Roman jurist, says, "the will of the prince has the force of law, because the people conferred on him all its power."¹ Later on, argument from Roman law could be made either to assert the omnipotence of the ruler or the sovereignty of the people. The debatable points were always whether the people had conferred all power on the ruler, and, if not, just how the people were to control the ruler if he violated his trust. These Stoic ideals were built solidly into the common stock of ideas and so became part of the whole tradition of the Occident.

From the practical experience of the Roman state, mediaeval thinkers derived the idea of a universal government ruled by a law of justice. The contribution of the Roman Empire to political thinking, as distinct from that of the Greeks, lay primarily in the designing of large-scale institutions and an all-embracing law that kept the peace over a wider area and for a longer time than did any other empire Europe has ever known. At the head of the Roman state there finally came to be an emperor who was exalted as a god, as had been Alexander and some of the Hellenistic kings. Mediaeval men, it is true, never worshipped their rulers, but from Greek and Roman imperial usages they derived a belief in "the divinity that doth hedge a king." And from these classical, as well as from Hebrew, sources descended the mediaeval idea that a king should head the government no matter how decentralized the state might be or how weak its control. So even in the most feudalized of mediaeval times men never dreamt of getting along without a king, and they never lost the concept of a state with political, as distinguished from feudal, private-law authority.

Much of the best of Rome's political experience was embodied in her law, the basis of which was the law of the city of Rome, *jus civile,* as it evolved through centuries of legislation and of decisions in the courts. Alongside this civil law, and deeply affecting its growth, were the laws of the peoples Rome conquered. From the third century B.C., a special judge had handled cases involving foreigners and foreign law. In his court, all sorts of old formalities had to be set aside and decisions made on the basis of the laws of the conquered peoples and on considerations of equity and common sense. Thus a body of law, called *jus gentium*, conforming to good business practice and to public utility, grew up beside the civil law. These cosmopolitan contacts and the adjustments to meet current situations made the civil law less narrow and provincial and informed it with a comprehensive ideal of justice.

Finally, a group of Roman Stoic writers, of whom Cicero was the most notable, and which later included all the leading writers on law, preached the idea of a natural law. This *jus naturale* represented the highest purposes of a divine order in the world and provided a norm for all human laws and governance. The belief that justice, right, equality, and fair dealing should underlie positive law became a commonplace in Western political and social thought.[2] In this way the old *jus civile* was modified first by *jus gentium*, and then by *jus naturale*. So varied was the long political experience of Rome, and so marked by legal genius had been her great statesmen and jurists, that men spoke of Roman law as "written reason." This Roman law was finally codified in the sixth century in the great *Corpus Juris Civilis* of Justinian. Much that was basic in Roman political and legal experience and thought reached the Middle Ages through the writings of Cicero, especially his *De Legibus* and his *De Republica*, for most of the later Roman jurists and the Justinian Code were neglected, in the West, until the twelfth century.

From the later Roman Stoics, Seneca and Marcus Aurelius, came, in part, the common mediaeval idea of two commonwealths: the civil state to which a man is subject and a greater society composed of all rational beings. This greater commonwealth is a moral and religious fellowship rather than a legal and political state. Through it the wise and good man can render a service to humanity even though he possesses no political power. Seneca (d. A.D. 65), unlike Cicero a century earlier, had ceased to believe that the state was an ethical institution and the highest that man had devised. He conceived the idea that man had once lived in a golden age of innocence, in which all goods were held in common and no government was necessary. This primitive golden age had been succeeded by ages of sophistication, luxury, and corruption, during which the institutions of government and of property had developed—a doctrine that the Church Fathers extended to mean that all human institutions were the result of sin.

From the Old Testament mediaeval men derived the idea of a divine plan in history, a plan of which the state was an instrument. The divine process was associated with a chosen people who were sent to earth to fulfill God's purposes. From the Hebrews came, also, the idea that sovereign power belongs to God, and that the state, property, and the family were all instituted by God, but those who control them are trustees and agents of God and are justified in his sight only if they exert their power to fulfill God's purposes. So men's rights and powers and possessions are purely relative, derivative, and conditional. God sets the value of persons much higher than the value of things, and the prophets were stern in their condemnation of the rich who ground the faces of the poor. The inevitable injustices of society must always be tempered by justice and by charity. After the Hebrew people had a king, they developed the idea that he was God's anointed and had a sacred character; he could not, however, tamper with the rites of the temple or the synagogue. This conception of the Hebrew state deeply influenced mediaeval political ideas. The Old Testament gave the ecclesiastical apologists a distinct advantage because the ancient record nearly always proved that the monarchs who were most subservient to priests and prophets were the most prosperous.

With the New Testament there came a renewal of the idea of the sovereignty of God, and the idea that all power and property are held in stewardship for him. There came also, in the field of social ideas, a deeper emphasis on pity for the unfortunate and on the duty of charity, and a greater hope for human regeneration. The good news of the Gospels irradiated all men's lives with the ideas of the love of God and the love of one's fellowmen. The great concern of Jesus was the Kingdom of Heaven on earth and in heaven, and mundane affairs and earthly governments were temporary expedients. Like the Hebrew prophets before him, he had a complete disregard of compromise. Statements like "Take no thought for the morrow" and "Render unto Caesar the things that are Caesar's and unto God the things that are God's" show that Jesus took ultimate values out of the political and social arena, and even more than Plato, set them in a timeless eternity. So Jesus left no definite theory of the church, of the state, or of property, though his emphasis on the respect for personality, and on treating individuals as ends remains, in all human history, the ultimate challenge. He "endowed mankind," as Whitehead said, "with its most precious instrument of progress, the impractical ethics of Christianity." [8]

The ideal community of Jesus was more comprehensive than that of Seneca, which included only the wise; Jesus' kingdom was for all men. With Jesus it is not a sharing of a life of reason that brings men together but the fact that all men have a common father in God. The first followers of Jesus, expecting the world soon to come to an end in the Last Judgment, were indifferent to all worldly concerns. When this end did not come, the Christian leaders became more interested in definite plans for human government and society. Plato, Aristotle, and Cicero had all believed that the state would give scope for the realization of the good life for all its citizens; they never separated the religious and political spheres. The early Christians, like the Stoics, found the state inadequate for the attainment of the good life. St. Paul transferred the Hebrew idea of a chosen people to the Christians and he borrowed from Stoicism the idea of a world community, a community that cut across every barrier of race and social status. In some of the later writers of the New Testament, it is clear that Christian teaching is moving away from the old local loyalties of the family, of the city-state, and of the Roman Empire.

With Plato, Aristotle, and Cicero the supreme virtue is service to the state; with the Fathers the supreme virtue is service to the church and to God. The great Christian corporation is the church, headed by Christ in heaven, and on earth guided by his agents, the clergy. The ideals of classical antiquity, and of the Bible, were reworked and reinterpreted by the Church Fathers. The sense of belonging to two worlds was, as we have seen, a common idea of both Stoics and Christians, though neither Seneca nor Marcus Aurelius envisaged an open conflict between loyalties to the state and to humanity at large. To the persecuted Christians this conflict became central, and the Church Fathers developed a theory of the state based on the assumption of a dual nature of man and a dual control over man's life. Gradually, in their theories, the Church Fathers came to regard the state as the necessary collaborator of the church. In controversies with the state authorities some of the Church Fathers, without producing an elaborated theory of the state, showed clearly the Christian position. Ambrose, for example, asserted that the church in spiritual matters had jurisdiction over all Christians, the emperor included, and, on several occasions, he forced the emperor to retract.

The first elaborated Christian theory of the state was that of Augustine. His writings, especially the *City of God*, were a mine of ideas from which later thinkers borrowed. His basic idea is a conception of the Christian commonwealth as the great community. The Christian is a citizen of two states, that into which he is born, and that into which he is reborn. As man's nature is twofold, he is both body and spirit, so he is, at once, a citizen of an earthly and of a heavenly state. Earthly states are corruptible and ever changing. The state is rooted in sin. "If justice be put to one side, what are kingdoms but instances of robbery on a large scale? What are robberies more than kingdoms on a small scale?" On the other hand, he does regard the state as a partial remedy for sin if it is aided by the supernatural society of the church. All history has been a conflict between these two states, and this conflict will continue until the Last Judgment.

Augustine never precisely defined the counterparts of his two societies. The Christian Roman Empire founded by Constantine is not exactly the picture of his secular state, nor is the church the exact counterpart of the Heavenly City. For it is not merely membership in the church, but also a God-fearing life, that constitutes citizenship in the state of God. For Augustine the two societies remain mingled until the Last Judgment. The formation of the concept of the Christian community, however, marked an era in the history of ideas. From now on for centuries, this world, in men's minds, remained the theater of a cosmic conflict between the powers of God and of Satan. Augustine did not believe that the state is merely the secular arm of the church, but he did insist that the state must be Christian. Government is only justified if it furthers the purposes of God. Such a theory of the state was bound to eventuate in the theocratic theories of the medieval church.

In economic doctrines, as in his political ideas, Augustine is first a theologian and a moralist. He agreed with most of the other early Christian writers in opposing the charging of interest, based on ideas of the Greek philosophers and on Biblical statements like that of Luke (vi, 35): "Lend hoping for nothing again, and your reward shall be great, and ye shall be children of the highest." ⁴ He exalted the benefits of labor as a means of moral perfection. To gain a livelihood men may engage in agriculture, and industry, and even in trade. But riches should never be made an end in themselves, and, in all transactions, honesty must prevail, and only a "just price"—based on the common estimation, that is, the market—should be asked for goods and services. Property, like the state, was made necessary by the fall of man and was to be tolerated if used to good ends. Wealth is a trust from God and it must be shared with the less fortunate. He held that it was not riches that damn a man, but pride, a covetous heart, and a failure to do justice to his fellows and to dispense charity for those in need. Justice must be the basis of all economic as well as of all political relations. Without justice, "which renders to each his due," a state or a society is but "a band of robbers." Property, like the state, was the result of the fall of man, but property and the state could also be used to work for man's regeneration if guided by the proper authorities and to the proper ends. And so human institutions both represent the fall of man from his primitive innocence, and may, at the same time, be the means by which the evils of human nature can be controlled. The distinctive character of later mediaeval thought as contrasted with the political theorizing of antiquity arose from this conception of a society devoted to the pursuit of a divine ideal.

The disappearance of the Roman imperial power in the West was followed by a period of small barbarian kingdoms, among which that of the Franks became the strongest and largest. At the same time, the bishop of Rome, without a powerful emperor such as ruled in the East, slowly gathered all the churches of Latin Christendom under his control and moved toward making the papacy the most powerful political force in the West. Partly out of earlier theories and partly out of the practical situation, the church writers in the four centuries after Augustine elaborated the idea of a dual organization of society. Spiritual interests of all sorts were to be in the hands of the church; secular interests, such as the maintenance of public order, were to be controlled by civil governments. Between these two orders, without trying to define exactly the limits of their powers, there was to prevail a mutual helpfulness. This doctrine of two coördinate powers was defined at the close of the fifth century by Gelasius I, the bishop of Rome. "There are two systems," Gelasius wrote, "under which this world is governed, the sacred authority of the priests and the royal power. Of these, the greater weight is with the priests in so far as they will answer to the Lord, even for kings, in the Last Judgment." [5] Each of these two powers is supreme in its sphere.

The case for the theocratic view of the state was strengthened in the ninth century by the *False Decretals*, a series of statements about the powers of the church which contained forgeries long believed to be genuine. The forgeries may have been the work of a Frankish priest; their purport was to prove the absolute power of the bishop of Rome in the church and to present him as the spiritual head of the whole of Christendom. Circulating at the same time with these forgeries was another, the *Donation of Constantine*, probably of the eighth century, a supposed grant of the first Christian emperor to the pope and his successors of temporal authority in the West. These documents were all accepted as genuine until the fifteenth century by many of the partisans and the enemies of the papacy, though no great use was made of the *Donation of Constantine* by the church before the thirteenth century.

While the learned writers of the Latin Church continued to discuss the problems that had concerned the Church Fathers, a new stream of political thought and experience entered the West through the Barbarian Migrations and the founding and development of Germanic states. One of the basic ideas which the early Germans brought with them was the notion that law was attached to the tribe rather than to a territory, a concept that fitted their primitive tribal organization and a more or less nomadic habit of life. In the course of time, this idea was gradually set aside, and the classical idea of the territoriality of law took its place. Much more enduring was the Germanic concept of law as custom perpetuated by word of mouth. The law was not supposed to have been made by anyone; it was conceived as permanent and unchangeable and rooted in the nature of things. When situations arose that seemed not to be covered by the old law, the

Germanic idea was that more investigation was needed to find out what the old law really meant. And so law is found rather than made, and the ruler or some authority sets forth the discovery in a statute or assize. Thus, the decrees of mediaeval rulers and assemblies were not usually regarded as legislation in the modern use of that word. They merely told what, in the opinion of the king and his council, the law had been discovered to mean.

The early Germanic theory of rulership combined a number of ideas not commonly held in classical times. One of these was the idea of consultation between the ruler and his people—"what touches all must be approved by all." Thus the enactments of mediaeval rulers frequently announce that a given decree had been made after its consideration by "our chief men," or by the "bishops and nobles," or even that the conclusion had been arrived at "by our whole people." Such agreement often meant merely that those consulted acknowledged that the law was actually as stated. All of these general ideas and usages did not imply a definite machinery of popular representation or of popular control of the ruler, and it was centuries before states like Spain, France, and England worked out the apparatus of representative government. This late development must not, however, obscure the fact that, ultimately, both limited monarchy and representative government descended, at least in part, from the ideas and usages of the Early Germans.

The Germanic ruler was not only bound to consult, in some form or other, with his people, but usage demanded also that he be subject to customary law. The ruler could not set aside rights that usage guaranteed to those under his rule or that earlier rulers had declared to be the law. Promises to uphold the law were often embodied in the coronation oath. In practice the ruler was often elected, though this procedure was usually combined with the idea of heredity and the theory that the king ruled by the "grace of God." The first two of these seemingly contradictory ideas came from Germanic usages and the last descended from the Old Testament. The Old Testament, likewise, contained the idea that there existed not only a pact between God and his people but also between the people and their earthly rulers. So a vague state of mind about kingship dominated mediaeval men: the ruler was elected to leadership; he inherited the throne, and he ruled by the grace of God. Add to this the idea of Jesus and St. Paul that men should always obey the powers that be, and the theory that a king who behaved in an unlawful way should be deposed, and it will be seen that the whole mediaeval idea of kingship showed a very mixed ancestry and contained, at one and the same time, ideas that could not easily be reconciled.

The power of the mediaeval ruler was not only hedged about by old theories and usages that came down from the past—classical, Christian, and Germanic—but it was likewise curbed, from the ninth century through the fifteenth, by feudal rights and usages. Feudalism was a rough and ramshackle form of government that grew up, in the ninth century, to fit the extreme agricultural localism and the need for local defense. In a period of anarchy, large political units were impossible. At the same time, society was economically organized into agricultural communities that were largely self-sufficing. Feudalism fitted such a society; it combined the rights of land ownership or land use with the rights of government. This meant that, in practice, the king's powers in matters of law enforcement, taxation, and the ability to build up an army were severely curbed, and the king was able to deal with the great majority of his subjects only at second or third hand. So far as feudal society was held together, its binding ties were the contractual relations of lord and vassal, rather than the power or prestige of the monarchy. From the eleventh century on, the king, often with the backing of the rising middle class, took from the feudal noble his right to enforce law and to go to war; slowly, the monarch was able to push the king's law and the king's peace, the king's right to raise troops for his army, and the king's right to collect taxes, into the local district. And in this process the political rights, though not the economic privileges nor the social prestige of the feudal aristocracy, diminished. Under the feudal regime, the king was always regarded as the head of the state and above even the greatest of the feudal lords. In practice, however, the monarch was often little more than a figurehead.

Most mediaeval states were never well centralized and well integrated. Side by side, even in a state as well centralized as was France in the fifteenth century, were a multitude of local law codes. The idea of a uniform national law is distinctly modern; the essence of mediaeval legal usage is local diversity. Moreover, the mediaeval state did not, like some modern states, possess a written constitution to form a norm of thought and action. This lack contributed greatly to the inherent contradictions in mediaeval political ideas. At the same time it must always be borne in mind that mediaeval men, having a profound respect for the past, collected out of all this past—Biblical, classical, and Germanic—a strange conglomeration of ideas which they cherished dearly though they often grossly misunderstood. They treasured them all, and tried, valiantly, and often vainly, to harmonize them.

2. MAIN CURRENTS OF POLITICAL AND SOCIAL THOUGHT, 1000–1500

THE ELEVENTH century, which in every field of activity saw western Europe moving forward, showed also a great resumption of political theorizing. The heart of the great volume of political writing from the eleventh through the fifteenth centuries lay in the protracted controversy over the relative powers of church and state. The starting point of this argument was, as we have seen, the theory of the two powers of Gelasius I. According to this view, human affairs are to be ruled by two authorities, the spiritual sphere by priests, the secular by lay rulers. Between the successors of Christ and of Caesar there should be co-operation and mutual aid. This theory rarely acknowledged a separate church and state but thought only of a single Christian society; the idea of complete separation of church and state is a modern rather than a mediaeval concept. To most mediaeval men any controversy between ecclesiastical and lay rulers, at least in theory, could only be between two officials of a single governance. Both sides shared some common concepts about the church; it was on the value of the state and on the limits of its jurisdiction that they differed profoundly. Both sides could find texts in the Bible and incidents from history to show that one power or the other, in this particular or that, was supreme. The Gelasian concept assumed that a line could be drawn between spiritual and secular matters, but as popes and kings tried to act they found themselves competing for control in many areas of power.

The inherent contradictions inside the system of thought were brought to the front in the eleventh century. Kings were more desirous to integrate their states than they had been before; they wished to capture and hold the loyalty of their subjects, especially of their more powerful feudal dependents among whom were the higher clergy. The lay powers saw with alarm the slipping away from their control of great estates which went into the episcopal and monastic holdings of the church, lands from which lay rulers had hoped to derive support in men and income. Unless lay rulers could, in some way, control the appointments to the higher positions in the church, they would lose one of the most valuable sources of their power. On the side of the church, there arose a radical attempt to free itself from abuses, especially from the really scandalous traffic in church offices. The higher positions in the church usually commanded large incomes and great prestige, and these honors and emoluments made such positions the object of ambitions far removed from religious considerations. According to the law of the church, the bishop should be chosen by certain of the clergy of the diocese, and the abbot by the members of the monastic house. In practice, these decisions were often controlled by some ruler or noble. The church was also fighting the marriage of the clergy, chiefly to prevent its properties from being alienated to wives and children.

If the church was to take the lead in improving the life of the faithful it had to be free from the social and economic entanglements of a married clergy, free from the miserable commercialism involved in the traffic in church offices, and free, above all, to place in positions of church leadership men of worthy character and purpose. The movement toward ecclesiastical reform was first spread by the Cluniac Order founded in Burgundy in 910. This new and highly centralized monastic order undertook a vigorous propaganda for the reform of the whole church. This included the raising of the papacy out of local Italian political bickering, and the setting up of an autonomous control of the pope over all the offices of the church. Much the same program was backed by the German emperor, Henry III, who intervened to aid a reforming party in Rome itself. All this resulted in 1059 in the founding of the College of Cardinals, which took the election of the pope out of the control of factions of central Italian nobles and vested it permanently in the hands of leading churchmen.

A member of the reforming party in Rome became Pope Gregory VII, who prohibited lay investiture, that is, the bestowing of high church offices by laymen. The emperor, Henry IV, tried then to secure Gregory's deposition. Gregory replied by excommunicating the emperor and by absolving his vassals from the feudal oaths of allegiance. The controversy dragged on till after both Gregory VII and Henry IV were dead and a temporary settlement was made with the *Concordat of Worms* (1122), by which both the church and the imperial authorities must be consulted in appointments to the higher positions in the church. This concordat, however, did not mark a real settlement and the controversies continued for centuries. The significance of the eleventh-century dispute lies in the fact that, by this time, the pope had the wealth, organization, and power to assume the tone of a Roman emperor. The church was now a great political power rather than a mere ideal as it had been with Augustine. This situation created for the faithful the problem of a divided loyalty. As long as the church was willing to accept some control from secular authority, a precarious collaboration was possible. But when the church demanded complete authority to fulfill its mission its demands became an attack on the power necessary to the function of the emperor.

The papal position in the eleventh century was set forth in the *Dictatus*, which Gregory VII may not have written himself, and in a series of state documents, most of which he certainly composed. In the church, Gregory declared, the pope was an absolute monarch superior to all church officials and church councils. The pope, in addition, was superior to all earthly rulers, and, while the pope would not rule directly, he maintained the right to intervene in state affairs when he felt it his duty. Gregory VII, with something of the temperament of a Hebrew prophet, was a born fighter with a great gift of attracting men to his program. His ideal, which he claimed had always been held by the church, was a purified ecclesiastical hierarchy as a necessary step to the reformation of the world. Society could never be improved by an institution as depraved as itself. The clergy were too much a part of the state, sharing its corruption; reform could only come by severing these entanglements and by setting up a caste that would offer a pattern of purity and devotion to all the laity. Then, all lay concerns, the family, education, culture, and the state, must be directed by the church. Those entrusted with souls were infinitely more important than those who regulated merely the earthly activities of men. There could be only one fundamental loyalty for the Christian, and that was to his church. As Ambrose had said, "the glory of princes was to the glory of bishops as the brightness of lead to the brightness of gold." Though Gregory VII used a very peremptory form of utterance, he probably intended to exercise only a moral discipline rather than to claim absolute sovereignty. Later on, however, ecclesiastical writers were to make such claims. What is new in Gregory is his policy rather than his theory.

The imperial position was a defensive one, and the appeal was made to passages in the Bible and to enactments of the Christian states of Constantine and Charlemagne. The apologists of the empire had as their fundamental conviction the divine origin of the state and the sacredness of the ruler. The political and legal terms used on both sides were, as yet, very imperfectly defined, and no one had any clear conception as to exactly what was secular and what was spiritual. Moreover, both sides began by agreeing to the principle of the two powers, though they were usually very prompt in advancing arguments which either undercut this theory or destroyed it entirely. Henry IV had stated the point of view of the secular ruler when, in 1076, he had informed the pope that he derived his powers from God directly and could be judged by God alone and could never be deposed except for heresy. The emperor and his backers insisted that the function of the prince was as divine in origin and character as that of the priest. Kings, whether good or bad, are instruments of a divine purpose. If kings are evil, God will punish them. Much was made, by the apologists for the emperor, of the sayings of Jesus, Paul, and Peter, all of whom had enjoined the faithful to submit to the powers that be. These direct injunctions were very useful to those defending the rights of kings and very annoying to their adversaries who exalted the powers of the pope. The church's interpretation of the doctrine that "the powers that be are ordained of God" was later made with the reservation that God acted through the instrumentality of the church.

The Gelasian theory had insisted that the two powers of *sacerdotum* and *imperium* could never be united, and Henry IV and his backers had maintained that that was exactly what the Vicar of Christ was doing.

Followers on both sides wrote treatises. Honorius of Augsburg, in his *Summa Gloria* (1123), defended the papal position. As the Hebrews had no royal ruler until the priest, Samuel, anointed Saul, so there was no Christian ruler before the bishop of Rome baptized Constantine. The Constantine, in the *Donation* which bears his name, had surrendered all political power in the West to the pope. Honorius then turned around and paid lip service to the doctrine of the two swords and declared that, in purely secular matters, kings should be honored and obeyed. Manegold of Lautenbach (d. 1119) defended the action of Gregory VII in deposing Henry IV because Henry, he claimed, had broken an implied contract with his own subjects and some of his nobles had rejected his rule. Secular governments are necessary and are derived from God, but Henry IV had acted like a tyrant and deserved deposition. This is the earliest known statement of the theory of a contract between the ruler and his subjects. The implications of popular sovereignty here, and the idea that subjects could depose their sovereign, must have been distasteful to the pope and his partisans; Manegold's argument proved too much. On the side of the German emperor, and of lay rulers in general, was Crassus' *Defense of King Henry IV* (1084), in which the author defended the emperor's right to hold his throne through the principle of inheritance of Roman law. In the *York Tracts* (1100), which came out of the controversy over investitures between King Henry I of England and Anselm, the author centered his attack on the tyrannical position the pope had taken inside the church. These tracts show the beginnings of an argument, much used later, that condemned the papacy for using its spiritual authority as a means of earthly aggrandizement rather than as a mission to preach and teach.

In the twelfth century a remarkable revival of the study of Roman law began at Bologna and soon spread elsewhere. The leading spirit was that of Irnerius (d. 1130), the first of a series of great commentators on the Code of Justinian. Irnerius' school of "Glossators," whose main interest was in achieving a correct understanding of

Roman law, was followed, in the thirteenth century, by a school of "Post-Glossators," who undertook a more philosophical study of this law and began to apply its principles to the social, political, and legal questions of their own time. The emphasis of this later school was often on the side of the state. The Code of Justinian naturally contained no references to feudalism and it treated the church as a department of the state; at the same time it looked to the monarch as the source of the whole institutional life of the state. Arguments from Roman law gradually became the stock in trade of those defending the rights of rulers against the church and against the feudality. At the same time, the study of Roman law began to modify the old ideas of law as custom and this brought back the Roman idea that it was possible to create new law. Finally, it revived the Roman idea of natural law as a norm for the interpretation and enforcement of all positive law.

The revived study of Roman law was, in part, responsible for a renewed interest in canon law, the law of the church. In the same twelfth century, Gratian, another teacher in Bologna, compiled his *Decretum*, the first great codification of this law of the church. The *Decretum* brought together regulations taken from the Bible, from the traditions and usages of the church, from precedents in Roman and Germanic law, and, most important of all, from the legislation of church councils and of the popes. Gratian's code came to be recognized as a standard work and remained the basis of all the later study and commentary on canon law. The simultaneous revival of interest in both Roman and canon law helped to define the terms used in political theorizing and, at the same time, it tended to cast political controversies in legal terms. It also reinforced the earlier mediaeval idea that government and law were inseparable, that is, that the government must act under either customary or natural law.

The revival of interest in legal studies stimulated a more profound examination of the local systems of law in various European states. Glanvill (d. 1190), or his nephew, wrote the first treatise on the common law developing in the king's courts in England, *The Laws and Customs of the English Kingdom*. A much more comprehensive work on the same subject was that of another English jurist, Bracton (d. 1268). More clearly than Glanvill, he shows the influence of Roman law, especially in a field like contracts, on which there was little in English law, and in his general terminology. No work of such deep understanding or such scope on English law appeared before Blackstone wrote in the eighteenth century. Bracton's vigorous defense of the supremacy of law in England became an effective weapon against royal arbitrariness in the struggles of the seventeenth century. Something of the same sort of thing that Bracton did for English law was done for law in France by the *Books of Customs and Usages of Beauvoisins* of Beaumanoir (d. 1296). The work shows the influence of Roman and canon law, but it is pervaded by a largeness of spirit that belonged to the author himself. Beaumanoir not only clearly described the laws but he also understood the principles underlying them; the work was lavishly praised by Montesquieu. Nearly all the treatises on Roman, canon, and national law written after the beginning of the twelfth century contain comments on government and on society, and any extended study of mediaeval political and social theory should consider the writers on law along with those more commonly classed as political theorists.

Before the full impact of the revival of the study of Roman and canon law and of the "new Aristotle" had been felt, two popular writers had added their contributions to the protracted controversy. The twelfth century mystic, St. Bernard (d. 1153), in his *De Consideratione*, attacked the papacy for spending so much energy on secular concerns. The function of the pope should be pastoral not princely. Bernard gave a cutting rebuke to the extravagance, frivolity, and worldly ambition of most of the prelates of his time. Political authority has its function, but it should not be in the hands of the church. John of Salisbury (d. 1180), an Englishman, once a student of Abelard and later a teacher and bishop at Chartres, wrote in his *Policraticus* the first extended political treatise since Augustine's *City of God*. The work is diffuse and abounds in digressions and is only partly concerned with political problems. Monarchy is the only type of government he considers, and his political interest is primarily ethical. Throughout this work the influence of ancient writers, especially of Plutarch, Cicero, and Seneca, is much more marked than that of the Bible and the Church Fathers. The author presents almost no comments on the practical organization of government, and, though he lived in a feudal world, he makes few references to feudalism. His insistence is on the necessity of subordinating the state and its ruler to divine law, on the obligation of the prince to obey the laws, and, finally, on the right of a people to be rid of a ruler who is a tyrant. That which distinguished the rightful ruler from the tyrant is his observance of law. He believes in tyrannicide, though he says it must be done without offence to religion, and that the best means of being rid of a tyrant is by prayer.

The political literature of the eleventh and twelfth centuries is indicative of the increase in interest in political questions, but, at the same time, it shows a great vagueness in the use of terms and arguments. Both the apologists for ecclesiastical and for lay authority ransacked the Bible and the Church Fathers, and both drew incidents from history to give what they considered infallible proofs of the rightness of their several positions. The arguments continued in the next three centuries with the terms more clearly defined and with the invention of new reasons to buttress each side.

The thirteenth century showed the church, and especially the papacy, greatly strengthened in power and prestige. The purpose of the church was to weld Christendom into one community, a world state under clerical guidance, each of its worldly rulers recognizing the supremacy of the pope. On the day of his consecration, Innocent III (d. 1216) preached on the text, "I have this day set thee over the nations, to destroy and to overthrow, to build and to plant." [6] Innocent III's activities were all based on his claims to spiritual power, but, in practice, he forced Philip II of France to take back a wife he wished to divorce and obliged John of England to hand over his crown and receive it back as a fief of the papacy. The church also developed in the Mendicant Friars and the universities powerful agents for the strengthening of its prestige among both the masses and the intellectuals. Certainly the thirteenth century seemed to realize all the dreams of both St. Augustine and of Gregory VII.

Another new element that affected political thinking was the recovery of Aristotle's *Politics*. Aristotle believed that the state had a value in and for itself. He also believed it was a law of nature that everything belongs to a hierarchy of values and that the lower exists for and is governed by the higher. These ideas had to be reconciled with the Christian theories of the state. Aquinas (d. 1274) undertook to synthesize the old and the new currents of political and social thought as part of his vast philosophical system.[7] In political theory he strove to harmonize the writers on Roman and on canon law, the theologians, Aristotle, Augustine, Isidore of Seville and others, and something of the political practices of his own time. He represents, as does no other single mediaeval writer, the totality of ten centuries of thought. All knowledge, according to Aquinas, exists in a hierarchy: at the base are fields of special knowledge, above these is philosophy, which seeks to formulate the basic principles of all human thought, and finally, at the top, is divine revelation as found in Christian theology. Revelation is above reason, and reason is above particular areas of knowledge, but these gradations of knowledge and understanding are not contradictory one to another. In the same way, nature forms a vast hierarchy reaching down from God to the lowest being. Each kind in this vast chain of beings seeks, by its own internal urges, to reach the perfection natural to itself. The higher forms of being rule over the lower as God rules over the world or the soul over the body. Everything should, in its place, contribute to the perfection of the whole. Society and the state in such a system exist to perform their special functions in the whole of existence. Aquinas followed Aristotle's belief that man is a social and political animal, and he thus regarded the state, not as the result of the fall of man, but as a natural and God-ordained organization. The state is rooted in nature rather than in sin.

Everywhere in the writings of Aquinas, Aristotle is used as far as he can be, but everywhere he receives a Christian completion. For example, what Aristotle says about nature, about ethical values, and about the state is repeated with approval, though in each case Aquinas goes on to point out that as the world of nature is not the whole world, and as ethical behavior can only be realized in the light of the doctrine of the fall of man and his redemption through Christ, so society and the state are only means toward realizing the kingdom of God. So Aristotle's theories, as applicable only to secular concerns, are accepted, but they are always subordinated to Christian ideas. In all his attitudes toward nature and the world, Aquinas did not share the hostility of many of the Church Fathers. With Aquinas, human experience and reason are not obliterated by revelation but are to be used as tools for building a Christian civilization.

Society and the state represent a mutual exchange of services to which each contributes, the peasant and the craftsman by supplying material goods, the priest and the monk by conducting religious work, and the ruler by governing—a theory first elaborated by John of Salisbury. Each must act in his place, and all relations between classes and individuals must be based on a distributive justice—"to each his due." The art of government is not a mere technique, nor can it be measured merely by its efficiency or apparent success. The means are never, as with Machiavelli, independent of the ends, and the ends are always Christian and ethical. The ruler has a trust from God, on the one hand, and an obligation to the whole community on the other. The ruler, thus, must act according to both human and divine laws. Aquinas seems to prefer an elective and limited monarchy to other forms of government as Aristotle preferred constitutional democracy, and he enlarged Aristotle's ideal city-state to a larger ideal kingdom that has a higher degree of self-sufficiency than a city-state and a greater resourcefulness for defense against enemies.

In spite of the fact that Aquinas' views on society and politics were a deduction from his first metaphysical premises, he often shows some spirit of realism and a consideration of the world about him not common in earlier mediaeval political thought. In some particulars he was quite modern; he believed in the organization of states on a national basis because such states would gain in cohesiveness through having common manners and customs; he believed that the states should provide for the education of their members, and finally that the states should see that no citizen suffers want. Aquinas disliked tyranny and he justified resistance to it, though he warned those who resist to be sure that their action is less injurious to the state than the abuses they endeavor to remove. Aquinas is insistent that the power of rulers must be limited, though he is nowhere explicit as to how this is to be done. What he apparently assumes is that not only will the king act under natural law but he will also consult with the principal men of his realm. In the controversy between the relative importance of ecclesiastical and temporal authorities, Aquinas took the position of a moderate papalist. He believed the church, under some circumstances, could depose a ruler and free his subjects from allegiance to him, but he also believed that the state was in God's plan and that the king was God's anointed. Aquinas, thus, differed from the canon lawyers of his time who were moving away from the Gelasian tradition and were attributing to the church a complete legal supremacy and a direct sovereignty in temporal matters.[8]

Aquinas' discussion of various types of law represents the most carefully elaborated part of his political theory. There are four kinds of law: first, the eternal law, God's reason. This is beyond the grasp of human reason; it is the perfect law that governs the universe. Next is divine law, which is found in the Bible and in the theology of the church; it is a gift of divine grace and could never have been found by reason alone. Beside this is natural law, which God implants in all beings, moving them to preserve themselves and to perceive the difference between good and evil and so to avoid evil. By this natural law men are inclined to organize society and to found states and to rear families. Natural law is common to all men, both Christian and pagan. Finally, human law is the law by which men try to make the other types of law definite and effective in human relations; theft, for example, is condemned by other types of law, but these higher types of law do not provide definite punishments for theft. No law can force the individual into entire absorption in the group, just as in an army a soldier can do certain things that would not be proper for the entire army. On the other hand, Aquinas believed the church should suppress heresy and that the state should aid the church in punishing or executing those convicted of heresy. "If it be just that forgers and other malefactors are put to death without mercy by the secular authority, with how much more reason may heretics not only be excommunicated, but also put to death, when once they are convicted of heresy."[9]

In economic thought, Aquinas, like many mediaeval writers, envisaged a hierarchical social structure based on agriculture. Everyone was assigned to his place by nature; individuals are differently endowed, but the endowment given to each individual is for the benefit of the whole. Any attempt to break away from this natural order was a revolt against what had been divinely ordained. This earthly hierarchy, like the heavenly one, has been established by God. There is, among men, as there is in the universe, a moral unity and solidarity. Every part of the whole must be connected with the whole as well as with every other part in ranks, conditions, and degrees. As Augustine said, "God ordained and made everything, and he ordained everything in different degrees." In a society that changed as slowly as did that of the Middle Ages, this belief that society was a static order of estates seemed reasonable enough; kings, clergy, and nobles above, craftsmen and peasants below should all carry out their reciprocal obligations and all human relations should be founded on the Christian principles of justice, "to each his due," and let all men treat each other as brothers. The main social question Aquinas kept raising was "What is justice?" —justice in the ownership and use of property, justice in trade, and justice between employer and employed.

In accepting the state as a natural institution, Aquinas also took over Aristotle's belief that property is in accordance with natural law. Property, however, must be used to foster the good life as it was defined by the church. Here he uses the old Aristotelian and the early Christian idea that property should be private in possession but should be used for the good of all. The owner is the administrator of his possessions in the general interest, though this administration is left to the judgment of each individual. Aquinas carried this idea so far as to justify theft in cases of extreme necessity. On the other hand, he held that charity, while an absolute obligation, should be left to the conscience of the individual and should be restricted so as to leave a residue sufficient to maintain a man in his status in life. Aristotle had tempered his realistic views of the economic process with metaphysical and ethical ideas. So Aquinas found no great difficulty in grafting Aristotle's economic ideas on traditional Christian thought. Like some of the writers on canon law before him, Aquinas accepted Aristotle's distinction between the natural economy of the household and the unnatural art of money making. With the evils inevitable in an imperfect world, the best that men could do was to apply to the world of trade such principles as would make it work toward good. The calling of the trader is so beset with opportunities for sin that anyone who engages in trading activities of any sort should be mindful of the peril to his soul.[10] Usury, which included both money lending and injustice in trade, is condemned with the backing of a number of quotations from the Bible. Aristotle had also condemned lending money for interest; money arose, he held, as a means of facilitating natural exchange. Usury used money, which was properly merely a means of exchange, as a device for making more money; this was contrary to nature and was unethical. Aquinas, however, recognized exceptions; when a loss had been incurred by a loan, or the chance of a profit missed, then a sum larger than the loan should be paid back. Later on, other exceptions were made. In practice these modifications were in time sufficient to break down the prohibition of usury.[11]

Everywhere, as we have seen, Aquinas' basis of judgment is justice. The whole organization of society is not based on equality, but on a hierarchy of classes and ranks; in this hierarchy each man, by what Aquinas calls the principle of "distributive justice," is entitled to a share of worldly goods. In his theory of price, however, "commutative justice" demands an absolute equality of all men as the determinant factor in fixing a price. Justice demands that the prices of goods and services must always square with their value. Thus it is unjust to sell anything at a higher price than it is worth or to buy anything at a lower price. Aquinas does not analyze the theory of the just price at any length; it was, perhaps, too common a concept of his time. He assumes that the price of an article should include the cost of the materials used and payment for the labor involved, including a fair, living wage. The just price, Aquinas declared, cannot be fixed with complete accuracy, but his insistence on the early Christian idea of the obligation of the seller to inform the purchaser of any defects in the thing sold shows clearly his fundamental idea that no one should take advantage of another. The later Scholastic writers accepted the right of the public authorities to regulate prices, in which case the legal, not the market, price became the just price. On the other hand, they condemned monopoly as a violation of "commutative justice," especially in the case of the guilds who restricted entrance by such devices as high entrance fees. The later Scholastics ceased to view the just price in static terms; they saw that the sources of value are two: scarcity and utility, which agrees with modern theory, the Marxians excepted. They saw clearly that prices were the result of the variable forces of the market, the result of the competition of buyers and sellers. Allowances should be made for differences in persons, places, and times. Actually, the just price was ordinarily the customary price, which did not change rapidly in a customary age.

Along with the theory of the just price went that of the just wage, that is, a wage that would enable the worker to live decently in the station of life in which he was placed. Aquinas, ignoring the elements of supply and demand and competition, refused to regard labor as a commodity to be bought and sold like wares. The remuneration of the worker was to be measured not by the market value of his product, but by the extent of his needs, a doctrine which, if effective, would have kept wages low. The doctrine of the just price hurt the merchant, and the doctrine of the just wage hurt the craftsman. In practice, the economic activities of the later mediaeval centuries, from at least 1100 on, were influenced by the teachings of the church, but they did not always follow them.

Nicholas Oresme, in the fourteenth century, wrote a powerful attack on the practice of debasing the coinage. He calls the prince who does this a "liar" and "a perjurer," and he shows how it drives wealth out of the community and ruins foreign trade. The bad money drives out the good (later called Gresham's Law) and creates economic anarchy. If the value of money is to be changed it should be changed by the Estates General, and not by the monarch. In the use of gold and silver coinage Oresme believed the mint ratio should follow the market ratio. Oresme, in parts of his argument, made a secular and detached analysis of economic phenomena and anticipated some of the modern orthodox monetary theory. The Scholastic arguments on economics were further elaborated in the later mediaeval centuries, though the greatest Scholastic works on economics did not appear until the sixteenth and seventeenth centuries, at the very time when the writings of Descartes and Leibniz were undermining the basic Scholastic ideas.

The political controversies between church and state authorities continued with unabated heat; on both sides more extreme claims were made. The writers on canon law, during the thirteenth century, elaborated the theory of the absolute sovereignty of the papacy, transforming the church's right of spiritual discipline into claims of complete legal supremacy. The theory of *plenitudo potestatis* set aside the theory of co-ordinate powers of Gelasius I until we hear in the bull, *Unam Sanctam*, of Boniface VIII that there is one final power on earth—the pope. The bull comes close to claiming that both swords, the temporal and the spiritual, belong to the pope. Boniface denounced as false the claim that he had asserted that Philip IV of France was answerable to him for his kingdom and was bound to recognize his suzerainty. The king, he claimed, was only subject to him on the ground of sin. The pope was a man of violent temper and unbridled speech, however, and he may well have said what he later denied and what he never would have put into an official document.

An extended statement defending the position of Boniface VIII, though written before the bull, *Unam Sanctam*, is the work of Aegidius Colonna (d. 1316) *Concerning the Power of the Church*. He uses the stock citations from scripture and history but depends mostly on the Aristotelian argument that by a law of nature the higher controls the lower. Political power and the ownership of property are only righteous if they serve good ends and only the church can determine these ends. No one has the right to hold political power or property unless he is in good standing with the church. So in all matters the church must be the final judge, and it may intervene in all cases where either political power or material goods are put to any use that involves mortal sin; "a power," adds the author, "so broad and ample that it includes all temporal cases whatsoever." The most elaborate statement of papal claims is the *Concerning Ecclesiastical Power* by Augustinus Triumphus, written when the papacy had been transferred to Avignon. Herein the pope is described as the representative of God; from his judgment there is no appeal, for the utterance of the pope is identical with that of God. The pope may depose emperors and kings and appoint new rulers if it is for the welfare of Christendom. The pope may exercise direct power over all states; all governments exist only by his permission. Laymen are bound to obey the pope rather than any secular ruler. Only in case the pope falls into heresy may he be deposed and this must be done by a church council. Earlier writers had made as strong claims for the papacy, but their claims had always been couched in less systematic terms. Now, in the fourteenth century, papal claims are set forth more systematically and in more definite and legal terms. It is curious that as the papacy in the fourteenth century declined rapidly in power and prestige, the most exaggerated statements of its claims were set forth.

At the same time, the claims of the papacy were vigorously assailed from a number of points of view. Dante in the *De Monarchia* (1313) revived the old arguments in favor of the independence of the emperor. The work contains little that is new and, like much mediaeval political theory, bears little relation to actual conditions; certainly the mediaeval empire he defends never existed outside of the imagination of its apologists. Dante opposes one set of impossible theories with another set equally impossible. He begins with arguments to show that a unified and universal monarchy, on the old Roman model, is the necessary basis for the advancement of human welfare. Various systems of law and custom are to be allowed to exist inside this universal monarchy, but only in the world monarch can there be found a final court of appeal to bring harmony and peace and order in the world. Dante's argument here is influenced by the anarchy of domestic Italian politics of his own time. Dante next shows, by the use of Roman history and law, that the Roman people acquired their right to rule the world by the will of God. After stringing together a good many rather far-fetched arguments to prove that the Roman people "triumphed by the judgment of God," he proceeds to show that the Holy Roman Empire is the direct successor of the ancient Roman Empire. The third part of the work attempts to prove that the Holy Roman Emperor holds his power from God alone, and to dismiss, with acrimonious remarks, any who would hold that the emperor derived his rights from the pope. Bryce speaks of Dante's treatise as an epitaph rather than a prophecy, but the work has interest because it is the best-known defense written of the imperialist tradition. "In its ideal of a universal empire realizing the notion of the *Civitas dei*," says Figgis, "in its scholastic argument, in its reverence for Rome, the *De Monarchia* is an epilogue, the last and noblest expression of that conception of the Kingdom of God upon earth which gave to the Middle Ages a touch of romance and redeemed its squalid brutality from contempt by its sense of the inherent dignity of human affairs." [12]

The most effective attacks on papal theory came from writers all of whom were, in some degree, motivated by a nationalist dislike of an international power, the papacy. From the twelfth century on there had begun to appear in all the states of Latin Christendom a pride in one's own nation as contrasted with others. This early nationalism was mostly concentrated on the warlike virtues of any given people, and, to a lesser degree, on the general superiority of one civilization above all the others. The nation is centered in its king, the chief of the nation in battle and the symbol of national unity. Loyalty to the ruler becomes a duty, and devotion to country becomes a real affection for one's native land. It is, of course, true that nationalism became much more marked in modern times, but it certainly cannot, from the twelfth century on, be left out of consideration. The growth of nationalist sentiment, the more extended study of Roman law, the growing power of the secular state, and the growth of the middle class all indicated that times were changing and with them the whole climate of opinion.

The emperor and the imperial party proved, in the end, less able to deal with papal pretensions than the monarchs of other states of Europe. From Philip IV of France at the opening of the fourteenth century through Henry VIII of England in the sixteenth century, the papacy had to meet a series of strong attacks from the monarchs of emerging nation-states. This attack was more confident and aggressive than that found in the earlier apologists for imperial and royal independence. The advocates of the rights of the secular state pass from the defensive to an offensive attitude. Backing Philip IV, in his quarrel with Boniface VIII, over matters such as the right of the king to tax the clergy, a quarrel that led to the death of Boniface and the transference for over seventy years of the papacy to southern France, were a number of publicists trained in the Roman law. Unlike most of the earlier mediaeval political writers, they were laymen of the middle class with a secular education and with practical experience in government administration.

John of Paris (d. 1306), in his *Of Royal and Papal Power*, defended the existence of kingdoms independent of the Holy Roman Empire. The church's authority, moreover, should be limited to spiritual matters and the church should use moral persuasion rather than force. The church is only a steward for the property it holds, and all ecclesiastical property should be under the legal control of the monarch. If the pope acts illegally, he may be deposed by a church council. He attacked the whole idea of universal empire, and said the ideal state is a national one. John of Paris tried to find a middle ground between the extremists, and he worked out a realistic and logical compromise which gave to both the church and the state its sphere. He was one of the greatest of mediaeval political thinkers, and later was much studied.

The most extreme of these writers who backed the king of France was Pierre Dubois (d. 1322), a former pupil of the Averroist, Siger of Brabant, and of Aquinas, who, about 1306, published his *On the Recovery of the Holy Land*. Dubois is more strongly nationalistic than any earlier mediaeval writer, and he says, at the outset, that in renewing the Crusades, as in other enterprises, France should take the place of the empire as the leader of Latin Christendom. To put an end to feudal wars, Dubois proposed a general league of nobles and clerics who would employ an economic boycott and, if need be, force to maintain the peace. Controversies between monarchs should be settled by an international court of nine, each side to choose three and the remaining three members to be selected by a board of arbitration. Emphasizing the importance of the state, Dubois insists that the pope and the clergy should confine themselves to spiritual ministrations. He then piles up a long series of proposals for reforms, many of them taken from other writers: the marriage of the clergy; the removal to the king's courts of cases in the church courts; the relinquishment of church lands for an annual pension to the clergy; state control of education for both boys and girls who were to be taught modern languages and science; the introduction of Greek, Hebrew, Arabic, and modern languages into the curriculum of the universities; and the reorganization of the courts, the army, and the coinage in France, all to increase the power of the French monarch who is to be made emperor and is to rule from Constantinople. The book is chiefly remarkable for its insistence on the supremacy of the secular power that was to conquer in the sixteenth century with Machiavelli, Luther, and Bodin.[13] For the first time the end of mediaeval universality, in its traditional form, is clearly and bluntly proclaimed.

After the controversies between the representatives of the king of France and the papacy had waned, a hot conflict flared up between the German emperor and the pope and between the British monarchy and what Ockham called "the Church of Avignon." Also, the papacy entered a controversy with a powerful part of the Franciscan Order, who believed that only enough property to maintain a bare subsistence was an absolute prerequisite to the proper performance of their spiritual work. Indeed, the further one goes into the fourteenth century, the more one sees of conflict of forces and ideals. The synthesis of the thirteenth century is everywhere breaking up. The critics of the existing order often had very little in common; society was becoming more diversified politically and economically, and an anarchy of divergent points of view was the result. In a conflict between two rival emperors in Germany, Pope John XXII refused to recognize either claimant and put forward a third candidate. Lewis the Bavarian, one of the original claimants, finally got the crown. The chief backers of the German emperor, Lewis of Bavaria, against the papacy were Marsiglio of Padua, an Italian at one time rector of the University of Paris, and William of Ockham, an English Franciscan and a famous Nominalist philosopher. The theories of Marsiglio precede his stay with Lewis the Bavarian, and the arguments of both writers were far more anti-papal than pro-imperial.

Marsiglio of Padua (d. 1343) summed up his political ideas in the *Defender of the Peace*, the most original political treatise of the whole Middle Ages.[14] The work shows a number of influences in the background of the author. He draws on the experience of the north Italian communes; he knew their struggles to achieve self-government and the difficulties put in their way by the interference of emperors and popes. He had studied Aristotle's *Politics*; at the same time he had been influenced by the Latin Averroists who relegated religious truth to the realm of faith and believed in studying worldly experience from a point of view independent of religious dogma. Secular questions must be decided on their own merits. Finally, it is evident that he was sympathetic with some of the arguments of the Spiritual Franciscans and with the French and German rulers in their several quarrels with the papacy. He writes in an involved, diffuse, and cumbersome style; he repeats himself, and cites, in a wearisome fashion, masses of quotations from the Bible and earlier writers. All this is characteristic of mediaeval political thought, as is also his curious ignoring of the whole of feudalism, which lay at the basis of so much of mediaeval life. But his ideas were very original, so original, in fact, that they are beyond the range of the current Latin vocabulary; for example, he manipulates phrases and struggles to express the idea of state sovereignty, now a common conception, but for which at the time there was no word. The lack of exact terms, familiarized by usage, is the surest sign of a thinker's originality.

Marsiglio begins by elaborating a theory of the state, based partly on Aristotle, but still more on his own observation. Sovereignty lies with the more substantial citizens meeting in an assembly which delegates the direction of the government to the ruler. For him the essence of the community's authority is the right to make law with coercive force. The vote, in the state, is not to go to every man, but to the *pars valentior*, the weightier part, in which class, position, and achievement are to be the criteria. Votes must not only be counted, but weighed. His own preference is for an elective monarchy, and, as the monarch is elected, so too may he be deposed. There is, logically, no place in his system for an emperor who would possess power outside Germany or for a universal state in a world of different civilizations and languages. The state has absolute sovereignty, and there is no superior power above it. The church should, in all secular matters, be subject to the law of the state. Having defined the position of the state chiefly to enable him to define the rightful place of the church, Marsiglio opens a great diatribe against the usurpations and pretensions of the papacy. The state, which exists primarily to secure internal peace, is everywhere balked by the meddling of the church.

Marsiglio defines the church, not as the clergy, but as the whole body of the faithful, *universitas fidelium*. While denying the desirability of a universal state, Marsiglio accepts the idea of a universal religion and a universal church, but he rejects most of the theory of the existing church, and having established a theory of limited monarchy for the state, Marsiglio set out to do the same for the church. The guiding body of the church should be a church council convoked by the civil authorities, and elected by laymen and ecclesiastics, each province or community to have delegates according to the "number and quality" of its inhabitants. Such a council should have the sole right to define Scripture and would make recommendations for ecclesiastical affairs to be enacted by the state. Marsiglio denies the divine origin of the church hierarchy; in the New Testament the words bishop and priest are used interchangeably. Moreover, St. Peter had no superiority over the other apostles, and it is uncertain that he ever was in Rome. The pre-eminence of the bishop of Rome is based on the historical chance that Rome was the leading city of the old empire. The church should persuade men, but it cannot force belief. God alone is the judge, and his judgment is only exerted in the life hereafter. Any law that involves an earthly penalty belongs only to earthly law and government; Marsiglio's theory abolished canon law as a distinct jurisdiction. In all secular affairs the control of the clergy by the state is in principle exactly like the control of trade or agriculture. The church is under the state in all temporal matters. A priest may warn and threaten; beyond this he has no competence though the state has the duty and the right to suppress heresy in so far as it is against the existing law of state. Marsiglio compares the duty of the clergy to the advice given by a physician. Little wonder that the pope who first read Marsiglio's treatise snorted that he'd never read so great a heretic! His ideas, however, lived after him, and he was often cited during the Conciliar Period, and later by the early Protestant reformers. The spirit of secularism that would free the state from clerical interference, his belief that the state is itself a *societas perfecta,* having within it all the means of the good life, and the spirit of historical criticism, give his work its unique position in mediaeval political literature. As in science and philosophy, so in political thought, the fourteenth century seems more original than the fifteenth.

William of Ockham (d. 1349) shared some of Marsiglio's views, though he is both more complex and less radical. His theories are hard to define exactly because they are spread out through a series of works which cover many subjects.[15] Moreover, his method of presentation is one that gives all sides of an argument full analysis, often without any very clear indication of his own belief. The Nominalism of Ockham, while avoiding the extremes of the Latin Averroists, held that many aspects of human experience could be understood by reason alone. Like Marsiglio, Ockham opposed the ideas of papal absolutism as a heretical innovation that did not belong to the early church, and he upheld the complete independence of the empire and the national kingdoms from the control of the papacy. Especially, he disliked the arbitrary use of power by either the church or the state; however, in the state he believed that the ruler was ultimately bound by customary, and natural, law, and by this common utility Ockham, like many thinkers of the fourteenth century, believed a reform of the church was only possible through a general church council. Marsiglio had proposed the introduction of laymen into church councils—apparently a novel suggestion. Ockham worked out an elaborate project of a whole series of councils starting with parish assemblies of all beliefs who would choose delegates to a larger district council representing all of Latin Christendom. At the basis of Ockham's thought is an extreme relativism and a despair of all institutions which make him end with a belief in the right of private judgment, that in the last analysis the judge of right can only be the mind and conscience of the individual.

Wyclif (d. 1384) in England took an anti-clerical and nationalist tone somewhat like that of the French publicists who backed Philip IV against Boniface VIII; he was also influenced by Ockham. Wyclif's basic principle is found in his theory of dominion. God is the supreme possessor of all things, and by God man is assigned his duties. The proper use of power and possessions and the performance of these duties legitimize men's actions before God. And upon God every individual is directly dependent. The position of the church is merely one of convenience. Wyclif defended the right of the monarch even to disendow the church and denied all the political claims of the clergy. Hus spread Wyclif's theories in Bohemia, which became a center of reformist ideas in central Europe. Both Wyclif and Hus show the fusion of nationalism, mysticism, and the desire for religious reform that was to dominate the Lutheran Revolt. Ockham's works seem to to have been more widely read than those of Marsiglio of Padua or Wyclif, though all were very influential in the whole Conciliar Movement and in the Protestant Reformation.

The fifteenth century politically and economically saw the modern world taking shape. Everywhere the national idea as against a universal empire and papacy was evident. Even the church councils were organized now by "nations." France and England became strongly centralized monarchies, Spain was united, and in Germany and Italy many highly centralized petty despotisms were set up. In each case, the power of the nobles and of the church was restricted by the monarch. The English Parliament, the French Estates General, and the Spanish Cortes were sharply curbed by energetic kings of the type of Henry VII, Louis XI and Ferdinand of Aragon. Alongside this striking growth of monarchy went the increasing significance of the middle class, which became the mainstay of the crown in limiting the political power of the nobility. The papacy, first in exile at Avignon as a puppet of the French monarchy, fell next into a schism with first two, then three popes pronouncing anathemas at one another and the various governments taking sides. After a series of church councils the schism was healed, but the church never again regained the power and prestige it had had before the downfall of Boniface VIII. A new political, economic, and cultural order was coming into being; this was only partly reflected in political theorizing which still concerned itself chiefly with questions about the organization of the church.

The spectacle of a divided Christendom deeply disturbed all thoughtful men and led them to devising remedies. Out of the Conciliar Movement came an enormous controversial literature, at the heart of which lay the question of the nature of sovereignty in the church. Gerson (d. 1429), the leading theorist connected with the Council of Constance (1414–18), was a reformer rather than a revolutionary. Only an overruling necessity in the condition of the church led him to propose remedies. He shows no sympathy with the radical theological doctrines of Wyclif and Hus, and he rejects the more revolutionary aspects of the theories of Marsiglio and Ockham. He believed that the government of the church should remain in the hands of the church hierarchy, though the supreme power in the church should reside in a general council, and the papacy should become a constitutional monarchy. The pope in his system shares his power with the council, and is, in some circumstances, subordinate to it. The pope should normally act under law, as, earlier, the arbitrary action of the papacy, in clear defiance of its own canon law, had undermined respect for both the law of the church and for its head. After a single pope was agreed upon at Constance, and the three other claimants disposed of, a reactionary papal party tried to destroy the changes made by the Council of Constance, especially the decree

Sacrosancta that declared a council the supreme governing body of the church. This drove the defenders of the Conciliarist theory of church government to take a more left-wing position.

On Catholic Concord by Nicholas of Cusa (d. 1464) is a more vigorous defense than that of Gerson of the limited monarchy idea for the church. According to Nicholas, the church is a perfect society which contains within itself the means to correct its errors. The *Donation of Constantine* is a forgery and the pope is not absolute master of the church. The acceptance of those to whom law applies is the only basis for validity in any law. So he carries on from his defense of the right of a church council to control the papacy to a full exposition of a general doctrine that authority must rest on the consent of the governed. "By nature," he says, "men are equally strong and equally free." His basic principle of a necessary harmony in all political, as in all human, relations leads him to insist that his idea of consent does not abolish the important and necessary role of the executive. Each power in the whole church must act in a co-ordinate way; no officer or body should take power that belongs to another. All derive their powers from the whole community. Even the most extreme partisans of the conciliar idea thought that power should be shared jointly by pope and council; none proposed to destroy all the monarchical power in the office of pope. In his theory of representation, Nicholas falls back on the stock mediaeval idea of representation by classes. So his popular sovereignty in practice means an assembly of nobles and higher clergy; the magnates stand for the lesser men. He makes the suggestion, as had Marsiglio and Ockham, that representatives be chosen in specific constituencies preferably by an election. By 1443 the Conciliar Movement had failed either to reform the church or to modify its government, and the ancient absolutism of the papacy had been reconstituted. From the end of the Conciliar Movement in 1443 to the outbreak of Luther's revolt in 1517 the papacy enjoyed a sort of Indian summer. The papacy was re-established by the middle of the fifteenth century as the first absolute monarchy, and the theory and practice of papal absolutism became the model for royal absolutisms in the sixteenth, seventeenth, and eighteenth centuries. At the same time the Conciliar Movement was the seed-ground of modern liberalism, for it was the first great public debate of the values of constitutionalism against absolutism. Its theory that power inheres in the body of the believers was ultimately transferred from the church to the state. The road from the church councils of the fifteenth century to 1688, to 1776, and to 1789 is a direct one.

During the five centuries between 1000 and 1500, all the western European states developed parliamentary institutions. England, however, proved, in the course of time, to be the only state that brought over from mediaeval into modern times the institutions of limited monarchy and a live and effective parliamentary tradition. For this reason, a special interest attaches to the last great mediaeval political theorist, Sir John Fortescue (d. 1476). This English judge wrote the first two treatises on the English constitution as distinct from the more purely legal expositions of earlier writers. His *Governance of England* and his *On the Praise of English Law* show how the law and the customary political usages of England prevent royal tyranny. "The king," he says, "has the delegation of power from the people, and he has no just claim to any power but this." Again he writes, "The king of England cannot alter nor change the laws at his pleasure, for he governeth his people by power, not only royall, but politique," or constitutional as we would say. He is curiously indifferent to problems of the relation of church and state; his outlook is secular and his argument is constructed largely without benefit of Scripture or theology. He is full of praise for the English polity where the monarchy is limited by parliament, the privy council, law, and the courts. He observes correctly that England is a limited monarchy, while France has become an absolute one. Living in the anarchy of the Wars of the Roses, he saw that the nobles would have to be curbed by the monarch, and he foreshadowed the policy later carried out, after 1485, by Henry VII. He is modern in that he writes realistically about English political usages; in this he shows new attitudes that became clearer in Machiavelli a half-century later. Looking beneath the surface of things, Fortescue realized that the causes of national difference in legal and political institutions must be sought in underlying difference of economic and social conditions; in this he is an important precursor of Bodin and Montesquieu. His defense of limited monarchy made him next to Bracton, the most quoted mediaeval writer in the struggles of the seventeenth century in England. Then, looming through the mists of time, Fortescue seemed to the generations from Coke to Locke a sort of Isaiah of modern liberty.

3. MEDIAEVAL SCHOOLS

AFTER the Barbarian Migrations of the fifth century, it was chiefly the Christian bishops who kept schools alive in the Latin West. Their efforts were aided by some surviving secular schools, especially in Italy and, for a time, in Gaul, and by schools conducted by the monasteries. By the sixth century, the secular schools of Gaul disappeared; Gregory of Tours writes: "The culture of liberal letters is declining, or rather perishing; one would not know how to find a single man instructed in dialectic or grammar." [16] In Italy, lay schools survived both the Ostrogothic and Lombard migrations; there seems to have been no real break in the history of these Italian schools which taught grammar, the art of drawing documents and writing letters, Latin literature, and law. Thus, there never ceased in Italy to be schools conducted by laymen for laymen. The teachers in these Italian schools, as in Roman times, were supported by the fees of their pupils and, sometimes, by payment from the state. In the bishops' schools, small groups of boys were admitted as boarders in the bishop's household, usually when they were about the age of seven. Here they remained as part of the episcopal household until the age of eighteen, by which time they were obliged to decide whether they would join the clergy. It was the intention of the church that youths so educated should take holy orders, and the majority did so in all the mediaeval centuries. In the cathedral churches, in monasteries, and in some parish churches, to secure boys for the choir, song schools were conducted. The boys usually were given board and elementary instruction in the elements of the faith, singing, spelling, and a little Latin grammar, all in return for their services as choristers. With the revival of town life, which became marked in Italy by the eleventh century, the towns began to set up more municipal schools to teach boys reading, writing, and arithmetic, all of them useful in business. From Italy, these municipal schools spread all over Latin Christendom until by the fourteenth century they had become common.

Literacy steadily improved after the Carolingian Renaissance and still more after 1100. Before 1100 it was exceptional for an English king to read or write Latin; in the twelfth and thirteenth centuries, the monarch was usually able to read Latin if not to write it; and, in the fourteenth and fifteenth centuries, the English monarchs were taught in their youth to read and write Latin, French, and English. The instruction of rulers and nobles was usually the work of the chaplain attached to the royal or noble establishment. Certainly from the twelfth century on large numbers of laymen could read. The idea that only clerics could read is a myth about the Middle Ages that dies hard. Actually some clerics, especially parish priests in country districts, could not read, though laymen could read. By the fifteenth century facilities for rudimentary instruction were so distributed as to reach even smaller towns and villages in most sections of Latin Christendom. Coulton estimates that, in the early sixteenth century, there were 26,000 pupils in schools in England out of a population of five million. In the monastic schools little attempt was made to educate anyone but prospective members of the order, though occasionally a layman or a man destined for the secular clergy received his early instruction in a monastic school. The greatest service of monastic schools to general education was in supplying learned monks to the episcopate where as bishops they were well-equipped to teach the youths of their households. In all such schools the teaching depended on the learning and capacity of the bishop or priest or monk.

Educational opportunities which were very uneven before Charlemagne had been extended and regularized during his rule. At his court, Charlemagne had maintained both an academy made up of the greatest men of learning he could find, and a palace school, which had been founded earlier, for the education of his own children and a selected group, some of whom later became important bishops and abbots in the empire. Charlemagne and his successors worked hard to increase the number of episcopal and monastic schools and to improve the instruction given in them. The capitularies of Charlemagne are filled with instructions for improving education even down to directions for every priest to run a school. The program was ambitious, but the lack of teachers and funds and the backwardness of the times meant that Charlemagne's orders were only in small part fulfilled.

Down into the twelfth century, which saw the beginnings of universities, the cathedral schools were the most important organs of instruction. After about 1000, the great cathedral schools of northern France and the Low Countries—Paris, Chartres, Laòn, Rheims, Tours, Orléans, Liège, and Utrecht—and schools of secular canons, especially that of St. Victor in Paris, produced more great scholars and more educated men than the monasteries.

In the eleventh and twelfth centuries, the cathedral school of Chartres was the finest in Latin Christendom. The teaching was primarily along literary and theological lines. In the teaching of Latin literature great emphasis was laid on stylistic matters, and the pupils were trained to write Latin prose and verse based on the great Roman classics. The spirit of the school of Chartres is shown in John of Salisbury, one of its greatest teachers: "Most delightful in many ways is the fruit of letters that, banishing the irksomeness of intervals of place and time, bring friends into each other's presence and do not suffer noteworthy things to perish. For the arts would have perished, laws would have vanished, the offices of religion would have fallen away, and even the correct use of language would have failed, had not the divine pity provided letters for mortals. Who would know the Alexanders and Caesars, or admire Stoics and Peripatetics had not writers signalized them? The light of fame endures for no one save through writing. Besides all this, solace in grief, cheerfulness in poverty, modesty among riches are bestowed by letters." [17] John of Salisbury was the master of all the Latin literature extant in the twelfth century. Virgil he regarded as the world philosopher who, in the form of an allegory, expressed the truth of all philosophy. He admired the flowing verses of Ovid and emphasized the ethical teaching of Horace, Juvenal, and Terence. Seneca he considered almost a Christian. Above all the others he admired Cicero. John's desire was to unite religious faith with classical culture. His literary taste was excellent, though his chief interests were in the ethical values of the ancients whose wisdom he believed was of great worth to society. John's point of view was that of an ardent Christian Platonist and humanist. After the twelfth century the universities took the lead in higher education, though the cathedral schools continued to instruct most of the candidates for the priesthood.

The curriculum in all the schools, high and low, was based on part or all of the seven liberal arts. These had been described by Martianus Capella, had been divided by Boethius into the *trivium* and the *quadrivium,* and named by Cassiodorus "the seven liberal arts," all in the early Middle Ages. They consisted of grammar, rhetoric and dialectic, the literary studies, and arithmetic, geometry, astronomy, and music, four scientific studies. There is no evidence that all seven were fully presented in any school between the time of Cassiodorus in the sixth century and the School of Chartres in the eleventh, but some parts of the seven liberal arts one would find in every school.

The young pupil began with grammar, "the science," says Rabanus, "which teaches us to explain the poets and historians, and the art which qualifies us to speak and write correctly." This meant first learning the Latin alphabet, pronunciation, and the parts of speech, and involved endless repetition and the committing to memory of a large number of rules. Explanations in Latin gradually took the place of those given in the vernacular; then manuals of conversation, and readers with fables, proverbs, bits from the Church Fathers, and the Psalms were introduced. And so the pupil acquired his first speaking and reading knowledge of Latin, and along with this he would memorize rules of grammar, commit passages of poetry to memory, and learn to write in Latin. Virgil being considered the chief master of style, the older students devoted much attention to his verses. John of Salisbury describes the teaching of grammar he received as a youth at Chartres. His teacher, Bernard of Chartres, he says, "not only read the authors with his pupils, but explained constructions, pointed out mistakes and beauties in the text, elucidated matters of antiquity, asked the pupils to judge and criticize, made them memorize passages and write original exercises in prose and verse." [18] The grammatical textbooks used were those of Donatus and Priscian; along with these, after 1100, the *Doctrinale* of Alexandre de Villedieu circulated extensively. It was all in verse and easy to memorize, and it recognized changes in Latin since the time of Priscian. In the course of the twelfth century, the study of grammar and rhetoric in advanced schools declined; the pupils were more interested in studying science, medicine, law, logic, and philosophy. This is shown in the decline in Latin style in the thirteenth and fourteenth centuries, which in turn led to a revival of interest in style in the humanist movement of the fourteenth and fifteenth centuries.

The study of rhetoric grew directly out of that of grammar, and, except for the first stages when the pupil was learning to read and write, went along with it. Roman rhetoric had laid its chief emphasis on oratory; mediaeval rhetoric was mainly interested in teaching the pupil to write letters and to prepare documents. In an age when the ability to write was not a common accomplishment the capacity to write a good letter and to make a contract, a will, or a bill of sale was of great importance. This art was commonly called "ars dictandi" or "dictamen," meaning training in how to write private and official prose. Handbooks with model letters and legal documents were the ordinary textbooks. The great development of "ars dictandi" in the eleventh century spread from Lombardy, where it apparently developed for business purposes. In Italy, an "ars notaria" also developed, especially for legal purposes; out of this came, in the twelfth century, the revived study of Roman law. In some schools rhetorical studies along more purely stylistic lines were pursued. The pupils spent much time in writing Latin prose and verse compositions; for school verses the favorite textbook was Bede's *De Arte Metrica*, an encyclopedia of metrical forms. Here again the most notable schools were the cathedral schools of northern France, above all those of Chartres, Paris, and Orléans. The study of logic, which completed the *trivium*, was hardly more than what would now be called a formal study of the means of clear and consistent thinking, including the power to detect identity of meaning under different expressions, the power to make fine distinctions, and the grasp of all a proposition implies. The favorite textbooks in dialectic were the logical manuals of Boethius and his translations of the *Categories* and the *De Interpretatione* of Aristotle. Usually metaphysical problems were not a part of the study of logic, or, as it was usually called, dialectic.

All parts of the *trivium* were restricted by the fact that the students were always working in a language that was removed from common speech. Even the greatest minds lost something in sharpness of perception and in suppleness of expression by having their ordinary concepts in one language and their professional thinking in another. The use of Latin meant that ideas could have a wide currency across all frontiers and it kept mediaeval men in contact with the sources of their culture, but, on the other hand, it may be doubted whether any half-dozen scholars ever met who could discuss in Latin with all the shades of thought as readily and completely as modern men can meet and discuss in their own vernacular.

While it is undoubtedly true that the *trivium* occupied the major part of the study of the liberal arts, the traditional opinion that the *quadrivium* was hardly pursued is far from being true. Especially after the twelfth century, more emphasis was placed on the *quadrivium*. Arithmetic consisted first of the simple processes of addition, subtraction, multiplication, and division. With the introduction of the abacus in the eleventh century—with Roman numerals at the top of vertical columns to show the order of units, tens, and hundreds—and of Arabic numerals in the twelfth and thirteenth centuries, the teaching of arithmetic could be speeded up. Arithmetic also usually included methods for determining Easter and the movable feasts of the church. Geometry was, at first, on a very elementary level, for before the twelfth century only the propositions of Euclid, without the proofs, were available, and only a few operations, such as the calculation of an angle, could be performed with these. The favorite textbooks in both arithmetic and geometry, before the twelfth century, were those of Boethius. From the twelfth century on, not only was all of Euclid recovered but Arab treatises on geometry were also introduced into the West. Along with these came a revival of Roman methods of surveying. As a result, pupils could be taught to compute the areas of triangles and circles and polygons. The study of geometry traditionally also included some rudimentary instruction in geography. The most popular subject in the *Quadrivium* was always astronomy. It consisted of instruction about the course of the sun, the moon, and the stars, and the change of seasons; often based on an outline of practical astronomy by Bede. As arithmetic usually contained some instruction about number symbolism, so the astronomy taught usually included a little astrology. Music, the last subject of the *Quadrivium,* was classed by mediaeval men as a theoretical science, mathematical in character. Boethius' *De Musica* was the favorite textbook. Along with theories of music, there was usually studied something of the art of choral singing, and sometimes the playing of an instrument.

Some elementary instruction was often given also in medicine; this consisted of recipes and various simple home remedies.

In all of the study of the liberal arts, many subjects were neglected which were taught elsewhere by mediaeval men and women to the young. The training of the gentleman and of the noble woman in the castle, the education of the youthful prince in statecraft, the intricacies of a skilled trade, and, among the peasants, the methods of farming and of running a household were all learned outside the schools. As a boy, a nobleman was left until the age of seven to be trained in good manners by the women of his father's household. From seven to fourteen the youth acted as a page either in his father's castle or in that of a neighboring lord. Menial services were expected of the boy, and he was taught to ride, to hunt, to jump, to swim, and to fight. The chaplain was supposed to teach religious principles, and he sometimes taught the boys, and more rarely the girls, to read and write. At fourteen the youth became a squire, at which time his outdoor training became more strenuous, and he might even be taken into some fighting. Girls were taught how to sew and embroider, to spin and weave, and to run a household. Some of them learned to read, and like the boys, some acquired from travelling musicians the ability to play a harp or viol and to improvise songs.

In the later Middle Ages, from the later thirteenth century through the fifteenth, schools increased in number and improved in quality. Now nearly every cathedral church had a song school, a grammar school in which some boys were taught to read and write Latin, and a higher school for the training of priests. Parish schools were also more numerous. A common form of piety was to found a chantry with an endowment for a priest to say masses for the souls of the founder and his family. It became a practice to add to the duties of such chantry priests gratuitous teaching of boys. The endowment of schools being regarded by the church as a good work, some schools were founded with the chantry feature either subordinate or absent. From the thirteenth century on, the curriculum was improved as new textbooks were available, such, for example, as the whole of Euclid, Arabic treatises on algebra and trigonometry, Ptolemy's *Almagest* and Arabic astronomical books and tables, Avicenna's *Canon of Medicine*, new dialogues of Plato, and much of the writings of Aristotle. The craze for the new Greek and Arabic science and philosophy, in the cathedral schools, drove grammatical and rhetorical studies into the background. Quarrels ensued between those who believed in a humanistic training and those who were more interested in dialectic and science. In this "battle of the seven liberal arts," as contemporaries named it, dialectic won the upper hand, though humanistic studies never disappeared.

In southern Germany, the Rhineland, and in France, grammar schools were founded by the guilds and by the town governments. In the Low Countries, the lead in improving education was taken by a new religious order, *The Brethren of the Common Life*, who began as popular preachers; gradually they came to enter the field of teaching. In the schools where they taught, and in those they influenced, great attention was given to selecting the headmasters and the teachers, and, in the instruction, much emphasis was laid on training the character of the boys. Out of the two most remarkable schools influenced by these Brethren, those at Deventer and Zwolle, came Thomas à Kempis, Nicholas of Cusa, Agricola, and Erasmus. The Mendicant Orders were both interested in scholarship, and in the thirteenth century they captured many of the teaching positions in the new universities. Like the monasteries, they educated few who were not to join the order, but their importance for the history of education lay chiefly in the thorough training they gave their own members.

The last new impetus to primary and secondary education in the later Middle Ages came from Italy. Petrarch and others in the fourteenth century revived the educational ideals of the School of Chartres. They attacked the great emphasis of the schools on logic, and their worship of Aristotle, and believed more attention should be placed on reading the literary masterpieces of Roman antiquity. Early in the fifteenth century, Quintilian's treatise on the training of the orator, Cicero's work on oratory, and Plutarch's treatise on eloquence were recovered. The emphasis of all of these works was on literary studies and on the attention to be given in education to moral training. Most of the Italian schoolmasters and writers on education take their ideas from these three treatises.

These Italian educators of the fifteenth century turned away both from the emphasis on dialectics that had prevailed in the schools since the thirteenth century and from the previous intellectual and physical asceticism. They wished to train men for this world and for service in the state. Guarino da Verona (d. 1460), a pupil of the great humanist Chrysoloras, spent some time in Constantinople where he learned Greek and collected a library of Greek works. After his return he set up a school for the Este family at Ferrara. Here great emphasis was placed on Greek and Latin literary studies. Among his methods was that of having his pupils write letters to him; these were carefully corrected and discussed in class. Greek and Latin literature, he believed, contained profound truths, and a close study of them would enable a youth to converse with the great intellects of antiquity and enter into their spirit. Guarino believed in reasoning with his students and in reducing sharply the amount of physical discipline used. Everywhere he tried to arouse the positive interest of his pupils and to bring them into active co-operation in the whole educative process. The first lessons in spelling were taught by movable letters; arithmetic was learned by games. Emphasis was laid on the necessity of studying the personality of the child and adjusting the teaching to it. As the students grew older, more music, mathematics, and natural science were studied. Guarino's school won fame all over Europe; even from faroff England came Grey, later the Bishop of Ely, Free, later the Dean of Wells, and Tiptoft, Earl of Worcester, to study his methods.[19]

Many of the same ideas were put into practice by Vittorino da Feltre (d. 1446) at a school set up for the Gonzagas of Mantua. Vittorino added an emphasis on regular physical exercises, on diet, and on personal habits, and so he threw over the whole mediaeval idea of the worthlessness of the body in favor of a program of securing a harmony of the flesh and the spirit. Schoolmasters of this type believed that a thorough training in the Greek and Latin classics was the most practical way to make a complete and useful citizen. The study of Aristotle, Demosthenes, Cicero, and Caesar would show them the problems of politics and administration. Classical literature, too, would mould character and personality, and would be a safeguard against self-indulgence and the vulgar idea that pleasure is the end of life. Long passages of classical poetry, of the Bible and the Church Fathers were learned by heart, and these were the basis of teaching both literary style and ethics.[20] Schools of this sort inspired some theoretical writing on education; these treatises and the schools themselves attracted wide attention. In the early sixteenth century, Erasmus helped to spread the new ideas, and it was from him that Colet got the inspiration for the reorganization of St. Paul's School in London.

4. THE RISE OF UNIVERSITIES

"UNIVERSITIES," writes Haskins, "like cathedrals and parliaments, are a product of the Middle Ages. Only in the twelfth and thirteenth centuries do there emerge in the world those features of education with which we are most familiar, all that machinery of instruction, examinations, and academic degrees. In all these matters we are the heirs, not of Athens and Alexandria, but of Paris and Bologna." [21] The oldest university or center of advanced studies was that of Salerno, which grew out of a medical school that may have descended from antiquity. From the tenth through the twelfth century, a number of remarkable teachers attracted students there, and the proximity of Salerno to the Muslim and Byzantine worlds evidently acted as a stimulus. The control of the school was in lay hands though ecclesiastics studied and taught there. By the twelfth century, the course was well-organized in a five-year cycle of studies. The first great seat of medical studies outside Italy appeared in the University of Montpellier, founded in the thirteenth century. In the same century, medical faculties were established at Bologna and Paris and in a few other centers. Here the study of medicine failed to fulfill the early promise of the School of Salerno, for it was severely restricted by the application of scholastic deductive methods and by the slavish acceptance of such Greek and Arabic medical textbooks as were available.

The University of Bologna grew out of a local law school, of which there were a number in northern and central Italy. Young men interested in the study of law began to flock to Bologna in the twelfth century to study Roman law with Irnerius and canon law with Gratian. The students organized into corporations to protect themselves against high rents and prices, and they laid down rules for their teaching. In the universities of Italy and Spain the students organized first and hired their teachers. If the professors did not live up to their regulations they were fined or dismissed. No professor could be absent a day, unless he were ill or wanted to be married, though only a single day's leave was allowed in the latter case. So much of the subject had to be covered in each specific term of the year. No teacher could spend weeks on introduction and bibliography—or, for that matter, on auto-biography. Regulations of this sort indicate that the students were paying their money to receive professional training which they expected to use shortly as teachers, lawyers, doctors, or priests.[22] This organization of students, which preceded any effective faculty organization, became a common practice in Italian, Spanish, and southern French universities. At Bologna, as at other Italian universities, the studies were primarily practical, such as medicine and law. Theology was not commonly taught in the Italian universities until the four-teenth century, and the control was usually in the hands of laymen. The teachers lived primarily on the fees paid by their students.

The mother of northern universities was the University of Paris, which grew, in the twelfth century, out of the cathedral school of Notre Dame. The recovery of Greek and Arabic learning and the brilliant teaching of Abelard, and others who just preceded him, at-tracted students in droves. The chancellor, the bishop's officer who controlled the school, found it hard to manage as it spread from the island in the Seine to the south bank of the river. To protect them-selves, the elementary faculty organized and appointed their own head, the rector. Thereupon a struggle ensued between chancellor and rector until the university finally got free of the bishop's control and became an autonomous body. Eventually the rector of the faculty of arts became the head of all the faculties. Four faculties were finally constituted: an elementary faculty of arts and advanced faculties of theology, canon law, and medicine. The organization of the Univer-sity of Paris became the model for northern universities. So famous did this university become that men said, "the Italians have the pa-pacy, the Germans have the empire, but the French have learning." To Paris came the Italians Bonaventura, Aquinas, and Dante, the German, Albertus Magnus, and the Scotsman, Duns Scotus. No uni-versity has ever had the international prestige that belonged to the University of Paris in the thirteenth and fourteenth centuries. The University of Oxford apparently arose out of a "migration" of discontented students who, about 1167, left Paris because of quarrels over the prices of books, clothing, and lodging. There was already a school at Oxford, but the migration transformed it into a "studium generale" or university. The University of Cambridge resulted from a similar migration from Oxford. Other universities were founded by princes and by prelates; the first university beyond the Rhine was that of Prague (1348), the first university in Germany was at Heidelberg (1386). By 1500, there were seventy-seven universities in Latin Christendom.

The earliest universities were slow growths. They had no definite founders, and the dates chosen for their beginnings are arbitrary. The first degrees given were certificates to teach, the master's and doctor's degrees; the bachelor's degree came later. Originally this last degree covered only studies in the *trivium*. The curriculum included most of the seven liberal arts in an advanced form, and, in the superior faculties, theology, medicine, and law. Among the advanced courses of study that in theology was the longest; at Paris it came to cover thirteen or fourteen years, and no student less than thirty-five could be made a doctor. Before the student, in the classroom, was his textbook, usually with wide margins in which he could write. This textbook was often the most expensive item in his budget. The professor then made a detailed commentary on this fundamental text. A teacher of law at Bologna gives a clear picture of the method. "First, I shall give you summaries of each chapter; secondly I shall give you a clear statement of the purport of each law included in the chapter; thirdly I shall read the text with a view to correcting it; fourthly I shall briefly repeat the content of each law; fifthly I shall solve apparent contradictions, adding any general principles of law." [23] The method trained students in thoroughness and taught them to make fine distinctions. It meant, on the other hand, taking learning too much on authority. Mediaeval men commented on their learning endlessly, but rarely doubted anything. Their learning was, at once, too disputatious, and too dogmatic. Moreover, the curriculum included no Greek or Hebrew until the end of the Middle Ages, no modern languages, no social sciences, and no laboratory work. Examinations were taken at the end of a four- or six-year course; no wonder the students compared them to the Last Judgment. [24]

The earliest universities had no buildings, except the hired rooms in which instruction was given. By the thirteenth century donors began to establish colleges, in which the students lived and, in some cases, in which instruction was also given. It remained only for the university to give examinations and to grant degrees. The Sorbonne, for example, takes its name from an endowed house for poor theological students established in Paris by Robert de Sorbon, a chaplain of St. Louis. On the Continent, wars and inflation ruined the endowments of the colleges and they died out; in Oxford and Cambridge they survive as the basis of the whole institution. Most university students outside Italy had taken the tonsure and were classed as ecclesiastics; as a result they were usually tried for offenses in church courts. The universities were always trying to free themselves from the control of both church and state and to direct completely their own affairs. This is one of the reasons that led the early universities to collect charters, confirming their rights and privileges, from kings and prelates.

From their letters and verses, from university and college statutes, and from conversation manuals to help students over their difficulties, we catch glimpses of student life. Town and gown squabbles and riots were common, the quarrels usually arising over love affairs or over prices charged the students by the townsfolk. Less blood was shed on many a battlefield than has been spilled on the main streets of old university towns like Bologna, Paris, Oxford, and Heidelberg. Many student letters beg for money; an Oxford student wrote home: "The city is expensive and makes many demands; I have to rent lodgings, buy necessities, and provide for many other things which I cannot now specify. Wherefore I respectfully beg your paternity that by the prompting of divine pity you may assist me, so that I may be able to complete what I have well begun. For you must know that without Ceres and Bacchus Apollo grows cold!" In turn, a letter of a father to his son says: "I have recently discovered that you live dissolutely, preferring play to work, and strumming a guitar while the others are at their studies."[25] More serious types of students are also represented, men who, by studying diligently and gaining the most from their university training, were later to make some important and distinguished contributions to the fields of medicine, law, and theology. On the other hand, a pretentious fledgling writes, "It took me two hours and a half to deliver my first lecture but no one showed the least sign of fatigue and the next day all the seats were taken by eleven o'clock though my lecture did not start till one!" Most of the students who flocked to the mediaeval universities were poor; it did not become fashionable to be educated till after 1500. They had hard times collecting the wherewithal to pay for their clothes and keep and their textbook. Some lived in colleges which began as endowed boarding halls established by well-to-do donors; others found quarters in such corners as they could afford. The houses of monastic orders and of the friars usually supported one or two of their members at a university. In the larger universities these students lived in Benedictine, Cluniac, Franciscan, and Dominican houses of study. They often represented the pick of the house which sent them, and were usually serious students.

A typical day at the University of Paris in the thirteenth century began at five or six o'clock in the morning when the great bells of the Cathedral of Notre Dame rang out the call to work. From the neighboring houses, the students would pour out into the narrow streets, and betake themselves to the bare lecture halls. Here the beadles saw that the straw on the floors was properly arranged, and in some of the halls, that the benches and seats were in order. The students, in the meantime, were filing in either to occupy the rows of hard benches, or to sit on the straw on the floor, their knees raised to serve as desks. The teacher entered, mounted the platform, and started a series of lectures that, with short interruptions, went on for hours. The students took notes on wax tablets, and then, later in the day, copied and reworked this material on parchment sheets. In the afternoons, the great playing meadows that stretched out beyond the city walls, along the banks of the Seine, were the busy scene of the games of all the nations of western Europe: running and jumping matches, wrestling, quoits, ninepins, ball games, swimming, and sometimes just plain fights. The evenings were spent at study, or in the taverns with which the university towns abounded. Except for late revellers, the curfew sent students and citizens to bed at nine o'clock. The hard-working youths left few records, just as the serious student of today rarely gets onto the pages of the newspapers. We know that the early universities trained large numbers of young men who soon became the leaders of their professions in law, medicine, and the church, but unfortunately we know little about their student days. Only here and there do we catch glimpses of the conscientious student. A professor from Bologna describes "a student who rises with morning bell, is the first to enter and the last to leave the classroom, who often spends days in his room reading, who ponders his lectures at mealtime, and even argues in his sleep." Then there's Chaucer's student, the clerk of Oxford, "who had long gone to lectures on logic. He had at his bed's head twenty volumes of Aristotle; of study he took most heed and care. Not a word spoke he more than was needful and that little was modest. All that he said tended toward moral virtue. Above all things he loved to learn and to teach." [26]

The evidence that does endure mostly portrays the wasters. Large numbers of university and college regulations survive; some of these give vivid glimpses of student deviltry, like the rules of New College, Oxford, against throwing stones in chapel, and those of the University of Leipzig which list fines for students who throw missiles at the professors. The students quarreled among themselves. At Paris groups of students often had pitched battles. As one writer says, they taunted each other thus: "Some affirmed that the English students were drunkards, the Germans obscene, the Normans boastful, the Burgundians stupid, the Romans slanderous, the Sicilians cruel, the Flemish fickle, gluttonous and slothful." If the students contended among themselves so did the professors; a preacher of the thirteenth century says, "professors are like fighting cocks, ever ready to fly at each other." A number of student letters and Latin exercise books, ranging from the twelfth into the sixteenth century, survive. By far the most common appeal was that for money. "There never will be a letter that does not ask for cash," writes a weary Italian father of the fourteenth century. Other letters assure papa and mamma that all goes well. "This is to inform you," write two youths from Orléans, "that we are living in good health and are devoting ourselves wholly to study mindful of the words of (the Roman) Cato, 'to know anything is praiseworthy.' We occupy a dwelling next door to the schools, so that we can go to school every day without wetting our feet."

Student pranks often appear in letters. Here's a picture of a student lodginghouse in Paris, five hundred years ago. "One day I saw the mistress of the house quarreling with the servant girl. Tongues clashed, the battle of hot words swayed to and fro. The girl then came to make the bed. I praised her courage for standing up so bravely. 'I would fight her gladly enough,' she said, 'if I were only strong enough.' 'Tear off her false hair,' said I, 'and seize hold of her own hair.' I thought no more about the matter. While we were at supper, in runs a man; he cries 'come and see a bloody piece of work.' We find maid and mistress struggling on the ground, handfuls of hair lying littered about. We separated them. I congratulate myself that I was not suspected" (of putting the maid up to such tricks). We catch glimpses of love affairs; one student writes, "I was at church and saw a certain girl, when she turned, and looked back at me; my heart melted; my whole being was set on fire, so that I did not know what to do." All sorts of other matters appear in letters. We hear about the fat Italian friar who came to preach, about begging at the doors of the wealthy, about singing or playing at parties for food and pay, about the juggler and the dancing bears in the marketplace, about the relative merits of veal and beans in one lodginghouse as against those in another, and about the student who quarreled with his roommate over a misplaced book. Letters and statements from parents and other older people often take a severe tone. One parent writes indignantly, "I have learned, not from your master, but from a certain trustworthy source, that you do not study, nor act in the schools as a good student should, but play and wander about, indulging in sport and in certain other dishonorable practices which I do not now care to explain by letter." The preachers were particularly severe on the subject of student behavior. One describes a student who had learned nothing, but started back home with a load of books with which he hoped to impress his family. His pack horse fell into a stream, and the books were lost, and, the preacher thunders, "what knowledge is this, which thieves may steal, mice or moths eat up, fire or water destroy?" Another preacher of the early thirteenth century flayed students of the University of Paris as "bandits, who, at night, run armed about the streets, and commit adultery, rape and robbery." Other preachers condemn the lazy students who wander from school to school, who care only for a good time, who go to classes but once or twice a week, choosing by preference those courses that allow them to sleep late in the morning. "They are wont," writes a monk, "to roam about the world, in Paris they seek liberal arts, in Orléans classics, at Salerno medicine, but nowhere manners and morals!" That the pranks of the students were not always severely judged appears in a letter of a professor at Orléans written to a student's father, "No doubt your son was one of a crowd that sang bawdy songs; what of it? The young man's general record is good, and he is making excellent progress in the law."

Student verse abounds, much of it of a very worldly tone; one jibe is of the "Gospel according to Marks of Silver." Many gay drinking songs have survived, including a parody on Aquinas' "Hymn to the Lord's Supper." Other verses tell of springtime and joy, of love, of poverty, and of sorrow. Here are verses in a gay mood:

> *"Cast aside dull books and thought;*
> *Sweet is folly, sweet is play;*
> *Take the pleasure spring has brought*
> *In youth's opening holiday.*
> *Right it is old age should ponder*
> *On grave matters frought with care;*
> *Tender youth is free to wander,*
> *Free to frolic, light as air."*

Now a few fragments from a drinking song:

> *"Topers in and out of season*
> *Pass the wine-cup; let it be*
> *Filled and filled for bout on bout!*
>
> *Those who cannot drink their rations*
> *Go, begone from these ovations!*
> *Here's no place for bashful boys;*
> *Like the plague, they spoil our joys.*
>
> *If there's here a fellow lurking*
> *Who his proper share is shirking,*
> *Let the door to him be shown.*

> *When your heart is set on drinking,*
> *Drink on without stay or thinking*
> *Till you cannot stand up straight,*
> *Nor one word articulate!"*

Another short drinking song runs thus:

> *"In the public house to die*
> *Is my resolution,*
> *Let wine to my lips be nigh*
> *At life's dissolution,*
> *That will make the angels cry,*
> *With glad elocution,*
> *'Grant this toper, God on high,*
> *Grace and absolution.'"* [27]

And now a student sings of spring and love:

> *"The woods are green with branches*
> *And sweet with nightingales,*
> *All flowered are the dales.*
> *Sweet it is to wander*
> *Sweeter to pluck roses,*
> *But dalliance with a lovely lass*
> *Far surpasseth these.*
>
> *And yet when all men's spirits*
> *Are dreaming on delight,*
> *My heart is heavy in me,*
> *And troubled at her sight.*
>
> *If she for whom I travail*
> *Should still be cold to me,*
> *The birds sing unavailing,*
> *'Tis winter still for me."*

Some fall in love and get over it; with others the darts of Cupid have struck deeper. Here is an echo of a forgotten tragedy of the twelfth century:

"Low in thy grave with thee
  Happy to lie
Since there's no greater thing left
  Love to do;
And to live after thee
  Is but to die.

Peace, O my stricken lute!
  Thy strings are sleeping.
Would that my heart could still
  Its bitter weeping!"

Coulton estimates the maximum number of students at Oxford as 1500, and at Paris as 2000, and Rashdall goes further and says there were two or three thousand at Oxford and four or five thousand at Paris. Then he makes the striking remark: "It is probable a larger proportion of the population received a university education at the close of the Middle Ages than is now the case in modern countries." [28] The students ranged from mere boys to high dignitaries of mature age. Probably two-thirds never graduated, and of those who took the bachelor's degree much less than half went on to take the master's degree. Only a handful went on to take a degree in theology, the most exacting of all mediaeval scholastic disciplines.

The universities nevertheless played a great role in European culture. They influenced the policies of governments and of the church. Canon law was chiefly the creation of Rome and Bologna, the theology and philosophy of the church was largely shaped at Paris, and early modern science, after 1200, was, to a great extent, the creation of the universities of Oxford, Paris, and Padua. The University of Paris took the lead in ending the Great Schism and in starting the Conciliar Movement. Through the influence of the universities, Roman law was made to supplant a good deal of the old customary law in northern France and in the German states. Everywhere the universities ended by putting much of the direction of public and private affairs into the hands of educated men. The university, too, was often the road that led upward for the poor youth who possessed energy and ability. Rashdall concludes:

"When all allowances are made for the mixed motives which drew men to the universities, when we have allowed for the coarseness and brutality of the life that was lived in them, when we have admitted the intellectual deficiencies of their most brilliant products, the very existence of the universities is evidence of a side of the Middle Ages to which scant justice has been done—their enormous intellectual enthusiasm. The popular conception of the Middle Ages is far too favorable on the side of religion and morality, far too grudging on the intellectual side. The universities represent one of the greatest achievements of the mediaeval mind, not only on account of the value of their intellectual products, but as pieces of institutional machinery. And the institution has outlived a large part of the culture which it originally imparted." [29]

CHAPTER IX

Literature (I)

1. THE EPIC TRADITION

2. LYRIC POETRY

3. CHIVALRIC ROMANCE

THE SURVIVING literature of the early Middle Ages in the West is all in Latin; only beginning with the eighth century has some vernacular literature been preserved. From this time on, all mediaeval literature may be regarded as Janus-headed: one mouth speaks types of Latin literature, out of the other proceeds the vernacular literatures. Back of both, however, there is a common civilization and very much of a common mentality. It has long been the custom to divide mediaeval literature by the languages in which it happens to be written.[1] A more reasonable classification is one that separates it into literary genres: the epic, the lyric, romances, the drama, the short story, history and biography, and symbolic literature. In such a classification it becomes clear that not only is the division of literature into genres more fundamental than the arbitrary division by languages, but also that such a division by literary forms corresponds, in a rough fashion, to its division by social classes. The cloister, the cathedral school, and the universities produced primarily devotional, historical, philosophical, and scientific works. From the home of the chieftain and, later, from the castle, came the epic, to be followed by the aristocratic love lyric and the chivalric romance. The town and its bourgeois world early be-

320]

came the patron of the drama and the fabliaux. As the middle class grew, learning came to be more diffused, and after 1300 the town became the home of literary geniuses of the type of Dante, Chaucer, Petrarch, and Villon, whose works often cut across a number of literary forms.

Alongside the Latin literature of the learned, vernacular literature developed, and each profoundly influenced the other. Many authors wrote in both Latin and their native speech, and, even for those who wrote exclusively in one language, there are everywhere evidences of the influence of writings in the parallel language. For example, stories, figures of speech, and systems of metrical construction move from Latin literature into the vernacular literatures, and also the other way around. The forms of mediaeval Latin were kept in an approximate uniformity through the study of grammar and the use of the old Roman classics as models of style. Of course, this usage varied considerably from century to century, and from one country to another. In contrast, whole families of vernacular dialects—Germanic, Romance, Celtic, and Slavic—grew and changed for centuries, without benefit of schools, dictionaries, or grammars. Any one of these dialects was spoken only by a comparatively small group of people. The dialect was useful to the group in daily life and in the telling of stories, but often people a few miles away could not understand it. The local dialects, until the later Middle Ages, also had variations in spelling and syntax and were without the vocabulary a scientist or a philosopher needed. This is one of the reasons why for so long—indeed into the seventeenth century—men frequently wrote in Latin. The influences of commerce, government, and schools, and sometimes of great books from the fourteenth century on, finally made one dialect dominant. So the dialect of the Ile de France came to be the national speech of France, that of Tuscany the national language of Italy, that of Castile the national speech of Spain, that of the Midlands the national language of England, and, after 1500, that of Saxony, the national speech of Germany.

This survey attempts to treat mediaeval literature, especially imaginative literature, as distinct from writing in the fields of philosophy, science, mysticism, and political thought, as a general cultural manifestation of Latin Christendom from the eleventh century through the fifteenth. From these five centuries a huge mass of writing, good, bad, and indifferent, has survived, out of which only a small selection can be described. This literature is interesting and often very beautiful; much of it, like Romanesque and Gothic art, remains as one of the great achievements of the West. It is important, also, because many of the literary forms of modern times, while influenced by the literatures of Greece and Rome, really had their beginnings in the mediaeval centuries. In this literature we see the whole range of mediaeval life from the gutter to the stars. "If," says one modern critic, "the Middle Ages conjure up in your mind glowing old folios of black letter with gilt initials, crimson, and green, and blue, in which slim ladies with spiked head-dresses walk amid spare flowers and trees like bouquets, or where men-at-arms attack walled cities no bigger than themselves, or long-legged youths, with tight waists and frizzed hair, kiss girls under apple-trees; or a king on a dais with gold lilies for his background, minstrels on their knees before him, lovers in the gallery, you get sheer beauty. Only there is another side. The Middle Ages comprised all these things—the knight-errant and the inquisitor, the altar and the witches' sabbath, loveliness and squalor. These centuries were, in the words of Rabelais, 'both enormous and delicate,'" and all of these things are reflected in their literature.[2]

I. THE EPIC TRADITION

IN the Middle Ages, as among the Greeks, the earliest extant native literature is the epic or tale of great deeds. These long narratives, in verse and later also in prose, combine history and folk-legends so that it is impossible to tell where one leaves off and the other begins. The earliest epics were intended to be heard rather than read, hence their stock repetitions which remind the hearer just where the story stands. Some of the Teutonic narratives are concerned with tales about the Germanic peoples before, during, and after the great migrations of the fifth and sixth centuries, and they use, as a common verse convention, alliteration and assonance, as we have already noticed in the case of *Beowulf*. Nearly all the epics are primarily stories of fighting. They show great admiration for physical courage and loathing of physical cowardice. In the earlier epics, little mention is made of women, and the epics apparently were addressed primarily to an audience of men. Most manifest some Christian coloring and also the influence of Virgil. All of them, as in the case of all literature until well into modern times, show the influence of patronage, clerical, royal, or noble. Indeed, much of mediaeval literature is marked by propaganda; it was written for persons and coteries and often for special occasions: victories, marriages, or great political events. A literature apart from patronage became possible only in the later Middle Ages with the rise of a middle-class reading public, and it was helped by the spread of printing and the cheap multiplication of books.

The performer of a mediaeval literary work, at least before a reading public arose in the thirteenth century, might be either an author or a professional entertainer, a minstrel or jongleur. In the center and north of Europe the climate did not encourage an open-air reciting of stories as frequently occurred in ancient Greece. The winter enforced longer hours of leisure, amusements were few, and men welcomed the storyteller whether he were a professional entertainer, a travelling pilgrim, a monk, or a friar, who, besides telling tales, was also the purveyor of rumors and news and the carrier of gossip. An account of the thirteenth century lists the sixteen pleasures of the feudal nobleman: hunting, fishing, fencing, jousting, playing chess, eating and drinking, listening to the minstrels in the castle hall, talking with the ladies, holding a court of justice, walking over his lands and observing his crops and flocks, being bled by the doctor, warming himself by the fire, attending church festivals, and watching the snow fall! No wonder the nobles got bored and wanted to hear stories and to go on fighting expeditions and to wander off on pilgrimages or crusades.

Next in time to the Anglo-Saxon lyrics and stories in early mediaeval Teutonic literature are the Scandinavian eddas and sagas in verse and prose. These stories of gods and men date from about 900 to 1250, and they survived only in Icelandic manuscripts. Probably the oldest in form is the *Elder or Poetic Edda*,[3] a collection of thirty-four poems, uneven in quality and dealing with Norse mythology, historic legends, and moral teachings. They seem to have been composed between 600 and 1100 and written down in the form in which they survive between 900 and 1150. The *Poetic Edda* is little influenced either by Graeco-Roman or Christian ideas, and brings us closer than any other work to the mentality of the early Germanic peoples. The collection opens with the *Sibyl's Vision* (*Völuspá*), sometimes called "the Scandinavian Genesis." In this poem, an inspired prophetess tells her revelations about the creation and the ultimate destruction of the world, how there will then arise a new green earth out of a purging fire, and in this new world the great hall of the gods will shine in splendor. It is a combination of the grandeur of Genesis and the imagery of the Book of Revelation. Evidently the work of a poet endowed with great imagination and a rare mastery of form, the poem implies an earlier literary development lost to us. The style is direct and virile, passionate, intense, glowing with color and full of ruthless action, with elemental passions working in elemental strength. The expression is often too condensed; all is movement, there is no pausing, no seeking for incidental beauties, and no elaboration of ideas.

The rest of the first part of the *Poetic Edda* concerns other affairs of the gods; here are the *Sayings of Odin* (*Hávamál*) a sort of Scandinavian "Book of Proverbs," and a powerful story of Thor (*Thrymskvitha*). The second part contains stories of heroes, including tales of Sigurd (Siegfried) which Wagner made the basis of his "Ring." The chief historic characters are Ermanaric, king of the East Goths, Attila the Hun, Gundobald the Burgundian, and Theodoric, the East Goth. Religion is elemental; love is often an animal urge. Hunting is both a diversion and a necessity; war is the business of life. A second form of Icelandic poetry is called *Skaldic* from *skald,* the name for poet; it was written mostly from the ninth through the thirteenth century. It is largely occasional poetry, praising kings and mighty men and celebrating events like the receipt of a shield, the events of a journey, and the death of a notable person. There is little about love and much about fighting. Vengeance, physical prowess, and pride are monotonously in the foreground. *Skaldic* poetry shows both Christian influence and some of the elaborate conventions developed by Irish Celtic poetry. There is little refinement in all this early culture, and few arts besides woodcarving and metalworking.

More epic in quality are the prose sagas, the best of which were written between 1175 and 1250. These are concerned chiefly with the tales of men who lived in Iceland from about 870 to 1025. The sagas mix history and mythology and legend; a few are love stories, but mostly they tell of fighting, of family life, and of adventures at sea. The outcome is often tragic, but there are usually touches of affection and humor. The common man often figures; in this way the sagas are more democratic and more concerned with the whole life of a people than is most mediaeval literature. When each character is introduced, his appearance and traits are described in summary fashion; all the rest is action with no reflections on character, motives, or situations. But in their actions the characters are highly individualized; some are lazy, some industrious, some quarrelsome, some shrewd, others stupid, some generous, and some stingy. Many of the sagas are magnificent narratives. They are full of marvellous imagery; a warrior is a "tree of battle," a ship is "ocean's high-stepping steed," and a sword is a "flame of light." Most sagas show marked organizing ability in handling the story; no saga is a jumble of unrelated facts as real life often is. Perhaps the finest of the sagas is the *Story of Burnt Njal*, written about 1220, a stirring tale of man's struggles with his fellows and with faith. Its sense of the dignity and pathos in the lives of ordinary men and women makes it universal in its appeal.

The last important work of Norse literature, the *Young or Prose Edda*, written in the thirteenth century by an Icelandic chieftain, Snorri Sturluson, consists of a collection of mythological stories and a handbook for writing poetry, with many examples. The latter shows a common belief among primitive peoples that the ability to make poetry is not so much a natural gift as the result of study and practice in which success can only be obtained by the careful observance of established rules of composition. The Norse peoples regarded the ability to make verse very highly; when the king of Norway, who died in 1066, enumerated his eight accomplishments, he put first "I know how to make poetry," placing it above his skill in riding, swimming, and fighting.

Comparable in its importance as a work of literature to *Beowulf* and the greatest Scandinavian stories in the early history of the Germanic literatures is the *Nibelungenlied*. It was written by an unknown Austrian poet about 1200, who worked over early Germanic legends and other tales about the Burgundians and the Huns of the fifth and sixth centuries and combined with these the style of chivalric romance newly introduced from France—a strange mixture. There is more here of court manners, of women, of love, and of Christian ideas than in *Beowulf*, the Norse stories, or the French *chansons de geste*. The poet was a man of genius and from these divergent materials he produced a masterpiece. The epic contains some powerful writing; everything is told in action, the diction is simple, and there is a quick brevity and lack of ornamentation about the great moments. When Siegfried dies, "the flowers on every side were wet with blood. With death he struggled, but not for long, since the sword had cut him all too sorely. Then a lusty warrior and a brave could speak no more." [4] After Siegfried's murder, his wife, Kriemhild, marries again. But her love for Siegfried, and her hatred of her own brother and his vassal, Hagen, who are responsible for Siegfried's death, eat into her soul. She has her second husband invite all of her own family on a visit. A terrible slaughter ensues, Kriemhild kills her brother, and, in turn, is herself slain; in the end "dead bodies lay stretched over all." The poem concludes on a note of profound melancholy: "At the last, all joy turneth to sorrow."

A second German epic, the *Gudrun*, probably written about 1240 in Austria or Bavaria, is related to the *Nibelungenlied* somewhat as the *Odyssey* is related to the *Iliad*. In the *Nibelungenlied* the tragic fate of Troy has its counterpart in the total destruction of the Burgundian royal house; in the *Gudrun*, as in the *Odyssey*, we have the adventures of various individuals and, through the whole poem, the ways of the sea and the beat of the waves. The tone is milder and more humane than that of the *Nibelungenlied*; it is also less well constructed and less a work of art. In both works women play a larger role than in *Beowulf* and the Norse stories.

The French *chansons de geste* belong to the twelfth and thirteenth centuries; over eighty have survived of which about thirty deal with Charlemagne and his ancestors, with their wars against the Saracens in Spain and Italy, and against rebellious nobles, and even with a wholly fictitious journey of Charlemagne to the Holy Land. Other *chansons* are about the Crusades, and some, like *Raoul de Cambrai*, about feudal wars; a few formed parts of a cycle. A number were composed to exalt the fame of a famous pilgrimage shrine, others to extol the reputation of a great baronial family. Many of them paint a lawless society, rude, ferocious, pious, and superstitious, a society with few arts except poetry. They show the inability of the church and the central government to keep the peace. Only occasionally is there mention of a woman. Sometimes there is an amusing touch, as when the pope, in one *chanson de geste,* appeals for help against the Saracens, and promises the prince that if he sends aid he may eat meat all the days of his life and take as many wives as he will.

The greatest of these French epics, and one of the supreme works of mediaeval literature, is the *Chanson de Roland,* which exalts Charlemagne as a great religious leader and which is undoubtedly influenced not only by the older epic tradition but also by the traditional saint's life. It was probably written by a monk in Normandy about 1100; besides telling a great story with edifying examples of heroism and Christian faith, it may have been composed to stir up interest in maintaining the new crusading states in Palestine. The epic has about four thousand ten-syllable lines, each with a pause after the fourth syllable; it uses alliteration and assonance, two traditional Germanic poetic conventions. The narrative is divided into sections—*laisses*—varying from five to eighty lines, to mark a unit in the action or in the poet's thought. These divisions also helped to avoid tediousness for the reciter and for his audience.

The *Chanson de Roland* describes events of the eighth century, mainly a fight at the pass of Roncesvalles in the Pyrenees where Charlemagne was backing one Moslem faction against another. This becomes a holy war of the cross against the crescent. The events took place in 778 but the whole atmosphere of the epic is of the eleventh century. Here we have the devotion of the feudal vassal to his lord, the ceremonies of knighting, and the Christian hatred of the Saracen that belongs to the age of the First Crusade. The poem throbs with crusading ardor. The atmosphere is stern; Roland is betrayed by Ganelon, one of his company, and is killed by the Saracens. Charlemagne then returns to avenge him. Whereas, later, the best of Arthur's Round Table is "the courtliest knight" and again "the gentlest man that ever ate in hall among the ladies," Charlemagne says of Roland: "for the arraying and winning of great battles never has the world seen the like; none are as brave as thou art." Roland, himself, sums it all up with the remark, "better be dead than a coward be called." Miraculous elements, borrowed from the saints' lives and passed on later to the chivalric romance, are scattered through the poem. Charlemagne is spoken of as two hundred years old, his campaign of a few months becomes one of seven years, the blast of Roland's horn carries for thirty leagues, and, when Roland is about to die, a tempest sweeps all France.

The *Roland* is written with a self-conscious art. It is a vast fresco of heroism, of the devotion of Roland and his men to their lord, Charlemagne, of devotion to the country, "la douce France," and, finally, of devotion to God.[5] All is action; there is only one simile and but a few lines of reflection and comment. Roland, the main character, is vividly portrayed, as he develops through suffering. He is rash and headstrong in the beginning but tired and compassionate at the end, when he speaks forgivingly even of his foes. The tale of Roland became one of the favorite mediaeval stories. When the Black Prince defeated John, the king of France, in 1356, men said, "if we had another Charlemagne, he would find a Roland." Chaucer describes a traitor as "a very Ganelon," and Dante thinks of Roland's horn in the *Inferno* when he hears a trumpet, "So loud it turned all thunder faint." Ganelon, Dante placed in hell, but Roland he set in Paradise. St. Francis praised Roland and his friend Oliver, who "died in battle holy martyrs for the faith of Christ." Men wove the story into tapestries, carved it on their churches, and, as at Chartres, told the tale in stained glass. So among both the intellectuals and the common people, the tale of Charlemagne and Roland lived on; as Dante says, they were heroes who "on earth were of so great fame that through them every muse was made rich." [6]

The great Spanish epic, the *Cid*, tells the story of a Christian hero who fought the Saracens through many vicissitudes and died in 1099. Within less than fifty years after his death, this warrior had passed out of history into legend. The Cid, the champion, became a legendary hero for Spain, as Arthur was for Britain, Siegfried for Germany, and Charlemagne for France. The author, who was evidently a priest and wrote in the Castilian dialect, had read Virgil's *Aeneid* and the *Song of Roland*. The hero was a historical character, as was also Roland, but the story follows the sequence of known events much more closely. The *Cid* is more matter of fact, and is not as fine a work of art as the *Chanson de Roland*. It stands as the first great work of Spanish literature.

Among the Celts of Ireland, and among the Slavic peoples of eastern Europe, especially the Russians, Poles, Czechs, Serbs, and Bulgarians, there was an early tradition of composing epics, and from each of these peoples, epic poems have survived. The earliest Irish literature, which parallels Anglo-Saxon literature, is preserved in manuscripts written in the eleventh century, but the works themselves seem to have changed little after the eighth or ninth century. The early Irish stories are told in prose, interrupted from time to time by verses intended to be sung as lyrics. In addition to a large number of hero tales, there have survived other narratives and some lyric verse. Early Irish prose and poetry is highly unreal; the writers are inclined to desert the natural and the possible for the supernatural and the impossible, and there is much fantastic exaggeration. Perhaps the most striking note of this early Irish literature is the vividness of imagination shown by the writers. Some of the Celtic stories, like that of Tristan, and the method of treating them entered the main stream of European literature in the twelfth century. The epics and hero tales, like the chivalric romances later, were spread by travelling entertainers who went from castle to castle, and, after the towns grew up, from one market place to another. In western Europe, the epics went out of fashion in the twelfth and thirteenth centuries, and their place was largely taken by the chivalric romances.[7]

Somewhat resembling the epic was the ballad, a popular verse form of the later Middle Ages. The ballads, of which a large number have survived in all the languages of western Europe, but of which the most interesting group is English, are anonymous poems less extensive than the epics and usually written in short stanzas of two or four lines. (The ballad stanzas were usually moulded to fit a recurrent melody.) The ballads ordinarily deal dramatically with a single situation and take a story at its climax. Often they use dialogue. Like the epics they are impersonal in tone, the interest is in the story, and little comment is ever added. Ballads, like other folk tales, have moved freely from country to country, and it is usually impossible to tell in what country and just when a ballad originated. The best ballads combine vigor, freshness, and artlessness; some of them rise to the level of great literature.

2. LYRIC POETRY

THE TWELFTH and thirteenth centuries, which were marked everywhere by a quickening of new activity, and which saw the birth of universities and Gothic art, saw also the transformation of old literary forms and the creation of new ones. By the eleventh century accentual verse and consistent rhyme schemes through a whole poem had become common in Latin poetry, though, alongside of this type of verse, some Latin poetry, following the old quantitative verse tradition, continued to be written. *Goliardic* verse is the most interesting secular Latin poetry. Much of it was written by men who later became ecclesiastics, doctors, lawyers, and teachers. As youths, they moved freely from one school to another, seeking small preferments and living off their wits. "They are wont," wrote a monk of the twelfth century, "to roam about the world and visit all its cities, till much learning makes them mad; for in Paris they seek liberal arts, in Orléans classics, at Salerno medicine, at Toledo magic, but nowhere manners and morals." The Goliardic poets mixed the language of the classical and Christian Latin poets with that of the market place and the barroom. Golias, a Rabelaisian figure, was the mythical head of an imaginary order devoted to gaiety and fast living. As we have seen, this verse reflects the student life of the older cathedral schools and of the growing universities. These contemporaries of the French troubadours and trouvères and of the German minnesingers showed great skill in their verse forms, preferring the stress rhythm and rhyme that had slowly crept into Latin poetry to older verse forms. The Goliardic poets hold their fame through their *joie de vivre* and through some of their verses which, as Raby says, are "of unmatched obscenity"; they deserve fame also for other types of verse, love-poetry, laments, and spring songs.

The religious poetry shows more contrasts with classical Latin poetry than is shown in the secular verse. Among the great religious poems of the twelfth century is Bernard of Morval's *On the Contempt of the World*, a favorite mediaeval title for books of devotion. From this poem of three thousand lines, comes our well-known hymn, *Jerusalem the Golden.*

> *Jerusalem the golden*
> *With milk and honey blest,*
> *Beneath thy contemplation*
> *Sink heart and voice oppressed.*
> *I know not, O I know not,*
> *What joys await us there,*
> *What radiance of glory,*
> *What light beyond compare.*
>
> *They stand, those halls of Zion*
> *Conjubilant with song,*
> *And bright with many an angel,*
> *And all the martyr throng;*
> *The prince is ever in them*
> *The daylight is serene;*
> *The pastures of the blessed*
> *Are decked in glorious sheen.*[8]

Abelard wrote a number of remarkable lyrics lamenting the loss of friends and a few hymns in which he created verse forms as bold as the new philosophical ideas he expounded in the schools. In both cases he broke away from tradition but left no immediate successors.

The supreme achievement of twelfth-century Latin religious poetry —and perhaps of all mediaeval Latin poetry—is the *Sequences* of Adam of St. Victor (d. 1180), a monk in a monastery in Paris famous for its cultivation of mysticism and for a number of writers including Hugo and Richard of St. Victor. These devotional poems of Adam of St. Victor are notable for their perfection of form and their closely packed content. They contain a great deal of symbolism and some rather abstruse theology. The whole visible universe appears to Adam as rich with hidden meanings. The return of spring is a symbol of the resurrection of Christ; nature is one vast allegory as are also the works of man. The subject is the feast of an apostle or a martyr, the festivals of the Virgin, Easter or Christmas; the author usually keeps strictly to his theme; and his verses have less obvious appeal than do those of the Franciscan poets of the thirteenth century. Adam of St. Victor, says a modern historian, "may indeed be considered the father of modern poetry, for he is the first writer who uses with any real art the two-syllabled rhyme on which most of our effects depend." [9] The supreme dogmatic poem of the Middle Ages is Aquinas' *Lauda Sion Salvatorem*, a doctrinal exposition of the doctrine of transubstantiation. Aquinas wrote other hymns; indeed, a number of great figures of the twelfth and thirteenth centuries, like St. Bernard and St. Bonaventura were as famous in their own time for their religious poetry as for their other activities.

The Franciscan movement, which was a rich inspiration to art, called out the most-known of all mediaeval Latin poems, the *Stabat Mater* and the *Dies Irae*. The *Stabat Mater*, the lament about Mary at the foot of the cross, is probably the work of Jacopone da Todi (d. 1306), who is also famous for some of his vernacular religious poems, the *Laudi*. No mediaeval hymn is more tender or more moving. The Franciscans humanized the Bible stories in both art and literature, especially those connected with the Virgin Mary and the sufferings of Jesus. These subjects were now handled with a personal and poignant touch. Christ is no longer the king, but the man of sorrows, with the thorns piercing his brow and the blood streaming from his wounds. No detail of his misery is spared, "for," as one writer said, "it ought not to weary us in meditating on these things, which it wearied not the lord himself to endure for us." Mary is presented as worn with sorrow, her eyes red with weeping, and her hands clasped in anguish.

> *By the cross, sad vigil keeping,*
> *Stood the mournful mother weeping,*
> *While on it the saviour hung;*
> *In that hour of deep distress*
> *Pierced the sword of bitterness*
> *Through her heart with sorrow wrung.*
>
> *Print, O mother, on my heart,*
> *Deeply print the wounds, the smart*
> *Of my saviour's chastisement;*

> *He who, to redeem my loss,*
> *Deigned to bleed upon the cross*
> *Make me share his punishment.*[10]

The *Stabat Mater*, later, became part of the liturgy of the church, and there are modern musical settings by Pergolesi, Haydn, Rossini, Verdi, and Dvorak.

The *Dies Irae* of Thomas of Celano (d. 1255), one of the early followers of St. Francis, a poem which concerns the Last Judgment, has been called the greatest poem in the Latin language. "This tremendous scene, pictured in stone above the doorway of so many churches, or in glorious colors in the western window, where the rays of the setting sun gave it an unearthly glamor, profoundly impressed the imaginations of generations of Christian people. The church built up the great drama of the graves opening at the sound of the trumpet, the resurrection of the body, and the appearance of all men in the flesh before the Judge." [11] The poem is a miracle of condensation and verse construction, combining sound and sense as do few poems in any language. A line like "Tuba mirum spargens sonum" (the trumpet sounding) is matchless. The poem consists of eighteen stanzas of three lines each, rhymed in triplets, except the last stanza which has six lines.

> *Dies irae, dies illa*
> *Solvet saeclum in favilla*
> *Teste David cum Sybilla.*

> *(The day of wrath, that dreadful day,*
> *Shall the whole world in ashes lay,*
> *As David and the Sibyls say.)* [12]

The fusion of sound and sense is, however, so complete that any translation seems faint beside the Latin original where blow follows blow like a hammer on an anvil. One writer translated the *Dies Irae* six times, but found that his last version had not carried him an inch beyond the first. The poem was later incorporated into the "Requiem Mass" of the Roman Church. The *Sequences* of Adam of St. Victor, the *Stabat Mater*, and the *Dies Irae* are worthy to stand beside the

Gothic cathedral and the *Divine Comedy* as representing the supreme achievements of the mediaeval genius. After the thirteenth century, Latin religious poetry, while still written in quantity, never again reached this high level. By the fourteenth century the Latin language could no longer compete with the vernacular languages of Europe, and the great talents from now on usually wrote in their own speech.

A new style of vernacular poetry arose in the south of France at the end of the eleventh century. In style and content this troubadour verse of Aquitaine, Gascony, Languedoc, and Provence dictated to much of the lyric poetry of the later Middle Ages and of modern times the course it was to follow. The immediate background of this flowering of poetry, which uses both stress rhythm and rhyme, is found in popular vernacular verse, in secular and religious Latin poetry, and in the Arab poetry of Spain. The earliest surviving lyric poetry of the south of France is religious and didactic. By the end of the eleventh century a passionate type of love poetry began to appear, written by men who called themselves troubadours (from a verb meaning to find or invent). The first troubadour, Count William of Poitiers, must have known the Latin poetry of Fortunatus which glorified women; he may have known Ovid's *Art of Love*, a treatise on the arts of seduction, and he may have learned something of the style of Arabic love verse.

For the twelfth century we know the names of nearly five hundred troubadours, about half of whom were nobles. Their verses show they were written for an aristocratic audience where wealth, refinement, and the influence of women were all marked. It is a sophisticated and self-conscious, even an artificial, world in which the poet writes, a world wonderfully portrayed in *Aucassin and Nicolette*, an early thirteenth-century, northern French tale written in prose and verse. The troubadours developed some nine hundred different forms of stanza construction; few schools of lyric poetry in all of world literature ever showed a more intense interest in technical perfection. As a result their poetry often falls into obscurity, artificiality, and excessive mannerisms. The poets were also musicians, and their verses were set to music which was often sung to a viol or lute accompaniment.

The favorite theme of the troubadours is love, but they also wrote short tales of adventure, funeral laments, satires on political persons and problems, and other sorts of occasional pieces. Hardly an aspect of love was left unexplored, though the favorite theme was one in which the lady was married and unhappy and the poet adored her secretly. This courtly love condones adultery, though the love it exalts is one that sought a union of hearts and minds and not of bodies. The lady is passive, though as the style moved to northern France and to other European states, the lady becomes more active and does not stand by merely to be adored. The devotion of the lover to the lady derives something from the devotion of the feudal vassal to his lord; indeed the troubadour love code has been called the "feudalization of love." It owes much to Latin poetry, especially that of Ovid, to the writings of the mystics, and to the cult of the Virgin which became more marked in the twelfth and thirteenth centuries. In the worship of "Our Lady" men saw the worship of all womanhood. Something came likewise from the Platonic idea of seeing in an earthly love the reflection of an eternal beauty and love; perhaps this idea came into southern France from Mohammedan culture. This aspect of the love motif played a great role in early Italian lyric poetry. On the negative side, the exaggerated interest in love themes came from the preaching of chastity by the church; this, in some minds, increased the desire for sexual gratification. Finally, the love interest arose from the nature of marriages among the aristocracy where everything was arranged by the parents and where marriages were little more than business contracts in which love had no place, and from which there was little chance of escape through divorce.

Love with these troubadour poets became both a science and a theology, the *gai sçavoir,* as they named it. Lovers took service in the army of Cupid, and in this service they became pale and sleepless. The love had to be kept secret, the lover could never use the lady's name openly. The four stages of love were, successively, that of aspirant, suppliant, recognized suitor, and accepted lover. The lover was then given a ring by the lady, he took an oath of fidelity to her, and the lady became the lover's suzerain. Obedience to his lady's slightest wish and silent acquiescence to her rebukes were the only virtues he dared to claim. The lover's enemy was less the husband than his rival lover. The lover was no light-hearted gallant; his love was represented as a despairing and tragic emotion.[18] Only the hearts of members of the noble classes could feel these sentiments. There is a tradition that courts of love were held; this probably never happened. The idea arose from verse dialogues in which various theories about love were debated and a judgment rendered on such questions as whether a lover could be in love with two ladies at once, and whether married or unmarried couples were more affectionate.

Some of the outstanding verse forms of the troubadours were the *canso,* a love song, and the *alba,* the song of a lover parting at dawn, as in the following:

> *When the nightingale is crying*
> *To his mate, and she replying,*
> *My true love and I are lying*
> *'Mid the flowers,*
> *Till the watcher from the towers*
> *Calls out, "Lovers, now arise;*
> *I see daylight in the skies."* [14]

Others were the *pastorela,* in which the heroine is a shepherdess and the lover usually a noble, and the *sirventes,* a satiric poem on social, political, or religious matters.[15] In spite of their elaborate rules and conventions there is a marvellous freshness about some of the troubadour poetry. Something of its quality may be caught in the following fragments from the work of Bernart de Ventadorn.

> *Whene'er the lark's glad wings I see*
> *Beat sunward 'gainst the radiant sky*
> *Till lost in joy so sweet and free,*
> *She drops forgetful how to fly—*
> *Oh, when I view such happiness*
> *Meseems for pain and sore distress*
> *My longing heart will straightway break.* [16]

Some of the troubadour poets were obscure and complicated like the English metaphysical poets, and like Valéry, Rilke, and Eliot in our time. The art of writing in this style they called *trobar clus.* Among the leading troubadours were Bernart de Ventadorn, a poor boy who rose to fame, went to the court of Eleanor of Aquitaine, and later lived at the court of the Count of Toulouse; his poetry is the most vivid and genuine the school produced; there were also Arnaut Daniel, who wrote in a complicated and veiled style, but was much admired by Dante, and, finally, Bertran de Born whose verses are chiefly in praise of fighting and the glory of war. The Albigensian Crusade of the early thirteenth century which ravaged the south of France (a war whose cruelty is characterized by the statement of the papal legate, who, when asked what to do with the people captured in one siege, said, "Kill them all, God will know his own") cut short this great literary flowering. The writing of the troubadours, however, had by 1200 already begun to degenerate through the growth of mannerisms. In the meantime the style was spreading into northern France, into Germany, Italy, England, Spain, and Portugal. The troubadour poets, with their lyric subjectivity and their ideas of romantic love, struck the most modern note in mediaeval literature. They were the first to express ideas of love about which poets and novelists have never since ceased to write. "They effected a change," says C. S. Lewis, "which has left no corner of our ethics, our imagination, or our daily life untouched, and they erected impossible barriers between us and the classical past or the Oriental present. Compared with this revolution, the Renaissance is a mere ripple on the surface of literature." [17]

In the early twelfth century a vigorous popular poetry appeared in northern France of which only about ten songs survive. By the middle of the century a court poetry influenced by the troubadours began to flourish. These court poets, who wrote in the *langue d'oïl,* were called trouvères; the earliest famous trouvère was Chrétien de Troyes at the court of the Countess of Champagne, a great granddaughter of William of Poitiers, the daughter of Louis VII of France and Eleanor of Aquitaine, and a half-sister of Richard, Coeur de Lion. Chrétien was also one of the early writers of chivalric romance, a literary form that was the creation of the trouvères. Their poetry resembles that of the troubadours though it is less original and less varied in style.

The court of the Countess of Champagne was also the home of Andrew the Chaplain who wrote, in Latin, a prose treatise on the *Art of Courtly Love* (about 1186). This curious work shows the influence of Ovid's *Art of Love,* which Chrétien de Troyes translated into French, and other shorter pieces of Ovid. With Ovid love is all extra-marital and does not contemplate matrimony. For men Ovid tells how to lure women into love, and for women he gives directions on how to hold men. The worshipful devotion of the lover to the lady is not in Ovid, and came, as we have seen, from other sources. Some of Andrew's rules, which were exemplified in the imaginative literature of courtly love, were: marriage is not a good excuse for rejecting love; who does not conceal, cannot love; it is love's way always to increase or to lessen, and the true lover constantly, without intermission, is engrossed with the image of the beloved. The code of love includes thirty-one rules of this type. In the last section of his work, Andrew the Chaplain turns around and rejects courtly love as evil. The church, which taught the sanctity of marriage, and held marriage as one of Christ's seven sacraments, denounced the whole idea of courtly love. But, as in the case of much of the Goliardic poetry, here was a current of emotional expression the church never succeeded in curbing.

In southern Germany and Austria, as in southern and northern France, a popular poetry in the vernacular was developing in the twelfth century. At the same time, a courtly poetry, deeply influenced by the new styles in France, grew up. The first mention of the German minnesingers is a sermon of about 1150 in which the preacher attacks sexual love and knightly prowess, two aspects of the new life of chivalry, as forms of vainglory and sin. "When knights are assembled, they compete in telling how many they have seduced. All their boast is of women. He who fails to win praise, thinks himself lowered in repute among his fellows. And, again, wherever some tribute is paid to a man's worth, no one mentions the strength he needs to resist the devil, but instead the most lawless deeds are the oftenest named; they say, 'such and such a one is a fine brave fellow he has killed so many.' " [18] The German and Austrian minnesingers filled their poetry with *Frauendienst* and exalted women more than did the troubadours and the trouvères. We hear much of the charm of women's glances, of secret adoration, of the tyranny of love, its ecstasies, and its tears of regret. There is the same joy in nature as with the French lyric poets, especially in the annual miracle of spring with its return of birds and flowers. The lyric poets of the twelfth and thirteenth centuries began to look at nature afresh as did the Gothic sculptors and scholars like Roger Bacon and Frederick II. The minnesingers, like their French counterparts, were musicians, and in their verses showed a love of intricate verse forms. Some of the minnesingers also wrote chivalric romances.

During the Hohenstaufen period in the thirteenth century, two of the greatest minnesingers, Wolfram von Eschenbach and Walther von der Vogelweide, lived at the Wartburg Castle in central Germany, the *feste Burg* where Luther in 1521 was to begin his magnificent translation of the Bible. The most powerful poetic satires of the Middle Ages and some of its best love lyrics were the work of Walther von der Vogelweide (d. 1228). Walther's *Sprüche* attack the pope and clergy in brilliant invective, though he seems to have been a devout Christian and he wrote a tender prayer to Christ. His lyrics have a range and a depth of feeling unmatched by anything the troubadours or trouvères or other German minnesingers ever wrote. Everything he touched he transfused with a freshness and a superb vitality; at the same time he was a consummate craftsman in verse forms. He sings not only of extra-marital love but also of the joys of married love; in one poem he speaks of a successful marriage as "the completion of two lives" in which "both lives are increased in price and worth." This same view of marriage lies at the heart of Wolfram von Eschenbach's *Parzival*. Walther remains one of Germany's half-dozen greatest poets. After his death minnesong degenerated in complicated mannerisms that hid the lack of genuine inspiration.

In the fourteenth century, versifiers in the towns organized themselves into societies of Meistersingers, in imitation of the guilds. For the next two centuries they held poetic contests in churches and town halls. Theirs was definitely a bourgeois art of artisans and tradesfolk, a mechanical poetic that could be learned by diligent study of the rules. The Meistersingers produced quantities of verse, but nothing that is of first quality. Most famous of their number was Hans Sachs, the cobbler of Nüremberg who in the sixteenth century made a poem out of everything but made nothing into a poem. This German bourgeois verse was paralleled in the later Middle Ages by that of the Rhétoriqueurs in France whose work was also too studied and over-elaborate. In this it resembles the contemporary flamboyant Gothic sculpture and architecture. Both the Meistersingers and the Rhétoriqueurs represented only the weakest side of the old troubadour tradition, namely an exaggerated interest in linguistic intricacies.

Italian literature developed late. Until 1200 Latin seems to have met all the writer's needs. The new style reached Italy from both France and Germany. The southern French dialects were near enough to the Italian dialects for troubadour poetry to be understood by the Italians. Close political and economic relations with Germany account for the influence of minnesong. The first Italian poet to show the influence of the troubadours was Sordello, who wrote in Provençal. The first poetry in an Italian dialect appeared in Sicily, to which refuge some of the troubadours driven out of France by the Albigensian Crusade had come as exiles. In Sicily, the sonnet was invented by Giacomo da Lentino, and various styles of songs, *canzoni*, were perfected by Frederick II (d. 1250) and several other poets. The Sicilian poets in the first half of the thirteenth century showed that Italian, which cultivated people regarded as inferior both to Latin and Provençal as a literary language, was really capable of being used as a vehicle of effective literary expression.

In the second half of the thirteenth century—as Dante points out in his *De Vulgari Eloquentia*, a defense of Italian as a literary language—Florence and Tuscany came to the fore. Here the religious vernacular lyric, like contemporary Latin poems and contemporary painting, showed the influence of the Franciscan movement. St. Francis and his early followers brought the stories of the Bible and the truths of the Christian faith to the common man, and breathed into them a great human tenderness and a warm emotionality. Francis himself, as a boy, had learned Provençal songs. Later he composed a *Hymn to the Sun*, and he called himself the "Jongleur of God." The most interesting of the early Franciscan poets is Jacopone da Todi, probably the author of the Latin *Stabat Mater*.[19]

The leading love poets, Folgore da San Gimignano, Guinicelli, Cavalcanti, and Dante (d. 1321), wrote in what Dante calls the "dolce stil nuovo." They fused troubadour and minnesinger elements, but their treatment of love was their own. To these Tuscan poets, love purifies the heart as with fire; it is a spiritual love that reflects the divine, and, in turn, leads the spirit back to the universal. The physical attraction of men and women recedes into the background. The poet wishes to contemplate and to worship the revelation of the divine; he wishes to pass from knightly homage to mystical devotion. This Platonic idea in poetry, which may have entered Latin Christendom from Spain, had earlier been only a minor current. With the Tuscan poets of the thirteenth century it became central and remained so in Italian poetry through the sixteenth century. The whole conception of Dante's Beatrice would have been impossible without this background. The *Vita Nuova* of Dante, a series of sonnets and *canzoni* linked by passages in prose, all of which tell of his adoring love of Beatrice, prepared the way for the *Divine Comedy*. At the end of the *Vita Nuova*, Dante declares he will celebrate Beatrice as no woman was ever celebrated, a promise which he richly fulfilled.

The styles of vernacular lyric poetry as developed by the troubadours spread from one end of Latin Christendom to the other, and affected, with certain variations, the local styles. And after 1200 there is a growing body of lyric poetry in all the vernacular languages of western Europe. The most gifted of all later mediaeval poets in northern Europe was François Villon (d. 1463), a contemporary of Louis XI of France. Everything Villon wrote is colored by his vivid personality and his vagabond existence. In turn he sins and is sinned against; he is sorrowful and gay, mystical and devout, and again blasphemous, but always deeply sincere and vivid. Many of his poems, like his *Testaments*, are about himself, and even when he writes of other subjects he injects a very subjective mood into the poem. His verses, which combine pathos and irony, remind one of some of those of Heine, though Villon has a greater range.

The styles of lyric poetry, as set by the troubadours, had begun to change in Italy in the fourteenth century. In the vernacular verses of Petrarch (d. 1374) there is both a more worldly outlook and a more deliberate attempt to imitate classical Latin poetry in subject matter, figures of speech, and vocabulary than had appeared earlier in any vernacular poetry. The spell of the Latin classics was heavy on Petrarch, and he grafted this love of antiquity and the attempt to imitate it onto the older troubadour and Tuscan traditions. A shift in point of view was already evident in Dante, who, though profoundly mediaeval in general outlook, showed the beginning of a new literary age in his deep respect for the great Greek and Latin writers, in his patriotism, and, above all, in his enthusiasm for the vernacular. Petrarch is definitely more modern; for an ethical consciousness he, in some degree, substituted an aesthetic consciousness. His attitude toward the style of the great Latin writers was one of almost slavish admiration, and he wrote what he considered his important works in a Latin as close as possible to that of the ancient Roman authors. He regarded his vernacular verses as of secondary importance, a view that posterity has reversed. Above all, Petrarch is modern in his almost childish desire for earthly fame. He humanized the "dolce stil nuovo" and classicized it, and wrote with a brilliant and impeccable technical finish. His poems include over three hundred sonnets, many of them addressed to his ideal lady, Laura. No fact is too slight if it touches his love for her, no conceit or pun the thought of her invokes is too trivial. At their best, however, his sonnets are the epitome of grace.

> *Oft as in pensive mood I sit and write,*
> *'Mid plaint of birds and whisp'ring leafy trees,*
> *Where betwixt flowery banks a river bright*
> *Laughs back in ripples at the ruffling breeze,*
> *She whom heaven hath stolen from my sight,*
> *Whose face though mortal eye no longer sees*
> *Earth cannot hide, in pity of my plight*
> *Rebukes my grief with words more sweet than these—*
> *Celestial words not breathed by mortal breath:*
> *Ah why consume thy strength ere yet 'tis night*
> *In barren tears and tempest of fierce sighs?*
> *Weep not for me, for by the boon of death*
> *My days were made immortal, and mine eyes,*
> *Closing, were opened on eternal light.*[20]

His sonnets, his *Canzoni*, and his *Triumphs* cast, for centuries, the same spell over European letters that the Latin classics themselves had cast over Petrarch. Indeed few literary forms ever had the wide influence possessed by the Petrarchian sonnet. Petrarch's culture, his admiration for antiquity, and his mastery of style set him beside Cicero and Virgil as a model of elegance. His poems became handbooks for poets, storehouses of literary stage properties. Even his shortcomings—his ignorance of, and contempt for, philosophy and science, and his meagerness of thought—were imitated for centuries. Gabriel Harvey, Spencer's friend, writing in far-off England in the sixteenth century, says of Petrarch's poetry that it is "the grace of art, a precious tablet of rare conceits, and a curious frame of exquisite workmanship; nothing but neat wit and refined elegance." [21]

The spell of the classics became so strong in Italy that for over a century after Petrarch's death the leading Italian authors wrote in Latin. They flooded the reading public with Latin histories, stories, orations, and nearly every genre of poetry. Not until the second half of the fifteenth century are there again important poets writing in the Italian vernacular. The chief lyric poets of the end of the fifteenth century in Italy were Lorenzo the Magnificent and his friend, the humanist, Poliziano. Their verses are polished and graceful like those of Petrarch, though they are even more worldly. At the same time they show the direct influence of a revival of Platonism. The beauty of a woman and of this world awakens in the soul the memory of a divine beauty; all the beauty that man knows is but the first round of a ladder that leads the soul back to the universal beauty. The poet remembers the lost fatherland of truth and beauty, and in his rapture tells of it. The Italian poets of the age of Dante held many of the same ideas, but they had limited them by traditional Christian ideas. Now Platonism is used to create a sort of secular religion of beauty. This aesthetic gospel of fifteenth-century Italy spread, in the next century, throughout Europe. By 1500, Italy held the place as the leader of art and literature that France had held in the thirteenth century.

3. CHIVALRIC ROMANCE

THE CHIVALRIC romances grew in the same aristocratic French circles in which the lyrics of the trouvères had first appeared. The usages of chivalry had developed earlier, in the eleventh century. They were based on an old Germanic coming of age ceremony, in which, as Tacitus described it, a youth was presented with a shield and a spear. The church took over this ceremony and elaborated it. As the idea of chivalry developed, it was a curious combination of four elements: adulthood, religion, war, and love. Common to all four were the ideas of duty, devotion, and service. The true hero of chivalry rendered voluntary, life-long, and unrestricted service, first to his family, then to his feudal lord, to his lady, and to God. The youth who joined the order of chivalry had to be well-born, gentle-mannered, truthful, courteous to women, open-handed in hospitality, at least, to his own class, fearless or "preux" (well-proved in combat), and with a high sense of honor, a conception unknown to the ancients.

The virtues of knighthood were courage and devotion to duty, charity to the weak, and generosity to one's equals. Its best sides are seen in works like Wolfram von Eschenbach's *Parzival* and in Joinville's *Life of St. Louis*. The vices of knighthood were quarrelsomeness, brutality, dishonesty, contempt for the masses, gross superstition, and adultery. Often the knight had an absurd desire for glory and a sense of honor that made him haughty and contentious. The knight would fast on Friday and go on long pilgrimages, and, on the other hand, he would freely slaughter the peasants on the next estate. Mediaeval men were usually virtuous or vicious by fits and starts. Did the continual preaching of the virtues of celibacy, fasting, and absolute poverty lead men to a mechanical round of committing sins and then expiating them? One virtue was stressed at a time, and carried to exaggerated limits. So the mediaeval nobleman often lacked both a well-balanced view of life and any deep sense of justice. The Black Prince, the perfect mirror of chivalry, treated his captive, King John of France, with exquisite courtesy, but calmly watched the butchery of women and children that followed the sack of Limoges.[22]

The whole idea of chivalry had been fostered by the church; here, as in the case of the "Peace of God," the "Truce of God," and the Crusades, the church had launched a movement intended to improve society. So the church made the ceremony of becoming a knight, with the vigil and the blessing of the youth's armor and weapons, and the sermon that accompanied the dubbing of the knight, a sort of extra sacrament, a kind of ordination for the aristocratic laymen. The same attempt to link religion and war was shown in the backing given by the church to the military monkish orders of the age of the Crusades. A link between religion and the new theories of love is shown in the cult of the Virgin. In all these matters the church tried, not too successfully, to turn the popular urges of the time toward religious ends. By the thirteenth century, however, churchmen frequently condemned chivalry, pointing out the laziness, cowardice, arrogance, brutality, and lechery of the knights. The growth of chivalry in the eleventh and twelfth centuries shows also the increasing influence of women in a wealthier aristocratic society. With all of its faults, knighthood and chivalry marked an advance over earlier usages; one has only to compare Gregory of Tours' account of the Franks in the sixth century with life as described by writers of the eleventh through the fifteenth century to realize the improvement, and, in this change, chivalry played a role. In the fourteenth and fifteenth centuries, with the growth of centralized governments and of towns, and with the decay of feudalism, chivalry became rather an empty ceremony and its ideals merely the observance of elaborate etiquette. In the same way, the old tournaments or mimic battles, which earlier had been lively and brutal and sometimes fatal, became harmless displays of armor, fine raiment, and horsemanship. The ideal of the gentleman, as modified in the sixteenth century, is reflected in works like Castiglione's *The Courtier*, in which the gentleman has a finer code of justice and is also a person of intellectual culture as well as of warlike prowess.

The chivalric romance which came out of this background was a tale of love and adventure; the word "romance" means a story written in one of the vernacular romance languages instead of in Latin, and so it is, by implication, less serious and less learned. The earlier romances of chivalry were written in verse; by the middle of the thirteenth century prose versions had become common. Unlike the earlier epics most of the romances seem to have been composed primarily for an audience of women, and written to be read rather than recited. They glorified the aristocratic way of life and tried to offset the monotony of feudal existence with fabulous adventures. The authors filled their stories with long descriptions of tapestries, jewels, fine raiment, and elegant buildings with many details from Byzantine and Saracenic sources, and long descriptions, too, of tournaments, weddings, feats, battles and funerals, and the doings of strange monsters like unicorns and basilisks.

The sources of the romances were the old Greek and Latin epics often known through late Latin prose versions, mediaeval stories and legends, and the troubadour theory of love. One thirteenth-century French writer classified the subjects of romance into the matters of France, of Brittany, and of Rome the Great. The first was centered on the stories of Charlemagne, the second, on tales chiefly of Celtic origin and on subjects like King Arthur, Parsifal, or Tristan, and the last concerned the whole mythology and history of Greece and Rome from the Trojan War down, all mixed together. The first chivalric romances were written in northern France in the twelfth century, in the same area in which Gothic art was arising. From there the new styles of literature and art spread until they reached Iceland, Norway, and Ireland, and, to the south and east, Spain, Italy, and the Holy Land. By the end of the thirteenth century, in art, literature, philosophy, science, education, and music, the whole of Latin Christendom was made up of a series of cultural provinces of northern France.

The earliest known romance, which mixes war, love, and adventure, is the northern French *Roman de Thèbes* written, about 1150, in eight-syllable lines which rhyme in couplets. The earlier romances, thus, overlap the period of the *Chansons de geste*. This tale, whose author is unknown, is about the family of Oedipus and revolves around a long siege of the Greek city of Thebes. The story is taken, in part, from a Latin prose summary of Statius' *Thebias*, with material from Ovid's *Metamorphoses* and other sources. Also by an unknown author is the *Roman d'Enéas*, written about 1160, based on Virgil's *Aeneid*, but highly embellished with fantastic adventures of young knights-errant and their sacrifices to win a woman's love. About 1184 Benoît de Sainte-More wrote the *Roman de Troie*, a poem of thirty thousand lines. Since Virgil had represented the Trojans as the ancestors of the Romans, and mediaeval men revered the Romans, it was intolerable to have the Trojans defeated. So certain Latin stories of the Trojan War were drawn upon, and Benoît portrays the Trojans as a noble and courageous race, and the Greeks as mean and treacherous; Achilles is only able to defeat Hector by stabbing him from behind. Benoît's poem is very discursive and utterly lacking in realism or intensity, but it became popular. About 1171 several unknown northern French authors produced a *Roman d'Alexandre*, written in twelve-syllable lines, from which the later French Alexandrine line was derived.

None of these early romances on classical subjects have high literary value. The plots are badly handled, the stories lack unity, the characters are poorly defined, and the general impression they give is one of dullness and monotony. The same may be said of the romances based on the stories of Charlemagne, his ancestors and descendants. All of them had or pretended to have Latin originals, just as later, in countries outside of France, writers like Malory claimed a French original for everything. There was in the first half of the twelfth century a great craze for new themes and new methods, and writers explored all possible sources to find them. Then, everything was given a fashionable chivalric setting; handsome knights in armor, afire with love and ready for any adventure, and ladies of fabulous allure in castles and bowers became the stock in trade of romance writers. Helen of Troy is a ravishing beauty, Dido a lovelorn queen, Medea a bewitching coquette, and the ladies of Charlemagne's entourage are seductive beyond words. The settings are often amusingly anachronistic, especially in the classical stories; the glamorous Achilles as a boy is hid away in a nunnery, in another romance his son is knighted; Alexander is made to visit the Bishop of Ammon; classical mythology and history are presented in fantastic disorder, and Alexander, Charlemagne, Arthur, and Julius Caesar are presented as belonging to the same generation.

The richest vein for romances proved to be the body of Celtic stories, especially those about Arthur and the Round Table. These legends have only slight historical foundations in events of the fifth and sixth centuries in England and in Brittany. They had been elaborated in Ireland and Wales and mixed with ancient Celtic tales, the whole having been given a strong coloring of Christianity and of magic: the grail, for example, was originally a heathen talisman in an Irish fairy palace, and finally it became the cup out of which Jesus drank at the Last Supper. Originally the stories of Parsifal and of Tristan, though Celtic in origin, had had nothing to do with the stories of King Arthur. First Wales, then Cornwall seem to have been the earliest homes of Arthurian stories. A ninth-century chronicle by Nennius, a Welsh priest, presents Arthur as a Christian leader fighting against the heathen Anglo-Saxons in the fifth century. A chronicle of William of Malmesbury of 1125 mentions Arthur only briefly. In the first half of the twelfth century, a mason carved on a door of the Cathedral of Modena figures of Arthur and of some of his knights. A more extended account is in Geoffrey of Monmouth of about 1148; Geoffrey's account is fantastic and is sheer romanticizing but it was enormously popular.

Arthur defeats all the Anglo-Saxons and overruns Scotland and Gaul. His ancestry is traced to Brut, the grandson of Aeneas, and so ties up the British past with the glories of ancient Rome. The chronicler is evidently trying to make a British hero of the stature of Charlemagne. Geoffrey makes no mention of the Round Table, of Lancelot, of Tristan, or of the Holy Grail. The popularity of Arthur was beginning to grow; by the thirteenth century he was ranked as one of the "Nine Worthies," along with Hector, Alexander, Caesar, Joshua, David, Judas Maccabaeus, Charlemagne, and Godfrey of Bouillon.

These tales reached northern France in the twelfth century, chiefly through Latin chronicles. A French poet, Wace, about 1155, put this Arthurian material into a mediocre poem called *Brut*; the poem is dedicated to Eleanor of Aquitaine. Wace adds the Round Table to prevent disputes over precedence and to bring other men and their stories into a cycle. Layamon, about 1205, prepared, in middle English, a version of Wace's *Brut* in unrhymed, alliterative verse. Finally the full cycle of Arthurian stories was made up of a galaxy of isolated personages, each the hero of adventures having little or no connection with the others. In the earlier Arthurian romances, Arthur is the universal protector, but we hear less of his adventures than of those of his knights. The only episode which made it possible to link all these personages together was the quest of the Holy Grail. The next handling was in the short *Lays* of Marie de France (d. 1189), who may have been a member of the French royal house. Her stories are charming and exquisite, and though they show no great force or emotional depth, they have a higher literary quality than any of the other romances so far mentioned.

The first handling of this Celtic material, and of all chivalric romance that is really excellent from a literary point of view, is by Chrétien de Troyes (d. 1180), a trouvère who lived at the courts, first of the Countess of Champagne then of the Count of Flanders. He was steeped in the troubadour theory of love, and, between 1165 and 1180, Chrétien wrote five long romances, four of them dealing with Arthurian stories. He probably chose this Celtic material rather than the "matter of France" or the "matter of Rome" because it was less hackneyed. Chrétien is not content merely to narrate events, but he also tries to interpret them. At the center of his romances and beneath all the descriptions of armor and costume, of tournaments and battles, and of castles and nature, there is a systematic analysis of love and of human action. A good example of all this is his *Yvain*. As one of the first great explorers of the human heart, he must be numbered among the founders of the modern novel. Another important twelfth-century writer of romances, Robert de Born, wrote the best stories about the Holy Grail. From Chrétien's writings and those of Robert de Born, the taste for chivalric romances swept Europe. They prescribed the chief characters and situations and they made the Arthurian stories the great vehicles of chivalry and love.

The most-read of all romances and one of the most popular books of the whole Middle Ages was the thirteenth-century French *Roman de la Rose*. The characters are nearly all abstractions, as in the morality plays: Hope, Evil-Tongue, Youth, Generosity, and the rest. The first four thousand lines were written in the early thirteenth century by Guillaume de Lorris, who left his work incomplete about 1237. To this, a Parisian bourgeois, Jean de Meun, added eighteen thousand lines about forty years later, dedicating his part to King Philip the Fair. The first part is aristocratic in tone and is the work of a sensitive literary artist who keeps the reader interested in the youthful hero and his struggles to pluck the rose, his love. The last part is tedious, prolix, and pedantic. It has the encyclopedic character of Latin writings of the period, with attacks on the church, especially the friars, on women, on the aristocracy, and on the government. It was the misfortune of Jean de Meun to have read and remembered everything, and nothing he remembered could he keep out of his poem; Gerson described it as "a work of chaos and Babylonian confusion." In Jean de Meun's praise of nature, however, in his interest in science, and in his glorification of man we find a foreshadowing of modern times. Yet basically the *Roman de la Rose* is "a mediaeval product, comparable to the enormous tapestries, the endless chronicles, the omniscient encyclopedias, the vast Gothic cathedrals which grew slowly up, altering their plan as they grew, and sometimes ending with two different kinds of spire on the same building." [23]

The *Roman de la Rose* was enormously popular in spite of its shortcomings as a work of art. Chaucer translated some of the first part into Middle English, and it was translated into German. Men defended and assailed its ideas and its style, and the clergy quoted from it as from the Bible. Part of its vogue was due to the fact that French was read all over Europe from the thirteenth century through the fifteenth, as it was again from 1680 on. This helped the circulation of all French books. Outside France, men and women not only read French, but foreigners sometimes wrote in French. St. Francis knew French songs, Marco Polo's travels were written in French, and Dante's teacher, Brunetto Latini, not only wrote his small encyclopedia, the *Trésor*, in French, but also declared: "The French speech is the most delectable and most common to all nations."

The taste for chivalric romances spread to all the states of Latin Christendom. Around 1200 Hartmann von Aue wrote four chivalric romances in German; all were inspired by Chrétien de Troyes except *Der Arme Heinrich*, which may be of his own invention. Another German poet, Gottfried von Strassburg, wrote the finest version of the famous story of Tristan and Yseult. Gottfried's style is urbane and smooth and full of understatement, but the story he tells is one of wild passion. His tale of Tristan inspired Wagner's opera, and poems by Tennyson, Swinburne, Robinson, and others. The greatest of all German romances, however, is Wolfram von Eschenbach's (d. 1220) *Parzival*, which may be based on an unfinished story of Chrétien de Troyes. The legend of the search for the grail may have come from Oriental sources which became united with Celtic legends. Wolfram made it all an epic struggle of the soul of man to find fulfillment and peace. Parzival, as a naïve youth, makes great mistakes, but, through suffering, he grows slowly wise. His life is like that of Oedipus in Sophocles' two dramas. In his experiences, Parzival hovers between faith and doubt, between the "everlasting yea" and "the everlasting nay" of Carlyle's *Sartor Resartus*. Here the Holy Grail is a sacred stone; in later romances it is identified with the cup used at the Last Supper which, according to legend, Joseph of Arimathea brought to Glastonbury Abbey in England. *Parzival* is a great poem of chivalry in which the romantic ideal has been combined with religion and yet the story does not become monkish nor does it lose its knightly character. The story stands in sharp contrast with the tale of Tristan where love is a wild, blind, and destroying passion.[24]

The finest English chivalric romance before Malory is the fourteenth-century *Sir Gawain and the Green Knight.* The work, whose author is unknown and which is written in alliterative verse, has a simple design and a great human appeal. To find an English work of such high value is surprising because most of the English romances are inferiór to those written in French and German. In their handling of French stories, the English writers of romance seem to have been indifferent to form and to artistic detail and seem to have catered to a taste that loved the grossest exaggeration. On the other hand, their moral tone is higher than that of most of the French romances.

In all countries many of the later chivalric romances, from the thirteenth century on, were written in prose. This is true of Sir Thomas Malory's *Morte d'Arthur.* Malory (d. 1471) was an English nobleman who fought in the Wars of the Roses and who had a strange career stained by violence and jail sentences. He tells us that his stories were all gathered from French sources, though for some of his tales no such sources have ever been discovered. He was an admirable storyteller; a manuscript discovered in 1934 shows that what Malory originally composed was a series of romances, and that the version that later circulated was put together by Caxton and printed in the fifteenth century. In Caxton's version we read about grown men and later about their birth, and we hear about the actions of some of Malory's characters long after they are dead. Malory is very old-fashioned; he believes in the chivalric code and wants to improve men's manners. To his own generation, his stories, as he handled them, probably seemed about as quaint and archaic as they do to us. Malory's originality shows itself chiefly in the directness of his approach; he substitutes simple speech and manner for the more complicated courtly etiquette of the French romances; he avoids magic and uses a more realistic setting than that of the conventional fairy-tale scenery. Though he writes with a good deal of insight into human behavior, he fails to see the central fault in the chivalric code, that is, the conflict between duty to Arthur and his marriage vows and devotion to an ideal lady. Herein lies the essential tragedy that wrecks the lives of Arthur, his wife, Guinevere, and Arthur's friend, Lancelot. There are some fine plots and much excellent narrative and character analysis in Malory; books 20 and 21 are magnificent in sweep.[25] In Malory one may clearly see how the chivalric romance is one of the sources of the modern novel. The taste for writing romances and for reading them was still strong even in the late fifteenth century, which saw the composition of the most-read of the Spanish romances, the *Amadis of Gaul.* This popular work in prose made the tour of Europe.

In estimating this aristocratic lyric poetry and chivalric romances we see, at once, that, on the one hand, both differed from the epics, and, on the other, from the rising bourgeois literature, the fabliaux and the popular drama. The romances lack the seriousness of purpose and the simplicity of the epics. They are highly sentimental and complex and are addressed primarily to an audience of women. "Charlemagne's very realistic entourage of virile barons is replaced by a court of elegant chevaliers and unemployed ladies. Charlemagne's setting is historical and geographical; Arthur's setting is ideal and in the air. In the oldest epic poems we find only God-fearing men and a few self-effacing women; in the Arthurian romances we meet gentlemen and ladies, more elegant and seductive than anyone in the epic poems, but less fortified by faith and a sense of duty against vice because breathing an enervating atmosphere of leisure and decadent morality." [26] Just as the *Song of Roland* resembles the rude power of Romanesque art, the best of the romances reminds one of the complexity and refinement of certain Gothic art. In both the lyric poetry and the romances, love is always the mainspring of action, and in the romances the atmosphere is often that of a strange supernatural world where stones, springs, and herbs, and indeed nearly everything, have magical properties, and where men live only for love and adventure. [27]

As lyric poetry took a new turn in the fourteenth century with Petrarch, the chivalric romance was modified by Boccaccio and Chaucer. [28] Boccaccio (d. 1375), who always regarded himself first as a humanist and a classical scholar, wrote what have been called the first modern novels. The best of these stories, the *Fiammetta*, takes its name from the ideal lady of his devotion; it is the first long story in a modern prose vernacular about contemporary characters. In this, as in his other novels, he draws from the storehouse of chivalric romance and from the Latin classics; there are long sections of the *Fiammetta* that are hardly more than paraphrases of Ovid and Seneca. Boccaccio's end is chiefly pure amusement and diversion for his readers, and the mood is very worldly. Indeed, Boccaccio is the first modern author

who ignores Christianity for a frankly pagan view of life. But his
longer stories contain some excellent character analysis, and he gives
us an interesting picture of the frivolous Neapolitan society in which
he lived as a young man.

Chaucer's *Troilus and Criseyde*, though a work of higher literary
quality than any of the longer stories of Boccaccio, is based on Boccaccio's narrative poem, the *Filostrato*; indeed nearly a third of Chaucer's poem is directly translated from Boccaccio's. The story itself
comes from a section of Benoît de Sainte-More's *Roman de Troie*, but
Boccaccio had made it into a novel of fourteenth-century Italian life.
Chaucer's handling is more serious in tone than Boccaccio's and, at
the same time, shows greater ability to deal with comic elements.
Above all, Chaucer is Boccaccio's superior in his ability to depict and
analyze characters. His skill in transforming and humanizing Boccaccio's story resembles the fashion in which Shakespeare later borrowed stories and gave them a marvellous reshaping. Chaucer's *Troilus*
was the most accomplished long poem yet written in English. The
long stories of Boccaccio and the *Troilus* of Chaucer have dropped the
exaggeration of the older chivalric romances, and have a much more
realistic atmosphere. Though Chaucer's *Troilus* remains within the
conventional attitudes of the age of chivalry, his analysis of situations
and of individuals is surprisingly modern, especially if one compares
the work to one of the romances of Chrétien de Troyes or of the German minnesingers.

The Italians had never cared much for either Gothic art or chivalric
romances; this gave both their artists and writers a freer hand to try
innovations in style. In literature, as we have seen, Petrarch and Boccaccio both found a new and fresh inspiration in classical literature
and became innovators in their vernacular writings. Most of the
Italian writers of the fifteenth century wrote in Latin; those who did
use Italian included several who wrote long narrative poems that lie
between the mediaeval chivalric romances and the modern novel.
Pulci (d. 1484), a friend of Poliziano and his circle, wrote a long narrative poem, *Morgante Maggiore*, based on the old *matière de France*.
His handling of the Charlemagne stories, however, is thoroughly
bourgeois and realistic. The tale is told in eight-line stanzas, which
were also used by Poliziano, and from them passed on to Ariosto and

Tasso, the two great Italian narrative poets of the sixteenth century. Pulci's hero is Roland, the name, Morgante, in the title of his tale being that of the giant whom Roland (here called Orlando) tamed. Pulci's tone is ironic and mocking, and, at times, boisterous and profane. This gives his work, which lacks all high seriousness, the atmosphere of a gay burlesque. Its utter worldliness reflects one side of the Florence of Lorenzo the Magnificent. Byron, who translated the first canto of the *Morgante Maggiore*, acknowledged that he owed the manner of his *Don Juan* to Pulci. More aristocratic in tone is Boiardo's (d. 1494) *Orlando Innamorato*. The author was himself a noble; he spent his mature years at the Este court at Ferrara, and the poem, while it uses the old Charlemagne legends and shows the influence of Homer and Virgil, is really a picture of Italian court life at the end of the fifteenth century. From Pulci and Boiardo, and their two great sixteenth-century successors, Ariosto and Tasso, the taste for romantic narrative poems spread across Europe. By the end of the fifteenth century, all of western Europe had begun to look on Italian culture with an ecstasy of admiration, and Italy was playing the role, as the leader of culture, that France had played earlier.

CHAPTER X

Literature (II)

I. THE DRAMA

2. FABLIAUX AND NOVELLE

3. HISTORY, BIOGRAPHY, AND SERMONS

4. SYMBOLIC LITERATURE

MOST of the literature, as well as the learning, so far considered reflects the interests of the church and the aristocracy. By the twelfth century, however, a middle class had come into existence in nearly all the states of Latin Christendom, and its interests and outlook began to appear in literature. The long period of relative peace that had followed the Viking, Magyar, and Saracen raids of the ninth and tenth centuries and the slow accumulation of an agricultural surplus had brought back into the society of western Europe a class that had all but disappeared in the five centuries that followed the Barbarian Migrations. In the midst of an agricultural world tied closely to the economic activities and the interests of small local districts, a new class, the bourgeoisie, developed alongside the clergy, the nobles, and the peasants, and so there was created a more varied and diversified society. The town not only offered new opportunities for experience in self-government and easier means of exchanging ideas, but also opened new careers in business—trade, handicraft, and banking—in medicine, in law, in teaching, and in government administration; and, although the power of the church remained strong, the rise of the middle class represented a more matter-of-fact and even cynical view of life than that which flourished in the cathedral school, the monastery, or the castle. The townsmen, like the peasants, had few intellectual interests, but they were shrewd. Occasionally they produced a scholarly writer like Dante or Chaucer, and in Italy, from the fourteenth century on, it became fashionable for the upper middle class to cultivate learning. Speaking, though, of the middle class in general, Taylor says: "Their thoughts did not represent the intellectually and spiritually best in the world, did not touch the higher reaches of the saint, the theologian-philosopher, or the romantic poet. The most typical and original elements of mediaeval life drew little inspiration from the towns." [1] The rising towns became the homes of the drama and the short story.

I. THE DRAMA

BOTH the Greek and the mediaeval drama developed out of religious ceremonies, though the mediaeval—and ultimately the modern— drama had an independent development and was not derived from Greek and Roman drama. In the early Middle Ages the church disapproved of plays, since they were too much a part of the paganism that the church was fighting. Among the people their place was taken by wandering minstrels and acrobats, commonly called "mimes." These entertainers often travelled with trained bears or other animals and sometimes with a troupe of children. They performed in castle halls or on the village street; such entertainment supplemented the recitation of narrative or lyric verses. The survival of these "mimes," and the survival of traditional dances, kept alive types of dramatic characterization and the traditions of pantomime and acting that reappear later in the mediaeval drama. At the same time there were a number of dramatic elements in the Latin services of the church. The mass itself is a sort of symbolic drama of the death and resurrection of Christ with chanting by the priest and responses by the choir. Sometimes two priests would give a sermon, either in Latin or in the vernacular, in dialogue form; hymns were occasionally arranged for two choirs. As early as the tenth century, and perhaps earlier, short dramatic pieces (tropes), began to be introduced, especially in monastic churches, in connection with the great festivals of Easter and Christmas.

One of the earliest surviving tropes, the *Quem Quaeritis*, is hardly more than a series of stage directions for a brief play inserted into the Easter matins. All the parts were in Latin and were chanted. The original play included a scene between the angels and the Marys at the tomb of Jesus, followed by a responsive chant between the Marys and the choir. In the course of time, tropes like *Quem Quaeritis* were extended by the addition of dialogue and of more dramatic action, producing plays with several different scenes. In time, tropes were arranged in series, the resurrection story was extended backwards to include the Crucifixion and then other events of the last days of Jesus. On Good Friday, for example, a swathed cross would be laid away in some part of the choir with lamentations, and then on Easter morning it would be taken out with appropriate words and action.

A second step in the development of the drama was to move it out of the church. Comic elements which crept in made the plays seem out of keeping with the church services. Moreover, the crowds who wished to see such presentations could not be accommodated in the dark and narrow interiors of the church. So it gradually became the custom to give the plays outside, in front of the church. Many new incidents from both the Old and the New Testaments were added. Other changes that came in were the use of laymen as actors and the use of the vernacular instead of Latin. A number of transitional plays survive in which the dialogue is written partly in Latin and partly in the vernacular. All this meant a growing secularity in the drama and a growing dramatic effectiveness, for plays given by laymen in the vernacular and outside the church encouraged acting that was more varied and more realistic. And new scenes and incidents were invented. Noah's wife became the typical nagging shrew; Herod was now a typical bully, and "to out-herod Herod" furnished a great opportunity for dramatic action. The life of Mary Magdalene before her conversion offered the chance to present scenes of profligacy.

In some towns the remains of a Roman theater or arena were used for plays; in others booths were built on a public square or in a field outside the town wall. Here the central structure, in three levels, represented paradise, this earth (with the walls of Jerusalem, Herod's palace, Noah's Ark, the hill of Golgotha, and the Garden of Eden), with Hell below. The scenery was very crude; the costuming was elaborate but completely unhistorical, as it was in mediaeval painting. God's traditional costume was of white with a gilt wig and beard. This was, likewise, the costume for Christ though he usually wore red shoes as one who "had trod the winepress." Saints also wore gilded wigs, angels had gilt wings, and the Virgin wore a crown. The saved were dressed in white; the damned, in black or black and yellow. Herod was often clothed as a Saracen. The devil and his attendant demons wore grisly masks, were dressed in suits covered with horsehair, and wore horns and forked tails. Sometimes, in such a setting, a series of sets would be arranged side by side and the actors would move from one set to another. The common method of presenting plays in England was to mount them on a series of wagons or "pageants," on each one of which one important Bible story could be acted. Usually one of these platforms with wheels had two sections or floors; the lower, hung with curtains, supplied a dressing room, and the upper, covered with a canopy open on four sides, was the stage. So arranged, the plays could be repeated at several points as they were moved through a town. The juxtaposition of a series of sacred scenes, and in the scenes the mixing of sacred, profane, and even farcical elements, created a sprawling confusion of incidents and personages exactly as they were presented in mediaeval romances or in the huge and cluttered Gothic tapestries and paintings. The settings of both mediaeval and Renaissance theaters were derived from the architecture, the painting, and the sculpture of the period, and many of the effects striven for were to turn into living pictures the conceptions of the plastic art of the time. Noah's ark was represented as a ship, and a dragon's mouth stood for the gates of hell. Into these gates the devil would throw a sinner; there would then be groaning and a great rattling of pans, and smoke would belch forth. Parts of the play were often given on the ground in front of a set; it was a common feature for devils to run about the audience and torment some of the spectators to the delight of the other onlookers. It was now possible to introduce real dramatic action both comic and tragic into the plays.

In many towns the guilds took over one scene or another in the long cycles of plays that were presented on important feast days. Sometimes there was a real appropriateness in all this; the wine merchants presented the Marriage at Cana, and the fishmongers either the story of Jonah or the miracle of the miraculous draught of fishes or the feeding of the five thousand. In the York Cycle, the plasterers' guild presented the building of the ark, and the bakers' guild put on the Last Supper. Whole cycles of plays were given which covered the main stories in the Bible from the fall of man in Eden, through the Crucifixion, to the Last Judgment; one cycle from York in England includes forty-eight plays. The actors were all amateurs who, for a time, would set aside their labors to perform the sacred stories. They did not look on their work as a regular profession, though the guild would usually pay them for their services. Account books speak of paying "20 pence to God, 21 pence to the demon, 3 pence to Fauston for cock crowing, and 16 pence to two worms of conscience." Sometimes plays were put on by companies of students or of townsmen, independent of the guilds. The plays and their performance were the creation of the townsmen. The first regular company with its own establishment was probably the "Confrérie de la passion" which began in Paris about 1402.

From the thirteenth century on, it became the custom to refer to plays based on the Bible as mysteries, a designation probably derived from *misterium*, meaning a liturgical ceremony; in Italy, mystery plays, which became common in the fifteenth century, were called *sacre rappresentazione*. Those based on saints' lives were called miracle plays. Often comic insertions with improvised antics and farce with some mockery of the clergy crept in. Students in the cathedral schools and universities dramatized romances and other stories, but no examples of their efforts have survived. In the fourteenth century morality plays became common; here the actors represented virtues and vices and other abstractions like the characters in the *Roman de la Rose*. The favorite theme of the morality plays was the pursuit of Everyman (mankind) by evil forces and his rescue by Conscience or Wisdom. The morality plays, which continued to flourish into the sixteenth century, always inculcated some lesson. They were much longer than earlier mystery and miracle plays, and they show more ecclesiastical influence and, sometimes, a more aristocratic tone; it is known that they were frequently presented in castle halls. The peculiar paradox is that in seeming to draw drama away from realism into allegory the writers of morality plays succeeded in linking drama closer to actual life and to contemporary types. The comic scenes provided by the Devil and Old Vice, a buffoon, have in them the sort of humor whch supplied the authors of the interlude with certain subjects and methods. In the tragic figures the authors discovered the secret of showing the development of character and the delineation of conflicting passions. In addition, the morality plays have more unity and show more skill in construction than was shown in the mystery or miracle plays. Thus, they form an important link between the earlier mediaeval and the modern drama. The most famous of the morality plays, *Everyman*, exists in a number of languages of which an English fifteenth- or early sixteenth-century version is the best. Of all serious plays of the Middle Ages, it has still the greatest power on the stage.

The final stage of the mediaeval drama is represented by the development of the interlude. This was originally put in between parts of a sacred play, but it came to be developed for itself. The first good interlude is one of Adam de la Halle, the *Jeu de Robin et de Marion*, written in French, and first presented about 1283 at the Court of Naples. The spoken dialogue, which is charming and sprightly, is interspersed with songs and dances; with some exaggeration it has been called "the first comic opera," though it has no historical connection with this later form. The wittiest interlude that has survived is *Patelin*, a fifteenth-century French farce, which is still occasionally performed. Sometimes interludes were performed by puppets; sometimes they were done in pantomime, or had merely a few general directions and the actors had to make up their speeches. Out of this last came the Italian *commedia dell' arte*. In the interlude the plot and the action were freer than in the religious plays, and there was more opportunity for humor and realistic treatment. No great writer appeared to handle the drama during the Middle Ages, but out of the morality play and the interlude came the great drama of the age of Shakespeare and Lope de Vega.

2. FABLIAUX AND NOVELLE

THE CHURCH is largely responsible for beginning the mediaeval drama, though the middle class took it over and shaped its development. The fabliaux and the novelle were purely the creation of the bourgeoisie; the earliest fabliaux appeared in towns in north-central France in the twelfth century. These short stories in verse are usually about three or four hundred lines long and were written by jongleurs for recitation in the market place. In most cases the name of the author has not come down. About 750 fabliaux have survived; a large number have been lost. Some of the fabliaux show a high degree of art in the arrangement of the plot and in the manner of telling. The ideas and sentiment are of the newly self-conscious bourgeoisie of the merchant, the craftsman, the shopkeeper, and the jolly host of the inn and his guests. These tales reflect a crowded world where no man could escape the scrutiny of his neighbors and fellow townsmen, and where everyone was sure to know another's faults. They bring before our eyes, like the paintings of Breughel and Jan Steen, a world far removed from both the cloister and the castle hall. The telling of the tale is often set in a mocking and satirical tone, which has been later named the *esprit gaulois*.

The authors of the fabliaux are especially severe on ecclesiastics and on women and, to a lesser extent, on the nobles; there is rarely a decent woman or an honest priest in one of these jocose tales. The tone is often coarse, but there is never any attempt to make vice attractive. They seem to have been written to raise a laugh rather than to accomplish a reform. Nothing could stand in greater contrast than the romantic highflown mood of the chivalric romances and the realistic and *terre-à-terre* mood of the fabliaux. The haughty heroine of romance gives place to the woman of the people, shrewd, tricky, and ready to deceive. These stories love to dwell on the cunning and two-facedness of mankind, and they delight to show the triumph of a shrewd wit over stupidity. Sometimes a moral is drawn; here the fabliaux are close to the *exemplum,* a pious type of tale used by the clergy to drive home some point of a sermon. A number of the fabliaux were based on old stories that had come down from classical times or had been imported from the Orient. Just as the townsmen sometimes listened to recitations of chivalric romances, and later loved to read them, the fabliaux were, on occasion, recited in castle halls and laughed over by great lords and ladies. Perhaps the best-known examples of the fabliaux genre are Chaucer's *Reeve's Tale*, his *Miller's Tale*, and many of the stories in Boccaccio's *Decameron*. The tales are filled with fascinating glimpses of the social life of the towns, just as the romances present details of the life of the nobility. All this literature has thus been of great usefulness to the modern students of mediaeval life.

Out of this background came the *Roman de Renard*, a long series of stories about animals who represent persons. Stories about animals were popular both in Latin and in the vernacular languages in the earlier Middle Ages. These legends and tales of Reynard the Fox were first brought together in the borderland between France and Flanders; they remained popular in France and the Low Countries, and spread from there into England, Germany, and other states. The best version is the French *Roman de Renard*, which is about forty thousand lines long, and seems to be the work of over twenty writers, chiefly churchmen, of twelfth- and thirteenth-century France. The chief characters are the fox, the wolf, the cat, the hen, the cock, the ass, the hare, and the lion. The beasts survive either by virtue of brute strength or by trickery. The fox is a miracle of slyness; accordingly he becomes the symbol of suppressed humanity trying to outwit stupid power. Unable to overcome his betters, he often outwits them, and, in the process, makes them ridiculous.

The Italian novelle resemble the fabliaux of France and of some of the other nations of northern Europe; they were probably originally influenced by French originals. Like the fabliaux, the novelle find their subjects in the real world of living townsmen; the tone is very earthy, and the interest is usually centered on the development of a single action. The earliest surviving collection of Italian novelle is the *Novellino*, of whose original hundred tales only sixty-six survive; it dates from the end of the thirteenth century. Its range is much greater than that of the French fabliaux and the collection includes chivalric, mythological, and moral tales as well as bourgeois stories of priests and women.

Boccaccio (d. 1375), the first great writer of novelle, did not write until the middle of the fourteenth century. He was, as we have seen, the author of a number of long stories, in prose and verse, which have been called "the first European novels." He was also the author of the first great collection of short stories, the *Decameron*. Boccaccio's father belonged to a well-to-do Florentine bourgeois family, though the son was brought up by his unmarried mother who lived in humble circumstances. As a young man he worked in Naples where he met his ideal lady, Fiammetta, an illegitimate daughter of the king of Naples and the wife of a nobleman. She, like Petrarch's Laura, died in the Black Death in 1348. Besides his enthusiasm for this lady, two other devotions held his heart, his admiration for his friend, Petrarch, and his passionate devotion to the classics. He was the first important European writer since John Scotus Erigena who knew Greek. His middle and later years were spent in Florence, where he wrote his *Life of Dante* and his *Genealogy of the Gods*, the first great piece of modern classical scholarship and the first general treatise on the whole of Greek and Roman mythology. Boccaccio considered himself primarily a classical scholar, but his place in world literature rests on his longer tales, and, above all, on the *Decameron* (the Greek word for ten days).

These tales in prose were told by a group of seven ladies and three gentlemen who had betaken themselves during the Black Death to a pleasant estate near Florence. In the city one heard nothing but the groans of the dying and the rattle of the death cart as it hauled away the corpses thrown into the streets.² While this went on, the group in the country passed the time telling tales of love, trickery, and adventure. Boccaccio's plots were drawn from many sources, from earlier fabliaux and novelle, from stories that had come westward from the bazaars of the Orient, and from incidents of contemporary life. The *Decameron* is a world in itself filled with a variety of types, each one carefully observed. The reader rubs elbows with the scum of the earth, thieves, hypocrites, and whores, but he also meets men of exquisite good breeding and of high ideals; there are plain folk, too, honest, generous, and hearty—a veritable *comédie humaine*. The tone is, in turn, ironic, amusing, and tragic. The book is full of living people and lascivious stories; these are the secret of its immortality. The mood of these stories is racy and worldly, even cynical. A typical story is that of the Jew who went to Rome, and, having seen all the abuses there, decided that any religion that could continue to exist with such outrages going on must be the true one, and so became a Christian! The *Decameron* is thoroughly pagan; the characters recognize the church, but scoff at it, and they show clearly that what they really admire are the cultural standards of classical antiquity. Boccaccio seems to wish to prove nothing, but, in the process, he proves a great deal, above all that this world, and nature, and love, and the flesh are all good, and those who deny it are hypocrites or blind men. Boccaccio's only ideal is an artistic one. At last, St. Anthony is avenged![8] The prose style is extremely varied, fitting whatever story is being told; often one catches the rhythm of Cicero or of one of the great Latin prose styles. So remarkable is Boccaccio's style in syntax and vocabulary that, as the poetic style of Petrarch became the standard one in Italy, Boccaccio's prose became the standard of elegance and precision for later Italian prose writing. The *Decameron* was not only popular in Italy—there were nearly a hundred Italian editions before 1600—but it was widely translated and was used by French, German, Spanish, and English writers for centuries.

Like Boccaccio, Chaucer (d. 1400) was a burgher. He spent most of his life in London living in comfortable circumstances which allowed him a good deal of time for reading and study. He fought in France, was sent on diplomatic missions, and, through travel and study, he knew France and Italy and their cultures. He may even have met Petrarch and Boccaccio in Italy. He held a series of important government positions and served a term in parliament. Out of all these experiences he came to know men and the world. Chaucer's reading covered the Bible, French, Latin, and Italian literature, and some of the history, science, and philosophy of his time. By the fourteenth century learned laymen, especially among the middle class, were becoming more common. Chaucer was the first great English writer who knew continental Europe at first hand; and he showed great skill in using his somewhat unsystematic Latin learning and his wide knowledge of French and Italian literature to improve and enrich English literature. The poem of *Troilus and Criseyde* was, as we have seen, the finest narrative tale that had been produced up to his time. It is the only one of his major works which he completed; its influence outside England would have been greater had it been written in Latin, Italian, or French. Chaucer is one of the greatest literary figures of the Middle Ages, but, writing in Middle English, he never had the wide influence and international reputation enjoyed by writers like Aquinas and Petrarch.

Chaucer's masterpiece is the *Canterbury Tales*, a collection of stories in verse somewhat like the *Decameron*, which, however, he seems never to have read. A motley collection of twenty-nine pilgrims are described in the matchless verses of the "Prologue." Each member of the pilgrimage was to relate four tales. After they are on their way to Canterbury most of the members of the party tell stories that are closely related to the description of the teller in the "Prologue." The whole plan was never carried through; there are only twenty completed stories and four that are unfinished. There are more pilgrims than tales. The tales range from an edifying saint's life and a miracle of the Virgin, through stories of dark human tragedy and of passionate romance, to mock-heroic fables, parody, and the gayest farce. The pilgrimage shows us mediaeval folk, as they were, as no other work of those long centuries; it also shows us mediaeval men and women as they thought they were. Here we have all their strength and all their failings, their conventions, their beliefs, their tastes, their fears, and their follies. The range of characters rivals Balzac's.

Chaucer's outlook is less pagan than Boccaccio's, and his insight into human behavior is more profound. In English, only Shakespeare has surpassed him in his portrayal of men and women. Matthew Arnold, comparing Chaucer to Dante, found the English poet lacking in "high seriousness." Chaucer is, however, a writer with a deep human sympathy and a great understanding of all sorts and conditions of men, and, among all mediaeval vernacular writers, he was next to Dante, the greatest master of verse form. They are among the few mediaeval poets capable of handling easily a highly-polished verse style and of writing, with sustained interest, long passages of description, elaborate comparisons, and complex and difficult thoughts. Mediaeval literature—except lyric poetry—often lacks form and structure; some of the best works sprawl. But Dante and Chaucer were both deeply influenced by Virgil and Ovid and learned from them the high art of writing long poems.[4] In Chaucer's time modern English as a fusion of the earlier French of the upper classes and the Anglo-Saxon of the masses was coming into universal usage, and Chaucer's writings were one of the contributory forces in this change. It would seem that it was largely a matter of chance that there appeared no great work in the field of the mediaeval drama, whereas out of the fabliaux and the novelle there came Boccaccio's *Decameron* and Chaucer's *Canterbury Tales.*

3. HISTORY, BIOGRAPHY, AND SERMONS

THE MEDIAEVAL outlook on history, and much of its interest in the past, came ultimately from Augustine's *City of God*. The Christian epic, as Augustine conceived it, traced the story of man from Eden through the Crucifixion and the Resurrection to the Last Judgment. Into this vast framework all the events of history had to be arranged. It is for this reason that many mediaeval historians start their works with a long survey of the past drawn from earlier accounts. They begin to be more detailed and more interesting only as they approach their own time. Only when their written sources failed them do many mediaeval historians become interesting. Even then, nearly all mediaeval historians are inclined to be episodical, and they make few attempts to analyze the deeper political, social, economic, and intellectual currents. Besides the influence of Augustine on the writing of history between 1000 to 1500, there was also that of Bede. His reputation as a writer of textbooks helped to create an audience for his famous history and his works on chronology. Bede's influence on historical writing was on the side of a careful search for facts, of order and system in the arrangement and presentation of these facts, and of sane judgment in interpreting them. Few writers, after 1000, achieved Bede's standards in all these matters.

Among the great mass of Latin and, later, of vernacular histories that were written, few attain high eminence as literature. Many mediaeval historical works have been carefully edited in the last two centuries and are still studied simply because they contain material for the modern historian which is not otherwise available. A revival of historical writing in the eleventh and twelfth centuries saw the creation of a number of outstanding Latin histories in England, Germany, and France. William of Malmesbury (d. 1142), in two works, carried the story of England from the Anglo-Saxon migration to 1142. He was impressed by Anselm's teaching, which emphasized the right handling of authorities and the use of careful reasoning in proving all ideas. He tells us, too, that he was deeply influenced by the historical works of Bede. His work is marked by unusual impartiality in dealing with Anglo-Saxon and Norman affairs; it is well organized and shows a fine sense for the dramatic. His contemporary, Ordericus Vitalis (d. 1143), in his *Ecclesiastical History*, wrote a world history from the time of Christ; his account is original only from the Norman Conquest on. His work lacks organization and he is careless about the correct dating of events, but his interests ranged over all types of subjects and over events in all of Europe, and he shows great insight in estimating men. The ablest of English mediaeval historians was Matthew Paris (d. 1259). As a young man he had studied at the University of Paris; on his return to England he became a monk, but he spent much time at the court of Henry III and was sent to Norway on a diplomatic mission by the pope. He began by rewriting, with changes, the *Flowers of History* of Roger of Wendover, a world history to 1235; he continued this work down to 1259. Matthew Paris was greatly interested in all political and constitutional problems, and his analysis of the changes in the English government from *Magna Carta* to the rise of parliament is remarkable for its understanding. His account includes many important documents; no other mediaeval English historian, except perhaps Bede, combined so well a capacity to collect facts and to interpret them. Matthew Paris was a born historian.

The most interesting Latin history in Germany during the twelfth century was the work of Otto of Freising (d. 1158), the uncle of Frederick Barbarossa. In his two most important works, the *Book of Two Cities* and *The Deeds of the Emperor Frederick I*, he tells the story of mankind from the creation to 1146. He is biased in favor of the church and is careless in the handling of details, but his work is written with real force. Otto knew St. Bernard, Anselm, Arnold of Brescia, and many other important people of his time; as a result, he presents a remarkable picture of Hohenstaufen Germany.

The first great historical work written in France after 1000 was

Guibert of Nogent's (d. 1124) *The Deeds of God through the French*, the story of the First Crusade. The work opens with a penetrating analysis of the economic and social situation in France at the end of the eleventh century.[5] In his account of the First Crusade itself, he points out that the motives of the Crusaders were mixed; "many deserted their possessions in a greedy struggle for those of others." But he is also able to see the ideal side of the Crusade. The Crusades were largely a French enterprise, and many of the histories of them, in both prose and verse, were the work of French writers.

The first great vernacular history and one of the first important pieces of prose writing in any of the Romance languages is Villehardouin's (d. 1213) *Conquest of Constantinople*. The author was present in the Fourth Crusade and saw the sack of Constantinople in 1204. He astutely omits much that is unfavorable to his side, but in what he does tell he is accurate, clear, and terse. This is all the more surprising because vernacular prose in all languages was, for centuries, prolix and verbose. In most of the vernacular languages, the earliest specimens of prose writing are legal documents or translations of parts of the Bible or of Latin works. Vernacular prose made its way slowly as education advanced and as more laymen learned to read. By the fourteenth century, prose was regarded as an obvious medium for all sorts of works, but it remained true, in all the vernacular literature, that an effective style in vernacular poetry was achieved centuries before such a style commonly appeared in prose. The longest and one of the most-read historical works written in France, was the section on history of Vincent of Beauvais' (d. 1264) *Speculum*. This historical part of his encyclopedia included about twenty volumes and covered all history from the Garden of Eden to the time of St. Louis (d. 1270). It was entirely a compilation, but a fairly skillful one. It included a mass of information on the literatures and religions of the peoples of antiquity; it had an immense vogue and was widely used and copied.

The most vivid stylist among the French historians of the Middle Ages was Froissart (d. 1410). He was already known as a poet when he published his vernacular *Chronicles of France, Flanders, England, Scotland, and Spain*, covering the years 1326 to 1399. He is a great snob and social climber—it is only the goings-on of kings and nobles that concern him; and he has no talent for analyzing the causes of events. He travelled widely in France, the Low Countries, England, and Italy; he knew Petrarch and perhaps Chaucer, and many of the notable political figures of his time, such as Robert Bruce, the Black Prince, and Edward III. And he could always change his mind to suit his patron; in fact, three different versions of his work survive, each prepared for a different patron. He especially loved to write about weddings, tournaments, battles, knightly adventures, and all the stately circumstance of fourteenth-century chivalry. Loyalty, courage, love of adventure, and elegant manners are the measure of a man. In the chivalric romances the lower classes are usually presented as ugly and stupid; Froissart is indifferent to, rather than contemptuous of, the common people. He is inaccurate in dates, and the names and places of persons, but he makes us see events as does no other mediaeval historian. His talent lay in his ability to evoke scenes in which he sometimes rivals Shakespeare. Walter Scott said it was from Froissart that he had learned his art.

The ablest of all the French mediaeval historians as an analyst of events was Philippe de Commines (d. 1509), whose *Memoirs* of the reigns of Louis XI and Charles VIII reflect the transition to a modern type of historical writing. He analyzes both men and institutions with unusual insight. He is impressed with the power of parliament in England and compares it favorably to the despotism in France. In a detached manner the author examines political intrigues and events to show their causes and meaning. He strongly advises men in political life to study history, "for it holds the master key to all types of frauds, deceits, and perjuries." His cynical view of men and their ways rather resembles the views of Machiavelli and Guiccardini in sixteenth-century Italy. The work was highly esteemed; Charles V called it his breviary, Melanchthon recommended it as useful to princes, and it was a favorite book of Henry IV of France.

From the eleventh to about the middle of the thirteenth centuries the lead in historical writing was taken by England, Germany, and France. During this period Italy had few historians of note, though nearly every large town had its local chronicler. In the second half of the thirteenth century, Salimbene (d. 1290) wrote, in Latin, a fascinating account of his times. Besides the great political events which he records with the touch of a born storyteller, he gives valuable descriptions of the manners, customs, and culture of thirteenth-century Italy. Around 1300 Florence became the cultural capital of Italy, and of this rapidly expanding city there is a remarkable account, in the Tuscan vernacular, by Giovanni Villani (d. 1348). Villani was a layman and a practical man of affairs, and, though he begins his history with the Tower of Babel, when he approaches his own time, he shows himself as an astute man capable of individual observation and judgment. Villani's scope is wide and he includes much material on the general history of Europe. His use of earlier authorities, his feeling for reality, and his range of interests, which covered not only politics but also trade, industry, and religion, make his work the outstanding piece of historical writing of the fourteenth century. His brother and his nephew carried the story of Florence from 1346 to about 1400.

In the fifteenth century, the Italian historians became deeply enamored of the methods and styles of the Greek and Roman historians. They all wrote in Latin and modelled their works on the classical historians. They dropped the idea of universal history in the tradition of Augustine and wrote with a worldly point of view. For the first time, too, the historians became aware of the value of archeology for their studies, and they discovered the usefulness of inscriptions, coins, and other finds which were now being unearthed and collected in the first museums. To dismiss the fifteenth-century Italian historians as mere toadies of noble houses and as empty rhetoricians does scant justice to their merits. Actually they are the founders of modern historical writing. These fifteenth-century Italian historians discovered the true nature of antiquity, and, as they were nearly all laymen and shared, at the same time, a contempt for mediaeval historical methods, they looked at the world about them with a worldly shrewdness. All this meant, in the end, a resecularization of historical studies. At the same time, the study of the politics and culture of the ancient world afforded the historians new standards of comparison with their own age. These new attitudes spread across Europe, and, in the end, led everywhere to a new approach to history.

The first important work of the humanist historians was Bruni's (d. 1444) *History of the Florentine People*. Bruni's work clearly marks the beginning of a more critical historical method. He collected documents and tried to evaluate them and see them in proper perspective, and from them he attempted to understand the underlying causes of events. His work shows careful organization and is very well written. The story is carried to 1444, the year of his death. Soon several others followed in Bruni's steps. Valla (d. 1457) proved that the *Donation of Constantine* was a forgery, a testimony to his courage rather than to his critical capacities, for it was, textually, an easy thing to do. But Valla called attention to the necessity of scrutinizing documents of all types. Blondus (d. 1463) published a long *History since the Decline of the Romans*. Blondus dropped the mediaeval idea of regarding the centuries since the Barbarian Migrations as a part of Roman history. He saw clearly that Rome had disintegrated; he describes her fall and then goes on to tell the story of the new peoples who supplanted Rome. Blondus swept aside all the fantastic rubbish about the Trojan origin of Italian cities and other groundless legends that had cluttered the writings on history for long centuries. His work contributed more to the proper understanding of the Roman and mediaeval past than any work produced since the end of the Roman Empire.[6] Blondus' Latin was clumsy and inelegant, and, unlike most of his fellow Italian historians, he made no effort to please a patron. So his work was not widely circulated. Other writers, however, paid him the tribute of borrowing from it. Blondus is the great precursor of Mabillon and, beyond him, of Ranke and of modern historical method.

The Middle Ages produced not only a large body of historical writing but also a good deal of biography and some autobiography. The commonest form of biography was, as we have seen, the saint's life. This literary genre had taken form in the early Middle Ages and had not been greatly changed in succeeding centuries. The materials for these saints' lives were usually drawn less from a personal knowledge of the subject than from legends. These grew as they passed from one oral reporter to another. As no disbelief blocked the acceptance of miracles, since they interested most people, their multiplication outdistanced other elements of the story. The tendency was to reproduce the same miracles for each saint and also to make the miracles correspond with wonders in the Bible.

After the year 1000, the first important biographical work is the memoirs of the historian Guibert of Nogent (d. 1124). He gives a vivid account of his youth, his education, the growth of his ideas, and the history of his own region in northern France. Guilbert shows himself as a man widely read in classical and early Christian Latin literature and of a skeptical turn of mind on the subject of popular religious superstitions. On the other hand, parts are written with the passionate eloquence and earnestness of Augustine's confessions. From the same twelfth century comes the short but extraordinary autobiographical account of Abelard's early life, *The Story of my Calamities.*

The first important biography in the vernacular was Joinville's (d. 1317) *Life of St. Louis.* Joinville knew the king well and admired him, though not to the extent of going with him on his last crusade in Tunis. Joinville was over eighty when he wrote the book, which is less a systematic biography than a collection of stories and incidents. He tells us that St. Louis wore a hair shirt, that, disliking beer, he always drank it during Lent to mortify the flesh, and that when the able and saintly Louis fell ill he told his son: "I beg thee to make thyself loved by the people of thy kingdom, for indeed I should prefer that a Scot from Scotland came and ruled the people well and faithfully rather than thou should rule them ill." [7] A biographical work of great popularity was the *Golden Legend,* a collection of nearly 250 saints' lives, of James of Voragine (d. 1298). Originally written in Latin, this collection was translated into a number of vernacular languages. It furnished, in popular form, for preachers, artists, and writers, the life stories of most of the principal saints of the Christian calendar and soon became one of the most read of mediaeval books. Another favorite thirteenth-century work was the *Travels* of Marco Polo (d. 1324), a sort of autobiography, dictated in a Genoese prison and written down, in several versions, in French. The best parts tell of what the author saw in China and northern India when he was there with his father and his uncle, two Venetian merchants. Marco Polo was a fascinating raconteur but he was also a somewhat credulous man. He is less accurate in what he says about Japan and other parts of the Orient, which he never saw, than he is about his long stay in China. The discovery of the overland routes to Asia was the outstanding geographical event of the thirteenth century. The taste for travel books about Asia was extensive, and besides Marco Polo's *Travels* there circulated a number of accounts by Franciscan and Dominican missionaries. Some of these influenced Columbus and other early explorers.

The greatest of mediaeval biographies is the anonymous *Little Flowers of St. Francis of Assisi*, written in the vernacular. The teller supplies the saint with the usual collection of miracles, but he is a man of high literary talents, and the subject, St. Francis, the most lovable of mediaeval saints. And here he is brought to life in the most vivid fashion; no other mediaeval biography is so fascinating. The interest in ancient biography as a literary form led two Florentine writers, first Giovanni Villani and later Vespasiano, to undertake collections of short biographies of eminent Florentines: poets, artists, scholars, and statesmen. Neither writer had marked literary talent and the biographies are pedestrian, though of great use to the modern historian. The same may be said of a number of official biographies written by humanists about popes, princes, prelates, rich bankers, and business men who were as eager to have their lives described as they were to have their portraits painted. This desire for earthly fame and this attempt to exalt the individual, which appears very markedly in the fifteenth century, especially in Italy, is clearly one of the notes of a new age.

The surviving body of mediaeval Latin and vernacular literatures is enormous, and any comprehensive account of them should also include some discussion of writings in the fields of science, philosophy, political and social thought, and education, as well as works of devotion. Most of these are discussed in other portions of this work. Students of mediaeval literature have lately called attention to still another important field, that of sermons. For the period beginning in the thirteenth century a mass of sermons has survived; they are much rarer for earlier periods. They form part of the hundreds of religious works which in sheer bulk outnumber any other type of mediaeval writings. In some of these moral and didactic works, and above all in the sermons, the modern student is often able to get as close as he ever can to the thoughts and feelings of the common man. If the literary quality of mediaeval sermons is not very high, this must not obscure the fact that for the study of mediaeval life and society they are invaluable.

For all types of writing, mediaeval men had a high opinion of the value of rules for literature, and they greatly esteemed books of rhetoric and poetics. In all mediaeval centuries the idea prevailed that the art of writing could be learned by anyone who had the patience to master its rules. As we have seen, the early Germanic peoples had this idea and it was later enforced by Latin grammarians and by textbooks for both Latin and the vernacular literatures. So the poet was regarded as a learned craftsman who had the technique of verse at his fingertips, not as a person upon whom inspiration had descended. Dante summed up centuries of mediaeval thought in all these matters when he wrote, in the *De Vulgari Eloquentia*: "Here let the folly of those stand confessed who innocent of art and knowledge, and trusting to genius alone, rush forward to sing of the highest subjects in the highest style."[8] Boccaccio expressed the same idea when he declared: "However deeply the poetic impulse stirs the mind to which it is granted, it very rarely accomplishes anything commendable, if the instruments by which its concepts are to be brought out are wanting; I mean, for example, the precepts of grammar and rhetoric."[9] Occasionally there were writers who were aware that inspiration was important. Bernart de Ventadorn said, "Song can be of little value if it rises not from the depths of the heart"; and Riquier declared, "In all other branches of learning, good teaching is precious, but if God does not endow a man at the outset with knowledge of poetry, he will never gain it."[10] This was decidedly a minority view, and, from the twelfth century on, rhetorics and books of poetics were much read. It was not until education had turned large numbers to reading, and the cheaper multiplication of books by lay copyists and then by printing (accompanied by a stabilization of spelling and grammar) had occurred, that it was possible for a reader to recognize that personal touch which is the basis of individual style.

The production of books increased in the later mediaeval centuries. Before the twelfth century almost all books were written in monastic *scriptoria*. With the growth of towns, a book-trade in the hands of laymen developed. This came gradually, as in the case of other trades, to be divided elaborately. By the fourteenth century, in the larger cities, there were separate guilds of parchment-makers, copyists, illuminators, and binders, though one concern might combine several of these processes. Where this happened, the shopkeeper was usually called a "stationer" from the fact that he had a settled place of business and did not move from town to town. Such a "stationer" was the mediaeval counterpart of a modern printer and publisher combined. He employed copyists, illuminators, and binders. He usually sold his own books and sometimes rented them. The universities regulated the book trade very strictly in the university towns. In centers like Paris, Florence, and Venice, the town governments also regulated the copying and selling of books. A lay reading public began to expand in the thirteenth century, judging from the fact that imaginative works in the vernacular languages, especially chivalric romances, were then written to be read rather than recited. Books became somewhat cheaper in the fourteenth and fifteenth centuries, but they remained relatively expensive and rare before the spread of printing. Bernard of Chartres in the twelfth century had left a personal library of twenty-four volumes; Accursius, a great law teacher of Bologna in the next century, left a library of sixty-three volumes. Chaucer's clerk, who spent all he could get on books, had only twenty volumes. Books were bequeathed in wills along with other property of high value; out of 7,600 English wills of the fifteenth century only 338 books appear as bequests. This makes it obvious that few individuals possessed books.

Access to libraries was not easy, nor were they well distributed. Libraries belonged to cathedrals, monasteries, colleges, and some large parish churches; kings, a few nobles, wealthy bourgeois, and university professors also collected books. The building up of a large library as a gentleman's accomplishment first appears to have become common in Italy in the fifteenth century, and from Italy the vogue of collecting books passed to the kings, prelates, and nobles in all European countries. By 1500 the finest libraries in Europe were those of the Republic of Venice, part of whose collection came from Bessarion, a prelate of the Eastern Church who became a cardinal of the Latin Church, the Medici Library in Florence, and the Vatican Library in Rome.[11]

4. SYMBOLIC LITERATURE

CLOSE to the heart of the Middle Ages was its love for allegory and symbolism. This had early come into Christian thought from Platonism and Stoicism, and, from the beginning, Christian writers and artists had always looked behind external reality to hunt the purposes of God's ways and will. God's universe was all of a piece, and the greater is always somehow reflected in the lesser. So all human experience is packed with meanings at various levels, and one function of the writer, the artist, the teacher, and the preacher was to try to interpret the unknown from the known. Behind every object and every event lay a spiritual implication of which the immediate experience was merely the imperfect reflection. God gave man two sources of knowledge, the Book of Scripture and the Book of Nature. Behind each are hidden meanings to be searched out; the universe is a vast cryptogram to be decoded. The history of Job's sufferings, for example, has, on the surface, a value as a great human story; secondly, it prefigures Christ's death; and thirdly, it represents the trials of the Christian soul. All that is red reminds artist and writer of the blood of Jesus, every stream brings a remembrance of rebirth through baptism, fishermen lowering their nets remind men of their redemption, the crab walking sideways makes one think of the fraudulent, and the pelican, which was supposed to nourish its young with its own blood, was the analogue of Christ. There was no end to this type of symbolism inside the mind of the Middle Ages.

It is for this reason that we so often find mediaeval men looking at the world about them not for what it was but for what it was not. Allegory might be explained or it might be left to be perceived imaginatively. We have already seen the role of allegory and symbolism in literary works like the *Romance of the Rose, Parzival,* and the morality plays. It figures in many other literary works, and, in a number of cases, lies at the heart of some of the greatest literary achievements of the Middle Ages. Of this current in mediaeval letters, three works may be taken as representative: the Latin *Anti-Claudianus,* the Middle English *Vision of Piers Plowman,* and the *Divine Comedy.*

The *Anti-Claudianus* was the work of Alanus de Insulis (or Alain of

Lille, d. 1202), a learned Flemish monk who had spent years in Paris. In a number of works he organized and rephrased much of the learning available in the first half of the twelfth century. The *Anti-Claudianus*, a poem of 4,400 hexameter lines, written in a lofty and epic style, takes its name from a classic Latin poem, Claudian's *In Rufinum*. Here was portrayed the creation of a man, Rufinus, by a conspiracy of the vices and the furies. Alanus' subject is the creation of the soul of man by God. The poet holds that Nature creates the human body out of the four elements, but the creation of the soul can only be an act of God. Nature is unsatisfied with her works and yearns to make a perfect man. She calls a council of the virtues in a beautiful garden. Here, in this garden where the conference is held, stands a glorious palace whose frescoes depict the great men of yore: Plato, Aristotle, Seneca, Ptolemy, Cicero, Virgil, Hercules, Ulysses, Hippolytus, and many others. Nature expounds her plan, and Prudence reminds the council that only God can provide a soul. At the suggestion of Reason, Prudence is delegated to proceed to heaven. Prudence's daughters, the Seven Liberal Arts, make a chariot. Its five horses are the Senses, the Reason is the driver.

As Prudence journeys through space, she learns the cause of snow, rain, and storm, passes the evil spirits of the fallen angels, and then observes the planets and the system of the universe. Reason, unable to proceed further, then turns over the chariot to Theology, and Prudence proceeds through the heavenly orders of Dionysius the Areopagite. She sees the doctors of the church, saints and martyrs, and, above all honored, the Virgin Mary. In a magnificent passage, the Virgin is referred to in a series of epithets derived from allegorical interpretations of the text of the Bible. "Our Lady" is referred to as "Star of the Sea," "Way of Life," "Port of Salvation," "Limit of Piety," "Mother of Pity," "Garden Closed," "Fruitful Olive," "Rose without Thorn," "Light of the Blind," and "Rest of the Tired." Her praises are unnumbered and the recitation of them flows along in magnificent hexameters.[12] The heavenly journey of Prudence overwhelms her and her driver, Reason, until Faith comes to their aid and brings them to the court of the Trinity. Prudence's request is granted, God creates a soul, and entrusts it to Prudence to take to earth. Nature fashions a glorious body to receive the soul, Concord unites the two, and the Virtues and the Arts bestow their gifts. The poem ends with the triumph of virtuous man over the powers of evil and with the transformation of earth into the likeness of heaven.

The materials of the poem came from many sources, but especially from Plato's *Timaeus*, Boethius, Martianus Capella, and many of the writers of Alanus' own twelfth century. Alanus, like Dante later, summarized a great deal of the thought of his time, and his contemporaries called him the "Doctor universalis." But, like Dante, he is a great poet rather than an original thinker. His *Anti-Claudianus* is the greatest didactic and narrative Latin poem of the Middle Ages. In spite of the elaborateness of the allegory and its abstraction the magnificent sweep of many passages in the poem remind one at times of both Dante and Milton.

Alain of Lille was a scholar as well as a poet. Our next book, the *Vision of Piers the Plowman*, is the work of a poor and humble man, probably in minor orders, who lived in fourteenth-century England. The fourteenth and fifteenth centuries, which displayed a great deal of ecclesiastical corruption and much moral slackness, such as one finds in Boccaccio and in the writings of humanists like Filelfo and Valla, witnessed also the later writings of Meister Eckhart, the activities of the "Brethren of the Common Life," and the publication of *Piers Plowman*, the *German Theology*, the *Imitation of Christ*, and the sermons of Savonarola. Apparently, as the centuries passed and the full implication of the teachings of Jesus became better understood by the mass of Christians, some rejected them and turned to worldliness while others took them more seriously and put them more fully into practice.

William Langland (d. 1395), the author of *Piers Plowman*, was evidently a man of simple but intense devotion. His allegorical poem, written in old-fashioned alliterative verse, takes us close to the life of the common people, to the tangled story of their joys and sorrows, to the dull routine and the disappointments that formed the daily life of the masses. He paints a picture of the world as it is, followed by a picture of the world as it might be if the Gospels were obeyed—a series of allegorical visions of the Kingdom of England and the Kingdom of Heaven standing side by side. One May morning the poet falls asleep by a stream in the hills. He sees, in a vision, a "field full of folk" rich and poor, worthy and unworthy, a motley crowd in mortal predicament between the Tower of Heaven and the Pit of Hell. Holy Church appears and exhorts all men to the Truth. But no one knows the way. Then Piers the Plowman appears and offers to be their guide. The story then proceeds through many episodes and digressions in which the world of affairs, of moral interpretation, and of the priestly and episcopal life are unfolded. The third section includes a splendid vision of the Incarnation, the Passion of Our Lord, the Descent into Hell, the Founding of the Church, and the attack on it by Anti-Christ. The life of the hero, Piers the Plowman, is a symbol of the good life as it should be lived, first by the laity, then by the priesthood, and, lastly, by the episcopate. Always a symbol, the hero appears in the poem first as a farmer, then as a priest where he is identified with Christ, and finally as a bishop with St. Peter and his successors.

Though he was a contemporary of Chaucer, the author seems to belong to a different world. He has evidently been somewhat influenced by the reforming spirit of Wyclif and the Lollards. The riches and pretensions of the clergy and the wealthy are condemned. The work clearly reflects the spirit of revolt of the Lollard verses:

When Adam delved and Eve span,
Who was then the gentleman? [13]

The characters are all abstractions, but they are sharply differentiated. They are never presented for their intrinsic interest alone but for their relation to God and his purposes. The poet's range is great; he is, in turn, visionary and realistic, angry and humorous, and, at times, sublime. The poem is written to edify; in intention the author is never artistic; but the author's earnestness and rude vitality make many of his scenes intensely alive and moving. The work exists in three different versions; of these the first and second versions are more effective than the last in which the poem is more than doubled, and the result is dull and chaotic. The great moral of the poem is that in all the evil of the world the righteous can build a better society. The maxims of Do-Well are to be God-fearing, honest, hard-working, charitable, and obedient to the church; those of Do-Better are to be all these things, and, in addition, to teach the ignorant, to heal the suffering, to practice always what one preaches, and to be long suffering in adversity. Finally, the purposes of Do-Best include those of Do-Well and Do-Better, and, beyond this, are to guide the church by such authority of righteousness that others may be saved from hell. The work is a strange one, but it must have met some spiritual need of its time, for it was widely read in England, and many manuscripts of it survive. John Ball, the Lollard agitator, referred to it in his letter of encouragement to the rebellious peasants led by Wat Tyler. Among all literary works in fourteenth-century England, only a few ballads and miracle plays were more widely known.

The great symbolic work of the Middle Ages, and the only achievement of that period to stand in world literature on the same height as the epics of Homer and the plays of Shakespeare, is the *Divine Comedy*. Dante was already well known as a lyric poet, and as a figure in the political life of Florence before he began work on the *Divine Comedy*. Most of its composition was accomplished in dreary years of exile, begun at Verona and ended at Ravenna. The whole work is divided into a hundred cantos; one is introductory, and thirty-three are then devoted to describing each of the three parts of the author's imaginary journey through hell, purgatory, and paradise. At the age of thirty-five, half the three score and ten allotted to man, he enters the other world. It is the Easter season of 1300, and everything he sees is dated from then. The journey occupies a week, from the Thursday evening before Easter, when he enters hell, to the Thursday after Easter, when he stands in the presence of God in paradise. Everything is allegorical: there are thirty-three cantos in each of the three sections as there were thirty-three years in the earthly life of Christ. In honor of the Trinity, there are nine circles in the pit of hell, nine divisions of the mountain of purgatory, and nine heavens in paradise before the empyrean. Also the complicated verse scheme, the *terza rima,* where the rhymes run aba, bcb, cdc, ded, etc., honor the Trinity. The beauty of the whole depends on its grand plan, whose vast sweep reminds one of the plan of Plato's *Republic* or of a Gothic Cathedral, or one of the great theological *Summas*. Some parts have only a slight interest; others speak of forgotten men. Still other parts are very abstract where, as he himself acknowledges, he puts into verse "things difficult to think." In the first two parts, Virgil, a poet rather than a philosopher, represents reason and is his guide. Later, Beatrice, symbolizing revelation, takes Virgil's place as Dante ascends in paradise.

The poem is planned so that it first moves away from God and then toward him. The poet's soul is only at peace when he, through love, is united with God. He begins with the turmoil of sin and a cry for help; this is all man can do until God's grace is extended to him. The realization of sin occupies the poet in hell. In purgatory a slow illumination and deliverance are accomplished. In Paradise, the poet realizes his hope of knowing God. The whole work is held together by the belief (and this idea is repeated many times) that good works without faith, and morality without religion do not suffice for salvation. "The *Inferno*," says Vossler, "may be characterized as the stern song of righteous retribution, the *Purgatorio* as the hopeful chant of merciful vindication, the *Paradiso* as the jubilant hymn of mystic love." [14]

The whole journey of Dante is a vast allegory representing "mankind, as, by its merits and demerits, it exposes itself to the rewards or the punishments of justice." Most punishments in hell are a symbol of the sin itself. The disciplines in purgatory correspond to stages of regeneration of the soul. And the heavens of paradise represent a hierarchy of states of beatitude. As the poet, led by Virgil, descends from one terrace to another in the vast funnel of hell, light, the symbol of truth, diminishes, and the sounds and smells grow more disagreeable. The name of Christ is never mentioned. The poets first meet some of the great philosophers, scientists, and heroes of antiquity among whom are Socrates, Plato, and Aristotle, "the master of those who know." As they go on, they meet a strange miscellany of folk: men and women of antiquity, figures from ancient and mediaeval legendry, and many of Dante's own contemporaries. Among the lustful, for example, are Paris, Dido, Cleopatra, Achilles, Helen of Troy, Tristan, and Paolo and Francesca, two figures near to Dante's own time. Everything is described with amazing vividness; we see and hear and smell with the poet. Some of the damned lie like dogs in the mire under a rain of hail; others burn in pits. Even the drawings of Botticelli and of Blake, inspired by Dante's lines, seem less vivid than his brief and "smiting words." At the bottom of hell, the two poets meet Lucifer, who in his three mouths chews Cassius and Brutus who slew Caesar, the founder of the Roman Empire, and Judas, who betrayed the divine founder of Christianity.

Virgil and Dante then leave hell and ascend the terraces of the lofty mountain of purgatory, "the second realm wherein the spirit of man is purified and becomes worthy to ascend to heaven." Stairs connect each terrace with the terrace above it; beside each stair stand angels most of whom chant "Beatitudes" to admonish the toiler as he mounts. The sights and sounds become more pleasant, the colors are those of sunrise and sunset, the birds sing, and the poets can see the stars. Here, as in hell, the poets meet great figures from the real or legendary past, notable contemporaries, and persons of whom we know little or nothing beyond their bare names like La Pia, a woman of whom Dante merely writes, "Siena gave me birth, Maremma undid me; he is privy to my death who had placed his ring on my finger in matrimony." In the *Purgatorio* Dante also expounds many points of philosophy and his own political views. At the top of purgatory, Dante bids farewell to Virgil, and Beatrice becomes his guide. When Beatrice appears, voices chant, "Blessed art thou who comest" (in the name of the Lord), the greeting of the multitudes to Jesus at his entry into Jerusalem; and then they sing, "Bear lilies with laden hands," the tribute of Anchises to the spirit of Marcellus in the *Aeneid*.

Dante and Beatrice then ascend through paradise. According to the Ptolemaic system—used by both Dante and, with modifications, by Milton—there are nine heavens that revolve about the earth. Each heaven corresponds to one of the emanations of the system of Dionysius the Areopagite: angels, archangels, principalities, and the rest. As in hell and purgatory, Dante discusses many points of philosophy and politics, and he meets a large number of notable persons and again some of his contemporaries. St. Thomas Aquinas, a Dominican, relates the life of St. Francis, and St. Bonaventura, a Franciscan, tells the story of St. Dominic. As Dante moves from one heaven to another, Beatrice grows more lovely, the matters discussed become more spiritual, and the light gradually increases in intensity. The poet is moving nearer to God. Beyond the ninth heaven is the unmoved empyrean wherein dwells God. Here there is no time and no motion, and the light is so bright he can see little; there in the dwelling place of the highest knowledge, power and love, "the natural law," he says, "in naught is relevant." Beatrice presents Dante to the mystic, St. Bernard, and St. Bernard presents him to the Virgin who brings him into the presence of God. Words fail him in the presence of "the love that moves the sun and other stars," and here, near to God, the poem ends.

The *Divine Comedy* is the most grandiose and cosmic creation in world literature ever written by a single hand. Only the *Republic* of Plato can even rival it. Tieck speaks of it as "the voice of ten silent centuries." Its power and beauty lie in its general plan, its sustained grandeur, and in its many superb details. Everything is highly finished; Dante was a superb craftsman. And yet at the same time it all seems inevitable. Carlyle, speaking of its lapidary quality, says Dante tells everything in a few smiting words, as at the end of the Paolo and Francesca incident he says simply "that day they read no further," and again at the end of the Ugolino story, "then hunger did what sorrow could not do." A line like "in his will is our peace" was chosen by Matthew Arnold as "a touchstone" of great poetry. It is, indeed, impossible for the power of man to approach nearer to the power of the divine and for earthly beauty to move nearer to divine beauty.

> *Ah! from what agonies of heart and brain,*
> *What exultations trampling on despair,*
> *What tenderness, what tears, what hate of wrong,*
> *What passionate outcry of a soul in pain,*
> *Uprose this poem of the earth and air,*
> *This mediaeval miracle of song!* [15]

CHAPTER XI

Art and Music

1. ROMANESQUE ART

2. GOTHIC ART

3. INNOVATION IN ITALY

4. MUSIC

THE HISTORY of mediaeval art, as we have seen, is primarily the story of church building. However, from the thirteenth century on, secular architecture becomes of more importance. And in the fourteenth and fifteenth centuries, sculpture and painting developed rapidly—especially in Italy—and began to have a life of their own apart from architecture. The art of the Latin West in the five centuries from 1000 to 1500 shows the same remarkable achievement that marks the development of philosophy, literature, education, and music. Western Europe is everywhere reaching out to create an original civilization of its own; it is no longer the stepchild of a decadent antiquity and of a barbaric German culture. In this evolution there are no sharp breaks; Romanesque art grew slowly out of the art of the Carolingian age; then, in the twelfth century, Gothic art gradually emerged out of the Romanesque, and in the fifteenth century, a new classical style slowly separated itself from the Gothic. First in Romanesque and then in Gothic architecture the tradition of an organic manner of construction, inherited from Roman antiquity, was subjected to long experimentation, and new types of construction were evolved. The Ro-

384]

manesque continued ancient types of building; the Gothic, which grew out of it, was essentially a new engineering departure. At the same time, painting and sculpture, which long remained under the spell of Byzantine styles, began, in the later twelfth century, to show more observation of nature; and so Gothic painting and sculpture turned to imitate nature forms, and, by the thirteenth century, both begin to attain realism. To this realistic urge in Gothic art, Italy added, in the generations from Niccolò Pisano to Donatello, an enthusiastic interest in classical models in sculpture and architecture. By the fifteenth century, the spell of antiquity, working with the desire for realistic representation, had moved Italy out of Gothic art into a new style.

Considering the technological and the economic backwardness of mediaeval Latin Christendom, its architectural achievements are phenomenal. Thousands of heavy stone and brick buildings were constructed: cathedrals, abbeys, parish churches, castles, and town halls. Village vied with village, and town rivalled town in the construction of great churches. Around these sanctuaries much of the life of the common people revolved; all the great events of the life of the individual, of his family, and of the community were centered in them. The churches were also used for many secular purposes. In time of war, men sought asylum there and the peasants might put their livestock in the church. And, even in peace-time, wine and beer, grain and hay were often stored there. The church was also the social and trading center. The itinerant merchants and peddlers set up their booths within the church porch or in front of it, and sometimes they spread out their wares on the flat tombs in the graveyard. When times were more secure, the market was extended out over a square in front of the church. Sometimes the local weights and measures were cut into the church wall so that every man might know them. The construction and decoration of these buildings often occupied generations. Many of these great structures stand today, defying time and its destructive forces; they seem like mighty outposts of eternity set down in a world where everything else passes. Like the great monuments of later Roman and of Byzantine architecture, huge Romanesque and Gothic churches seem built not to the measure of man and this world but to the measure of infinity and eternity.

I. ROMANESQUE ART

THE ELABORATION of Romanesque architecture in the tenth century, like the contemporary rise of feudalism, was partly due to the raids of Vikings, Slavs, Magyars, and Muslims, who pillaged and destroyed wherever they went. The churches with their wooden roofs were often ruined, and the saints' relics in them were destroyed. As a result, there was a desire to build fireproof buildings that could better resist such destruction. There was, likewise, a widespread urge to build on a more sumptuous scale to the greater glory of God. Thus, in the tenth century small churches were constructed, parts or all of which were vaulted with round barrel vaults. Not until the eleventh century were any large vaulted churches built. These appeared over wide areas in western Europe, but were especially remarkable in Catalonia, northern Italy, in parts of France, and in the Rhineland. Whether the buildings got their inspiration from surviving Roman buildings in Italy and France, or from parts of the Near East can probably never be settled. And, also, because of the lack of documents, no agreement has ever been reached on the dates of some of the most important Romanesque buildings. So, not knowing exactly which building preceded which, the earliest development of Romanesque architecture must remain uncertain.

The Romanesque churches of the eleventh and twelfth centuries, in both their ground plan and decoration, show the development of changes that had already begun to be marked in the Carolingian period. The common ground plan was cruciform, sometimes with apses at each end. Within, an ambulatory or walk ran around the apse and gave access to chapels used for the display of relics and for the cult of the saints. To support the vaulting above, the walls had to be heavy— for a barrel vault rests continuously on the whole length of the side wall—and the nave and aisles had to be narrow. At the same time, to support the walls of the nave, heavy compound piers supplanted round columns. There was great variety and ingenuity in the handling of these vaults, though sometimes wooden ceilings replaced vaulting. On the outside, two towers at the western front, polygonal towers and cupolas rising from the roof, sculpture about the doors, and arcades and decorative bands were added, all in contrast to the early Christian basilicas whose exteriors were starkly bare.

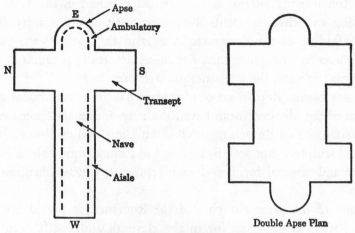

ROMANESQUE GROUND PLANS

CROSS SECTION OF ROMANESQUE CHURCH, TWELFTH
CENTURY

Romanesque buildings, with their heavy walls and piers, their dark interiors—the walls had to support the heavy vaults and so could be pierced only with small windows—and their vaults high above, have a rude power and vigor. The broad, spacious, and well-lighted interiors of the early Christian basilicas, with their emphasis on horizontal lines, are exchanged for dim, narrow interiors with massive walls. The Romanesque interior is the first achievement in the West of a building style that represents the mystic spirit of Christianity. Thus, the unfolding of the Romanesque style in the Latin West, though much later in emergence than Byzantine art, really parallels it. Both the Byzantine and the Romanesque styles resulted from the penetration into Graeco-Roman art of ideas external to the traditional classical art of the Mediterranean basin. Both Byzantine and Romanesque art were based on Roman methods of building, and on Roman painting and sculpture, but both Byzantine and Romanesque styles achieved a new and original form, and each represents a new Christian synthesis.

Many of the great churches of the Romanesque period are connected with monasteries, for in the eleventh and twelfth centuries the monastic clergy were superior in wealth, ability, and prestige to the secular clergy. The monasteries were, in these two centuries, still the great centers of learning and craftsmanship, and they were, in an otherwise localized society, places that exchanged ideas with other monastic centers. It was this exchange among monasteries, and the movement of men along pilgrimage roads, that formed the chief means of spreading ideas. Later on, Gothic architecture was primarily connected with the growing towns.

In the development of Romanesque architecture, the engineering demands of the vaulting determined a good deal of the designing and construction of the lower parts of the building. To harmonize with the round barrel vaults above, Romanesque windows and doors were usually rounded at the top instead of being either square or pointed. The style varied from district to district; for example, six to ten local Romanesque styles have been distinguished in France and similar provincial divisions have been noted in other western European states. But many common features cut across all these local variants. The earlier vaulted naves often used one long, unbroken barrel vault. It was discovered that the use of occasional cross arches broke the monotonous line of the long barrel vault. Also the use of regularly-spaced transverse arches made it possible to build the vault in sections; this saved on the wooden centering which was set up on scaffolding, and on top of which the vaults were built up from each side, stone by stone. Another device was the use of a groined vault placed over a square area by running barrel vaults at right angles to each other. Only squares could be so vaulted with round arches, for if round vaults of different diameters start from the same level they will rise to different heights and cannot be made to intersect in the middle.

These groined vaults, once commonly used by the ancient Romans, were extensively revived in the eleventh century. The stone cutting for the intersections of groined vaults was very hard to handle, and if the edges of the vaults were not sharp the vault was likely to be ragged and ugly in appearance. To handle this problem some masons utilized the old Roman device of building groined vaults with ribs. It was some time before they learned to build the ribs first and then to fill in the spaces with thinner stones. This was a stronger way to build, and the ribs concealed the inequalities of the masonry. When this was fully comprehended one basic feature of Gothic construction was already under way. The first long nave vaulted with ribs was probably that of the *Cathedral of Durham*, one of the greatest of all mediaeval churches, though the masons who built the vaults at Durham did not realize the technical possibilities of the methods they were using. Also in the twelfth century, while the ribbed vault was being developed, pointed barrel vaults and pointed windows were being tried. Pointed arches are easier to build than round ones, for more of the curve is near the perpendicular; also, pointed vaults and arches have less side thrust than round ones. The Hindus have a saying that "an arch or a vault never sleeps," that is, it always exerts pressure both downward and outward. With the use of pointed arches and pointed ribbed vaults it was possible to vault not only rectangular spaces but spaces where no two sides were the same without ever getting into trouble about the level heights for the arches.

Once the builders learned to combine the ribbed vault, the pointed arch, and the pointed vault into one integrated system, Gothic architecture was born, and the whole structure and feeling of the church was in for a thorough modification. The *Abbey Church of St. Denis* was begun in 1140. The Abbot Suger got together the best masons, painters, and stained glass makers he could find. Their collaboration resulted in the apse and choir of a church which, though intended to be the summation of the Romanesque building art, became instead the first great Gothic construction. If northern France did not invent the ribbed and pointed vault it was the first country to realize its possibilities.

The stone castle also developed in the same eleventh and twelfth centuries. Before this time places of defense were often wooden stockades. Gradually stone walls and towers replaced wooden ones. The first stone towers were square; then it was discovered that round towers could be more easily defended. Inside the castle walls, the main structure was the hall, which came from the early Germans. It was a huge room with an open, beamed roof, with a hole to let out the smoke from the fire in the middle of the floor. By the thirteenth century, fireplaces against the wall were used instead. At one end of the hall was a raised dais for the lord and his family; at the other end was a minstrels' gallery. On the floor, usually covered with rushes, stood trestle tables; against the wall were iron-bound wooden chests with cushions for loungers. Above, on the bare walls, were sometimes bright tapestries or great wall paintings with scenes of battles and tournaments. The master's bedroom had painted chests of drawers, cupboards, and a huge bed, hung with curtains. One found in the castle few comforts and little privacy. In the towns, from about 1200 on, the houses were often cozy, with glazed windows and small rooms that could be heated in the winter by fireplaces, rooms small enough so that they could be kept cleaner than were those in the castles. The interiors shown by the Flemish and Italian painters of the later Middle Ages prove that the town was the home of comforts. The peasantry lived in houses built of stone rubble, or of heavy squared beams with the open spaces filled with mud plastered on woven branches or reeds, or again, of wattle work: stakes, sticks, and mud. They had usually one large room, containing a chest, a trestle table, stools, and a bed. Peasant houses usually had only shutters at the windows. The principal buildings in the peasant village were the church, with an open place in front of it, and the lord's castle, or the manor house of his agent.

The sculpture, painting, and minor arts of the Romanesque period are full of the influence of Byzantine and Carolingian ivories, metal work, and manuscript illuminations. All of these arts show the same transcendental character with much abstraction and stylization and no direct observation of nature. The sculpture, in adapting designs from Byzantine objects, copied their stylistic devices such as concentric folds of drapery over chest and knees. Sometimes the inspiration came from antique sculpture; this was especially true in Italy and southern France. So the influence of Roman, Byzantine, and Carolingian art on Romanesque art varied from the approximation to ancient Roman sculpture in southern France and parts of Italy to the almost purely primitive art of the portals of Norman churches in England. Whatever their models, the Romanesque sculptors put them to such original and varied uses and infused them with so much spirit that they created a magnificent new decorative art.

Much the same thing happened in painting, though except for a few wall frescoes and some manuscript illuminations, little of this art has survived. It is curious that both Romanesque sculpture and painting began with highly sophisticated Roman and Byzantine designs and moved, in some areas, gradually toward simplicity and naturalness—ideals not realized before the Gothic period. At times, the artist deliberately distorted the form to emphasize some quality of the subject, as is done in much twentieth-century art. Both painting and sculpture, so far as they formed part of the decorations of buildings, are subordinated strictly to the architecture. The sculpture is usually embedded in the thickness of the building material and rarely violates the mass of the structure. Bodies are flattened and elongated and, on the capitals of columns, they are twisted and arranged so as to emphasize the structural lines of the architectural forms. Subjects are chosen partly for their decorative effect, and partly for their religious and symbolic significance. Events in the Old Testament are set beside subjects in the New in order to indicate how the one foreshadows the other. Into vast decorative schemes, especially about the doors on the western front, are worked the signs of the zodiac, the labors of the months, the seven liberal arts, the great thinkers of antiquity, the lives of the saints, scenes from daily life, and large numbers of animals, both real and fabulous.[1] The large sculpture, the wall paintings, the enamels, stained glass, the manuscript decorations, and the ivory and metalwork have the same power and monumentality that Romanesque buildings possess. About all of Romanesque art there is an air of primeval vigor which reminds one of the rude strength of the *Song of Roland.*[2]

2. GOTHIC ART

I N the later twelfth century, while Latin Christendom was being covered with great Romanesque buildings, advanced experimentation in the construction of churches led to the first building in the Gothic style. Sometimes it is difficult to differentiate clearly between the two styles, for the steps from Romanesque construction to Gothic are gradual. Gothic art, of course, had nothing to do with the Goths of history. The expression was first used as a term of opprobrium for a style that in the sixteenth century was out of fashion. Actually, Gothic architecture, painting, and sculpture arose first in northern France, and from there spread through Latin Christendom. As in the case of Romanesque art, there were many local variations in the Gothic style. In France the Gothic builders laid great emphasis on the relative height of their interiors—the vaulting in the choir of the *Cathedral of Beauvais* is 157 feet high—in England, emphasis was rather on the length of the interior. In Italy, where the style was neither well understood nor deeply rooted, the buildings are often badly designed, poorly constructed, and held together only by iron tie-rods. The Gothic style, however, lasted long enough to affect every phase of art, from the design of vast cathedrals to that of a page of a manuscript or even to the style of writing a letter of the text.

Gothic architecture, as we have seen, was a natural development out of the Romanesque; it was the last stage of an organic type of construction that had begun to develop in Latin Christendom by the tenth century. The essential features of Gothic engineering are vaults laid on ribs and so constructed that the weight of the vaulting is carried to a series of piers at the sides of the structure. The side walls then become screens to keep out the weather. Having little to do with supporting the vaults above, they can then be replaced with vast areas of glass. To strengthen the building, buttresses were built at the points where the ribs carry the weight of the vaulting into the piers below;

these buttresses may consist only of a thickening of areas along the side wall or they may mean a series of flying buttresses that carry part of the thrust of the vault onto piers outside the building. In such a building, the whole structure is in an elaborate equilibrium of thrust and counter-thrust. This vast armature of stone, more like an engine than a monument, must be kept in repair or it will collapse. Later schools of architecture said that a Gothic church, with its long rows of flying buttresses, was like an animal that carried part of its bony framework outside. In Gothic architecture the interior and the exterior are closely integrated. A Gothic architect would have been horrified and perplexed by Wren's work at St. Paul's in London where he put up a high blank wall on top of the walls of the side aisles to hide the flying buttresses of the nave.

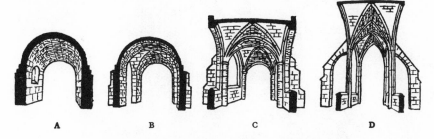

A   B   C   D

EVOLUTION OF MEDIAEVAL VAULTING

A. A very early Romanesque barrel vault. B. Section through piers of an early Romanesque round-arched groin vault. C. Section through window showing later round-arched and ribbed groin vault. D. Section through window bay showing typical Gothic pointed arch vault with ribs, piers, and flying buttresses.

The golden age of Gothic was the thirteenth century. To this period belong the great cathedrals and sculpture of northern France at Paris, Chartres, Rheims, and Amiens, all of which are dedicated to the Virgin. The façades of Paris and Rheims and the nave of Amiens represent the most successful combination of strength and grace in the whole history of the style. In later Gothic architecture, the decorated and perpendicular styles in England, and the flamboyant style in France, both of which were paralleled in other countries, the great emphasis is laid on intricacy of decorative features. The supports are reduced to the lowest possible size to support the structure. Everything

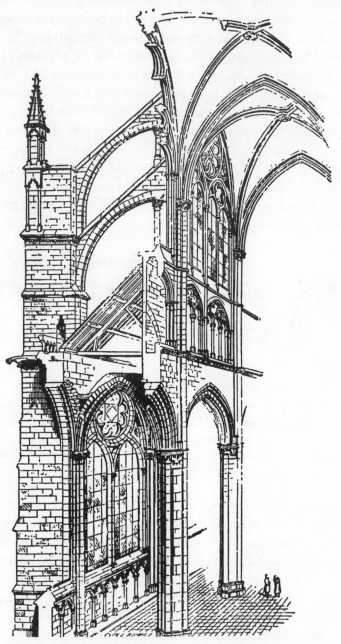

STRUCTURAL FRAMEWORK OF GOTHIC CATHEDRAL,
THIRTEENTH CENTURY

becomes more complex, just as in philosophy one moves from Aquinas to Duns Scotus and Ockham. The tracery in the windows was now very elaborate and above there were often complicated vaulting schemes, like the lierne and fan vaults in England. As in the case of

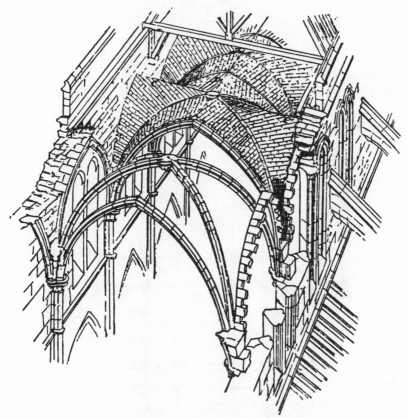

GOTHIC VAULTS, THIRTEENTH CENTURY

the Rococo style in the eighteenth century, what was gained in grace and skill of execution was lost in power and dignity.

In Gothic decoration it was the custom, as it had been in Romanesque art, to paint the sculpture and the interiors with subdued colors. The sculpture of both human figures and plant and animal forms shows a careful observation of nature and often amazing realism. Painting, in manuscript illumination, in frescoes and panel pictures, and designs for stained glass and tapestry remained longer under the

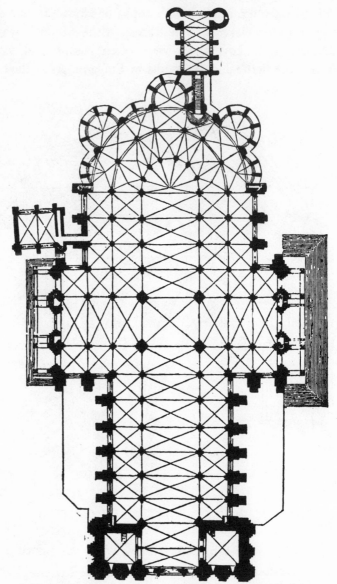

GROUND PLAN OF CHARTRES CATHEDRAL

spell of Byzantine and Romanesque forms than did sculpture. For a time, as the architecture became more transcendental and other-worldly, the sculpture became more worldly and realistic. Among the minor arts, such as ivory and metal work, tapestry, and enamels, stained glass stands as one of the great arts of the Gothic period. Romanesque builders had used some stained glass but not till the Gothic thirteenth century did the art come to full flowering. The windows were built up of small, but thick and uneven, pieces of glass, leaded together to form designs. All the color is in the glass; painting is rarely done on the glass except to put in, in black, folds of drapery and features. The small designs, in turn, were fitted into iron armatures and fastened then into stone tracery. With the large amount of leading, metal frame, and stone tracery, nearly a fifth of the surface of the window is black. And the brilliant points of color are seen against a dark background. The effect is incredibly rich; these windows form a sort of incense of color. These screens of colored fire are more ecstatic as a wall decoration than fresco or oil painting, tapestry or mosaic.[3]

The decoration of Gothic churches in France, and to a lesser extent in other countries, followed an elaborate plan; usually, this is based on Vincent of Beauvais' *Speculum.* A large Gothic cathedral might have as many as 10,000 figures in glass and stone and on painted walls; as Victor Hugo said, in effect, the Middle Ages never had an idea they did not express in glass or stone. There were characters and stories from the Old and New Testament, from the legends of the saints and from history. The labors of the seasons, the seven liberal arts, bits of plant and animal life, incidents from daily life and the devils of hell were all worked into vast schemes in which didactic and artistic purposes combine. Here, on the church, was a symbolic summation of all the knowledge one needed for salvation, a summary for the common man, as Aquinas made a summary in philosophy, and as Dante created one in poetry. Out of infinite variety and universal diversity, churchmen and artists made a vast harmony.[4]

Beginning with the Gothic period, it is possible to know something about the actual conditions of building. As building operations were often in the country, away from towns, workmen in the building trades were, before the fourteenth century, not as commonly organized in guilds as were other types of workers. Each type of craftsman trained his own apprentices. The master mason made the plans for the building; and the names of several thousand of these mediaeval architects are known. The building operations were supervised either by the master mason or by a clerk of the works appointed by the patron, a bishop, an abbot, a noble, or a town government. From the thirteenth century on, the building of castles, town and guild halls, and even fine bourgeois residences, like the house of Jacques Coeur at Bourges, occupied vast numbers of workers. The master mason was usually very well paid, and the position was one that commanded respect. An elaborate notebook of a thirteenth-century French master mason, Villard de Honnecourt (and others) has survived. It has a fascinating collection of sketches of plans, sculptures, and details of buildings of France and Switzerland. It also shows designs for a sawmill, an arrangement for lifting heavy weights, and other mechanical devices. This work proves that a master mason would usually be a man of wide knowledge, inventive capacity, and experience of men and materials.

In off-seasons the master mason or the clerk of the works travelled about looking after the preparation of lumber, the quarrying and cutting of stone, and the baking of brick. Back on the job, he had to provide plans, hire and pay the workers, and supervise the construction. Sometimes a master mason owned his own quarry. On the buildings themselves there were usually two groups of masons at work, the rough masons who hewed the heavy stones, mixed mortar, and laid the stones, and the free masons who worked with chisel and mallet on decorative sculpture, door and window moulding, on ribs of the vaults, and on window tracery. They were called "free-masons," for the stone they used could be worked freely in all directions or sawed clean with a toothed saw; such stone could be deeply undercut and lent itself to elaborate carving, and to the exact cutting needed in vaulting ribs and tracery. Their work demanded skill, for a slight error in one section would ruin the whole plan. In the later Middle Ages, elaborate drawings and wooden models of whole buildings and of parts of buildings were sometimes used in planning and construction.

The free masons were the sculptors for doorways, altars, and tombs. Sometimes they received the stones from the quarry already roughly shaped, and only needing finishing. Some quarries employed free masons who turned out sculpture at the quarry. In the fourteenth and fifteenth centuries more work was done at the quarry; this saved greatly in the cost of transport. Quarrying was usually done, on a small scale, from escarpments on hillsides, for quarrying or mining to any depth was impossible, as they had only buckets to take out the water. The work was done laboriously with picks, axes, and chisels. Next in importance to the masons were the carpenters. They were needed to build frames, scaffoldings, and centering for the use of the masons, and, in finishing the building, they added choir stalls and other types of furniture; finally the roof was their work. Except in Sicily, southern Spain, and a few other places where it did not freeze in the winter, the vaults had to be covered to keep off the weather. A huge wooden framework was constructed on top of the vaults, and this was, in turn, covered with plates of lead, copper, thin stones, or tiles. Many mediaeval buildings were never vaulted, and the only roofs they had were those made of wood.

Workmen did much of their preliminary work in large wooden sheds called lodges. Sometimes, if there was no town to house the workers, workmen had to live in sheds. A lodge was a place where work was done; here the workers also ate their noonday meal and stored their tools and supplies. Churches were usually slow in being built because only part of each year's income was set aside for building. On a large church a skeleton staff would be kept between building seasons. Castles, town halls, and other secular buildings were usually put up more rapidly. Transportation was easier by water than by land, but was in any case always difficult. The huge mediaeval buildings, constructed without the use of steam or electric derricks or of reinforced concrete or of any other modern building devices, must have presented appalling difficulties. Little wonder that they called out the devotion and energy of mediaeval communities for many generations.[5]

The Gothic sculptor borrowed ideas from his Romanesque forerunners, but he largely gave up using as models miniatures and ivories, and the sculptor looked about and began to imitate nature. Everything the artist saw in creation reflected God, but the attitude of the artist toward nature was changing. In the eleventh century Peter Damian declared: "The world is so filthy with vices that any holy mind is befouled by even thinking of it." In the thirteenth century Vincent of Beauvais said: "How great is even the humblest beauty of this world.

I am moved with spiritual sweetness toward the creator of this world, when I behold the magnitude and beauty of his creation." [6] It is not yet the mere beauty of this world that is praised; it is the beauty of the Lord's creation as in St. Francis' *Hymn to the Sun*. Sculptures are now done more in the round, and with more independence of the building behind them. Besides the plastic sense and the correctness in representing human, animal, and plant forms, the Gothic sculptors of the thirteenth century achieved a wonderful simplicity and idealization. It was one of the supreme periods in the history of sculpture, and there is a striking similarity between the draped figures of the Parthenon pediments and those from the west front of the cathedral of Rheims. In both cases, there is an amazing skill in using the flow of drapery to indicate the body underneath, and in both there is also a great force and loftiness.

The fourteenth and fifteenth centuries were a period when the Gothic sculptors were busied in making altar pieces, devotional statues, and tombs. The style became much more realistic, and, at the same time, more emotional. Details of the physical suffering of Jesus and the saints and the agonies of the mourning "Mother of God" are emphasized; the art of the time often seems a commentary on the Biblical line "Jesus wept." Much of this came from the preaching and teaching of the Franciscans; some of it was derived from the religious drama. At the same time, macabre subjects like the "Dance of Death" where skeletons invite the living, high and low, to dance, became popular in art and literature. This emotionality was carried even further in painting, where it reached its climax in the early sixteenth century in the *Isenheim Altar Piece* of Grünewald (d. 1528). The increasing skill of the stone and wood workers often led to the display of ingenuity, and to an over-fussiness of detail. What sculpture gained in subtlety it lost in idealism and monumentality. The sculpture of various countries became more clearly differentiated. Two later Gothic sculptors in the north of Europe developed a style of great realistic power. Claus Sluter (d. 1406), a Hollander, who worked chiefly at the brilliant court of the Duke of Burgundy at Dijon, and Till Riemenschneider (d. 1531), a Saxon active in southern Germany, gave to their figures a vigorous realism and a dramatic force rarely attained by Gothic sculpture. To this growing realism of Gothic sculpture, there was added first in Italy a self-conscious imitation of classical models. And as in poetry, so in sculpture and architecture, this combination marked the dawn of a new age.

Gothic painting in Italy, France, Germany, and the Low Countries reached a high level in the last two mediaeval centuries. Already in the thirteenth century, the painters, like the sculptors, cease to depend on earlier models, and begin to look at the world about them. They made less advance than the sculptors, for the sculptor does not need foreshortening or modelling in light and shade to create an illusion of depth, as his work stands in real space and in real light. But in both composition and drawing the painters produce more life-like, and less transcendental results. In the drawing of a figure the artist definitely tries to convey a sense of form. The first great school of Gothic painters was that of Siena. Here, first Duccio (d. 1339) and then Simone Martini and others took the old Byzantine designs and rehandled them in a less rigid way. Simone Martini went to Avignon, where he met Petrarch and painted a portrait of Laura. Portraits of individuals done from life increased in number in the fourteenth century. In general, however, the Sienese painters looked backward. Their compositions, usually set against a gold background, and making no attempt to represent depth, are very subtle and sophisticated. And their pictures are executed with marvellous finish. The Sienese school is weak in power, but many of its best pictures have a sophisticated and exquisite delicacy unmatched in mediaeval painting. Siena, famed for her mystic saints and for her spendthrift club of gilded youths, lives in many of these pictures as it does also in some of the verses of Folgore da San Gimignano. The work of the early Sienese painters represents the last great flowering of Byzantine painting rather than a new departure.

In Florence, Giotto (d. 1336) begins to get on the flat surface of a painting something of a three dimensional effect. He also shows great skill in foreshortening. This meant a change in the whole conception of painting, for with these devices—modelling in light and shade, precision in drawing, and foreshortening—the painter could create the illusion of an event happening before the spectator's eyes. Most effective in his large frescoes at Padua and Florence is his dramatic skill in composing a whole scene and his power of creating a mood by effective gestures of the main figures of a composition. Giotto conceived a picture as a single unit, not as a series of scattered figures or incidents. His style was worked out chiefly for large fresco paintings for the bare walls of Italian Gothic churches. These had to be executed rapidly, and had to be so handled that the general effect would carry at a distance. Men so revered Giotto that all art was long supposed to have turned a corner with his career. Poliziano, later on, wrote an epitaph for his tomb: "Lo, I am he by whom painting was restored to life, to whose right hand all was possible." For nearly a century after Giotto, the painters of Florence imitated his style. Only with Masaccio did painting move far ahead; even in the fifteenth century, Fra Angelico was still, in many ways, painting inside the same mediaeval traditions.

In nearly all the states of Latin Christendom native schools of painting flourished. They all borrowed a great deal from one another, and in the late fourteenth century formed what has been called the "international style." In the fifteenth century, of all the schools of Gothic art outside that of Italy, the most remarkable is that of Flanders. It first attracted attention through its effective use of an oil technique, and through the completion of a great altarpiece, the *Adoration of the Lamb* by Hubert and Jan van Eyck in 1432.[7] The Flemish school combined, from the van Eycks on, an amazing realism with intense religious devotion. The early Flemish painters showed no influences of classical literature and of classical sculpture, which were casting such a spell over the Italian painters of the fifteenth century. Nor were they much interested in technical experiments in perspective, foreshortening, and the representation of movement. Theirs was a native, homespun art which, according to Michelangelo, should only appeal to children and old women. But they were magnificent craftsmen in painting details. They strung together vividly painted items according to decorative rather than pictorial principles. Painting in oil, they could endlessly work over a picture; this was less possible with tempera painting, and hardly possible at all in fresco painting where the color had to be put on the wet plaster before it dried. With infinite patience, the Flemish painters seem to paint in every blade in the grass, every hair on a horse's mane, on the head of a man, or on the fur-trimming on costumes. They took a naïve delight in seeing the objects of their own craftsmanship in their paintings. No detail, however homely, came amiss, and they thought nothing of having the Annunciation of the Virgin take place inside a cozy Flemish sitting room. Their pictures were so solidly built that the tooth of time has gnawed at them in vain; their colors are today bright and glowing. They are still mediaeval in their spirit of religious devotion; this is particularly true of Roger van der Weyden (d. 1464), and Hans Memling, among the greatest painters of the Flemish school, whose devotional paintings represent the same mood as the work of other famous Flemings, the mystic, Thomas à Kempis, and the composers, Dufay and Josquin des Prés. They are still mediaeval, too, in their interest in telling a story. In the handling of light and shade and in the use of an oil technique the Flemish painters in the early fifteenth century were, for a time, in advance of the Italians, who collected Flemish paintings and studied them.

The Gothic painters of France, Spain, Austria, and Germany were often men of high gifts. In each country there was no common style, but rather a series of local schools which became very productive in the fifteenth century. The last great figure in mediaeval painting in the north of Europe, Albrecht Dürer (d. 1528) of Nuremberg, handled the traditional Gothic themes with matchless skill. His paintings and woodcuts, though they show the new currents from Italy, still echo the last enchantments of the Middle Ages. By the beginning of the sixteenth century the Italians, especially the Florentines, had forged so far ahead of the rest of Europe in technical devices that the talents began flocking to Italy to study. In the sixteenth century most of the local schools of painting outside Italy became very Italianate in manner; Italian compositions, classical ruins, Italian buildings, and Italian types and landscapes were everywhere.

3. INNOVATION IN ITALY

GOTHIC art had moved rapidly, after 1200, toward a style of sculpture and of painting based on a close observation of natural forms. This shift away from Byzantine and Romanesque designs had first become clearly defined in France, and had spread, from there, across Latin Christendom. To this growing naturalism the Italians added a self-conscious imitation of classical forms. This is first manifested in the home of the earliest school of Italian poetry in southern Italy and Sicily. Here, sculptors in the thirteenth century were trained by copying and adapting ancient Roman models. From this background, it seems, came Niccolò Pisano (d. 1278). In a number of works, especially in reliefs on a pulpit in Pisa, he combines a close observation of natural forms in men and animals with a deliberate adaptation of details from Roman sculpture, in modelling, poses, costume, and setting. Many of these details were suggested by Roman sarcophagi. After Niccolò's time, most sculptures for over a century reverted to more or less traditional Gothic lines.

The movement so tentatively started by Niccolò Pisano began to move rapidly ahead in the fifteenth century. Here the great initiator was the architect Brunelleschi (d. 1446). As a youth, he was trained as a goldsmith; then he spent some time in Rome, part of it, according to an old tradition, in the company of Donatello. Here he had measured the ruins and made sketches of them.[8] When he returned to Florence he began to adapt this material to the needs of his native city. In a series of buildings, including the cathedral dome, he took from traditional building methods and from his classical studies what he needed, and combined them into an essentially new style. His use of classical columns, pilasters, and arches began a type of building that, with many modifications, lasted for five centuries. In addition, Brunelleschi discovered the mathematical laws of perspective including the one by which objects diminish in size as they recede into the background. Wherever perspective had been used before in art it had been based on rule-of-thumb methods. This momentous discovery of Brunelleschi revolutionized all the major arts.

His influence on architecture appears in the later fifteenth century in the work of Alberti and Bramante. Alberti (d. 1472) was a scholar and writer as well as an artist; a Latin comedy of his was mistaken for an original work of Terence. Alberti wrote important treatises on education, politics, painting, architecture, and sculpture—the last three are the first important modern aesthetic treatises. In his writings on architecture he adopted many of the ideas of Vitruvius, whose work had been discovered by Alberti's friend, the humanist, Poggio. We see in his writings that there were growing up in fifteenth-century Italy certain new ideas: the idea of style as something to be created by the individual artist devoted to the production of things beautiful and interesting in themselves, and the idea of the art lover for whom art was an intellectual diversion. In his writings and in the buildings he designed, Alberti conceived of ornament and decoration apart from symbolism, and also somewhat apart from the engineering structure of the building. He was essentially a theorist and an amateur; he prepared plans, but always left the actual building to others. Like Brunelleschi he is less the successor of the mediaeval master mason than the precursor of the modern architect. Thus, Alberti helped to give to architecture a certain papery and inorganic quality which it was to have for centuries. There is often little integration of the exterior and interior, and much architectural design is simply a sort of external decoration, that, compared with Romanesque and Gothic building, seems superficial. The spell of classical architecture on Alberti is strong; according to him the essence of beauty lies in classical balance and proportion: "The harmony and concord of all parts achieved in such a manner that nothing could be added or taken away or altered except for the worse." A Gothic building was rarely completed, and additions could always be made. Buildings now, for the first time since the fall of Rome, were conceived as aesthetic wholes in which no changes or additions were possible. Bramante (d. 1514) began the practice of designing buildings on a colossal scale that marked the transition to the grand style of the sixteenth century. His plan for St. Peter's in Rome, though it was never carried through, was "to place the Pantheon on top of the Basilica of Constantine." When Bramante, Raphael, and Michelangelo went to live in Rome, the papal capital replaced Florence as the art center of Italy.

Brunelleschi's ideas not only turned architecture to new ideals, but they also modified sculpture and painting. His interest in classical models and in perspective appears in the sculptures of Ghiberti (d. 1455), especially those on the second set of doors he made for the *Baptistery* in Florence. Here the figures in relief, in a series of scenes from the Old Testament, are carefully observed from nature, though the proportions of the bodies, the gestures, and the groupings show the influence of Roman sculpture. Perspective is very skillfully used in the backgrounds. The influence of Ghiberti is evident on both the painters and the Florentine sculptors of the fifteenth century; especially is it marked on the art of Brunelleschi's friend, Donatello (d. 1466), the most gifted of all Italian sculptors before Michelangelo. His work has an enormous range and vitality. Like the other sculptors of his time he is a careful student of nature, and his most outstanding characteristic is his realism—in which he is continuing a Gothic tradition. Most of the artists now made endless sketches from natural objects and their sketch-books were later drawn on for ideas for their pictures and sculptures. In addition, Donatello, like the artists and writers of his time, was deeply interested in the achievements of the classical past. And it is evident that he had studied what Roman sculpture was available. He combined all of these interests in a vivid style of his own, a style full of nervous energy. As Vasari said of one of Donatello's figures, "life seems to move within the stone." One of his most original creations was the *Gattamelata* at Padua, the first equestrian bronze statue since the fall of Rome. In his *David* he made the first nude bronze statue that had been made in Italy for ten centuries. Indeed, Donatello is the first sculptor since antiquity to treat sculpture as an art independent of architecture. His close friendship with Cosimo de' Medici shows that the sculptor was no longer, as in the Middle Ages, regarded as a mere craftsman but a man to be honored in the highest degree, and a fit friend for a prince. The artist now became the social equal of the scholar and the composer of music. Cosimo de' Medici and Donatello are buried in the same tomb in *San Lorenzo* in Florence. Donatello's work not only influenced later Italian sculpture, but it either directly or indirectly influenced much of the sculpture of the rest of western Europe. We are now in a time when all of Latin Christendom is rapidly becoming a series of cultural provinces of Italy.

The changes made in Italy in architecture and sculpture were paralleled by new developments in painting. Alberti says in his treatise on painting, written in 1436: "The function of the painter is to render, with lines and colors, the visible surface of any body or thing so that it appears in relief and just like the body itself." [9] This had been, evidently, one of the purposes of Giotto. Not until Masaccio (d. 1428), however, were further important advances made. He showed great skill in drawing, in handling perspective, in which he was influenced by Brunelleschi, and in using light and shade on the figures. Masaccio, though he died when he was only about twenty-seven years old, left a phenomenal achievement. He used a single source of light to pull his compositions together and to give them depth. His drawing is very skillful, but there are no sharp lines in the coloring; one color merges into another. He also uses aerial (atmospheric) perspective, where objects like rocks and trees lose the intensity of their color in the distance, along with linear perspective to give his pictures depth. Each figure seems to have a substantial existence and to press solidly onto the ground. As a result, his paintings have what Berenson calls "tactile values," and Roger Fry names "plasticity," that is, they clearly produce a three-dimensional effect. There were no classical models for painting as there were for sculpture and architecture, and Masaccio's accomplishment is one of the most revolutionary in the history of art. The Brancacci Chapel in Florence, where his frescoes of the Fall of Man and the life of Peter were painted, became a school where the greatest geniuses went to learn their art.

In the next generations, after the great triumvirate of Brunelleschi, Donatello, and Masaccio, there was a great deal of popular interest in art. Competitions were held more frequently for commissions, and the sample works of the contestants were exhibited to the public. And works when completed attracted people in large crowds. Town governments, princes, nobles, and wealthy burghers vied each with the other in giving commissions to the growing number of men who turned to art as a profession. This patronage was less confined to the church, and artists, more and more, executed works of art for lay patrons. Records show that ever since 1300 the town councils in Italy spent a great deal of time on art projects, and that the towns were willing to devote much wealth to their adornment. Art works were collected and exhibited now more as works of art than as devotional objects. Not since Athens in the fifth century B.C. were men of all ranks so interested in art as they were in fifteenth-century Florence and in many other cities of north and central Italy. Youths who wished to become artists were apprenticed, at the age of ten or twelve, to a master artist who was a member of a guild. In the master's studio the youth was given menial jobs and gradually he worked up from sweeping the studio and grinding colors to learning to draw, to paint, and to model in clay. Finally he would do minor parts of a commission, such as painting in backgrounds, transferring the master's drawing to a panel or a wall, and painting minor figures until such time as he might become a full member of the guild and set up as a master.

One of the traditional types of painting was to put a picture on a wooden panel, which was first covered with gesso, a mixture of glue and fine plaster, and then polished down to a marble-like surface. On this surface the subject was drawn and the underpainting was put in brown or green tones with shading to model the forms. This underpainting reappears in old pictures whose upper layers have flaked off. The final color was then applied. The color was mixed with white of egg which dried quickly and could not easily be repainted. The result was a hard enamel-like surface. The gold was usually gold leaf glued on. In fresco painting, also an old technique, the design was drawn on a section of wet plaster, the picture was painted in colors mixed in water, and plaster and paint dried together. With an oil technique, the colors were mixed with linseed oil, the painting was done on a wooden panel or on canvas. Much repainting was possible, and more brilliant and translucent colors could be attained than with a tempera or fresco technique. After the oil painting was finished it was covered, for its protection, with a transparent varnish. These methods are described in a number of contemporary Italian treatises.

Experimentation in methods of drawing and painting continued through the fifteenth century in Italy. Pollaiuolo (d. 1498) made a more careful study of anatomy than had been made before, particularly of human figures in action, and, in his drawing of nudes, surpassed any of his predecessors. Mantegna (d. 1506) worked in the university town of Padua, famous for its scientific studies and for an interest in classical archeology, and then for the Gonzaga family at Mantua. He loved Roman subjects and excelled in painting Roman soldiers and Roman architecture in a hard, firm style. A greater genius was Piero della Francesca (d. 1492), who discovered enormous new possibilities in lighting his figures. His style represented a long evolution beyond earlier mediaeval paintings, which had taken less notice of light; their flat figures cast no shadows. Masaccio and, still more, Piero della Francesca, used light not only to model their figures, but found it equal in value to perspective in creating the illusion of depth.

Botticelli (d. 1510) handled both religious and mythological subjects in an exquisite and lyrical style that has more charm than strength. Like Fra Angelico, he was less interested in painting the appearances of things than in presenting his own subjective visions. His sad-eyed Venuses and sad-eyed madonnas reflect the sensitive and uneasy soul of the most subtle and subjective of painters.[10]

The summation of all the artistic experiments of fifteenth-century Italy is seen in the work of Leonardo da Vinci (d. 1519). No man in history, since Plato, had shown, at once, so many talents. His training was that of an artist, but he reached out to take all knowledge as his province.[11] In every field he panted for the concrete. His experiments in anatomy and mechanics, and his writings on a wide variety of subjects lay buried in his notebooks, and few were ever published until the nineteenth century. His own time knew him as a painter of portraits and of Biblical subjects. In works like the *Mona Lisa* and the *Last Supper* everything seems as inevitable as in a play of Sophocles. There was no technical device in painting that he did not manipulate with perfect sureness. In what he actually saw in the human body, in animals, in plants, and in rocks he entirely outstripped all his contemporary artists and scientists. He had a direct and objective apprehension of external reality, and he believed that being lies not behind things but in life itself. By this close study of natural appearances he discovered that not only do colors run into one another along the borders of forms, but also that the outlines, if left vague and as though disappearing into shadow, make the figure become more life-like. All impression of dryness and stiffness disappears. The famous invention of Leonardo, called by the Italians "sfumato," meant that something is always left to the imagination of the spectator as he looks at the picture. Leonardo, too, added his own psychological insight and consummate taste. "One has two things to paint" he wrote, "man and his point of view. The first is easy; the second verges on the impossible." What Leonardo had won in his ability to draw, to color, and to compose, and in his capacity to make visible the various ideas and passions of men, became a birthright to his successors like Raphael, Michelangelo, and Titian.

4. MUSIC

MUSIC, the youngest of the arts, had, as we have seen, begun to change in the ninth century, a century that saw also the first development of sequences and of the liturgical drama. Alongside the unharmonized chant of the church and secular songs, there was developing the first harmonized music of which there remains definite evidence. Such a new style came to involve the use of staff lines to indicate pitch. First a single line representing "F" was drawn horizontally across the page to assist in the reading of the neumes. Soon a second line, representing "C," was added above this; the lines were marked "F" and "C." Two more lines were added to produce the four-lined staff; this method of indicating pitch by lines became a permanent usage in Western music. Many of the changes in musical usage that occurred between 850 and 1100 came to be attributed to an Italian monk, Guido of Arezzo (d. 1050). What seems to have happened was that, while Guido added little to musical theory or practice, as a teacher and as a writer on music, he helped to clarify and to spread certain ideas that were more or less common by his time. He was critical of the slovenly practices he heard in the churches—"when the service is celebrated it often sounds not as if we are praising God but as if we were having a quarrel"—and he wished to reform the musical practice of the church.[12] Guido's writings are based on a six-tone system, with a half-tone between the third and fourth tones, and each tone indicated by syllables (called solmization). After Guido's time it is known that this "hexachord" was used in teaching singing. It did not replace the older modes, but was simply a method of teaching them.

By the second half of the eleventh century there was, as yet, no uniformity in musical notation. The old neumes continued to be employed to indicate the rise and fall of the voice and the style of singing to be used. In addition to this vague type of notation, one to four staff lines and clefs were used, and some writers also tried to indicate the duration of notes. The further development of harmonized music depended on the gradual acceptance of the use of staff lines to indicate pitch and the development of a notation that indicated the relative length of the notes. In the eleventh century the style of organum also changed. In the earlier organum the melody of the chant was given to the higher voice. By 1100 it moved, on occasion, to the lower voice. Also, instead of a mere parallel setting of notes, the second voice introduced oblique and contrary motion, and sometimes two or more notes were set against a leading note to produce a more complicated harmony. Organum was changing to counterpoint. Likewise, by the end of the twelfth century, there grew up in France a system of mensural notation. The semi-breve (equal to our whole note) became the common unit of measurement. Notes of shorter duration were the minim (a half-note) and the semi-minim (a quarter-note). To lengthen a note a breve was used, equal to two semi-breves; also the longa and the maxima, two longer types of notes, were employed. All of these experiments in harmonized music, from the ninth through the twelfth centuries, created a musical style of increasing complexity.

While these changes in church music were gaining acceptance, through the later eleventh and twelfth centuries, a phenomenal flowering of secular music appeared first in southern and then in northern France, in Germany, and in other parts of Latin Christendom. The melodies of the southern French troubadours, like their verses, strike a modern note; they are full of variety and imagination and strongly forecast the later major and minor modes. The various musical forms developed by the troubadours and later by their followers depended upon the form of the poetry, though only the "rondo," with its reiteration of the first notes, became a fixed musical form that survived into later usage. The change from the modality of the Gregorian chants toward the tonality of the troubadour songs parallels the substitution of the vernacular language for Latin in poetry. The probabilities are that the whole musical style of the secular musicians had long been in existence outside church circles, but it is only from the end of the eleventh century that records have been preserved. The history of church music in the Middle Ages, like that of Latin literature, can be studied from surviving documents; documents for the history of secular music and of vernacular literature are much more fragmentary.

It is known that the troubadours, the trouvères, and the minnesingers used accompaniments of viols, lutes, harps, wood-winds, and other instruments, but there is no clear evidence that these accompaniments were harmonized. The secular musicians borrowed melodies from the music of the church, and by the fourteenth century, church composers were using tunes from secular music.[18] Of course, some parts of compositions could be performed on instruments, and sometimes all the parts of a choral composition were played on them. But it was the secular musicians, attached to the courts of kings and nobles, who wrote the first compositions for instruments alone, the earliest of which that survive are from the thirteenth century. These were performed at coronations, tournaments, baptisms, weddings, feast days, and other great occasions. In the eleventh, twelfth, and thirteenth centuries such groups of players probably were rarely larger than ten to twenty. The types of instruments used included viols, harps, zithers and beaten dulcimers, recorders, oboes, trumpets, and drums imported from the Islamic world. By the fourteenth century large numbers of instrumentalists were assembled to play. Guillaume de Machaut, a notable French poet and musician, tells about an orchestra of thirty-six kinds of instruments, some with a number of men playing the same part. In the same fourteenth century, four hundred players performed at the court in Mantua, and four hundred and fifty entertained the German Diet at Frankfort in 1397. From the ninth century on we know that the jongleur or minstrel was a professional singer and entertainer who usually could play at least four instruments. The church condemned their calling as too worldly, but each mediaeval century after the ninth saw an increase in the number of these reciting and singing performers.

By 1200 northern France had not only become the center of secular music, but also the principal home of new developments in church music. Organum had, in the twelfth century, been transformed by discant wherein the voices no longer move up or down parallel-wise but spread out in contrary motion. Also in the twelfth century, two-part writing began to be supplemented by combinations of three or more voices. These more elaborate settings for parts of the liturgy and for hymns were chiefly the creation of French musicians, especially those connected with the cathedral of Notre Dame in Paris. Here the leading composers and teachers of singing were Leoninus and Perotinus. As this counterpoint became more elaborate, one part might sing a melody to a text totally different from that of the other voices.

In this way popular melodies and secular texts were sometimes woven into church music. Motets of this type, which used measured rhythm, show extraordinary ingenuity in weaving together voices that were both melodically and rhythmically independent.[14] The harmony was frequently rough and without euphony, but the whole movement, in the end, was to result in an extraordinary enrichment of music.

These changes of the first half of the thirteenth century are summed up in the most remarkable musical treatise of the period, Franco of Cologne's *Ars Cantus Mensurabilis*, of about 1260. Franco laid down the rule that the ear was the judge of dissonance and consonance. Perfect harmony occurs where two tones blend so well that they can hardly be distinguished. Imperfect consonance appears when two tones are sounded together and each maintains its independence, as with major and minor thirds. Finally, intermediate consonance occurs with two notes sounding halfway between perfect and imperfect as the fourth and fifth. Franco is less clear in his distinctions between various kinds of dissonant intervals. In the late fourteenth century a special kind of discant, *faux bourdon* (false bass) came into use. Probably used first in England, it spread from there to the Continent. *Faux bourdon* is based on parallel sixth chords and its acceptance as a device greatly enriched the possibilities for composers of polyphonic music.

By 1300 we begin to find a remarkable development of secular music, and, exactly as in literature, there begins to appear a series of composers who are laymen. From the close of the preceding century, there are the musical settings of poems and of dramatic pieces by Adam de la Halle. Soon after 1300 an English monk wrote the famous round *Sumer is icumen in*, a six-part setting for a Middle English secular poem. This work is based on strict melodic imitation in the upper four voices while the two basses support them with an independent melody in canon. This is the earliest polyphonic composition that seems immediately attractive to the modern listener. From now on the influence of secular music on sacred music becomes more marked; discoveries and changes in one field are promptly transferred to the other. New rhythmic procedures, and more elaborate harmonic arrangements that came into vogue after 1300, were called "Ars nova" after a treatise by this name, written about 1325, by Philippe de Vitri. The "Ars nova" was so named to distinguish it from the "Ars antiqua" of earlier centuries. The two momentous innovations of the "Ars nova" of the fourteenth century were the introduction of smaller time-values and a wider scope of rhythmic expression.

In the field of church music the changes toward a more complex system of harmony and rhythm met opposition from the church authorities. Indeed, beginning in the twelfth century, there is much evidence that some of the church authorities disapproved of any harmonized music. They considered it too worldly, and, as harmony came to be used in secular music, they wished to keep the traditional plain chant unharmonized to distinguish ecclesiastical from secular music. In 1324 Pope John XXII condemned the ornamentation of the traditional Gregorian chants. Speaking of the prevailing musical style, the Pope declared: "They truncate the melodies with hockets; they deprave them with discants; they stuff them with upper parts made out of secular songs; so that often they must be losing sight of the fundamental sources of our melodies in the 'antiphonal' and 'gradual.' Their voices are incessantly running to and fro, intoxicating the ear. As a consequence of all this, devotion, the true end of worship, is little thought of. Yet it is not our intention to forbid occasionally the use of such consonants, for example, the eighth, fifth, and fourth which heighten the beauty of the melody, soothe the hearer and rouse his devotion." [15] In spite of this papal condemnation, the musical style of the fourteenth century became increasingly elaborate.

The leading composer in France was the poet Guillaume de Machaut (d. 1377), who wrote different types of secular part songs, church motets, and at least one complete mass. In his monophonic songs he showed himself a gifted composer of melodies. He says of his secular songs, "he who writes and composes without feeling spoils both his words and his music." In his polyphonic secular songs he abandoned the older, stiff, note-by-note harmony and created a style of a melody with accompaniment. He wrote thirds frequently and used, occasionally, bold dissonance. His usual method is one in which the parts begin and later converge in perfect consonances, octaves, fourths or fifths, while in between cadence points the lines move with little regard for euphony. The only mass of Guillaume de Machaut was a four-part work, probably written for the coronation of Charles V at Rheims where the composer was a canon. It is less original and more archaic in style than his secular works, but is interesting as the first complete polyphonic mass written by one composer that survives. A great deal of music of other fourteenth-century French composers has been preserved.

In Italy, Florence became the great musical center in the fourteenth century. Much of this Italian music resembles the French music of the same time, though the Italians had an independent musical tradition, and the Italian composers had more success than the French in the invention of beautiful melodies. In the Italian composers of the fourteenth century, the older crude successions of fifths and octaves have vanished; the thirds and sixths have been definitely accepted, and the harmonic system has become one attractive to modern listeners. The literature and painting of the period show that there was much development of instrumental music. Growing in popularity were the clavichord, on which the strings were struck by brass wedges, and the virginal, on which they were plucked. The Italians added several new compositional forms, the most interesting of which were the madrigal and the "caccia," a composition for two voices in canon usually accompanied by a third voice. The early Italian madrigals, written in two or three parts, show a tendency to emphasize the melody in the top voice. As with other types of polyphonic choral music, one part was sometimes sung and the other parts played on instruments. The leading Italian composer, Landini (d. 1397), besides choral compositions, wrote some interesting music for the organ. Landini was everywhere given the highest honors; at Venice he was feted as a composer and performer on the lute and the organ, and, for his achievement in poetry, the King of Cyprus crowned him with laurel in the presence of Petrarch.

The musician, by the fourteenth century, had become as socially esteemed as the poet and the artist. Music had come to play a great role in life. Not only were church services accompanied by music, but no important occasion seems to have been without music. A person returning from foreign lands was greeted with music, a visitor approaching his host was welcomed by music. Tournaments, weddings, and holidays were celebrated with music; armies went to war with music. Singers and musical instruments became common in paintings. Music was taught in the schools, the playing of instruments was widely diffused among the aristocracy and the middle class, and everyone sang.

The fifteenth century was marked by a phenomenal musical development which began in England, and came to its full flowering in Burgundy, northern France, and Flanders. This was, in part, due to the increased patronage offered musicians, especially in the royal chapels, established all over Latin Christendom by kings and princes in imitation of the papal choir in Rome. Dunstable (d. 1453) was the leader of an English school of composers, though he spent much of his life on the Continent. The composers of the fourteenth century had made important advances in the definition of discord and in the use of the third and sixth, but Dunstable is the first musician who fully realized the possibilities of these discoveries. Dunstable alternated the third with the sixth, avoided hard discords and ineffective perfect concords. He thus avoided both the monotony and the harshness of earlier music and produced works of a smooth texture. He shows great skill in handling a group of independent melodies tied together in a single composition; each voice is of as great interest and importance as any other, yet at the same time is a necessary part of the whole. The result has been described as a "kind of tonal communism," and it became the dominant style up to the seventeenth century.

The new style used by Dunstable and some of his English contemporaries was perfected by the Burgundian-Flemish school. In three generations the musicians of Burgundy, northern France, and Flanders came to dominate the music of Europe. So remarkable was their achievement that a Flemish musician in 1477 dared to write, "there is no music worth hearing save only in the last forty years," and in the early sixteenth century the Italian historian, Guicciardini, referred to them as "the true masters of music." The first to win a wide fame was Dufay (d. 1474). As a young man he had sung in the papal choir in Rome; he then entered the service of the duke of Burgundy, and finally ended his days as a canon of the *Cathedral of Cambrai*. His fame was so great that he was invited to write a motet for the dedication of Brunelleschi's dome in Florence. This contemporary of Claus Sluter and Jan van Eyck borrowed heavily from the musical style of Dunstable and carried it to a greater subtlety. Dufay developed the "canon," a form in which the same melody is sung by several voices, in such a manner that one voice announces the melody, a second comes in somewhat later, followed by a third, and so on. Thus all voices sing the same melody, but never the same phrase at the same time. In Dufay's canon the second voice may merely repeat what the first has sung, but may repeat it at a different interval, and even sing it backwards.

Dufay borrowed some themes from secular songs and wrote masses on the melodies of popular tunes like *The Armed Man, If My Face Is Pale, Gentle Memory,* and others. Exactly opposite to the practice of the twentieth century, mediaeval musicians did not strive for originality and seem to have regarded it as a somewhat reprehensible eccentricity. That a composer should provide all his thematic material would have appeared as strange to them as to demand that an architect should manufacture his own bricks. Most admired was the composer who could take any theme at hand and draw out of it rich and unexpected possibilities. Dufay left a remarkable series of masses and of secular part songs, the best of them written after 1437 when he came under the influence of Dunstable. Dufay's special contribution to the art of music was his development of the device of imitation and his common use of four rather than three voices. He deliberately pursues euphony for its own sake, and his works have a somewhat effeminate quality. His is a style that lacks great force but has a vague and dreamy charm.

The most original composer of the next generation was Okeghem (d. 1495), who, though educated in Antwerp, spent much time in Italy and France. Some of his elaborate compositions appear to have been problems which he set himself in the technique of composition. One of his canons, the *Deo gratias,* is written in thirty-six parts; it is in nine-fold canonical form, nine voices repeat from time to time, each at the interval of one measure, the same melody. Such complex devices do not leave much opportunity for free artistic expression, though, in spite of its complexity, much of Okeghem's music is very beautiful. And it is a mistake to consider him a mere technician. Okeghem, as no one before him, showed the possibilities of thematic augmentation, diminution, and inversion.[16]

In the work of his pupil, Josquin des Prés (d. 1521), the music of the Flemish school reached new heights. It is interesting to notice that in this phenomenal musical development of the north as in the contemporary flowering of painting there were no available classical models as there were in literature, architecture, and sculpture. The influence, however, of the Italian humanist movement led to one important change in musical style. Due to ideas found in ancient writers, above all in Plato, the composers tried to integrate words and music more closely. At the same time, composers first in Italy then in the North began to think and compose "harmonically" rather than in relation to a *cantus firmus,* or some fixed melody. Many of the leading northern composers, like Dufay and Josquin, spent time in Italy, and from thence northward carried these new stylistic ideas. It is interesting, also, to note that while the painters and sculptors were developing the use of perspective and other three-dimensional devices the composers were extending the range of harmony and of musical expression in general. As a youth, Josquin studied with Okeghem in Paris, and then spent a long period in Italy in the time of Lorenzo the Magnificent. At the very end of the fifteenth century he returned to Paris to the royal chapel of Louis XII. He came at a fortunate period in the development of the art; by his time music had the capacity for a rich and varied expressiveness. He loosened the tongue of an old polyphonic art and made it speak with an unmatched eloquence in masses, motets, and secular part songs. Luther said of Josquin, "other composers do what they can with the notes; Josquin alone does what he wishes." In his music there is no stress and strain; everything seems easy and inevitable. A number of his contemporaries were almost equally famous; the Low Countries and northern France were richly supplied with musical genius. Through the Flemish style, music regained a definite tonal center about which the whole musical structure is organized. It had not had such a focus since the Gregorian chants had been formulated. Now there again existed a musical art fully rounded and integrated. As Italy, in the fifteenth century, was the great center of cultural influence in art, literature, and scholarship, so the Flemings commanded the field in music to such an extent that by 1500 all schools of music in Europe were but provincial imitations of that of the Low Countries. For strength and sublimity these fifteenth-century Netherlandish composers were not rivalled until the time of Bach.

CHAPTER XII

Underlying Attitudes

1. THE WAY OF THE MYSTICS

2. THE INTERESTS OF THE HUMANISTS

BEHIND the great cultural achievements of the mediaeval centuries lay certain basic attitudes of both mysticism and humanism. In some mediaeval minds these attitudes lived together harmoniously, but oftener they were in conflict. Some examination of the writings of the mystics and humanists should bring us close to the heart of mediaeval ways of feeling and thinking. The traditions of both mysticism and humanism had their origins in antiquity; both were an inheritance of the Middle Ages rather than its own creation. But to each of these currents mediaeval men made significant contributions.

1. THE WAY OF THE MYSTICS

THE ESSENCE of mysticism lies in the surrender of a human personality to a spiritual power beyond itself, by which process the personality gains a greater harmony and force. The mystic hopes to arrive at a feeling of deliverance from the world and the flesh, and, free from the chain of causality, to enter into the knowledge of God and into God's very existence. This is what Bonaventura means when he defines mysticism as "the reaching out of the soul to God, through the yearning

[419

of love." The mystic's mind seeks to reach God by sympathetic intuition which can penetrate to him through the visible world. Such a mind finds in all familiar objects a reflection of the divine, and inevitably the language of the mystics resorts to symbolism in its attempt to express spiritual reality and the ineffable. The mystic often begins where thought ends, and tries to grasp the divine in a single vision in which all detail is lost. God ceases to be an object of worship and becomes rather an experience. "This highest stage of union," wrote Suso in the fourteenth century, "is an indescribable experience, in which all ideas of images and forms and differences have vanished. All consciousness of self and of all things has gone, and the soul is plunged into the abyss of the Godhead and the spirit has become one with God." [1] The first stage of mysticism is a conviction of the existence of a supernatural reality, accompanied with a sense that this world is an illusion; the next stage is a sense of immediate contact with this supersensuous reality; and the final stage is an absorption of the soul in God.[2] The mystic's way is the flight of the alone to the alone; the external world is shut out; the soul, rising above reason and self-consciousness, is absorbed in God. The earlier mediaeval mystics speak of this last phase as a revelation of light and knowledge; the later mystics from the twelfth century on often speak of being lost in darkness and negation.

The great currents of mysticism in Greek philosophy and religion entered Christianity at least as early as the time of St. Paul, and, as we have seen, mysticism plays a great role in the New Testament and in the writings of the Church Fathers. In Latin Christendom, new chapters of the history of mysticism begin with the introduction of the writings of Dionysius the Areopagite into the West in the ninth century, though not till the twelfth century did these writings gain great influence. His glowing language described how all things come from God and return to him. This world is evolved from the Son (the "word" of St. John's Gospel and the "nous" of Plotinus). The mind can know God only through symbols, but the soul may directly behold the divine image. Through the searching of prayer and through purification, the soul gains first an enraptured vision, and then, abandoning all and being set free from all, the soul finally achieves an ecstatic union with the divine.

"By laying aside all mental energies," says Dionysius, "and by pure contemplation, the soul shares in that super-essential light in which all knowledge pre-exists, and enters into a union above thought, above states of consciousness, above knowledge. Leave behind the senses and the operations of the intellect and all things that the senses or the intellect can perceive and strain upwards in unknowing toward the union with him who is above all being and knowledge. For by unceasing and absolute withdrawal from thyself and all things thou wilt be borne up to the divine darkness that surpasseth all being. Unto this darkness which is beyond light we pray that we may come, and, through loss of sight and knowledge, may see and know that which transcends sight and knowledge by the very fact of not seeing and knowing, for this is real sight and knowledge." [3]

The mystics of whom we have records were mostly educated men and women, and their writings show that they were fed by tradition as well as by direct experience. "Any carefully annotated mystical text," says Evelyn Underhill, "will show the close dependence on authority even of the most apparently personal outpourings. We have constantly to be on guard against discovering novelty in sayings and doctrines which are often adopted from an earlier source." [4] The language of the Bible, especially of the Psalms and the Song of Songs, and of earlier mystics is constantly used, though often in such a way as to show a fresh significance. Mysticism imparted a more vivid meaning to traditional religious concepts and did much to revitalize religious ideas and practices. Mystics like St. Francis of Assisi breathed new life and fervor into the church; the pope, who in a dream saw Francis upholding the tottering walls of his Lateran Palace, had prophetic insight. On the other hand, mystics like the leaders of the Cathari, the Albigensians, the Waldensians, and other sects, and like Wyclif and Luther, all of whom sought a more intense spiritual life than they saw in the church about them, became heretics. These opposing tendencies in mysticism run all through the mediaeval centuries.

The great monastic revivals of the tenth and eleventh centuries, out of which came the Cluniac, the Cistercian, and Carthusian orders, produced a setting in which mysticism was fostered, and from this period dates the beginning of the golden age of mysticism in the Latin church. The most outstanding mystical writers of the eleventh century were the Italian monk Peter Damian (d. 1072) and Anselm (d. 1109), the archbishop of Canterbury. Peter Damian was a fierce ascetic to whom life was a ceaseless preparation for death, a tormented soul who lived in a world of phantoms. The terror of judgment hung over him, and in a series of treatises and poems he painted the horrors of hell and the glories of paradise. Anselm, like St. Bernard later, combined the contemplative and the active life; the strength and courage he derived from the one helped to carry him through the trials of the other. Anselm's mystical writings show the influence of Augustine though not of Dionysius. His clear and critical mind rejected the exaggerated symbolism that clutters many mystical works; and he writes in a simple and convincing way of his own experiences.

The twelfth century and each successive century through the fifteenth saw an extension of mystical writing. St. Bernard (d. 1153), as an abbot at the Cistercian house of Clairvaux, and as a preacher and reformer, touched many sides of the life of his time. No churchman, before or after him, ever wielded so unquestioned an authority over prelates and rulers, an authority grounded on personal charm, on eloquence, and on saintliness. His mystical writings show him as very conservative; he distrusted the intellectual revival in the French cathedral schools and viewed with deep apprehension the rationalism of the philosophers and theologians. Especially he despised pride of the intellect, and the pursuit of knowledge for its own sake was, to him, a disgraceful inquisitiveness. Bernard's ideal was not the objective demonstration of truth by systematic means, but the subjective apprehension of it in direct contemplation. Love grows with the knowledge of God until self-love is so fused with love for God that we love ourselves only for God's sake.[5] He was a severe critic of men like Abelard, who, in his mind, turned Christian souls from their true vocation, that is, the discovery of God through prayer and ascetic practices.

St. Bernard, like many other of the mystical writers, likes to dwell on the steps of progress on the mystic way to the divine. In the *Twelve Steps of Humility* he describes how the mystic's road begins with a profound pessimism about the physical world, and in this state of humility, in which man is aware of his own misery and wretchedness, he may, with God's grace, start upward in his endeavor to achieve righteousness and purity of heart. Finally, as he mounts toward the highest, he becomes dead to the body and to this world, and in an ecstatic vision is gathered up in God. The perfect and enduring union with God comes only after death. "How could God be all in all if in man anything of man remained?" The mysticism of St. Bernard is non-scholastic, without imaginative visions and without thought of the devil. It is a mysticism purely religious and unalloyed, centered on the thought of Jesus. Bernard added nothing new to the stock of mystical ideas, but his vivid way of writing left its impress on much of later mystical writing. His treatise *On the Love of God* and his *Sermons on the Canticles*, the most read of his works, gave him an enormous reputation. The position given him by Dante in the *Paradiso* represents fairly the mediaeval respect for him.

Hugo (d. 1141) and his pupil, Richard (d. 1173), of St. Victor, both contemporaries of St. Bernard, and both members of the celebrated monastery of St. Victor in Paris, elaborated on the stages of mystic purification. Richard made the first extended attempt to give a psychological analysis of the experience of the mystic, and he is the originator of some of its most important distinctions. His remarkable analysis of the stages in the unfolding of the contemplative consciousness exercised a decisive influence on later mystical writers. Dante praises Richard as "superhuman in contemplation." Unlike St. Bernard, however, the Victorines were interested in theology and philosophy and desirous of bringing together sacred studies and mystical attitudes. Much of their teaching was embodied in commentaries on the Scriptures and in the poetic *Sequences* of Adam of St. Victor (d. 1192). In all of these writings there is an abundant use of symbolic imagery, some of which is borrowed from Dionysius the Areopagite whose influence the Victorines helped to extend. Their fusion of theology and mysticism reappears in some of the greatest scholastics of the thirteenth and fourteenth centuries, and even influenced Luther and Calvin and their followers.

The twelfth and thirteenth centuries also produced a number of mystical writings by women, chiefly in Germany; the inspiration came mostly from Augustine, from the Song of Songs, and the Book of Revelation. Elizabeth of Schönau, Hildegard of Bingen, Mechthild of Magdeburg, and others have left a series of books of mystic meditations and visions. Hildegard of Bingen (d. 1179)—like St. Catharine of Siena later—wrote to many of the leading men of her time, including popes and emperors, denouncing the corruption of the world and speaking of herself as "an agent of the Living Light." The mystic outpourings of these women tell of strange sense perceptions, of the stench of hell, the sweet perfumes of paradise, the gentle touch of angels, and the pain of blows. They heard voices and saw glowing visions. Their language is frequently very erotic. Their works had a wide circulation, and they helped to create a taste for this type of writing which later centuries were not slow to supply.[6]

The ascetic and mystical ardors of the eleventh and twelfth centuries stirred large numbers of people to crave for a spiritual perfection which the average institutionalism did not satisfy. The appearance of new tensions and new social problems in the growing towns of northern Italy, southern France, the Rhine Valley, and Flanders was another cause of the growth of popular mystical movements. Social and political aims are usually tied up with religious aspirations in attacks on the powers who tried to uphold the *status quo*. Various types of heretics and infidels held certain radical ideas; all were very ascetic and condemned marriage; they were opposed to oaths, to killing men and animals, and to the possession of wealth. They were especially bitter against the wealth and immorality of the clergy, and they harked back to the simple faith of Jesus and of the early church, though it should be noted that no single group possessed all of these ideas. Some of these ardent souls became merely heretics, like the Waldensians who believed that a direct approach to God without the sacraments was possible, who wanted to bring the Bible, in translation, to the common man, and who wished to return to the apostolic life of poverty. Besides the Waldensians, there were other heretical movements in Italy, the Rhineland, and Flanders. Some groups, like the Cathari in Italy and the Albigensians in France, left Christianity entirely, and embraced a dualistic system of stern asceticism that came ultimately from the Zoroastrianism of Persia. In these groups of heretics and infidels there appears for the first time a large role played by the laity, the freeing of mysticism from purely monastic circles, the formation of free associations of the devout, and, finally, the use of the vernacular for popular religious writings. The craving for spiritual realities was now assuming a more democratic form. The support given by the papacy to the Mendicant Friars, early in the thirteenth century, was undoubtedly inspired by a realization of the importance of recognizing these changes, and a desire to bring them into the main stream of Catholic life.

In the later twelfth century there appeared in southern Italy a mystic, Joachim of Flora (d. 1204), who profoundly influenced the religious history of Latin Christendom. In his *Eternal Gospel*, Joachim declared that the epochs of Father and Son, corresponding to the Old and the New Testaments, were about over, and a new epoch of the Holy Spirit would soon begin. In this new age, the church would be ruled by its contemplative spirits; in other words, institutional Christianity would be supplanted by mystical Christianity. This new age, to begin about 1260, would be established by two new orders, one for laymen and the other for priests, who would live in apostolic poverty. The church condemned Joachim's ideas after his death, but, in the minds of many, the Mendicant Orders fulfilled his prophecies. He was very widely read; Dante placed him high in his *Paradiso*, the only non-Biblical prophet to appear there. After the death of St. Francis, the writings of Joachim became the chief support of the Spiritual Franciscans.

Many of the great scholastics of the thirteenth and fourteenth centuries were at the same time great mystics. Bonaventura, Albertus Magnus, Aquinas, and Ockham—above all Bonaventura and Ockham—cannot be understood if approached only from the formal side of their philosophy. The sources of their mysticism lay not only in the intense devotional lives they led, but also in the inspiration of the mystical writers they read and in the example of saintly lives that stirred the thought and emotion of their times. Outstanding among these saints was Francis of Assisi (d. 1226), who gave the mysticism of the thirteenth century its most original characteristics. If he is compared with St. Bernard of the preceding century, it will be seen that, though both shared the monkish spirit, Francis was of a more joyous frame of mind, and he never felt himself an exile from the cloister as he worked out in the world. Francis and his followers showed the common man the spiritual satisfactions that lay hidden within the Catholic fold. With him mysticism emerges from the monastery into the everyday world. Bernard was always the great churchman; Francis was not troubled by political or doctrinal questions. Bernard was like Ambrose, the scourge of evildoers, while Francis, like Jesus, moved the hearts of the people. He speaks the language of the common man, and gains inspiration from the literature of romance, and from the rediscovery of the beauty and wonder of the world that characterized the Gothic age. Yet Francis retains his connection with the great Catholic tradition which had been broken by the heretical sects. He conserves the best values of the democratic reaction against the formalities of religion but never becomes enmeshed in its vagaries. To his own generation the life of Francis seemed a perfect re-creation of the life of Jesus. And though his followers could not maintain his level of spirituality, the life and sayings of Francis lived on as an inspiration to restore, within the church, the spirit of Jesus and of early Christianity. Above all, the example of Francis spread far and wide an adoring devotion to all the events of the life of Jesus, especially those connected with his passion.

The Franciscan movement produced a number of Latin and vernacular lives of the founder and a large amount of devotional literature. Most outstanding of these devotional works were several treatises by St. Bonaventura (d. 1274) and an anonymous *Meditations on the Life of Christ*. The note of this Franciscan devotional literature can be caught in the words of Bonaventura: "Have always the eyes of your mind toward Jesus crucified, crowned with thorns, having drunk the vinegar and gall, spit upon and abused, blasphemed of sinners, pierced by the spear, buried of mortal men." [7] Bonaventura describes the mystic's way as a progress through a series of stages of contemplation "through love of the crucified." The *Meditations* follows step by step the sorrows of both Jesus and the Virgin. The passion of Jesus grows by feeding on his mother's sorrow; her grief grows as she sees the sufferings of her son. The simple narrative of the Bible is elaborated with a thousand details. The *Meditations* is a work of great depth of feeling; it is, indeed, one of the masterpieces of mediaeval mystical writing. Its influence on literature and art and on the writings of later mystics was enormous. [8]

The Spiritual Franciscans differed from the main body of the order and tried to maintain the strict rule of poverty of the founder. The pope condemned them, but after a long struggle their point of view brought, in the fourteenth century, the great "Reform of the Strict Observance." Among the Spiritual Franciscans the leading writer was Jacopone da Todi (d. 1306), the author of the *Stabat Mater* and of a large number of Italian devotional poems. He was a man of fierce enthusiasms and of great literary talents, and he gave expression to every aspect of mystical fervor. Some of his vernacular *Laude* show how, under the pressure of emotion, language as a medium of expression breaks down; in each stanza of a long devotional poem, he repeats the word "love," as many as twenty times. Jacopone defines God as "love beyond all language, imageless good." As a result of the whole Franciscan movement, religion had come to find its expression in a personal experience and in a direct relation between the human soul and Christ. Christ was now no longer the solemn Redeemer who appears on the sculptured doorways of the Romanesque and early Gothic churches. Nor is he the divine logos of the theologians. He has become the Son of Mary, the Man of Sorrows, close to the heart of the common people.

Something of the same emphasis can be found in the growth of Dominican mysticism, which arose in an attempt to adapt the learning of the church to unlearned folk, especially nuns. In Italy, St. Catharine of Siena (d. 1380) felt a call to bring the pope back from Avignon to Rome. Though only a poor Dominican nun, she corresponded with monarchs and prelates, travelled to Avignon, and finally got the pope to return to Rome. For this militant mystic no task was too difficult, nor was any vested interest powerful enough to deter her. Her writings, including four hundred letters, are among the masterpieces of early Italian literature. By the early fourteenth century there were more Dominican convents for women in the Rhineland than in any other part of Europe. It was in this area that there developed what Goethe called "the scholastic of the heart." The first great German mystic, the Dominican, Meister Eckhart (d. 1327), was a learned teacher of theology who used a scholastic terminology though he tried—often in vain—to bring his ideas to the level of the common man. He strives to combine bold theological speculation and mystical fervor in a system that does justice alike to the intellect and to religious emotion. Eckhart begins with a conception of God like that of Erigena; God is so great he is beyond name and definition, and he is both in the universe and above it. Eckhart's thought is close to pantheism, and some of his ideas were condemned by the pope after his death. Eckhart's intentions were strictly orthodox, but he offered ideas that were soon taken up by heretical sects like the "Brethren of the Free Spirit," which flourished in the Rhineland in the fourteenth century. It was a time of stress: the papacy was in exile at Avignon; England and France were at war by 1337; in 1348–49 the Black Death swept Europe; and, in the schools, the "treaty of peace between reason and faith," made by the thirteenth-century Scholastics, was being dissolved by Ockham and the Nominalists. Men were seeking for assurance, and the mysticism of men like Eckhart showed them how to commune with God. Eckhart recommended to his followers an active Christian ministry. "Even were one in a rapture like St. Paul," he declared, "if he saw a sick man who needed help it were much better that out of love he should abandon the rapture and serve the needy one in greater love." His idea that, at the apex of the mind there is a divine spark which is one with God, expressed in Eckhart's saying, "The eye with which I see God is the same as the eye with which God sees me" was especially abhorrent to the orthodox. This idea of the divine spark, the *Seelenfünklein*, was taken up, with modifications, by his pupils, Suso and Tauler, and by the Fleming, Ruysbroek. At times the eloquence of Eckhart reaches exuberant heights, and there are traces of the language of the minnesingers and of the phrases of Joachim of Flora.

The teaching of Eckhart was carried on by two other Dominicans whom he influenced: Tauler and Suso. Tauler (d. 1361) was less of a philosopher than Eckhart, and he is best known through his powerful sermons; he was the greatest German preacher of his time. Suso (d. 1366) was a tortured ascetic who wrote in a poetic style. His chief work, the *Book of Eternal Wisdom*, is an imaginary conversation between Jesus and his servant, especially about his passion. The beauty of Suso's language led one writer to refer to him as "the minnesinger of the love of God." Suso's devotion is to the "Eternal Wisdom," but he expresses it in the glowing language of romance.[9] The German mystics of the fourteenth century did much to inspire the devotion of a new informal society of clerics and laymen, the "Friends of God," as well

as that of the older Beghards and Beguines, societies for devout laymen and laywomen. These societies penetrated all ranks and brought
together merchants, friars, agitators, monks, nuns, and visionaries in
an effort to revive the Christian way of life. The movement produced
an extensive devotional literature of which Merswin's *Book of the
Nine Rocks* and the anonymous *German Theology* were the most
read. Merswin's treatise presents, in a series of visions, the steps upward
that must be taken by the "Friends of God" who wish to avoid the corruption of the official church. It shows that the members of the society,
though they remained orthodox, regarded themselves as an inner
fortress of spiritual power within the church. The *German Theology*,
which became a favorite book of Luther's, lays its emphasis on the
practice of a personal religion and an intense religious life close to
God. A third writer influenced by Eckhart was Ruysbroek (d. 1381),
a Flemish priest, who wrote in a popular style about the mystic's life
of contemplation. One of his followers, Gerard Groot (d. 1384),
founded at Deventer the "Brethren of the Common Life," who taught
"the new devotion," a simple and undogmatic Christianity, and who
had great influence in the fifteenth century as teachers and preachers
in the Low Countries and the Rhineland. Thomas à Kempis, Nicholas
of Cusa, Hegius, Agricola, and Erasmus were all taught by members of
"the Brethren."

It is interesting to notice that the mystics differed among themselves
not only in their approach to the divine and in the different things
they emphasized, but also on basic doctrine. St. Bernard and Aquinas
believed that the full realization of God could never occur in a mortal
mind and that only in death could the mystic union take place. On
the other hand, the School of St. Victor and most of the German mystics of the fourteenth century held that the soul in this life could be
united with God. Also, according to most mystics before the fourteenth century, it was believed that only a few men had a capacity for
the mystic experience. But the German mystics believed that God
grants a mystic vocation to all men without distinction and that all
men should be urged to use this God-given faculty.

Mysticism flourished in England in the fourteenth and fifteenth
centuries, though most of the English mystics, except Rolle and Wyclif, were connected with the solitary life, and had little influence on

the mass of the faithful. Much of English mysticism is concerned only with the spiritual perfection of the individual. As on the Continent, however, the mystics wrote in both Latin and the vernacular, and they helped to stimulate the growth of vernacular literature. Rolle (d. 1349), the best-known English mystic, studied at Oxford and Paris where he came into contact with the writings of the French, Italian, and German mystics. His own works, which are direct and unencumbered with difficult ideas or abstractions, were widely read for the next two centuries. He attacked the corruption of the monasteries and called for a reform of the clergy. His cult of the "Holy Name of Jesus" survived the Reformation, and much of Rolle's shrewd advice and homely imagery, especially that which comes from his best-known work, the *Fire of Love*, reappeared in English devotional books of the fifteenth, sixteenth, and seventeenth centuries. An anonymous contemporary of Rolle wrote the *Cloud of Unknowing*, which is filled with the ideas and phrases of Dionysius the Areopagite. Hilton (d. 1396), also influenced by Rolle, was the author of the *Scale of Perfection*, a devotional classic second in popularity only to the *Imitation of Christ*. These works show that in England, as on the Continent, there was an intense devotional life inside the church. Out of these same currents came the teaching of Wyclif and the preaching of the Lollards. Their emphasis on the corruption of the church, the need of a direct approach to God, and the value of reading the Bible in the vernacular simply carried further, into open heresy, the intense religious emotion and the moral and reforming zeal of the mystics. The church may have gone to "sleep in Zion," but among the faithful the miseries of society and the many disorders in the church aroused a burning devotion to Christian ideals.

Among the leading thinkers of the fifteenth century there were currents of mysticism even in Italy where secular and aesthetic interests were strong. Ficino and Pico della Mirandola, among the philosophers, St. Bernadino of Siena and Savonarola, the two Dominican preachers, Fra Angelico, the painter, and a series of minor writers show the continuity of profound mystical interests. In the north, Gerson (d. 1429), chancellor of the University of Paris, was, like Bonaventura in the thirteenth century, both a mystic and a philosopher. He was an enemy of religious exaggerations of all sorts and distrusted the visionaries who were, by his time, common in France, Flanders, and Germany. On the other hand, he believed that the voices heard by Joan of Arc (d. 1431) were genuine and he defended some of the "Brethren of the Common Life" who had been charged with heresy. The basic doctrines in his mystical writings are chiefly derived from the Victorines and Bonaventura, but he writes in a personal and direct style. He was long believed to be the author of the *Imitation of Christ*. Cardinal Nicholas of Cusa (d. 1464) was a deeply learned man interested in science, philosophy, politics, and religion, a type of universal genius, by no means confined to the homeland of Leonardo da Vinci. As a student at Deventer, he had read the Neo-Platonists, and Eckhart and the German and Low Country mystics. In the midst of an active career he found time for a life of intense devotion out of which came the little masterpiece *On the Vision of God*. It is the work of a deep and subtle thinker, too profound to be popular, but full of a quiet wisdom distilled from a life of scholarship, religious devotion, and practical struggle with men who had, as he said, allowed "Christianity to degenerate into an appearance."

Out of the great currents of northern mysticism in the fifteenth century came the *Imitation of Christ*, edited and partly written by Thomas à Kempis (d. 1471), a Low Country monk. More remarkable for the beauty of its language than for the originality of its ideas, the *Imitation* is a monkish book. The Jesus who went about the world doing good is ignored. On the other hand, the voice of dogma is silent; there are only the voices of the beloved and the one who seeks him. The stress is laid on how one may alleviate his inner conflicts. Its doctrine is to seek God first; "consider that you and God are alone in the universe and you will have a great peace in your heart"; conquer yourself where you are. The admiration for the work has been without limit; no Christian book, except the Bible, has ever had so wide a circulation.[10] The popularity of mystic literature of the fourteenth and fifteenth centuries shows the decline of an interest in scholasticism. Men now seek the proof of God less in logic and reason and more in an inner illumination of the soul and a direct experience of God which brought peace and power. They yearn to return to Jesus and to the ardors of the early church. This is the message of men as different as Ockham, Wyclif, Thomas à Kempis, and Luther. So the later mediaeval mystics by their dislike of a too formal and too rationalized Christianity and by their desire to find a direct approach to God helped prepare the way for Luther. Indeed mysticism is not only one of the deepest currents in mediaeval civilization but it is also the tap-root of the Protestant Reformation.

2. THE INTERESTS OF THE HUMANISTS

MEDIAEVAL men were, as we have seen, the inheritors of a double antiquity; they were the heirs of Graeco-Roman culture as well as of the traditions of Judaism and early Christianity. They never lost contact with either tradition, though, after the fall of Rome, it was not until the eleventh and twelfth centuries that they began fully to understand and to use their inherited riches. So while the mystics and reformers were rediscovering the legacy of early Christianity, the humanists were entering more thoroughly into the cultural heritage which had been left to them by the great centuries of classical antiquity.

Humanism may be defined as an enthusiasm for the literature of Greece and Rome, both for its style and for its ideas. While in no mediaeval century had such enthusiasm been entirely quenched, it was stronger at times than at others. There had been a great revival of interest in the Latin classics in the schools of the Carolingian and Ottonian periods. The Barbarian raids of the tenth century had created chaos in many areas of western Europe, and not until the eleventh and twelfth centuries does another revival appear. This so-called "Renaissance of the Twelfth Century" was particularly marked in the cathedral schools of Chartres, Paris, and Orléans. Of these the School of Chartres, as we noted, became the most famous. Here in the eleventh century, Fulbert, a pupil of Gerbert of Aurillac, had introduced an improved study of the seven liberal arts. The students spoke of Fulbert, their chief teacher, as "a venerable Socrates." The teaching at Chartres was very thorough though by no means revolutionary. In literary subjects, the chief authors studied were Cicero, Livy, Ovid, Horace, Virgil, and Statius, and the Christian classics of Augustine, Boethius, Fortunatus, and Bede, always with the aid of the grammarians, Donatus and Priscian. Evidently great attention was paid to teaching the students to write effective Latin prose and verse.[11] The pupils we know were taught to write both verse with a stress rhythm and verse based on the ancient Roman system of quantity.

In the twelfth century, Bernard of Chartres, Thierry, and John of Salisbury raised the instruction at Chartres to a level beyond that of any other school in Latin Christendom. John of Salisbury describes the methods used by Bernard of Chartres:

> By citations from the authors, he brought into relief the grammatical figures, the rhetorical colors, the artifices of sophistry, and pointed out how the text in hand bore on other studies. He inculcated correctness of diction, and a fitting use of figures. Realizing that practice strengthens memory and sharpens faculty, he urged his pupils to imitate what they had heard. The evening exercise was filled with such an abundance of grammar that any one, by attending it for a year, would have at his fingers' end the art of writing and speaking. For those boys who had to write exercises in prose or verse, he selected the poets and orators, and showed how they should be imitated in the linking of words. Yet Bernard pointed out to awkward borrowers that whoever imitated the ancients should himself become worthy of imitation by posterity. He impressed upon his pupils the virtue of economy, and the values of words. He explained where a meagerness of diction was fitting, and where copiousness should be allowed, and the advantage of due measure everywhere. He admonished them to go through the histories and poems with diligence, and daily to fix passages in their memory.[12]

The teaching at Chartres in the first half of the twelfth century probably differed in quality rather than in kind from what was taught in other schools. From a pupil of the cathedral school of Paris, where literary studies and a fine style in Latin verse and prose were also cultivated, came the famous grammar and rhetoric, the *Doctrinale*, of Alexander de Villedieu. The work is fuller and more systematic than that of Priscian, and it has the advantage of using the *Vulgate* and the Christian Latin writers as examples, and of conforming to contemporary usage. For the next three centuries it remained the common textbook for the teaching of grammar all over Latin Christendom. In Italy the schools also laid great emphasis on the art of writing, the *ars dictaminis,* though the purpose was sometimes only to teach pupils to write official letters and to draw up legal documents. In many Italian schools the study of grammar and rhetoric became hardly more than a short business course. The Italian *ars dictaminis* and *ars notaria* (for drafting legal documents) in the later twelfth and thirteenth centuries spread over France and other parts of western Europe.

The flowering of Latin literary studies centering in northern France in the first half of the twelfth century promised to lead to a great revival of classical literary studies. Students from these northern French cathedral schools taught all over western Europe, and some of them carried the gospel of the study of humane letters far and wide. That the humanism of the twelfth century was on the way to a real comprehension of classical civilization is shown in the writings of John of Salisbury. Very rarely does any reference of his to the ancient world startle the modern reader as fantastic or fabulous as do those of most mediaeval writers, including Dante. John shows also a just understanding of the character of many of the leading men of antiquity. The humanism of the twelfth century was a clerical humanism in opposition to the growth of ascetic idealism. It showed a new awareness of this world, and, through this awareness, it came to understand better the world of Greece and Rome. But this humanistic movement was cut short by the growing interest in dialectical and theological studies stimulated by the recovery of Greek and Arabic learning. Literary studies did not disappear, but they did not continue to fulfill the promise of the French cathedral schools of the earlier part of the twelfth century. Already by 1215 the classical authors are absent from the arts course in the University of Paris, and a curriculum of 1255 prescribes only Donatus and Priscian among Latin authors, and throws all its emphasis on the new versions of Aristotle. In the *Battle of the Seven Liberal Arts,* a poem of 1250, the dialectians of Paris defeat the grammarians of Orléans. Literary form came to be despised, and logic professed to be able to supply any defects in a man's grammatical studies. By the later thirteenth century grammar had become a logical science.

What the "Renaissance of the Twelfth Century" had been on the verge of accomplishing was achieved by Italy in the fourteenth and fifteenth centuries. The Italian humanists came to be the heirs and successors of the mediaeval rhetoricians. These Italian humanists, however, did not invent a new field of learning nor did they create a new profession. All types of Italian humanist oratory, for example, had their antecedents in earlier mediaeval literature: wedding and funeral orations, academic speeches, and judicial and political orations. The origins of Italian humanism seem to be connected with the growth of towns and with the revived study of Roman law. The rise of an urban civilization in Italy and the revival of the study of Roman law which it brought about made the life and literature of ancient Rome seem more vital. So the study of ancient civilization began to seem less a matter of books to be piously preserved from the past than a live and contemporary issue. In the latter part of the thirteenth century there began to appear writers on Roman law who show clearly that they were reading Roman history and literature with greater insight and understanding. It is evident that they are beginning to see Roman civilization as a living thing. These Italian legal writers of the late thirteenth and early fourteenth centuries also sensed the distance which had developed between the civilization of the classic past and their own time. Thus, the earliest Italian humanism was not initially a scholarly reaction against scholasticism or a self-conscious desire to restore ancient culture, but a spontaneous and natural interest in Roman civilization. These attitudes began to affect imaginative literature in Italy in the early fourteenth century. Among a number of works, the Latin play, the *Ecerinis* of Mussato of 1314, shows the growth of new interests. The plot concerns an adventurer who threatened Padua in the thirteenth century, but the whole handling of the play was based on the tragedies of Seneca. Italian humanism, thus, was already in existence before Petrarch was born, and it was a direct outgrowth of classical studies as pursued by the later Middle Ages.

The first age of Italian humanism, the fourteenth century, was a period of discovery and inspiration. After the movement was under way, it was pushed ahead dramatically by Petrarch (d. 1374). He discovered two speeches and the *Letters to Atticus* of Cicero and started a craze for ransacking monastic and cathedral libraries for other lost works. Many classical works were "lost" in the sense that only a few, or even one copy, survived, that hardly anyone read them, and that they were not part of the stream of culture. Petrarch tried in vain to find someone who could teach him Greek, though when he did find a teacher he did not persevere long enough to master the language. However, he carried about with him a copy of Homer, as one might have carried a saint's relic. Petrarch's enthusiasm for the civilization of antiquity was without bounds. "Among the subjects which interested me I dwelt especially on antiquity, for our own age has always repelled me, so that, had it not been for the love of those dear to me, I should have preferred to have been born in any other period than our own." [13] Like many others later, he discovered in antiquity a great authority for a partial break with the mediaeval spirit. He found in Latin literature a natural and wholesome enjoyment of the goods of human life, and a worldly wisdom full of sanity and the spirit of the golden mean. He imitated Cicero in prose and Virgil in verse, and he thought that later times would remember him for his Latin writings, above all for his unfinished Latin epic, *Africa*. In his vernacular verses, which posterity has much preferred, he took words, methods of sentence structure, figures of speech, and stories from the great Latin writers, and gave them a new life in European letters.

In Petrarch can be seen a revitalizing of classical studies that was to sweep Europe. Like Niccolò Pisano, and, later on, Brunelleschi, Donatello, and the Italian fifteenth-century painters, he reactivated classical concepts. As Panofsky says: "The Jupiters and Perseuses in the Carolingian manuscripts are classical enough in appearance, yet they have not attained the status of free agents. They are confined as an insect in a piece of amber in the prison of an established context. The Carolingians salvaged the classical concepts, but they were able to use them only by way of quotation. It was beyond their power and their wish to activate them. This process of activation began with the twelfth century. But with this there also went the practice of dressing persons of classical tradition in contemporary costumes as courtly ladies and knights in mediaeval settings. It took the energies of Mantegna, Pollaiuolo, and other determined classicists to stop this." [14] The same thing happened in scholarship and literature. Everywhere classical concepts were to be taken out of the quotation status and were to be given a chance to grow, to change, and to multiply. On the other hand, it must always be borne in mind, the humanists in shifting the center of their interest made no fundamental break with mediaeval thought.

The classical humanism of the fourteenth through the seventeenth century remained fundamentally Christian, scholastic, and mediaeval. Only the emphasis changed.

Petrarch is so important a figure in the history of thought that even his weaknesses and his foibles are significant. He was contemptuous of philosophy and ignorant of science, and in his scholarship and in his creative writing he had far too large a faith in a purely stylistic ideal. Words alone have power. Cicero he held in the highest esteem, but he censured Aristotle for his lack of rhetoric. Petrarch began the humanistic attack on scholasticism, and, beyond it, on the whole of mediaeval culture. He denounced the scholastics because they wasted their time over trivialities, and because they wrote in a crabbed and unclassical Latin. They were ignorant of classical art and history and had no proper understanding of classical literature. He set up classical culture as the standard by which to judge all civilizations, and he dismissed the thousand years between 300 and 1300 as centuries of barbarism and darkness. Personally Petrarch was extremely vain; he wrote a series of letters to the great men of antiquity whom he alone recognized as his equals. He had a great appetite for flattery, which later humanists seem to have caught from him, and he moved about restlessly from place to place seeking admirers.[15] But he plays a large role in the history of culture. By his passion for collecting manuscripts and inscriptions, by his enthusiasm for classical studies, by his use of classical models in his own writing, and, finally, by his perception that the future of letters depended on recovering Greek imaginative literature, Petrarch set the pattern of a new scholarship and a new literary revival.

Petrarch's secretary, John of Ravenna, by his lectures at Florence, Padua, and Venice spread the master's ideas. Poggio, Filelfo, Bruni, Guarino da Verona, and Vittorino da Feltre were all his pupils. The ideas of Petrarch were also furthered by his devoted friend, Boccaccio (d. 1375), who was a great collector of forgotten Latin authors. He "discovered" Martial, a complete text of Ausonius, a minor work of Ovid, and, above all, a large section of Tacitus.[16] He found a teacher of Greek and mastered the language and thus became the first important man of letters to know Greek since John Scotus Erigena in the ninth century. Petrarch was still influenced by Christianity. Though less ardently religious than Dante, he was a close student of Augustine whom he quotes hundreds of times, and his later works, written after he was fifty, are strongly colored with religious ideas. Boccaccio, on the other hand, is the first important writer who renounced Christianity for paganism. Though he was converted late in life, in his best-known works he rejected Christian doctrine and morality and turned to the paganism of Greece and Rome as to a better world. Boccaccio believed his reputation would rest on his works on classical mythology and on other ancient subjects. However, as with Petrarch, it was his vernacular writings that have kept his name alive. At the end of the fourteenth century, a Greek, Manuel Chrysoloras, began to lecture on Greek literature in Florence. Crowds of students came to hear these lectures and his teaching marks the advent of the great enthusiasm for classical culture that began now to sweep through the whole intellectual life of Italy.[17] This humanistic movement that was now gathering momentum in Italy was based on the development of a more secular point of view which, in turn, was stimulated by a growth of town life and of wealth more rapid than anywhere else in Europe. It was a bustling world of business and politics of which the Italian humanists and writers were the mouthpiece.

The first half of the fifteenth century was an age of translation and of book collecting. Pope Nicholas V in Rome, the Medici in Florence, and Cardinal Bessarion and the city government in Venice were developing great libraries of Greek and Latin pagan and Christian literature. And following these examples, many of the petty tyrants, the nobles, and the leaders of the middle class became ardent book collectors. Nicholas V hired the best scholars he could find to turn the great works of Greek literature into Latin. Among these was Laurentius Valla, a brilliant scholar but a vain and lewd man. In spite of his evil reputation, the pope called him to Rome and loaded him with honors. He translated Herodotus, Thucydides, and Demosthenes into Latin, but he won greater fame by showing that the *Donation of Constantine* was a forgery.

The universities were not always cordial toward the humanists who, however, did not lack for patronage. Some taught in the universities, others found employment as tutors, librarians, and secretaries. They were often flattered and badly spoiled by their rich patrons. Their ideal was that of eloquence; "great is eloquence," wrote Pope Pius II, "nothing so much rules the world; political action is the result of persuasion." The worst of all the vain humanists were Poggio (d. 1459) and Filelfo (d. 1481). Both were very learned, and Filelfo's boast that no one but himself had mastered Greek and Latin literature and could wield the prose of Cicero, the verse of Horace and Virgil, and the Greek of Homer and Xenophon was not entirely an empty vaunt. Both were brilliant, reckless, and conceited, and they took great joy in small triumphs over rival scholars, in doubtful witticisms, and in filthy stories. Filelfo and Poggio quarrelled for years. Both exhausted the resources of the Latin language to befoul each other's characters and explored the lowest depths of human nature to find fresh accusations. And the learned world stood by and applauded. Piling up literary dunghills of this sort, unhappily, became, for centuries, a tradition of humanist scholarship.

It was during this first half of the fifteenth century that Guarino da Verona established his famous school at the Este Court at Ferrara. He was a pupil of Chrysoloras and had spent some time in Constantinople. His school was visited by men from all over Europe. A similar school was established by Vittorino da Feltre at the court of the Gonzagas at Mantua. In these schools the classics became the basis of instruction, and the curriculum included physical exercise as recommended by Plato in the *Republic*. The work of the humanist scholars and educators was greatly aided by the introduction of printing into Italy about 1465. In this same fifteenth century the enthusiasm for classical studies led many of the talents to write in Latin, and vernacular writing almost disappeared until the latter part of the century.

The second half of the fifteenth century takes the center of humanism back to Florence where the "Platonic Academy," established in 1459 by Cosimo de' Medici, attracted some of the greatest scholars of the time, among them Marsilio Ficino (d. 1491), Pico della Mirandola (d. 1494), and Poliziano (d. 1494). The spirit of Plato and the Neo-Platonists dominated the group; indeed so esteemed did Plato become that candles were burned before his bust in some of the Florentine palaces. The tone of the "Platonic Academy" was more definitely Christian and philosophical and less critical of the great scholastics than had been most of the earlier humanists. Ficino took his metaphysical terminology, the logical method of his argument, and many of his general ideas from the earlier Scholastics, especially Aquinas. He sought to harmonize Moses and Pythagoras, Plato and Aristotle, Christ, and Plotinus. To this synthesis Pico added the Jewish *Cabbala*, Arabic thought, and Zoroastrianism. Christianity became part of a universal religious tradition. The general ideal of this Florentine academy was an undogmatic Christianity, not unlike that of the contemporary "Brethren of the Common Life" in the North. The writing and teaching of the members of the "Platonic Academy" not only affected Italian literature and art, but had a profound influence on a series of northern humanists. Grocyn, Linacre, and Latimer came from England to Florence to study with Poliziano, and Reuchlin came from Germany. Beyond this, the ideas of the "Platonic Academy" influenced Melanchthon, Lefèvre d'Etaples, Erasmus, Colet, More, and Zwingli. In the sixteenth century, Italian humanism espoused a sterile literary purism; as Cardinal Bembo said, "Avoid the 'Epistles of St. Paul' lest his barbarous style should spoil your taste." And the humanists produced a narrow, classicistic school of rules for writing both in Latin and in the vernacular.

The enthusiasms of the Italian humanists had begun to influence northern scholars and writers by the end of the fourteenth century. Many contacts between northern and Italian scholars were made during the Councils of Constance and of Basel. During the later fifteenth century, there were humanist circles in nearly all the larger cities and in the university towns. Monarchs and nobles collected libraries, established printing presses, and lectureships, and young men of talent flocked to Italy to study the classics as they were also going there to study art and science. The learned public in northern Europe was greatly aroused by a great controversy over John Reuchlin (d. 1522). Reuchlin had come to be recognized as a great Hebrew scholar. Though primarily a scholar and not a controversialist, he got into a furious dispute with the Dominicans at Cologne, in the years 1508 to 1510, over his right, fearlessly, to examine the text of the Old Testament and to comment freely on it and on certain matters in the Jewish *Talmud* and *Cabbala*. Reuchlin was backed by most of the leading writers of the time, and he published their approving letters as the *Letters of Eminent Men*.

Soon there appeared two series of *Letters of Obscure Men* apparently written by pious and earnest souls who inquired about all sorts of sacred matters, such as what should be done if one eats a cherry on Friday and there is a worm in the cherry which one eats inadvertently. Is this a mortal sin? The letters, written to the Dominican fathers of Cologne, were composed in atrocious Latin, and were full of pious nonsense. All the learned in Europe were soon laughing, for the letters were a hoax written by Ulrich von Hutten and a group of lively young German humanists. The *Letters of Obscure Men* are coarse and vulgar in tone, but they hit hard, and they served to bring together many of the more hopeful and forward-looking elements of northern humanism. Sebastian Brandt's (d. 1521) *Ship of Fools*, though written in German, is another characteristic work of northern humanism. Under the form of an allegory—a ship laden with fools and steered by fools to a fools' paradise—Brandt lashes out at the vices of the age, including those in the church. The author was widely read in classical and humanist literature, and, like most northern humanists in contrast with those of Italy, he combined a love of classical culture with an earnest desire for reform in church, state, and society.

The prince of northern humanists was Erasmus of Rotterdam (d. 1536). He found the scholastics inadequate and their disputes fruitless. He would have agreed heartily with Melanchthon's remark, "What wagon loads of trifling, what pages he fills with disputes whether there can be horsiness without a horse, and whether the sea was salt when God made it." [18] Erasmus' greatest work, his edition of the New Testament, called men's attention to the Bible text.[19] No one since the death of Augustine was a finer Latinist. Though he saw that the attempts of the Italian Latinists to write a pure Ciceronian style that spoke of Jesus as "Jupiter optimus maximus" and of the twelve Disciples as the "conscript fathers" was a folly, he also saw clearly that the return to paganism of some of the Italian humanists was due to their failure to grasp the fact that, in many ways, Christianity was an advance over paganism. His great interests were less in stylistic concerns and in pure scholarship than in moral and religious reform. He believed in a simple, undogmatic piety, and he loved reason and hated violence. His irony and his earnestness are best shown in his popular *Praise of Folly*. It was his fate to be widely read and then to be repudiated by both the Catholics and the Protestants. His point of view be-

longs rather to the attitude taken by Liberal Christians in the nineteenth century than to his own time. Erasmus, like other humanists,
saw too many problems in the development of mankind to be able to
postulate one absolute and obey it. He saw good and evil on both sides
and he believed in progress through the gradual penetration of humanist ideas among the masses, for all of which both the Protestants
and the Catholics hated him.

The whole humanist movement in the north of Europe was one,
though by no means the deepest, root of the Protestant Reformation.
All over Europe it set up classical models in art and literature, and
the humanist teachers and critics ushered in the classical period of European culture. Their work began as an inspiration to artists, writers,
and scholars, and ended as a school of rules, as one can easily see if he
compares the classical influences in Shakespeare, Milton, and Pope or
in Mantegna, Raphael, and Canova. In these classical influences on art
and letters, too often it is Roman and Latin models rather than Greek
ones that were followed. Even if many of the humanists had a foolish
contempt for both science and philosophy, nevertheless by their emphasis on worldly concerns and by preparing an intellectual setting
in which both science and philosophy could grow they aided the
growth of each. Finally, the humanists in the end completely transformed secondary and university education. Through them began the
reign of the Greek and Latin classics in the schools which has not
ended in the twentieth century. So while the great mass of Latin humanist literature, poems, histories, and orations are no longer read—
Symonds compares the writings of the humanists to vast glacial mo-
raines left on the landscape of early modern culture—nevertheless
they brought an enormous enrichment to nearly every phase of Western culture, and they left a profound mark on this culture, particularly
in the centuries between 1300 and 1850.

Epilogue*

I. THE MIDDLE AGES, CENTURY BY CENTURY

IN a topical discussion of this sort and in one that is centered on intellectual history and omits nearly all political and economic matters, the general movement of history is often lost. To restore the balance, and to pull the various threads together, let us view the whole mediaeval age century by century.

The great Roman Empire, which had made an economic, political, and cultural unity of the whole Mediterranean basin, began, in the third and fourth centuries A.D., to show evidences of decline and of transformation. The old economic prosperity and the traditions of honest and efficient government that had once characterized the most successful empire of history steadily deteriorated and disintegrated. The ancient religion of the state and the family was supplemented by Stoicism and Neo-Platonism for the intellectuals, and by the mystery religions and Christianity for the masses. Nearly all interest in experimental science had disappeared. The literature and art of the pagan world became reminiscent; its creative energy was weakening. The vital intellectual forces, outside the Neo-Platonic School, lay with the

* This epilogue may also be read as an introduction to the book.

[443

Christians. First in the Greek East with a number of great thinkers, including Origen, then in the Latin West, with Tertullian, and later Ambrose, Jerome, and Augustine, the basic ideas of the Christian faith were combined with Greek philosophy into a new Christian theology. In art, the rising Christian church took over the styles of the later Roman Empire, but, in using them, the Christians emphasized those features of Roman art that were other-worldly and transcendental. The Christian church made its peace with the Roman state, and the institution that had earlier been persecuted was now favored and was loaded with riches. More ardent souls among the Christians took refuge in monasteries.

The fifth century is the age of the Germanic Migrations. Rome had earlier shown an unmatched capacity to assimilate all sorts of cultures. In her weakened condition, there was, in the fifth century, presented to her the greatest problem in assimilation in her long history. And the solution of it was now beyond Rome's powers. These Barbarians broke down the enfeebled Roman government and trade, and pushed western Europe downward into a crude agricultural economy. The towns decayed, and the Barbarians set up a number of small kingdoms, the most important of which was that of the Franks on both sides of the lower Rhine. Learning was represented by elementary compends like that of Martianus Capella, and there was now little stone or brick building in Latin Christendom. The Celtic and Germanic peoples, however, had traditions of art, literature, and government of their own, which were later to be impressed on European culture. Missionaries from Ireland and Rome reintroduced Roman Christianity into western Europe; the missionaries, in trying to save the Barbarians from their heathendom, also began to rescue them from their savagery. In the east of Europe, centering in Constantinople, the old economic, political, and cultural life of the Roman world went on in the Byzantine Empire. The traditions of classical education, literature, and philosophy were continued, though only in art did the Byzantine world make important new contributions.

The sixth, seventh, and eighth centuries saw the Latin West still in a backward economic and cultural situation. The Barbarians were settling down to a fixed agricultural life, but manners, as described by writers like Gregory of Tours, were still savage and brutal, and the level of culture was low. Learning, now mostly confined to monasteries, was represented by men like Boethius and Cassiodorus, Benedict, Gregory the Great, Isidore of Seville, and Bede; only Boethius in the sixth century and Bede in the seventh show much originality. Indeed, not only did the most learned minds contribute little that is new, but some of the most respected thinkers of the period, like Gregory the Great, were even unable to understand Augustine. After Boethius, the knowledge of Greek all but disappeared in the West. The atmosphere of these centuries is murky, with only an occasional gleam of light. The first great work of vernacular literature, the Anglo-Saxon epic *Beowulf*, was written down in the seventh century. At the opening of the same century the chants of the Latin church were reorganized, and tradition has long attributed this to Gregory the Great. The first great new artistic creation of Christianity in the West was this plain song which used Jewish and classical elements but was in itself essentially a new style that expressed the inner spirit of Christianity.

In the East, the Byzantine Empire reached its greatest prosperity and territorial extent under Justinian in the sixth century. During his reign, the Roman law was given a great codification and Byzantine art came to its first flowering. In the seventh century, Mohammedanism, a new religion, and with it a new cultural synthesis, began in Arabia. From the eighth century through the eleventh, in the Near East, in Africa, and in Spain, the sons of Islam produced a brilliant material civilization, brought important agricultural, manufacturing, and cultural ideas west from India and Persia, and themselves made significant contributions in science, philosophy, and art. They revived the Greek scientific and philosophical works and developed an experimental method; the main line in the history of science passed from the Greeks to the Mohammedans, to be taken up again by the Latin West in the twelfth and thirteenth centuries. No contrasts could have been more striking in this period than those between the Latin West and the East, which though divided in religion was highly urbanized and supported a brilliant material and intellectual culture.

While in Spain and in the east of Europe, strong states, an urban civilization, and a high level of culture continued for centuries, the Latin West moved slowly upward in the eighth century and the first part of the ninth. The Frankish rulers, over several centuries, built up the first large state since the fall of Rome. They brought a return of peace and more effective government, and, through their patronage of monasteries, they also fostered a revival of learning, "the Carolingian Renaissance." If this created little that was new, it at least insured the copying, and thus the survival, of the ancient Latin authors. It brought into the Latin West a revival of early Christian church architecture, and, in sculpture and painting, reintroduced the figural art of the Mediterranean Basin. The greatest writer was John Scotus Erigena, who lived at the court of Charlemagne's grandson in France. Under the German Ottos, this revival of art and learning spread across western and central Germany. During this same period, the religious drama, the Latin poetic sequence, and polyphonic music began. The peace established by the Carolingian dynasty was disturbed in the ninth century by new barbarian raids of Vikings, Slavs, and Magyars, and by attacks from the Mohammedans in the Mediterranean. The central government could not protect the inhabitants. Men turned to local strong men for defense, feudalism developed, and western Europe came to be divided into a multitude of small and petty feudal holdings.

In the East, the great cultural centers were Constantinople, Damascus, Bagdad, and Cairo. The Mohammedan centers were most remarkable for their science and philosophy both of which were later to influence the West. From the ninth through the twelfth centuries, there was a second great flowering of Byzantine art, though in science and philosophy Byzantium lagged far behind her Islamic neighbors. Byzantium was now playing in eastern Europe something of the role Rome played in the West; Byzantine missionaries were carrying Christianity to the Slavic peoples in the Balkans and in Russia.

The tenth and eleventh centuries saw the beginning of a revival in the West. This is shown by the growth of the Cluniac, Cistercian, and Carthusian Orders, by the great effort of the Germans to expand toward the east and spread Christianity eastward and northward, and by the beginnings of a revival of town life and the middle class in Italy. From the eleventh century on, Latin Christendom was producing an original civilization of its own. In France, under the Capetians, in Germany, under the early Franconian emperors, in England after the

Norman Conquest, in Spain following the capture of Toledo by the Christians, strong states were developing, states in which the monarch was striving to curb the feudal nobles and to impose the king's law and the king's peace on his subjects. The papacy consolidated its power and, in the Crusades, Latin Christendom started to expand. As the secular states and the Roman church both gained in power, clashes between them were inevitable. In culture, Anselm produced the first important philosophic writing since Erigena, the Romanesque style developed, and a great body of Latin poetry and history was written. Alongside this flowering of Latin literature, vernacular epics were composed in northern France, Germany, Scandinavia, and Ireland, and in the south of France the first troubadour poetry appeared.

The last four mediaeval centuries, the twelfth through the fifteenth, witnessed a great increase in the power and wealth of the middle class, the rapid growth and then the slow decline of papal power, the beginnings of representative government in the towns and in the national assemblies of England, France, Germany, and the Spanish states. The development of culture in Latin Christendom was so remarkable in the twelfth and thirteenth centuries, that they, rather than the fifteenth century, seem to represent the beginning of modern civilization. In its cultural expansion, France was the leader from the twelfth into the fourteenth century when Italy began to take the lead. From the twelfth century on, the movement is continuous; in the first two centuries the church was able to dominate nearly every aspect of intellectual life. But after 1300, the lay world had sufficiently developed to remove some currents of thought and expression from ecclesiastical control. Also from the twelfth century on, the Latin West furnished the initiative in new cultural currents, and both the Byzantine and the Islamic civilizations, at least in comparison with their earlier achievements, made few advances.

In the twelfth century the schools of northern France were the leaders; here one found men like John of Salisbury at Chartres and Abelard and Peter Lombard in Paris. Until the twelfth century, the great centers of learning were the monasteries which usually had more wealth and attracted men of greater ability than did the secular clergy of priest and bishop. In the twelfth century, with the growth of towns, the secular church gained greatly in wealth and in prestige. To the cathedral school of Paris (and to other centers) came, after 1150, a stream of new translations of Aristotle and other Greek philosophers and scientists together with their Arabic commentators. This cathedral school of Paris was gradually reorganized into the greatest mediaeval university, which attracted to its classrooms men like Albertus Magnus from Germany, Roger Bacon from England, and Bonaventura, Aquinas, and Dante from Italy. At the same time, the study of medicine and of Roman and canon law were being renewed in Italy. Northern France, however, kept the lead not only in theological studies, but also in art, literature, and music. By the end of the twelfth century Romanesque art had evolved into Gothic, and out of the epic had grown the chivalric romance. The lyric and narrative poets of northern France, in both Latin and the vernacular, were now the leaders of Europe. And the same was true of the Gothic art and of the organum and counterpoint of northern France. The church dominated much of this civilization, though it met opposition from the secular governments of England, France, and Germany, and it had to face extended heretical movements in northern Italy, and in central and southern France.

The thirteenth century represented the supreme attempt of the Roman church to direct the whole life of society in all its reaches. The Mendicant Friars did much, through preaching and charitable work, to renew the faith of the masses, while in the universities they undertook the work of making Christianity acceptable to the intellectuals. The supreme cultural achievements of the thirteenth century are best represented in the Gothic cathedral, the theological "Summas," the *Roman de la Rose*, *Parzival*, and the *Divine Comedy*. Everywhere the middle class is now powerful and is beginning to join forces with the growingly effective monarchs in curbing the power of the turbulent nobility. The king is extending his law-enforcing and taxing power into the local community. Beneath the apparent unity of the culture of the thirteenth century there were, however, important minor currents of nationalism, skepticism, and secularism that were to come to the fore in the future.

The fourteenth century was one of restlessness and criticism. At the opening of the century, the king of France removed the papacy from Rome to Avignon, and the Vicar of Christ lost some of his prestige. Attacks on the papacy from a number of angles begin to appear; the criticisms of Dante, Marsiglio of Padua, William of Ockham, Wyclif, and Hus were all partly inspired by nationalism. In some of these attacks can be found the origins of the Reformation. Toward the middle of the century, France and England entered on what was to be a Hundred Years' War, and all Europe was ravaged by the Black Death. France no longer dominated culture. In Italy, the classical enthusiasm of Niccolò Pisano in the preceding century was followed by phenomenal changes in the traditional styles of painting inaugurated by Giotto. Italy also became a leader in music; Landino in Florence was the leading composer of the fourteenth century. Petrarch and Boccaccio turned the attention of scholars and poets to rich new veins of inspiration, first in the Latin then in the Greek classics. A second great center of culture was England, indications of which are the poetry of Chaucer, the philosophy of Ockham, the reforming ideas of Wyclif and the Lollards, and the music of Dunstable.

The last mediaeval century, the fifteenth, saw the end of the Hundred Years' War, and strong monarchy—limited in England but absolute in France—becoming the pattern of the future. The papacy, having weathered the Babylonish Captivity and the Conciliar Movement, was back in Rome enjoying a sort of Indian summer before the storm of the Protestant Reformation. Everywhere the middle class was willing to defy church and state authorities and the nobility to extend its political and economic rights. The whole tone of Italian society became secularized. The spell of classical culture was strong on the Italians; Brunelleschi, Donatello, the painters, the humanists, and the poets all show a deliberate attempt to create new styles inspired by what they knew of ancient civilization. The most remarkable scientific genius in Europe was Leonardo da Vinci, like Dante, Petrarch, Boccaccio, Giotto, and Landino, a Florentine. Every large Italian city was the center now of an intense artistic and cultural activity. In the north of Europe, the Gothic style in architecture, painting, and sculpture still held sway. Jan Van Eyck, Villon, the German meistersingers, Josquin des Prés, and Thomas à Kempis still belong to a mediaeval world. Only Dürer, Erasmus, and some of the humanists show much of the influence of the new Italian currents. Flanders is the great center of northern painting, and in music it is the leader of all Europe.

Slowly an old culture that, for centuries, had been agricultural, feudal, and ecclesiastical had had growing up in it a new culture that was urban, national, and secular. Gradually the balance was shifted toward the newer forces. The old did not disappear, but, by the fifteenth century, especially in Italy, what had earlier been the minor currents had come to be the major ones, and the older forces of peasant, noble, and priest were challenged. Slowly there was forming what was to be the pattern of the early modern world: political absolutism, which came to mean not only monarchs who were absolute or nearly so in government, but also a state-directed religion; mercantilism, a state-controlled economy; and a state-patronized classicism in the fine arts and literature. As the old declines the new rises within it; there are in history no beginnings and no ends in the whole sequence of things.

2. THE TRANSITION FROM MEDIAEVAL TO MODERN TIMES

BY the end of the twelfth century, many of the changes that were to move Europe from mediaeval to modern times were under way. First among these was the rise and expansion of the middle class. The founding and development of towns, the emancipation of the serfs, and the growth of commerce, banking, and manufacture restored to Europe the class that had been the backbone of the Roman Empire. After the eleventh century, wealth in capital steadily grew alongside the older feudal wealth in land. The town opened up new careers in craftsmanship, business, medicine, law, teaching, and government administration. It introduced a more worldly point of view and shifted the whole balance in society. The decline and disappearance of the middle class in the later Roman Empire and the early Middle Ages and its reappearance after the tenth century seem to be more fundamental than any other changes in the history of the West in the Christian Era.

Another great change that separates the period before and after the eleventh and twelfth centuries was the rise of a series of well-centralized national states. This process of national consolidation under kings took place on a large scale in England and France and in the Spanish,

Hungarian, Polish, and Scandinavian kingdoms and, on a smaller scale, in the petty principalities and city-states of Italy and Germany. These national monarchies differed from both the old Roman Empire, which made no allowances for national differences, and the makeshift feudal governments that had grown up in the ninth and tenth centuries. In the later mediaeval and early modern period, the monarchs and the leaders of the middle class often made common cause against the nobility. Both wanted uniform coinage and courts, good roads, the opening up of wider markets, and the enforcement of peace. In time, the leaders of the middle class got titles for themselves, and they began to imitate the cultural patterns of the landed aristocracy. This new plutocracy intermarried with the old nobility, and, in the end, the two became fused. This is first evident in Italy, though by the later fifteenth century it is beginning to be seen in most of the states of western Europe. The new nation-states grew up between the church universal on the one hand and the local feudal powers on the other. The growth of national royal power can be traced in the increase of the king's ability locally to enforce his law, collect his taxes, and raise troops for his army. It can also be seen in the departmentalizing of the central government and the growth of an administrative bureaucracy. The first gains made by the state were at the expense of the nobility. In spite of severe clashes with the church, no permanent gains were made by the state against the church until the sixteenth century after the start of the Protestant Reformation. Then Protestant monarchs broke with the papacy, seized church lands, curbed or abolished ecclesiastical church courts, made themselves heads of the church within their own states, and, beyond this, gained for themselves a halo of sanctity which blossomed in the seventeenth century into the theory of the divine right of kings. The unity of Christendom broke down, and peace was now maintained only by an unstable balance of a power system which was already in existence before Machiavelli so brilliantly described it in the early sixteenth century.

All these changes meant a decline in the political influence and, to a lesser extent, in the economic power and the social prestige of the nobility. It should, however, be remembered that while, by 1500, the nobles had lost much of their political power, they still had control of great economic resources and commanded an immense social prestige.

The church steadily declined, especially after 1300, as an organization and as an intellectual and spiritual force. The church had, in the early Middle Ages, taken the place of the Roman Empire in holding many national and cultural groups together under the leadership of the bishop of Rome. It had also taken the lead in education and in charitable work of all sorts, and had assumed extensive powers of government. The church had come to be the most powerful of all mediaeval states with the best system of local administration, tax collection, and law enforcement, and with the most elaborately organized central administration in Europe in its capital at Rome. After 1300 it was evident that national monarchies had grown so strong that they were destined to assume all the powers of government and to confine the clergy largely to spiritual functions. So, as the middle class and the nation-state rose in power, the feudal nobility and the church declined. The process was so gradual that it only became evident in the perspective of later ages.

Another line of transition from mediaeval to modern times is shown in the growth of vernacular literature and the fact that learning, art, and music become, with each century after 1200, less the monopoly of the clergy. Secular subjects push into art and literature and into the curriculum of the schools. By the thirteenth century some scholars cease to be satisfied with the results of the thinking of Aristotle and the Greeks, and they are aware that human knowledge can be expanded by the efforts of men. Science begins again to advance. The old never disappears, but the new comes in alongside it, and in the course of time the balance is shifted. As we have seen, the first great flowering of culture in the Latin West in the twelfth and thirteenth centuries was largely domination by the clergy and by the ideals of the church, and it centered in northern France. On the other hand, the cultural movement of the fourteenth and fifteenth centuries, dominated chiefly by northern Italy, was more under the influence of laymen and represented more secular ideals.

At the close of the mediaeval period, the Spanish and Portuguese, by the discovery of the Americas and of a new sea route to India, pushed onward and outward an expansion of Europe that had begun in the eleventh century with the trade of the Italian communes in the Near East. European civilization was finally to be carried around the globe.

Before the voyages of Columbus and Vasco da Gama, this civilization was shut in to the south and southeast by the Islamic peoples spread out from Morocco to the Balkans and beyond the Balkans to India and Malaysia. On the east, was the Tartar Empire now falling to pieces, but long the terror of the civilized world from China and India through Russia to the borders of Latin Christendom. Europe now began to outflank these barriers by the discovery of new sea routes until the ends of the earth stood face to face. The mediaeval voyages and discoveries, in the end, meant that commerce and civilization, which had for millennia centered in the Mediterranean, were to be shifted to the North Atlantic. Thus the whole geographical axis of Western civilization began to change as Europe moved from mediaeval into modern times.

Finally, some more intangible changes mark this transition. There is some growth of individualism, though again this can be exaggerated, and if there is a change it should be dated from twelfth-century France, rather than from fifteenth-century Italy. There is also some decline of conservatism, a growth of self-reliance, and a spirit of adventure. In many of these fields, what had appeared as a ripple in the twelfth century or earlier became almost a tidal wave by the close of the fifteenth century. On the other hand, it should always be remembered that the growth of modern political and religious liberty owes more to the struggles of the sixteenth and seventeenth centuries than it does to the Middle Ages.

Many mediaeval institutions and ideas are still alive in the modern world. First among these are the Roman Catholic Church and the Eastern Orthodox Churches which have kept—with some modification—their organization, their liturgy, and their theology. What the Roman Church lost, as a result of the Reformation, it gained later in new communicants in the Americas, Asia, and Africa. A second mediaeval creation, unknown to classical antiquity, is that of representative government. In its world influence this was chiefly the creation of England, and, to a much lesser extent, of France and some of the continental states. The universities of the modern world are again, in origin, a mediaeval contribution to civilization. Courses of study, academic degrees, and the whole machinery of higher education were fashioned not by ancient Athens, Alexandria, and Rome, but by mediaeval Bologna, Paris, and Oxford. Germanic law, and its offshoots in the common law and the jury system, came into the modern world from our mediaeval ancestors. They also bequeathed to us Byzantine, Romanesque, and Gothic architecture which since the eighteenth century have inspired the designing of many modern buildings. And out of the revival of a great mediaeval functional style, the Gothic, modern functional architecture found its inspiration. Harmonized music was the invention, from the ninth century on, of mediaeval men, as were also the vernacular languages and literatures which have long served and enriched the modern world. Modern times owe to the Middle Ages an esteem for women and a respect for the dignity of labor unknown to classical antiquity.

Finally, harder to define is the Romantic element in literature and life which, while it arose in the later ages of pagan antiquity, was deepened by the mediaeval centuries. To realize this, one has only to compare a passage, describing the coming of evening, in Homer's *Odyssey* (XIII, 31 ff.) with one from the *Divine Comedy* of Dante (*Purgatory* VIII, 1–6). "As when a man," writes Homer, "longs for his supper, for whom, all day long, two dark oxen drag through the fallow field the jointed plow, and welcome to such an one the sunlight sinketh, so that he may get him to supper, for his knees wax faint by the way." Dante, speaking of the same sunset hour writes: "It was now the hour that turns back desire in those that sail the sea, and softens their hearts, the day when they had said to their sweet friends farewell, and which pierces the new pilgrim with love, if he hears from afar a bell that seems to deplore the dying day."

Every age will judge the Middle Ages by its own standards and ideals. To many modern thinkers, the greatest weaknesses of mediaeval thought were its lack of desire to spread the bounds of knowledge, its lack of a spirit of free inquiry in the Greek or the modern sense, and its failure to clear up a mass of superstitions that flourished among the masses. If in these particulars, certainly important ones, the modern world has made progress, other ideals of the Middle Ages will indicate the measure of what has been lost. In religion, mediaeval thinkers taught that the things of the spirit are supreme; in philosophy, they held there was an infinite disparity between the substance and its accident, between appearance and reality, and they had all the authority of Plato and Aristotle to back them. In art and literature they believed that supreme beauty lies in limitless aspiration and in the attempt of man to represent the infinite power and goodness of the divine. They also believed that both the life of the common people and their language were worthy of use in painting, sculpture, poetry, and prose. In education, their aim was to develop character and to train men to live with their fellows, rather than merely to train them to earn their bread and butter.

In society, the great mediaeval thinkers held that all men are equal in the sight of God and that even the humblest has an infinite worth. In economics, they taught that work is a source of dignity not of degradation, that no man should be used for an end independent of his welfare, and that justice should determine wages and prices. In politics, they taught that the function of the state is moral, that law and its administration should be imbued with Christian ideas of justice, and that the relations of ruler and ruled should always be founded on reciprocal obligation. The state, property, and the family are all trusts from God to those who control them, and they must be used to further divine purposes. Finally, the mediaeval ideal included the strong belief that all nations and peoples are part of one great community. As Goethe said, "Above the nations is humanity," or as Edith Cavell wrote in 1915 in the margin of her *Imitation of Christ* the night before she was executed, "Patriotism is not enough."

Notes

CHAPTER I

[1] G. L. Laing, *Survivals of roman religion* (New York, 1931) esp. pp. 8–15 for lists of saints and special curative function of each, one for toothache, one for child-birth, and the rest, and their relation to gods of the ancient world; also cf. V. D. Macchioro, *From Orpheus to St. Paul* (New York, 1930), pp. 23–5.

[2] "The shortest cut to the study of the philosophy of the Middle Ages is to commit the 'Timaeus' to memory," P. Shorey, *Platonism, ancient and modern* (Berkeley, 1938), p. 105.

[3] Interesting modern examples of the Platonic theory of reality are the following:

a) from a sonnet of Michelangelo:

> Heaven-born, the soul a heavenly course must hold;
> Beyond the visible world she soars to seek
> (For what delights the sense is false and weak)
> Ideal form, the universal mould.
> The wise man, I affirm, can find no rest
> In that which perishes; nor will he lend
> His heart to aught that doth on time depend.
>   ——R. W. Livingstone, ed., *The legacy of Greece*
>   (Oxford, 1921), p. 27.

b) from Shelley's *Adonais*, stanza 52:

> The one remains, the many change and pass;
> Heaven's light forever shines, earth shadows fly;
> Life like a dome of many colored glass,
> Stains the white radiance of eternity,
> Until death tramples it to fragments.

c) and finally from Proust:

There are two worlds, one the world of time, where necessity, illusion, suffering, change, decay, and death are the law; the other the world of eternity, where there is freedom, beauty, and peace. Normal experience is in the

456]

world of time, but glimpses of the other world may be given in moments of contemplation or through accidents of memory. It is the function of art to develop these insights and to use them for the illumination of life in the world of time.

——Cited in H. March, *The two worlds of Marcel Proust* (Philadelphia, 1948), p. 1.

⁴ For an excellent brief definition of the mystic's attitude cf. E. R. Good- enough, *An introduction to Philo Judaeus* (New Haven, 1940), pp. 27–8.

⁵ A. O. Lovejoy, *The great chain of being* (Cambridge, Mass., 1936). p. 24.

⁶ Plato was twenty-eight years old when Socrates was executed, and sixty years old when he first met Aristotle. Aristotle was in close relations with Plato for twenty years.

⁷ Lovejoy, *op. cit.,* p. 63.

⁸ This "failure of nerve" is a long story.

Anyone who turns from the great writers of classical Athens, say Sophocles or Aristotle, to those of the Christian Era must be conscious of a great differ- ence in tone. The new quality is not especially Christian; it is just as marked in the Gnostics and Mithra worshippers as in the Gospels, in Plotinus as in Jerome. It is a rise of asceticism, of mysticism, of pessimism, a loss of self confidence, of hope in this life and of faith in normal human effort; a despair of patient inquiry, a cry for infallible revelation; an indifference to the wel- fare of the state. It is an atmosphere in which the aim of the good man is not so much to live justly, to help the society to which he belongs; but rather, by means of a burning faith, by contempt for the world and its standards, by ecstasy, suffering and martyrdom, to be granted pardon for his unspeakable unworthiness, his innumerable sins. There is an intensifying of certain spiritual emotions; an increase of sensitiveness, a failure of nerve.

——G. Murray, *Five stages of Greek religion* (2nd ed., Oxford, 1925), p. 155.

⁹ Found scratched on a wall in Herculaneum. W. W. Hyde, *Paganism to Christianity in the Roman Empire* (Philadelphia, 1946), p. 30 note.

¹⁰ *Cambridge ancient history,* XI, pp. 690–6.

¹¹ E. Bevan, ed., *Later Greek religion* (London, 1927), p. 111.

¹² S. H. Mellone, *Western Christian thought in the Middle Ages* (Lon- don, 1935), p. 20.

¹³ Seneca said: "The mind unless it is pure and holy comprehends not God." St. Matthew says: "Blessed are the pure in heart for they shall see God." Seneca wrote: "Let us give as we wish to receive"; St. Matthew says: "Whatso- ever ye would that men do unto you do ye even so unto them." Many of the Stoic ideas, especially the doctrine of the inner light and the idea of the brother- hood of man were independently reproduced in Quakerism.

¹⁴ The great passage in Augustine's *Confessions* (IX, 10) which tells of his farewell to his mother, Saint Monica, is based on Plotinus' *Enneads*, V, i, 2; beyond this Augustine's whole outlook is deeply penetrated with Neo-Platonism.

¹⁵ J. Hussey, *Church and learning in the Byzantine Empire 867–1185* (Oxford, 1937), p. 79.

¹⁶ Bidez in *Cambridge ancient history*, Vol. XII, p. 653, calls Iamblicus a "nincompoop"; T. Whittaker, *The Neo-Platonists* (2nd ed., Cambridge, 1918), pp. 124–5, defends him. Gibbon called the whole Neo-Platonic school "the second childhood of human reason." This charge may, perhaps, be applied to Iamblicus, but it hardly fits the commentators and systematizers, Porphyry and Proclus, and it is absurd if applied to Plotinus, who was one of the world's important religious philosophers and the greatest philosophical mind between Aristotle and Aquinas.

¹⁷ F. Cumont, *Oriental religions in Roman paganism* (Chicago, 1911), p. 100.

¹⁸ J. Frazer, *Adonis, Attis, and Osiris* (2nd ed., London, 1922), p. 347.

¹⁹ Cumont, *op. cit.*, pp. vii–viii.

CHAPTER II

¹ Amos v, 21–4.

² Isaiah i, 10–17; Micah vi, 8.

³ Job xxiv, 2–4, 7, 9–10; for earlier denunciation of the same vices, cf. Amos vi and viii.

⁴ Twelve books of later inspiration were classed together by St. Jerome as the Apocrypha, "things hidden." The Roman Catholics, the Anglicans, and the Lutherans still include these in their Old Testament. Most other sects have dropped them from their text of the Old Testament.

⁵ Isaiah xxxiv, 8–13. Each reader will think of other magnificent passages; in such a consideration do not omit the Eighteenth Psalm.

⁶ If [says Philo] any yearning enters into thee, O soul, of inheriting the good things of God, thou must leave not only thy country, that is the body, and thy kindred, sense perception, and the house of thy father, reason, but thou must run away from thyself. For the mind, no longer in itself, but exalted by heavenly love, led along by the One Really Real, pulled upwards toward him, while truth goes in advance and removes impediments —behold, that is thy inheritance.

———E. R. Bevan and C. Singer, eds., *The Legacy of Israel* (Oxford, 1928), p. 46.

This is the mystic's story through the ages. "I was free," writes Thomas Merton in 1947. "I had recovered my liberty; I belonged to God, not to myself, and to belong to him is to be free, free of all the anxieties and worries that belong to this earth." T. Merton, *The seven story mountain* (New York, 1948), p. 370.

⁷ On the inconsistencies in the accounts of Jesus in the New Testament cf. D. W. Riddle and H. H. Hutson, *New Testament life and literature* (Chicago, 1946), p. 60.

Books on the life of Jesus are numerous. They vary from works of pious imagination to writings that deny the reality of Jesus as a historical figure. Verbal descriptions of Jesus and his mission are as diverse as the artists' conceptions of him. He has been seen as a fighter by the militaristic and as a peacemaker by the pacifist; as conservative by the fundamentalist and as revolutionary by the radical; as emaciated by the ascetic and as vigorous by the athletic.

———Riddle and Hutson, *op. cit.,* p. 56.

[8] Jesus' messianic consciousness was the central fact of His life. No treatment of the subject which tries to evade or to deny that fact can hope to do justice to it. Jesus was the spiritual heir of a long line of Jewish eschatologists. The messianic framework of the Gospels cannot be proved to reflect the beliefs of Jesus throughout, but its central features antedate the crucifixion. And these central features are the belief that the Messiah is both Son of Man and Son of God, and that he is to suffer death at the hands of his own people, for whom he will shed his blood as a vicarious sacrifice. It is true that most New Testament scholars have tried to date the introduction of these basic features of Christology to the Apostolic Age, or later. Against this, however, is the whole weight of early Christian literature. Paul and Peter fought bitterly over the question of the extension of ancient Jewish ritual to gentile converts; they would certainly have fought much more bitterly over any supposed innovations with respect to the person of their Lord.

———W. F. Albright, *From the Stone Age to Christianity*
(Baltimore, 1940), p. 305.

For the belief that the idea of Jesus as the Son of God and a Messiah who would bring a sudden change was the interpretation not of Jesus but of his first followers cf. Riddle and Hutson, *op. cit.,* Ch. VIII.

[9] The constricted Jesus of Christian theology does not belong to modern times. He is dated. He is the product of the early centuries A.D., when men believed in Olympus, and drenched its altars with blood. Magic plays about him like lightning. He walks upon the waters, ascends into the air, is obeyed by the tempests, turns water into wine, blasts the fig tree, multiplies loaves and fishes, raises the dead. All these marvels made him God incarnate to the thinkers of the First Century; all these marvels make him a conventional myth to those of the Twentieth.

———A. Weigall, *The paganism in our Christianity*
(New York, 1928), pp. 18–19.

[10] For reasons why Jews of Palestine would not accept Christianity cf. Riddle and Hutson, *op. cit.,* Ch. IX.

[11] 1 Corinthians VII, 9; Galatians III, 26, 28.

[12] Gospel according to St. John I, 1–4.

[13] Gospel according to St. John XI, 25–6, VI, 53–4. The logos doctrine came originally into Judaism from Sumerian, Canaanite, and Egyptian sources; the influence of Platonism merely strengthened a concept already known. Cf. W. F. Albright, *op. cit.,* pp. 285–6.

[14] 1 Corinthians III, 19.

CHAPTER III

¹ A. D. Nock in *Cambridge ancient history*, Vol. XII, p. 449.

² For fantastic stories in the *Physiologus*, read the tales of the lion, the unicorn, and the pelican in W. Rose, *The epic of the beast* (London, n.d.), pp. 186–9, 199–200, 229–30; for exaggerations in the literature of the Christian Apochrypha cf. E. J. Goodspeed, *History of early Christian literature* (Chicago, 1942), pp. 120–2. A large mass of this early Christian writing, to which references are made in extant works, has been lost.

³ C. W. Jones, *Saints lives and chronicles in early England* (Ithaca, 1947), pp. 2–3.

⁴ W. R. Inge, "Origen" in *Pro. of the British Academy*, Vol. 32, 1946, p. 1.

⁵ Inge, *op. cit.*, pp. 4–5.

⁶ "It is my object to annihilate a paltry conception of God [writes Origen,] the conception of those people who regard God as localized in heaven. I will not permit it to be said that God sojourns in a material place. You might as well say that he himself is corporeal. This would result in the most impious doctrines." E. de Faye, *Origen and his work* (New York, 1929), pp. 56–7.

⁷ The *Mystical Theology* opens with the following rhapsody:

Trinity, which exceedeth all Being, Deity and Goodness! Thou that instructeth Christians in Thy heavenly wisdom! Guide us to that topmost height of mystic love, Super-Essential, Super-Divine, Super-Excellent, which exceedeth light and more than exceedeth knowledge, where the simple, absolute, and unchangeable mysteries of heavenly Truth lie hidden in the dazzling obscurity of the secret Silence, outshining all brilliance and surcharging our blinded intellects with the utterly impalpable and invisible fairness of glories which exceed all beauty! Such be my prayer; and thee I counsel that, in the earnest exercise of mystic contemplation, thou leave the senses and the activities of the intellect and all things that the senses or the intellect can perceive, and all things in this world of nothingness, and that, thine understanding being laid to rest, thou strain (as far as thou mayest) towards a union with Him, whom neither being nor understanding can contain. For, by the unceasing and absolute renunciation of thyself and all things, thou shalt in pureness cast all things aside, and be released from all, and so shall be led upwards to that which exceedeth all existence. These things thou shalt not disclose to any of the uninitiated, by whom I mean those who cling to the objects of human thought.
——C. E. Rolt, ed., *Dionysius the Areopagite on the divine names*, etc. (new ed., London, 1940), pp. 191–2.

Dionysius, at one place, describes God as follows:

Super-essential indetermination, the unity which unifies every unity, the absolute no-thing which is above all reality. No monad or triad can express the all-transcending hiddenness of the all-transcending super-essentially, super-existing super-Deity.

——W. R. Inge, *The philosophy of Plotinus*
(3rd ed., 2 vols., London, 1929), Vol. II, p. 112.

By A.D. 500, when Dionysius was writing, the atmosphere is definitely mediaeval. Here some dates are interesting: 393, last Olympic games; 396, last Eleusinian rites; 404, last gladiatorial contests in the Colosseum; 476, last Roman Emperor in the West; 529, schools of Greek philosophy closed; 533, last theatrical exhibition in Rome; 549, last race in the circus in Rome.

⁸ F. Lear, "Mediaeval attitude toward history," in *Rice Institute Pamphlets*, 1933, p. 105.

⁹ H. O. Taylor, *The mediaeval mind* (3rd ed., 2 vols., New York, 1919), Vol. I, p. 73.

¹⁰ One of the most quoted letters of Jerome is on the monastic life:

Though your little nephew twine his arms around your neck; though your mother, with disheveled hair, point to the breast with which she nourished you, though your father fall down before you, pass on. Fly with tearful eyes to the banner of the cross. O solitude whence are brought the stones of the city of the Great King! What would you, brother, in the world? How long are the shades of roofs to oppress you? Do you fear poverty? Christ called the poor "blessed." Are you terrified at labor? No athlete without sweat is crowned. Does the infinite vastness of the forest affright you? In the mind walk abroad in Paradise. In a word, hear the apostle as he answers, "The sufferings of the present time are not worthy to be compared with the glory which shall be revealed in us!"

——F. A. Wright, ed., *Select letters of St. Jerome*
(New York, 1933), pp. 31–3, 49–51

¹¹ F. R. M. Hitchcock, ed., *The city of God* (London, 1922), p. v.

¹² The passages of the *Confessions* describing his conversion and his leavetaking of his mother are too familiar to be quoted. Anyone not familiar with them will find them in *Confessions*, VIII, 11–12, and IX, 10, in the Everyman edition, Pusey translation, pp. 168–71, 194–6.

¹³ W. W. Hyde, *Paganism to Christianity in the Roman empire* (Philadelphia, 1946), p. 199.

¹⁴ Augustine sums up his argument as follows in Book XIV, Ch. 28:

These two states have been created by two different sets of affections, the earthly by the love of self to the contempt of God; the heavenly by the love of God to the contempt of self. That one glories in self; this one in God. The one lifts up its own head in its pride; the other says to its God, "Thou art my Pride and the Lifter-up of my head." In the one, the princes are actuated by a thirst for ruling; while in the other the princes and the subjects serve one another in love, the former by their care, the latter by their obedience. In that city, the wise live according to man, and seek profit for their own bodies or souls. While in this state the only human wisdom is piety, which offers true worship to God, and looks for its reward to the society of the saints, consisting of both men and angels, that "God may be all in all."

Cf. Santayana's brilliant summary of this whole "Christian epic" in his *Reason and religion* (New York, 1906), pp. 92–7.

[15] The historians of Christian Latin poetry disagree on the subject of the origin of stress rhythm. For the point of view presented here cf. M. Manitius, *Geschichte der Lateinischen Literatur des Mittelalters* (Munich, 1911), Vol. I, p. 20, and F. Brittain, *The mediaeval Latin and Romance lyric to A.D. 1300* (2d ed., Cambridge, 1951), pp. 1–3. Raby insists that there was no stress rhythm in early Latin poetry and that rhythm came into Christian Latin poetry from Syria. F. J. E. Raby, *History of Christian Latin poetry* (Oxford, 1927), pp. 21–5. P. de Labriolle, *Histoire de la littérature Latine Chrétienne* (3rd ed., 2 vols., Paris, 1947), Vol. I, pp. 265–8, finds nothing in so-called stress rhythm of Commodian except barbarized Latin. Anyone interested in metrics is advised to look at these passages. If the theory of the origin of rhythm of Manitius is rejected, that discussed by Raby, *op. cit.*, pp. 20–2, is, I believe, the next best choice.

[16] To appreciate a Latin hymn, with all its flavor we must take it not merely for itself, but as part of something larger. First of all, it is wedded to music, which makes its own appeal. Then it is caught up into the large atmosphere of some religious office. Finally, the service is celebrated in a church, which, however humble, puts the altar in the place of reverence. As we listen to the Latin words, we hear the deep voice of the organ, and glance upward in imagination at the vaulting. This is the whole body of the hymn, which loses flesh and blood if you tear it away, if we merely read the hymns.

——E. K. Rand, *Founders of the Middle Ages* (2nd ed., Cambridge, Mass., 1929), pp. 214–15.

[17] Whether the basilica plan came from the Roman assembly hall, or the Roman house, or Roman buildings of the imperial cult, or the sanctuaries of the mystery cults, or the synagogue, or from other sources is still uncertain; for a summary of the literature cf. P. Lavedan, *Histoire de l'art* (2 vols., Paris, 1950), Vol. II, pp. 50–2. In Rome, typical basilicas are *Santa Maria Maggiore, San Lorenzo fuori le mura,* and *San Paolo fuori le mura* (rebuilt after fire in 1823); typical round churches are *Santa Costanza* and *San Stefano Rotundo.*

CHAPTER IV

[1] E. Gibbon, *History of the decline and fall of the Roman Empire,* ed. by J. B. Bury (7 vols., London, n.d.), Vol. V, pp. 169–70.

[2] Diehl writes:

From every province in the Empire and every country in the world men flocked to Byzantium for business, for pleasure, and for litigation. There were Asiatics with hooked noses, almond eyes under thick eyebrows, pointed beards, and long black hair; Bulgars with shaved heads and dirty clothes, wearing an iron chain round their waists by way of belt; fur-clad Russians with long, fair mustaches; Armenian or Scandinavian adventurers who had come to seek their fortunes in the great city; Muslim merchants from Bagdad or Syria, and western merchants, Italians from Venice or Amalfi, Pisa or Genoa, Spaniards and Frenchmen, and Varangians [Russians] "tall as palm trees."

——*Cambridge mediaeval history*
(Cambridge, 1927), Vol. IV, p. 750.

³ *Cambridge mediaeval history*, IV, pp. 746, 750. A westerner, Luidprand, sent by Otto I in 949, describes the splendors of the imperial palace:

Adjoining the imperial palace there is a hall of extraordinary size and beauty. In front of the emperor's throne stood a tree of gilded iron, whose branches were filled with birds of various kinds, made of iron and gilded, which gave forth the various sorts of birds' notes. The throne was so cunningly constructed that at one instant it looked low, the next, higher, and a moment later had risen to a great elevation. It was guarded on either side by huge lions, covered with gold, which lashed their tails and roared aloud. At my entrance, the lions roared, and the birds sang. When I raised my head, after prostrating myself before the emperor, I beheld him whom before I had seen seated at a moderate height elevated almost to the roof of the hall. In a hall of extraordinary height and magnificence nineteen tables were spread. Only golden dishes were used. After dinner fruit was served in three golden vessels of such enormous weight that they could not be carried by men but were brought in on little carts decked with purple coverings. It would take too long to describe all the performances which followed, but I must mention one. There was a man who carried on his forehead, without touching it with his hands, a pole twenty-four feet long on which a cross piece was fastened. Then two little boys, naked, climbed up the pole, and performed all sorts of gymnastic feats.

Luidprand hated the Byzantines, and what he says of the emperor will pass for the usual view of the Latin Christians on the Byzantines in general: "lying, crafty, merciless, proud, falsely humble, and greedy; he eats garlic, onions, and leeks," and he found Constantinople magnificent, but a city "half-starved, lying, wily, rapacious and vainglorious." F. A. Wright, ed., *The works of Luidprand of Cremona* (London, 1930), pp. 207–10, 259.

⁴ This estimate is based largely on Diehl, who seems to have entered into their mentality with more insight and sympathy than any modern scholar, cf. esp. Book II, "Les éléments de faiblesse" of his *Byzance* (Paris, 1919) and *Cambridge mediaeval history*, Vol. IV, Ch. 24.

⁵ The lot of the Byzantines was not a happy one:

The more one studies the life of the East Romans, [says Baynes] the more one is conscious of the weight of care which overshadowed it; the fear of the ruthless tax-collector, the dread of the arbitrary tyranny of the imperial governor, the peasant's helplessness before the devouring land-hunger of the powerful, the recurrent menace of barbarian invasion: life was a dangerous affair, and against its perils only supernatural aid, the help of saint, or magician, or astrologer could avail.

———N. H. Baynes and H. Moss, eds., *Byzantium*
(Oxford, 1948), p. xxix.

⁶ Luke xɪv, 26.

⁷ The Essenes did not share in the common life of the Jewish people but lived apart in communities. They renounced marriage and shunned riches. They dressed in white as a mark of purity. They taught absolute obedience to their director, and provided, for new candidates, a three-year probationary period before vows were taken. They combined a practical life of working in the fields and preaching with prayer and contemplation. There were other Jewish recluses besides the Essenes. The Essenes were famed for their prophecies. Founded about 150 B.C., Josephus estimates their number as about 4,000. John the Baptist and even Jesus himself may have been a member of the Essenes.

⁸ There is a strange life of Paul the hermit by Jerome. Jerome tells how Paul, a learned and cultivated man, fled the world to live in a cave in Egypt. When Paul was a hundred and ten years old, he was visited by St. Anthony, who was directed to the lonely spot by friendly beasts. St. Anthony entered the cave but Paul heard him and closed the door. At length he admitted Anthony. Then, said St. Paul of Thebes, "how fares the human race? Are new homes springing up in the ancient cities? What government directs the world? Are there still some remaining for the demons to carry away." At supper time a raven brought twice the usual ration it was wont to bear to St. Paul alone. St. Anthony then went to fetch the cloak of St. Athanasius in which to wrap the body of St. Paul, who thought he was nearing death. On his return, St. Anthony saw St. Paul in "robes of snowy white ascending on high amid bands of angels." He wrapped the body of St. Paul in the cloak and prepared to bury it when there came with manes flying two lions. They came to the corpse, lay down at St. Paul's feet, roared out their mourning and then pawed the desert sand until they had dug out a grave. St. Anthony gave the lions his blessing and they departed. St. Jerome ends his tale with a monastic reflection: "I may be permitted to ask those who do not know the extent of their possessions, who adorn their houses with marble, who string house to house and field to field, what did this old man in his nakedness ever lack? Poor though he was, Paradise is open to him; you with all your gold will be received into Gehenna." St. Jerome, *Life of Paul the Hermit* in *Nicene and Post-Nicene Fathers*, 2nd series, Vol. VI, p. 300.

⁹ The regulations of Theodore of Studius for the copying of manuscripts are very detailed; punishments for slipshod work are severe:

> The monk who failed to keep his copy and the original clean, to mark exactly the stops and accents, and to observe lines and spaces was subjected to a penance of one hundred and thirty prostrations. If he wandered from the text of the original, the penalty was three days exclusion from the community; if he read the text carelessly, he was compelled to live on bread and water for three days.

———J. W. Thompson, *The medieval library*
(Chicago, 1939), p. 316.

[10] J. B. Bury, *History of the Eastern Roman Empire* (London, 1912), pp. 448-9.

[11] J. M. Hussey, *Church and learning in the Byzantine Empire 867-1185* (Oxford, 1937), p. 34.

[12] N. H. Baynes and H. Moss, eds., *Byzantium* (Oxford, 1948), p. 242. I have not discussed here collections of sermons, orations, and of letters that have survived; they are very useful to the historian in search of details about all aspects of Byzantine civilization.

[13] Occasional passages of the *Digenes Akritas* remind one of the *Roman de la Rose* or the close of Dante's *Purgatory*:

The ground was embroidered with radiant flowers. There were trees and tall reeds. A fresh spring welled up in the midst of the meadow, and near it were deep pools in which the flowers and the trees were reflected. The wood was full of birds which sang sweetly.

———J. B. Bury, *Romances of chivalry on Greek soil* (Oxford, 1911), p. 20.

[14] J. F. Scott and others, eds., *Readings in mediaeval history* (New York, 1933), p. 94.

[15] The origins of the Byzantine use of the squinch and the pendentive have produced a great controversial literature; cf. D. T. Rice, *Byzantine Art* (Oxford, 1935), pp. 47-52, and P. Lavedan, *Histoire de l'art*, Vol. II (2nd ed., Paris, 1950), pp. 58-62.

[16] C. R. Morey, *Mediaeval art* (New York, 1942), p. 104.

[17] *Cambridge mediaeval history*, Vol. IV, p. 752.

[18] N. H. Baynes and H. Moss, eds., *Byzantium* (Oxford, 1948), pp. 390-1.

[19] W. R. Lethaby, *Mediaeval art* (2nd ed., London, 1948), p. 34.

[20] A very effective description of this type of lavish display will be found in Morey, *op. cit.*, pp. 108-09.

[21] D. T. Rice, *Byzantine painting* (London, 1948), p. 3.

CHAPTER V

[1] Whatever may be the theories of various scholars on the correct use of terms, the author has found that, in practice, the following words and their derivatives are used practically interchangeably: Moslem, Muslim, Mohammedan, Arab, Islam, and Saracen. The following distinctions may be made, however: The faithful object to Mohammedan because, unlike the Christians, they say they do not worship their founder; the faithful prefer Muslim. Arab refers to the country of the origin of the faith and to the common language of the Mohammedan world. Many Arabs are not Mohammedans and most Mohammedans are not Arabs. Islam is the name given to the new faith by Mohammed, and means "submission to God," and is used also to designate the body of the faithful. The submission of Abraham and Isaac to the will of God, expressed in the

Arab verb *aslama,* was the situation that provided Mohammed with his name for the new faith. The present use of the word Saracen includes both the religion and the whole culture.

² The whole question of what Mohammed got from Jewish and Christian sources is still debated, cf. C. C. Torrey, *Jewish foundations of Islam* (New York, 1933); Torrey is very detailed, though he exaggerates the Jewish element in Islam. A. Guillaume, "Influence of Judaism on Islam" in E. R. Bevan and C. Singer, eds., *The legacy of Israel* (Oxford, 1928), takes something of the same position. On the other hand, R. Bell, *The origin of Islam in its Christian environment* (London, 1926), ignores the influence of Judaism. A compromise position is that of J. Obermann, "Islamic Origins" in N. A. Faris, ed., *The Arab heritage* (Princeton, 1944); H. A. R. Gibb, in his *Mohammedanism* (Oxford, 1949), says (p. 37): "Earlier scholars postulated a Jewish source with some Christian additions. More recent research has conclusively proved that the main external influences (including the Old Testament materials) can be traced back to Syriac Christianity." No one believes that Mohammed had "direct, first-hand acquaintance with Scripture—notwithstanding his constant appeal to matters and persons of Biblical history and the bona fide implications that his familiarity with things Biblical were of the most intimate kind. Not only the Hebrew original but any sort of translation would surely have precluded the gross discrepancies, inaccuracies, and delusions he exhibits, almost invariably, when his revelation involves data from the Old Testament, or, for that matter, from the New Testament. The decisive thing is that in a great many instances where a Biblical element appears misrepresented or distorted in the revelation of Mohammed, the very same misrepresentation and distortion can be shown to recur in post-Biblical sources as embellishments characteristic of the treatment of Scripture in both the Jewish Synagogue and the Christian Church." Obermann, *op. cit.,* 94–5. Most medieval Christians in both the East and the West regarded Mohammedanism as a heretical sect rather than as a separate religion. Dante consigns Mohammed to a lower circle of Hell with all the "sowers of scandals and schisms."

³ At first the Mohammedans were told by their Prophet to turn toward Jerusalem when they prayed; later when he abandoned all hope of a religious alliance with the Jews, the faithful were told to turn toward Mecca when they prayed.

⁴ Mohammed sometimes refers to the Christians as the "People of the Evangel." He denies that Christ can be the "Son of God," but he accepts the idea of the Virgin Birth. Mohammed is ignorant of the facts of Christ's life. He condemns the Jews for asserting that Jesus was put to death, and the fact that the Christians believed in the Crucifixion is ignored. Evidently Mohammed got his information from some sect of Christian heretics.

⁵ D. G. Hogarth, *Arabia* (Oxford, 1922), p. 52.

⁶ P. Hitti, *History of the Arabs* (4th ed., New York, 1949), p. 122.

⁷ H. A. R. Gibb, *Mohammedanism* (Oxford, 1949), p. 49.

⁸ J. W. Thompson, *Economic and social history of the Middle Ages 300–1300* (New York, 1928), p. 193.

⁹ The famous "Throne verse" shows Mohammed's utterance in its grandest style.

God, there is no God but He, the Living, the Self-Sufficient. Slumber seizeth Him not, nor sleep. To Him belongeth whatsoever is in the Heavens and whatsoever is in the Earth. Who is there that shall intercede with Him save by His will. He knoweth what is present with men, and what shall befall them. His throne is wide as the Heavens and the Earth, and the keeping of them wearieth Him not. And He is the High, the mighty One. Koran, Sura II, v. 256.

¹⁰ A bird's-eye view of the Moslem world at the hour of prayer (ignoring the difference caused by longitude and latitude) would present the spectacle of a series of concentric circles of worshippers radiating from the *Kah'bah* at Mecca and covering an ever widening area from Sierra Leone to Canton and from Tobolsk to Cape Town.

———Hitti, *op. cit.*, pp. 130–1.

¹¹ The month of *Ramadān* was chosen because Mohammed's revelations began in that month, and his first military victory occurred in the same month. Fasting was unknown in Pre-Islamic Arabia; Mohammed took the idea from the Jews and the Christians.

¹² Koran, Sura IX, v. 5, 29.

¹³ The economic interpretation of the Arab conquests is not entirely modern; a number of contemporaries pointed it out. One wrote:

No, not for paradise didst thou the nomad life forsake;
Rather, I believe, it was the yearning after bread and dates.

———Hitti, *op. cit.*, p. 144.

¹⁴ H. Lammens, *Islam, belief and institutions* (New York, n.d.), p. 140.

¹⁵ Some of the important mystic statements of Mohammed are collected in T. Arnold and A. Guillaume, eds., *The legacy of Islam* (Oxford, 1931), pp. 211–12.

¹⁶ In religious courts, and often in other courts, it became a common practice to ask an eminent scholar, usually called a *mufti,* for an opinion on an important case. The *mufti* was ordinarily not attached to the administration, though in the Ottoman Empire he was a state official.

¹⁷ D. de Santillana, "Law and Society" in T. Arnold and A. Guillaume, eds., *The legacy of Islam* (Oxford, 1931), p. 286.

¹⁸ The Koran allows four lawful wives and an unlimited number of slave concubines; divorce was easy for the husband. Women were allowed to inherit and to dispose of property. There were saints, preachers, and scholars among the women of Islam, but, in general, women were kept out of public and social life by custom rather than by law. It meant that, as through much of Greek and Roman history, educated men shared their tastes and enjoyments with other men or with women not connected with his family life. Muslim society used many slaves, but free workers existed alongside them; the population was less sharply divided between freemen and slaves than in classical antiquity, and, everywhere, the tendency was toward kindliness in the treatment of slaves, an attitude expressly enjoined in the Koran.

[19] The great mystic and reformer al-Ghazālī made concessions to changed conditions:

The concessions made by us are not spontaneous, but necessity makes lawful what is forbidden. We know it is not allowed to feed on a dead animal; still it would be worse to die of hunger; of those that contend that the caliphate is dead forever and irreplaceable, we should like to ask; which is to be preferred, anarchy and the stoppage of social life for lack of a properly constituted authority, or acknowledgment of the existing power, whatever it be? Of these two alternatives, the jurist cannot but choose the latter.

Writing in the fourteenth century, another theorist says:

The sovereign has a right to govern until another and stronger one shall oust him from power and rule in his stead. The latter will rule by the same title and will have to be acknowledged on the same grounds; for a government, however objectionable, is better than none at all; and between the two evils we must choose the lesser.

——G. E. von Grunebaum, *Medieval Islam*
(Chicago, 1946), pp. 168–9.

[20] Because of limitations of space, any discussion of orthodox Muslim theology is omitted.

[21] B. Russell, *History of western philosophy* (New York, 1945), p. 427.

[22] E. Renan, *Averroès et l'Averroïsme* (Paris, n.d.), Part I, Ch. I, Sec. VII.

[23] This account of Islamic science omits any discussion of the basic framework that lies back of all mediaeval science; this will be discussed later in the chapter on science in Latin Christendom, 1000–1500.

[24] The careful observation of Islamic diagnoses is shown in the following passage from Rhazes.

The outbreak of smallpox is preceded by continuous fever, aching in the back, itching in the nose, and shivering during sleep. The main symptoms of its presence are: back-ache with fever, stinging pain in the whole body, congestion of the face, pain in the throat accompanied by difficulty of respiration, dryness in the mouth. Excitement, nausea, and unrest are more pronounced in measles than in smallpox, while the aching in the back is more severe in smallpox than in measles.

——T. Arnold and A. Guillaume, eds., *The legacy of Islam*
(Oxford, 1931), pp. 323–4.

[25] D. C. Munro, *Essays on the Crusades* (Burlington, 1903), pp. 19–20.

[26] Much of the apparatus of modern chemistry came from the Greek alchemists of Alexandria who produced over eighty different pieces of apparatus including furnaces, lamps, water baths, ash baths, dung-beds, reverberatory furnaces, scorifying pans, crucibles, beakers, filters, etc. Cf. F. S. Taylor, *The alchemists* (New York, 1949), Ch. IV.

[27] The identity of Jabir and Geber has produced a great controversial literature. The problem has two parts: first, who is the author of the large number of Arabic treatises ascribed to Jabir, and second, who is the author of the Latin

treatises ascribed to Geber? The answer to the first question seems to be that they were composed in the late ninth and early tenth centuries by members of a Shi'ite sect. In the case of the Latin works ascribed to Geber, it is impossible to be sure that they are translations from the Arabic. The question is important in the history of chemistry because it is only in the Latin treatises of Geber that there is any consistent use of mineral acids. Cf. G. Sarton, *Introduction to the history of science* (Baltimore, 1927), Vol. I, Ch. II, pp. 532–3; and P. Kraus, *Jabir* (Cairo, 1943).

[28] E. J. Holmyard, *The great chemists* (London, 1929).

[29] The *Arabian Nights* exist in many versions, and the stories are of many countries and times. They have a great vitality, but they never found a finished stylist to put them into good form. They have, thus, never been highly regarded as works of art by Muslim critics.

[30] No extended treatment of Islamic literature is given here, because, unlike Muslim philosophy, science, and art, it had little influence on the culture of the West.

[31] The question of the origin of the mosque is much debated; for the various theories cf. works referred to in P. Lavedan, *Histoire de l'art* (Paris, 1950), Vol. II, pp. 71–2.

[32] The chief surviving monuments, west of Persia, are, first from the Ommiad period, the splendid "Dome of the Rock" in Jerusalem, a huge timber dome set above an octagonal base (built about 691), the Great Mosque of Damascus in which horseshoe arches and a tall minaret are first used, and the mosque at Kairouan in Tunis (built about 730). In the "Dome of the Rock" and the Mosque at Damascus, Byzantine mosaic workers and sculptors were employed. The great monuments of the Abbasid period (750–1258), in and about Bagdad, were deeply influenced by Persian art. Those in Bagdad were destroyed in the Tartar sack of the city in 1258, but the style can be seen in the ruins of the mosque and palace at Sāmarra, the mosque of ibn-Tūlūn at Cairo (built about 876), and the great mosque of Cordova with its 1,293 columns. The mosques of the ninth century introduced the brick dome and the extensive use of glazed tiles. To the tenth century belongs the Fātimid mosque of al-Azhar at Cairo in which are found some of the earliest arabesques. The "Giralda" of Seville, now the bell-tower of the cathedral, was built in the twelfth century. The finest surviving buildings of the twelfth through the fourteenth century are some of the mosques and palaces of Cairo and Damascus, the fortifications of Aleppo and Cairo, and the Alhambra in Spain. Closely allied to these Muslim buildings in the West are the Mozarabic churches of Spain and the extreme south of France, some of the churches of Sicily, and the Mudejar churches and palaces of the later Middle Ages in Spain.

[33] T. Arnold and A. Guillaume, *op. cit.*, p. 395.

[34] A fuller account of the translation into Latin of Greek and Arabic philosophical and scientific works in the eleventh through the thirteenth century is given in a later chapter on mediaeval science in the West.

[35] For the influence of Islamic poetry on the troubadours see references

p. 534.

CHAPTER VI

¹ G. M. Trevelyan, *History of England* (New York, 1926), pp. 38–40, and W. D. Foulke, tr., *History of the Langobards of Paul the Deacon* (New York, 1906), pp. 57–8. For a different interpretation of the results of the Germanic migrations cf. A. Dopsch, *The economic and social foundations of European civilization* (New York, 1937). Dopsch finds less destruction and change and more continuity in the period of the migrations and after than most historians. Something of the same view is represented by H. Pirenne, *Mohammed and Charlemagne* (London, 1939), who also believes that the Mohammedan conquests mark the beginning of the Middle Ages in the West. R. A. Dennet, "Pirenne and Muhammad" in *Speculum*, 1948, denies Pirenne's thesis.

² H. O. Taylor, *Classical heritage of the Middle Ages* (3rd ed., New York, 1911), p. 51, and C. S. Lewis, *The allegory of love* (Oxford, 1936), p. 79.

³ The early history of monasticism is discussed in Chapter IV.

⁴ E. Gibbon, *Decline and fall of the Roman Empire*, Bury ed. (London, n.d.), Vol. IV, p. 201.

⁵ In the preface to his *On the soul*, Cassiodorus describes his method, which is prophetic of that of the later Scholastics:

> Let us first learn why it is named soul; second its definition, third its substantial quality, fourth whether any form should be attributed to it, fifth what are its moral virtues, sixth its natural forces by which it holds the body together, seventh its origin, eighth the place of its seat, ninth the body's form, tenth the souls of sinners, eleventh the souls of the just, and twelfth, the resurrection.
>
> ———J. Migne, *Patrologia Latina*
> (Paris, 1841–86), Vol. 70, column 1281.

⁶ Robert Bridges, ed., *The spirit of man* (London, 1919), no. 20.

⁷ For a specimen of Gregory's allegorizing cf. M. L. W. Laistner, *Thought and letters in Western Europe 500–900* (London, 1931), pp. 76–7; and for his type of moral tales cf. J. H. Robinson, *Readings in European history* (2 vols., Boston, 1904), Vol. I, pp. 76–7.

⁸ Christianity remained a very superficial veneer for the masses. In the next century we hear still of pagan rites such as human sacrifices and reading the future from the flight of birds. A formula for renouncing these practices in Germany has survived:

> Question, Forsaketh thou the devil?
> Answer, I forsake the devil.
> Q. And all the devil's works?
> A. And I forsake all the devil's works. Thor and Odin and all the evil spirits.
> Q. Believest thou in God the Almighty Father?
> A. I believe in God the Almighty Father.
> Q. Believest thou in Christ the Son of God?
> A. I believe in Christ the Son of God.

Q. Believest thou in the Holy Ghost?
A. I believe in the Holy Ghost.

Evidently accepting Christianity was like changing allegiance from one ruler to another.

————E. Emerton, *An introduction to the study of the Middle Ages* (Boston, 1916), pp. 155–6.

⁹ Einhard describes Charlemagne's love of learning:

While dining he listened to music or reading. Histories and the deeds of the ancients were read to him. He delighted in the works of St. Augustine, especially in his *City of God*. He was a zealous promoter of liberal studies, and greatly revered their teachers upon whom he bestowed the highest honors. He tried to learn to write, and used even to put his tablets and writing books under his pillow, so that when he should have leisure he might accustom his hand to forming the letters, but in this task too long postponed and begun too late in life, he had but little success.

————Einhard, *Life of Charlemagne*
(New York, 1880), Chs. 24–5.

¹⁰ In a letter written between 780 and 800 Charlemagne says:

Be it known that we have considered it expedient that the bishoprics and monasteries entrusted by the favor of Christ to our government, in addition to the rule of monastic life and the intercourse of holy religion, ought to be zealous also in the culture of letters, teaching those who by the gift of God are able to learn, so that just as the observance of the monastic rule imparts order and grace to moral conduct, so also zeal and teaching may do the same for the use of words. In recent years, when letters have been written to us from various monasteries to inform us that the brethren were offering up in our behalf holy and pious prayers, we noted in most of these letters correct thoughts but uncouth expressions. We, therefore, began to fear lest perchance, as the skill in writing was wanting so also the wisdom for understanding the Holy Scriptures might be much less than it rightly ought to be. Therefore, we exhort you not only not to neglect the study of letters, but also to pursue it earnestly that you may be able more easily and more correctly to penetrate the mysteries of the divine Scriptures.

————D. C. Munro, ed., *Selections from the laws of Charles the Great*
(Philadelphia, 1900), pp. 12–13.

These injunctions were often repeated by Charlemagne; cf. Munro, *op. cit.*, pp. 12–14. Charlemagne's interest in education figures in his legend after his death; thus the Monk of St. Gall writing in 883 describes a visit of the Emperor to a school, how he tested the boys, praised those who had learned, and denounced those who had not. A. J. Grant, ed., *Early lives of Charlemagne* (London, 1926), pp. 62–5.

¹¹ An elementary knowledge of Greek existed from the fifth century on in Irish monasteries. In the seventh century, Theodore of Tarsus introduced a more thorough study of Greek into some English monasteries. From there an interest in more advanced types of Greek studies spread to Ireland, but in the

eighth century the interest in England diminished. Bede knew some Greek but Alcuin, an English scholar of the eighth century knew none, and, in turn, Erigena, an Irishman of the ninth century, knew Greek well. After the ninth century, the interest in Greek studies died out throughout Latin Christendom. Boccaccio, in the fourteenth century, is the next important European man of letters, after Erigena, who knew Greek well.

[12] J. Migne, *Patrologia Latina*, Vol. 122, *De divisione naturae* I, 69. For a Catholic defence of Erigena cf. F. Coplestone, *History of philosophy* (2 vols., London, 1947–50), Vol. II, pp. 132–5. A number of legends about Erigena circulated in the later Middle Ages. One claimed he had, in his youth, known Bede and Alcuin, another said he had travelled in Greece and in the Orient, and a third made him a founder of the University of Paris.

[13] There is also a legend that Erigena went to the monastery of Malmesbury in England, where he was attacked by his students who stabbed him to death with their pens. H. Bett believes this story. H. Bett, *Erigena* (Cambridge, 1925), pp. 15–16.

[14] In 953 Otto I sent John of Gorze in Lorraine to Cordova. Here he spent three years, learned the Arabic language, and brought back some Muslim books to Lorraine. There is no record of what they were, and we know of no translations made at the time.

[15] F. J. E. Raby, *A history of secular Latin poetry in the Middle Ages* (2 vols., Oxford, 1934), Vol. I, p. 85.

[16] Raby says of the sixth and seventh centuries:

> The monastic theory despaired of the world and pictured it as a stormy sea upon whose waves floated the ark of the monastery, the only hope of safety and shelter. In those troubled times a strange darkness fell over the human spirit. The wildest superstitions were accepted as the truth. The veneration of relics and images, the belief in their magical power, the immense growth of stories of miracles which went side by side with the increasing popular worship of the saints, the systematization of demonology, that terrible science which revealed an unseen world of horror—all these were forces powerful in forming the intellectual and emotional quality of the first centuries of the Middle Ages.
>
> ——F. J. E. Raby, *A history of Christian Latin poetry* (Oxford, 1927), pp. 121–2.

[17] The whole poem in Latin (with English translation, part of which is quoted here) is in F. A. Wright and T. A. Sinclair, *A history of later Latin literature* (London, 1931), pp. 284–5; another translation is in J. Lindsay, *Mediaeval Latin poets* (London, 1934), pp. 120–1.

[18] Saintsbury writes amusingly of the scholarly labors expended on *Beowulf*, and for that matter on some other aspects of mediaeval culture:

> Scholarly conjecture has for the better part of a century let itself loose over the date, scene, meaning and composition of the piece. Whether it was brought from Jutland by the Saxon invaders and Anglicised or was composed in England itself; whether the scenery is that of the east or west coasts of the North Sea; whether it is an entire poem or a congeries of ballads;

whether it is literal history embellished poetically or a myth—all the questions have been asked with pains, answered with confidence, and the answers all pooh-poohed with disdain. It has been wildly and unreservedly praised and has been made to bear all sorts of meanings and messages.

——G. Saintsbury, *Short history of English literature*
(New York, 1924), pp. 3–6.

[19] The descriptions of nature are very effective:

> *Wild and lonely the land they live in,*
> *Wind-swept ridges and wolf-retreats,*
> *Dread tracts of fen where the falling torrent*
> *Downward dips into gloom and shadow*
> *Under the dusk of the darkening cliff.*
> *Not far in miles lies the lonely mere*
> *Where trees firm-rooted and hung with frost*
> *Overshroud the wave with shadowing gloom.*
> *And there a portent appears each night,*
> *A flame in the water; no man so wise*
> *Who knows the bound of its bottomless depth.*
> *The heather-stepper, the horned stag,*
> *The antlered hart hard driven by hounds,*
> *Will turn at bay and die on the brink*
> *Ere ever he'll plunge in that haunted pool.*
> *'Tis an eerie spot!*

——C. W. Kennedy, tr., *Beowulf*
(Oxford, 1940), p. 44.

[20] One of the most quoted passages in Bede's history is a marvellous picture of the time; Bede is describing the discussion of the advisors of the Anglo-Saxon King Edwin as to whether they should accept Christianity, and one of the king's chief men said:

So seems the life of man, O king, as a sparrow's flight through the hall when you are sitting at meat in winter-time with the warm fire on the hearth, but the icy storm without. The sparrow flies in at one door, and tarries for a moment in the heat of the fire, and then flying forth vanishes into the wintry darkness whence it came. So tarries for a moment the life of man, but what is before it, what after it we know not. If this new teaching tells us ought of these, let us follow it.

——Bede, *Ecclesiastical history of the English nation,*
Book II, Ch. XIII.

[21] In the *Book of Kells*, as in other Celtic manuscripts, the complicated abstract designs are amazing in their skillful handling, but alongside them the human figures of holy men are as surprisingly crude; they are treated as one big ornament wholly and imperturbably superhuman. In Ireland, Christianity finally surrendered to the barbarian style; in England and on the Continent the opposite took place. "The apparently limitless meandering of these Irish interlaces (in manuscript illumination) remind one of the Irish sagas with their ef-

fect of non-arrival; the hero forgets the purpose with which his wanderings commenced, and the poem ends on a theme, plot, and destination quite foreign to that with which it started." C. R. Morey, *Mediaeval art* (New York, 1942), p. 184.

[22] P. H. Láng, *Music in western civilization* (New York, 1941), p. 76.

[23] G. M. Trevelyan, *History of England* (New York, 1926), p. 2.

[24] V. Duruy, *A short history of France* (2 vols., London, n.d.), Vol. I, pp. 162-3.

CHAPTER VII

[1] E. Renan, *Averroës et l'Averroïsme* (Paris, 1869), pp. 201–02.

[2] Much of this comes from Greek thought. In Plato's *Timaeus*, as summarized by Aristotle, "Timaeus tries to give a physical account of how the soul moves its body. The soul is in movement and the body moves because it is interwoven with it. The motions of the heavens are the motions of the soul." C. Singer, *Short history of science* (Oxford, 1941), p. 37.

[3] Here are some samples of popular science in the twelfth century from Alexander Neckham's *On the nature of things:*

The eagle, on account of its great heat, mixeth very cold stones with its eggs when it sitteth on them, so that the heat shall not destroy them. In the same way, our words, when we speak with undue heat, should later be tempered with discretion. The wren is a little bird. Who has not wondered to hear a note of such volume proceeding from so trifling a body? By such things, we are taught that the virtues of little things should not be scorned. When the body of the wren is put upon the spit before the fire it need not be turned for the wren will turn itself. [On the other hand, Neckham gives a good description of the compass.] Sailors, when in cloudy weather, they can no longer profit by the light of the sun, or when the world is wrapped in darkness, and they are ignorant whither the ship's course is directed, touch a needle to the magnet. The needle will then whirl around until its point is directed to the north.

Writing in the thirteenth century, Bartholomew Anglicus describes many marvellous beasts:

Satyrs be somewhat like men and have horns in the forehead, and are like to goats in their feet. St. Anthony saw such an one in the wilderness. Some of them have heads as hounds, and some be called cyclops because each of them hath but one eye, and some be headless and noseless and their eyes be in the shoulders. And others have only one foot so large that they beshadow themselves with the foot when they lie in the sun, and yet they be so swift that they be likened to hounds in swiftness. [On the other hand, the author gives a shrewdly observed description of the cat.] The cat is a lecherous beast in youth, swift and pliant, and is led by a straw and playeth therewith, and is a right heavy beast in age and full sleepy. He lieth slyly in wait for mice, and is aware where they be more by smell than by sight. In time of love is hard fighting for wives, and one scratcheth the other grievously. Nor is he hurt when he is thrown down off an high place.

——T. Wright, ed., *Alexander of Neckham, De naturis rerum* (London, 1863), Book I, Ch. 23, Book II, Ch. 98; and R. Steele, *Mediaeval lore.* (London, 1924), pp. 156, 165.

A lapidary will tell you this sort of thing: a sapphire held in the hand during prayer would secure a favorable answer from God, an opal folded in a bay leaf rendered its holder invisible, and an amethyst made one immune from intoxication.

⁴ The Muslim contributions to science, which should be considered here, are discussed in Chapter V.

⁵ In the *Opus tertium*, a brief summary of his ideas, Bacon speaks of one Peter of Maricourt:

One man I know, and one only who can be praised for his achievements in experimental science. Of battles of words he takes no heed. What others strive to see dimly, like bats blinking at the sun, he gazes at in the full light of day, because he is master of experiment. Through experiment he gains knowledge of natural things, medical, chemical, indeed of everything in the heavens and on earth. He is ashamed that things should be known to laymen, old women, soldiers, plowmen, of which he is ignorant. Therefore he has looked closely into the doings of those who melt metals; he knows everything relating to the art of war, the making of weapons and the chase; he has looked carefully into agriculture; he has even taken note of remedies, lot-casting, and charms used by old women; so that nothing which deserves investigation should escape him. If philosophy is to be carried to its perfection, his aid is indispensable. As a reward, he neither receives it nor looks for it. He puts honor and wealth aside.

In a curious letter, Bacon predicts the uses of science:

I will now enumerate the marvellous results of art and nature which will make all kinds of magic appear trivial. Instruments for navigation will be made which will do away with the necessity of rowers, so that great vessels shall be borne about with only a single man to guide them and with greater speed than if they were full of men. And carriages can be constructed to move without animals to draw them, and with incredible velocity. Machines for flying can be made in which a man sits and turns an ingenious device by which skillfully contrived wings are made to strike the air. Then arrangements can be devised, compact in themselves, for raising and lowering weights infinitely great. Bridges can be constructed ingeniously to span rivers without supports.

——J. H. Robinson, ed., *Readings in European history* (2 vols., New York, 1904), Vol. I, pp. 460-1.

⁶ A. G. Little, *Roger Bacon* (London, 1928), pp. 4-5.

⁷ Petrarch, earlier, had dismissed the scientists because "they in no way help toward a happy life, for what does it advantage us to be familiar with the

nature of animals, birds, fishes and reptiles when we are ignorant of the race of man to which we belong?" R. M. Setton, "Some recent views of the Italian Renaissance" in *Report of the annual meeting of the Canadian Historical Association* (Toronto, 1947), p. 27.

⁸ Speaking of the "Scientific Revolutión" and of its mediaeval beginnings, Butterfield writes:

> Since that revolution overturned the authority in science not only of the Middle Ages but of the ancient world—since it ended not only in the eclipse of scholastic philosophy but in the destruction of Aristotelian physics—it outshines everything since the rise of Christianity and reduces the Renaissance and the Reformation to the rank of mere internal displacements within the system of mediaeval Christendom. Since it changed the character of men's habitual mental operations even in the conduct of the non-material sciences, while transforming the whole diagram of the physical universe and the very texture of human life itself, it looms so large as the real origin both of the modern world and of the modern mentality that our customary periodisation of European history has become an anachronism and an encumbrance.
>
> ——H. Butterfield, *Origins of modern science 1300–1800*
> (London, 1949), p. vii.

⁹ L. White, Jr., "Technology and invention in the Middle Ages" in *Speculum*, 1940, p. 156.

¹⁰ B. Russell, *History of western philosophy* (New York, 1945), p. 463.

¹¹ G. G. Coulton, *Studies in medieval thought* (London, 1940), pp. 96–7.

¹² Because of lack of space no discussion of the history of purely theological questions is included here.

¹³ No Christian [says Anselm] ought in anyway to dispute the truth of what the Catholic Church believes in its heart and confesses with its mouth. But always holding the same faith unquestioningly, loving it and living by it, he ought himself as far as he is able to seek the reason for it. If he can understand let him thank God. If he cannot let him not raise his head in opposition but bow in reverence.

> ——A. G. McGiffert, *History of Christian thought*
> (2 vols., New York, 1932–3), Vol. II, p. 186.

¹⁴ A. Weber, *History of philosophy* (New York, 1896), p. 221.

¹⁵ Here are sample questions from Abelard's *Sic et non*:

Should human faith be based on reason, or no?
Is God one, or no?
Is sin pleasing to God, or no?
Is God the author of evil, or no?

> ——J. H. Robinson, *Readings in European history*
> (2 vols., New York, 1904), Vol. I, pp. 451–2.

¹⁶ H. O. Taylor, *The mediaeval mind* (4th ed., 2 vols., New York, 1925), Vol. I, p. 416, and Henry Adams, *Mont St. Michel and Chartres* (New York,

1904), p. 315. The famous correspondence of Abelard and Heloise all dates from a period long after their separation; the first letter, written by Abelard, called the *Historia calamitatum*, is a dramatic retelling of the love affair.

[17] All of Aristotle's logical treatises were available in Latin translations before 1150; the other works became current at the following dates: *Physics* about 1180; *De caelo* and *De anima* about 1210; the *Metaphysics* became available in three portions between 1175 and 1270; the *Ethics* came in sections between 1200 and 1245; and the *Politics* began to circulate about 1260. It is clear that the reception of Aristotle was a gradual process. The earlier division of thinkers into those who did and did not use Aristotle has now been given up for a three-fold division, first, those who used Aristotle in an eclectic manner along with other authorities, second, those who used him as the Muslims interpreted him, and finally, those who tried to use his work in its original form. M. D. Knowles, "Some recent advance in the history of mediaeval thought" in *Cambridge historical journal*, 1947, pp. 33–4.

[18] Aquinas, *Summa contra gentiles*, Book I, Ch. 12.

[19] Pierre Duhem, the distinguished historian of science, A. D. Sertillanges, *Aquinas and his work* (London, 1932), p. 88.

[20] J. N. Figgis, *Political thought from Gerson to Grotius* (2nd ed., Cambridge, 1916), p. 9.

[21] S. D. Mellone, *Western Christian thought in the Middle Ages* (Edinburgh, 1935), pp. 289–90.

[22] Pico, the prince prodigy, who died at the age of thirty-one, says in his famous *Oration on the dignity of man*:

> Then the supreme maker declared that unto man, on whom he would bestow naught singular, should belong in common whatsoever have been given to his other creatures. Then he took man, made in his own image, and having placed him in the center of the world spake to him thus, "Neither a fixed abode, nor a form in thine own likeness, nor any gift peculiar to thyself alone, have we given thee, O Adam, in order that what abode, what likeness, what gifts thou shalt choose, may be thine to have and to possess. The nature allotted to all other creatures, within laws appointed by ourselves, restrains them. Thou, restrained by no narrow bounds, according to thy own free will, in whose power I have placed thee, shall define thy nature for thyself."
>
> ——J. A. Symonds, *The revival of learning* (3rd ed., London, 1897), p. 35.

CHAPTER VIII

[1] C. Bailey, ed., *The legacy of Rome* (Oxford, 1923), p. 71.

[2] In the *De Republica* Cicero declares:

> There is, in fact, a true law—namely, right reason—which is in accordance with nature, applies to all men, and is unchangeable and eternal. By its commands this law summons men to the performance of their duties; by its pro-

hibitions it restrains them from doing wrong. To invalidate this law by human legislation is never morally right. Neither the senate nor the people can absolve us from our obligation to obey this law. It will not lay down one rule at Rome and another at Athens, nor will it be one rule today and another tomorrow. But there will be one law, eternal and unchangeable, binding at all times upon all peoples, and there will be one common master and ruler of men, namely God, who is the author of this law.
———G. H. Sabine and S. B. Smith tr., Cicero, *On the commonwealth* (Columbus, 1929), III p. 22.

    3 A. N. Whitehead, *Adventures of ideas* (Cambridge, 1933), p. 20.
    4 Augustine's economic theories are less original than his political ideas. The idea of the "just price" was inherited from Greek thought; the best discussion of it is in Aristotle's *Nicomachean Ethics*, Book V. The Christians took over the idea, and backed it with a long series of injunctions from the Bible, including St. Paul's statement (in 1 Thessalonians IV: 6), "let no man go beyond and defraud his brother in any matter." Lactantius had developed the doctrine so far as to insist it was the duty of the seller to indicate to the buyer any defects of a commodity, and likewise that the buyer should never seek to profit by a mistake of the seller. In his *De Trinitate*, Augustine illustrated these ideas with a story, which most writers for a thousand years repeated. It tells of the sale of a manuscript to a buyer (presumably Augustine himself) who knew its value and paid a higher price than was asked. Augustine, like most early Christian and mediaeval writers, borrows from ancient thought, though he bases everything on quotations from the Bible. An interesting example of the long continuity in these matters is shown in the chapter on "Monasticism" in the *Cambridge mediaeval history*, Vol. I, p. 520, by the learned Benedictine, Dom Butler; here the author finds no other sources for monasticism than a few quotations from the New Testament!
    5 W. A. Dunning, *A history of political theories, ancient and mediaeval* (New York, 1902), p. 166.
    6 *Cambridge mediaeval history* (Cambridge, 1936), Vol. VI, p. 3.
    7 Aquinas' political and social ideas are found chiefly in *Commentary on the Politics of Aristotle*, the *Rule of Princes*, of which he completed only one book and a part of another out of four, and, above all, in sections of the *Summa Theologica*. His pupil, Aegidius Colonna, in a work of the same name as one of Aquinas, the *Rule of Princes*, sets forth Aquinas' views and adds many of his own.
    8 "In order," says Aquinas, "that the spiritual be kept separate from the earthly, the office of this kingdom is committed not to earthly kings but to the priests, and above all to the chief priest, the successor of Peter, the vice regent of Christ, the Roman bishop, to whom is due the subjection of all kings." R. Lane-Poole, *Illustrations of the history of mediaeval thought* (2nd ed., London, 1920), p. 211.
    9 A. P. D'Entrèves, ed., *Aquinas, selected political writings* (Oxford, 1948), pp. xxii–xxiii.
    10 Aquinas is, in general, not very favorable to trade:

There are two ways [he says] in which it is possible to increase the prosperity of a commonwealth. The more worthy is the production of an abundance of necessities by virtue of the fertility of the land; the other is by means of commerce. The former is the more desirable condition, since it is better that a state should produce an abundance of riches from its own soil, for when merchants are necessary to maintain the people, injury may result in time of war. Also the coming of foreigners is apt to corrupt morals. If the citizens devote themselves to commerce there is opportunity for many vices. A state should restrict its commercial pursuits.

——E. S. Davidson, *Forerunners of St. Francis*
(Boston, 1927), pp. 341–2.

Some of the Church Fathers had condemned all trade; by the time of Aquinas, the church writers had come to accept trade if it were for the public good and for the necessities of life and not for the sake of gain.

11 The Roman Church held onto the concept of usury, in one form or another, for centuries; it remained a thorny subject for confessors until about 1830 when the pope forbade priests to make inquiries in the confessional as to the penitents' investments.

12 J. N. Figgis, *From Gerson to Grotius* (2nd ed., Cambridge, 1916), p. 32.

13 At times Dubois talks like Montesquieu or even more recent writers:

It is scarcely possible to discover anything in the world that will prove good and desirable in every time and place. So that laws should vary with places, times, and people. Many philosophers have taught the expediency of this, and the lord of all sciences has not feared to proclaim it, since many things he appointed in the Old Testament he changed in the New.

——M. Langlois, ed., *P. Dubois De Recuperatione Terrae Sanctae*
(Paris, 1891), p. 39.

In another treatise, Dubois makes a blunt statement of his extreme nationalist bias: "It is a peculiar merit of the French to have a surer judgment than other nations, not to act without consideration, nor to place themselves in opposition to right reason." R. Lane-Poole, *Illustrations of Mediaeval Thought* (2nd ed., Oxford, 1920), p. 225.

14 I have not mentioned John of Jandun as a possible co-author. He may have given advice to Marsiglio but he apparently wrote none of the *Defensor pacis*. Cf. A. Gewirth, "John of Jandun and the 'Defensor Pacis'" in *Speculum*, 1948.

15 The best introductions to Ockham's political ideas are the *Eight questions concerning the power and dignity of the pope*, the incomplete though long treatise which he called *The Dialogue*, and the short and lucid, *On imperial and papal power*.

16 *Cambridge mediaeval history*, Vol. V, p. 766. It was always regarded as part of the duty of the parish priest to see that every child was taught the Apostle's Creed and the Lord's Prayer in Latin. After 1000, bishops repeatedly charged the parish clergy to instruct their flocks also in the Articles of Faith, the

Ten Commandments, the Seven Virtues, the Seven Deadly Sins and the meaning of the Sacraments; much of this instruction could be given in the vernacular.

[17] H. O. Taylor, *The mediaeval mind* (4th ed., 2 vols., New York, 1925), Vol. II, pp. 140–1.

[18] P. Abelson, *The seven liberal arts* (New York, 1906), p. 32.

[19] In picturing to ourselves the method pursued by the humanists in the instruction of their classes, we must divest our minds of all associations with the practice of modern professors. Very few of the students whom the master saw before him, possessed more than meagre portions of the text of Virgil or of Cicero; they had no notes, grammars, lexicons, or dictionaries of antiquities and mythology, to help them. It was therefore necessary for the lecturer to dictate quotations, to repeat parallel passages at full length, to explain geographical and historical allusions, to analyse the structure of sentences in detail, to provide copious illustrations of grammatical usage, to trace the stages by which a word acquired its meaning in a special context, to command a full vocabulary of synonyms, to give rules for orthography, and to have the whole Pantheon at his fingers' ends. In addition to this, he was expected to comment upon the meaning of his author, to interpret his philosophy, to point out the beauties of his style, to introduce appropriate moral disquisition on his doctrine, to sketch his biography, and to give some account of his relation to the history of his country and to his predecessors in the field of letters. In short, the professor of rhetoric had to be a grammarian, a philologer, an historian, a stylist, and a sage in one. He was obliged to pretend at least to an encyclopaedic knowledge of the classics, and to retain whole volumes in his memory. All these requirements, which seem to have been satisfied by such men as Filelfo and Poliziano, made the profession of eloquence—for so the varied subject matter of humanism was often called— a very different business from that which occupies a lecturer of the present century. Scores of students, old and young, with nothing but pen and paper on the desks before them, sat patiently recording what the lecturer said. At the end of his discourses on the "Georgics" or the "Verrines," each of them carried away a compendious volume, containing a transcript of the author's text, together with a miscellaneous mass of notes, critical, explanatory, ethical, aesthetical, historical, and biographical. In other words, a book had been dictated, and as many copies as there were attentive pupils had been made.

——J. A. Symonds, *The revival of learning* (3rd ed., London, 1897), pp. 90–1.

[20] In one of the educational treatises, Aeneas Silvius Piccolomini's *De liberorum educatione*, we have interesting glimpses of these new educational ideas:

> As regards a boy's physical training, we must bear in mind that we aim at implanting habits which will prove beneficial during life. So let him cultivate a certain hardness which rejects excess of sleep and idleness in all its forms. Habits of indulgence, such as the luxury of soft beds or the wearing of silk instead of linen next the skin, tend to enervate both body and mind. Too much importance can hardly be attached to right bearing and gesture.

Childish habits of playing with the lips and features should be early con-trolled. A boy should be taught to hold his head erect, to look straight and fearlessly before him, and to bear himself with dignity, whether walking, standing, or sitting. In ancient Greece we find that both philosophers and men of affairs—Socrates, for instance, and Chrysippus, or Philip of Mace-don—deemed this matter worthy of their concern, and therefore it may well be thought deserving of ours. Games and exercises which develop the mus-cular activities and the general carriage of the person should be encour-aged by every teacher. For such physical training not only cultivates grace of attitude, but secures the healthy play of our bodily organs and estab-lishes the constitution. . . . In respect of eating and drinking, the rule of moderation consists in rejecting anything which needlessly taxes digestion and so impairs mental activity. At the same time fastidiousness must not be humored. A boy, for instance, whose lot it may be to face life in the camp or in the forest, should . . . discipline his appetite. . . . The aim of eating is to strengthen the frame; so let vigorous health reject cakes or sweets, elaborate dishes or small birds or eels, which are for the delicate and the weakly. . . . What but disease and decay can result from appetite habit-ually overindulged? To the Greeks of the best age eating and drinking were only means to living, not the chief end and aim of it. For they recog-nized . . . that in this capacity for bodily pleasures we are on the same level with lower creatures. . . .

In religion I may assume from your Christian nurture that you have learnt the "Lord's Prayer," the "Salutation of the Blessed Virgin," the "Creed," the "Gospel of St. John," and certain "Collects." You have been taught in what consist the chief commandments of God, the gifts of the Spirit, the deadly sins, the way of salvation, and the doctrine of the life of the world to come. This latter truth was, indeed, taught by Socrates, as we know from Cicero.

——F. Schevill, ed., *The first century of Italian humanism* (New York, 1928), pp. 73–6.

[21] C. H. Haskins, *The rise of universities* (New York, 1923), pp. 3–4. The original term for a university was *studium generale;* the word "university" comes from the Latin, *universitas,* originally used for any body of men or large organization.

[22] According to the student regulations:

A professor might not be absent without leave, and if he desired to leave town he had to make a deposit to insure his return. If he failed to secure an audience of five, he was fined as if absent. He must begin with the bell and quit within one minute after the next bell. He was not allowed to skip a chapter in his commentary or postpone a difficulty to the end of the hour, and he was obliged to cover the ground systematically, so much in each spe-cific term of the year.

——C. H. Haskins, *op. cit.,* p. 75.

[23] F. P. Graves, *A history of education during the Middle Ages* (New York, 1910), p. 91.

²⁴ After the examination was over one young master wrote to his parents:

Sing unto the Lord a new song, praise him with stringed instruments, rejoice upon the high sounding cymbals, for your son held a glorious disputation. He answered all questions without a mistake, and no one could prevail against his arguments. Moreover, he celebrated a famous banquet, at which both rich and poor were honored as never before, and he has duly begun to give lectures which are already so popular that others' classrooms are deserted and his own are filled.

—C. H. Haskins, *Studies in mediaeval culture*
(Oxford, 1929), p. 87.

For an example of university dissertation cf. A. O. Norton, ed., *Readings in the history of education, mediaeval universities* (Cambridge, Mass., 1909), pp. 112–20; for examples of other questions discussed cf. P. S. Allen, *The age of Erasmus* (Oxford, 1914), pp. 107–12.

²⁵ Haskins, *op. cit.*, pp. 10, 15. Martin Luther, who was both a preacher and a professor, has some harsh words about whining students: "Some get ulcers from their school satchels, others colic from their books, others gout from the paper. The ink of the rest has dried up, or they have devoured long letters from their mothers and so get homesickness and nostalgia." P. Smith, *Life and letters of Luther* (2nd ed., Boston, 1911), p. 332.

²⁶ J. U. Nicholson, tr., *Chaucer's Canterbury Tales in modern English* (New York, 1934), p. 10.

²⁷ J. A. Symonds, tr., *Wine, women and song* (London, 1925), p. 69.

²⁸ G. G. Coulton, "Student numbers at mediaeval Oxford" in *History*, 1935, and *Cambridge mediaeval history*, Vol. VI, p. 601.

²⁹ *Cambridge mediaeval history*, Vol. VI, p. 601.

CHAPTER IX

¹ Edward Dowden writes:

Had I my way in the teaching of English literature, I would have the student start with a general sketch of European literature. I would fix an outline map in the mind of the student. It is essential that he should know where were the headquarters of literature in each successive period. When Boccaccio is spoken of in connection with Chaucer, when Tasso or Ariosto is spoken of in connection with Spencer, or Boileau in connection with Dryden or Pope, or Goethe in connection with Carlyle, he ought to be able to place Boccaccio and Tasso and Ariosto and Boileau and Goethe aright in the general movement of European literature, and to conceive aright the relation of each to the literary movement in our own country.

—L. Magnus, *A general sketch of European literature in the centuries of
romance*
(London, 1918), p. vi.

So far as mediaeval literature is concerned, Dowden's wish remains a "pious hope."

² E. Mason, ed., *Aucassin and Nicolette and other mediaeval romances* (New York, 1910), p. viii.

³ *Edda* is derived either from "Oddi," a famous manor in Iceland, or from a word which means the art of literary composition.

⁴ D. B. Shumway, tr., *The Nibelungenlied* (Boston, 1909), p. 135.

⁵ At the end of the first half of the *Chanson de Roland*, the hero dies and offers himself as a vassal to God:

> Roland lies on a high peak, looking toward Spain; he feels that his time is spent, and with one hand he beats upon his breast, "Oh God, I have sinned; forgive me through Thy might the wrongs, both great and small, which I have done from the day I was born even to this day on which I am smitten." With his right hand he holds out his glove to God; and lo, the angels of heaven come down to him.
>
> ——I. Butler, tr., *The song of Roland*
> (Boston, 1904), p. 87.

⁶ I. Butler, tr., *op. cit.*, pp. xviii–xx.

⁷ We have cherished these books which have upheld the vision of man's emergence from cave and jungle, kindled our wonder at our own mettle and helped to mould us into a more humane gregariousness. These stories have defeated time because they call upon us to admire the strength in man which is more than human, because they assert that the race can transcend its physical limits. Implicit in this conclusion is the conviction that humanity is neither imbecile nor futile, that its struggle for self-realization has meaning, and that the literature which aligns its force with this endeavor has the best chance to be remembered.

> ——*Saturday review of literature*, July 14, 1945.

Lack of space makes it impossible to get far off the main-travelled roads of literature; this is especially to be regretted in the case of mediaeval Irish and of mediaeval Spanish literature.

⁸ Anon., *The seven great hymns of the mediaeval church* (7th ed., New York, 1868), pp. 22–3.

⁹ F. A. Wright and T. A. Sinclair, *A history of later Latin literature* (London, 1931), pp. 309–10.

¹⁰ Anon., *Great hymns, op. cit.*, pp. 103, 107.

¹¹ F. J. E. Raby, *A history of Christian Latin poetry* (Oxford, 1929), p. 443.

¹² Anon., *Great hymns, op. cit.*, pp. 56, 76.

¹³ The poetry which expresses such a state of mind is usually idealised and pictures the relationship rather as it might have been than as it was. The troubadour who knew his business would begin with praises of his beloved; she is physically and morally perfect, her beauty illuminates the night, her presence heals the sick, cheers the sad, makes the boor courteous and so forth. For her the singer's love and devotion is infinite: separation

from her would be worse than death; her death would leave the world cheerless, and to her he owes any thoughts of good or beauty that he may have. It is only because he loves her that he can sing. Hence he would rather suffer any pain or punishment at her hands than receive the highest favours from another. The effects of this love are obvious in his person. His voice quavers with supreme delight or breaks in dark despair; he sighs and weeps and wakes at night to think of the one subject of contemplation. Waves of heat and cold pass over him, and even when he prays, her image is before his eyes. This passion has transformed his nature: he is a better and stronger man than ever before, ready to forgive his enemies and to undergo any physical privations; winter is to him as the cheerful spring, ice and snow as soft lawns and flowery meads. Yet, if unrequited, his passion may destroy him; he loses his self-control, does not hear when he is addressed, cannot eat or sleep, grows thin and feeble, and is sinking slowly to an early tomb. Even so, he does not regret his love, though it lead to suffering and death; his passion grows ever stronger, for it is ever supported by hope. But if his hopes are realised, he will owe everything to the gracious favour of his lady, for his own merits can avail nothing. Sometimes he is not prepared for such complete self-renunciation; he reproaches his lady for her coldness, complains that she has led him on by a show of kindness, has deceived him and will be the cause of his death; or his patience is at an end, he will live in spite of her and try his fortune elsewhere.

————H. J. Chaytor, *The troubadours*
(Cambridge, 1912), pp. 17–18.

[14] B. Smythe, *Troubadour poets* (London, 1911), p. 184.

[15] For an example of the "sirventes" cf. Chaytor, *op. cit.*, pp. 85–7.

[16] J. H. Smith, *The troubadours at home* (2 vols., New York, 1890), Vol. II, p. 162.

[17] C. S. Lewis, *The allegory of love* (Oxford, 1938), p. 4; the student should read the whole of Ch. 1.

The position of woman had changed; she was no longer the medium of satisfaction of the male impulse or for the rearing of children as in antiquity, no longer the silent drudge or the devout sister of the first Christian millenary, no longer the devil of the monkish conception; transcending humanity she had been exalted to the heavens, and had become a goddess. She was loved and adored with a devotion not of this earth; no metaphor was sufficiently ecstatic to express the full fervor of admiration; a new religion was created and she was the presiding deity.

————E. Lucka, *Eros*
(New York, 1915), p. 130.

The theories of love in troubadour poetry are well summarized in T. A. Kirby, *Chaucer's Troilus* (University, La., 1940), Ch. 2; in fact the whole of Part I of Kirby's book is an admirable survey of all the romantic theories of love from Ovid through Dante.

[18] M. F. Richey, *Essays on the mediaeval German love lyric* (Oxford, 1943), p. 1.

[19] There are some examples of Jacopone's Italian verses in translation in J. A. Symonds, *The Renaissance in Italy* (2nd ed., 7 vols., London, 1898), Vol. IV, pp. 468–78. In the same volume, pp. 461–4, there are some superb sonnets of Folgore da San Gimignano. Rossetti's translation of Guinicelli's famous *Canzone, on the gentle heart*, which summarizes the theory of love of the Tuscan poets is in M. Van Doren, *Anthology of world poetry* (2nd ed., London, 1939), pp. 424–6.

[20] R. Rendel, *An anthology of Italian lyrics* (London, 1925), p. 35. Some idea of Petrarch's sonnets and other verses can be obtained from H. H. Blanchard, ed., *Prose and poetry of the Continental Renaissance* (New York, 1949).

[21] J. B. Fletcher, *Literature of the Italian Renaissance* (New York, 1934), p. 69.

[22] Walter Scott regarded chivalry as next to Christianity itself; Bishop Stubbs said, "is not chivalry the gloss put by fine manners on vice and selfishness and contempt for the rights of man?"

The fact is [says Coulton] no institution displays more clearly the contrast between theory and practice which was so characteristic of mediaeval society. In the cathedral the saint stood side by side with the demon or grinning buffoon. In chivalry we have the same contrast of splendor and squalor, dresses of brocade of which the sleeves might dip into a sauce, or the train drag in the filth of the streets, and beneath the table dogs fighting for the bones.

——G. G. Coulton, *Mediaeval panorama* (Cambridge, 1939), pp. 235–6.

Here is a picture from an account of the eleventh century:

My uncle Geoffrey became a knight in his father's lifetime and began his knighthood by two wars against his neighbors. He also carried on war against his own father in the course of which he committed many evil deeds of which he afterwards bitterly repented. [Then follows a long list of wars.] Because of all these wars and the prowess he showed he was called the Hammer, as one who hammered down his enemies. In the last year of his life he made me, his nephew, a knight. And in the night which preceded his own death, laying aside all care of knighthood and secular things, he became a monk in the monastery of St. Nicholas which his father and he had built with much devotion and endowed with their goods.

——C. H. Haskins, *The Renaissance of the twelfth century* (Cambridge, Mass., 1927), pp. 248–9.

[23] G. Highet, *The classical tradition* (Oxford, 1949), p. 67. There is a convenient summary of the story of the *Roman de la rose* in U. T. Holmes, *A history of old French literature* (2nd ed., New York, 1948), pp. 304–7.

[24] If in Wolfram's "Parzival" we observe how the intense development of chivalric morals leads to the heightening of individual morality, and how the heightening of individual morality in turn leads to a still further development of chivalric morals, we see a process diametrically opposite in the "Tristan" of Gottfried von Strassburg. Here the overstraining of chivalric

culture leads to a revolt of the individual against the barriers of society and thereby to a dissolution of the moral foundations both of social and individual life. While Wolfram with soul-stirring power calls up to view the gradual rounding out and persistent upbuilding of a character clinging to the chivalric ideal, Gottfried with the finest psychological art depicts the delight and the woe, the demoniac charm and the consuming fire and the curse of destructive passion. No other work of mediaeval poetry impresses us so deeply with the tragedy of human civilization which by its striving for ever higher refinement again and again is driven to self-destruction and to the annihilation of all true culture.

——K. Francke, *Personality in German literature before Luther* (Cambridge, Mass., 1916), pp. 36–7.

²⁵ Malory can evoke a scene; one side of his genius is well described by E. K. Chambers:

> You may regard the whole thing as a tapestry; half close your eyes, and watch a pleasant landscape, full of running waters, and moated castles and hermitages and green lawns, among which move bright little figures in blue and white and red armour, every now and again stopping to lay spears in rest and upset one another, and then swearing eternal friendship, and riding away again. Here is a ford perilous, and at the door of a pavilion a dwarf watches a shield. There a tired knight sleeps under an apple tree and by sweep four queens and cast an enchantment upon him.
>
> ——E. K. Chambers, *Malory* (London, 1922), p. 6.

²⁶ W. W. Comfort, tr., *Arthurian romances by Chrétien de Troyes* (New York, n.d.), pp. xvi–xvii.

²⁷ The absurdities in the romances arise partly from the peculiar character of Celtic story. Celtic magic and mystery is of a peculiar sort. In Germanic stories, when supernatural beings appear, the wind still blows off the rocky headlands. Such beings are more gruesome because they are revealed in a world of everyday things. In the Arthurian stories, however, we move in a world where natural phenomena are not only suspended but not to be expected. Adventures have the inconsequence of dreams, a Turk changes to a knight when his head is cut off; water is cast upon a magic stone and a storm arises. Matthew Arnold, in seeking to discover the distinguishing qualities of Celtic literature, quoted Henri Martin's phrase, "always ready to act against the despotism of fact."

——W. W. Lawrence, *Mediaeval story* (2nd ed., New York, 1926), pp. 107–08.

The democratically-minded modern critics have been severe in their judgment of the romances:

> What do we care for these enchanted castles, these miraculous fountains near which terrific battles are fought for nothing, these dwarfs and giants defying courtly manners, these caves of love and fairy groves, these bold seduc-

tions and strange deliverances? How wearisome are these incessant descriptions of garments, of hair dress, of the riding, sitting, and curtseying of the knights and ladies. Even the best of the romances are spoiled by fashionableness and artificiality.

——K. Francke, *op. cit.,* pp. 20–1.

²⁸ Boccaccio and Chaucer are discussed at greater length in Ch. X.

CHAPTER X

¹ H. O. Taylor, *The mediaeval mind* (4th ed., 2 vols., New York, 1925), Vol. I, pp. 344–5. This judgment is contradicted by H. Adams, *Mont St. Michel and Chartres* (Boston, 1913), esp. Ch. VI.

² Some passages from the introduction to the *Decameron* will give a vivid picture of the Black Death of 1348–49:

In the year then of our Lord 1348, there happened at Florence, the finest city in all Italy, a most terrible plague; which, whether owing to the influence of the planets, or that it was sent from God as a just punishment for our sins, had broken out some years before in the Levant; spite of all the means that art and human foresight could suggest, as keeping the city clear from filth, and excluding all suspected persons; notwithstanding frequent consultations what else was to be done; nor omitting prayers to God in frequent processions: it began to show itself in a sad manner, here there appeared certain tumours in the groin, or under the armpits, some. as big as a small apple, others as an egg; and afterwards purple spots in most parts of the body: the usual messengers of death. To the cure of this malady, neither medical knowledge nor the power of drugs was of any effect; few or none escaped; but they generally died the third day from the first appearance of the symptoms. And the disease, by being communicated from the sick to the well, seemed daily to get ahead, and to rage the more, as fire will do by laying on fresh combustibles. One instance of this kind I took particular notice of, namely, that the rags of a poor man just dead, being thrown into the street, and two hogs coming by at the same time and rooting amongst them, and shaking them about in their mouths, in less than an hour turned round and died on the spot. These accidents, and others of the like sort, occasioned various fears and devices amongst those people that survived, all tending to the same uncharitable and cruel end; which was to avoid the sick, and everything that had been near them; expecting by that means to save themselves. And some holding it best to live temperately, and to avoid excesses of all kinds, made parties, and shut themselves up from the rest of the world; eating and drinking moderately of the best, and diverting themselves with music, never listening to anything from without, to make them uneasy. Others maintained free living to be a better preservative, and would baulk no passion or appetite they wished to gratify, drinking and revelling incessantly from tavern to tavern, or in private houses; which were frequently found deserted by the owners, and therefore common to every one. A third sort of people chose a method between these two; not confining themselves to rules of diet like the former, and yet avoiding the intemperance of the latter; but eating and drinking what their appetites required, they walked everywhere with odours and nosegays to smell to; for they supposed the whole atmosphere to be tainted with the stink of dead bodies. Others fled into the country. Every place was filled with the dead. A method now was taken, as well out of regard to the living, as pity for the dead, for the neighbours, assisted by what porters they could meet with, to clear all the houses, and lay the bodies at the doors; and every morning great numbers might be seen brought out in this manner; from whence they were carried away; it has been observed also, whilst two or three priests have walked before a corpse with their crucifix, that two or three sets of porters have fallen in with them; and where they knew but of one, they have buried six, eight, or more: nor was there any to follow and shed a few tears over them; for things were come to that pass, that men's lives were no more regarded than the lives of so many beasts. The consecrated ground no longer containing the numbers which were continually brought thither, especially as they were desirous of laying every one in the parts allotted to their families; they were forced to dig trenches and to put them in by hundreds, piling them up in rows, as goods are stowed in a ship, and throwing in little earth till they were filled to the top. Between March and July following, it is supposed, and made pretty certain, that upwards of a hundred thousand souls perished in the city only. What magnificent dwellings, what noble palaces were then depopulated to the last person! what families extinct! what riches and vast possessions left, and no known heir to inherit! what numbers of both sexes in the prime and vigour of youth, whom in the morning neither Galen, Hippocrates, nor Aesculapius himself, but would have declared in perfect health, after dining heartily with their friends here, have supped with their departed friends in the other world!

——*Decameron*
(New York, 1925), pp. xix–xxiv.

⁸ [Boccaccio] was the first who frankly sought to justify the pleasures of the carnal life. His romances, with their beautiful gardens and sunny skies, fair women and luxurious lovers, formed a transition from the chivalry of the early Italian poets to the sensuality of Beccadelli. He prepared the nation for literary and artistic paganism, by unconsciously divesting thought and feeling of their spiritual elevation. Dante had made the world one in Christ. Petrarch put humanity to school in the lecture room of the Roman sagas. A terrestrial paradise of sensual delight, where all things were desirable, contented the poet of the *Fiametta*. To the beatific vision of the *Divine Comedy*, to the *Trionfo della morte* of Petrarch, succeeded the *Amorosa visione*, a review of human life, in which Boccaccio begins by invoking Dame Venus and ends with earthly love.

——J. A. Symonds, *The revival of learning*
(3rd ed., New York, 1897), p. 71.

⁴ [Chaucer seems to have been a man who was] passionately aroused in the presence of beautiful objects, fresh May flowers, busy larks singing salutations to the rising sun, stars following their prescribed courses, or dewdrops sparkling upon the grass. He was not greatly affected by the joys or sorrows of humanity in general, but he seems to have been profoundly touched by the experience of particular persons whom he created. His poetical world was a world of concrete perceptions filled with a variety of individual human beings, and all the elements which he employed in his creations were carefully subordinated to one outstanding purpose, the concrete representation of life.

——W. C. Curry, *Chaucer and the mediaeval sciences*
(Oxford, 1926), p. viii.

⁵ The following passage from Guibert of Nogent's history of the First Crusade will give a first-hand idea of mediaeval historiography at its best:

The French at this time suffered from famine; bad harvests, coming blow after blow, had raised the price of grain to an excessive rate. Avaricious merchants speculated according to their custom upon the misery of all. There was little bread, and it was dear. The poor supplied the place of it by eating roots and wild herbs. All of a sudden the cry of the Crusade, resounding everywhere at the same time, broke the locks and chains which kept the granaries. Then provisions which formerly had been beyond price, which no one could buy, were sold for nothing when every one was aroused and wanted to go. Then one might have seen seven sheep sold for five pence. The famine disappeared and was followed by abundance. As every one was eager to take the road of the cross, each hastened to convert into money everything which he did not need on the journey; the price of sale was fixed, not by the seller, but by the buyer. Things which cost most were objects necessary for the road, but the residue was sold for nothing.

——J. W. Thompson, *A history of historical writing*
(2 vols., New York, 1942), Vol. I, p. 233.

⁶ Burckhardt says of Blondus, his work alone "would entitle us to say that it was the study of antiquity which made the study of the Middle Ages possible, by first training the mind to habits of impartial historical criticism." J. Burckhardt, *The Renaissance in Italy* (London, 1878), p. 246.

⁷ F. Marzials, tr., *Memoirs of the Crusades* (London, 1908), p. 139.

⁸ H. J. Chaytor, *From script to print* (Cambridge, 1945), p. 50.

⁹ C. G. Osgood, *Boccaccio on poetry* (Princeton, 1930), p. 40.

¹⁰ Chaytor, *op. cit.,* pp. 51, 78.

¹¹ The Medicean Library is described by Vespasiano, a fifteenth-century Florentine:

When Cosimo had finished the residence, he began to reflect how he might have the place peopled with goodly men of letters; and presently he hit upon the plan of founding a fine library. One day when I happened to be with him in his room, he said to me: "How would you go about this library?" I replied that as for buying the books it would be impossible, for they were not to be had. Thereupon he said: "How can it be done?" When I told him that it would be necessary to have the books copied, he asked if I would be willing to undertake the task. I answered that I was. Then he told me to set about the work and that he would leave everything to me. The library was begun at once, for it was his will that no time should be lost. And as I was given all the money I needed, I assembled quickly forty-five writers and finished two hundred volumes in twenty-two months. We made use of the excellent plan of the library of Pope Nicholas.

As for the contents of the library, in the first place there are the Bible and the Concordances with all their commentaries, ancient and modern. And the first writer who commented on the Holy Scriptures and showed the manner of commenting to all the others was Origen. He wrote in Greek and St. Jerome translated that part of his work which deals with the five books of Moses. Then there are the works of St. Ignatius the martyr, who wrote in Greek. Further, there are the works of St. Basil, those of St. Gregory of Nazianzen, of Gregory of Nyssa, his brother, of St. John Chrysostom, of St. Athanasius. All the works of the Greek doctors which have been translated into Latin are there. Then follow the holy doctors and writers in Latin; St. Cyprian of Carthage, most elegant and saintly; the works of Tertullian, a very learned Carthaginian. Further, the four doctors of the Latin Church are represented by all their works; and no other library has these works complete. Next come the works of St. Bernard as well as those of Hugh of St. Victor, of St. Anselm, of St. Isidore of Seville, of Bede, of Rabanus Maurus. On coming to the modern doctors we note St. Thomas Aquinas, Albert the Great, Alexander of Hales, St. Bonaventura.

Turning to the philosophers, we list of the works of Aristotle both his Moral and Natural Philosophy; all the commentaries of St. Thomas and Albert the Great as well as of others on the philosophy of Aristotle; Aristotle's Logic and other modern systems of logic. In Canon Law there are the Decretals. Of histories there will be found all the Ten Books of Livy, Caesar's Commentaries, Suetonius on the Lives of the Emperors, Plutarch's Lives, Sallust on *De bello Jugurthino et Catilinario.* The Library contains also all the works of Tully in three volumes; all the works of Seneca in one volume; Quintilian, *De institutione oratoria.* Of poets the following are represented: Virgil, Terence, Ovid, Lucan, Statius, Seneca, Plautus; and of grammarians, Priscian. And all the other works necessary to a library were there, not one being missing. And since there were not copies of all these works in Florence, we sent to Milan, to Bologna, and to other places, wherever they might be found. Cosimo lived to see the library completed as well as the cataloguing and the arranging of the books. In all of which he took great pleasure, everything being done, as was his custom, with great promptness.

——F. Schevill, ed., *First century of Italian humanism* (New York, 1928), pp. 60–2.

¹² Something of the flavor of the Latin original can be caught in the verses quoted in F. J. E. Raby, *A history of Christian Latin poetry* (Oxford, 1927), p. 300.

¹³ The combination of religious devotion and a desire for social justice, which appears often in the history of English civilization, lies back of a passage like the following from the 7th section of *Piers Plowman*:

> *The needy are our neighbors, if we note rightly;*
> *As prisoners in cells, or poor folks in hovels,*
> *Charged with children and overcharged by landlords,*
> *What they may spare in spinning they spend on rental,*
> *On milk, or on meal to make porridge*
> *To still the sobbing of children at meal time.*
> *Also they themselves suffer much hunger*
> *They have woe in winter time, and wake at midnight*
> *To rise and rock the cradle at the bedside,*
> *To card and to comb, to darn clouts and wash them,*
> *The woe of these women who dwell in hovels,*
> *Is too sad to speak of or to say in verse.*
> ——H. W. Wells, tr., *The vision of Piers Plowman*
> (London, 1938), p. xiv.

¹⁴ K. Vossler, *Mediaeval culture* (2 vols., New York, 1929), Vol. I, p. 79. Dante, not understanding the nature of the drama, called Virgil's *Aeneid* a "tragedy" and his own poem a "comedy," because it ends happily. Later generations added the "Divine."

¹⁵ From H. W. Longfellow's sonnet sequence, *Divina commedia*, the greatest tribute to Dante in English.

CHAPTER XI

¹ Romanesque art represents the fulfilment of the task undertaken by artists when, at the end of the classical period, they began to lose touch with reality and broke up the harmonies created by the Greeks, in order to give expression to new creeds such as the cult of the emperor and the Christian religion. A long and arduous path had to be trodden before the new transcendental tendencies, which at first seemed almost entirely negative and merely a symptom of decadence, had assumed stylistic forms which are a complete and positive expression of a new conception of the world. The decisive moment came when in the Carolingian age the Mediterranean heritage was taken over by the peoples of the North, whose tradition of wholly abstract and ornamental art enabled them to give visible form to purely transcendental relationships. By applying in the following centuries the principles of this art to the descriptive paintings and sculptures taken over from

the South, a perfect subordination of matter to abstract harmony was effected, and that is the essence of Romanesque art.

——E. Kitzinger, *Early mediaeval art*
(London, 1940), p. 96.

In fact [writes Hamlin] to read aright the mental state of the Roman-
esques centuries (10th–12th) we must study its buildings as well as its literature. In them both we can read a story of idealism, of frustration, of
naïveté, of ignorance and of vision which together produced the extraordinary vitality of the time. The conflict between luxury and asceticism, between bestiality and idealism, between unbridled imagination and disciplined thought, was far from solved. Indeed, in the cloister it was perhaps
raised to a higher pitch. For the monk, the ancient gods persisted as living
devils, and the legends show that Satan himself was conceived of as a very
real entity. Fear and hope fight in these sometimes tortured sculptures, as
they fought in the minds of their makers; cruelty and sadism show in the
terrible beasts devouring men or other animals, just as mercy is shown in the
lovely carvings of many of the Biblical stories. And the fear of the end of
the world and of an eternal Hell, pictured in very physical terms, is always
haunting in the background.

——T. Hamlin, *Architecture through the ages*
(New York, 1940), p. 251.

² The large number of magnificent Romanesque churches which survive makes any selection difficult, but among the greatest are the following: the
cathedrals of Pisa in Italy, of Compostella in Spain, of Mainz and Speyer in Germany, and of Durham in England. Close in style to the cathedral of Compostella is the church of St. Sernin at Toulouse. Every student should know these
six churches. The supreme achievement of Romanesque sculpture are the west
portals of the Cathedral of Chartres. The word "Romanesque" was first used by
the French archeologist Chaumont in 1825.

³ I am forced to say [writes Lethaby] that the window of dyed glass is
the most perfect art form known. So anyone must feel who has watched the
changing hues of the windows of Chartres or Bourges, through a summer's
afternoon, from the hour when the shadows of the flying buttresses fall in
great bands across the burning glass, to the twilight when they fade and
hardly glimmer in the gloom of the vaults.

——W. R. Lethaby, *Mediaeval art*
(rev. ed., London, 1949), p. 133.

⁴ There are a number of contemporary writings which indicate what mediaeval men thought of their churches. In the tenth century, the monk Theophilus wrote:

"The house of God decorated with the utmost beauty; ceilings and
walls showing forth with different colors a likeness of the paradise of God,
glowing with various flowers and verdant with herbs and leaves, and the
saints with crowns. You have, after a fashion, shown to beholders everything
in creation praising God, its creator. If the eye of man beholds the ceilings,

they glow; if it regards the walls, there is the appearance of paradise; if it marks the windows it admires the inestimable beauty of the glass. If it regards how much rejoicing is in heaven, and how much suffering in the flames of hell, it is animated by hope for its good actions, and is struck with fear by the consideration of its sins." Abbot Suger wrote of the jewelled liturgical objects of St. Denis, "Thus, when, out of my delight in the beauty of the house of God, the loveliness of the many colored gems has called me away from external cares and worthy meditation has induced me to reflect, then it seemed that I saw myself dwelling in some strange region of the universe which exists neither in the slime of earth nor in the purity of heaven, and that by the grace of God I can be transformed from this inferior to that higher world." Writing in the thirteenth century, Durandus says, "Pictures and ornaments in churches are the lessons and scriptures of the laity. For what writing supplied to him who can read, that doth a picture supply to him which is unlearned, and can only look. But we worship not images nor account them to be gods yet we adore them for the remembrance of things done long ago."

———E. G. Holt, ed., *Literary sources of art history*
(Princeton, 1947), pp. 10, 27, 61.

The symbolism of the mediaeval church, as discussed by a number of mediaeval writers, is well summarized by Huysmans:

In considering the system of symbolism it is necessary to study the significance of numbers. The secrets of church building can only be discerned by recognizing the mysterious idea of the unity of the figure I., which is the image of God Himself. The suggestion of II., which figures the two natures of the Son, the two dispensations, and, according to Saint Gregory the Great, the twofold law of love of God and man. Three is the number of the Persons of the Trinity, and of the theological virtues. Four typifies the cardinal virtues, the four Greater Prophets, the Gospels and the elements. Five is the number of Christ's wounds, and of our senses, whose sins He expiated by a corresponding number of wounds. Six records the days devoted by God to the creation. Seven is the number of the gifts of the Holy Ghost, of the Sacraments, of the words of Jesus on the Cross. Eight recalls the idea of the eight Beatitudes. Nine is the number of the angelic hierarchy, of the special gifts of the Spirit as enumerated by Saint Paul; and it was at the ninth hour that Christ died. Ten is the number of laws given by Jehovah. And this might be repeated to infinity.

Well, then, after having pointed out the natural and very proper interpretation that may be applied to this vessel, as representing the Body of Our Lord, while the incense signifies His Divinity, and the fire is the Holy Spirit within Him; and after having defined the various interpretations of the metal of which it is made—if of gold, it answers to the perfection of His Divinity; if of silver, to the matchless excellence of His Humility; if of copper, to the frailty of the flesh He assumed for our salvation; if of iron, to the Resurrection of that Body which conquered death.

Jesus is dead; His head is at the altar; His outstretched arms are the

two transepts; His pierced hands are the doors; His legs are the nave where
we are standing; His pierced feet are the door by which we have come in.
        ——J. K. Huysmans, *The Cathedral*
        (London, 1922), pp. 86–7, 88–9, 108.

Huysmans' account is based on Durandus (d. 1296), *Rationale divinorum officiorum*, a thirteenth-century summary of liturgical lore.

⁵ A famous contemporary account of the building of the Cathedral of
Chartres appears in a letter written by the Archbishop of Rouen:

> Who has ever seen! Who has ever heard tell, in times past, that powerful princes of the world, that men brought up in honour and in wealth, that nobles, men and women, have bent their proud and haughty necks to the harness of carts, and that, like beasts of burden, they have dragged to the abode of Christ these wagons, loaded with wines, grains, oil, stone, wood. and all that is necessary for the wants of life, or for the construction of the church? But while they draw these burdens, there is one thing admirable to observe; it is that often when a thousand persons and more are attached to the chariots,—so great is the difficulty,—yet they march in such silence that not a murmur is heard, and truly if one did not see the thing with one's eyes, one might believe that among such a multitude there was hardly a person present. When they halt on the road, nothing is heard but the confession of sins, and pure and suppliant prayer to God. At the voice of the priests who exhort their hearts to peace, they forget all hatred, debts are remitted, the unity of hearts is established. There one sees old people, young people, little children, calling on the Lord with a suppliant voice, and uttering to Him, from the depth of the heart, sobs and sighs with words of glory and praise! After the people, warmed by the sound of trumpets and the sight of banners, have resumed their road, the march is made with such ease that no obstacle can retard it. When they have reached the church they arrange the wagons about it like a spiritual camp, and during the whole night they celebrate the watch by hymns and canticles.
>   ——H. Adams, *Mont St. Michel and Chartres*
>   (Boston, 1913), pp. 104–05.

For other contemporary descriptions of church building cf. E. G. Holt, *op. cit.*, pp. 20–58. For the whole question of the origin of ribbed vaults cf. P. Lavedan, *Histoire de l'art*, (2 vols., Paris, 1950), Vol. I, pp. 204–10.

⁶ N. Pevsner, *An outline of European architecture* (2nd ed., London, 1945), p. 58.

⁷ On the controversies on the Van Eycks, cf. Lavedan, *op. cit.*, p. 278.

⁸ [In Rome, Brunelleschi] gave himself so exclusively to his studies [his biographer tells us] that he took no time either to eat or sleep; his only thought was of architecture which was then extinct,—I mean the good old manner and not the barbarous one [Gothic] which was much practiced at the period. He also well examined and made careful drawings of all the vaults and arches of antiquity; and if by chance the artists found fragments of capital, columns, cornices, or basements of buildings buried in the earth,

they set laborers to work and caused them to be dug up. Nor did he rest until he had drawn every description of fabric, temples, basilicas, aqueducts, baths, arches, and amphitheaters. The different orders were divided by his cares, each order, Doric, Ionic, and Corinthian, being placed apart. And such was the effect of his zeal in that study, that he became capable of entirely reconstructing the city in his imagination, and of beholding Rome as she had been before she was revived.

——F. P. Chambers, *The history of taste*
(New York, 1932), pp. 32–3.

⁹ A. Blunt, *Artistic theory in Italy 1450–1600* (Oxford, 1940), p. 11.

¹⁰ There came to be a strange mingling of the pagan and the Christian in Italian art and later in the art of all Europe. The same painter would turn from representing the love of Venus and Mars to Mary swooning on the hill of Calvary.

The old gods [says Symonds] lent a portion of their charm even to Christian mythology, and showered their beauty bloom on saints who died renouncing them. Sodoma's Sebastian is but Hyacinth or Hylas, transpierced with arrows so that pain and martyrdom add pathos to his poetry of youthfulness. Leonardo's St. John is a faun of the forest, ivy-crowned and laughing, on whose lips the word "repent" would be a gleeful paradox. Roman martyrs and Olympian deities were alike burghers of one spiritual city, the city of the beautiful.

——J. A. Symonds, *Renaissance in Italy, the fine arts*
(new ed., London, 1906), p. 25.

¹¹ In a letter to Ludovico Sforza, the tyrant of Milan, Leonardo described his talents:

Most illustrious Lord, Having now fully studied the work of all those who repute themselves masters and artificers of the instruments of war, and found that these inventions in their mode of operation in no way differ from those in common use, I will endeavour, without disparaging others, to explain myself. I will lay before your Lordship my secret inventions, and then offer them to you to carry into execution at your pleasure.

(1) I have a sort of extremely light and strong bridge, so contrived as to admit of being carried with the greatest ease, and with the aid of which one may pursue, and at any time flee from, the enemy; and others secure and indestructible by fire and battle, easy and convenient to remove and set up. Also contrivances for burning and destroying those of the enemy.

(2) During the siege of a town I understand how to draw off the water from the trenches, and make an endless variety of bridges, battering rams, scaling ladders, and other instruments appertaining to such expeditions.

(3) Moreover, even if by reason of the height of the ramparts, or on account of the strength of the place or its position, it should not be possible during the siege of a place to avail oneself of bombards, I have nevertheless means of demolishing any fortress, even if it were built on a rock.

(4) I have also a kind of bombards, extremely convenient and easy to transport; with these it is possible to hurl forth showers of small stones, a perfect whirlwind, and with the smoke of it to strike the enemy with terror.

(5) Further, I have methods for quite noiselessly constructing mines and secret winding passages, whereby one can reach any given point, even if it were necessary to pass under trenches and rivers.

(6) Further, I can make covered wagons, secure and indestructible, which, when they are introduced among the enemy, manned with shooters, can break through even the largest army of armed men; behind them the foot-soldiers can follow.

(7) Further, I can, as occasion requires, make bombards, mortars, and light ordnance of the most beautiful and serviceable forms, quite unlike those in common use.

(8) When bombards will not serve, I will contrive catapults, mangonels, *trabocci,* and other instruments not now in use, of marvellous efficacy; in short, according to the variety of circumstances, I will contrive various and endless instruments of offence and defence.

(9) Should the encounter be at sea, I can construct many different machines and instruments admirably adapted both for defence and attack, and ships which can resist the attack of the largest bombards and powder and smoke.

(10) In time of peace I believe myself able to vie successfully with any in the designing of public and private buildings and in conducting water from one place to another.

Further, I can execute in sculpture,—marble, bronze, and terra-cotta, —and likewise also in painting, anything that is at all possible of accomplishment and against any competitor whatsoever.

——O. Sirén, *Leonardo da Vinci*
(New Haven, 1916), pp. 59–60.

[12] T. Finney, *History of music* (2nd ed., New York, 1947), p. 70. For the method of Guido of Arezzo for handling melodies of greater than the hexachord cf. Curt Sachs, *Our musical heritage* (New York, 1948), pp. 74-7.

[13] Over three hundred and fifty troubadour and eight hundred trouvère melodies have been preserved, but none of them in a notation that indicates the rhythm of the music. For the differences of troubadour, trouvère, and minnesinger music and for the role of the minstrels cf. W. Apel, ed., *Harvard dictionary of music* (Cambridge, Mass., 1950), articles on these subjects.

[14] A writer of the later thirteenth century, Johannes de Grocheo, describes this style of music:

> The motet is a song made up of several interwoven voices, voices either have their own texts or their own sort of syllable division, and which sound together in consonances. The part upon which the others are built, in the manner in which a house is built upon its foundations, is called the tenor, and it determines and regulates the composition. The voice immediately about the tenor is called the "motetus," and it usually begins on the fifth above the tenor and maintains about that relationship to it, though it can at times go

to the octave. The voice which begins at the octave above the tenor and usually remains in about that range is called the "triplum." When the harmony makes it necessary the "triplum" may go either above or below this range. The "quadruplum" is a voice which may be added to make the whole perfect.

——H. Leichtentritt, *Geschichte der Motette* (Leipzig, 1908), p. 5.

¹⁵ T. M. Finney, *A history of music* (2nd ed., New York, 1947), pp. 112–13.

¹⁶ The complexities of the musical style of Okeghem and Obrecht (d. 1505) and others of their generation parallel the developments of art in the flamboyant style and of poetry in the complicated manner of the French Rhétoriqueurs and the German Meistersingers. In music, art, and literature there was, in the fifteenth century, a sort of Gothic Baroque period.

CHAPTER XII

¹ M. Smith, *An introduction to the history of mysticism* (London, 1930), p. 10.

² The final stage of the mystic's absorption in the divine has been repeatedly described; St. Augustine says: "With the flash of one glance, my mind arrived at that which is." "When the Lord comes," writes St. Bernard, "there is a consuming fire and his presence is understood in the power by which the soul is changed, and by the love by which it is inflamed; there ensues a certain sudden and unwonted enlargement of mind, an inpouring of light." Richard of St. Victor says: "When the mind of man is rapt into the abyss of the divine light, so that, utterly oblivious of all external things, it knows not itself and passes wholly into its God, and so, in this state, is held in check and lulled into deep sleep the crowd of carnal desires. In this state, while the mind is alienated from itself, while it is, on all sides, encircled by the conflagration of divine love, it puts on a certain divine condition, and passes into a new kind of glory." Rolle writes: "When the mind now beginning to burn in desire of its Maker, is made able to receive uncreated light, and is so inspired and filled with gifts of the Holy Ghost, so that so far as mortals may, it is raised to the sweetness of everlasting life. And, while the soul is filled with sweetness of the Godhead, oh, love strong, ravishing, burning, wilful, unslaked." And finally, according to Suso, "The spirit soars up, now flying on the summitless heights, now swimming in the bottomless depths of the sublime marvels of the Godhead." M. Smith, *op. cit.*, pp. 51, 70, 72–3, 78, 91.

³ C. E. Rolt, tr., *Dionysius the Areopagite, Concerning the divine names* I, 4, and *Mystical theology* I, 2 (new ed., London, 1940).

⁴ *Cambridge mediaeval history*, Vol. VII, p. 778.

⁵ As the little water drop [wrote St. Bernard] poured into a large measure of wine seems to lose its own nature entirely and to take on both the

taste and the color of the wine, or as iron heated red-hot loses its own appearance and glows like fire, or as air filled with sunlight is transformed into the same brightness so that it does not so much appear to be illuminated as to be itself light, so must all human feeling toward the Holiest be self-dissolved in unspeakable wise, and wholly transfused in the will of God.

—— S. H. Mellone, *Western Christian thought in the Middle Ages* (Edinburgh, 1935), pp. 129–30.

⁶ Elizabeth of Schönau describes a typical vision:

On the Sunday night following the festival of St. James (in the year 1153), drawn from the body, I was borne into an ecstasy. And a great flaming wheel flared in the heaven. Then it disappeared, and I saw a light more splendid than I was accustomed to see; and thousands of saints stood in it, forming an immense circle; having palms and shining crowns and the titles of their martyrdoms inscribed upon their foreheads. From these titles, as well as from their pre-eminent splendour, I knew them to be the Apostles. At their right was a great company having the same shining titles. At the left of the Apostles shone the holy order of virgins, also adorned with the signs of martyrdom, and behind them another splendid band of maidens, some crowned. Below it was another circle of great brilliancy, which I knew to be of the holy angels. In the midst of all was a Glory of Supreme Majesty, and its throne was encircled by a rainbow. At the right of that Majesty I saw one like unto the Son of Man, seated in glory; at the left was a radiant sign of the Cross. At the right of the Son of Man sat the Queen of Kings and Angels on a starry throne circumfused with immense light.

Jacques de Vitry describes the more exaggerated type of mystics:

You saw some of these women dissolved with such a particular and marvellous love toward God that they languished with desire, and for years had rarely been able to rise from their cots. They had no other infirmity, save that their souls were melted with desire of Him, and, sweetly resting with the Lord, as they were comforted in spirit they were weakened in body. The cheeks of one were seen to waste away, while her soul was melted with the greatness of her love. Another's flow of tears had made visible furrows down her face. Others were drawn with such intoxication of spirit that in sacred silence they would remain quiet a whole day, with no sense or feeling for things without them, so that they could not be roused by clamour or feel a blow. I saw another whom for thirty years her Spouse had so zealously guarded in her cell, that she could not leave it herself, nor could the hands of others drag her out.

—— H. O. Taylor, *The mediaeval mind* (3rd ed., 2 vols., New York, 1919), Vol. I, pp. 460–1, 477–8.

⁷ Bonaventura, *Selecta scripta* (Quaracchi, 1898), p. 220.

⁸ The scene of the scourging is pictured in detail. He stands naked in the presence of all, that youth so gracious and modest, "fairer than the children of men"; that flesh so innocent, so tender, so pure and so beauteous,

endures the rude and dòlorous scourges of shameful men. That royal blood flows on every side from every part of his body. So each detail of the long agony is dwelt upon, and the growing anguish of the Mother is depicted, until, when the centurion pierces the side of her Son, she faints in the arms of Mary Magdalene. Then verily the sword of that spear pierced the body of the Son and the heart of the Mother. But the sorrows of Mary are not over. When Joseph, as the day grows late, would wrap Jesus in the shroud for His burial, her grief breaks out anew. "O my friends," she cries, "do not take away my Son so quickly, nay, bury me with Him." But the last parting must come. "Now therefore, O my Son, our companionship is severed, and I must be parted from Thee, and I thy mother most sorrowful must bury Thee; but thereafter whither shall I go? Where shall I abide, my Son? How can I live without Thee? I would more gladly be buried with Thee, that wherever thou wert, I might be with Thee. But as I may not be buried with Thee in the body, I will be buried in the heart; I will bury my soul in the tomb with Thee, to Thee I give it up, to Thee I commend it. O my Son, how full of pain is this separation from Thee!"

——F. J. E. Raby, *History of Christian Latin poetry*
(Oxford, 1927), pp. 420–21.

⁹ Suso wrote in German. He declared he had received his revelations from God, but he added:

One thing a man should know, that there is as great a difference between hearing himself the sweet accords of a harp and hearing another speak of them as there is between the words received in pure grace and those that flow through a living mouth. And those same words when they come to be set down on dead parchment, especially in the German tòngue; for then are they chilled, and they wither like plucked roses; for the sprightliness of their delivery, which moves the heart of man, is then extinguished, and in the dryness of dry hearts are they received. Never was there a string, how sweet soever, but it became dumb when stretched on a dry log. A joyless heart can as little understand a joyful tongue as a German can an Englishman.

——G. G. Coulton, *Mediaeval panorama*
(Cambridge, 1939), pp. 523–4.

¹⁰ To the student not acquainted with the writings of the mystics a good introduction would be the following parts of the *Imitation of Christ*, Book I, Chs. 1, 2, and 20, Book II, Ch. 1, Book III, Chs. 1, 2, 12, 16, and 27, Book IV, Chs. 8, 11, 13, and 18.

¹¹ The study of Latin grammar and literature was, says Taylor,

"a chief means by which mediaeval civilization could maintain its continuity with its source. Grammar was most instrumental in preserving mediaeval Latin from violent deflections, which would have left the ancient literature as the literature of a forgotten tongue. Had mediaeval Latin failed to keep itself veritable Latin; had it instead suffered transmutation into local Romance dialects, the Latin classics and all that hung from them, might have become

as unknown to the Middle Ages as the Greek and even been lost forever."
———H. O. Taylor, *op. cit.*, Vol. II, p. 149.

[12] A. O. Norton, ed., *Reading in the history of education* (Cambridge, Mass., 1909), pp. 31–3.

[13] J. H. Robinson and H. Rolfe, *Petrarch* (2nd ed., New York, 1914), p. 64.

[14] E. Panofsky, "Renaissance and renascences" in *Kenyon review*, 1944, pp. 219–22. Panofsky concludes that the Middle Ages, which "had left antiquity unburied, alternately galvanized and exorcised its body. The Renaissance stood weeping at its grave, and tried to resurrect it." The sentimentalism of the humanists and their indifference and often their open contempt of science and philosophy are emphasized by L. Thorndike, "Renaissance or prerenaissance" in *Journal of the history of ideas*, 1943, and by G. Sarton, "Science in the Renaissance" in J. W. Thompson and others, *The civilization of the Renaissance* (Chicago, 1929).

[15] Some of Petrarch's attitudes have been passed on to many later professors of literature, i.e., his ignorance of, and contempt for philosophy and science, and his belief that somehow he was sort of a reliquary of culture, who, if approached with proper reverence, would impart a bit of his precious possession to a student.

[16] Boccaccio's biographer described his visit to the library of Monte Cassino:

He said that when he was in Apulia, attracted by the celebrity of the convent, he paid a visit to Monte Cassino. Desirous of seeing the collection of books, which he understood to be a very choice one, he modestly asked a monk to open the library, as a favour, for him. The monk answered stiffly, pointing to a steep staircase, "Go up; it is open." Boccaccio went up gladly; but he found that the place which held so great a treasure, was without a door or key. He entered, and saw grass sprouting on the windows, and all the books and benches thick with dust. In his astonishment he began to open and turn the leaves of first one tome and then another, and found many and divers volumes of ancient and foreign works. Some of them had lost several sheets; others were snipped and pared all round the text, and mutilated in various ways. At length, lamenting that the toil and study of so many illustrious men should have passed into the hands of most abandoned wretches, he departed with tears and sighs.

Poggio described the discovery of a codex of Quintilian at Constance in 1414:

I verily believe that, if we had not come to the rescue, he [Quintilian] must speedily have perished; for it cannot be imagined that a man magnificent, polished, elegant, urbane, and witty could much longer have endured the squalor of the prison-house in which I found him, the savagery of his jailers, the forlorn filth of the place. He was indeed right sad to look upon, and ragged, with rough beard and matted hair, protesting by his countenance and garb against the injustice of his sentence. He seemed to be stretching out his hands, calling upon the Romans, demanding to be saved from so unmerited a doom. Hard indeed it was for him to bear, that he, who had preserved the lives of many by his eloquence and aid, should now find no saviour from the unjust punishment awaiting him. In the middle of a well-stocked library, too large to catalogue at present, we discovered Quintilian, safe as yet and sound, though covered with dust and filthy with neglect and age. The books, you must know, were not housed according to their worth, but were lying in a most foul dungeon at the very bottom of a tower, a place into which condemned criminals would hardly have been thrust. From the convent libraries of Italy, [says Symonds] from the museums of Constantinople, from the abbeys of Germany and Switzerland and France, the slumbering spirits of the ancients had to be evoked. The chivalry of learning, banded together for his service, might be likened to Crusaders. As the Franks deemed themselves thrice blest if they returned with relics from Jerusalem, so these new Knights of the Holy Ghost, seeking not the sepulchre of a risen God, but the tombs wherein the genius of the ancient world awaited resurrection, felt holy transports when a brown, begrimed, and crabbed copy of some Greek or Latin author rewarded their patient quest. Days and nights they spent in carefully transcribing it, comparing their own MS. with the original, multiplying facsimiles, and sending them abroad with free hands to students who in their turn took copies, till the treasure-trove became the common property of all who could appreciate its value.

——J. A. Symonds, *The revival of learning*
(3rd ed., London, 1897), pp. 96–9.

[17] Bruni, who became the first great humanist historian, describes the influence of Chrysoloras' teaching:

I was then studying Civil Law, but . . . I burned with love of academic studies, and had spent no little pains on dialectic and rhetoric. At the coming of Chrysoloras, I was torn in mind, deeming it shameful to desert the law, and yet a crime to lose such a chance of studying Greek literature; and often with youthful impulse I would say to myself, "Thou, when it is permitted thee to gaze on Homer, Plato and Demosthenes, and the other poets, philosophers, and orators, of whom such glorious things are spread abroad, and speak with them and be instructed in their admirable teaching, wilt thou desert and rob thyself? Wilt thou neglect this opportunity so divinely offered? For seven hundred years, no one in Italy has possessed Greek letters; and yet we confess that all knowledge is derived from them. There are doctors of civil law everywhere; and the chance of learning will not fail thee. But if this one and only doctor of Greek letters disappears, no one can be found to teach thee. Overcome at length by these reasons, I gave myself to Chrysoloras, with such zeal to learn, that what through the wakeful day I gathered, I followed after in night, even when asleep.

——H. O. Taylor, *Thought and expression in the 16th century*
(2 vols., New York, 1920), Vol. I, p. 36.

The intense, almost excessive enthusiasm for classical culture can be explained only by the fact that it was perfectly designed to meet the needs of educated, urban laymen, of a society that had ceased to be predominantly either feudal or ecclesiastical, yet had in its own immediate past nothing to draw upon for inspiration.

——W. F. Ferguson, "The interpretation of the Renaissance" in *Journal of history of ideas,* 1951, p. 494.

[18] P. Smith, *Erasmus* (New York, 1931), p. 23.

[19] John Colet, Erasmus' English friend, in urging men to read the neglected Bible, said of even the most eminent theologians: "They are wont to look on no more scripture than they find in their *Duns Scotus.*" F. Seebohm, *The Oxford reformers* (London, n.d.), p. 18. In his lecture on St. Paul, Colet used Suetonius and the Roman writers to help explain the teachings of Paul. He abandoned all allegory and scholastic dialectic and tried to see directly what Paul meant. Erasmus declared:

Do not interpret what I have said as directed against theology itself, which I have singularly cultivated, but against the theologasters of our age, unsurpassed by any in the murkiness of their brains, in the barbarity of their speech, the stupidity of their natures, the thorniness of their doctrine, the harshness of their manners, and the hypocrisy of their lives.

——Smith, *op. cit.,* p. 23.

Bibliographical Notes*

THESE NOTES *are in a very summary form; nearly all comments and, at least, a third of the works consulted by the author have been omitted. Preference has always been given to more recent works and to those written in English and French. Many of the books and articles cited contain bibliographies. To save space, titles have sometimes been shortened. Under any given topic, the list of titles starts with general works and moves on to more detailed studies. Works that the author found of unusual value are starred.*

SOME GENERAL WORKS. *Cambridge mediaeval history* (2nd ed., 8 vols., 1924–36) with elaborate bibliographies; W. H. Allison and others, eds., *Guide to historical literature* (New York, 1931); L. J. Paetow, *Guide to the study of mediaeval history* (2nd ed., New York, 1931); C. P. Farrar and A. P. Evans, *Bibliography of English translations from mediaeval sources* (New York, 1946); F. S. Smith, *The classics in translation, an annotated guide* (New York, 1930); A. Baudrillart, *Dictionnaire d'historie et de géographie ecclésiastique* (Paris, 1912–23); F. Cabrol and H. Leclerq, *Dictionnaire d'archéologie chrétienne et de liturgie* (Paris, 1913 ff.); A. Vacant and E. Mangenot, *Dictionnaire de théologie catholique* (Paris, 1909 ff.); H. F. Williams, ed., *Index of mediaeval studies published in Festschriften 1865–1946* (Berkeley, 1951); J. Delorme, *Chronologie des civilisations* (Paris, 1949); S. H. Steinberg, *Historical tables 58 B.C. –A.D. 1945* (3rd ed., London, 1953); H. O. Taylor, *The mediaeval mind* (4th ed., 2 vols., New York, 1925) still the best single book on intellectual history of the Middle Ages, though it does nothing with the Byzantine and Islamic culture or with art, music, and other topics, and it stops with Dante; G. Schnürer, *L'église et la civilisation au moyen âge* (3 vols., Paris, 1933–8); *Speculum* (Cambridge, Mass., 1926 ff.), its bibliographies are the best means of keeping abreast of new studies, and these bibliographies keep those in the *Cambridge mediaeval history* and in Paetow's manual up to date; cf. also *Progress of mediaeval and Renaissance studies in the United States and Canada* (Boulder, Colo., 1923 ff.).

SOME ANTHOLOGIES. C. W. Jones, ed., *Mediaeval literature in translation* (New York, 1950); J. B. Ross and M. M. McLaughlin, eds., *The portable mediaeval reader* (New York, 1949); and G. G. Coulton, ed., *Life in the Middle Ages* (4 vols., Cambridge, 1930); and, finally, for pictures to illustrate mediaeval

---

* There are three supplements to this list of works, printed at the end.

[503

culture: W. Goetz, ed., *Propyläen Weltgeschichte* (10 vols., Berlin, 1929–33), Vols. 2–4 inclusive; and *Propyläen Kunstgeschichte* (16 vols., Berlin, 1923–9), Vols. 5, 6, 7, 8, and 10.

CHAPTER 1

GENERAL. M. Cary and others, *The Oxford classical dictionary* (Oxford, 1949); *The Cambridge ancient history* (12 vols., Cambridge, 1923–39); R. W. Livingstone, ed., *The legacy of Greece* (Oxford, 1921); C. Bailey, ed., *The legacy of Rome* (Oxford, 1923); the separate chapters or articles of these works are not listed below. W. W. Jaeger, *Paideia, the ideals of Greek culture* (2nd ed., 3 vols., Oxford, 1943–5); W. W. Hyde, *From paganism to Christianity in the Roman Empire* (Philadelphia, 1946); and C. N. Cochrane, *Christianity and classical culture* (Oxford, 1940).

TRADITIONAL RELIGION. E. O. James, *The beginnings of religion* (London, 1948).

GREEK RELIGION. M. P. Nilsson, *A history of Greek religion* (2nd ed., Oxford, 1949), by the same author, *Greek popular religion* (New York, 1940) and *Greek piety* (Oxford, 1948); W. K. Guthrie, *The Greeks and their gods* (London, 1950); M. Gorce and R. Mortier, eds., *Histoire générale des religions: Grèce-Rome* (Paris, 1948); G. Murray, *Five stages of Greek religion* (2nd ed., Oxford, 1925); and two volumes of texts with comments: F. M. Cornford, ed., *Greek religious thought from Homer to Alexander*, and E. Bevan, ed., *Later Greek religion* (New York, 1923–7); A. B. Cook, *Zeus* (3 vols., Cambridge, 1914–40); and W. W. Hyde, *Greek religion and its survivals* (New York, 1923).

ROMAN RELIGION. A. Grenier, *Les religions étrusque et romaine* (Paris, 1948); F. Altheim, *History of Roman religion* (London, 1944); A. Grenier, *The Roman spirit in religion, thought and art* (London, 1926); and C. L. Lang, *Survivals of Roman religion* (New York, 1931).

PHILOSOPHY. L. Robin, *Greek thought and the origins of the scientific spirit* (New York, 1928); A. H. Armstrong, *An intro. to ancient philosophy* (3rd ed., London, 1957); A. Rivaud, *Histoire de la philosophie* (Paris, 1948), Vol. I; A. O. Lovejoy, *The great chain of being* (Cambridge, Mass., 1936); J. Burnet, *Early Greek philosophy* (4th ed., London, 1948); K. Freeman, *The pre-Socratic philosophers* (Cambridge, Mass., 1947), and by the same author, a collection of texts, *Ancilla to the pre-Socratic philosophers* (Cambridge, Mass., 1948); W. W. Jaeger, *The theology of the early Greek philosophers* (Oxford, 1947); A. E. Taylor, *Plato, the man and his work* (6th ed., London, 1952), and by the same author, *Platonism and its influence* (New York, 1932); R. Klibansky, *The continuity of the Platonic tradition* (London, 1939); W. W. Jaeger, *Aristotle, fundamentals of the history of his development* (Oxford, 1934); J. L. Stocks, *Aristotelianism* (New York, 1925); G. H. Clark, ed., *Selections from Hellenistic philosophy* (New York, 1940); R. H. Hicks, *Stoic and Epicurean* (New York, 1910); E. R. Bevan, *Stoics and Skeptics* (Oxford, 1913); T. Whittaker, *The Neo-Platonists* (2nd ed., Cambridge, 1918);

W. R. Inge, *The philosophy of Plotinus (3rd ed., 2 vols., London, 1948); E. Bréhier, *La philosophie de Plotin* (new ed., Paris, 1948); P. W. Pistorius, *Plotinus and Neo-Platonism* (London, 1952); L. J. Rosán, *The philosophy of Proclus* (New York, 1949); T. Whittaker, *Macrobius, or philosophy, science and letters in the year 400* (Cambridge, 1923); W. H. Stahl, ed., *Macrobius commentary on the dream of Cicero* (New York, 1952); and E. de Faye, *Gnostiques et gnosticisme* (2nd ed., Paris, 1925).

MYSTERY RELIGIONS. F. Cumont, *Oriental religions in Roman paganism* (Chicago, 1911), there is a 4th ed. in French of 1929; H. R. Willoughby, *Pagan regeneration* (Chicago, 1929); A. D. Nock, *Conversion* (Oxford, 1933); S. Angus, *The religious quests of the Graeco-Roman world* (New York, 1929); R. Reitzenstein, *Die Hellenistischen Mysterien-Religionen* (3rd ed., Leipzig, 1927); W. K. C. Guthrie, *Orpheus and Greek religion* (London, 1935); I. M. Linforth, *The arts of Orpheus* (Berkeley, 1941), critical of older accounts of Orphism; M. Brillant, *Les mystères d'Eleusis* (Paris, 1920); J. G. Frazer, *Adonis, Attis, Osiris* (new ed., 2 vols., London, 1922); A. J. Festugière, *La révélation d'Hermes Trismégiste* (4 vols., Paris, 1944–57); F. Cumont, *Les mystères de Mithra* (3rd ed., Brussels, 1913; English tr. of an earlier ed., Chicago, 1903); A. S. Geden, *Select passages illustrating Mithraism* (London, 1925); E. Hatch, *The influence of Greek ideas and usages on the Christian church* (new ed., New York, 1921), exaggerates claims for Greek influences.

CHAPTER II

GENERAL. *Cambridge ancient history* (12 vols., Cambridge, 1923–39), and *Cambridge mediaeval history* (2nd ed., Cambridge, 1924), Vol. I, indispensable (the individual chapters on Judaism and Christianity are not listed separately in this bibliography); W. F. Albright, *From the Stone Age to Christianity* (Baltimore, 1940); W. W. Hyde, *Paganism to Christianity in the Roman Empire* (Philadelphia, 1946); E. R. Bevan and C. Singer, eds., *Legacy of Israel* (2nd ed., Oxford, 1928); W. F. Albright, *The archeology of Palestine* (London, 1949); and T. Finegan, *Light from the ancient past 5000 B.C.–500 A.D.* (Princeton, 1946), a survey of archeological finds.

OLD TESTAMENT. R. H. Pfeiffer, *Introduction to Judaism and the Old Testament* (new ed., New York, 1948), the most useful general work; H. H. Rowley, *Growth of the Old Testament* (London, 1950); G. F. Moore and L. H. Brockington, *Literature of the Old Testament* (Oxford, 1948); S. H. Hooke, ed., *Myth and ritual* (Oxford, 1933), and by the same editor, *The labyrinth* (London, 1935); A. S. Peake, ed., *The people and the book* (Oxford, 1925); H. H. Rowley, ed., *The Old Testament and modern study* (Oxford, 1951); H. W. Robinson, *The Old Testament, its making and meaning* (London, 1936); W. O. Oesterley and T. H. Robinson, *Hebrew religion, its origin and development* (2nd ed., London, 1937); A. Lods, *Israel from its beginnings to the middle of the eighth century* (London, 1932), and by the same author, *The prophets and the rise of Judaism* (London, 1937); C. C. Torrey, *The*

Apocryphal literature (New Haven, 1945); and R. H. Pfeiffer, *History of New Testament times with introduction to the Apocrypha* (New York, 1949).

PHILO THE JEW. G. F. Moore, *Judaism in the first centuries of the Christian era* (3 vols., Cambridge, Mass., 1927–30); H. A. Wolfson, *Philo, the founder of religious philosophy in Judaism, Christianity and Islam* (2 vols., Cambridge, Mass., 1947); E. R. Goodenough, *By light, light, the mystic gospel of Hellenistic Judaism* (New Haven, 1935); H. Lewy, ed., *Philo, philosophic writings, selections* (London, 1946); E. Bréhier, *Les idées philosophiques et religieuses chez Philon d'Alexandrie* (new ed., Paris, 1950); E. R. Goodenough, *An introduction to Philo Judaeus* (New Haven, 1940).

NEW TESTAMENT. C. Guignebert, *Christianity* (New York, 1927), a brief survey, liberal; E. F. Scott, *The literature of the New Testament* (New York, 1932); T. Henshaw, *The New Testament in the light of modern scholarship* (London, 1952); A. E. Barnett, *The New Testament, its making and meaning* (New York, 1946); C. H. Dodd, *The present task in New Testament studies* (Cambridge, 1936); M. Dibelius, *A fresh approach to the New Testament and early Christian literature* (New York, 1936); K. Lake, *Landmarks in the history of early Christianity* (New York, 1920); H. Lietzmann, *Beginnings of the Christian Church* (4 vols., London, 1937–51); C. N. Cochrane, *Christianity and Classical culture* (Oxford, 1940); D. W. Riddle and H. H. Hutson, *New Testament life and literature* (Chicago, 1946); S. J. Case, *The origins of Christian supernaturalism* (Chicago, 1946); A. C. McGiffert, *History of Christian thought* (2 vols., New York, 1932–3); J. F. Bethune-Baker, *An introduction to the early history of Christian doctrine* (7th ed., London, 1942); and the best summary of present views on the first three Christian centuries: M. Goguel, *Origines du Christianisme* (3 vols., Paris, 1946–7).

JESUS. Two works by C. A. H. Guignebert, *Jesus* (New York, 1935) and *Jewish world in the time of Jesus* (New York, 1939); M. Dibelius, *Jesus* (Philadelphia, 1949), and T. S. Kepler, ed., *Contemporary thinking about Jesus* (New York, 1944).

PAUL. G. A. Deissmann, *Paul, a study in social and religious history* (2nd ed., London, 1926); A. D. Nock, *St. Paul* (London, 1938); C. H. Dodd, *"The mind of Paul"* in *Bull. of John Rylands Library* (1933–4); A. Schweitzer, *Paul and his interpreters* (London, 1912), surveys the controversies over Paul; A. von Harnack, *The mission and expansion of Christianity in the first three centuries* (2nd ed., 2 vols., London, 1908), a classic; E. Hatch, *The influence of Greek ideas and usages on the Christian Church* (new ed., New York, 1921); and T. S. Kepler, ed., *Contemporary thinking about Paul* (New York, 1950).

LATER NEW TESTAMENT. R. G. Bury, *The Fourth Gospel and the logos doctrine* (Cambridge, 1940); C. H. Dodd, *An interpretation of the Fourth Gospel* (Cambridge, 1952); C. H. Dodd, *The Johannine Epistles* (London, 1946); H. Leisegang, *Die Gnosis* (Leipzig, 1924).

EARLY CHURCH. A. Fliche and V. Martin, eds., *Histoire de l'église* (Paris, 1934 ff.); A. Alföldi, *The conversion of Constantine and pagan Rome* (Oxford, 1949); and P. Charanis, *Church and state in the later Roman Empire* (Madison, 1939).

CHAPTER III

GENERAL. J. B. Lightfoot, ed., *The Apostolic Fathers* (5 vols., London, 1885–90); A. Roberts and J. Donaldson, eds., *The Anti-Nicene Fathers* (10 vols., New York, 1896–9); P. Schaff, ed., *The Nicene and Post-Nicene Fathers* (28 vols., New York, 1889–1900); The *Cambridge ancient history* and the *Cambridge mediaeval history*, as noted above under Chapter II, both contain admirable chapters which are not separately listed here; A. Fliche and V. Martin, eds., *Histoire de l'église* (vols. 1–6, Paris, 1934 ff.); A. von Harnack, *Dogmengeschichte* (6th ed., 3 vols., Tübingen, 1922), the English translation of Harnack and of several other German works noted here are not made from the latest editions; F. Wiegand, *Dogmageschichte* (3 vols., Berlin, 1928–9), summarizes best scholarship; O. Bardenhewer, *Geschichte der alt-kirchlichen Literatur* (2nd ed., 5 vols., Freiburg, 1913–22); E. J. Goodspeed, *A history of early Christian literature* (Chicago, 1942); B. Altaner, *Précis de patrologie* (Mulhouse, 1941); F. Cayré, *Manuel of patrology* (2 vols., Paris, 1936–40); J. Quasten, *Patrology* (Brussels, 1951 ff.), the last three are good Roman Catholic manuals; A. C. McGiffert, *History of Christian thought* (2 vols., New York, 1932–3); J. F. Bethune-Baker, *An introduction to the early history of Christian doctrine* (7th ed., London, 1942); H. Lietzmann, *The era of the Church Fathers* (London 1951), the last three are Protestant handbooks; M. Grabmann, *Die Geschichte der Scholastischen Methode* (Freiburg, 1909), Vol. I; E. Gilson and P. Böhmer, *Geschichte der Christlichen Philosophie* (Paderborn, 1937); E. Gilson, *La philosophie au moyen âge* (2nd ed., Paris, 1944), a masterpiece; F. Ueberweg, *Die patristische und scholastische Philosophie* (11th ed., Berlin, 1928); C. M. Cochrane, *Christianity and classical culture* (Oxford, 1940); M. L. Laistner, *Christianity and pagan culture* (Ithaca, 1951); H. M. Relton, *A study in Christology; the problem of the relation of the two natures of Christ* (London, 1934); A. L. Williams, *Adversus Judaeos, a bird's eye view of Christian apologiae* (Cambridge, 1935); E. de Faye, *Gnostiques et Gnosticisme* (2nd ed., Paris, 1925); and A. D. Nock, *Conversion, the old and the new in religion from Alexander to Augustine* (Oxford, 1933).

GREEK FATHERS. A. Peuch, *Histoire de la littérature Grecque Chrétienne* (3 vols., Paris, 1928–30); W. Bousset, *Kyrios Christos, Geschichte des Christus Glaubens* (3rd ed., Göttingen, 1926); E. R. Goodenough, *The theology of Justin Martyr* (Jena, 1923); J. Lawson, *The biblical theology of Iranaeus* (London, 1940); C. Mondésert, *Clément d'Alexandrie* (Paris, 1943); E. de Faye, *Origène* (3 vols., Paris, 1923–8), of which there is a summary in *Origen and his works* (New York, 1929); J. Daniélou, *Origène* (Paris, 1948); D. Armand, *L'ascèse monastique de St. Basil* (Maredsous, 1949); W. K. L. Clarke, *St. Basil* (Cambridge, 1913); P. Gallay, *Vie de Saint Grégoire de Naziance* (Paris, 1943); and J. Daniélou, *Platonisme et théologie mystique, essai sur Grégoire de Nysse* (Paris, 1944).

THE LATIN FATHERS. P. de Labriolle, *Histoire de la littérature latine chrétienne* (3rd ed., 2 vols., Paris, 1947), the best survey, there is an English translation of an earlier edition (New York, 1925); M. Manitius, *Geschichte der lateinischen Literatur des Mittelalters* (3 vols., Munich, 1911–31); E. M. Pickman, *Mind of Latin Christendom* (Oxford, 1937); H. O. Taylor, *The classical heritage of the Middle Ages* (3rd ed., New York, 1911); H. O. Taylor, *The mediaeval mind* (3rd ed., 2 vols., New York, 1919); E. K. Rand, *Founders of the Middle Ages* (2nd ed., Cambridge, Mass., 1929); F. A. Wright and T. A. Sinclair, *A history of later Latin literature* (London, 1931); E. S. Duckett, *Latin writers of the fifth century* (New York, 1930); S. Dill, *Roman society in the last century of the western empire* (2nd ed., London, 1899); P. Courcelle, *Les lettres Grecques en Occident* (new ed., Paris, 1948); J. Morgan, *The importance of Tertullian in the development of Christian dogma* (London, 1928); F. H. Dudden, *Life and times of St. Ambrose* (2 vols., Oxford, 1935); F. Cavallera, *St. Jérôme* (2 vols., Louvain, 1922), incomplete; F. X. Murphy, ed., *A monument to St. Jerome* (New York, 1952); E. Gilson, *Introduction à l'étude de St. Augustin* (new ed., Paris, 1949), indispensable; H. I. Marrou, *St. Augustin et la fin de la culture antique* (2nd ed., 2 vols., Paris, 1950); J. N. Figgis, *Political aspects of St. Augustine's "City of God"* (London, 1921); J. T. Shotwell, *Introduction to the history of history* (2nd ed., New York, 1939); W. J. Oates, ed., *Basic writings of St. Augustine* (2 vols., New York, 1948); J. W. Raymond, tr., *Orosius, seven books against the pagans* (New York, 1936); and E. M. Sanford, tr., *Salvian, on the government of God* (New York, 1930).

POETRY. Besides the general histories of Puech, Labriolle, and Manitius mentioned above, cf. K. Krumbacher, *Geschichte der Byzantinischen Literatur* (2nd ed., Munich, 1897); G. Soyter, *Byzantinische Dichtung* (Athens, 1938); E. Wellesz, *History of Byzantine music and hymnography* (Oxford, 1949); and F. J. E. Raby, *History of Christian Latin poetry* (Oxford, 1927), and his *History of secular Latin poetry in the Middle Ages* (2 vols., Oxford, 1934).

ART. P. Lavedan, *Histoire de l'art* (2nd ed., Paris, 1950), Vol. II, with best available recent bibliography; C. R. Morey, *Early Christian art* (Princeton, 1942); L. Bréhier, *L'art chrétien* (2nd ed., Paris, 1928); O. Marucchi, *Manual of Christian archeology* (Patterson, 1935); O. M. Dalton, *East Christian art* (Oxford, 1925); J. Strzygowski, *Origins of Christian church art* (Oxford, 1923); M. J. Rostovtzeff, *Dura-Europos and its art* (Oxford, 1938); W. Lowrie, *Art in the early church* (New York, 1947); A. Grabar, *Le martyrium* (Paris, 1946); E. B. Smith, *The dome* (Princeton, 1950), and by the same author, *Early Christian iconography* (Princeton, 1918); F. Cabrol and H. Leclercq, *Dictionnaire d'archéologie chrétienne et de liturgie* (27 vols., Paris, 1907–37); and E. de Bruyne, *L'Esthétique du moyen âge* (Louvain, 1947).

MUSIC. E. Wellesz, *History of Byzantine music and hymnography* (Oxford, 1949); G. Reese, *Music in the Middle Ages* (New York, 1940); J. Chailley, *Histoire musicale du moyen âge* (Paris, 1950); W. Apel, ed., *Harvard dictionary of music* (6th ed., Cambridge, Mass., 1950); P. H. Láng, *Music in western civilization* (New York, 1941); W. Apel, *"Early history of the organ"* in *Speculum,* 1948; A. T. Davison and W. Apel, *Historical anthology of music* (2nd ed., Cambridge, Mass., 1949), Vol. I; J. A. Dunney, *The mass* (New York, 1941); L. Duchesne, *Christian worship, its origin and evolution* (5th ed., London, 1925); E. Wellesz, *Eastern elements in western chant* (Oxford, 1947);

C. Sachs, *History of musical instruments* (New York, 1940); C. Sachs, *The rise of music in the ancient world* (New York, 1943); and K. Geiringer, *Musical instruments* (Oxford, 1945).

CHAPTER IV

GENERAL. *Cambridge mediaeval history* (Cambridge, 1923) Vol. IV; M. Gaudefroy-Demombynes, *Le monde musulman et byzantin jusqu'aux Croisades* (Paris, 1931); C. Diehl and others, *Le monde oriental de 395 à 1453* (2 vols., Paris, 1944–5); A. A. Vasiliev, *Histoire de l'Empire byzantin* (2 vols., Paris, 1932), there is an inferior English version of Vasiliev (2 vols., Madison, 1928–9); G. Ostrogorsky, *Geschichte des byzantinischen Staates* (Munich, 1940); N. H. Baynes and H. Moss, eds., *Byzantium* (Oxford, 1948), a volume in the Oxford Legacy series; two excellent works by J. B. Bury, *History of the later Roman Empire 395–565* (2 vols., London, 1923), *History of the Eastern Roman Empire 802–867* (London, 1912); L. Bréhier, *Le monde byzantin* (3 vols., Paris, 1947–50), of great value. Then some brief manuals: C. Diehl, *Byzance* (Paris, 1919); C. Diehl, *History of the Byzantine Empire* (Princeton, 1925); C. Diehl, *Les grands problèmes de l'histoire byzantine* (Paris, 1943); N. H. Baynes, *The Byzantine Empire* (new ed., Oxford, 1943); and S. Runciman, *Byzantine civilization* (London, 1933). Five other works of general import are: N. Jorga, *Histoire de la vie byzantine* (3 vols., Bucharest, 1934); C. Diehl, *Justinian et la civilisation byzantine au VIe siècle* (Paris, 1901); G. Schlumberger, *L'épopée byzantine à la fin du dixième siècle* (3 vols., Paris, 1896–1905), a magnificent work; S. de Nersessian, *Armenia and the Byzantine Empire* (Cambridge, Mass., 1945); and C. Diehl, *Figures byzantines* (2 vols., Paris, 1906–08). Much new material on Byzantine civilization appears in the following periodicals: *Byzantion* (Brussels, 1924–   ); *Revue des études byzantines* (Paris, 1943–   ); *Byzantina-Metabyzantina* (New York, 1946–   ), and *Dumbarton Oaks papers* (Washington, 1941–   ); and *Dumbarton Oaks studies* (1950–   ).

CHURCH. Besides general works already cited, J. Pargoire, *L'église byzantine 527–847* (3rd ed., Paris, 1923); G. Every, *The Byzantine patriarchate 451–1204* (London, 1947); L. Oeconomos, *La vie religieuse dans l'empire byzantin 1081–1204* (Paris, 1918); E. J. Martin, *A history of the iconoclast controversy* (New York, 1931); E. Dawes and N. Baynes, trs., *Three Byzantine saints* (London, 1947).

MONASTICISM. E. C. Butler, *"Monasticism"* in *Cambridge Mediaeval history* (2nd ed., Cambridge, 1934), Vol. I, Ch. 18; D. U. Berlière, *L'ordre monastique des origines au XIIe siècle* (3rd ed., Paris, 1924); H. B. Workman, *Evolution of the monastic ideal* (2nd ed., London, 1927); H. Waddell, ed., *Desert fathers* (New York, 1936); K. Heussi, *Der Ursprung des Mönchtums* (Tübingen, 1936); J. M. Hussey, *"Byzantine Monasticism"* in *History* (1939); W. K. L. Clarke, *St. Basil* (Cambridge, 1913); W. K. L. Clarke, ed., *Ascetic works of St. Basil* (Cambridge, 1925); M. G. Murphy, *St. Basil and Monasticism* (Washington, 1930); and A. Gardner, *Theodore of Studium* (London, 1905).

EDUCATION. L. Bréhier, "L'enseignement supérieur à Constantinople" in *Byzantion*, Vols. 3 and 4; L. Bréhier, *L'enseignement classique et religieux à Byzance* in *Revue d'histoire et de philosophie religieuse* (1941); F. Fuchs, *Die höheren Schulen von Constantinople im Mittelalter* (Leipzig, 1926).

LEARNING. J. E. Sandys, *History of classical scholarship* (3rd ed., Cambridge, 1921), Vol. I; B. Tatakis, *La philosophie byzantine* (Paris, 1949); J. M. Hussey, *Church and learning in the Byzantine Empire 867–1185* (Oxford, 1937); S. K. Padover, "Byzantine libraries" in J. W. Thompson, *The mediaeval library* (Chicago, 1939).

LITERATURE. A. Puech, *Histoire de la littérature grecque chrétienne* (3 vols., Paris, 1928–30); K. Krumbacher, *Geschichte der byzantinischen Literatur* (2nd ed., Munich, 1897), the great work; G. Montelatici, *Storia della letteratura bizantina* (Milan, 1916), contains some material not available to Krumbacher; G. Soyter, *Byzantinische Dichtung* (Athens, 1938); N. Jorga, "La littérature byzantine" in *Revue du Sud-Est Européen* (1925); J. W. Thompson, *A history of historical writing* (2 vols., New York, 1942), Vol. I; G. Buckler, *Anna Comnena* (Oxford, 1929); E. A. S. Dawes, tr., *Alexiad* (London, 1928); G. La Piana, "Byzantine theater" in *Speculum* (1936); G. R. Woodward and H. Mattingly, tr., *Barlaam and Joasaph* (New York, 1914); J. B. Bury, *Romances of chivalry on Greek soil* (Oxford, 1911); E. H. Haight, *Essays on Greek romances* (2 vols., New York, 1943–5); H. Gregoire, "The historical element in western and eastern epics" in *Byzantion* (1944); and J. N. Neale, *Hymns of the eastern church* (new ed., London, 1939); for other references to articles on Byzantine epics cf. N. H. Baynes and H. Moss, eds., *Byzantium* (Oxford, 1948), pp. 413–14.

ART. P. Lavedan, *Histoire de l'art* (2nd ed., Paris, 1950), Vol. II, the best bibliographical guide; C. Diehl, *Manual d'art byzantin* (2nd ed., 2 vols., Paris, 1926), the standard work; also highly valuable are the two general works of O. M. Dalton, *East Christian art* (Oxford, 1925), and his earlier *Byzantine art and archeology* (London, 1911); D. T. Rice, *Byzantine art* (Oxford, 1935); and P. Lemerle, *Le style byzantin* (Paris, 1943) are the two best brief manuals; cf. also the relevant parts of W. R. Lethaby, *Mediaeval art* (2nd ed., London, 1949), and C. R. Morey, *Mediaeval art* (New York, 1942); on iconography, L. Bréhier, *L'art chrétien* (2nd ed., Paris, 1928); A. Grabar, *L'empereur dans l'art Byzantin* (Paris, 1936); and G. Millet, *Recherches sur l'iconographie de l'évangile, XIV–XVI⁰ siècles* (Paris, 1916). ARCHITECTURE: J. A. Hamilton, *Byzantine architecture and decoration* (London, 1933); A. Grabar, *Le martyrium* (Paris, 1946); two of the many works of J. Strzygowski are important: *Origins of Christian church art* (Oxford, 1923), and *L'ancien art chrétien de Syrie* (Paris, 1936) with a summary of his views by Millet; H. C. Butler, *Early churches in Syria* (Princeton, 1929); E. B. Smith, *The dome* (Princeton, 1950); E. H. Swift, *Hagia Sophia* (New York, 1940), contains description of recent cleaning of mosaics; G. Downey, "Byzantine architects, their training and methods" in *Byzantion* (1948); *Mosaics and Painting*, O. Demus, *Byzantine mosaic decoration* (London, 1948) has modified all earlier views; C. Diehl, *La peinture byzantine* (Paris, 1933); and D. T. Rice, *Byzantine painting* (London, 1948), brief. SCULPTURE: L. Bréhier, *La sculpture et les arts mineurs byzantins* (Paris, 1936). MINOR ARTS: Two works by J. Ebersolt, *Les arts somptuaires de Byzance* (Paris, 1923), and *La miniature byzantine* (Paris, 1926); K. Weitzmann, *Illustration in roll and codex* (Princeton, 1947); H. Gerstinger, *Die griechische Buchmalerei* (Vienna, 1926); A. Goldschmidt and K. Weitzmann, *Die byzantinischen Elfenbeinskulpturen* (2 vols., Berlin, 1930–4); and M. L. Gothein, *History of garden art* (2 vols., London, 1928).

MUSIC. H. J. W. Tillyard, *Byzantine music and hymnography* (London, 1923), and E. Wellesz, *History of Byzantine music and hymnography* (Oxford, 1949).

INFLUENCES OF BYZANTIUM. GENERAL: N. Jorga, *Byzance après Byzance* (Bucharest, 1935); J. Ebersolt, *Orient et occident* (2 vols., Paris, 1928–9); J. P. Fallmerayer, *Byzanz und das Abendland* (Vienna, 1943); and A. Vasiliev, *Byzance et les Arabes* (2 vols., Brussels, 1935–50). INFLUENCE ON SLAVIC WORLD: J. S. Roucek, ed., *Slavonic encyclopedia* (New York, 1949); L. I. Strakhovsky, ed., *Handbook of Slavic studies* (Cambridge, Mass., 1949); L. Niederle, *Manuel de l'antiquité slave* (2 vols., Paris, 1923–6); S. H. Cross, *Slavic civilization* (Cambridge, Mass., 1948), brilliant short essay; Obolensky, "Russia's Byzantine heritage" in *Oxford Slavonic papers* (1951); M. Spinka, *History of Christianity in the Balkans* (Chicago, 1933); F. Dvornik, *Les Slaves, Byzance et Rome au IXe siècle* (Paris, 1926); F. Dvornik, *The making of central and eastern Europe* (London, 1949); T. Uspensky, *L'art byzantin chez les Slaves* (4 vols., Paris, 1930–2). BULGARIA: B. Filov, *Geschichte der alt-bulgarischen Kunst* (Berlin, 1932), there is an English version (Bern, 1919), and a French version (Sofia, 1925). SERBIA: C. Jirecek, *La civilisation serbe au moyen âge* (Paris, 1920); G. Millet, *L'ancien art serbe, les églises* (Paris, 1919); and Vercors, ed., *L'art médiaéval Yugoslave* (Paris, 1950). ROUMANIA: N. Jorga and G. Balz, *Histoire de l'art roumain ancien* (Paris, 1922), and L. Réau, *L'art roumain* (Paris, 1947). RUSSIA: G. Vernadsky, *Ancient Russia* and *Kievan Russia* (2 vols., New Haven, 1943–8), of greatest usefulness; B. Leib, *Rome, Kiev, et Byzance à la fin du XIe siècle* (Paris, 1921); G. P. Fedotov, *Russian religious mind, Kievan Christianity* (Cambridge, Mass., 1946); G. P. Fedotov, ed., *Treasury of Russian spirituality* (New York, 1948); Y. M. Sokolov, *Russian folklore* (New York, 1950); N. K. Gudzy, *History of early Russian literature* (New York, 1949); D. R. Buxton, *Russian mediaeval architecture* (Cambridge, 1934); S. H. Cross, *Russian mediaeval churches* (Cambridge, Mass., 1949); L. Réau, *L'art russe* (Paris, 1945); N. P. Kondakov, *L'icon russe* (4 vols., Prague, 1928–33); and D. T. Rice, *Russian icons* (London, 1947), a popularization.

CHAPTER V

GENERAL. J. Sauvaget, *Introduction à l'histoire d'orient musulman* (Paris, 1946), the most useful general bibliography on Islam; H. W. Hazard, ed., *At-

las of Islamic history (Princeton, 1951); M. T. Houtsma and others, eds., **The encyclopedia of Islam* (4 vols., London, 1913–36; supplement 1938), indispensable; T. P. Hughes, ed., *Dictionary of Islam* (London, 1895); T. Arnold and A. Guillaume, eds., **The legacy of Islam* (Oxford, 1931); A. J. Arberry, **The legacy of Persia* (Oxford, 1952); T. C. Young, ed., *Near Eastern culture and society* (Princeton, 1951); and N. A. Faris, ed., *The Arab heritage* (Princeton, 1944), the different articles in these last four books are not separately listed here; P. K. Hitti, **History of the Arabs* (6th ed., London, 1956), admirable; C. Brockelmann, *History of the Islamic peoples* (New York, 1947), very brief on Middle Ages; C. Huart, *Histoire des Arabes* (2 vols., Paris, 1912–13); C. Diehl and G. Marcais, *Le monde oriental de 395 à 1081* (Paris, 1936), C. Diehl and others, *L'Europe septentrionale et orientale de 1081 à 1453* (Paris, 1945), and M. Gaudefroy-Demombynes, *Le monde musulman et byzantin jusqu'aux Croisades* (Paris, 1931), three good French manuals; H. A. R. Gibb, **Mohammedanism* (Oxford, 1949), excellent brief introduction; R. Levy, **An introduction to the sociology of Islam* (new ed., Camb., 1957); J. Goldziher, **Le dogme et la loi de l'Islam* (Paris, 1920), the work of one of the great Islamic scholars; H. Lammens, *Islam, belief and institutions* (New York, 1929), and M. Gaudefroy-Demonbynes, *Muslim institutions* (London, 1950), two convenient handbooks; G. E. von Grunebaum, **Medieval Islam* (Chicago, 1946), a series of essays; D. L. O'Leary, *Arabic thought and its place in history* (rev. ed., London, 1939); Carra de Vaux, *Les penseurs de l'Islam* (5 vols., Paris, 1921–6), the last two works contain much information but are not well organized; L. Lévi-Provençal, **La civilisation arabe en Espagne* (2nd ed., Paris, 1948); A. Mazahéri, *La vie quotidienne des musulmans au moyen âge* (Paris, 1951); and J. Finegan, *Archeology of world religions* (Princeton, 1952), Ch. IX.

RELIGIOUS SYSTEM. F. Buhl, **Das Leben Mohammeds* (Berlin, 1930), the standard life; Tor Andrae, **Mohammed, the man and his faith* (new ed., London, 1957), good account; R. Blachère, **Introduction au Coran* (Paris, 1947); T. W. Arnold, **The preaching of Islam* (2nd ed., London, 1913); A. Guillaume, *The traditions of Islam* (Oxford, 1924); A. J. Wensinck, *The Muslim creed* (Cambridge, 1932); A. S. Tritton, *Muslim theology* (London, 1947); J. E. Archer, *Mystic elements in Mohammed* (New Haven, 1924); A. J. Arberry, *Sufism* (London, 1950); R. A. Nicholson, **The mystics of Islam* (London, 1914), and by the same author, **Studies in Islamic mysticism* (Cambridge, 1921) and *Rumi, poet and mystic 1207–1273* (New York, 1950); Margaret Smith, *Al-Ghazālī, the mystic* (London, 1944); A. J. Wensinck, **La pensée de Ghazzali* (Paris, 1950); W. M. Watt, *The faith and practice of Al-Ghazālī* (London, 1951); Margaret Smith, ed., *Readings from the mystics of Islam* (London, 1950).

EDUCATION. K. A. Totah, *The contribution of the Arabs to education* (New York, 1926); and M. Khan, **"Muslim theories of education during the Middle Ages" in *Islamic culture* (1944); also F. Rosenthal, **The technique and approach of Muslim scholarship* (Rome, 1947), explains how Muslims regarded all problems of scholarship; S. K. Padover, "Muslim libraries" in J. W. Thompson, *The mediaeval library* (Chicago, 1939).

LAW. D. R. MacDonald, **Development of Muslim theology, jurisprudence* *and constitutional theory* (New York, 1903), masterful study; J. Schacht, *Origins of Muhammaden jurisprudence* (Oxford, 1950).

PHILOSOPHY OF MUSLIMS AND JEWS. D. L. O'Leary, *How Greek science passed to the Arabs* (London, 1949), a disorderly but still useful book; M. Horten, *Die Philosophie des Islams* (Munich, 1924); T. J. de Boer, *History of philosophy in Islam* (2nd ed., London, 1933); L. Gautier, *Introduction de la philosophie musulmane* (Paris, 1923); G. Quadri, **La philosophie arabe dans l'Europe médiévale* (Paris, 1947); A. M. Goichon, *La philosophie d'Avicenne* (Paris, 1951); L. Gauthier, *Ibn Rochd* (Averroes) (Paris, 1948); J. Husik, *A history of mediaeval Jewish philosophy* (4th ed., Philadelphia, 1944); G. Vajda, **Introduction à la pensée juive au moyen âge* (Paris, 1947); L. G. Lévy, *Maimonide* (2nd ed., Paris, 1932).

SCIENCE. G. Sarton, *Guide to history of science* (Waltham, 1951); J. Lindsay, ed., *Early history of science, a short hand list* (London, 1950); H. Guerlac, ed., *Selected readings in the history of science* (Ithaca, 1950), Vol. I; G. Sarton, **Introduction to the history of science* (3 vols., Baltimore, 1927–47), for reference; L. Thorndike, **History of magic and experimental science* (6 vols., New York, 1923–41, Vols. 1 and 2 in 2nd ed. of 1929); W. C. Dampier, *History of science* (4th ed., Cambridge, 1949), and C. Singer, *A short history of science before 1800* (Oxford, 1941), the two best short introductions in English; W. P. Wightman, *Growth of scientific ideas* (New Haven, 1951); A. Mieli, *La science arabe et son rôle dans l'évolution scientifique mondiale* (Leyden, 1938), only a fair book but valuable till a better one appears.

ALCHEMY. T. L. Davis, "Introduction to an ancient Chinese alchemical classic" in *Proceedings of the Am. Acad. of Arts and Sciences* (1935); H. H. Dubs, "The beginnings of alchemy" in *Isis* (1937); J. Ruska, "Alchemy in Islam" in *Islamic culture* (1937); F. S. Taylor, *The alchemists* (New York, 1949), the best introduction; M. Berthelot, **Introduction à l'étude de la chimie des anciens et du moyen âge* (new imp., Paris, 1938); P. Kraus, *Jabir* (Cairo, 1943); A. J. Hopkins, *Alchemy, child of Greek philosophy* (New York, 1934); John Read, *Prelude to chemistry* (2nd ed., London, 1939), and by the same author, *The alchemist in life, literature, and art* (London, 1947).

MEDICINE. A. Castiglioni, **A history of medicine* (2nd ed., New York, 1947); D. Campbell, *Arabian medicine and its influence on the Middle Ages* (2 vols., London, 1926); E. G. Browne, **Arabic medicine* (Cambridge, 1921), also in a French edition (Paris, 1933) contains revisions; E. Elgood, *The medical history of Persia* (Cambridge, 1951).

ASTRONOMY, PHYSICS, AND MATHEMATICS. J. L. Dreyer, *History of the planetary systems from Thales to Kepler* (Cambridge, 1906); T. O. Wedel, *The mediaeval attitude toward astrology* (New Haven, 1920); E. Hoppe, *Histoire de la physique* (Paris, 1928); F. Cajori, **History of mathematics* (2nd ed., New York, 1919).

GEOGRAPHY. C. R. Beazley, **The dawn of modern geography* (3 vols., Oxford, 1897–1906), a classic; G. H. T. Kimble, *Geography in the Middle Ages* (London, 1928); E. G. R. Taylor, *Ideas on the shape, size, and movements of the earth* (London, 1943); B. Trapier, *Les voyageurs Arabes au moyen âge* (Paris, 1937).

TECHNOLOGY. R. J. Forbes, *Man the maker, a history of technology and engineering* (New York, 1950).

LITERATURE. H. A. R. Gibb, *Arabic literature, an introduction* (Oxford, 1926); J. Abd-el-Jalil, *Brève histoire de la littérature arabe* (2nd ed., Paris, 1946); C. Huart, *La littérature arabe* (4th ed., Paris, 1931); C. Brockelmann, **Geschichte der arabischen Literatur* (2 vols., Weimar, 1901–9; supplement, Leyden, 2 vols., 1936–41), the fundamental work; R. A. Nicholson, **A literary history of the Arabs* (2nd ed., Cambridge, 1941), excellent; and by the same author, **Translations of eastern poetry and prose* (Cambridge, 1922), an admirable anthology; E. G. Browne, **Literary history of Persia* (new ed., 4 vols., Cambridge, 1928–30); D. S. Margoliouth, *Lectures on Arabic historians* (Calcutta, 1930); C. Issawi, **An Arab philosophy of history, selections from Ibn Khaldun* (New York, 1950).

ART. G. Marçais, **L'Art de l'Islam* (Paris, 1946), the best introduction; P. Lavedan, **Histoire de l'art* (Paris, 1950), Vol. II for bibliography; the best collection of pictures is in H. Glück and E. Diez, *Die Kunst des Islam* (Berlin, 1925); H. Saladin, G. Migeon, and G. Marçais, **Manuel d'art musulman* (6 vols., Paris, 1907–27). ARCHITECTURE: K. A. C. Cresswell, **Early Muslim Architecture* (2 vols., Oxford, 1932–40), a masterpiece; and by the same author, **Muslim architecture of Egypt* (Oxford, 1951); also E. T. Richmond, *Moslem architecture 623–1516* (London, 1926); M. S. Briggs, *Muhammadan architecture in Egypt and Palestine* (Oxford, 1924). THE MINOR ARTS: A fine survey is M. D. Dimand, **A handbook of Muhammadan art* (2nd ed., New York, 1944). PAINTING: Cf. T. W. Arnold, **Painting in Islam* (Oxford, 1928); and two works of E. Blochet, *Les enlumineurs des manuscripts orientaux* (Paris, 1926), and *Musulman Painting* (London, 1929); R. Ettinghausen and E. Schroeder, eds., *Iranian and Islamic Art* (Newton, Mass., 1941), an invaluable series of prints illustrating Islamic art.

MUSIC. J. Ribera, **Music in ancient Arabia* (Oxford, 1929); H. G. Farmer, *A History of Arabian music* (London, 1929).

INFLUENCES IN CHRISTENDOM. *Legacy of Islam* already cited; T. C. Young, "Christendom's Cultural Debt to Islam," a survey in *Moslem world* (1945); J. W. Sweetman, *Islam and Christian theology* (3 vols., London, 1945–52); R. L. Devonshire, *Quelques influences islamiques sur les arts de l'Europe* (Cairo, 1935).

CHAPTER VI

GENERAL. L. Halphen, **Les barbares, des grandes invasions au XIe siècle* (4th ed., Paris, 1940), F. Lot, **La fin du monde antique et les débuts du moyen âge* (Paris, 1927, English tr. New York, 1931), both indispensable; also H. S. Moss, **Birth of the Middle Ages 395–814* (Oxford, 1935).

GENERAL INTELLECTUAL HISTORY. H. O. Taylor, **The mediaeval mind* (3rd ed., 2 vols., New York, 1919), a great work whose interest is centered on literature and on "the growth of thought and emotion"; J. E. Sandys, **A history of* *classical scholarship* (3rd ed., Cambridge, 1921), Vol. I; F. A. Wright and T. O. Sinclair, *History of later Latin literature* (London, 1931), thin, but only general work available in English; A. C. McGiffert, **A history of Christian thought* (2 vols., New York, 1932-3), a fine, brief survey; M. Manitius, **Geschichte der Lateinishen Literatur des Mittelalters* (3 vols., Munich, 1911-31), one of the greatest works available in any field of mediaeval studies; P. de Labriolle, **Histoire de la littérature Latine chrétienne* (2nd ed., 2 vols., Paris, 1947), admirable but stops with Isidore of Seville; E. K. Rand, *Founders of the Middle Ages* (2nd ed., Cambridge, Mass., 1929); H. O. Taylor, **Classical heritage of the Middle Ages* (3rd ed., New York, 1911), like a number of other works cited, these last two cover only part of period; J. de Ghellinck, **Littérature latine du moyen âge* (2 vols., Paris, 1939), brief but good, stops in eleventh century; M. L. W. Laistner, **Thought and letters in Western Europe 500-900* (London, 1957); P. Kletler, *Deutsche Kultur zwischen Völkerwanderung und Kreuzzügen* (Potsdam, 1934); L. Bréhier, **Grégoire le grand, etc.*, Vol. V of A. Fliche and V. Martin, *Histoire de l'église* (Paris, 1938); M. J. James, "Learning and literature to the death of Bede" and "Learning and literature till Pope Sylvester II" in *Cambridge mediaeval history*, Vol. III; L. Friedländer, "Das Nachleben der Antike im Mittelalter" in *Erinnerungen, Reden, und Schriften* (2 vols., Strasbourg, 1905); C. W. Jones, ed., **Mediaeval literature in translation* (New York, 1950) our best anthology; R. Latouche, ed., **Textes d'histoire médiévale, V^e-XIe siècle* (Paris, 1951).

EDUCATION. H. I. Marrou, **Histoire de l'éducation dans l'antiquité* (2nd ed., Paris, 1950); M. Roger, **L'enseignement des lettres classiques d'Ausone à Alcuin* (Paris, 1905); T. Haarhoff, *Schools of Gaul* (Oxford, 1920); P. R. Cole, *Later Latin Education in Ausonius, Capella and the Theodosian code* (New York, 1909); E. Lesne, *Les écoles de la fin du VIIIe siècle à la fin du XIe siècle* (Lille, 1940), and by the same author, *Les livres, scriptoria, et les bibliothèques VIIe-XIe siècles* (Lille, 1938); P. Courcelle, **Les lettres Grecques en Occident* (new ed., Paris, 1948), a thorough study; F. Cumont, "Pourquoi le Latin fut la seule langue liturgique" in *Mélanges Fredéricq* (Brussels, 1904); F. Lot, "A quelle époque a-t-on cessé de parler Latin?" in *Bulletin Du Cange* (1931); J. W. Thompson and others, *The mediaeval library* (Chicago, 1939); B. Ullman, "Classical authors in certain mediaeval *Florilegia*" in *Classical philology* (1932).

TRANSMITTERS OF ANCIENT AND PATRISTIC LEARNING 500-1000. E. S. Duckett, *The gateway to the Middle Ages* (New York, 1938); W. J. Chase, ed., *The "Ars minor" of Donatus* (Madison, 1926); J. Chapman, **St. Benedict and the sixth century* (London, 1929); C. Butler, **Benedictine monachism* (2nd ed., London, 1924); M. A. Schroll, *Benedictine monasticism, with commentaries on the rule* (New York, 1941); H. M. Barrett, *Boethius* (Cambridge, 1940), an excellent introduction. On Boethius' relations with Theodoric, two articles by W. Bark, "Theodoric vs. Boethius" in *American historical review* (1944), and "The legend of Boethius' martyrdom" in *Speculum* (1946), Bark is convinced of Boethius' treason; H. R. Patch, "The beginning of the legend of Boethius" in *Speculum* (1947), is not so convinced; H. R. Patch, *The tradition of Boethius* (Oxford, 1935), on Boethius' influence; L. W. Jones, ed., *Cassiodorus' "Introduction to divine and human readings"* (New York, 1946), with a long introduction on Cassiodorus; also a good introduction on Cassiodorus is in T. Hodgkin, ed., *The letters of Cassiodorus* (London, 1886); W. H. Hatton, "Gregory the Great" in *Cambridge mediaeval history*, Vol. II; F. H. Dudden, *Gregory the Great* (2 vols., New York, 1905); E. Brehaut; *An encyclopedist of the Dark Ages, Isidore of Seville* (New York, 1912); J. L. Romero, *San Isidoro de Sevilla* (Buenos Aires, 1947).

CELTIC AND ANGLO-SAXON LEARNING. L. Gougaud, *Christianity in Celtic lands* (London, 1932); J. Ryan, *Irish monasticism* (Dublin, 1931); F. M. Stenton, *Anglo-Saxon England* (2nd ed., Oxford, 1947), a general work in the *Oxford history of England*; F. O'Brian, *"Expansion of Irish Christianity to 1200"* in *Irish historical studies* (1943-4), two important bibliographical articles; S. J. Crawford, *Anglo-Saxon influence on western Christianity 600–800* (Oxford, 1938); W. Levinson, *England and the continent in the eighth century* (Oxford, 1946), an excellent work; J. D. Ogilvy, *Books known to Anglo-Saxon writers 670–804* (Cambridge, Mass., 1936); D. E. Martin-Clarke, *Culture in early Anglo-Saxon England* (Baltimore, 1947); G. R. Stephens, *Knowledge of Greek in England in the Middle Ages* (Philadelphia, 1933); E. S. Duckett, *Anglo-Saxon saints and scholars* (New York, 1947); C. W. Jones, *Saints lives and chronicles in early England* (Ithaca, 1947), contains the best account of Bede as an historian.

BEDE. A. H. Thompson, ed., *Bede, essays in commemoration* (Oxford, 1935); G. F. Browne, *Venerable Bede* (new ed., London, 1930); M. L. W. Laistner, "Bede as a scholar" in *Transactions of Royal Historical Society* (1933); R. Davis, "Bede's early reading" in *Speculum* (April, 1933); C. W. Jones, ed., *Bede, opera de temporibus* (Cambridge, Mass., 1943), with a very valuable introduction; C. Plummer, *Life and times of Alfred the Great* (Oxford, 1902).

MEROVINGIAN TIMES. S. Dill, *Roman society in Gaul in the Merovingian Age* (London, 1926); E. Salin, *La civilisation merovingienne* (3 vols., Paris, 1949–57), important archeological work; H. F. Muller, *L'époque mérovingienne* (New York, 1945), mostly philological.

CAROLINGIAN RENAISSANCE AND LATER. E. Patzelt, *Die Karolingische Renaissance* (Vienna, 1924); H. Naumann, *Karolingische und Ottonische Renaissance* (Frankfort, 1926); A. Kleinclausz, *Charlemagne* (Paris, 1934); L. Halphen, *Charlemagne* (Paris, 1947); A. Kleinclausz, *Eginhard* (Paris, 1942), and by the same author, *Alcuin* (Paris, 1948); E. S. Duckett, *Alcuin* (New York, 1951); F. L. Ganshof, "Eginhard" in *Bibliothèque d'humanisme et Renaissance* (1951); G. Brunhes, *La foi chrétienne et la philosophie au temps de la renaissance carolingienne* (Fribourg, 1904); E. K. Rand, *Survey of the manuscripts of Tours* (2 vols., Cambridge, Mass., 1929); W. S. Howell, tr., *The rhetoric of Alcuin and Charlemagne* (Princeton, 1941); H. Bett, *Erigena* (Cambridge, 1925); M. Cappuyns, *Erigène* (Louvain, 1933); W. N. Pittenger, "The Christian philosophy of Erigena" in *Journal of religion* (1944); three studies by E. von Erhardt-Siebold, "Atheniensis Sophista" in *Isis* (1944), on Neo-Platonic ideas in Charlemagne's circle, *The astronomy Erigena*, and *More light on Erigena's astronomy* (2 vols., Baltimore, 1940); J. M. Clark, *The abbey of St. Gall as a center of art and literature* (Cambridge, 1936); J. Lestocquoy, *"The tenth century"* in *Economic history review* (1947); R. S. Lopez, *"Still another Renaissance?"* in

American historical review (1951), valuable summaries of new views; Guy de Valous, *Le monachisme clunisien* (2 vols., Paris, 1935); J. Leflon, *Gerbert* (St. Wandrille, 1946); O. G. Darlington, "Gerbert the teacher" in *American historical review* (1947); J. W. Thompson, "Introduction of Arabic science into Lorraine in the Tenth Century" in *Isis* (1929).

LATIN POETRY. Besides the books cited under General Works, cf. F. J. E. Raby, *History of Christian Latin poetry* (Oxford, 1927), and by the same author, *History of secular Latin poetry in the Middle Ages* (2 vols., Oxford, 1953), both very discursive, but useful; R. de Gourmont, *Le Latin mystique* (Paris, 1922), work of an aesthete, contains some valuable comments; P. S. Allen, *The Romanesque lyric 50–1050 A.D.* (Chapel Hill, 1928), uneven; H. Waddell, *The wandering scholars* (7th ed., London, 1934), an over-written and overpraised book; F. Brittain, *The mediaeval Latin and Romance lyric (to 1300 A.D.)* (2nd ed., Cambridge, 1951), and S. Gaselle, *Oxford book of mediaeval Latin verse* (new ed., Oxford, 1937) are two admirable anthologies with excellent notes with references to where translations of many poems can be found; for hymns, J. Julian, ed., *Dictionary of hymnology* (2nd ed., London, 1907), an extraordinary work; for translations, cf. M. Britt, ed., *Hymns of the breviary and missal* (new ed., New York, 1936), with comments; O. J. Kuhnmuench, *Early Christian Latin poets from the fourth to the sixth century* (Chicago, 1929); J. Lindsay, tr., *Mediaeval Latin poets* (London, 1934); H. Waddell, tr., *Mediaeval Latin lyrics* (4th ed., London, 1933).

SPECIAL POETS. O. M. Dalton, tr., *The letters of Sidonius* (2 vols., Oxford, 1915); C. E. Stevens, *Sidonius Apollinaris and his age* (Oxford, 1933); A. Loyen, *Sidone Apollinaire et l'esprit précieux en Gaule* (Paris, 1943); D. Tardi, *Fortunat* (Paris, 1927); E. H. Zeydel, "The authenticity of Hroswitha's works" in *Modern language notes* (1946); E. H. Zeydel, "Were Hroswitha's dramas performed during her lifetime?" in *Speculum* (1945); W. von den Steinen, *Notker der C chter und seine Welt* (2 vols., Berne, 1948).

VERNACULAR LITERATURE. There are three recent bibliographies of great value: F. W. Bateson, ed., *Cambridge bibliography of English literature* (Cambridge, 1941), Vol. I; J. Körner, *Bibliographisches Handbuch des Deutschen Schriftums* (Berne, 1949); U. T. Holmes, ed., *A critical bibliography of French literature* (Syracuse, 1947), Vol. I; a brief handbook and chronology is M. Edwardes, *A summary of literatures of modern Europe* (to 1400) (London, 1907).

ANGLO-SAXON AND GERMAN LITERATURE. V. Grönbech, *The culture of the Teutons* (3 vols., Oxford, 1932); F. B. Gummere, *Founders of England* (new ed., New York, 1930). ANGLO-SAXON LITERATURE: R. H. Hodgkin, *History of the Anglo-Saxons* (2nd ed., 2 vols., Oxford, 1939), for general background; G. K. Anderson, *The literature of the Anglo-Saxons* (Princeton, 1949); F. Klaeber, ed., *Beowulf* (3rd ed. with supplement, New York, 1940), with a very fine introduction; R. W. Chambers, *Beowulf, an introduction* (2nd ed., Cambridge, 1932); W. W. Lawrence, *Beowulf and the epic tradition* (Cambridge, 1940); D. Whitelock, *The audience of Beowulf* (Oxford, 1951); J. R. Hulbert, "The genesis of Beowulf, a caveat" in *pub. mod. lang. ass.* (1951); and R. K. Gordon, tr., *Anglo-Saxon poetry* (London, 1926), a good prose translation of whole corpus of Anglo-Saxon verse. Brief introductions to the early phases of German and

French literature are in J. G. Robertson, *History of German literature* (new ed., London, 1947), and U. T. Holmes, Jr., *History of Old French literature* (2nd ed., New York, 1948).

HISTORY. Besides works cited above: J. W. Thompson, *History of historical writing* (2 vols., New York, 1942); J. T. Shotwell, **Introduction to the history of history* (2nd ed., New York, 1939); R. L. Poole, *Chronicles and annals* (Oxford, 1926); P. Courcelle, **Histoire littéraire des grandes invasions germaniques* (Paris, 1948); M. L. W. Laistner, "Value and influence of Cassiodorus' Ecclesiastical history" in *Harvard theological review* (1948); R. Meunier, *Grégoire de Tours* (2 vols., Poitiers, 1946); O. M. Dalton, tr., **Gregory of Tours, history of the Franks* (2 vols., Oxford, 1927), with excellent introduction and notes; J. Wallace-Hadrill, "The work of Gregory of Tours in the light of modern research" in *Transactions, Royal Historical Society* (1950); F. A. Wright, tr., *The works of Luidprand of Cremona* (London, 1930); H. Delehaye, **Les légendes hagiographiques* (3rd ed., Brussels, 1927), the best work on mediaeval biography as a literary genre.

ART. For bibliography P. Lavedan, **Histoire de l'art* (Paris, 1950), Vol. II; C. R. Morey, **Mediaeval art* (New York, 1942), a luminous survey; E. Kitzinger, **Early mediaeval art in the British Museum* (London, 1940), brief but first-rate; M. Harttmann, **Die Kunst des frühen Mittelalters* (Berlin, 1929), the best collection of pictures; the two stimulating works of J. Strzygowski in English represent his revolutionary views fairly well, **Origin of Christian church art* (Oxford, 1923), and **Early church art in northern Europe* (London, 1928); H. Picton, **Early German art (to about 1050)* (London, 1939), shows influence of Strzygowski, excellent pictures; W. A. von Jenney and W. Volbach, *Germanischer Schmuck des frühen Mittelalters* (Berlin, 1933); D. T. Rice, **English art 871–1100* (Oxford, 1952); T. D. Kendrick, **Anglo-Saxon art* (London, 1938), and by the same author, **Late Saxon and Viking art* (London, 1949); R. A. S. MacAlister, **The archeology of Ireland* (new ed., London, 1950), a standard work; F. Henry, *Irish art in the early Christian period* (London, 1940); P. Jacobsthal, **Early Celtic art* (2 vols., Oxford, 1944). ART IN GAUL: E. Enlart, **Manuel d'archéologie française* (2nd ed., 3 vols., Paris, 1919–24), a classic; E. Mâle, *La fin du paganisme en Gaule et les plus anciennes basiliques* (Paris, 1950); L. Bréhier, *L'art en France des invasions barbares à l'époque romane* (Paris, 1930); J. Hubert, **L'art pré-roman* (Paris, 1938); G. Plat, *L'art de bâtir en France des Romains à l'an 1100* (Paris, 1939); R. Rey, *L'art roman et ses origines* (Paris, 1945); J. Baum, *La sculpture figurale en Europe à l'époque Merovingienne* (Paris, 1937). SPECIAL STUDIES ON LATER PHASES: R. Hinks, **Carolingian art* (London, 1935); R. Krautheimer, "The Carolingian revival of Early Christian architecture" in *Art Bulletin* (1942); H. Jantzen, *Ottonische Kunst* (Munich, 1947); A. W. Clapham, **English romanesque architecture before the conquest* (Oxford, 1930); on ivory carving, A. Goldschmidt, **Die Elfenbein Skulpturen, 8–14 Jahrhundert* (4 vols., Berlin, 1914–26), the fundamental work; on painting, L. Réau, **Histoire de la peinture au moyen âge, La miniature* (Paris, 1947), Vol. I; T. Köves, *Les problèmes de la peinture chrétienne du IVe au IXe siècle* (Paris, 1927); E. Sullivan, *The book of Kells* (London, 1927), with fine color reproductions.

MUSIC. In addition to references to music in Bibliographical Notes to Chapter III, the following should be noted: W. Apel, *The notation of polyphonic music 900–1600* (4th ed., Cambridge, 1949); E. Wellesz, *Eastern elements in Western chant* (Oxford, 1947), both the work of Apel and that of Wellesz are very important contributions to the history of music; O. Strunk, ed., *Source readings in music history* (New York, 1950); three articles on musical theory: L. Ellinwood, "Ars musica" in *Speculum* (1948); M. F. Bukofzer, *"Speculative thinking in mediaeval music" in *Speculum* (1942); L. Schrade, "Music in the philosophy of Boethius" in *Musical quarterly* (1947).

CHAPTER VII

SCIENCE. For the general works on the history of science that pertain to the Middle Ages cf. first the bibliographical notes on science, Chapter V. In addition, attention is called to the following: F. R. Johnson and X. Larkey, "Science in the Renaissance" in *Modern language quarterly* (1941), a bibliographical article; C. H. Haskins, *Renaissance of the twelfth century* (Cambridge, Mass., 1927); C. H. Haskins, *"The spread of ideas in the Middle Ages" in *Studies in mediaeval culture* (Oxford, 1929); C. Singer, ed., *Studies in the history and method of science* (2 vols., Oxford, 1917–21), a valuable collection of separate essays; C. Singer, *From magic to science* (New York, 1928); L. Thorndike, *Science and thought in the fifteenth century* (New York, 1929), supplements some of later volumes of Thorndike's history of science; L. Thorndike and P. Kibre, *Incipits of mediaeval scientific writings in Latin* (Cambridge, 1937), an indispensable guide to research; H. Butterfield, *The origins of modern science 1300–1800* (London, 1949), a brief and brilliant introduction; P. Duhem, *Le système du monde de Platon à Copernic* (5 vols., Paris, 1913–17), a great work though it needs correcting at some points, and it tends to overemphasize the originality of mediaeval scientists; it should be used with Thorndike's history, for Thorndike is wary of isolated geniuses and "great precursors" and likes to push thinkers back into the context of their age; J. Sageret, *Le système du monde de Pythagore à Eddington* (Paris, 1931), brief; E. Whittaker, *From Euclid to Eddington, a study of concepts of the external world* (Cambridge, 1949); L. Thorndike, *"Survival of mediaeval interests into early modern times" in *Speculum* (1927), a fecund study. SYMBOLISM: G. P. Conger, *Theories of macrocosms and microcosms in the history of philosophy* (New York, 1922); R. Allers, *"Microcosmus from Anaximander to Paracelsus" in *Traditio* (1944); V. F. Hopper, *Mediaeval number symbolism* (New York, 1938).

POPULAR SCIENCE. G. Storms, *Anglo-Saxon magic* (Hague, 1948); P. Studer and J. Evans, *Anglo-Norman lapidaries* (Paris, 1924), J. Evans, *Magical jewels of the Middle Ages and the Renaissance* (Oxford, 1922); C. V. Langlois, *La connaissance de la nature et du monde d'après les écrits français* (2nd ed., Paris, 1927); and R. R. Steele, ed., *Mediaeval lore* (London, 1924). TRANSLATORS: S. D. Wingate, *The mediaeval Latin versions of the Aristotelian scientific cor-*

pus (London, 1931); G. Lacombe, *Aristotelis latinus* (Rome, 1939); M. Grabmann, "Aristoteles im zwölften Jahrhundert" in *Mediaeval studies* (1950); R. Walzer, "Arabic transmission of Greek thought to mediaeval Europe" in *Bulletin of John Rylands Library* (1945); C. H. Haskins, *Studies in the history of mediaeval science* (2nd ed., Cambridge, Mass., 1927), a basic work. Additional works, to those given for Chapter V, ALCHEMY AND ASTRONOMY: W. Ganzenmüller, *L'alchimie au moyen âge* (Paris, 1940); T. M. Lowry, *Historical introduction to chemistry* (2nd ed., London, 1936); M. Davidson, *The stars and the mind* (London, 1947); F. R. Johnson, *Astronomical thought in Renaissance England* (Baltimore, 1937), and D. C. Allen, *The star-crossed universe* (Durham, 1941), both are concerned with the sixteenth century but are of use because astrology in the later Middle Ages was much the same; N. De Vore, *Encyclopedia of astrology* (New York, 1947). ENCYCLOPEDIAS: M. de Boüard, "Encyclopédies médiévals" in *Revue des questions historiques* (1930); E. M. Sanford, "Famous Latin encyclopedias" in *Classical journal* (1949). Additional titles on HERBALS AND BOTANY: H. Bales, *Albertus Magnus als Zoologe* (Munich, 1928), a valuable study; L. Thorndike, ed., *The herbal of Rufinus* (Chicago, 1946); W. Blunt, *Art of botanical illustration* (London, 1950).

SOME OF THE GREAT SCIENTISTS 1200–1500. D. E. Sharp, *Franciscan philosophy at Oxford in the 13th century* (Oxford, 1930); S. H. Thomson, *The writings of Grosseteste* (Cambridge, 1940), a survey of manuscripts; J. C. Russell, *"Phases of Grosseteste's intellectual life"* in *Harvard theological review* (1950); A. G. Little, ed., *Essays on Roger Bacon* (Oxford, 1914); R. B. Burke, tr., *The opus maius of Roger Bacon* (2 vols., Philadelphia, 1928); M. Bouyges, "Bacon, a-t-il lu les livres arabes?" in *Archives d'histoire doctrinale et littéraire du moyen âge* (1930), the answer is no, Bacon could not read Arab books; C. H. Haskins, *"Science at the court of Frederick II," *"Michael Scot," and *"The 'De arte venandi' of Frederick II" in *Studies in the history of mediaeval science* (Cambridge, Mass., 1924), the basic studies on Frederick II; also cf. E. Kantorowicz, *Frederick II* (London, 1931), and C. A. Wood and F. M. Frye, eds., *Art of falconry* (Stanford University, 1943); E. A. Peers, *Ramon Lull* (London, 1929); A. Maier, *Die Vorläufer Galileos im 14. Jahrhundert* (Rome, 1941); D. B. Durand, *"Oresme and the mediaeval origins of modern science" in *Speculum* (1941); M. Clagett, *"Some general aspects of physics in the Middle ages" in *Isis* (1948); M. Clagett, *Marliani and late mediaeval physics* (New York, 1941); R. Creutz and E. Hoffmann, *Medizinisch-physikalisches Denken bei Nikolas von Cues* (Heidelberg, 1939); J. H. Randall, Jr., *"Development of scientific method in the School of Padua" in *Journal of History of Ideas* (1940), a very important study; E. Gilson, *Etudes sur le rôle de la pensée médiévale dans la formation du système cartésiene* (Paris, 1930). LEONARDO DA VINCI: P. Duhem, *Etudes sur Léonardo da Vinci* (3 vols., Paris, 1913 ff.); B. Dibner, "Da Vinci, military engineer" in M. F. Montagu, ed., *Studies offered to George Sarton* (New York, 1947); I. B. Hart, *The mechanical investigations of Leonardo da Vinci* (London, 1925); J. P. McMurrich, *Leonardo da Vinci, the anatomist* (Baltimore, 1930); there are two excellent collections from the writings of Leonardo, J. P. Richter, ed., *Literary works of Leonardo da Vinci* (2nd ed., 2 vols., Oxford, 1939), and E. MacCurdy, ed., *Notebooks of Leonardo da*

Vinci (2 vols., New York, 1938). The student should read in the writings of Roger Bacon, Frederick II, and Leonardo da Vinci.

TECHNOLOGY. L. White, *"Technology and invention in the Middle Ages" in *Speculum* (1940), a brilliant introduction to the subject with an extraordinary bibliography; R. J. Forbes, *Man the maker, a history of technology and engineering* (New York, 1950); J. F. Finch, *Engineering and western civilization* (New York, 1951); W. B. Parsons, *Engineers and engineering in the Renaissance* (Baltimore, 1939); A. P. Usher, *A history of mechanical inventions* (New York, 1929); L. Olschki, *Geschichte der neusprachlichen Wissenschaft* (3 vols., Halle, 1919–27), esp. Vol. I, a great work; G. Casestrini, *Arte militaire meccanica medievale* (Milan, 1946); F. Lot, *L'art militaire et les armées au moyen âge* (2 vols., Paris, 1948); L. Thorndike, "Introduction of the mechanical clock about 1271 A.D." in *Speculum* (1941), and by the same author, "Sanitation in the Middle Ages" in *Speculum* (1928). PRINTING: T. F. Carter, *Invention of printing in China and its spread westward* (new ed., New York, 1955); P. Butler, *Origin of printing in Europe* (Chicago, 1940); C. P. Winship, *Printing in the 15th century* (Philadelphia, 1940); E. P. Goldschmidt, "Mediaeval texts and their first appearance in print" in supplement to the *Bibliographical society transactions* (1943).

TRAVEL, NAVIGATION, AND RELATED SUBJECTS. A. P. Newton, ed., *Travel and travellers of the Middle Ages* (New York, 1926), an admirable introduction; J. K. Wright, *The geographical lore of the time of the Crusades* (New York, 1925); L. Olschki, *Marco Polo's precursors* (Baltimore, 1943); H. H. Hart, *Venetian adventurer* (3rd ed., Stanford University, 1947), a good introduction to Marco Polo; M. Letts, *Sir John Mandeville* (London, 1949); E. Prestage, *The Portuguese pioneers* (London, 1933); S. E. Morison, *Portuguese voyages to America in the 15th century* (Cambridge, Mass., 1940); E. Sanceau, *Henry the navigator* (New York, 1947); S. E. Morison, *Admiral of the Ocean Sea* (2 vols., Boston, 1942), now the standard life of Columbus; F. J. Pohl, *Amerigo Vespucci* (New York, 1944); L. A. Brown, *The story of maps* (Boston, 1949), a first rate work; R. V. Tooley, *Maps and map makers* (2nd ed., London, 1952).

PHILOSOPHY. GENERAL WORKS: The most important of these are: M. Grabmann, *Die Geschichte der scholastischen Methode* (3 vols., Freiburg, 1909–10); E. Gilson, *La philosophie au moyen âge* (2nd ed., Paris, 1941), admirable; F. Ueberweg, *Grundriss der Geschichte der Philosophie* (11th ed., Berlin, 1928), Vol. II, the English translation of Ueberweg is of an early edition; M. Manitius, *Geschichte der lateinischen Literatur des Mittelalters* (3 vols., Munich, 1911–31), goes only through the twelfth century; unfortunately none of these four basic works (except an old edition of Ueberweg) is available in an English translation. Other works of high value are: M. Grabmann, *Mittelalterliches Geistesleben* (2 vols., Munich, 1926–36); E. Gilson, *Etudes de philosophie médiévale* (Strasbourg, 1921); other general interpretive works by the same author are: *The spirit of mediaeval philosophy* (New York, 1936), *Reason and revelation in the Middle Ages* (New York, 1938), *Unity of philosophical experience* (New York, 1938), and *Being and some philosophers* (Toronto, 1949); Gilson is also the chief editor of *Archives d'histoire doctrinale et littéraire du moyen âge* (Paris, 1926 ff.). M. de Wulf, *Histoire de la philosophie médiévale* (7th ed., 3 vols., Louvain, 1947), of which part is available in English translation; E. Bréhier, *La philosophie au moyen âge* (Paris, 1937); and A. Rivaud **Histoire de la philosophie* (Paris, 1950), Vol. II. Some brief histories in English are: B. J. Hawkins, *A sketch of mediaeval philosophy* (London, 1946); S. H. Mellone, *Western Christian thought in the Middle Ages* (Edinburgh, 1935); A. C. McGiffert, *History of Christian thought* (2 vols., New York, 1932–3); S. J. Curtis, *A short history of western philosophy in the Middle Ages* (London, 1950); M. H. Carré, *Realists and nominalists* (Oxford, 1946); F. Copleston, S.J., **Mediaeval philosophy, Augustine to Scotus* (London, 1950); R. McKeon, ed., *Selections from mediaeval philosophers* (2 vols., New York, 1929–30), the best anthology of source material. SPECIAL ASPECTS OF MEDIAEVAL PHILOSOPHY: G. Boas, *Essays on primitivism and related ideas in the Middle Ages* (Baltimore, 1948); R. Lane-Poole, **Illustrations of the history of mediaeval thought* (2nd ed., London, 1920); C. C. J. Webb, **Studies in the history of natural theology* (Oxford, 1915); M. D. Knowles, **"Some recent advances in the history of mediaeval thought"* in *Cambridge historical journal* (1947); F. Solmsen, "Discovery of the syllogism" in *Philosophical review* (1941); P. Boehmer, *Mediaeval logic 1250–1400* (London, 1951). STUDY OF THE BIBLE: B. Smalley, **The study of the Bible in the Middle Ages* (2nd ed., Oxford, 1951); C. Spicq, *Esquisse d'une histoire de l'exégèse latine au moyen âge* (Paris, 1944); G. B. Hatfield, "The Bible in mediaeval civilization" in *Historia Judaica* (1943). PLATO AND ARISTOTLE IN THE MIDDLE AGES: R. Klibansky, *Continuity of the Platonic tradition during the Middle Ages* (London, 1939); H. Kantorowicz, "Plato in the Middle Ages" in *Philosophical review* (1942); A. E. Taylor, *Platonism and its influence* (New York, 1932); G. T. Muckle, "Greek works translated into Latin before 1350" in *Mediaeval studies* (1942); H. Buttenwieser, "Popular authors in the Middle Ages: the testimony of the manuscripts" in *Speculum* (1942); two articles by J. S. Beddie, "Libraries of the twelfth century" in *Haskins anniversary essays* (Boston, 1929), and "The ancient classics in mediaeval libraries" in *Speculum* (1930); J. L. Stocks, *Aristotelianism* (New York, 1925); F. van Steenberghen, *Aristote en Occident* (Louvain, 1946); further references to Aristotle's influence appear above in the bibliographical notes on science in this section.

DOCTRINAL HISTORY. M. Grabmann, **Die Geschichte der Katholischen Theologie* (Freiburg, 1933), the best general account of the history of mediaeval theology; A. H. Thompson, "Mediaeval doctrine to 1215" in *Cambridge mediaeval history*, Vol. VI, a convenient, short account; E. Gilson, **"Doctrinal history and its interpretation"* in *Speculum* (1949), a discussion of questions of editing and interpreting mediaeval theological and philosophical texts.

SPECIAL PERIODS AND INDIVIDUAL PHILOSOPHERS. G. B. Burch, *Early mediaeval philosophers* (New York, 1951), from Erigena through Abelard; J. de Ghellinck, S.J., **Le mouvement théologique du XIIe siècle* (2nd ed., Louvain, 1948); F. Picavet, *Roscelin* (Paris, 1911); C. Filliatre, *La philosophie de Saint Anselme* (Paris, 1920); A. Koyré, *L'idée de Dieu dans la philosophie de St. Anselme* (Paris, 1923); J. G. Sikes, **Abailard* (Cambridge, 1932); J. R. McCallum, *Abelard's Christian theology* (Oxford, 1949); E. Gilson, **Heloise and Abelard*

(Chicago, 1951); J. Cottiaux, "La conception de la théologie chez Abélard," in *Revue d'histoire ecclésiastique* (1932); and C. K. Scott-Moncrieff, tr., *Abelard's letters* (New York, 1926); J. de Ghellinck, S.J., "La carrière de Pierre Lombard" in *Revue d'histoire ecclésiastique* (1931); C. C. J. Webb, *John of Salisbury* (London, 1932); S. Painter, "John of Salisbury and the Renaissance of the twelfth century" in G. Boas, ed., *The Greek tradition* (Baltimore, 1939). REFERENCE WORKS ON PERSONS TEACHING IN OXFORD AND PARIS: D. E. Sharp, *Franciscan philosophy at Oxford* (Oxford, 1930); A. G. Little and F. Peltser, *Oxford theology and theologians 1282–1302* (Oxford, 1934), contains a first-hand account of actual problems discussed; D. A. Callus, "Introduction of Aristotelian learning to Oxford" in *Proceedings of the British Academy* (1943); P. Glorieux, *Répertoire des maîtres en théologie de Paris au XIIIᵉ siècle* (2 vols., Paris, 1933–4), continued in V. Doucet, "Maîtres franciscans de Paris" in *Archivum franciscanum historicum*, Vol. 26. MYSTIC PHILOSOPHERS: E. Gilson, *The mystic theology of St. Bernard* (London, 1940); E. Gilson, *The philosophy of St. Bonaventura* (New York, 1938; new ed. in French, Paris, 1953). LATIN AVERROISTS: P. Mandonnet, *Siger de Brabant et l'averroëisme latin au XIIIᵉ siècle* (2nd ed., Louvain, 1911); F. van Steenbergher, *Siger de Brabant d'après ses oeuvres inédites* (Louvain, 1931), vol. I, supplements Mandonnet; M. Grabmann, *Der Lateinische Averroismus des 13 Jahrhunderts* (Munich, 1931). ALBERTUS MAGNUS AND AQUINAS: A. G. Sertillanges, *Foundations of Thomist philosophy* (London, 1931); M. Grabmann, *Der hl. Albert der Grosse* (Munich, 1932); M. Grabmann, *Aquinas* (New York, 1928); E. Gilson, *The philosophy of Aquinas* (2nd ed., Cambridge, 1939), there is a more recent edition in French (Paris, 1944); M. C. D'Arcy, *Aquinas* (Oxford, 1930); M. de Wulf, *Mediaeval philosophy illustrated from the system of Aquinas* (Cambridge, Mass., 1922); A. Pegis, ed., *The basic writings of Aquinas* (2 vols., New York, 1945). LATER SCHOLASTICS: E. A. Peers, *Ramon Lull* (London, 1929); C. R. S. Harris, *Duns Scotus* (2 vols., Oxford, 1927), considers Duns Scotus "the greatest of mediaeval philosophers"; B. Landry, *Duns Scotus* (Paris, 1922); E. Longprée, *La philosophie de Duns Scotus* (Paris, 1924), attacks Landry; Berand de St. Maurice, *Duns Scotus* (Paris, 1948); E. Gilson, *Jean Duns Scotus* (Paris, 1952). The literature on WILLIAM OF OCKHAM is even more controversial than that on Duns Scotus: E. Moody, *The logic of William of Ockham* (New York, 1935); S. C. Tornay, *The nominalism of William of Ockham* (New York, 1936), and by the same author, *Ockham, studies and selections* (La Salle, Ill., 1938); two articles by A. C. Pegis, *"Concerning William of Ockham" in *Traditio* (1944), and *"Some recent interpretations of Ockham" in *Speculum* (1948); P. Boehmer, "A reply to Pegis" in *Franciscan studies* (1945), attacks the almost universally held conclusion that Ockham was a skeptic; R. Guelluy, *Philosophie et théologie chez Ockham* (Louvain, 1947), minimizes his modernity; L. Baudry, *Guillaume d'Occam* (Paris, 1950), Vol. I.

RENAISSANCE PHILOSOPHIES. J. O. Riedl, ed., *Catalogue of Renaissance philosophers 1350–1650* (Milwaukee, 1940), an excellent reference work; P. O. Kristeller and J. H. Randall, Jr., *"The study of the philosophies of the Renaissance" in *Journal of history of ideas* (1941), a basic bibliographical article. NICHOLAS OF CUSA: M. Patronnier de Gandillac, *La philosophie de Nicolas de Cues* (Paris,

1941); T. Whittaker, *"Nicholas of Cusa" in *Mind* (1925); H. Bett, *Nicholas of Cusa* (London, 1932). ITALIAN PHILOSOPHERS: G. Saitta, *Il pensiero Italiano nell'umanismo e nel Rinascimento* (Bologna, 1949), Vol. I; C. Carbonara, *Il secolo XV* (Milan, 1943); E. Garin, *Filosofi italiani del quattrocento* (Florence, 1942); P. O. Kristeller, *"Humanism and scholasticism in the Italian Renaissance" in *Byzantion* (1945); E. Cassierer and others, eds., *The Renaissance philosophy of man* (Chicago, 1948), a collection of sources with admirable commentary; A. H. Douglas, *The philosophy and psychology of Pomponazzi* (Cambridge, 1910); E. Weil, *"Die Philosophie des Pomponazzi" in *Archiv für Geschichte der Philosophie* (1932). There is a special issue of the *Revue internationale de philosophie* (1951) devoted to the philosophy of the Renaissance, which contains a rich bibliography. FLORENTINE PLATONISTS: N. A. Robb, *Neo-Platonism of the Italian Renaissance* (London, 1935); P. O. Kristeller, *The philosophy of Ficino* (New York, 1943); E. Cassirer, *"Ficino's place in intellectual history" in *Journal of history of ideas* (1945), and by the same author, *"Pico della Mirandola" in *Journal of history of ideas* (1945); P. Kibre, *The library of Pico della Mirandola* (New York, 1936). NEO-SCHOLASTICISM: J. L. Perrier, *The revival of scholastic philosophy* (New York, 1909); J. S. Zybura, *Present day thinkers and the new scholasticism* (2nd ed., St. Louis, 1927); C. A. Hart, ed., *Aspects of the new scholastic philosophy* (New York, 1932); and R. Phillips, *Modern Thomistic philosophy* (London, 1934), a good introduction.

CHAPTER VIII

GENERAL HISTORY OF POLITICAL THOUGHT. P. Janet, *Histoire de la science politique dans ses rapports avec la morale* (3rd ed., 2 vols., Paris, 1887), and G. H. Sabine, *A history of political theory* (3rd ed., New York, 1950), both surveys of high value; F. M. Watkins, *The political tradition of the west* (Cambridge, Mass., 1948); J. W. Gough, *The social contract, a critical study of its development* (Oxford, 1936); H. Higgs, ed., *Palgrave's dictionary of political economy* (3 vols., London, 1923–6); E. R. A. Seligman, ed., *Encyclopedia of the social sciences* (15 vols., New York, 1930–5), extraordinarily useful; F. W. Coker, ed., *Readings in political philosophy* (2nd ed., New York, 1938), a brief collection of texts.

MEDIAEVAL POLITICAL THOUGHT. W. A. Dunning, *A history of political theories, ancient and mediaeval* (New York, 1902), excellent summaries of ideas of main thinkers, little comment; W. H. V. Reade, "Political thought to 1300," and H. Laski, *Political theory in the later Middle Ages" in *Cambridge mediaeval history*, Vols. VI and VIII; two volumes of lectures edited by F. J. C. Hearnshaw, *The social and political ideas of some great mediaeval thinkers* (London, 1923), and *The social and political ideas of some great thinkers of the Renaissance and Reformation* (London, 1925), each essay is on a different thinker, the titles of the different essays are not listed separately in these notes; R. W. and A. J. Carlyle, *History of mediaeval political theory in the west* (6 vols., London, 1903–6), very discursive and uneven, but still an extraordinary work; O. Gierke, *Political theories of the Middle Ages* (Cambridge, 1900), a long essay; C. H. McIlwain, *Growth of political thought in the west* (New York, 1932), the work of a master; A. P. d'Entrèves, *The mediaeval contribution to political thought* (Oxford, 1939). A number of interpretative essays should be noted: J. W. Allen, "Politics" in F. J. C. Hearnshaw, ed., *Mediaeval contributions to modern civilization* (New York, 1922); F.. M. Powicke, "Reflections on the mediaeval state" in *Transactions, Royal Historical Society* (1936); C. H. McIlwain, "Mediaeval institutions in the modern world" in *Speculum* (1941); W. Ullman, "The development of the mediaeval idea of sovereignty" in *English historical review* (1949); A. M. Stickler, "Political theories of the mediaeval canonists" in *Traditio* (1951); E. Lewis, "Natural law and expediency in mediaeval political theory" in *Ethics* (1940); E. Lewis, *"Organic tendencies in mediaeval political thought" in *American political science review* (1938), a study of unusual insight; H. Kohn, *"The dawn of nationalism in Europe" in *American historical review* (1947); E. M. Sanford, "The study of ancient history in the Middle Ages" in *Journal of the history of ideas* (1944).

ST. AUGUSTINE. N. H. Baynes, *The political ideas of Augustine's 'De Civitate Dei'* (London, 1936); J. N. Figgis, *Political aspects of Augustine's City of God* (London, 1921); H. Combès, *La doctrine politique de St. Augustin* (Paris, 1927); H. X. Arquillière, *L'Augustinisme politique* (Paris, 1934).

BACKGROUND OF FEUDALISM. C. Stephenson, *Mediaeval feudalism* (Ithaca, 1942), M. Bloch, *La société féodale* (2 vols., Paris, 1939), and F. L. Ganshof, *Feudalism* (London, 1952), admirable introductions; and four articles: H. A. Cronne, "The origins of feudalism" in *History* (1939); C. Stephenson, "The origin and significance of feudalism" in *American historical review* (1941); F. M. Stenton, "The changing feudalism of the Middle Ages" in *History* (1935); and C. S. Lobingier, "The rise and fall of feudal law" in *Cornell law quarterly* (1933).

ECONOMIC AND SOCIAL DOCTRINE. A. Gray, *The development of economic doctrine* (New York, 1935), the best brief introduction; W. J. Ashley, *"An introduction to English economic history and theory"* (4th ed., 2 vols., London, 1906–9); A. Fanfani, *Storia delle dottrine economiche* (2nd ed., Como, 1939); R. Gonnard, *Histoire des doctrines économiques* (3 vols., Paris, 1927–8); E. Troeltsch, *The social teachings of the Christian churches* (2 vols., New York, 1931), a classic work; the following three works are useful but all three distort mediaeval economic thought to make it too anti-capitalistic: G. O'Brien, *An essay on mediaeval economic teaching* (London, 1920); Bede Jarrett, *Social theories of the Middle Ages 1200–1500* (Boston, 1926); and R. H. Tawney, *Religion and the rise of capitalism* (London, 1926), Ch. 1; C. Gore, ed., *Property, its duties and rights* (2nd ed., 1922), of which two chapters discuss Biblical and mediaeval theories of property; B. N. Nelson, *The idea of usury* (Princeton, 1949), now the best work on the subject; C. F. Taeusch, "History of the concept of usury" in *Journal of the history of ideas* (1942); J. J. Rabinowitz, "Some remarks on the evasion of the usury laws" in *Harvard theological review* (1944); T. P. McLaughlin, "The teaching of the canonists on usury" in *Mediaeval studies* (1939–40); M. Mandonnet, "Albert le grand et les 'Economiques d'Aristotle" in *Archives d'histoire doctrinales et littéraires du moyen âge* (1933); A. P. Evans, "Problem of control in mediaeval industries" in *Political science quarterly* (1921); R. de Roover, "The theory of monopoly prior to Adam Smith, a revision" in *Quarterly journal of economics* (1951); R. Linhardt, *Die Sozialen Prinzipien des hl. Thomas von Aquin* (Freiburg, 1932; E. Schreiber, *Die volkswirtschaftlichen Anschauungen der Scholastik seit Aquinas* (Jena, 1913), a first-rate work; A. E. Monroe, ed., *Early economic thought* (Cambridge, Mass., 1924), a collection of texts.

LAW AND KINGSHIP. H. D. Hazeltine, *Roman and canon law in the Middle Ages" in *Cambridge mediaeval history*, Vol. V; A. H. Chroust, "The function of law and justice in the ancient world and the Middle Ages" in *Journal of the history of ideas* (1946); A. H. Chroust, "The philosophy of law from St. Augustine to St. Thomas Aquinas" in *New Scholasticism* (1946); H. Cairns, *Legal philosophy from Plato to Hegel* (Baltimore, 1949); W. Ullman, *The mediaeval idea of law* (London, 1946); Munro Smith, *The development of European law* (New York, 1928); F. Schulz, *History of Roman legal science* (Oxford, 1946); A. Calisse, *A history of Italian law* (London, 1928); W. Holdsworth, *History of English law* (3rd ed., 12 vols., London, 1924–38); J. Declareuil, *Histoire générale du droit français* (Paris, 1925); H. Brunner, *Deutsche Rechtsgeschichte* (2nd ed., 2 vols., Leipzig, 1906–28); A. d'Entrèves, *Natural law* (London, 1950), a brilliant, brief introduction to the subject; F. Pollock, *"History of the law of nature" in *Essays in the law* (London, 1922); D. Lottin, *Le droit naturel chez St. Thomas et ses prédécesseurs* (Bruges, 1928); P. Vinogradoff, *Roman law in mediaeval Europe* (2nd ed., Oxford, 1929); M. P. Gilmore, *Argument from Roman law in political thought 1200–1600* (Cambridge, Mass., 1941); E. Levy, "Reflections on the first reception of Roman law in Germanic states" in *American historical review* (1942); E. Levy, "The vulgarization of Roman law in the early Middle Ages" in *Medievalia et humanistica* (1943); Q. Breen, "The twelfth century revival of Roman law" in *Oregon law review* (1945); S. Kultner, "The scientific investigation of mediaeval canon law" in *Speculum* (1949); S. Brie, *Die Lehre vom Gewohnheits Recht* (Breslau, 1899), Vol. I; F. Schulz, "Bracton on kingship" in *English historical review* (1945); C. H. McIlwain, *"Bracton" in *Constitutionalism, ancient and modern* (new ed., Ithaca, 1947); F. Kern, *Kingship and law in the Middle Ages* (Oxford, 1939); A. Lane-Poole, *Obligations of society in the 12th and 13th centuries* (Oxford, 1946); L. K. Born, "The perfect prince, a study of 13th and 14th century ideals" in *Speculum*, 1928; G. von Below, *Der deutsche Staat des Mittelalters* (Leipzig, 1914), Vol. I; P. Viollet, *Histoire des institutions politiques et administratives de la France* (3 vols., Paris, 1890–1903), Vol. II.

CONTROVERSIES BETWEEN CHURCH AND STATE 500–1200 A.D. R. Hull, *Mediaeval theories of the papacy* (London, 1934); K. Voigt, *Staat und Kirche von Konstantin bis zum Ende der Karolingerzeit* (Stuttgart, 1936); V. Martin, *Les origines du gallicanisme* (2 vols., Paris, 1939), contains a full discussion of theories from Gregory VII on; W. Ullman, *Mediaeval papalism, the political theories of the canonists* (London, 1949); A. Fliche, *La querelle des investitures* (Paris, 1946); P. Fournier, "Etudes sur les fausses décrétals" in *Revue d'histoire ecclésiastique* (1906–7); H. X. Arquillière, "Sur la formation de la théocratie pontificale" in *Mélanges d'histoire du moyen âge offerts à M. Lot* (Paris, 1925); Z. N. Brooke, "Gregory VII" in *Cambridge mediaeval history*, Vol. V; G. Tellenbach, *Church, state, and Christian society at the time of the investiture contest* (Oxford, 1940); C. Mirbt, *Die Publizistik im Zeitalter Gregors VII* (Leipzig, 1894), a basic work which is well summarized in P. Imbart de la Tour, *La polémique et les publicistes à l'époque de Grégoire VII* (Paris, 1907); P. Jaochimsen, "The Investiture Contest and the German constitution" in G. Barraclough, ed., *Mediaeval Germany 911–1250* (2 vols., Oxford, 1938); E. Voosen, *Papauté et pouvoir civil à l'époque de Grégoire VII* (Gembloux, 1927); J. P. Whitney, *Hildebrandine essays* (Cambridge, 1932); G. B. Borino, *Studia Gregoriana* (2 vols., Rome, 1947); H. X. Arquillière, *Grégoire VII, essai sur sa conception du pouvoir pontifical* (Paris, 1934); and E. Bernheim, ed., *Quellen zur Geschichte des Investiturstreits* (2nd ed., Leipzig, 1913), a collection of documents; C. C. J. Webb, *John of Salisbury* (London, 1932); H. Liebeschütz, *Mediaeval humanism in the life and writings of John of Salisbury* (London, 1950), the *Policraticus* is partly translated by *J. Dickinson (New York, 1927), with interesting introduction, and partly by J. B. Pike (Minneapolis, 1938).

FROM 1200 TO THE CONCILIAR MOVEMENT. E. F. Jacob, "Innocent III" in *Cambridge mediaeval history*, Vol. VI; M. Grabmann, *"Studien über den Einfluss der aristotelischen Philosophie auf die mittelalterlichen Theorien über das Verhältnis von Kirche und Staat" in *Sitzungsberichte der Bayrischen Akademie der Wissenschaften* (1934); R. Lane-Poole, *Illustrations of the history of mediaeval thought and learning* (2nd ed., London, 1920); B. Roland-Gosselin, *La doctrine politique de Saint Thomas d'Aquin* (Paris, 1928); A. d'Entrèves, ed., *Aquinas, political writings* (Oxford, 1948); W. H. V. Reade, "The political theory of Dante" in E. Moore, ed., *Dante's De Monarchia* (Oxford, 1916); A. d'Entrèves, *Dante as a political thinker* (London, 1952); C. S. Woolf, *Bartolus of Sassoferrato* (Cambridge, 1913), brilliant and penetrating; G. de Lagarde, *La naissance de l'esprit laïque au déclin du moyen âge* (6 vols., St. Paul-Trois Chateaux, 1934–46); J. Rivière, *Le problème de l'église et de l'état au temps de Philippe le Bel* (Louvain, 1926); W. L. Brandt, "Pierre Dubois, modern or mediaeval?" in *American historical review* (1930); A. Kämpf, *Pierre Dubois* (Berlin, 1935); C. K. Brampton and C. Previté-Orton, *"Marsiglio of Padua" in *English historical review* (1922–3); two articles by R. Scholz, *"Marsilius von Padua" in *Historische Zeitschrift* (1936), and "Marsilius von Padua und die Genesis des moderne Staatsbewusstseins" in *Historische Zeitschrift* (1937); there is a translation of the *Defensor pacis* and also a treatise on Marsiglio, both by A. Gewirth (2 vols., New York, 1951); L. Baudry, "La philosophie et la politique dans Ockham" in *Archives d'historie doctrinale et littéraire du moyen âge* (1939); M. A. Shepherd, *"William of Occam and the higher law" in *American political science review* (1932); R. Scholz, *Wilhelm von Ockham als politischer Denker* (Leipzig, 1944); C. C. Bayley, "Pivotal concepts in the political philosophy of Ockham" in *Journal of the history of ideas* (1949); B. L. Manning, "Wyclif" in *Cambridge mediaeval history*, Vol. VII; H. B. Workman, *Wyclif* (2 vols., Oxford, 1926).

CONCILIAR MOVEMENT. J. N. Figgis, *Political thought from Gerson to Grotius* (2nd ed., Cambridge, 1916), an original and basic work; E. F. Jacob,

Essays in the conciliar epoch (2nd ed., Manchester, 1951); two articles by H. X. Arquillière, "L'origine des théories conciliaires" in *Séances et travaux de l'académie des sciences morales et politiques* (1911), and "L'Appel au concile sous Philippe le Bel" in *Revue des questions historiques* (1911); J. T. McNeill, "The emergence of conciliarism" in J. L. Cate and E. N. Anderson, eds., *Essays in honor of James Westfall Thompson* (Chicago, 1938); L. R. Loomis, "Nationality at the Council of Constance" in *American historical review* (1939); J. L. Connolly, *Gerson* (Louvain, 1938); H. Bett, *Nicholas of Cusa* (London, 1932); E. Vansteenberghe, *Nicolas de Cues* (Paris, 1920); A. Posch, *Die 'Concordantia' des Nikalaus von Cusa* (Paderborn, 1930).

ITALY IN THE LATER MIDDLE AGES. E. Emerton, *Humanism and tyranny, studies in the Italian trecento* (Cambridge, Mass., 1925); D. Cantimori, "Rhetoric and politics in Italian humanism" in *Journal of the Warburg Institute* (1937); and E. W. Nelson, "Origins of modern balance of power politics" in *Medievalia et humanistica* (1943).

FORTESCUE AND HIS GENERAL BACKGROUND. C. H. McIlwain, *"Mediaeval estates" in *Cambridge mediaeval history*, Vol. VII; G. Post, *"Plena potestas and consent in mediaeval assemblies" in *Traditio* (1943); H. Mitteis, *Der Staat des Hohen Mittelalters* (2nd ed., Weimar, 1944), a valuable, comparative constitutional history; S. B. Chrimes, *English constitutional ideas in the fifteenth century* (Cambridge, 1936); M. A. Shepherd, "The political and constitutional theory of Fortescue" in C. F. Wittke, ed., *Essays in honor of C. H. McIlwain* (Cambridge, Mass., 1936); E. F. Jacob, "Fortescue and the law of nature" in *Bulletin of the John Rylands library* (1934); F. Gilbert, Fortescue's 'dominium regale et politicum' " in *Mediaevalia et humanistica* (1944), C. J. Skeel, "The influence of the writings of Fortescue" in *Transactions, Royal historical society* (1916); the standard editions of Fortescue are C. Plummer, ed., *Governance of England* (Oxford, 1885), and S. B. Chrimes, ed., *De laudibus Legum Anglie* (Cambridge, 1942).

MEDIAEVAL SCHOOLS. GENERAL WORKS: H. J. Marrou, *Histoire de l'éducation dans l'antiquité* (2nd ed., Paris, 1950), excellent compend, comes down into early Middle Ages; P. Monroe, ed., *A cyclopedia of education* (4 vols., New York, 1911–13); Foster Watson, ed., *An encyclopedia of education* (4 vols., London, 1921–2); M. Deanesly, *"Mediaeval schools to ca. 1300," and G. H. Potter, *"Education in the 14th and 15th centuries," in *Cambridge mediaeval history*, Vols. V and VIII, an admirable survey; F. P. Graves, *History of education during the Middle Ages* (New York, 1910); E. P. Pride, "Ecclesiastical legislation on education 300–1200" in *Church history* (1943); P. Abelson, *The seven liberal arts* (New York, 1906); L. Maître, *Les écoles épiscopales et monastiques en Occident 768–1180* (Paris, 1924), and E. Lesne, *Les écoles de la fin du VIIIe siècle à la fin du XIIe siècle* (Paris, 1940), two very good studies; L. Thorndike, "Elementary and secondary education in the Middle Ages" in *Speculum* (1940); G. G. Coulton, "From school to university" in *Mediaeval panorama* (Cambridge, 1939); G. Manacorda, *Storia della scuola in Italia, il medio evo* (2 vols., Milan, 1914); J. E. Sandys, *A history of classical scholarship* (3rd ed., Cambridge, 1920), Vol. I; J. Adhémar, *Les influences antiques dans l'art du moyen âge français* (London, 1939), the first three chapters are an admirable survey of the study and use of Latin writers, 5th–15th centuries. MORE SPECIALIZED STUDIES: M. Roger, *L'enseignement des lettres classiques d'Ausone à Alcuin* (Paris, 1905), a classic work; P. R. Cole, *Later Latin education in Ausonius, Capella, and the Theodosian Code* (New York, 1909); T. Haarhoff, *Schools of Gaul in the last century of the Western Empire* (Oxford, 1920); G. Bardy, "L'église et l'enseignement, 1–4 siècles" in *Revue des sciences religieuses* (1932–5); U. Berlière, "Les écoles claustrales au moyen âge" in *Bulletin de l'académie royale de Belgique, classes des lettres* (1921); G. G. Coulton, "Monastic schools in the Middle Ages" in *Mediaeval studies* (London, 1913); G. G. Coulton, "Religious education before the Reformation" in *Ten mediaeval studies* (3rd ed., Cambridge, 1930); A. Franklin, *La vie privée d'autrefois, écoles et collèges* (Paris, 1892); G. Paré and others, *La renaissance du XIIᵉ siècle, les écoles et l'enseignement*, a basic work; P. Delhaye, "L'organisation scolaire au XIIᵉ siècle" in *Traditio* (1947); R. Limmer, *Bildungszustände und Bildungsideen des 13 Jahrhunderts* (Munich, 1928); A. H. Thompson, *Song schools of the Middle Ages* (London, 1942). LITERACY: J. W. Thompson, *The literacy of the laity in the Middle Ages* (Berkeley, 1936); V. H. Galbraith, "The literacy of the English kings" in *Proceedings of the British Academy* (1935); J. W. Adamson, *The illiterate Anglo-Saxon and other essays* (Cambridge, 1946); J. W. Adamson, "The extent of literacy in England in the 15th and 16th centuries" in *The Library* (1930). GRAMMAR AND RHETORIC: C. S. Baldwin, *Mediaeval rhetoric and poetic* (New York, 1928); R. H. Robbins, *Ancient and mediaeval grammatical theory* (London, 1951); R. McKeon, "Rhetoric in the Middle Ages" in *Speculum* (1942); C. H. Haskins, *"The early artes dictandi in Italy"* in *Studies in mediaeval culture* (Oxford, 1929); H. Wieruszowski, "Ars dictaminis in the time of Dante" in *Medievalia et humanistica* (1943). EDUCATION OF WOMEN: C. Jourdain, Mémoire sur l'éducation des femmes au moyen âge" in *Excursions historiques et philosophiques* (Paris, 1888). ENGLISH SCHOOLS: A. F. Leach, *Schools of mediaeval England* (2nd ed., London, 1916); Foster Watson, *The English grammar schools to 1600* (Cambridge, 1908); G. A. Plimpton, *The education of Chaucer* (Oxford, 1935); C. P. McMahon, *Education in 15th century England* (Baltimore, 1947). NEW TYPES OF SCHOOLS AFTER 1400: W. H. Woodward, *Vittorino da Feltre and other humanist educators* (Cambridge, 1897); W. H. Woodward, *Studies in education 1400–1600* (Cambridge, 1906); cf. also references under humanism, Chapter XII. LIBRARIES: J. W. Thompson, *The mediaeval library* (Chicago, 1939); F. Milkau and G. Leyh, *Geschichte der Bibliotheken* (2 vols., Leipzig, 1940), the fundamental work; J. de Ghellinck, "Progrès récents en histoire des bibliothèques" in *Revue d'histoire ecclésiastique* (1942); N. R. Ker, *Mediaeval libraries of Great Britain* (London, 1941). CATHEDRAL SCHOOLS: A. Clerval, *Les écoles de Chartres au moyen âge* (Paris, 1895); D. D. McGarry, "Educational theory in the 'Metalogicon' of John of Salisbury" in *Speculum* (1948); L. J. Paetow, ed., *Battle of the seven arts* (Berkeley, 1914); C. H. Haskins, "A list of textbooks from the close of the twelfth century" in *Studies in the history of mediaeval science* (Cambridge, Mass., 1924); R. F. Seybolt and P. Monroe, eds., *Autobiography of Butzbach* (Ann Arbor, 1933), a fascinating document.

UNIVERSITIES. S. d'Irsay, *Histoire des universités* (2 vols., Paris, 1933–5), and H. Rashdall, *The universities of Europe in the Middle Ages* (2nd ed., 3 vols., Oxford, 1936), both works of great value; also cf. the older H. Denifle, *Die Enstehung der Universitäten des Mittelalters* (Berlin, 1888); C. H. Haskins, *The rise of universities* (New York, 1923), three brilliant, brief lectures; H. Rashdall, "The mediaeval universities" in *Cambridge mediaeval history*, Vol. VI, a convenient summary of Rashdall's ideas; A. O. Norton, *Readings in the history of education, mediaeval universities* (Cambridge, Mass., 1909); L. Thorndike, ed., *University records and life in the Middle Ages* (New York, 1944), a collection of documents in translation; L. J. Paetow, *The arts course at mediaeval universities* (Champaign, 1910); P. Kibre, *The nations in mediaeval universities* (Cambridge, Mass., 1948); several essays in F. M. Powicke, *Ways of mediaeval life and thought* (London, 1950); F. M. Powicke, "Some problems in history of the mediaeval university" in *The Christian life in the Middle Ages and other essays* (Oxford, 1935); L. Halphen, "Les universités au XIIIᵉ siècle" in *Revue historique* (1931); P. O. Kristeller, *"The school of Salerno" in *Bulletin of the history of medicine* (1945); A. Sorbelli, *Storia della università di Bologna* (Florence, 1940), Vol. I; H. Denifle, ed., *Cartularium universitatis Parisiensis* (4 vols., Paris, 1889–97), continued by Van Moé and others (Paris, 1935–8), basic documents on the University of Paris 1163–1452; also cf. M. Fournier, *Les statuts des universités françaises* (4 vols., Paris, 1890–4); C. Gross, "The political influence of the University of Paris in the Middle Ages" in the *American historical review* (1901); C. E. Mallet, *A history of the University of Oxford* (3 vols., London, 1924–8); J. B. Mullinger, *The University of Cambridge* (2 vols., Cambridge, 1873–84); R. Dumoulin-Eckart, *Geschichte der deutschen Universitäten* (Stuttgart, 1929); G. Reynier, *La vie universitaire dans l'ancienne Espagne* (Paris, 1902); J. B. Coissac, *Les universités d'Ecosse* (Paris, 1915). STUDENT LIFE: three essays by C. H. Haskins, "Life of mediaeval students as seen in their letters," "The University of Paris in the sermons of the 13th century," and *"Manuals for students," all in *Studies in mediaeval culture* (Oxford, 1929); R. F. Seybolt, *Renaissance student life* (Urbana, 1927); R. F. Seybolt, ed., *Manuale scholarium* (Cambridge, Mass., 1921); A. S. Rait, *Life in the mediaeval university* (Cambridge, 1912).

CHAPTER IX

The bibliographical notes for this chapter and the next (Chapter X) should be considered together.

GENERAL WORKS. BIBLIOGRAPHIES: F. Baldensperger and W. P. Friederich, *Bibliography of comparative literature* (Chapel Hill, 1950); C. P. Farrar and A. P. Evans, *Bibliography of English translations of mediaeval sources* (New York, 1946); H. Hermannsson, *Old Icelandic literature* (Ithaca, 1933); R. I. Best, *A bibliography of Irish philology and printed literature* (Dublin, 1913); F. W. Bateson, *The Cambridge bibliography of English literature* (Cambridge, 1941), Vol. I; U. T. Holmes, *A critical bibliography of French literature, the mediaeval period* (Syracuse, 1947); R. Bossuat, *Manuel bibliographique de la littérature française du moyen âge* (Melun, 1951); J. Körner, *Bib-*

liographisches Handbuch des Deutschen Schrifttums (Bern, 1949); B. Q. Morgan, *A critical bibliography of German literature in English translation* (2nd ed., Palo Alto, 1938). DICTIONARIES, ANTHOLOGIES, AND GENERAL HISTORIES: L. Magnus, *A dictionary of European literature* (2nd ed., London, 1927); A. Franklin, *Dictionnaire des noms, surnoms, et pseudonymes Latins de l'histoire littéraire du moyen âge 1100–1520* (Paris, 1875); L. Spence, *Dictionary of mediaeval romance and romance writers* (London, 1913); H. L. Ward and J. A. Herbert, *Catalogue of romances in the British Museum* (3 vols., London, 1883–1910); A. Langfors, *Les incipits des poèmes français antérieurs au XVIᵉ siècle* (Paris, 1917), Vol. I; E. Langlois, *Table des noms propres de toute nature compris dans les chansons de gestes imprimées* (Paris, 1904); W. Stammler and K. Langosch, *Die deutsche Literatur des Mittelalters, Verfasser-lexicon* (3 vols., Berlin, 1931–43); C. W. Jones, ed., **Mediaeval literature in translation* (New York, 1950); H. H. Blanchard, ed., **Prose and poetry of the continental Renaissance in translation* (New York, 1949); L. Olschki, **Die romanischen Literaturen des Mittelalters* (Potsdam, 1928), covers all literatures in Romance languages; M. Edwardes, **A summary of the literatures of modern Europe to 1400* (London, 1907); A. Ebert, *Histoire générale de la littérature du moyen âge* (3 vols., Paris, 1883–4), only goes into 11th century; L. Magnus, *The centuries of romance* (London, 1918); H. Hallam, *Introduction to the literature of Europe in the 15th, 16th and 17th centuries* (2 vols., New York, 1854); G. Cohen, **"Le mouvement intellectuel, moral et littéraire"* in H. Pirenne and others, *La civilisation occidentale au moyen âge, XIᵉ–XVᵉ siècles* (Paris, 1933); N. Ségur, *Histoire de la littérature Européenne*, Vol. II, *Moyen âge et Renaissance* (Paris, 1949); these two surveys are the only ones that systematically combine Latin and vernacular literatures. L. Réau and G. Cohen, **L'art du moyen âge (arts plastiques, art littéraire) et la civilisation française* (Paris, 1935); R. Schneider and G. Cohen, *La formation du génie moderne dans l'art de l'Occident (arts plastiques, art littéraire)* (Paris, 1936), both confined largely to France.

INTRODUCTIONS TO LITERATURE IN VARIOUS LANGUAGES. M. Manitius, **Geschichte der lateinischen Literatur des Mittelalters* (3 vols., Munich, 1911–31), stops in twelfth century; F. A. Wright and T. A. Sinclair, *A history of later Latin literature* (London, 1931); J. Ghellinck, **L'essor de la littérature latine au XIIᵉ siècle* (2 vols., Brussels, 1946); J. Vendryès and others, **Les religions des Celtes, Germains, et Slavs* (Paris, 1948); J. A. MacCulloch, *The Celtic and Scandinavian religions* (London, 1948); M. Dillon, **Early Irish literature* (Chicago, 1948); R. Flower, *The Irish tradition* (Oxford, 1947); M. L. Sjoestedt, *Gods and heroes of the Celts* (London, 1949); S. O. Súilleabháin, *Handbook of Irish folklore* (Dublin, 1942); H. Jackson, ed., **A celtic miscellany* (London, 1951); T. P. Ellis and J. Lloyd, trs., *The Mabinogion* (2 vols., Oxford, 1929); G. Bach and others, *History of the Scandinavian literatures* (New York, 1938); E. Bredsdorff and others, *An introduction to Scandinavian literatures* (Cambridge, 1951); A. Tilley, ed., **Mediaeval France, a companion to French studies* (Cambridge, 1922); K. Voretsch, *Introduction to the study of old French literature* (New York, 1931); U. T. Holmes, **A history of old French literature* (2nd ed., New York, 1948); R. Bossuat, *Histoire de la littérature française, le moyen âge* (Paris, 1931); H. A. Hatzfeld, **Literature through art* (New York, 1952), a new approach to French literature 1100–1940; F. P. Wilson and B. Dobrée, eds., *Oxford history of English literature* (Oxford, 1945 ff.), still incomplete; A. C. Baugh and others, *A literary history of England* (New York, 1948); W. L. Renwick and H. Orton, *The beginnings of English literature to Skelton* (2nd ed., London, 1950); R. M. Wilson, *The lost literature of mediaeval England* (London, 1952); H. S. Bennett, *English books and readers, 1475–1557* (Cambridge, 1952); J. Bithell, ed., *Germany, a companion to German studies* (London, 1932); J. G. Robertson, *History of German literature* (new ed., London, 1947); H. De Boor, *Geschichte der deutschen Literatur, Vol. I, 770–1170* (Munich, 1949, more vols. promised); E. Gardner, *Italy, a companion to Italian studies* (London, 1934); A. Pompeati, *Storia della letteratura italiana* (2 vols., Turin, 1946); H. Hauvette, *La littérature italienne* (6th ed., Paris, 1924); R. A. Hall, Jr., *A short history of Italian literature* (Ithaca, 1951); A. Gaspary, *History of early Italian literature to the death of Dante* (London, 1901); G. Bertoni, *Il Duecento* (2nd ed., Milan, 1930); N. Spageno, *Il Trecento* (3rd ed., Milan, 1942); V. Rossi, *Il Quattrocento* (2nd ed., Milan, 1933); E. A. Peers, ed., *Spain, a companion to Spanish studies* (4th ed., London, 1948); E. Mérimée and S. G. Morley, *History of Spanish literature* (New York, 1930); and G. Brenan, *The literature of the Spanish people* (Cambridge, 1951).

FOLKLORE. H. A. Guerber, *Legends of the Middle Ages* (New York, 1896); S. Thompson, *The folk tale* (New York, 1946); S. Thompson, *Motif-index of folk literature* (6 vols., Bloomington, 1932–6); C. G. Loomis, *White magic, an introduction to the folk lore of Christian legend* (Cambridge, Mass., 1948), concerns only saints legends; and M. Leach, ed., *Standard dictionary of folk-lore, mythology, and legend* (2 vols., New York, 1949–50), a very valuable work.

THE EPIC TRADITION. M. Bowra, *Heroic poetry* (London, 1952); B. S. Phillpots, *Edda and saga* (London, 1931); H. Koht, *The old Norse sagas* (New York, 1931); H. G. Leach, ed., *A pageant of old Scandinavia* (Princeton, 1946); H. A. Bellows, tr., *The poetic Edda* (New York, 1923); A. C. Brodeur, tr., *The prose Edda* (New York, 1916); E. Tonnelat, *La chanson des Nibelungen* (Strasbourg, 1926); K. Bartsch, ed., *Nibelungenlied* (8th ed., Leipzig, 1923); D. B. Shumway, tr., *Nibelungenlied* (Boston, 1909); M. Armour, tr., *Gudrun* (New York, 1949); C. H. Bell, ed., *Peasant life in old German epics* (New York, 1931), three useful translations; J. Crosland, *The old French epic* (Oxford, 1951); J. Bédier, *Les légendes épiques* (3rd ed., 4 vols., Paris, 1926–9), the great classic work on the French epics, though all of its conclusions are no longer accepted; J. Siciliano, *Les origines des chansons de geste* (Paris, 1951) presents recent views; J. Horrent, *La chanson de Roland dans les littératures française et espagnole au moyen âge* (Paris, 1951); E. Lewis, "Personality in the chansons de geste" in *Philological quarterly* (1936); M. A. Pei, *French precursors of the Chanson de Roland* (New York, 1948); C. A. Knudson, "The problem of the Chanson de Roland" in *Romance philology* (1950); I. Butler, tr., *The Song of Roland* (Boston, 1904), a fine translation; R. Folz, *Le Souvenir de Charlemagne dans l'Empire Germanic médiéval* (Paris, 1950); J. Bédier, *Les chansons de croisade* (Paris, 1909); A. Hatem, *Les poèmes épiques des Croisades* (Paris, 1932); H. J. Chaytor, *The Provençal chanson de geste*

(London, 1946); E. Lévi-Provençal, "Le Cid et l'histoire" in *Revue historique* (1937); R. Menendez-Pidal, *The Cid and his Spain* (London, 1934); A. M. Huntington, tr., *Poem of the Cid* (3 vols., New York, 1921).

BALLADS. W. J. Entwistle, *European balladry* (Oxford, 1939); G. Gerould, *The Ballad of tradition* (Oxford, 1932); and M. J. C. Hodgart, *The ballads* (London, 1950).

CHIVALRY. C. Stephenson, *Mediaeval feudalism* (Ithaca, 1942); A. Abram, "Chivalry" in *Cambridge mediaeval history*, Vol. VI; E. Prestage, ed., *Chivalry* (London, 1928); S. Painter, *French chivalry* (Baltimore, 1940); G. Cohen, *Histoire de la chevalerie en France au moyen âge* (Paris, 1949); R. L. Kilgour, *The decline of chivalry* (Cambridge, Mass., 1937); H. Dupin, *La courtoisie au moyen âge d'après les textes du XIIᵉ et du XIIIᵉ siècle* (Paris, 1931); C. Ffoulkes, *European arms and armour* (London, 1932); F. H. Cripps-Day, *History of the tournament in England and France* (London, 1918); R. C. Clephan, *The tournament* (London, 1919); N. Denholm-Young, "The tournament in the 13th century" in R. W. Hunt, ed., *Studies in mediaeval history presented to Powicke* (Oxford, 1949); R. H. Cline, "The influences of romances on tournaments" in *Speculum* (1945).

LYRIC POETRY. SOME ANTHOLOGIES: S. Gaselee, ed., *The Oxford book of mediaeval Latin verse* (new ed., Oxford, 1937); H. Waddell, tr., *Mediaeval Latin lyrics* (London, 1929); J. Lindsay, tr., *Mediaeval Latin poets* (London, 1934); F. Brittain, ed., *The mediaeval Latin and Romance lyric to 1300* (2nd ed., Cambridge, 1951); for further translations of hymns cf. *The English hymnal* (many editions), and *Hymns, ancient and modern* (new ed., London, 1950). LATIN POETRY: The two works by F. J. E. Raby, *History of Christian Latin poetry* (Oxford, 1927), and *History of secular Latin poetry in the Middle Ages* (2 vols., Oxford, 1934), are indispensable; cf. also R. de Gourmont, *Le Latin mystique* (new ed., Paris, 1912). Two stimulating works whose conclusions have not been widely accepted are by P. S. Allen, *The romanesque lyric* (Chapel Hill, N. C., 1928) and *Mediaeval Latin lyrics* (Chicago, 1931). HYMNS: J. Julian, *Dictionary of hymnology* (rev. ed., London, 1908); S. Singer, *Die religiöse Lyrik des Mittelalters* (Bern, 1933), on both Latin and vernacular religious poetry; A. K. MacGilton, *A study of Latin hymns* (Boston, 1918); M. Britt, ed., *The hymns of the breviary and missal* (rev. ed., New York, 1936); R. E. Messenger, "Recent studies in mediaeval Latin hymns" in *Trans. Amer. Philol. Ass.* (1940); W. J. Ong, "Wit and mystery, a reevalulation in mediaeval Latin hymnody" in *Speculum* (1947); W. B. Sedgwick, "Origin of rhyme" in *Revue Bénédictine* (1924); D. S. Wrangham, tr., *The liturgical poetry of Adam of St. Victor* (3 vols., London, 1881); G. Wdzieczy, "Life and works of Thomas of Celano" in *Franciscan Studies* (1945). GOLIARDS: H. Brinkmann, *Geschichte der lateinischen Liebesdichtung im Mittelalter* (Halle, 1925); M. Manitius, *Vagantenlieder* (Jena, 1927); O. Dobiache-Rojdesvensky, *Les poésies des Goliards* (Paris, 1931); J. H. Hanford, "The progenitors of Golias" in *Speculum* (1926); J. L. Heller, "A note on the confession of Golias" in *Speculum* (1933); two remarkable volumes of translation: J. A. Symonds, tr., *Wine, women and song* (London, 1925), and G. F. Whicher, tr., *The Goliard poets* (Norfolk, 1949).

VERNACULAR LYRICS. TROUBADOURS: C. S. Lewis, *The allegory of love* (Oxford, rev. ed., 1938); R. R. Bezzola, *Les origines et la formation de la littérature courtoise 500–1200, Pt. I to 1100 A.D.* (Paris, 1944); A. J. Denomy, *Heresy of courtly love* (New York, 1947), all general works covering several branches of literature; A. Pillet and H. Carstens, eds., *Bibliographie der troubadours* (Halle, 1933); J. Boutière and A. Schutz, eds., *Biographies des troubadours* (Toulouse, 1950); A. Jeanroy, *La poésie lyrique des troubadours* (2 vols., Paris, 1934), a basic work; A. Jeanroy, *Histoire sommaire de la poésie occitane* (Paris, 1945), a brief introduction; J. Anglade, *Histoire sommaire de la littérature méridonale au moyen âge* (Paris, 1921), covers all southern French literature including poetry; H. J. Chaytor, *The troubadours* (Cambridge, 1912), and J. Anglade, *Les troubadours* (2nd ed., Paris, 1919), two popular introductions; K. Axhausen, *Die Theorien über den Ursprung der Provenzalischen Lyrik* (Düsseldorf, 1937), and G. Errante, *Sulla lirica romanza della origine* (New York, 1943), survey all the theories of origins of troubadour poetry; E. Rodeti, "Critical principles of the troubadours" in *American bookman* (1944); S. Stronski, *La poésie et la réalité aux temps des troubadours* (Oxford, 1943); G. von Grunebaum, "The Arab contribution to troubadour poetry" in *Bulletin of the Iranian Institute* (1946); the literature on the possible Arab influences on troubadour poetry is too extensive to summarize here; G. Paris, "Les cours d'amours du moyen âge" in *Mélanges de littérature française du moyen âge* (Paris, 1912), best summary of arguments for and against existence of courts of love. A few texts: R. T. Hill and T. G. Bergin, eds., *Anthology of Provencal troubadours* (New Haven, 1941); I. Farnell, *Lives of the troubadours* (London, 1896); J. H. Smith, *The troubadours at home* (2 vols., New York, 1890); and B. Smythe, tr., *Troubadour poets* (London, 1911); the last three contain excellent translations. H. J. Chaytor, *The troubadours and England* (Cambridge, 1923), and J. Audian, *Les troubadours et l'Angleterre* (new ed., Paris, 1937), show troubadour influence on one country. TROUVÈRES: A. Jeanroy, *Les origines de la poésie lyrique en France au moyen âge* (3rd ed., Paris, 1925), a basic work; C. C. Abbott, tr., *Early mediaeval French lyrics* (London, 1932); W. P. Jones, *The pastourelle* (Cambridge, Mass., 1931); J. J. Parry, tr., *The art of courtly love of Andreas Capellanus* (New York, 1941); T. Silverstein, *"Andreas, Plato and the Arabs"* in *Modern philology* (1949). GERMAN LYRIC: A. Moret, *Les débuts du lyrisme en allemagne (à 1350)* (Paris, 1951); M. F. Richey, *Essays on the mediaeval German love lyric* (Oxford, 1943); A. Closs, *The genius of the German lyric* (London, 1938); N. Naumann, *Die Minnesänger* (Leipzig, n.d.), with colored illuminations of the Manesse manuscript at Heidelburg; W. Stammler, *Die deutsche Dichtung 1400–1600* (2nd ed., Stuttgart, 1950), a great work; three translations of Minnesinger are: F. C. Nicholson, tr., *Old German love songs* (Chicago, 1907); J. Bithell, tr., *The minnesingers* (London, 1909); and W. A. Phillips, tr., *Walther von der Vogelweide, selected poems* (London, 1896); on meistersingers cf. A. Taylor, *The literary history of meistergesang* (Oxford, 1937). ENGLISH LYRICS: 3 volumes by C. F. Brown, ed., *English lyrics of the 13th century* (Oxford, 1932); *Religious lyrics of the 14th century* (Oxford, 1924), and *Religious lyrics of the 15th century* (Oxford, 1939); A. K. Moore, *The secular lyric in Middle English*

(Lexington, Ky., 1951); and R. H. Robbins, ed., *Secular lyrics of the 14th and 15th centuries* (Oxford, 1952). ITALIAN POETS: two important articles by E. H. Wilkins, "The invention of the sonnet" and *"The derivation of the canzone" in *Modern philology* (1915); E. F. Langley, *The poetry of Giacomo da Lentino* (Cambridge, Mass., 1935); J. E. Shaw, *Cavalcanti's theory of love* (Toronto, 1949); D. G. Rossetti, tr., *Early Italian poets* (London, many eds.); Villon: L. Cons, *L'état présent des études sur Villon* (Paris, 1936); two studies by P. Champion, *Histoire poétique du XVᵉ siècle* (2 vols., Paris, 1927), and *Villon* (2nd ed., 2 vols., Paris, 1933); E. F. Chaney, *Villon and his environment* (Oxford, 1947); J. Siciliano, *Villon et les thèmes poétiques du moyen âge* (Paris, 1934), a fundamental work. ITALIAN LYRIC POETS OF 14TH AND 15TH CENTURIES: J. B. Fletcher, *Literature of the Italian Renaissance* (New York, 1934); N. A. Robb, *Neo-Platonism of the Italian Renaissance* (London, 1935); P. Van Tieghem, *La littérature Latine de la Renaissance* (Paris, 1944); E. H. Wilkins, "An introductory Petrarch bibliography" in *Philological quarterly* (1948), and by the same author, *Petrarchian studies* (Rome, 1951); H. Hauvette, *Les poésies lyriques de Pétrarque* (Paris, 1931); A. Lipari, *The dolce stil nuovo according to Lorenzo de' Medici* (New Haven, 1936).

CHIVALRIC ROMANCES. A. B. Taylor, *An introduction to mediaeval romance* (London, 1930), of great usefulness; J. D. Bruce, *The evolution of Arthurian romance* (2nd ed., 2 vols., Göttingen, 1928); the literature on Arthurian romance is enormous and very controversial; a bibliography of the year's work appears each year in the *Modern language quarterly*; among some of the important works are E. Faral, *La légende arthurienne, études et documents* (3 vols., Paris, 1929); M. Wilmotte, *Origines du roman en France* (Brussels, 1940); R. S. Loomis, *Arthurian tradition and Chrétien de Troyes* (New York, 1949); and J. S. Tatlock, *The legendary history of Britain* (Cambridge, Mass., 1950); J. Marx, *La légende Arthurienne et le graal* (Paris, 1952); J. Bédier, "Les lais de Marie de France" in *Revue des deux mondes* (Vol. 107); G. Cohen, *Chrétien de Troyes* (new ed., Paris, 1948); W. W. Comfort, tr., *Arthurian romances of Chrétien de Troyes* (London, n.d.); G. Paré, *Les idées et les lettres au XIIIᵉ siècle; le Roman de la Rose* (Montreal, 1947); A. M. Gunn, *The mirror of love, a reinterpretation of the 'Roman de la rose'* (Lubbock, Texas, 1952); F. S. Ellis, tr., *Romance of the rose* (3 vols., London, 1900); J. Anglade, ed., *Le roman de Flamenca* (Paris, 1926); M. F. Richey, *The story of Parzival and the grail* (Oxford, 1935); S. O. Andrew, tr., *Sir Gawain and the green knight* (London, 1929); E. Vinaver, ed., *The works of Sir Thomas Malory* (3 vols., Oxford, 1947), with valuable introduction; R. S. Loomis, *Arthurian legends in mediaeval art* (Oxford, 1938); E. Gardner, *The Arthurian legend in Italian literature* (New York, 1930); W. J. Entwistle, *The Arthurian legend in the literatures of the Spanish peninsula* (London, 1925); C. S. Northrup and J. Parry, "The Arthurian legends, modern retellings, a bibliography" in *Jour. of Eng. & Ger. philology* (1944); W. A. Nitze, *Arthurian romance and modern poetry and music* (Chicago, 1940); M. J. Reid, *The Arthurian legend; comparison of treatment in modern and mediaeval literature* (London, 1938). ROMANCE IN LATER MIDDLE AGES: H. Hauvette, *Boccace* (Paris, 1914); R. K. Gordon, tr., *The story of Troilus* (London, 1934); T. A. Kirby, *Chaucer's Troilus* (University,

La., 1940); R. K. Root, ed., *The book of Troilus and Creseyde* (Princeton, 1926); P. Grillo, *Two aspects of chivlary, Pulci and Boiardo* (Providence, 1942); there are further references to Boccaccio and Chaucer in the bibliography of the next chapter.

CHAPTER X

These notes should be used with those for Chapter IX since some of the works listed there, especially those classified as "general works," also contain useful material for the topics discussed in Chapter X.

THE DRAMA. P. Hartnoll, ed., *The Oxford companion to the theater* (Oxford, 1951), an admirable handbook; E. K. Chambers, *The mediaeval stage* (2d ed., 2 vols., Oxford, 1903), and K. Young, *The drama of the mediaeval church* (2 vols., Oxford, 1933), two basic works; other general works on the drama are: W. Creizenach, *Geschichte des neueren Dramas* (5 vols., Halle, 1909–23); L. Dubech and others, *Histoire générale du théâtre* (5 vols., Paris, 1931–4); K. Mantzius, *A history of theatrical art* (6 vols., New York, 1937); A. Nicoll, *World drama* (London, 1949); A. Nicoll, *The development of the theater* (3rd ed., New York, 1948), on history of stage construction, etc.; A. Nicoll, *Masks, mimes, and miracles* (New York, 1931); D. J. Grout, *A short history of opera* (New York, 1947). MEDIAEVAL THEATER IN PARTICULAR: G. R. Kernodle, *From art to theater* (Chicago, 1944), shows relations of mediaeval art and the theater; R. S. Loomis and G. Cohen, *"Were there theaters in the 12th and 13th centuries?"* in *Speculum* (1945), answered by "no" by D. Bigongidri in an *article with the same title in *Romanic review* (1946); H. C. Gardiner, *Mysteries end* (New Haven, 1946), shows how Reformation ended mystery plays in 16th century; cf. also M. Henshaw, "Studies in mediaeval drama 1933–1950" in *Progress of mediaeval and Renaissance studies* (No. 21, Boulder, 1951); and *Mélanges d'histoire du théâtre du moyen âge et de la Renaissance offerts à Gustave Cohen* (Paris, 1950). DRAMA BY COUNTRIES: E. Faral, *Mimes français du XIIIᵉ siècle* (Paris, 1910); G. Cohen, *Le théâtre en France au moyen âge* (2 vols., Paris, 1928–31); G. Cohen, *Histoire de la mise en scène dans le théâtre religieux français du moyen âge* (2nd ed., Paris, 1926); E. K. Chambers, *English literature at the close of the Middle Ages* (2nd ed., Oxford, 1947), Ch. 1; A. Nicoll, *British drama* (New York, 1925); J. Q. Adams, ed., *Chief pre-Shakesperean dramas* (Boston, 1924), excellent anthology; M. J. Rudwin, *An historical and bibliographical survey of the German religious drama* (Pittsburgh, 1924; J. S. Kennard, *The Italian theater* (2 vols., New York, 1932).

FABLIAUX. J. Bédier, *Les fabliaux* (4th ed., Paris, 1925), the essential work; L. Foulet, *Le roman de Renard* (Paris, 1914); W. Rose, ed., *Reynard the fox* (New York, 1924), Caxton's translation of a Flemish version put into modern English.

BOCCACCIO. H. Hauvette, *Boccace* (Paris, 1914); J. Luchaire, *Boccace* (Paris, 1951); T. C. Chubb, *Life of Boccaccio* (New York, 1930); E. Hutton, *Some aspects of the genius of Boccaccio* (London, 1922); P. Poirier, *Boccace, moraliste de la chair* (Brussels, 1943); F. N. Jones, *Boccaccio and his imitators in German, English, French, Spanish and Italian literature* (Chicago, 1910).

CHAUCER. The literature on Chaucer as on Dante is enormous; some good introductions to Chaucer are: R. D. French, *A Chaucer handbook* (2nd ed., New York, 1947); N. Coghill, *The poet Chaucer* (Oxford, 1949); H. S. Bennett, *Chaucer and the fifteenth century* (Oxford, 1947); J. L. Lowes, *Chaucer and the development of his genius* (Boston, 1934); R. K. Root, *The poetry of Chaucer* (new ed., Boston, 1934); H. R. Patch, *On rereading Chaucer* (Cambridge, Mass., 1939); a few other useful works on Chaucer are W. C. Curry, *Chaucer and the mediaeval sciences* (Oxford, 1926); M. E. Thomas, *Mediaeval skepticism and Chaucer* (New York, 1950); G. G. Coulton, *Chaucer and his England* (6th ed., London, 1937); E. Rickert, ed., *Chaucer's world* (New York, 1948); M. Bowden, *A commentary on the general prologue to the Canterbury Tales* (New York, 1948); W. F. Bryan and G. Dempster, eds., *Sources and analogues of Chaucer's Canterbury Tales* (Chicago, 1941); C. F. Spurgeon, *Five hundred years of Chaucer criticism and allusion 1357–1900* (3 vols., Cambridge, 1935); and A. C. Baugh, "Fifty years of Chaucer scholarship" in *Speculum* (1951).

HISTORY. J. W. Thompson, *History of historical writing* (2 vols., New York, 1942), very comprehensive; H. Richter, *Englische Geschichtschreiber des 12 Jahrhunderts* (Berlin, 1938); V. H. Galbraith, *Historical research in mediaeval England* (London, 1951), a penetrating lecture on English mediaeval historians; L. Keeler, *Geoffrey of Monmouth and the late Latin chroniclers 1300–1500* (Berkeley, 1946); V. H. Galbraith, *Roger of Wendover and Matthew Paris* (Glasgow, 1944); C. C. Mierow, ed., *The two cities of Otto of Freising* (New York, 1928); J. Longnon, *Recherches sur la vie de Villehardouin* (Paris, 1939); F. S. Shears, *Froissart* (London, 1930); G. G. Coulton, *Chronicler of European chivalry* (London, 1930), on Froissart. ITALIAN HISTORIANS OF 14TH AND 15TH CENTURIES AND THEIR INFLUENCE: E. Feuter, *Histoire de l'historiographie moderne* (Paris, 1914); W. F. Ferguson, *The Renaissance in historical thought* (Boston, 1948), Ch. 1; P. Van Tieghem, *La littérature Latine de la Renaissance* (Paris, 1944); B. L. Ullman, "Bruni and humanistic historiography" in *Medievalia et humanistica* (1946); C. B. Coleman, *The treatise of Valla on "the Donation of Constantine"* (New Haven, 1922); W. R. Trimble, "Early Tudor historiography" in *Journal of the history of ideas* (1950).

BIOGRAPHY. J. C. Russell, "An introduction to the study of mediaeval biography" in *Modern Language quarterly* (1943), primarily on how to construct a biography of a mediaeval figure from existing sources. SAINTS LEGENDS: three basic studies: P. Meyer, *"Légendes hagiographiques en Français"* in *Histoire littéraire de la France* (Paris, 1906) Vol. 33; H. Delehaye, *Les légendes hagiographiques* (3rd ed., Brussels, 1927), and by the same author, *Cinq leçons sur la méthode hagiographique* (Brussels, 1934); also G. H. Gerould, *Saints legends* (Boston, 1916); J. D. M. Ford, "The saints life in the vernacular literature of the Middle Ages" in *Catholic historical review* (1931), mostly a summary of Meyer; F. G. Holweck, ed., *A biographical dictionary of the saints* (St. Louis, 1924); F. S. Ellis, ed., *The golden legend of Jacques de Voragine* (7 vols., London, 1900); E. G. Gardner, *"The little flowers of St. Francis"* in

W. W. Seton, ed., *St. Francis of Assisi 1226–1926, essays in commemoration* (London, 1926). JOINVILLE: Two articles by A. Foulet, "When did Joinville write?" in *Romanic review* (1941), and "The archetype of Joinville's Vie de St. Louis" in *Modern language quarterly* (1945); J. Evans, tr., *History of St. Louis by Joinville* (Oxford, 1938); E. Faral, *La vie quotidienne au temps de St. Louis* (Paris, 1942).

SERMONS. C. Langlois, *"L'éloquence sacrée au moyen âge" in *Revue des deux mondes* (1893); L. Bourgain, *La chaire française au XII⁰ siècle* (Paris, 1879); A. Lecoy de la Marche, *La chaire française au moyen âge, spécialement au XIII⁰ siècle* (2nd ed., Paris, 1886); J. T. Welter, *L'exemplum dans la littérature réligieuse et didatique du moyen âge* (Paris, 1927); H. Caplan, *Mediaeval artes praedicandi, a hand list* (2 vols., Ithaca, 1934–6), a list of rhetorical treatises on preaching; T. M. Charland, *Artes praedicandi* (Paris, 1936), a discussion of such treatises; two very valuable works by C. R. Owst, *Preaching in mediaeval England* (Cambridge, 1926), and *Literature and pulpit in mediaeval England* (Cambridge, 1933).

SYMBOLIC LITERATURE. W. H. Cornog, ed., *The Anti-Claudian of Alain of Lille* (Philadelphia, 1935); G. R. de Lage, *Alain de Lille* (Montreal, 1952); M. W. Bloomfield, *"Present state of 'Piers Plowman' studies" in *Speculum* (1939); N. Coghill, *Visions from "Piers Plowman"* (London, 1949), skillful translation of parts of poem with comments; H. W. Wells, tr., *Vision of Piers Plowman in modern English* (London, 1938); D. W. Robinson, Jr., and J. Huppe, *Piers Plowman and scriptural tradition* (Princeton, 1951); E. T. Donaldson, *Piers Plowman, the C text and its poet* (New Haven, 1949).

DANTE. E. Gardner, *Dante* (2nd ed., New York, 1923), and U. Cosmo, *A handbook to Dante studies* (Oxford, 1950), two excellent introductions; K. Vossler, *Mediaeval culture, an introduction to Dante and his times* (2 vols., New York, 1929), indispensable; H. R. Patch, *The other world according to descriptions in mediaeval literature* (Cambridge, Mass., 1950); E. Gilson, *Dante, the philosopher* (New York, 1949); M. Asin-Palacios, *Islam and the "Divine Comedy"* (New York, 1926), and the same author's answer to his critics, "L'influence musulman dans la 'Divine Comédie'" in *Revue de la littérature comparée* (1924); H. L. Stewart, "Dante and the schoolmen" in *Journal of history of ideas* (1949); P. Wicksteed, *Dante and Aquinas* (London, 1913); E. Gardner, *Dante and the mystics* (London, 1913); P. Toynbee, *Dictionary of proper names and notable matters in the works of Dante* (Oxford, 1898), reissued in a revised and brief form as a *Concise dictionary of Dante* (Oxford, 1914); W. P. Friederich, *Dante's fame abroad 1350–1850* (Chapel Hill, 1950).

MEDIAEVAL RHETORICAL AND CRITICAL WRITINGS. E. de Bruyne, *L'esthétique du moyen âge* (Louvain, 1947); R. H. Robins, *Ancient and mediaeval grammatical theory* (London, 1951); C. S. Baldwin, *Mediaeval rhetoric and poetic* (New York, 1928), and by the same author, *Renaissance literary theory and practice* (New York, 1939); E. Faral, *Les arts poétiques du XII⁰ et XIII⁰ siècles* (Paris, 1924); E. Lobel, *Mediaeval Latin poetics* (Oxford, 1932); E. R. Curtius, *Dichtung und Rhetorik im Mittelalter* (Halle, 1938); M. F. Patterson, *Three centuries of French poetic theory 1328–1620* (2 vols., Ann Arbor, 1935); J. W. Atkins, *English literary criticism, the mediaeval phase* (Cambridge, 1942);

C. G. Osgood, *Boccaccio on poetry* (Princeton, 1930); R. McKeon, "Poetry and philosophy in the twelfth century, the renaissance of rhetoric" in *Modern philology* (1946).

CONDITIONS OF PUBLICATION AND CIRCULATION OF BOOKS. K. J. Holzknecht, *Literary patronage in the Middle Ages* (Philadelphia, 1923); R. Crosby, *"Oral delivery in the middle ages" in *Speculum* (1936); E. Faral, *Les jongleurs en France* (Paris, 1910); R. K. Root, "Publication before printing" in *Pub. mod. lang. ass.* (1913); H. S. Bennett, "The production and dissemination of vernacular manuscripts in the 15th century," in *Library* (1947); H. J. Chaytor, *From script to print* (Cambridge, 1945); G. Cohen, *La vie littéraire en France au moyen âge* (Paris, 1949); E. P. Goldschmidt, *Mediaeval texts and their first appearance in print* (Oxford, 1943); G. H. Putnam, *Books and their makers in the Middle Ages* (2 vols., New York, 1896-7); F. Milkau and Layh, *Geschichte der Bibliotheken* (2 vols., Leipzig, 1940), now the standard work; J. W. Thompson, *The mediaeval library* (Chicago, 1939); N. R. Ker, *Mediaeval libraries of Great Britain* (London, 1941); J. de Ghellinck, "Progrès récents en histoire des bibliothèques" in *Revue d'histoire ecclésiastique* (1942); two studies by P. Kibre, "The intellectual interests reflected in libraries of the 14th and 15th centuries" in *Journal of the history of ideas* (1946), and *The library of Pico della Mirandola* (New York, 1936); L. Delisle, *Recherches sur la librairie de Charles V* (2 vols., Paris, 1907).

MISCELLANEOUS WORKS ON ASPECTS OF MEDIAEVAL LITERATURE. G. Highet, *The classical tradition, Greek and Roman influences on western literature* (Oxford, 1949); W. P. Ker, *Epic and romance* (London, 1908), and by the same author, *Essays in mediaeval literature* (New York, 1905); W. W. Lawrence, *Mediaeval story* (2nd ed., New York, 1931); G. Cohen, *Tableau de la littérature médiévale, idées et sensibilités* (Paris, 1950); A. Pauphilet, *Le legs du moyen âge, études de littérature médiévale* (Paris, 1950); F. Tupper, *Types of society in mediaeval literature* (New York, 1926); B. Swain, *Fools and folly during the Middle Ages and the Renaissance* (New York, 1932); D. Comparetti, *Virgil in the Middle Ages* (London, 1908); E. K. Rand, *Ovid and his influence* (Boston, 1925); L. K. Born, *"Ovid and allegory" in *Speculum* (1934); J. M. Clark, *The dance of death in the Middle Ages and the Renaissance* (Glasgow, 1950); L. Olschki, *The genius of Italy* (Oxford, 1949); and finally two remarkable works, J. Huizinga, *Waning of the Middle Ages* (London, 1924), and E. R. Curtius, *Europäische Literatur und Lateinisches Mittelalter* (Bern, 1948; Eng. tr., New York, 1952).

CHAPTER XI

ART. GENERAL WORKS: F. Cabrol and H. Leclerc, *Dictionnaire d'archéologie chrétienne et de liturgie* (Paris, 1913 ff.); Viollet-le-Duc, *Dictionnaire raisonné de l'architecture du XIe au XVIe siècle* (10 vols., Paris, 1875); A. Michel, ed., *Histoire de l'art depuis les premiers temps chrétiens* (8 vols., Paris, 1905-29); P. Lavedan, *Histoire de l'art* (2nd ed., Paris, 1950), Vol. II, the best brief general history of art, as Michel is still the best of the longer accounts; Lavedan contains a remarkable bibliography and special sections called "état des questions" on controversial topics; E. L. Lucas, ed., *The Harvard list of books on art* (new ed., Cambridge, Mass., 1952); A. Hauser, *The social history of art* (2 vols., New York, 1951), very suggestive; W. R. Lethaby, *Mediaeval art* (new ed., London, 1949), stresses architecture; H. Focillon, *Art d'Occident, le moyen âge, roman et gothique* (Paris, 1938); C. R. Morey, *Mediaeval art* (New York, 1942), omits architecture, a great work; L. Réau and Cohen, *L'art du moyen âge et la civilisation française* (Paris, 1935), continued in R. Schneider and G. Cohen, *La formation du génie moderne dans l'art de l'Occident* (Paris, 1936); P. Deschamps and Thibout, *La peinture murale en France* (Paris, 1951); J. Huizinga, *The waning of the Middle Ages* (London, 1924); A. Brutalis, *Précis d'archéologie du moyen âge* (3rd ed., Paris, 1936); V. Gay, *Glossarie archéologique du moyen âge et la Renaissance* (2 vols., Paris, 1887-1928). Two excellent volumes of plates in *Propyläen-Kunstgeschichte*: M. Hauttmann, *Die Kunst des frühen Mittelalters* (Berlin, 1929), and H. Karlinger, *Die Kunst der Gotik* (Berlin, 1927).

GENERAL WORKS ON DIFFERENT COUNTRIES. A. Venturi, *Storia dell'arte italiana* (11 vols., Milan, 1901-40), the standard work; P. Toesca, *Storia dell'arte italiana* (Turin, 1927), Vol. I; J. Alazard, *L'art italien des origines à fin du XVe siècle* (2 vols., Paris, 1948-52), other volumes are to bring story of Italian art to the present; C. Enlart, *Manuel d'archéologie française* (2nd ed., 3 vols., Paris, 1919-24), a basic work; V. Flipo, *Memento pratique d'archéologie française* (Paris, 1930); G. Dehio, *Geschichte der deutschen Kunst* (2nd ed., 3 vols., Berlin, 1921-31); *Ars Hispaniae* (Madrid, 1947 ff.); R. dos Santos, *L'art portugais* (Paris, 1938). ARCHITECTURE AND SCULPTURE: B. Fletcher, *A history of architecture on the comparative method* (11th ed., London, 1943); T. Hamlin, *Architecture through the ages* (New York, 1940), two standard manuals; K. J. Conant, *A brief commentary on early mediaeval church architecture* (Baltimore, 1942); V. Mortet and P. Deschamps, eds., *Recueil des texts rélatifs à l'histoire de l'architecture, XIe-XIIIe siècles* (2 vols., Paris, 1911-29); A. Gardner, *An introduction to French church architecture* (Cambridge, 1938); J. Evans, *Art in mediaeval France* (Oxford, 1948), studies various types of patron; O. E. Saunders, *A history of English art in the Middle Ages* (Oxford, 1932); W. Oakeshott, *The sequence of English mediaeval art* (London, 1950), two works on painting, sculpture, and the minor arts; H. Batsford and C. Fry, *The greater English church* (2nd ed., London, 1944), and by the same authors, *The cathedrals of England* (8th ed., London, 1950); J. Evans, *English art 1307-1461* (Oxford, 1949), the first published volume of *The Oxford history of English art*; C. A. Cummings, *History of architecture in Italy from Constantine to the Renaissance* (new ed., 2 vols., Boston, 1927); B. Bevan, *History of Spanish architecture* (London, 1938); L. Gál, *L'architecture religieuse en Hongroie du IXe au XIIIe siécles* (Paris, 1929); E. B. Smith, *The dome* (Princeton, 1950); A. H. Thompson, "Military architecture" in *Cambridge mediaeval history*, Vol. VI; H. Braun, *The English castle* (London, 1936); J. Baum, *Malerei und Plastik des Mittelalters* (Potsdam, 1930); G. H. Chase and C. R. Post, *History of sculpture* (New York, 1925); L. Réau, *L'art religieux du moyen âge, la sculpture* (Paris, 1946); P. Vitry and G. Brière, eds., *Documents de sculpture française du moyen âge* (3 vols., Paris, 1904); M. Aubert, **La sculpture au moyen âge* (Paris, 1947), best general work on mediaeval sculpture; A. Gardner, *Mediaeval sculpture in France* (Cambridge, 1931), and by the same author, *English mediaeval sculpture* (new ed., Cambridge, 1951); A. L. Mayer, *Mittelalterliche Plastik in Spanien* (Munich, 1922).

ROMANESQUE ART. GENERAL: L. Bréhier, **Le style roman* (Paris, 1942), good brief introduction, but, like most French books, hardly concerns itself with anything outside France; more extended are: G. T. Rivoira, **Lombardic architecture* (2nd ed., Oxford, 1933); A. W. Clapham, **Romanesque architecture in western Europe* (Oxford, 1936); L. Lefrançois-Pillion, *L'art roman en France* (Paris, 1947); R. Rey, *L'art roman et ses origines* (Paris, 1945); J. Puig y Cadafalch, **Le premier art roman* (Paris, 1928), and by the same author, **La géographie et les origines du premier art roman* (Paris, 1935); J. Strzygowski, *Early church art in northern Europe* (London, 1928); these three books have done much to modify earlier views of the origins of Romanesque art; R. de Lasteyrie, **L'architecture religieuse en France à l'époque romane* (2nd ed., Paris, 1929), the basic work on its subject; two works by A. W. Clapham, *English romanesque architecture before the conquest* (Oxford, 1930), and *English romanesque architecture after the conquest* (Oxford, 1934); C. Ricci, *Romanesque architecture in Italy* (London, 1925); W. M. Whitehill, *Spanish Romanesque architecture of the 11th century* (Oxford, 1941); H. Schaefer, "Origins of the two-tower façade in Romanesque architecture" in *Art bulletin* (1945); L. C. MacKinney, "Pre-Gothic architecture, a mirror of the social and religious renaissance" in *Speculum* (1927). SCULPTURE: H. Focillon, **L'art des sculpteurs romans* (Paris, 1931); L. Lefrançois-Pillion, *Les sculpteurs français du XIIe siècle* (Paris, 1931); K. Porter, **Romanesque sculpture of the pilgrimage roads* (10 vols., Boston, 1923), does for art something of the same thing Bédier did for the "Chansons de geste"; J. Evans, *Cluniac art of the Romanesque period* (Oxford, 1950); E. Mâle, "Les influences arabes dans l'art roman" in *Revue des deux mondes* (1923); E. Lüthgen, *Romanische Plastik in Deutschland* (Leipzig, 1923); E. Panofsky, **Die deutsche Plastik des XI–XIII Jahrhunderts* (Munich, 1924); R. Jullian, *La sculpture romane dans l'Italie du nord* (Paris, 1945); G. Gaillard, *La sculpture romane espagnole* (Paris, 1946). PAINTING: E. W. Anthony, *Romanesque frescoes* (Princeton, 1951); P. H. Michel, *Fresques romanes des églises de France* (Paris, 1949); T. Borenius and E. W. Tristan, *English mediaeval paintings* (Florence, 1926); works on miniature painting are listed under "minor arts."

GOTHIC ART. W. G. Constable, **"Painting, sculpture and the arts"* in *Cambridge mediaeval history*, Vol. VIII; L. Réau, *L'art gothique en France* (Paris, 1946); E. Lambert, **Le style gothique* (Paris, 1943), almost entirely on French Gothic; J. Harvey, **The Gothic world 1100–1600* (London, 1950), discusses Gothic architecture all over Europe and Latin America; R. de Lasteyrie, **L'architecture religieuse en France à l'époque Gothique* (2 vols., Paris, 1926–7), a basic work; L. Lefrançois-Pillion, **Les sculpteurs françaises du XIIIe siècle* (2nd ed., Paris, 1931); E. Lambert, *L'art gothique en Espagne* (Paris, 1931); E. Panofsky, **Gothic architecture and scholasticism* (Latrobe, Pa., 1951); H. David, **De Sluter à Sambin* (Paris, 1933); L. B. Bridaham, ed., *Gargoyles,* *chimères and the grotesque in French Gothic sculpture* (New York, 1930). PAINTING (works on miniature painting listed under "minor arts"): C. G. Blunt, *Gothic painting 1200–1500* (London, 1947), excellent brief introduction, as is also C. Sterling, *Les peintres primitives* (Paris, 1949); C. Sterling, *La peinture française, les primitifs* (2nd ed., 1947); G. Ring, ed., *A century of French painting 1400–1500* (New York, 1949); G. Bazin, *Primitifs français* (Paris, 1948), superb color plates; A. Stange, *Deutsche Malerei der Gotik* (4 vols., Berlin, 1934–50), of which there is a poor condensed version in English, *German primitive painting* (New York, 1950); C. Glaser, *Les peintres primitifs allemands* (Paris, 1931); E. Panofsky, *Dürer* (3rd ed., 2 vols., Princeton, 1947); C. Post, *History of Spanish painting* (Cambridge, Mass., 1930 ff.), a work of great erudition; and J. Lassaigne, *Spanish Painting* (Geneva, 1952), Vol. I, with superb illustrations.   FLEMISH PAINTING: M. F. Friedländer, *Die altniederländische Malerei* (14 vols., Berlin and Leyden, 1924–37), the fundamental work; H. Fierens-Gevaert, *Histoire de la peinture flamande des origines à la fin du XVᵉ siècle* (3 vols., Paris, 1927–9); F. J. Mather, *Western European painting of the Renaissance* (New York, 1939); E. Panofsky, *The origin and character of early Flemish painting* (Cambridge, Mass., 1952); L. van Puyvelde, *The Flemish primitives* (New York, 1948); M. Conway, *The Van Eycks and their followers* (London, 1921); E. Renders, *Jan Van Eyck et le polyptyque* (Brussels, 1950); L. Baldass, *Jan Van Eyck* (London, 1952); E. Lotthe, *La pensée chrétienne dans la peinture flamande et hollandaise 1432–1669* (2 vols. Paris, 1952); J. Destrée, *Roger de la Pasture* (2 vols., Paris, 1930).   ITALIAN PAINTING: T. Borenius, *Italian painting* (2 vols., London, 1946); F. J. Mather, *A history of Italian painting* (New York, 1923), two useful brief introductions; R. van Marle, *The development of the Italian schools of painting* (19 vols., The Hague, 1923–38), a fundamental work; B. Berenson, *The Italian painters of the Renaissance* (Oxford, 1928), a landmark; P. d'Ancona, *Les primitifs italiens du XIᵉ au XIIIᵉ siècle* (Paris, 1935); L. Hautecoeur, *Les primitifs italiens* (Paris, 1931); L. Venturi, *Italian painting, the creators of the Renaissance* (Paris, 1950), superb color plates; G. H. Edgell, *History of Sienese painting* (New York, 1932); M. Meiss, *Painting in Florence and Siena after the Black Death* (Princeton, 1951); I. V. Pouzyna, *La Chine, l'Italie et les débuts de la Renaissance* (Paris, 1935); O. Sirén, *Giotto and some of his followers* (2 vols., Cambridge, Mass., 1917).

ITALIAN ART OF 14TH AND 15TH CENTURIES. W. Bode, *Die Kunst der Frührenaissance in Italien* (Berlin, 1926), for pictures; W. Weisinger, "Renaissance theories of the revival of the fine arts" in *Italica* (1943); H. Thode, *Franz von Assisi und die Anfänge der Renaissance* (2nd ed., Berlin, 1904); P. Sabatier and others, *L'influence de Saint François d'Assise sur la civilisation italienne* (Paris, 1926); W. Bode, *Florentine sculptors of the Renaissance* (2nd ed., New York, 1928); two works by P. Schubring, *Die italienische Plastik des Quattorcento* (Berlin, 1919), and *Die Architektur der italienischen Frührenaissance* (Munich, 1924); R. Wittkower, *Architectural principles in the age of humanism* (London, 1949); P. H. Michel, *La pensée de Léon Baptiste Alberti* (Paris, 1930); J. Mesnil, *Masaccio et les débuts de la Renaissance* (The Hague, 1927);

K. Clark, *Piero della Francesca* (Oxford, 1951); R. L. Douglas, *Leonardo da Vinci* (Chicago, 1944); K. Clark, *Leonardo da Vinci* (2nd ed., Cambridge, 1952); E. MacCurdy, ed., *The notebooks of Leonardo da Vinci* (2 vols., New York, 1941-2).

MINOR ARTS. MINIATURES: E. Aeschlimann, *Dictionnaire des miniaturistes du moyen âge et de la Renaissance* (Milan, 1949); L. Réau, *Histoire de la peinture au moyen âge,* Vol. I. *La miniature* (Paris, 1947), the best general work; J. A. Herbert, *Illuminated manuscripts* (2nd ed., London, 1912), only good general work in English; H. M. Martin, *La miniature française du XIIIᵉ au XVᵉ siècle* (Paris, 1913); E. G. Millar, *English illuminated manuscripts from Xth to XIIIth century* (Paris, 1926), and by the same author, *English illuminated manuscripts of the XIVth and XVth centuries* (Paris, 1928); P. Durrieu, *La miniature flamande (1415-1530)* (Paris, 1921); A. Goldschmidt, *German illumination* (2 vols., New York, 1928); P. Ancona, *La miniature italienne* (Paris, 1925); and J. Domínguez-Bordona, *Spanish illumination* (Florence, 1929). GLASS: J. L. Fischer, *Handbuch der Glasmalerei* (Leipzig, 1914); J. Verrier, *L'histoire du vitrail; vitraux de France aux XIᵉ et XIIIᵉ siècles* (Paris, 1949); B. Rackham, *A guide to the stained glass, Victoria and Albert Museum* (London, 1936); J. D. Le Couteur, *English mediaeval painted glass* (London, 1920), Chs. 1–5 incl., best description of technique of making windows; M. Aubert, *Le vitrail en France* (Paris, 1946); P. Claudel and M. Aubert, eds., *Vitraux des cathédrales de France* (Paris, 1937), finest color reproductions; and E. W. Anthony, *History of mosaics* (Boston, 1935). FABRICS: G. Migeon, *Les arts du tissu* (Paris, 1909); J. Marquet de Vasselot and R. Weigert, *Bibliographie de la tapisserie* (Paris, 1935); S. J. Demotte, *La tapisserie gothique* (New York, 1924). MISCELLANEOUS: H. S. Cunynghame, *European enamels* (London, 1906); A. Goldschmidt, *Die Elfenbein-Skulpturen, VIII–XIII Jahrhunderts* (4 vols., Berlin, 1914–26); R. Koechlin, *Les ivoires gothiques français* (3 vols., Paris, 1924); J. Natanson, *Gothic ivories* (London, 1951); E. Hutton, *The Cosmati, Roman marble workers* (London, 1950); E. R. Goddard, *Women's costume in French texts of the 11th and 12th centuries* (Baltimore, 1927); D. Hartley, *Mediaeval costume and life* (New York, 1931); M. L. Gothein, *History of the garden art* (2 vols., London, 1928); F. Crisp, *Mediaeval gardens* (2 vols., London, 1924); E. P. Goldschmidt, *The printed book of the Renaissance* (Cambridge, 1950), and by the same author, *Gothic and Renaissance bookbindings* (2 vols., London, 1928); C. Ffoulkes, *European arms and armour* (London, 1932), and by the same author, *Decorative iron-work from the XIth to the XVIIIth century* (London, 1913); J. Evans, *Magical jewels of the Middle Ages and the Renaissance* (Oxford, 1922), and by the same author, *Pattern, a study of ornament in western Europe 1180–1900* (2 vols., Oxford, 1931).

THEORIES OF ART. F. P. Chambers, *History of taste* (New York, 1932); A. Goldwater and Treves, eds., *Artists on art* (2nd ed., New York, 1947); E. G. Holt, ed., *Literary sources of art history* (Princeton, 1947); L. Venturi, *History of art criticism* (New York, 1936); K. E. Gilbert and H. Kuhn, *History of esthetics* (Bloomington, 1952); two works by E. de Bruyne, *Etudes d'esthétique médiévale* (3 vols., Bruges, 1946), and a briefer summary *L'esthétique du moyen âge* (Louvain, 1947); A. Blunt, *Artistic theory in Italy, 1450-1600* (Oxford, 1940); K. Clark, *Alberti on painting* (London, 1944); F. H. Taylor, *The taste of angels, history of art collecting* (New York, 1949), Vol. I.

PRACTICAL CONDITIONS OF WORKING. G. G. Coulton, *Art and the Reformation* (New York, 1928); two works by M. S. Briggs, *The architect in history* (Oxford, 1927), and *Short history of the building crafts* (Oxford, 1925); two studies by D. Knoop and Jones, *The mediaeval mason, an economic history* (Manchester, 1933), very useful, and *A short history of free-masonry* (Manchester, 1940); L. Lefrançois-Pillion, *Maîtres d'oeuvres et tailleurs de pierre des cathédrales* (Paris, 1949); F. H. Crossley, *English church craftsmanship* (London, 1941); C. Bauchal, *Nouveau dictionnaire biographique des architectes français* (Paris, 1887); J. H. Harvey, *Yevele, life of an English architect* (2nd ed., London, 1950); M. D. Anderson, *The mediaeval carver* (Cambridge, 1935); L. F. Salzman, *Documentary history of building in England to 1540* (London, 1951); P. Frankl, *"The secret of the mediaeval mason"* in *Art bulletin* (1945); J. Ackerman, *"Ars sine scientia nihil est"* in *Art bulletin* (1949); G. Kubler, *"A late Gothic computation of rib vault thrusts"* in *Gazette des beaux arts* (1944); M. Aubert, "Building yards and master builders in the Middle Ages" in *Liturgical arts* (1951); E. Panofsky, ed., *Abbot Suger on the abbey of St. Denis* (Princeton, 1945); T. F. Tout, "Mediaeval town planning" in *Bulletin of John Rylands library* (1917-18); F. L. Ganshof, *Etude sur le développement des villes entre Loire et Rhin au moyen âge* (Paris, 1943); H. R. Hahnloser, *Villard de Honnecourt* (Vienna, 1935); F. Antal, *Florentine painting and its social background* (London, 1948), valuable material but unreliable in its conclusions; H. Ruhemann and E. M. Kent, *The artist at work* (London, 1951), clever survey of methods of painting; Theophilus, *Traité des divers arts* (Paris, 1924), most important early mediaeval treatise on techniques; D. V. Thompson, Jr., and G. H. Hamilton, trs., *De arte illuminandi* (New Haven, 1933), anonymous treatise on manuscript illumination; D. V. Thompson, Jr., "Mediaeval parchment making," in *Library* (1935); D. V. Thompson, Jr., tr., *The craftsman's handbook of Cennini* (2 vols., New Haven, 1932-3), and by the same author, *The practice of tempera painting* and *Materials of mediaeval painting* (both, New Haven 1936); G. Loumeyer, *Les traditions techniques de la peinture médiévale* (Liège, 1943); W. G. Grüneisen, "La perspective, esquisse de son evolution" in *Mélanges de l'école française de Rome* (1911); G. M. Richter, "Perspective, ancient, mediaeval and Renaissance" in *Scritti in onore di B. Nogara* (Rome, 1937); M. S. Bunin, *Space in mediaeval paintings and the forerunners of perspective* (New York, 1940), and by the same author, "Further notes on space in mediaeval painting" in *Speculum* (1947); R. Grinnel, "The theoretical attitude toward space in the Middle Ages" in *Speculum* (1946); W. Goetz, *"Entwicklung des Wirklichkeitssinnes"* in *Archiv für Kulturgeschichte* (1937); A. P. Laurie, *The technique of the great painters* (London, 1950); J. Lestocquoy, "Le commerce des oeuvres d'art au moyen âge" in *Mélanges d'histoire sociale* (1943); and H. Wieruszowski, "Art and the commune in the time of Dante" in *Speculum* (1944).

ICONOGRAPHY. *Three great works of E. Mâle, *L'art religieux du XIIe siècle en France* (3rd ed., Paris, 1928), *du XIIIe siècle* (7th ed., Paris, 1935;

English ed., London, 1913), and *de la fin du moyen âge* (5th ed., Paris, 1949); selections from these have been published in English (New York, 1949); L. Bréhier, *L'art chrétien, son développement iconographique* (2nd ed., Paris, 1928); C. Terrasse, *La cathédrale miroir du monde* (Paris, 1946), useful survey; R. van Marle, *Iconographie de l'art profane au moyen âge et à la renaissance* (2 vols., The Hague, 1931-2); E. Panofsky and F. Saxl, *Classical mythology in mediaeval art" in *Metropolitan museum studies* (1933); J. Adhémar, *Influences antiques dans l'art du moyen âge français* (London, 1939); J. Seznec, *La survivance des dieux antiques* (London, 1940); J. M. Clark, *The dance of death in the Middle Ages and the Renaissance* (Glasgow, 1950).

MUSIC. GENERAL WORKS: R. D. Darrell, ed., *Schirmer's guide to works on music* (New York, 1951); W. Apel, ed., *Harvard dictionary of music* (6th ed., Cambridge, Mass., 1950); P. A. Scholes, ed., *The Oxford companion to music* (8th ed., Oxford, 1950); *Grove's dictionary of music and musicians* (5th ed., 9 vols., London, 1954); H. Riemann, *Musikgeschichte in Beispielen* (4th ed., Leipzig, 1929); A. T. Davison and W. Apel, eds., *Historical anthology of music*, Vol. I, to 1600 (2nd ed., Cambridge, Mass., 1949); C. Parish, ed., *Masterpieces of music before 1750* (New York, 1951); J. A. Westrup, *The meaning of musical history* (Oxford, 1946), essay on method; J. Combarieu, *Histoire de la musique* (3 vols., Paris, 1913-19); H. Riemann, *Geschichte der Musiktheorie im IX-XIX Jahrhunderten* (2nd ed., Berlin, 1920); *Oxford history of music* (2nd ed., 7 vols., Oxford, 1929-38); A. Schering, *Tabellen zur Musikgeschichte* (4th ed., Leipzig, 1934); G. Kinsky, ed., *A history of music in pictures* (New York, 1930); M. Sauerlandt, *Die Musik in fünf Jahrhunderten der Europäischen Malerei 1450-1850* (Leipzig, 1922); O. Strunk, ed., *Source readings in music history* (New York, 1950), very useful; C. Sachs, *History of musical instruments* (New York, 1940); K. Geiringer, *Musical instruments, their history* (Oxford, 1945), convenient reference work. GENERAL WORKS ON MUSIC IN THE MIDDLE AGES: T. Gérold, *Histoire de la musique, des origines à la fin du XIVe siècle* (Paris, 1936); A. Machabey, *Histoire et évolution des formules musicales au XVe siècle* (Paris, 1928); H. Besseler, *Die Musik des Mittelalters und der Renaissance* (Potsdam, 1931); G. Reese, *Music in the Middle Ages* (New York, 1940); J. Chailley, *Histoire musicale du moyen âge* (Paris, 1950), and by the same author, *La musique médiévale* (Paris, 1951); F. M. Turner, "Mediaeval music," Vol. I of F. Bonaira, ed., *History of English music* (London, 1948); C. de Coussemaker, *Histoire de l'harmonie au moyen âge* (Paris, 1852); W. Apel, *The notation of polyphonic music 900-1600* (4th ed., Cambridge, Mass., 1949); W. Tappolet, *La notation musicale et son influence sur la pratique de la musique* (Neuchatel, 1947); C. Sachs, "Some remarks about old notation" in *Musical quarterly* (1948), on transcribing old music; M. F. Bukofzer, *Studies in mediaeval and Renaissance music* (New York, 1950); L. Ellinwood, "Ars musica" in *Speculum* (1945), survey of mediaeval writing on music; on same subject is M. F. Bukofzer, "Speculative thinking in mediaeval music" in *Speculum* (1942); H. Panum, *Stringed instruments of the Middle Ages* (London, 1939); G. S. Bedbrook, *Keyboard music from the Middle Ages to the beginning of the Baroque* (London, 1949); W. Apel, *"Early history of the organ"* in *Speculum* (1948), an important article; N. Dufourcq, *Esquisse d'une histoire de l'orgue en France* (Paris, 1935); H. Klotz, *Über die Orgelkunst der Gotik, der Renaissance und des Barock* (Kassel, 1934); Y. Rokseth, **La musique d'orgue au moyen âge* (Paris, 1940). OTHER ASPECTS OF MEDIAEVAL MUSIC: P. Wagner, *Einführung in die gregorianische Melodien* (3 vols., Fribourg, 1901; Vol. I in Eng. trans., London, 1907); E. Dickinson, **Music in the history of the western church* (new ed., New York, 1925); L. Duchesne, **Christian worship* (5th ed., London, 1925); J. A. Dunney, *The mass* (New York, 1941); A. Hughes, **Latin hymnody* (London, 1922); E. Wellesz, *Eastern elements in western chant* (Oxford, 1947); Van Doren, *Etude sur l'influence musicale de l'abbaye de St. Gall* (Louvain, 1925); J. Beck, **La musique des troubadours* (Paris, 1910), and by the same author, *Le chansonnier de Noailles* (Paris, 1927); P. Aubry, *Trouvères and troubadours* (London, 1914); M. F. Bukofzer, **Sumer is icumen in, a revision* (Berkeley, 1944); A. Einstein, **The Italian madrigal* (3 vols., Princeton, 1948); H. E. Bush, "The recognition of chordal formation" in *Musical quarterly* (1946); W. Apel, ed., *French secular music in the late 14th century* (Cambridge, Mass., 1950); H. Besseler, **Bourdon und Fauxbourdon* (Leipzig, 1950); E. Dannemann, **Die Spätgotische Musik-Tradition im Frankreich und Burgund* (Strasbourg, 1936); A. Pirro, *Histoire de la musique de la fin du XIVe siècle à la fin du XVIe siècle* (Paris, 1940); C. van den Borren, **Dufay* (Brussels, 1926), and by the same author, **Etudes sur le XVe siècle musical* (Antwerp, 1941); P. O. Kristeller, **"Music and learning in the early Italian Renaissance"* in *Journal of Renaissance and Baroque music* (1947); and O. Kinkeldey, "Music printing in incunabula," in *Papers, bibliographical society of America* (1932).

SOME RECORDINGS OF EARLY MUSIC. COLLECTIONS: Curt Sachs, ed., **L'Anthologie sonore* (13 vols., detailed list of compositions obtainable from The Gramophone Shop, New York 17); the author has found the following records, from *L'Anthologie sonore*, particularly valuable; 16, 18, 27, 35, 59, 63, 65, 67, 71, 91, 98, 99, and 100. MUSIC OF THE GOTHIC PERIOD AND EARLY RENAISSANCE: Four records, "Allegro" 14 and "Allegro" 72, *Music of the 12th and 13th centuries* (EMS 201); the best records of Gregorian chant are those by the Solesmes monks ("Victor musical masterpieces," 87) *Perotinus* ("Concert hall society," 112), "Italian Madrigal, ars nova and 16th cen." (Allegro 3029). MEDIAEVAL AND RENAISSANCE CHORAL MUSIC: ("Victor musical masterpieces," M-379); **Liturgical music* by choir of Dijon cathedral ("Victor musical masterpieces," 212); in the French series *Discophiles français*: Brumel, *Messe*; Josquin des Prés, *Chansons and Motets*; Guillaume de Machaut, *Mass* ("Concert hall society," 1107); Dufay and Josquin des Prés, **Secular songs* (2 vols., EMS 206 and EMS 213); and Josquin des Prés, **De profundis* ("Concert hall society," 47).

CHAPTER XII

MYSTICISM. GENERAL WORKS: J. de Marquette, *Introduction to comparative mysticism* (New York, 1949), and M. Smith, *An introduction to the history of mysticism* (London, 1930), two very brief surveys; P. Pourrat, **La spiritua-

lité chrétienne (new ed., 4 vols., Paris, 1927–31; Eng. trans. of first 3 vols., London, 1922–7); E. Underhill, *Mysticism* (14th ed., London, 1944), and by the same author, *"Mediaeval mysticism" in *Cambridge mediaeval history*, Vol. VII; W. R. Inge, *Christian mysticism* (3rd ed., London, 1913); E. C. Butler, *Western mysticism* (London, 1922); von Hügel, *The mystical element in religion* (2nd ed., 2 vols., London, 1923), a great work, based on the life of St. Catharine of Genoa, but a profound study of the mystical attitude in general; P. E. More, *Christian mysticism* (London, 1932); R. Otto, *Mysticism, east and west* (New York, 1932), a comparison of Christian and Oriental mysticism; J. Bernhart, *Die philosophische Mystik des Mittelalters* (Munich, 1922); R. M. Jones, *Studies in mystical religion* (4th ed., London, 1923); M. A. Ewer, *A survey of mediaeval symbolism* (New York, 1933); L. Gougaud, *Devotional and ascetic practices in the Middle Ages* (London, 1927); J. T. McNeill, *A history of the care of souls* (New York, 1951); W. James, *The varieties of religious experience* (New York, 1902); and J. H. Leuba, *The psychology of religious mysticism* (New York, 1925), Freudian.

USEFUL COLLECTIONS OF SOURCES. T. S. Kepler, ed., *The fellowship of the saints* (New York, 1948), very comprehensive; J. Chuzeville, ed., *Les mystiques italiens* (Paris, 1942), and by the same editor, *Les mystiques allemands* (Paris, 1935); W. R. Inge, ed., *Light, life and love, selections from the German mystics* (3rd ed., London, 1935); M. Noetinger, ed., *Les mystiques anglais* (Paris, 1928); E. A. Peers, ed., *The mystics of Spain* (London, 1952); J. T. McNeill and H. Gamer, eds., *Mediaeval handbooks of penance* (New York, 1938).

BACKGROUND OF MYSTICISM AND ASPECTS OF ITS DEVELOPMENT, 1000–1500. G. G. Coulton, *Five centuries of religion* (4 vols., Cambridge, 1923–50), a work of vast erudition and scope, severely critical of the church; J. A. MacCulloch, *Mediaeval faith and fable* (New York, 1932), excellent introduction to the faith of the masses; cf. also R. Bernheimer, *Wild men in the Middle Ages* (Cambridge, Mass., 1952), and K. Seligmann, *The mirror of magic* (New York, 1948); A. H. Thompson, *"The monastic orders" in *Cambridge mediaeval history*, Vol. V; A. S. Turberville, *"Heresies and the Inquisition," in *Cambridge mediaeval history*, Vol. VI, two good surveys; A. P. Evans, "Social aspects of mediaeval heresy" in *Essays in honor of G. L. Burr* (New York, 1931); S. Runciman, *The mediaeval Manichee, a study of heresy* (Cambridge, 1946); J. Mackinnon, *The origins of the Reformation* (London, 1939); B. Smalley, *The study of the Bible in the Middle Ages* (2nd ed., Oxford, 1951); O. J. Blum, *St. Peter Damian* (Washington, 1947); W. Williams, *St. Bernard* (Manchester, 1935); E. Vacandard, *Vie de St. Bernard* (new ed., 2 vols., Paris, 1927); E. Gilson, *The mystical theology of St. Bernard* (London, 1940; new ed. in French, Paris, 1947); G. B. Burch, ed., *Steps of humility* (Cambridge, Mass., 1940); E. Gebbart, *Mystics and heretics in Italy* (New York, 1922); E. S. Davidson, *Forerunners of St. Francis* (Boston, 1927); G. La Piana, *"Joachim of Flora, a critical survey" in *Speculum* (1932); H. Bett, *Joachim of Flora* (London, 1931); H. Grundmann, *Neue Forschungen über Joachim von Flora* (Marburg, 1950); A. G. Little, *"The mendicant orders" in *Cambridge mediaeval history*, Vol. VI, the best introduction to the subject; R. F. Bennett, *The early Dominicans* (Cambridge, 1937); A. G. Little, *Guide to Franciscan studies* (London, 1920);

P. Gratien, *Histoire de l'ordre des frères mineurs au XIIIe siècle* (Paris, 1928); O. Englebrecht, *St. Francis of Assisi* (New York, 1950); E. E. Underhill, *Jacopone da Todi* (London, 1919); E. Gilson, *The philosophy of St. Bonaventura* (New York, 1938); P. Misciattelli, *The mystics of Siena* (Cambridge, 1929); G. G. Scholem, *Major trends in Jewish mysticism* (rev. ed., New York, 1946), useful for comparison; E. L. Schellenberg, *Die deutsche Mystik* (2nd ed., Berlin, 1927); W. Stammler, *Von der Mystik zum Barock 1400–1600* (2nd ed., Stuttgart, 1950), a remarkable history of German literature and culture; P. Hoesl, *La vie d'amour de St. Elisabeth d'Hongrie* (2nd ed., Paris, 1947); X. de Hornstein, *Les grands mystiques allemands du XIV siècle, état présent des problèmes* (Lucerne, 1922); H. Delacroix, *Essai sur le mysticisme spéculatif en Allemagne* (Paris, 1900); J. M. Clark, *The great German mystics, Eckhart, Tauler, and Suso* (Oxford, 1949); R. B. Blankney, *Meister Eckhart, a modern translation* (New York, 1941); M. d'Asbeck, *La mystique de Ruysbroeck* (Paris, 1930); A. G. Seesholtz, *Friends of God* (New York, 1934); R. M. Jones, *The flowering of mysticism, the Friends of God* (New York, 1939); A. Hyma, *The Christian Renaissance, a history of the 'devotio moderna'* (Grand Rapids, 1924), and by the same author, *The Brethren of the Common Life* (Grand Rapids, 1950); E. F. Jacob, "The Brethren of the Common Life" in E. F. Jacob, *Essays in the conciliar epoch* (2nd ed., Manchester, 1951); S. Winkworth, tr., *Theologica Germanica* (London, 1907); J. L. Connolly, *Gerson* (Louvain, 1928); A. Combes, *Gerson* (Paris, 1940); G. Bullett, *The English mystics* (London, 1950); H. E. Allen, ed., *Writings attributed to Rolle* (New York, 1927); W. Butler-Bowdon, ed., *The book of Margery Kempe* (London, 1936); K. Cholmeley, *Margery Kempe* (London, 1947); H. Workman, *Wyclif* (2 vols., Oxford, 1926); M. Deanesly, *The Lollard Bible* (Cambridge, 1920); G. G. Coulton, *"Scholastics and the Bible," *"Fight for the Bible," and *"The open Bible" in *Mediaeval panorama* (Cambridge, 1939); M. Spinka, *Hus and the Czech reform* (Chicago, 1941).

HUMANISM: FROM THE ELEVENTH THROUGH THE THIRTEENTH CENTURY. J. E. Sandys, *A history of classical scholarship* (3rd ed., Cambridge, 1921), Vol. I; C. S. Baldwin, *Mediaeval rhetoric and poetic* (New York, 1928); C. H. Haskins, *Renaissance of the 12th century* (Cambridge, Mass., 1927); G. Paré and others, *La renaissance du XIIe siècle, les écoles et l'enseignement* (Paris, 1933); A. Clerval, *Les écoles de Chartres au moyen âge* (Chartres, 1895); L. Delisle, "Les écoles d'Orléans" in *Annuaire-bulletin de la société de l'histoire de France* (1869); C. C. Webb, *John of Salisbury* (London, 1932); H. Liebeschütz, *Mediaeval humanism in the life and writings of John of Salisbury* (London, 1950); S. Painter, "John of Salisbury" in G. Boas, ed., *The Greek tradition* (Baltimore, 1939); E. K. Rand, *The classics in the 13th century" in *Speculum* (1929); E. Boutaric, "Vincent de Beauvais et la connaissance de l'antiquité classique au 13e siècle" in *Revue des questions historiques*, 1875, and L. J. Paetow, ed., *The battle of the seven arts* (Berkeley, 1914).

ITALIAN HUMANISM: QUESTION OF THE NATURE OF THE "RENAISSANCE." W. F. Ferguson, *The Renaissance in historical thought, five centuries of interpretation* (Boston, 1948), a basic work; J. Burckhardt, *Renaissance in Italy* (Phaidon ed., London, 1937), this edition of the classic work of the Swiss historian contains a superb collection of pictures. The literature is very extensive; here are a few useful articles: E. Panofsky, *"Renaissance and Renascences" in *Kenyon review* (1944); J. Huizinga, *"Le problème de la renaissance" in *Revue des cours et conferences* (1938-9); four articles by H. Baron, "A sociological interpretation of the early Renaissance in Florence" in *South Atlantic quarterly* (1939); "The historical background of the Florentine Renaissance" in *History* (1938); "Articulation and unity in the Italian Renaissance" in *Annual report, American historical association* (1942); and "Toward a more positive evaluation of the 15th century Renaissance" in *Journal of history of ideas* (1943); M. de Filippis, "The Renaissance problem again" in *Italica* (1943); R. M. Setton, *"Some recent views of the Italian Renaissance" in *Report of the annual meeting of the Canadian historical association* (1947); E. F. Jacob and A. S. Turberville, "Changing views of the Renaissance" in *History* (1931-2); N. Nelson, *"Individualism as a criterion of the Renaissance" in *Journal of English and German philology* (1933); five articles by H. Weisinger, "Ideas of history during the Renaissance" in *Journal of history of ideas* (1945); "Renaissance theories of the revival of the fine arts" in *Italica* (1943); "The self-awareness of the Renaissance" and "Who began the revival of learning?" in *Papers of the Michigan academy of science, arts, and literature* (1944); and "The Renaissance theory of the reaction against the Middle Ages" in *Speculum* (1945); D. B. Durand and H. Baron, "Tradition and innovation in the fifteenth century Renaissance" in *Journal of history of ideas* (1943), L. Thorndike, "Renaissance or Prerenaissance?" in *Journal of history of ideas* (1943); P. O. Kristeller, *"Humanism and scholasticsm in the Italian Renaissance" in *Byzantion* (1945), an important discussion.

GENERAL WORKS ON ITALIAN HUMANISM. BIBLIOGRAPHY AND COLLECTIONS OF SOURCE READINGS: D. C. Allen, "Latin literature of the Renaissance" in *Modern language quarterly* (1941); D. P. Lockwood and R. Bainton, "Classical and Biblical scholarship in the Renaissance" in *Church history* (1941); P. O. Kristeller and J. H. Randall, Jr., "The study of the philosophies of the Renaissance" in *Journal of history of ideas* (1941); J. O. Riedl, ed., *Catalogue of Renaissance philosophies, 1350-1650* (Milwaukee, 1940); M. Whitcomb, ed., *Literary source book of the Renaissance* (rev. ed., Philadelphia, 1903); F. A. Gragg, ed., *Latin writings of the Italian humanists* (New York, 1927); F. Schevill, ed., *The first century of Italian humanism* (New York, 1928); E. Cassirer and others, eds., *The Renaissance philosophy of man* (Chicago, 1948). OTHER GENERAL WORKS: A. Tilley, "The early Renaissance" in *Cambridge mediaeval history*, Vol. VII; R. C. Jebb, *"The classical Renaissance," and M. R. James, "The Christian Renaissance," in *Cambridge modern history*, Vol. I; J. E. Sandys, *History of classical scholarship*, Vol. II (2nd ed., Cambridge, 1908); J. S. Fletcher, *Literature of the Italian Renaissance* (New York, 1934); H. O. Taylor, *Thought and expression in the sixteenth century* (2 vols., New York, 1920); J. A. Symonds, *The revival of learning* (3rd ed., London, 1897), a great work; R. Schneider and G. Cohen, *La formation du génie moderne* (Paris, 1936); P. Van Tieghem, *La littérature Latine de la Renaissance* (Paris, 1944); N. A. Robb, *Neoplatonism of the Italian Renaissance* (London, 1935); J. E. Spingarn, *History of literary criticism in the Renaissance* (5th ed., New York, 1925); C. S. Baldwin, *Renais-

sance literary theory and practice (New York, 1939); V. Hall, Jr., *Renaissance literary criticism* (New York, 1945); G. Toffanin, *Storia dell'umanesimo* (3rd ed., Bologna, 1943), strongly Roman Catholic; E. Garin, *Der italienische Humanismus* (Berne, 1947); W. Ruëgg, *Cicero und der Humanismus* (Zurich, 1946); P. O. Kristeller, *"The philosophy of man in the Italian Renaissance" in *Italica* (1947); N. Spageno, *Il Trecento* (Milan, 1934); C. Carbonara, *Il secolo XV* (Milan, 1943); P. Monnier, *Le quattrocento* (new ed., 2 vols., Paris, 1924); A. von Martin, *Sociology of the Renaissance* (Oxford, 1944), a short work of great insight; C. M. Ady, "Morals and manners of the Quattrocento" in *Proceedings of British Academy* (1942); T. F. Crane, *Italian social customs of the 16th century* (New Haven, 1920). SPECIAL ASPECTS OF ITALIAN HUMANISM: R. Weiss, *Dawn of humanism in Italy* (London, 1947), and by the same author, *Il primo secolo dell'umanesimo* (Rome, 1950); E. H. Wilkins, "An introductory Petrarch bibliography" in *Philological quarterly* (1948); E. Tatham, *Petrarch* (2 vols., London, 1925-6); J. H. Robinson and H. Rolfe, *Petrarch* (2nd ed., New York, 1914); P. de Nolhac, *Pétrarque et l'humanisme* (new ed., 2 vols., Paris, 1907); M. E. Cosenza, ed., *Petrarch's letters to classical authors* (Chicago, 1910); T. E. Mommsen, *"Petrarch's conception of the Dark Ages" in *Speculum* (1942); H. Hauvette, *Boccace* (Paris, 1914); P. O. Kristeller, *The philosophy of Ficino* (New York, 1943), a fundamental work, also by the same author, *"The scholastic background of Ficino" in *Traditio* (1944), and *"Florentine Platonism in its relations with humanism and scholasticism" in *Church history* (1939); E. Cassirer, "Ficino's place in intellectual history" in *Journal of history of ideas* (1945), a long review of Kristeller's book on Ficino; E. Cassirer, *"Pico della Mirandola" in *Journal of history of ideas* (1942); G. S. Gutkind, *Cosimo de' Medici* (Oxford, 1938); L. Mohler, *Kardinal Bessarion* (2 vols., Paderborn, 1923-7); E. Robertson, "Aldus Manutius, scholar printer," in *Bulletin John Ryland's library* (1950), two works of W. H. Woodward, *Vittorino da Feltre and other humanist educators* (Cambridge, 1897), and *Studies in education 1400-1600* (Cambridge, 1906); S. G. Santayana, *Two Renaissance educators* (Boston, 1930).

NORTHERN HUMANISM. A. Tilley, "The Renaissance in Europe" in *Cambridge mediaeval history*, Vol. VIII; J. Mackinnon, *Origins of the Reformation* (London, 1939), especially Chs. 22-4; W. Andreas, *Deutschland vor der Reformation* (2nd ed., Stuttgart, 1934); A. Hyma, *The Christian Renaissance* (New York, 1925), and by the same author, *The Brethren of the Common Life* (Grand Rapids, 1950); W. S. Lilly, "Reuchlin" in *Renaissance types* (New York, 1901); H. Holborn, *Ulrich von Hutten* (New Haven, 1937); F. G. Stokes, ed., *Epistolae obscurorum virorum* (New Haven, 1925); P. Smith, *Life and letters of Luther* (2nd ed., Boston, 1914); F. Hildebrandt, *Melanchthon* (Cambridge, 1946); W. F. Schirmer, *Der englische Frühhumanismus* (Leipzig, 1931); R. Weiss, *Humanism in England during the fifteenth century* (Oxford, 1941); D. Bush, *Renaissance and English humanism* (Toronto, 1939); R. J. Mitchell, *John Tiptoft* (London, 1938); P. S. Allen, *The age of Erasmus* (Oxford, 1914); P. Smith, *Erasmus* (New York, 1923); A. Hyma, ed., *Erasmus and the humanists* (New York, 1930); N. Bailey, ed., *The colloquies of Erasmus* (2 vols., London, 1878); P. Smith, *Key to the colloquies of Erasmus* (Cambridge, Mass.,

1927); H. H. Hudson, tr., *Erasmus' praise of folly* (Princeton, 1944); E. H. Zeydel, ed., *Brandt's Ship of fools* (New York, 1944); also cf. A. Hyma, *Youth of Erasmus* (Ann Arbor, 1930); F. Seebohm, *The Oxford reformers* (2nd ed., London, 1869); and R. W. Chambers, *Thomas More* (New York, 1935).

Supplementary Note (January, 1954)

The following titles have come to the author's notice since the book first went to press. A few were inadvertently omitted in the first edition. A small number are new editions of works listed in the main bibliography.

GENERAL WORKS: *Life's picture history of western man* (New York, 1951), excellent pictures; a better work is F. van der Meer, *Atlas de la civilisation occidentale* (Paris, 1952); R. M. Hutchins and M. J. Adler, eds., *Great books of the western world* (54 vols., Chicago, 1952), cf. review by G. Highet in *New York Times*, Sept. 14, 1952; F. B. Artz, *The intellectual history of Europe from St. Augustine to Marx, a guide* (Boston, 1941); A. W. Mitchell, *Historical charts of the humanities* (New York, 1939); C. W. Previté-Orton, *The shorter Cambridge mediaeval history* (2 vols., Cambridge, 1952), largely political; R. W. Southern, *The making of the Middle Ages* (London, 1953), an original treatment of life and thought in the 11th and 12th centuries; J. Seznec, *The survival of the pagan gods* (New York, 1953), very important work for both art and literature; Will Durant, *The age of faith* (New York, 1950), and by the same author, *The Renaissance* (New York, 1953), good popularizations.

CLASSICAL BACKGROUNDS: Nairn, *Handlist of books relating to the classics* (3rd ed., Oxford, 1953); H. Bengtson, *Einfuhrüng in die alte geschichte* (2nd ed., Munich, 1953); M. Huxley, ed., *The root of Europe* (Oxford, 1952), good brief essays on Greek influences on later European culture; M. P. Nilsson, *Geschichte der griechischen Religion* (2 vols., Munich, 1941, 1950), a basic work; H. Frankfort & others, *Before philosophy* (new ed., London, 1949), on primitive thought, admirable; C. Kerényi, *The gods of the Greeks* (London, 1951); M. P. Nilsson, *Greek piety* (2nd ed., Oxford, 1949); W. K. C. Guthrie, *Orpheus and Greek religion* (2nd ed., London, 1952); L. R. Farnell, *Cults of the Greek city states* (5 vols., Oxford, 1896–1909), very valuable; B. Snell, *The discovery of the mind, Greek origins of European thought* (Cambridge, Mass., 1953); L. Robin, *La pensée grecque* (2nd ed., Paris, 1948); F. M. Cornford, *Principium sapientiae, the origins of Greek philosophical thought* (Cambridge, 1952); J. Burnet, *From Thales to Plato* (London, 1914), a first-rate work; M. Untersteiner, *The Sophists* (London, 1953); P. Lachieze-Rey, *Les idées morales, sociales, et politiques de Platon* (2nd ed., Paris, 1951); D. J. Allan, *The philosophy of Aristotle* (Oxford, 1952); P. Merlan, *From Platonism to Neo-Platonism* (The Hague, 1953), emphasizes similarities and shows Neo-Platonism developed before Plotinus; C. Bailey, *The Greek atomists and Epicurus* (London, 1928); M. Pohlenz, *Die Stoa* (2 vols., Göttingen, 1948-9); A. H. Armstrong, ed., *"Plotinus"* (London, 1953), a volume of selections; M. de Gandillac, *La sagesse de Plotin* (Paris, 1952); and E. Goodenough,

*"Religious aspirations" in *Age of Diocletian* (Metropolitan Museum, New York, 1952), a brilliant article.

BIBLICAL AND PATRISTIC BACKGROUNDS: G. A. Buttrick and others, eds., *The interpreter's Bible* (12 vols., New York, 1951 ff.), indispensable; A. G. Barrois, *Manuel d'archeologie biblique* (2 vols., Paris, 1939–53), a masterpiece; W. A. Irwin, *The Old Testament, keystone of human culture* (New York, 1952), now the best brief introduction to Old Testament thought; H. H. Rowley, *The Zadokite fragments and the Dead Sea Scrolls* (Oxford, 1952), good introduction to a new field of studies; R. H. Pfeiffer, *History of New Testament Times* (New York, 1949); K. S. Latourette, *A history of Christianity* (New York, 1953), amazingly comprehensive, useful for all periods of history of Christianity; A. H. McNeile, *An introduction to the study of the New Testament* (2nd ed., Oxford, 1953); R. K. Bultmann, *Theology of the New Testament* (2 vols., New York, 1951–4), new points of view in higher criticism; M. Goguel, *Life of Jesus* (London, 1933), and by the same author, *The birth of Christianity* (London, 1953), translations of first two (of the three) parts of Goguel's masterly work; M. Dibelius & W. Kümmel, *Paul* (Philadelphia, 1953); C. H. Dodd, *The interpretation of the Fourth Gospel* (Cambridge, 1953); A. D. Nock, "Hellenistic mysteries and Christian sacraments" in *Mnemosyne,* 1952; J. G. Davies, *Daily life of the early Christians* (New York, 1953); J. Baillie and others, eds., *Early Christian fathers* (Philadelphia, 1953 ff.), texts with commentaries, important; R. Seeberg, *Textbook of the history of doctrines* (new ed., 2 vols. in one, Grand Rapids, 1952), an older work but still very useful; H. Bettenson, ed., *Documents of the Christian Church* (Oxford, 1943), convenient collection; P. Antin, *Essai sur St. Jérome* (Paris, 1951); E. Barker, *"St. Augustine's theory of society" in *Essays on government* (2nd ed., Oxford, 1951), admirable; and O. Chadwick, *Cassian, a study in primitive monasticism* (Cambridge, 1950).

BYZANTINE CIVILIZATION: P. Lemerle, "La civilisation byzantine" in *Journal des savants,* 1950, and *Revue historique,* 1953, bibliographical articles; S. Galahad, *Byzance* (Paris, 1948); A. A. Vasiliev, *History of the Byzantine Empire* (new ed., Madison, 1952), indispensable; W. K. Medlin, *Moscow and East Rome, relations of church and state in Muscovite Russia* (Geneva, 1952); C. Zervos, *Un philosophie neoplatonicien du XIᵉ siècle, Psellus* (Paris, 1920); M. V. Anastos, *"Byzantine literature" in *Collier's Encyclopedia,* 1951; J. Sonet, ed., *Le roman de Barlaam et Josaphat* (2 vols., Paris, 1953); A. Grabar, *Byzantine painting* (Geneva, 1953); P. Meyer, ed., *Byzantine mosaics in Italy* (Oxford, 1952), the last two with superb color plates; W. R. Zaloziecky, *Die Sophienkirche* (Freiburg, 1936); E. W. Anthony, *History of mosaics* (Boston, 1935), convenient summary; P. Schweinfurth, ed., *Russian icons* (Oxford, 1953), with good plates; M. Merlier, *Etudes de la musique byzantine* (Paris, 1935); H. J. Tillyard, "Byzantine music about A.D. 1100" in *Musical Quarterly,* 1953; F. Dvornik, *The Slavs, their early history and civilization* (Cambridge, Mass., 1954); M. Rouet de Journel, *Monachisme et monastères russes* (Paris, 1952); D. Cizevsky, and others, *Outline of comparative slavic literatures* (Boston, 1952 ff.); and V. V. Zenkovsky, *History of Russian philosophy* (2 vols., London, 1953.)

ISLAMIC CIVILIZATION: H. A. R. Gibb, *Mohammedanism (2nd ed., Oxford, 1952); H. A. R. Gibb & J. H. Kramers, *Shorter encyclopedia of Islam (Leyden, 1953); F. M. Parejo, Islamologia (Rome, 1951), a general handbook of Islamic studies; E. Jackh, ed., Background of the Middle East (Ithaca, 1952); A. Syed, The spirit of Islam, a history of the evolution and ideas of Islam (6th ed., London, 1952); G. von Grunebaum, *Medieval Islam (2nd ed., Chicago, 1953); W. M. Watt, Muhammed at Mecca (Oxford, 1953); M. Pickthall, ed., *The meaning of the glorious Koran, an explanatory translation (New York, 1953), now the most useful English version; A. Jeffry, *The Qu'rān as scripture (New York, 1952), how the parts of the Koran were assembled; L. Gardet & M. Anawati, Introduction à la théologie musulmane (Paris, 1948); D. M. Donaldson, Studies in Muslim ethics (London, 1953); A. J. Arberry, *Sufism (London, 1950); G. M. Wickens, ed., *Avicenna, a symposium (London, 1952); L. Gardet, La pensée religieuse d'Avicenne (Paris, 1951); F. Rahman, ed., Avicenna's psychology (Oxford, 1952); A. Fyzee, Outlines of Muhammadan law (London, 1949); F. J. Carmody, ed., Michael Scot, De notibus celorum (Berkeley, 1953), critical edition of a Latin translation of important Muslim work on astronomy; R. Blachère, *Histoire de la littérature arabe (Paris, 1952); A. Rosenthal, *History of Muslim historiography (Leyden, 1952); A. S. Tritton, "Muslim education in the Middle Ages" in Muslim World, 1953; and K. A. Creswell, *"Problems in Islamic architecture" in Art bulletin, 1953.

LATIN CHRISTENDOM, A.D. 500–1000 (also a few titles that bear on later periods as well as on these five centuries): E. R. Curtius, *European literature and the Latin Middle Ages (New York, 1953), very suggestive and interesting work; F. J. E. Raby, *History of Christian Latin poetry (2nd ed., Oxford, 1953), the standard work; P. Renucci, L'aventure de l'humanisme européen, IVᵉ–XIVᵉ siècle (Paris, 1953), a good short account; K. Edwards, "Use of classical authors by mediaeval writers" in Aberdeen Univ. review, 1952; R. E. Messenger, *The mediaeval Latin hymn (Washington, 1953); M. E. Nicolau, L'origine du cursus rhythmique et les débuts de l'accent d'intensité en Latin (Paris, 1930); J. M. Wallace-Hadrill, *The Barbarian West, 400–1000 (London, 1952), convenient summary of present views; R. H. Hodgkin, *History of the Anglo-Saxons (3rd ed., 2 vols., Oxford, 1953), a basic work; C. W. Kennedy, tr., Early English Christian poetry (London, 1952); E. Salin, *La civilisation merovingienne (2 vols., Paris, 1949–52); A. K. Porter, *The crosses and culture of Ireland (New Haven, 1931); W. A. Phillips, History of the Church of Ireland, Vol. I (Oxford, 1933); M. Esposito, "Latin learning in mediaeval Ireland" in Hermatheia, 1930; M. L. Laistner, *"Some early mediaeval commentaries on the Old Testament" in Harvard theological review, 1953; M. and C. Quennell, Everyday life in Anglo-Saxon, Viking, and Norman times (London, 1953); A. Cabaniss, Agobard of Lyons (Syracuse, 1953); R. E. Sullivan, "The Carolingian missionary and the pagan" in Speculum, 1953.

SCIENCE, A.D. 1000–1500: I. B. Cohen, "Some recent books in the history of science" in Journal of History of ideas, 1954; G. Sarton, History of science (Cambridge, Mass., 1953 ff.), a survey of Sarton's life work; H. Guerlac, *Science in western civilization (New York, 1952), a syllabus, very useful; H. Guerlac, Selected readings in the history of science (through Galileo) (New York,

1954); A. P. Usher, *History of mechanical inventions (2nd ed., Cambridge, Mass., 1954); C. Singer, *History of technology (Oxford, 1954 ff.); S. F. Mason, *A history of the sciences (London, 1953); A. C. Crombie, *Augustine to Galileo, A.D. 400–1650 (London, 1952), a fine introduction; P. Doig, A concise history of astronomy (London, 1950); C. Singer, History of biology (2nd ed., New York, 1950); C. J. Jung, Psychology and alchemy (New York, 1953); G. Abelli, History of astronomy (New York, 1952); R. Dugas, *Histoire de la mécanique (Paris, 1952), important; M. Graubard, Astrology and alchemy, two fossil sciences (New York, 1953); P. P. Wiener, "The tradition behind Galileo's methodology" in Osiris, 1936; P. O. Kristeller, "Mediaeval and Renaissance Latin translations and commentaries" in Scriptorium, 1952; R. W. Lunt, "English learning in the late 12th century" in Trans. Royal Hist. Soc., 1936; A. C. Crombie, *Grosseteste and the origins of experimental science (London, 1952); S. E. Easton, *Roger Bacon (Oxford, 1952); E. Westacott, Roger Bacon in life and legend (London, 1953); E. A. Moody and M. Clagett, eds., *The mediaeval science of weights (Madison, 1952), some treatises with excellent commentary; M. Clagett, "Mediaeval latin translations of Euclid" in Isis, 1953; G. W. Coopland, Oresme and the astrologers (Cambridge, Mass., 1952); E. Zechlin, Maritime Weltgeschichte (Hamburg, 1947); A. P. Newton, ed., *The great age of discovery (London, 1932); B. Penrose, Travel and discovery in the Renaissance, 1420–1620 (Cambridge, Mass., 1952); D. B. Durand, *The Vienna-Klosterneuburg map corpus (Leyden, 1952); A. Arber, Herbals (2nd ed., Cambridge, 1953); J. H. Randell, Jr., *"The place of Leonardo da Vinci in the emergence of modern science" in Journal of the history of ideas, 1953, admirable; I. A. Richter, ed., Selections from the notebooks of Leonardo da Vinci (Oxford, 1952), a "World's classics" volume; G. Sarton, *The appreciation of ancient and mediaeval science in the Renaissance (Philadelphia, 1955), and two interesting interpretive articles: F. R. Johnson, *"Preparation and innovation in the progress of science" in Journal of the history of ideas, 1943; and E. Zilsel, *"The sociological roots of science" in American journal of sociology, 1942.

PHILOSOPHY: F. C. Copelston, Mediaeval philosophy (New York, 1952), a brief introduction; E. Gilson and P. Boehmer, *Geschichte der christlechen Philosophie (2nd ed., Paderborn, 1952); M. de Wulf, History of mediaeval philosophy, Vol. III (new ed., London, 1953); F. C. Copelston, *History of Philosophy, Vol. III, Ockham to Suarez (London, 1953), continuation of a fine history by an English Jesuit; E. Gilson, *Abélard et Héloïse (new ed., Paris, 1948; Eng. trans., London, 1953); R. de Vaux, "Notes et textes sur l'avicennisme Latin au XIIIe siècles" in Bibliothèque Thomiste, 1934; M. D. Chenu, Introduction à l'étude de St. Thomas d'Aquin (Paris, 1950); O. Bird, *"How to read an article of the Summa" in New Scholasticism, 1953; and E. Cassirer, *Individuum und Kosmos in der Philosophie der Renaissance (Leipzig, 1927), important work, emphasizes role of Nicholas of Cusa and of Florentine Neo-Platonists in 15th century thought.

POLITICAL AND SOCIAL THOUGHT: J. A. Schumpeter, History of economic analysis (2 vols., Oxford, 1954); E. Lewis, *Mediaeval political ideas (London, 1954), important; M. E. Reesor, The political theory of the old and middle Stoa

(New York, 1951); M. Hammond, *City state to world state in Greek and Roman political theory (Cambridge, Mass., 1951); C. Wirzubski, Libertas at Rome (Cambridge, 1950), good; J. Le Cler, *The two sovereignties, study of the relations of church and state (New York, 1952); W. Ullman, *"Development of mediaeval idea of sovereignty" in English historical review, 1949; R. C. Mortimer, Western canon law (London, 1953); J. M. Powicke, "Early history of canon law" in History XVIII (Munich, 1947); R. Folz, L'idée d'empire en Occident, Ve-XIVe siècle (Paris, 1953); W. Berges, *Die Fürstenspiegel des hohen und später Mittelalters (Leipzig, 1938), on treatises on training and duties of rulers; N. Lenkeith, *Dante and the legend of Rome (London, 1953); C. Previté-Ortou, "Marsiglio of Padua" in Pro. British Academy, 1935; F. Ganshof, *Histoire des relations internationales, I, Le moyen âge (Paris, 1953); H. Cam, *"Theory and practice of representation in mediaeval England" in History, 1953, a survey of present state of knowledge; and *Etudes presentées à la commission pour l'histoire des assemblées d'états (8 vols., Paris-Louvain, 1937-1949), a fundamental work.

EDUCATION: H. H. Lucas, ed., Rutebeuf, poèmes concernant l'université de Paris (Paris, 1952); F. Harrison, Life in a mediaeval college (London, 1952); and J. Heckscher, "Education of the aristocracy in the Renaissance" in Journal of modern history, 1950.

LITERATURE IN LATIN CHRISTENDOM: S. H. Steinberg, ed., *Cassel's Encyclopedia of literature (2 vols., London, 1953); E. Sykes, ed., Dictionary of non-classical mythology (New York, 1952); V. E. Hopper and B. D. N. Grebanier, *Essentials of European literature, Vol. I (New York, 1952), admirable, brief introduction; H. Haydn and J. C. Nelson, eds., A Renaissance treasury (New York, 1953), an anthology; R. S. Loomis, An introduction to mediaeval literature, chiefly in England, a reading list (new ed., New York, 1948); B. Woledge, Bibliographie des romans et nouvelles du moyen âge (Geneva, 1954); E. H. Wilkins, History of Italian literature (Cambridge, Mass., 1954); A. T. Holmes, *Critical bibliography of French literature, Vol. I (2nd ed., Syracuse, 1952); A. Fuchs, *Les débuts de la littérature allemande, 8e-12e siècle (Strasbourg, 1952); G. Turville-Petre, Origins of Icelandic literature (Oxford, 1953); E. O. Sveinsson, Age of the Sturlungs, Icelandic civilization in the 13th century (Ithaca, 1953); T. P. Cross, Motif-index of early Irish literature (Bloomington, 1952); E. Tonnelat, La légende des Nibelungen en Allemagne au XIXe siècle (Paris, 1953); M. Fleu, "Recent study of the Nibelungenlied" in Journal of Eng. and Ger. philology, 1953; L. R. Lind, ed., Lyric poetry of the Italian Renaissance (New Haven, 1954), with translations by various hands: C. Brown, ed., Religious lyrics of the Fourteenth Century (2nd ed., Oxford, 1952); B. Nagel, Der Deutsche Meistersang (Heidelberg, 1952); S. E. Scammell, "The historical Arthur" in Cambridge journal, 1952; J. M. Love, The forerunners of the French novel (London, 1954); T. Prideaux, World theater in pictures (New York, 1953); G. Frank, *The mediaeval French drama (Oxford, 1954); N. M. Henshaw, "The attitude of the church toward the stage to the end of the Middle Ages" in Medievalia et humanistica, 1952; R. Aigrain, *L'hagiographie (Paris, 1953); P. Lehmann, "Autobiographies of the Middle Ages" in Trans. Royal historical soc., 1953; four studies in French daily life: U. T. Holmes, *Daily *living in the 12th century* (Madison, 1952); E. Faral, *La vie quotidienne au temps de St. Louis* (Paris, 1948); M. Defourneaux, *La vie quotidienne au temps de Jeanne d'Arc* (Paris, 1952); A. Lefranc, *La vie quotidienne au temps de la Renaissance* (Paris, 1938); A. Renaudet, *Dante humaniste* (Paris, 1952); A. Masseron, *Dante et St. Bernard* (Paris, 1953); M. Rodinson, "Dante et l'Islam d'après les travaux récents" in *Revue de l'histoire des réligions*, 1952; C. A. Robson, *Maurice de Sully and the mediaeval homily* (Oxford, 1952); and D. Bush, *Classical influences in Renaissance literature* (Cambridge, Mass., 1952), an excellent lecture; cf. also works by Curtius, Raby, Seznec, and Renucci cited earlier in this supplementary note.

ART IN LATIN CHRISTENDOM: K. Gilbert and H. Kuhn, *History of esthetics* (2nd ed., Bloomington, 1952), useful for both art and literature; the same is true of A. Masseron, *L'influence de St. François d'Assise sur la civilisation italienne* (Paris, n.d.); T. Hamlin, *Architecture through the ages* (2nd ed., New York, 1953); P. Lavedan, *Histoire de l'urbanisme* (3 vols., Paris, 1926–1952); S. Giedion, *Space, time and architecture* (3rd ed., Cambridge, Mass., 1953); H. Focillon, *The life of forms in art* (New Haven, 1942), both very stimulating; C. R. Morey, *Early Christian art* (2nd ed., Princeton, 1954); E. H. Swift, *Roman sources of Christian art* (New York, 1951); J. G. Davies, *The origin and development of early church architecture* (London, 1952); R. Krautheimer, *"The beginning of early Christian architecture" in *Review of religion*, 1939, an important article; R. Krautheimer, ed., *Corpus basilicarum christianarum Romae* (Rome, 1937 ff.); J. W. Crowfoot, *Early Christian churches in Palestine* (London, 1941); E. Hempel & others, *Deutsche Kunstgeschichte* (5 vols., Munich, 1953 ff.); S. Toy, *Castles, a short history of fortification, 1600 B.C.– 1600 A.D.* (London, 1939), a standard work; H. Swarzenski, *Monuments of Romanesque art* (Chicago, 1954); S. M. Crosby, *L'abbaye de St. Denis* (Paris, 1953); W. S. Stoddard, *The west portals of St. Denis and Chartres, theory of origins* (Cambridge, Mass., 1952); M. Schapiro, *"On the aesthetic attitude in Romanesque art" in K. B. Iyer, ed., *Art and thought, in honor of A. Coomaraswamy*, on opinions of contemporary opinion, valuable study; L. Gischia and L. Mazenod, eds., *Les arts primitifs français* (Paris, 1953), especially useful for pictures; R. Dos Santos, *L'art portugais* (Paris, 1953); T. S. R. Boase, *English art 1100–1216* (Oxford, 1953); P. Deschamps and M. Thibout, *La peinture murale en France* (3 vols., Paris, 1952 ff.); M. Rickert, *Mediaeval painting in England* (London, 1954); E. Sandberg-Vavala, *Sienese studies* (Florence, 1953), and by the same author, *Uffizi studies* (Florence, 1948), excellent introductions; E. Panofsky, *Early Netherlandish painting* (2 vols., Cambridge, Mass., 1953); *Corpus de la peinture des anciens pays-bas meridionaux au XVᵉ siècle* (Antwerp, 1951 ff.), important and comprehensive work; A. Burkhard, *Grünewald* (Cambridge, Mass., 1936); A. Tenenti, *La vie et la mort à travers l'art du XVᵉ siècle* (Paris, 1952); G. G. Coulton, *Art and the Reformation* (2nd ed., Cambridge, 1953); G. P. Jones, *"Building in stone in mediaeval western Europe" in *Cambridge economic history of Europe*, Vol. II (Cambridge, 1952); J. Harvey, *Dictionary of mediaeval architects* (London, 1954); P. de Colombier, *Les Chantiers des cathedrales* (Paris, 1953); two works on restoration of medieval monuments: M. S. Briggs, *Goths and Vandals, a study of the* *preservation of historic buildings in England* (London, 1953), and P. Léon, *La vie des monuments français* (Paris, 1951); D. Ancona-Aeschlimann, *Dictionnaire des miniaturistes* (2nd ed., Milan, 1949); J. Evans, *The history of jewelry, 1100–1870* (London, 1953); J. Evans, *Dress in mediaeval France* (Oxford, 1952).

MUSIC IN LATIN CHRISTENDOM: E. H. Krohn, *The history of music, an index to the literature in musicological publications* (St. Louis, 1952); G. Reese, *Music in the Renaissance* (New York, 1954); C. Sachs, *Rhythm and tempo, a study in music history* (New York, 1953); H. Leichtentritt, *Musical form* (Cambridge, Mass., 1951), a standard work; W. L. Sumner, *The organ* (2nd ed., London, 1953); E. Walker, *A history of music in England* (3rd ed., Oxford, 1951); A. Geering, *Organa und mehrstimmigen Conductus, 13–16 Jahrhundert* (Munich, 1953); E. Krenek, *Ockeghen* (New York, 1953); F. F. Clough and C. J. Cuming, eds., *World's encyclopedia of recorded music* (London, 1952); some recent recordings are: Gregorian chants by monks of Solesmes now on long-playing records (Victor LCT–6011 and London–LLA, 14); *Masterpieces of music before 1750* (3 records, Haydn Society 2071–3), to illustrate the examples in the C. Parrish and J. F. Ohl anthology; G. Abraham, ed., *The history of music in sound* (London, 1953 ff.), with printed booklets; *Seven centuries of sacred music* (Decca, DL–9653); and *Music of the Middle Ages* (Vox–PL 8110), mostly songs of troubadours, trouvères, and minnesingers; *Spanish music* (ca. 1500) (E.M.S. 219).

MYSTICISM IN LATIN CHRISTENDOM: F. Gaynor, ed., *Dictionary of mysticism* (New York, 1953); H. Thurston, *The physical phenomena of mysticism* (Chicago, 1952); then a series of new editions of mystical writings: L. Menzies, tr., *The revelations of Mechthild of Magdeburg* (London, 1953); T. Merton, ed., *Bernard of Clairvaux* (Paris, 1953); C. Colledge, tr., *Spiritual espousals of Ruysbroek* (London, 1952); J. McCann, ed., *The cloud of unknowing* (London, 1952); R. Hudleston, ed., *Revelations of Juliana of Norwich* (London, 1952); J. M. Clark, ed., *Suso's little book of eternal wisdom* (London, 1952); T. S. Kepler, ed., *Theologia Germanica* (Cleveland, 1952); J. Chuzeville, ed., *Les mystiques espagnoles* (Paris, 1952); and some special studies: G. Dumeige, *Richard de Saint Victor et l'idée chrétienne de l'amour* (Paris, 1952); W. Williams, *St. Bernard* (2nd ed., Manchester, 1953); A. Hyma, *From Renaissance to Reformation* (Grand Rapids, 1951); M. Spinka, ed., *Advocates of reform: from Wyclif to Erasmus* (New York, 1953), important documents in translation; and J. H. Dahmus, *The prosecution of Wyclyf* (New Haven, 1952).

HUMANISM IN LATIN CHRISTENDOM: K. Burdach, *Reformation, Renaissance, Humanismus* (2nd ed., Leipzig, 1926), emphasizes continuity of Middle Ages and Renaissance; P. Renucci, *L'aventure de l'humanisme européen, IVe–XIVe siècle* (Paris, 1953); M. P. Gilmore, *The world of humanism 1453–1517* (New York, 1952), admirable; M. M. McLaughlin and J. B. Ross, eds., *The portable Renaissance reader* (New York, 1953); H. Hadyn, *The Counter-Renaissance* (New York, 1950), esp. Ch. I; M. Wegner, *Altertumskunde* (Freiburg, 1951) on classical studies 1300–1900; Bedarida, ed., *Pensée humaniste et tradition chrétienne, XVe–XVIe siècles* (Paris, 1950); S. H. Thomson, *"Pro saeculo IV" in Speculum* (1953); Metropolitan Museum of Art, *The Renais-*

sance, a symposium (New York, 1953), very valuable historical interpretations; and some special studies: R. Weiss, *"Greek culture of southern Italy in later Middle Ages" in *Pro. British Academy*, 1951; P. O. Kristeller, *"The place of classical humanism in Renaissance thought" in *Journal of the history of ideas*, 1943; and H. Baron, "Struggle for liberty in the Renaissance" in *American historical review*, 1953.

Second Supplementary Note (April, 1958)

GENERAL: L. Halphen, *Initiation aux études d'histoire du moyen âge* (3rd ed. rev., Paris, 1952), admirable; H. F. Williams, ed., *Index of mediaeval studies published in Festschriften* (Berkeley, 1951); H. Schleiffer and R. Crandall, eds., *Index to economic history essays in Festschriften* (Cambridge, Mass., 1933); F. van der Meer, *Atlas of western civilization* (London, 1955), fascinating; Bolgar, *The classical heritage and its beneficiaries* (Cambridge, 1954), a basic work on the reappropriation of classical culture by Byzantine and Latin Christian civilizations, cf. review in *Sat. Rev.*, 1 Jan., 1955; G. B. Ladner, ed., "History of ideas in the Christian Middle Ages, 1940–52, bibliographical survey" in *Traditio*, 1953; J. Chevalier, *Histoire de la pensée* (3 vols., Paris, 1955 ff), mostly history of philosophy; J. Mantinband, ed., *Dictionary of Latin literature* (to 1500) (New York, 1955); and L. White and others, *"Symposium on the 10th century" in *Medievalia et humanistica*, 1955.

CLASSICAL BACKGROUNDS: G. Harkness, *The sources of western morality* (New York, 1954); V. Ferm, ed., *Ancient religions* (New York, 1950); A. Festugière, *Personal religion among the Greeks* (Berkeley, 1954); F. C. Grant, ed., *Hellenistic religions* (New York, 1953); F. G. Grant, ed., *Ancient Roman religion* (New York, 1957), short source readings; H. I. Bell, *Cults and creeds in Graeco-Roman Egypt* (New York, 1953); A. J. Festugière, *Epicurus and his gods* (London, 1955); N. W. DeWitt, *Epicurus* (Minneapolis, 1954), now the best English account; A. H. Armstrong, *Plotinus* (London, 1953); and A. Winston, *Apollonius of Tyana* (New York, 1954). Also, E. Barker, ed., *From Alexander to Constantine* (Oxford, 1956); C. G. Star, *Civilization and the Caesars* (Ithaca, 1954); G. Sarton, *Hellenistic science and culture* (Cambridge, Mass., 1958); and M. L. Clarke, *The Roman mind, Cicero to Marcus Aurelius* (London, 1956).

BIBLICAL AND PATRISTIC BACKGROUNDS: W. F. Albright, *From the Stone Age to Christianity* (2nd ed., New York, 1957); S. W. Baron and J. L. Blau, eds., *Judaism, ancient and mediaeval* (2 vols., New York, 1954–5), source readings; M. Noth, *History of Israel* (London, 1958); W. F. Albright, *Archeology and the religion of Israel* (3rd ed., Baltimore, 1953); G. E. Wright, *Biblical archeology* (Philadelphia, 1957); S. B. Frost, *Old Testament Apocalyptic* (London, 1952); M. Burrows, *The Dead Sea Scrolls* (New York, 1955); T. H. Gaster, ed., *Dead Sea Scriptures in English translation* (New York, 1956); R. M. Grant, *The sword and the cross* (New York, 1955), excellent study of relations of Roman government and new religions; W. D. Davies and D. Daube, eds., *Back-*

ground of the New Testament and its eschatology (Cambridge, 1956); N. W. DeWitt, *St. Paul and Epicurus* (Minneapolis, 1954); A. Freemantle, ed., *Treasury of early Christianity* (New York, 1954), brief texts and comments; E. K. Barrett, ed., *New Testament background, select documents* (London, 1957); F. L. Cross, ed., *Oxford dictionary of the Christian Church* (Oxford, 1957), invaluable; G. Schnürer, *Church and culture, 350–814 A.D.* (Patterson, 1956) (translation of first volume of a famous German Catholic work); B. Stewart, *The development of Christian worship* (London, 1953); R. Bultman, *Primitive Christianity* (New York, 1957), and by same author, *Theology of the New Testament* (Vol. II, New York, 1955); E. Gilson, *History of Christian philosophy in the Middle Ages* (New York, 1955), a basic work; P. Böhner and E. Gilson, *Christliche Philosophie* (3rd ed., Paderborn, 1954), goes to Nicholas of Cusa, includes theology; H. Bettenson, ed., *Early Christian fathers* (Oxford, 1956); R. Payne, *The Holy Five, story of fathers of Eastern Church* (New York, 1956), a popularization; E. F. Osborn, *Clement of Alexandria* (Cambridge, 1957); R. J. Deferrari, ed., *Anthology of the Latin Fathers* (Milwaukee, 1955); H. A. Wolfson, *Philosophy of the Church Fathers* (3 vols., Cambridge, Mass., 1955 ff); J. Quasten, *Patrology* (4 vols., London, 1955 ff); R. L. Milburn, *Early Christian interpretations of history* (New York, 1954); J. Danielou, *Origen* (London, 1955); R. W. Battenhouse, ed., *A Companion to St. Augustine* (Oxford, 1955), excellent; L. Marrou, *St. Augustine et Augustinisme* (Paris, 1956); R. Roques, *L'Univers Dionysien* (Paris, 1954); H. F. Dondaine, *Le corpus dionysien au XIII siècle* (Paris, 1953), on influence of Dionysius; B. M. Peebles, *Prudentius* (Boston, 1951); and D. T. Rice, *Beginnings of Christian art* (London, 1957).

BYZANTINE CIVILIZATION: C. Diehl, *Byzantium* (New Brunswick, 1957), translation of a French classic; C. Ostrogorsky, *History of the Byzantine state* (London, 1956), best short history; J. M. Hussey, *The Byzantine world* (London, 1957); N. H. Baynes, *Byzantine studies* (London, 1954); E. Barker, ed., *Social and political thought in Byzantium* (Oxford, 1957); S. Runciman, *The Eastern schism* (Oxford, 1955); J. Mavrogodato, tr., *Digenes Akrites* (Oxford, 1956); P. N. Ure, *Justinian and his age* (London, 1951); D. T. Rice, *Byzantine art* (rev. ed., London, 1951); P. A. Micheles, *An aesthetic approach to Byzantine art* (London, 1955); D. V. Ainalov, *Hellenistic bases of Byzantine art* (New Brunswick, 1958), J. A. Hamilton, *Byzantine architecture and decoration* (new ed., London, 1956); F. Dvornik, *The Slavs, early history and civilization* (Boston, 1956); L. Ouspensky and W. Lossky, *The meaning of icons* (New York, 1956); D. T. Rice and S. Radojac, *Yugo-Slavian Byzantine frescoes* (London, 1955); J. Millet, *La peinture du moyen age en Yougoslavie* (Paris, 1955), O. Powstenko, *St. Sophia in Kiev* (New York, 1955); I. Grabar and others, *History of Russian art* (3 vols., Moscow, 1954 ff), wonderful illustrations; G. H. Hamilton, *Art and architecture of Russia* (London, 1954), best recent work; A. Stender-Petersen, ed., *Anthology of Old Russian literature* (New York, 1955); A. Stender-Petersen, *Geschichte der Russichen Literatur* (2 vols., Munich, 1957); and K. M. Setton, *Byzantine background to the Italian Renaissance* (Philadelphia, 1956); and R. P. Verdeil, *La musique byzantine chez les Bulgares et les Russes* (Copenhagen, 1953).

ISLAMIC CIVILIZATION: *Encyclopedia of Islam (new ed., 5 vols., Leyden, 1953 ff), invaluable; H. A. R. Gibb, ed., Shorter encyclopedia of Islam (Ithaca, 1956); R. Roolvink, ed., Historical atlas of Muslim peoples (London, 1957); A. Guillaume, Islam (London, 1954), brief; A. Jeffery, Islam (New York, 1955), short source readings; E. Schroeder, ed., *Muhammed's people (Portland, Maine, 1955), an excellent anthology; M. Gaudefroy-Demombynes, *Muslim institutions (London, 1954); G. von Grunebaum, "Islam, growth of a tradition" in American Anthropologist, 1955; P. K. Hitti, *"Life of Muhammed" in Jewish quarterly review, 1956, a review article; W. M. Watt, Mohammed at Medina (Oxford, 1956), a continuation of his Mohammed at Mecca; J. J. Saunders, "Mohammed in Europe, western interpretations" in History, 1956; A. J. Arberry, *The Koran, interpreted (2 vols., London, 1955); two works of G. von Grunebaum, Unity and variety in Muslim civilization (Chicago, 1955) and Islam, essays of a cultural tradition (Menasha, Wisc., 1955); G. H. Bosquet, ed., *al-Ghazalis' verification des sciences (Paris, 1955); L. A. Meyer, Islamic astrolabists (Geneva, 1956); H. J. Winter, Eastern science (London, 1952); F. J. Carmody, ed., Arabic astronomical literature in Latin translation, a bibliography (Berkeley, 1955); R. Blachère and H. Darmaun, eds., Extraits des geographes arabes du moyen âge (Paris, 1958); R. C. Dentan, ed., Idea of history in ancient Near-East (New Haven, 1955); E. I. Rosenthal, ed., Averroes' commentary on Plato's 'Republic' (Cambridge, 1956); H. Gibb, *"Influence of Islamic culture on mediaeval Europe" in Bull. J. Rylands Library, 1955; A. I. Katsh, Judaism in Islam (New York, 1954); M. Aga-Oglu, *"Remarks on the character of Islamic art" in Art bulletin, 1954, valuable study; G. Marcais, *L'architecture musulmane d'Occident (Paris, 1955); L. A. Mayer, *Islamic architects (Geneva, 1956); K. A. Creswell, Bibliography of painting in Islam (Cairo, 1953); A. Godard, ed., Iran, Persian miniatures (New York, 1956); and E. Perroy, "Encore Mahomet et Charlemagne" in Revue historique, 1954.

WESTERN EUROPE CA. A.D. 400–1000: Four general views: M. Deanesley, Early mediaeval Europe, 476–911 (London, 1956); S. Katz, The decline of Rome and the rise of mediaeval Europe (Ithaca, 1955); R. S. Lopez, Naissance de l'Europe (Paris, 1957); R. Latouche, *Les origines de l'economie occidentale, IVe–XIe siècle (Paris, 1956); F. J. E. Raby, *History of secular Latin poetry in the Middle Ages (2nd ed., Oxford, 1956), this and the author's one volume work on religious Latin poetry, both now in revised editions, are standard; L. F. Benson, Hymnody of the Christian Church (new ed., Richmond, 1956); H. Hubert, Les Germains (Paris, 1952); M. L. Laistner, *Intellectual heritage of early Middle Ages (Ithaca, 1957), series of special studies; G. E. McCracken, ed., Early mediaeval theology (Philadelphia, 1957), texts; N. K. Chadwick, Poetry and letters in early Christian Gaul (Cambridge, 1955); A. Momigliano, "Cassiodorus" in Pro. of British Academy, 1955; W. Bouser, ed., *Anglo-Saxon and Celtic bibliography (2 vols., London, 1956), a valuable tool; P. H. Blair, Introduction to Anglo-Saxon England (Cambridge, 1956), summarizes recent work; M. D. Knowles, ed., Heritage of early Britain (London, 1952); R. K. Gordon, Anglo-Saxon poetry (rev. ed., London, 1955); E. S. Duckett, *Alfred the Great (Chicago, 1956), best life; A. Grabar and C. Nordenfalk, Early mediaeval painting (Geneva, 1957), explores new ground; W. Holmquist, Germanic art (to

A.D. *1000*) (Stockholm, 1955); K. J. Conant, *Carolingian and Romanesque architecture* (announced, London, 1958); and W. Apel, *Gregorian chant* (Bloomington, 1957).

SCIENCE CA. 1000–1500: R. Taton, ed., *Science antique et médiévale* (Paris, 1957); M. Clagett, *Greek science in antiquity* (New York, 1956); L. Thorndike, *History of magic and experimental science*, Vols. VII & VIII (New York, 1956); E. S. Underwood, ed., *Science, medicine, and history, essays in honor of Charles Singer* (2 vols., Oxford, 1953); W. Bonser, *Anglo-Saxon medicine* (Oxford, 1955); D. de Virville, *Histoire de la botanique* (Paris, 1954); T. H. White, ed., *The book of beasts* (New York, 1955), good introduction to popular bestiaries; C. Singer, ed., *History of technology*, Vol. II, 700 B.C.–A.D. 1500 (Oxford, 1956); M. Clagett, *Mechanics in the Middle Ages* (Philadelphia, 1958); C. Wilson, *Heyesterburg; mediaeval logic and rise of mathematical physics* (Madison, 1956); F. S. Taylor, *The alchemists* (London, 1951); E. J. Holmyard, *Alchemy* (London, 1957); F. M. Powicke, "Grosseteste" in *Bull. J. Rylands Library*, 1953; D. A. Callus, ed., *Grosseteste* (Oxford, 1954), essays; G. Sarton, *Appreciation of ancient and mediaeval science during the Renaissance* (Philadelphia, 1956); L. Febvre and others, *Da Vinci et l'expérience scientifique* (Paris, 1953); A. Koyré, *From the closed world to the infinite universe* (Baltimore, 1957); S. E. Morison, *Columbus* (new ed., Boston, 1955); and N. B. Baker, *Vespucci* (New York, 1956).

PHILOSOPHY: G. Varet, *Manuel de bibliographie philosophique* (2 vols., Paris, 1956); B. Wuellner, ed., *Dictionary of scholastic philosophy* (Milwaukee, 1956); W. T. Jones, *History of western philosophy* (New York, 1952), the best one volume compend; A. Freemantle, ed., *The age of faith, the mediaeval philosophers* (New York, 1954), brief texts with comment; E. Gilson, *History of Christian philosophy in the Middle Ages* (New York, 1955), superb; M. Grabmann, *Mittelalterliches Geistesleben* (new ed., Munich, 1956); A. Dempf, *Hauptform mittelalterlichen Weltanschauung* (Munich, 1925); F. van Steenberghen, *Origins of Latin Aristotelianism* (Louvain, 1955); M. D. Chenu, *La théologie comme science au XIIIe siècle* (Paris, 1957); F. van Steenberghen, *Philosophical movement in the 13th century* (London, 1955); E. Gilson, *The Christian philosophy of Aquinas* (New York, 1956); F. C. Coplestone, *Aquinas* (London, 1955), a restatement; F. van Steenberghen, "Siger of Brabant" in *Modern Schoolman*, 1951; S. MacClintock, *Perversity and error, studies in the Averroist, John of Jandun* (Bloomington, 1956); P. Boehmer, ed., *Ockham, Philosophical writings* (Edinburgh, 1957), presents Ockham's ideas in first adequate English translation; P. Vignaux, *Nominalisme au XIVe siècle* (Paris, 1948); E. A. Moody, *Truth and consequence in mediaeval logic* (Amsterdam, 1953); P. Kibre, *"Intellectual interests reflected in libraries of 14th and 15th centuries" in *Journal of the history of ideas*, 1946.

POLITICAL AND ECONOMIC THOUGHT: T. P. Jenkin, *The study of political theory* (New York, 1955); W. Ullman, *Growth of papal government in the Middle Ages* (London, 1955); M. David, *La soveraineté et les limites du pouvoir monarchique, IXe–XVe siècle* (Paris, 1954); H. M. Cam and others, *"Mediaeval representation in theory and practice" in *Speculum*, 1954; T. Gilby, *Political theory of Aquinas* (Chicago, 1958); W. I. Brandt, *Dubois' recovery of* *the Holy Land* (London, 1956); C. T. Davis, *Dante and the idea of Rome* (Oxford, 1957); T. Brian, **Foundations of concilar theory* (Cambridge, 1955), on canonists; E. Lewis, **"Contributions of mediaeval political theory to American political tradition,"* in *American Political Science Review*, 1956; S. J. Miller, "Position of the king in Bracton and Beaumanoir" in *Speculum*, 1956; E. H. Kantorowicz, *King's two bodies, study of mediaeval political theology* (Princeton, 1957); R. de Roover, **"Scholastic economics, survival and influence"* in *Quarterly journal of economics*, 1955; C. Johnson, ed., *De Moneta of Orsme* (London, 1956); and J. T. Noonan, *Scholastic analysis of usury* (Cambridge, Mass., 1957).

EDUCATION: M. L. Clarke, *Rhetoric at Rome* (London, 1953); R. R. Bolgar, cf. under heading *General*; J. R. Williams, **"School of Rheims"* in *Speculum*, 1954, important study; D. McGarry, ed., *Metalogicon of John of Salisbury* (Berkeley, 1955); L. C. Mackinney, *Fulbert of Chartres* (South Bend, 1957); M. M. McLaughlin, "Paris masters of the 13th and 14th centuries and ideas of intellectual freedom" in *Church history*, 1955; W. J. Millor and H. E. Butler, trs., *The letters of John of Salisbury* (2 vols., Oxford, 1955–56); A. L. Gabriel, *Student life in the Ave Maria College* (South Bend, 1955); I. Haunal, *L'enseignement de l'écriture aux universités médiévals* (Budapest, 1954); P. Kibre, "Scholarly privileges" in *American Historical Review*, 1954; and D. D. McGarry, "Renaissance educational theory" in *Historical Bulletin*, 1954.

LITERATURE: C. S. Brown, ed., *Reader's companion to world literature* (New York, 1956), very brief, but excellent; S. Thompson, ed., *Motif-index of folk-literature* (new ed., 5 vols., Bloomington, 1955–7); C. Brooks, *Tragic themes in western literature* (New Haven, 1955); L. Kukenheim and H. Roussel, *Guide de la littérature française du moyen âge* (Leyden, 1957); S. D. Brown, ed., *Dictionary of French literature* (New York, 1957); J. Crosland, **Mediaeval French literature* (Oxford, 1956); R. Levy, **Chronologie de la littérature française du moyen âge* (Tubingen, 1957), a fundamental tool; J. Schwietering, *Die deutsche Dichtung des Mittelalters* (Darmstadt, 1957); M. Schauch, **English mediaeval literature and its social foundations* (Warsaw, 1956); M. Neumark, ed., *Dictionary of Spanish literature* (New York, 1956); H. Beyer, *History of Norwegian literature* (New York, 1956); S. Einarsson, *History of Icelandic literature* (London, 1957); J. H. Hannesson, *Sagas of Icelanders* (Ithaca, 1957), a bibliography; J. L. Young, tr., *The prose Edda* (Cambridge, 1955); R. Bossuat, **Le moyen âge* (new ed., Paris, 1955), considered by some the best general account of mediaeval French letters; J. Rychner, *La chanson de geste* (Geneva, 1955), emphasizes oral tradition; P. Le Gentil, *La chanson de Roland* (Paris, 1955); L. B. Simpson, tr., **The Cid* (Berkeley, 1957), best English version; T. Parry, *History of Welsh literature* (Oxford, 1955); G. Murphy, tr., *Early Irish lyrics* (Oxford, 1956); R. S. Loomis, ed., *History of Arthur literature in the Middle Ages* (announced, Oxford, 1958); H. L. Savage, *The Gawain poet* (Chapel Hill, 1956); M. F. Richey, *Studies of Wolfram von Eschenbach* (London, 1957); G. Cary, *The mediaeval Alexander* (Cambridge, 1956); J. Frappier, **Chrétien de Troyes* (Paris, 1957); F. E. Guyer, *Chrétien de Troyes* (New York, 1957); H. J. Wiegand, *Courtly love in Arthurian France and Germany* (Chapel Hill, 1956); E. Vinaver, ed., **Malory, Death of Arthur*

(Oxford, 1955); P. Nykrog, *Les fabliaux* (Copenhagen, 1957); R. Bossaut, *Roman de Renard* (Paris, 1957); D. G. Griffith, ed., *Bibliography of Chaucer 1908-53* (Seattle, 1955); F. N. Robinson, ed., *Works of Chaucer* (2nd ed., Boston, 1957), standard version; C. Muscatine, **Chaucer and the French tradition* (Berkeley, 1957); J. Speirs, *Mediaeval English poetry, the non-Chaucerian tradition* (London, 1957); W. F. Lehman, *Development of German verse form* (Austin, 1956); P. Le Gentil, *La poésie lyrique espagnole et portugaise à la fin du moyen âge* (Rennes, 1949 ff); B. Woledge, ed., *Bibliographie des romans et nouvelles en prose à 1500* (Geneva, 1954); C. J. Stratman, ed., **Bibliography of mediaeval drama* (Berkeley, 1954), indispensable; P. Zumthor, *Histoire littéraire de la France médiévale* (Paris, 1954), incorporates recent studies; D. Norberg, *La poésie latine rhythmique du haut moyen âge* (Stockholm, 1954); J. K. Bostock, **Old High German literature* (Oxford, 1955); M. Thorp, *Study of the Nibelungenlied, 1755-1931* (Oxford, 1940); E. M. Tillyard, *The English epic* (Oxford, 1953); A. G. Brodeur, "The structure of Beowulf" in *P.M.L.A.*, 1953; U. T. Holmes, "Post-Bédier theories of the Chansons de geste" in *Speculum*, 1955; C. F. Bayerschmidt and L. M. Hollander, trs., *Njal's Saga* (New York, 1954); P. Hartnoll, **Oxford companion to the theater* (2nd ed., Oxford, 1957); J. Gassner, *Masters of the drama* (3rd ed., New York, 1954); H. Craig, **English religious drama of the Middle Ages* (Oxford, 1955); B. Hunninghen, *Origins of the theater* (Hague, 1955); G. Cohen, **Etudes d'histoire du théâtre en France au moyen âge* (Paris, 1956); E. Heopffner, **Les troubadours* (Paris, 1954), now the most useful introduction; A. J. Denomy, "The accessibility of Arabic influences to the earliest troubadours" in *Mediaeval Studies*, 1953; J. M. Ferrier, *Forerunners of the French novel* (Manchester, 1954); G. Weber, **Gottfried von Strassburg's Tristan und die Krise des Weltbildes um 1200* (2 vols., Stuttgart, 1953); N. C. Starr, *King Arthur today* (Gainesville, 1954), discusses Arthurian legend in English and American letters, 1901-1953; A. M. Gunn, *The mirror of love, reinterpretation of Roman de la Rose* (Lubbock, 1952); R. Bossaut, ed., *Alain de Lille's 'Anticlaudianus'* (Paris, 1955); G. Reynaud de Lage, *Alain de Lille* (Montreal, 1951); D. Vittorini, **Age of Dante* (Syracuse, 1957); T. G. Bergin, ed., *Rhymes from Petrarch* (Edinburgh, 1956); E. H. Wilkins, **Studies in Petrarch* (Cambridge, Mass., 1955); H. G. Wright, *Boccaccio in England* (London, 1957); E. W. Edwards, *Orlando Furioso and its predecessor* (Cambridge, 1924); M. Barbi, **Life of Dante* (Berkeley, 1954); E. Gilson, **Dante et la philosophie* (Paris, 1954); F. Ferguson, *Dante's dawn of the mind, a modern reading of the Purgatorio* (Princeton, 1953); H. H. Blanchard, ed., *Poetry and prose of the Continental Renaissance* (2nd ed., New York, 1955); B. Ford, ed., *The age of Chaucer* (London, 1954), uneven; F. Desonay, *Villon* (2nd ed., Geneva, 1947); and F. de Roover, "Financing and marketing of early printed books" in *Bulletin Business History Society*, 1953.

ART, CA. 1000-1500: L. Réau, **Dictionnaire polyglotte des termes d'art et d'archéologie* (Paris, 1953), very useful; E. H. Gombrich, **Story of art* (8th ed., New York, 1957), the best one volume survey; E. G. Holt, ed., **Documentary history of art* (2 vols., New York, 1957-8), revision of an earlier work; E. Panofsky, **Meaning in the visual arts* (New York, 1955), a collection of essays; L. Réau, **Iconographie de l'art chrétien* (5 vols., Paris, 1955 ff); E. B. Smith,

Architectural symbolism of Imperial Rome and the Middle Ages (Princeton, 1956); J. Baltrusaitis, *Le moyen âge fantastique* (Paris, 1955), on the bizarre and fabulous; G. Ferguson, *Signs and symbols of Christian art* (Oxford, 1954), a good introduction to iconography; J. Harvey, *Cathedrals of Spain* (London, 1957); S. Toy, *History of fortifications* (London, 1955); R. Ritter, *Chateaux, donjons et places fortes, l'architecture militaire française* (Paris, 1953), excellent brief compend; J. Harvey, *Dictionary of English mediaeval architects (to 1550)* (London, 1954); A. Bugge, *Norwegian stave churches* (Oslo, 1954); C. B. Crichton, *Romanesque sculpture in Italy* (London, 1954); C. Terrasse, *La cathédrale, miroir du monde* (new ed., Paris, 1952); G. Webb, *Architecture in Britain, the Middle Ages* (London, 1956); P. Brieger, *English art 1216–1307* (Oxford, 1957); G. Zarnecki, *English Romanesque sculpture* (2 vols., London, 1951–3); H. Focillon, *Peintures romanes de France* (2nd ed., Paris, 1950); E. W. Anthony, *Romanesque frescoes* (Princeton, 1950); A. Grabar and C. Nordenfalk, *Romanesque painting* (Geneva, 1958); F. Saxl, *English sculptures of the 12th century* (London, 1954); C. H. Crichton, *Italian Romanesque sculpture* (London, 1955); J. Gartner and M. Pobé, *Romanesque art in France* (London, 1956), superb photographs; P. Frankl, *Gothic architecture* (London, 1956), and by the same author, *Gothic architecture, interpretations through eight centuries* (Princeton, 1957); O. von Simon, *The Gothic cathedral* (New York, 1956), conjectural but stimulating; O. Lehmann-Brockhaus, ed., *Lateinishe Shriftsquellen zur Kunst in England* (5 vols., Munich, 1956 ff); Y. Bonnefoy, *Peintures murales de la France Gothique* (Paris, 1954); P. Lavedan, *Représentations des villes dans l'art du moyen âge* (Paris, 1954); L. François-Pillion and J. Lafond, *L'art du XIVᵉ siècle* (Paris, 1954); J. Pope-Hennesy, *Italian Gothic sculpture* (London, 1955); L. Stone, *Sculpture in Britain, the Middle Ages* (London, 1955); J. Dupont and C. Gaudi, *Gothic painting* (Geneva, 1954), and G. Argan and J. Lassaigne, *Fifteenth Century* (Geneva, 1955), both with superb color reproductions; M. Rickert, *Painting in Britain, the Middle Ages* (London, 1954); W. Constable, *Painter's workshop* (Oxford, 1955), on techniques of painting; M. Friedlander, *From van Eyck to Bruegel* (New York, 1956), important; E. Carli, *Sienese painting* (New York, 1957), best color reproductions; D. Diringer, *The illuminated book* (New York, 1958); D. Miner, *The mediaeval illustrated book* (Philadelphia, 1958); M. Salmi, *Italian miniatures* (New York, 1957); *Central European miniatures in the Morgan Library* (New York, 1957), a sequel to volume on Italian miniatures of 1953; R. Sowers, *The lost art, a 1000 years of stained glass* (London, 1954); C. J. Connick, *Adventures in light and color* (New York, 1937), modern stained glass; C. Woodforde, *English stained and painted glass* (Oxford, 1954); L. Grodecki, *Vitraux de France XIᵉ–XVIᵉ siècle* (Paris, 1955); H. Read, *English stained glass* (London, 1926); H. Arnold, *Stained glass of the Middle Ages in England and France* (2nd ed., New York, 1955); G. Marchini, *Italian stained glass* (New York, 1957); F. Rossi, *Italian jeweled arts* (New York, 1957); L. van Puyvelde, *Le siècle des Van Eyck* (Paris, 1953); M. W. Brockwell, *The van Eyck problem* (London, 1955); E. Panofsky, *Dürer* (4th ed., Princeton, 1955); J. Alazard, *L'art et la pensée de Léonard de Vinci* (Paris, 1954); D. Dos Santos, *Nuno Goncalves* (New York, 1956); R. Krautheimer, *Ghiberti* (Princeton, 1957); H. W. Janson, *Donatello (2 vols., Princeton, 1957); *Leonardo da Vinci (New York, 1956), a huge collection of studies, with 1600 illustrations; and K. Clark, The Gothic revival (2nd ed., London, 1950).

MUSIC: E. C. Krohn, ed., History of music, an index to literature in musicological publications (St. Louis, 1952), and four works that try to tie up music history and general history; P. H. Láng, Music in western civilization (New York, 1951); H. Leichentritt, Music, history and ideas; C. Sachs, *Our musical heritage (2nd ed., New York, 1955); P. Garvie, ed., Music and western man (London, 1957); W. D. Allen, Philosophies of music history (New York, 1939); J. A. Westrup, Introduction to musical history (London, 1955), both discuss problems of study of history of music; P. Scholes, ed., *Oxford companion to music (9th ed., Oxford, 1955); E. Blom, ed., *Grove's dictionary of music (5th ed., 9 vols., London, 1954); E. Blom, ed., Everyman's dictionary of music (2nd ed., London, 1954); J. A. Westrup, ed., *New Oxford history of music (11 vols., Oxford, 1954 ff.), there will eventually be ten volumes of long playing records, The history of music in sound, to accompany this work, each volume supplied with an admirable pamphlet published by the Oxford University Press (nine volumes appeared before April, 1960), this series, the extensive Decca Archive Production series, and the three records made in Denmark to illustrate Parrish and Ohl's anthology have supplanted C. Sachs, ed., L'Antologie sonore; R. Stevenson, Music before the Classic Era (New York, 1955), brief survey; A. Harman, Mediaeval and Early Renaissance music (Fairlawn, N. J., 1958); C. Parrish, Notation of mediaeval music (New York, 1957); E. A. Bowles, Grouping of musical instruments in the Middle Ages (Cambridge, Mass., 1954); D. Boalch, Makers of the harpsichord and clavichord 1440–1840 (London, 1950); J. Jacquot, ed., La musique instrumentale de la Renaissance (Paris, 1955); N. C. Carpenter, Music in the mediaeval and Renaissance universities (Norman, 1957); E. Wellesz, Christian chant (London, 1956); E. Wellesz, "Recent studies in western chant" in Musical quarterly, 1955; W. G. Waite, The rhythm of 12th century polyphony (New York, 1954); S. Levarie, Guillaume de Machaut (New York, 1954); M. F. Bukofzer, "Dunstable, a quincentenary report" in Musical quarterly, 1954; R. L. Green, "Dunstable, a supplement" in Musical quarterly, 1954; B. Murray, "New light on Obrecht" in Musical quarterly, 1957; E. Lowinsky, *"Music in the culture of the Renaissance" in Journal of history of ideas, 1954; and P. O. Kristeller, *"Music and learning in the early Italian Renaissance" in Journal of Renaissance and Baroque music, 1947.

MYSTICISM AND HUMANISM: O. Chadwick, ed., Western asceticism (Philadelphia, 1957); F. Dressler, Petrus Damiani, Leben und Werk (Rome, 1954); R. C. Petry, Late mediaeval mysticism (Philadelphia, 1957); J. Chuzeville, ed., Les mystiques allemands (new ed., Paris, 1957); J. M. Clark, Meister Eckhart (London, 1957); E. W. McDonnell, The Beguines and Begards in mediaeval culture (New Brunswick, 1954); C. Dumeige, Richard de St. Victor et l'idée chrétienne de l'amour (Paris, 1951); S. Axters, The spirituality of the Old Low Countries (London, 1955); G. Heron, tr., Nicholas of Cusa, Of learned ignorance (London, 1954), good translation of one of most important works of 15th century; G. R. Potter, ed., The Renaissance (Cambridge, 1957); W. F. Ferguson, "Revival of classical antiquity or the first century of Humanism, a reappraisal" in *Report, Canadian Historical Association*, 1957; P. O. Kristeller, **Classics and Renaissance thought* (Cambridge, Mass., 1955) and by the same author, **Studies in Renaissance thought* (Rome, 1955); G. Post and others, **"The mediaeval heritage and the humanistic ideal" in *Traditio*, 1955; R. Marcel, ed., *Ficino's commentary sur le Banquet de Platon* (Paris, 1956); H. Bédarida, *Pensée humaniste et traditio chrétienne* (Paris, 1950); E. Pellegrin, *La bibliothèque des Visconti-Sforza* (Paris, 1955); A. G. Keller, "Bessarion" in *Cambridge historical journal*, 1955; R. Weiss, **Humanism in England during the fifteenth century* (2nd ed., Oxford, 1957); E. W. Hunt, **Colet* (London, 1946); P. A. Duhamel, "Oxford lectures of Colet" in *Journal of history of ideas*, 1953; H. Weisinger, "Attack on the Renaissance in theology today" in *Studies in the Renaissance*; G. Toffanin, *History of humanism* (New York, 1955), useful but too favorable to religious orthodoxy of humanists; A. Chastel, *Marsile Ficin et l'art* (Geneva, 1954); A. Renaudet, *Erasme et l'Italie* (Geneva, 1954); R. T. Mitchell, *John Free* (London, 1955); H. Baron, **Humanistic and political literature in Florence and Venice at the beginning of the Quattro-cento* (Cambridge, Mass., 1955) and by the same author, **The crisis of the early Italian Renaissance* (2 vols., Princeton, 1955); and G. Mattingly, **Renaissance diplomacy* (Boston, 1955), though the last three works deal partly or mainly with politics they contain material of interest to the student of humanism.

Third Supplementary Note (May, 1964)

CLASSICAL BACKGROUND: A Bonnard, **Greek civilization* (2 vols., New York, 1957–9), excellent introduction to classical Greek culture; W. K. Guthrie, *The Greek philosophers* (London, 1950); E. Havelock, *A preface to Plato* (Cambridge, Mass., 1963); J. K. Feibleman, *Religious Platonism, influence of religion on Plato and the influence of Plato on religion* (London, 1959); J. H. Randall, Jr., **Aristotle* (New York, 1960), good survey; E. Bréhier, **The philosophy of Plotinus* (Chicago, 1958), and by the same author, *La philosophie de Plotin* (new ed., Paris, 1961).

BIBLICAL BACKGROUND: J. B. Pritchard ed., **Ancient Near East,* text and pictures, and by the same author **Archeology and the Old Testament* (Princeton, 1958), fine introductions to Old Testament backgrounds; B. Mazur and others, eds., *Illustrated world of the Bible* (5 vols., New York, 1961); L. H. Grollenberg, *Atlas of the Bible* (London, 1956); J. Finegan, **Light from the Ancient East* (rev. ed., Princeton, 1959); G. E. Wright, *Biblical archeology* (Philadelphia, 1957); J. Bright, *A history of Israel* (Philadelphia, 1959); H. M. Orlinsky, **Ancient Israel* (2nd ed., Ithaca, 1960), a fine introduction; G. W. Anderson, *A critical introduction to the Old Testament* (London, 1959); R. K. Harrison, *History of Old Testament Times* (Edinburgh, 1957); E. Jacob, *Theology of the Old Testament* (New York, 1958); M. Burrows, **More light on the Dead Sea Scrolls* (New York, 1958), discusses discoveries since the author's earlier work of 1955; E. Stendahl, ed., **The scrolls and the New Testament* (New York, 1957), contributions by twelve specialists; and S. Neill, *The interpretation of the New Testament, 1861–1961* (Oxford, 1964).

THE PATRISTIC AGE: W. Walker, **History of the Christian church* (new ed., New York, 1959), a standard work; E. Van der Meer and C. Mohrmann, *Atlas of the early Christian world* (London, 1958), valuable for maps and pictures to about 600 A.D.; R. H. Bainton, *Early Christianity* (to A.D. 500), an introductory survey with selected texts; B. Altaner, *Patrology* (London, 1959); J. N. Kelley, *Early Christian doctrines* (London, 1958) largely replaces Bethune-Baker; R. M. Grant, *Gnosticism and early Christianity* (New York, 1959); R. M. Grant, ed., *Gnosticism* (New York, 1961), a useful collection of texts; R. M. Wilson, *The Gnostic problem* (London, 1958), mainly on Judaism and Gnosticism; H. von Campenhausen, *The fathers of the Greek church* (London, 1963); G. H. Ladner, *Idea of reform in the Age of the Fathers* (Cambridge, Mass., 1959); W. W. Jaeger, *Early Christianity and Greek Phaideia* (London, 1961); H. Marrou, *Augustine and his influence* (New York, 1959); D. S. Wallace-Hadrill, *Eusebius* (London, 1960); A. Momigliano, ed., *Conflict between paganism and Christianity in the Fourth Century* (Oxford, 1962); H. Marrou, *St. Augustin et la fin de la culture antique* (new ed., Paris, 1959); H. A. Deane, *Political and social ideas of St. Augustine* (New York, 1963); E. Gilson, *The Christian philosophy of St. Augustine* (London, 1960); E. Portalié, *Guide to the thought of St. Augustine* (London, 1961); O. Chadwick, ed., *Western asceticism* (London, 1958); M. Laurent, *L'Art chrétien des origines à Justinian* (Brussels, 1956); D. T. Rice, *Beginnings of Christian art* (New York, 1957), goes to about 1150 A.D.; W. F. Vollbach and M. Hirmer, *Early Christian art* (London, 1961); E. Syndicus, *Early Christian art* (London, 1962); and E. Mâle, *Early churches of Rome* (London, 1959).

BYZANTINE CIVILIZATION: J. M. Hussey, ed., *The Byzantine Empire* (2nd ed., Cambridge, 1963), a volume in the new edition of *Cambridge Medieval History;* H. W. Haussig, *Kulturgeschichte von Byzanz* (Stuttgart, 1959); M. V. Anastos, *The mind of Byzantium* (New York, 1960); P. Lemerle, ed., *Traité d'études byzantines* (9 vols., Paris, 1958 ff), a valuable series of handbooks treating varied aspects of Byzantine civilization; E. Dölger, *Byzanz und die europäische Staatenwelt* (Ettal, 1953), studies of Byzantine influences on Europe; Ohnsorge, *Abendland und Byzanz* (Darmstadt, 1958); D. T. Rice, *The Byzantines* (London, 1962); G. Downey, *Constantinople in the age of Justinian* (Norman, 1960); A. Grabar, *L'iconoclasme byzantin* (Paris, 1957), skillful synthesis of politics, religion, and art A.D. 550–900; N. Zernov, *Eastern Christendom* (London, 1960), fine survey of Eastern churches (London, 1960); V. Lossky, *The mystical theology of the Eastern Church* (London, 1957); G. Vernadsky, *Origins of Russia* (Oxford, 1959); D. Obolensky, "Russia's Byzantine heritage" in *Oxford Slavonic papers,* 1950; O. M. Dalton, *Byzantine art and archeology* (new ed., London, 1961), a standard work; D. T. Rice, *Art of Byzantium* (New York, 1959), for pictures, concerned only with art of the city of Constantinople; and by the same author, *Art of the Byzantine era* (London, 1963); J. Beckwith, *Art of Constantinople* (London, 1961), a Phaidon book with excellent pictures, omits architecture; C. Stewart, *Byzantine legacy* (London, 1947), for pictures; D. V. Ainalov, *Hellenistic origins of Byzantine art* (New Brunswick, 1961); G. Mathew, *Byzantine aesthetics* (London, 1963); P. A. Michelis, "Neo-Platonic philosophy and Byzantine art" in *Jour. of aesthetics and art criticism,* 1952; K.

Onasch, *Icons* (London, 1963); and E. Wellesz, *History of Byzantine music and hymnography* (2nd ed., Oxford, 1960), a fundamental work.

ISLAMIC CIVILIZATION: J. D. Pearson, ed., *Index Islamicus* (London, 1958), lists articles on Islamic subjects 1906–55; W. de Bary and A. T. Embree, eds., *Guide to Oriental classics* (New York, 1964); P. K. Hitti, *History of the Arabs* (new ed., New York, 1959), a basic work; R. H. Davison, *Near and Middle East, introduction to history and bibliography* (Washington, 1959); R. Landau, *Arab contribution to civilization* (San Francisco, 1958); A. Jeffery, *Islam, Mohammed and his religion* (New York, 1958), a collection of passages from early Mohammedan literature with useful commentary; J. A. Williams, ed., *Islam* (New York, 1961), also a collection of texts; R. Brunschvig and G. von Grunebaum, eds., *Classicisme et déclin culturel de l'Islam* (Paris, 1958); I. Goldziher, *Le dogme et la loi de l'Islam* (2nd ed., Paris, 1958), a classic work; A. Mez, *The renaissance of Islam* (London, 1937), a basic study; N. Daniel, *The concept of Islam* A.D. *1100–1350* (Edinburgh, 1950), ideas about Islam in Latin Christendom; R. W. Southern, *Western ideas of Islam in the Middle Ages* (Cambridge, Mass., 1962); P. K. Hitti, *Islam and the West* (Princeton, 1962); A. S. Tritton, ed., *Materials on Muslim education in the Middle Ages* (London, 1957); W. M. Watt, *Islamic philosophy and theology* (Edinburgh, 1962); E. I. Rosenthal, *Political thought in medieval Islam* (Cambridge, 1958); F. Rosenthal, ed., *Ibn Khaldûn's Introduction to history* (3 vols., New York, 1959), greatest Islamic work in the social sciences; S. M. Afnan, *Avicenna* (London, 1958), the best study; H. Corbin, *Avicenna and the visionary recital* (New York, 1960), study of mysticism in Islam; R. C. Zaehner, *Hindu and Muslim mysticism* (London, 1960); H. Gibb, *Arabic literature* (2nd ed., London, 1963); K. A. Creswell, ed., *Bibliography of the arts of Islam* (Oxford, 1962), and by the same author, *Short account of early Muslim architecture* (a Penguin book, London, 1958); J. D. Hoag, *Western Islamic architecture* (London, 1963); D. Hill and O. Grabar, *Islamic architecture and its decoration, 800–1500* (London, 1964); R. Ettinghausen, *Arab painting* (New York, 1962); B. Gray, *Persian painting* (Geneva, 1961); and H. G. Farmer, "Music of Islam" in *New Oxford history of music*, Vol. I (Oxford, 1957).

WESTERN EUROPE CA. A.D. *400–1000*: W. C. Bark, *Origins of the medieval world* (Stanford, 1958), challenges traditional views; H. Arbman, *The Vikings* (New York, 1961); T. G. Powell, *The Celts* (London, 1958); M. and L. de Paor, *Early Christian Ireland, 400–1200* (London, 1959); L. Bieler, *Ireland, harbinger of the Middle Ages* (Oxford, 1963); M. Hurlimann and W. Guyan, eds., *Art of the Celts* (London, 1958), a collection of pictures; P. Riché, *Education et culture dans l'occident barbare, VI–VII siècles* (Paris, 1962); J. Fontaine, *Isidore de Séville et la culture classique* (2 vols., Paris, 1959), a definitive study; E. Salin *La civilisation mérovingienne*, Vol. 4 (Paris, 1959), concludes an important work; A. F. Havighurst, ed., *The Pirenne thesis* (New York, 1958); H. Fichteneau, *The Carolingian Empire* (Oxford, 1957); L. Wallach, *Alcuin and Charlemagne* (Ithaca, 1959); E. S. Duckett, *Carolingian portraits* (Ann Arbor, 1962); H. P. Lattin, ed., *Letters of Gerbert* (New York, 1961); R. S. Lopez, ed., *Tenth century* (New York, 1959), excellent selection of texts; R. W. Chambers, *Beowulf* (3rd ed., Cambridge, 1959); A. G. Brodeur, *Art of Beowulf* (Berkeley, 1959); L. E. Nicholson, ed., *Anthology of Beowulf criticism* (Notre Dame, 1963); L. M. Hollander, tr., *The Poetic Edda* (2nd ed., Austin, 1962); P. Hallberg, *The Icelandic saga* (Lincoln, 1962); E. A. Fisher, *Anglo-Saxon architecture and sculpture* (London, 1959); F. Stenton, ed., *The Bayeux tapestry* (London, 1957); K. Conant, *Carolingian and Romanesque architecture* (London, 1959); and L. Grodecki, *L'architecture ottonienne* (Paris, 1958).

SCIENCE AND TECHNOLOGY *1000–1500*: M. Daumas, ed., *Histoire de la science* (Paris, 1958); R. Taton, ed., **Ancient and medieval science to 1450* (New York, 1963), crammed with facts, little interpretation; A. C. Crombie, **Augustine to Galileo* (2nd ed., 2 vols., Cambridge, Mass., 1961); C. Singer, *Short history of scientific ideas (to 1900)* (Oxford, 1959); M. Clagett, **Critical problems in the history of science* (Madison, 1959), studies by sixteen authorities, valuable; W. H. Stahl, *Roman science* (Madison, 1962), continues story into Twelfth Century; S. Sambursky, *The physical world of late antiquity* (London, 1962); R. M. Palter, ed., *Toward modern science* (2 vols., New York, 1961), series of essays; J. H. Randall, Jr., **School of Padua and emergence of modern science* (New York, 1960); B. L. Gordon, *Medieval and Renaissance medicine* (New York, 1960); T. K. Derry and T. I. Williams, *Short history of technology* (Oxford, 1960); F. Klemm, *History of western technology* (London, 1959); L. White, **Medieval technology and social change* (Oxford, 1962), very valuable; and J. F. Scott, *History of mathematics* (London, 1958).

PHILOSOPHY: D. Knowles, **Evolution of medieval thought* (Baltimore, 1962); A. Maurer, *Medieval philosophy* (New York, 1960); G. Leff, *Medieval thought* (London, 1958); P. Vignaux, *Philosophy in the Middle Ages* (New York, 1959); J. Le Goff, *Les intellectuels au moyen âge* (Paris, 1957); D. Knowles, *Saints and scholars, twenty-five medieval portraits* (Cambridge, 1962); J. Leclercq, *The love of learning and the desire for God, a study of monastic culture* (New York, 1961); M. Clagett and others, *Twelfth Century Europe and the foundations of modern society* (Madison, 1961); M. Seidlmayer, *Currents of medieval thought* (London, 1959), mainly on German thought; P. Delhaye, *Pierre Lombard* (Montreal, 1961); M. Chenu, *La théologie au XII siècle* (Paris, 1958); F. van Steenberghen, **Aristotle in the West* (Louvain, 1955); E. Gilson, **Jean Duns Scot* (Paris, 1952); E. Bettoni, *Duns Scotus* (London, 1961); L. Baudry, *Occam* (Paris, 1950); and F. L. Utley, ed., *Forward movement of the Fourteenth Century* (Columbus, 1961), contains studies in a number of fields.

POLITICAL AND ECONOMIC THOUGHT: G. H. Sabine, **History of political theory* (3rd ed., New York, 1961); M. Prélot, *Histoire des idées politiques* (2nd ed., Paris, 1961); J. Touchard & others, **Histoire des idées politiques* (2 vols., Paris, 1959); S. S. Wolin, **Politics and vision* (Boston, 1960), one of best interpretative works on political thought; J. B. Morrall, *Political thought in medieval times* (New York, 1962), admirable survey; W. Ullmann, *Principles of government and politics in the Middle Ages* (London, 1961); M. Pacaut, *La théocratie, l'église et le pouvoir au moyen âge* (Paris, 1957); M. Wilks, *Problem of sovereignty in the later Middle Ages* (Cambridge, 1963); E. Lewis, **"The 'positivism' of Marsiglio of Padua"* in *Speculum,* 1963; L. J.

Daly, *The political theory of Wyclif* (Chicago, 1962); B. Tierney, *Conciliar theory* (Cambridge, 1958); M. Watanabe, *Political ideas of Nicholas of Cusa* (Geneva, 1963); P. E. Sigmund, *Nicholas of Cusa and medieval political thought* (Cambridge, Mass., 1963); B. Tierney, *Medieval poor law* (Berkeley, 1959); J. W. Baldwin, *"Medieval theories of the just price" in *Trans. Amer. Philosophical Soc.*, 1959; and R. de Roover, "The concept of the just price" in *Jour. of economic history*, 1958.

EDUCATION: L. J. Daly, *Medieval university, 1200–1400* (New York, 1961); P. Kibre, *Scholarly privileges in the Middle Ages* (Cambridge, Mass., 1962); J. Kerer, *Statuta collegii sapientiae* (Lindau, 1958), with 80 reproductions of miniatures illustrating student life; A. Taylor, ed., *The philobiblon of Richard de Bury* (Berkeley, 1948); and L. Hajnal, *L'enseignement de l'ecriture aux universités médiévals* (2nd ed., Paris, 1960).

LITERATURE: K. Vossler, *Medieval culture* (new ed., 2 vols., London, 1958); W. T. H. Jackson, *Literature of the Middle Ages* (New York, 1960); G. Watson, *Cambridge bibliography of English literature, supplement* (Cambridge, 1957); P. Harvey and J. Heseltine, eds., *Oxford companion to French literature* (Oxford, 1958); F. J. E. Raby, ed., *Oxford book of medieval Latin verse* (new ed., Oxford, 1959); M. O. Walshe, *Medieval German literature* (Cambridge, Mass., 1962); R. E. Chandler and K. Schwartz, *New history of Spanish literature* (Baton Rouge, 1961); A. de Mandach, *Naissance et développement de la chanson de geste,* Vol. I (Geneva, 1961); M. de Riquer, *Les chansons de geste françaises* (2nd ed., Paris, 1958); F. Lot, *Etudes sur les légendes épiques françaises* (Paris, 1958); G. F. Jones, *The ethos of the 'Song of Roland'* (Baltimore, 1963), emphasizes pagan elements; W. A. Mueller, *The Nibelungenlied Today* (Chapel Hill, 1962); M. Valency, *In praise of love* (New York, 1958), admirable study of love lyric from troubadours through Dante; A. Flores, ed., *Anthology of medieval lyrics* (New York, 1962); H. Creekmore, ed., *Lyrics of the Middle Ages* (New York, 1959); W. Beare, *Latin verse and European song* (London, 1957); J. F. Benton, "The court of Champagne as a literary center" in *Speculum,* 1961; A. T. Hatto and R. J. Taylor, eds., *Songs of Neidhart von Reuental* (Manchester, 1958), study of both poetry and music of a leading minnesinger; D. Norberg, *Introduction à l'étude de la versification latine médiévale* (Stockholm, 1958); I. Frank, *Répertoire mètrique de la poèsie des troubadours* (2 vols., Paris, 1958); M. F. Richey, tr., *Medieval German lyrics* (London, 1958), a representative selection; R. S. Loomis, *Development of Arthurian romance* (London, 1963), excellent brief introduction; R. S. Loomis, ed., *Arthurian literature in the Middle Ages* (Oxford, 1959), studies by thirty specialists; R. S. Loomis, *The grail from Celtic myth to Christian symbol* (New York, 1963); H. Adolf, *Holy city and grail* (University Park, 1960); M. J. Reid, *The Arthurian legend* (London, 1960); R. W. Barber, *Arthur of Albion, introduction to the Arthurian literature of England* (London, 1961); R. Bezzola, *Les origines de la littèrature courtoise, 500–1200* (Vols. 2 and 3, Paris, 1963); W. Sacker, *Introduction to Wolfram's 'Parzival'* (Cambridge, 1963); W. T. Jackson, "Andreas Capellanus and the practice of love at court" in *Romantic review,* 1958; S. Bayraw, *Symbolisme médiéval* (Istanbul, 1956), concerned chiefly with chivalric romances; J. A. W. Bennett, ed., *Essays on Malory* (Oxford, 1963); A. C. Baugh, *"Fifty years of Chaucer scholarship" in *Speculum*, 1951; D. W. Robertson, Jr. *Preface to Chaucer* (Princeton, 1962); P. F. Baum, *Chaucer* (Durham, 1958), critical of overpraise of Chaucer; B. H. Bronson, *In search of Chaucer* (Toronto, 1960); W. C. Curry, **Chaucer and the medieval sciences* (new ed., London, 1960); R. J. Schoeck and J. Taylor, eds., **Chaucer criticism* (2 vols., Notre Dame, 1962); A. Nicoll, **Development of the theater* (4th ed., New York, 1958); J. D. Ogilvy, "Entertainers of the early Middle Ages" in *Speculum*, 1963; R. B. Donovan, *Liturgical drama in medieval Spain* (Toronto, 1958); G. Wickham, **Early English stages*, Vol. I, 1300–1576 (New York, 1959), revises many ideas about medieval drama; A. Williams, *The drama of medieval England* (East Lansing, 1961); J. Lawlor, **Piers Plowman* (New York, 1962), best introduction; R. W. Frank, Jr., *Piers Plowman and the scheme of salvation* (New Haven, 1958); M. A. Bloomfield, *Piers Plowman as a 14th century apocalypse* (New Brunswick, 1962); J. Fox, *Poetry of Villon* (London, 1962); G. R. Owst, **Literature and pulpit in medieval England* (2nd ed., Oxford, 1961); T. Welter, *L'exemplum dans la littérature du moyen âge* (Paris, 1957); R. Vaughan, *Matthew Paris* (Cambridge, 1958); and F. Wormald and C. E. Wright, eds., *The English library before 1700* (London, 1958).

ART: **Encyclopedia of world art* (15 vols., New York, 1960 ff), indispensable; R. Huyghe, ed., *Larousse encyclopedia of Byzantine and medieval art* (London, 1963); W. Oakeshott, **Classical inspiration in medieval art* (London, 1959); G. Cohen and L. Réau, *L'art du moyen âge et la civilisation française* (new ed., Paris, 1958); G. Cohen and R. Schneider, *La formation du génie moderne: arts plastiques, art littéraire* (new ed., Paris, 1958); E. Panofsky, **Renaissance and Renascences in Western art* (2 vols., Stockholm, 1960); H. R. Hitchcock, ed., *World architecture* (New York, 1963); H. Focillon, **Art of the West in the Middle Ages* (2 vols., London, 1963), a basic work; G. Ferguson, *Signs and symbols in Christian art* (Oxford, 1961); H. Busch and D. Lohse, eds., *Romanesque Europe* (London, 1960), useful collection of pictures; M. Aubert and others, **L'art roman en France* (Paris, 1961); H. Decker, *Romanesque art in Italy* (New York, 1959), valuable for illustrations; H. Busch and B. Lohse, eds., *Gothic Europe* (London, 1959), useful collection of pictures; J. Gimpel, *The cathedral builders* (New York, 1961); J. F. Fitchen, **Construction of Gothic cathedrals* (Oxford, 1960); P. Frankl, **Gothic architecture* (London, 1963); O. von Simon, **The Gothic cathedral* (2nd ed., New York, 1962); G. Lesser, *Gothic cathedrals and sacred geometry* (2 vols., London, 1957), very conjectural; P. Frankl, **The Gothic, literary sources and interpretations through eight centuries* (Princeton, 1959); H. Jantzen, *High Gothic* (New York, 1962); G. H. Cook, *The English cathedral through the centuries* London, 1957); T. Bowie, ed., *The sketchbook of Villard de Honnecourt* (Bloomington, 1959); L. Grodecki, ed., *Le vitrail français* (Paris, 1958); M. Aubert and others, **Le vitrail français* (Paris, 1958); D. V. Thompson, *Materials and techniques of medieval painting* (new ed., New York, 1958); L. Marcussi and E. Micheletti, *Early medieval painting* (to 1300) (London, 1960); L. Venturi and A. Mauiri *Painting in Italy before 1200* (Geneva, 1959); R. H. Wilenski, *Flemish painters* (2 vols., London, 1960); P. Descargües, *German painting 14–16th centuries* (London, 1958); N. Pevsner and M. Meier, *Grünewald* (London, 1958); E. Ruhmer, ed., *Grünewald, the paintings* (London, 1958); J. Porcher, *French medieval miniatures (New York, 1960); R. A. Weigert, *French tapestry (London, 1962); H. Delahaye, *Legends of the saints (Notre Dame, 1961); *Flanders in the 15th Century (Detroit, 1960), catalogue of an important exhibition; P. Kidson and U. Pariser, eds., Sculpture at Chartres (London, 1958); and F. B. Artz, From the Renaissance to Romanticism, trends in style in art, literature, and music, 1300–1830 (Chicago, 1962).

MUSIC: N. Dufourcq, ed., Larousse de la musique (2 vols., Paris, 1958); P. Collaer and A. van der Linden, eds., *Atlas historique de la musique (Paris, 1960); M. Pincherle, Illustrated history of music (New York, 1959), valuable for pictures; B. C. Cannon and others, *The art of music (New York, 1960), an excellent short history of musical styles; D. J. Grout, *History of Western music (New York, 1960), admirable; H. Riemann, *History of music theory, 9th–16th centuries (Lincoln, 1962); F. A. Kuttner and J. M. Barbour, eds, History of the theory of music, series of records with descriptive booklets (New York, 1960 ff); D. Stevens and A. Robertson, eds., Pelican history of music, Vol. I (London, 1960); E. Werner, The sacred bridge, interdependence of liturgy and music (to A.D. 1000) (New York, 1959); S. Corbin, L'Eglise et la conquête de sa musique (Paris, 1960); G. Reaney, *Medieval music (London, 1960), a good survey; A. Hughes and others, *New Oxford history of music, Vols. II and III (Oxford, 1954, 1959); C. Parrish, ed., A treasury of early music (New York, 1958); F. L. Harrison, Music in medieval Britain (London, 1958); and E. A. Bowles, "Role of musical instruments in medieval sacred drama" in Musical Quarterly, 1959.

MYSTICS: D. Baumgardt, *Great western mystics (New York, 1961); E. Colledge, ed., Medieval mystics of England (London, 1962); D. Knowles, *English mystical tradition (London, 1961), work of a great scholar; B. S. James, St. Bernard (New York, 1957); J. Ancelet-Hustache, Eckhart and the Rhineland mystics (New York, 1958); K. Pond, ed., Spirit of the Spanish mystics (New York, 1958).

HUMANISTS: F. B. Artz, Renaissance Humanism, 1300–1550, an introduction (Cambridge, Mass., 1965); W. J. Bouwsma, ed., The interpretation of Renaissance Humanism (Washington, 1959); B. Smalley, *English friars and antiquity in the early 14th century (New York, 1961), shows continuity of Humanist tradition; J. J. Murphy, "The arts of discourse, 1050–1400" in Medieval studies, 1961; A. Chastel, *The age of Humanism (New York, 1963); a series of Petrarch studies by E. H. Wilkins, *Life of Petrarch (Chicago, 1961), Studies in Petrarch (Cambridge, Mass., 1955), Petrarch's eight years in Milan (Cambridge, Mass., 1958), Petrarch at Vaucluse (Chicago, 1958), and Petrarch's later years (Cambridge, Mass., 1959); M. Bishop, Petrarch and his world (Bloomington, 1963); D. J. Geanakopolos, Greek scholars in Venice (Cambridge, Mass., 1962); L. Martines, *The social world of the Florentine Humanists, 1390–1460 (Cambridge, Mass., 1963); A. Chastel, Art et Humanism à Florence au temps de Laurent le Magnifique (Paris, 1959); L. W. Spitz, *The religious renaissance of the German Humanists (Cambridge, Mass., 1963); E. Wind, *Pagan mysteries in the Renaissance (London, 1958), study of classical influences in painting; and E. F. Rice, Jr., Renaissance idea of wisdom (Cambridge, Mass., 1958).

FOURTH SUPPLEMENTARY NOTE (1979)

GENERAL WORKS: C. Brinton, *European intellectual history* (New York, 1964), invaluable; J. M. Powell, ed., *Medieval Studies, an introduction* (Syracuse, 1976); J. L. Toley, *History of ideas, a bibliographical introduction* Vol. 2, (Santa Barbara, 1977); M. A. Ferguson, *Bibliography of English translations from medieval sources, 1944–1968* (New York, 1973); R. R. Bolgar, ed., *Classical influences on European culture, A.D. 500–1500* (Cambridge, 1971); J. Larner, *Culture and society in Italy, 1220–1420* (New York, 1971); F. H. Baumi, *Medieval Civilization in Germany, 800–1273* (New York, 1969); S. R. Packard, **Twelfth Century Europe* (Amherst, 1973); C. W. Hollister, ed., *Twelfth century renaissance* (New York, 1968); G. Constable, *Medieval monasticism, a select bibliography* (Toronto, 1976); L. D. Reynolds and N. J. Wilson, *Scribes and scholars, a guide to the transmission of Greek and Latin literature* (new ed., Oxford, 1974); G. Leff, *Dissolution of the medieval outlook, 14th century* (New York, 1976); M. Lambert, *Medieval heresy* (New York, 1977); D. J. Geanakoplos, *Interaction of Byzantine culture and the west in the Middle Ages* (New Haven, 1976); M. Schachner, *Medieval universities* (New York, 1938); M. Colish, *The mirror of language* (New Haven, 1968).

BIBLICAL AND CLASSICAL BACKGROUNDS: J. H. Hexter **The Judaeo-Christian tradition* (New York, 1966); **Cambridge history of the Bible* (3 vols., Cambridge, 1972); B. W. Anderson, *The living world of the Old Testament* (3rd ed., London, 1978); B. Reicke, *New Testament era* (London, 1970); F. F. Bruce, *New Testament history* (London, 1970); R. M. Grant, *Early Christianity and society* (San Francisco, 1977); H. von Campenhausen, *The fathers of the Latin Church* (Stanford, 1969); H. Battenson, ed., *Early Christian fathers* (Oxford, 1978); L. Edelstein, *The meaning of Stoicism* (Cambridge, Mass., 1966); A. H. Armstrong, ed., *Cambridge history of later Greek and early medieval philosophy* (Cambridge, 1966); H. Chadwick, *Early church* (Baltimore, 1967).

BYZANTIUM: P. Whitting, ed., **Byzantium, an introduction* (New York, 1971); G. Ostrogorsky, *History of the Byzantine state* (new ed., New Brunswick, 1969); D. A. Miller, *The Byzantine tradition* (New York, 1966); H. W. Haussig, *History of Byzantine civilization* (London, 1971); J. M. Hussey and others, eds., *The Byzantine Empire, part 2; Church and civilization* (2nd ed., Cambridge, 1967); W. Vollach, ed., *Byzanz und der Christliche Osten* (Berlin, 1969); R. Krautheimer, *Early Christian and Byzantine architecture* (London, 1965); K. Weitzmann, **The icon* (London, 1978); E. Kitzinger, *Byzantine art in the making, 3rd–7th century* (Cambridge, Mass., 1977); E. Kitzinger, *The Art of Byzantium and the medieval west* (Bloomington, 1976); A. Demus, *Byzantine art and the west* (London, 1971); C. Cavarnos, *Byzantine thought and art* (Belmont, Mass., 1968); A. Grabar, *Christian iconography, a study of origins* (Princeton, 1969); A. Voyce, *Art and architecture of medieval Russia* (Oklahoma, 1967); J. Meyerdorff, *Byzantine theology* (New York, 1974); O. Strunk, *Music in the Byzantine world* (New York, 1977); F. Dvornik, *Early Christian and Byzantine political philosophy* (2 vols., Washington, 1966).

ISLAM: C. Cahen, ed., *Sauvaget's introduction to the history of the Muslim east, a bibliographical guide* (Berkeley, 1965); S. N. Fisher, **The Middle East*

(3rd ed., New York, 1978); R. M. Savory, ed., *Introduction to Islamic civilization* (Cambridge, 1976); P. M. Holt and others, eds., *The Cambridge history of Islam* (2 vols., Cambridge, 1970); J. J. Saunders, *History of medieval Islam* (New York, 1965); P. Crone and M. Cook, *The making of the Islamic world* (Cambridge, 1977); S. H. Nasr, *Science and civilization in Islam* (Cambridge, Mass., 1968); D. T. Rice, *Islamic art* (London, 1965); G. Mitchell, ed., *Architecture of the Islamic world* (London, 1978); O. Grabar, *Formation of Islamic art* (New Haven, 1973); R. Ettinghausen, *Arab painting* (Cleveland, 1962); F. Rosenthal, *Classical heritage in Islam* (Berkeley, 1974); W. M. Watt, *The influence of Islam on medieval Europe* (Edinburgh, 1972); M. Fakhry, *History of Islamic philosophy* (New York, 1970); W. M. Watt, *Islamic political thought* (Edinburgh, 1968); M. Nakosteen, *Islamic origins of western education* (Boulder, 1964).

LATIN CHRISTENDOM A.D. 400–1000: A. Lewis, *Emerging medieval Europe* (New York, 1967); G. Duby, *The making of the Christian west* (London, 1967); P. H. Blair, *The world of Bede* (London, 1970); P. Riché, *Education and culture in the barbarian west, 6th–8th century* (Columbia, So. Car., 1976); J. T. McNeill, *The Celtic churches, A.D. 200–1200* (Chicago, 1974); A. F. Havinghurst, ed., *The Pirenne Thesis* (new ed., Lexington, 1969); D. Bullough, *Age of Charlemagne* (London, 1965); K. McKitterick, *Frankish church and the Carolingian reform, A.D. 789–895* (London, 1977); C. E. Lutz, *Schoolmasters of the 10th century* (Hamden, Conn., 1977); F. Souchal, *Art of the early Middle Ages* (New York, 1968); J. Hubert, *Carolingian art* (London, 1970); D. T. Rice, ed., *The dark ages* (London, 1965); R. S. Hoyt, ed., *Life and thought in the early Middle Ages* (Minneapolis, 1968).

SCIENCE: E. Grant, ed., *Source book in medieval science* (Cambridge, Mass., 1974); D. C. Lindberg, ed., *Science in the Middle Ages* (Chicago, 1978) very important; R. C. Dales, *Scientific achievement of the Middle Ages* (Philadelphia, 1973); W. A. Wallace, *Causality and scientific explanation* (Vol. I, Ann Arbor, 1972) and S. Rubin, *Medieval English medicine* (New York, 1975).

PHILOSOPHY: E. Bréhier, *The Middle Ages and the Renaissance, Vol. III of "History of philosophy"* (Chicago, 1965); J. R. Weinberg, *Short history of medieval philosophy* (Princeton, 1964) includes Jewish, Islamic, and Christian philosophies; F. C. Copleston, *History of medieval philosophy* (New York, 1974); R. McInerny, *St. Thomas Aquinas* (Boston, 1977) and G. Verbeke, *Aquinas and the problems of his time* (The Hague, 1976).

POLITICAL AND ECONOMIC THOUGHT: W. Ullmann, *History of political thought, the Middle Ages* (London, 1965); W. Ullmann, *Law and politics in the Middle Ages* (Ithaca, 1975); W. Ullmann, *Individual and society in the Middle Ages* (Cambridge, 1966); B. Smalley, ed., *Trends in medieval political thought* (Oxford, 1965); R. de Roover, *La pensée económique des scholastiques* (Montreal, 1971); A. S. Mcgrade, *Political thought of Ockham* (Cambridge, 1974).

VERNACULAR LITERATURE: C. S. Lewis, *An introduction to medieval and Renaissance literature* (Cambridge, 1964); J. H. Fisher, ed., *Medieval literature, a review of research 1930–1960* (New York, 1966); C. J. Stratman, *Bibliography of medieval drama* (2nd ed., 2 vols., New York, 1972); R. Briffault, *The troubadours* (Bloomington, 1965); J. T. Topsfield, *Troubadours and love* (Cambridge, 1975); J. Fleming, *Roman de la rose* (Princeton, 1970); H. Bekker, *The Nibelungenlied, a literary analysis* (Toronto, 1971); J. J. Murphy, *Medieval rhetoric, a select bibli-*

ography (Toronto, 1975); J. J. Murphy, *Rhetoric in the Middle Ages* (Berkeley, 1974); P. Bec, *La lyrique française au moyen age* (Paris, 1977); P. Le Gentil, *Chanson de Roland* (Cambridge, Mass., 1969); T. G. Bergin, **Dante* (Boston, 1965); P. Bortani, *Chaucer and Boccaccio* (Oxford, 1977); M. Lambert, *Malory* (New Haven, 1975); B. Smalley, *Historians in the Middle Ages* (London, 1974); J. Fox, *A literary history of France in the Middle Ages* (London, 1974); D. C. Fowler, *Literary history of the popular ballad* (Durham, 1968); P. Dronke, *Medieval Latin and the use of the European love lyric* (2nd ed., 2 vols., Oxford, 1969); O. B. Hardison, *Christian rite and drama in the Middle Ages* (Baltimore, 1965); M. Schauch, *English medieval literature and its social foundations* (Oxford, 1967); P. Salmon, *Literature in medieval Germany* (London, 1967); B. Rowland, *A companion to Chaucer studies* (Oxford, 1968); V. Branca, *Boccaccio* (New York, 1976) and J. H. Fox, *The poetry of Villon* (London, 1962).

ART: F. Van der Meer, *Early Christian art* (London, 1967); J. Beckurth, **Early medieval art* (London, 1964); A. Grabar, *L'art du moyen age en Europe orientale* (Paris, 1968); A. Grabar, *Christian iconography, a study of its origins* (Princeton, 1969); M. Meiss, *French painting in the time of Duc de Berry* (2 vols., London, 1967); L. R. Shelly, **Role of the master mason in medieval English building* in *Speculum* (1964); S. Halliday, *Stained glass* (New York, 1976); E. von Witzleben, **French stained glass* (London, 1968); P. de Colombar, **Les chantiers des cathédrales* (new ed., Paris, 1973); J. Harvey, **Medieval craftsmen* (London, 1975); D. Knoop and J. P. Jones, *The medieval mason* (3rd ed., Manchester, 1967); J. Pope-Hennessy, ed., *History of western sculpture* (4 vols., London, 1965); V. W. Egbert, *Medieval artist at work* (Princeton, 1967) and E. de Bruyne, *Esthetics of the Middle Ages* (New York, 1969).

MUSIC: A. Hughes, *Medieval music, a bibliography* (Toronto, 1974); H. Raynor, *Social history of music* (London, 1972); R. H. Hoppin, ed., *Anthology of medieval music* (New York, 1978); J. Caldwell, *Medieval music* (Bloomington, 1978); A. J. Bescond, *Le chant grégorien* (Paris, 1972); H. van der Weif, *Chansons of the troubadours and trouvères* (Utrecht, 1972); and B. G. Seagrak and W. Thomas, *Songs of the meister-singers* (Urbana, 1966).

MYSTICISM: C. Butler, *Western mysticism* (new ed., New York, 1968).

HUMANISM: A. Gerlo, **Bibliographie de l'humanisme* (Brussels, 1965); R. Pfeiffer, *History of classical scholarship 1300–1850* (Oxford, 1976); W. von Wilamovitz-Moellendorff, *History of classical scholarship* (London, 1976); R. W. Southern, *Medieval humanism* (New York, 1970); W. Ullmann, *Medieval foundations of Renaissance humanism* (London, 1977); G. Holmes, *The Florentine enlightenment 1400–1450* (London, 1969); H. Baron, *From Petrarch to Bruni* (Chicago, 1968); J. Gadol, *Alberti* (Chicago, 1969) and C. L. Stenger, *Humanism and the Church fathers* (Albany, 1977).

FAITH OF THE COMMON MAN: G. A. MacCulloch, **Medieval myth and fable* (Boston, 1932) basic; and R. C. Finucane, *Popular beliefs in medieval England* (Totowa, N. J., 1978).

Index

✺